EMPLOYMENT LAW

EMPLOYMENT LAW

General Editor
Jane Moffatt

UNIVERSITY PRESS

OXFORD
UNIVERSITY PRESS

Great Clarendon Street, Oxford OX2 6DP

Oxford University Press is a department of the University of Oxford.
It furthers the University's objective of excellence in research, scholarship,
and education by publishing worldwide in

Oxford New York

Auckland Cape Town Dar es Salaam Hong Kong Karachi
Kuala Lumpur Madrid Melbourne Mexico City Nairobi
New Delhi Shanghai Taipei Toronto

With offices in

Argentina Austria Brazil Chile Czech Republic France Greece
Guatemala Hungary Italy Japan Poland Portugal Singapore
South Korea Switzerland Thailand Turkey Ukraine Vietnam

Oxford is a registered trade mark of Oxford University Press
in the UK and in certain other countries

Published in the United States
by Oxford University Press Inc., New York

British Library Cataloguing in Publication Data
Data available

Library of Congress Cataloging in Publication Data
Data available

Typeset by RefineCatch Limited, Bungay, Suffolk
Printed in Great Britain
on acid-free paper by
Ashford Colour Press, Gosport, Hampshire

ISBN 0–19–9258022–3   978–0–19–928922–3

1 3 5 7 9 10 8 6 4 2

Disclaimer
While every care has been taken in the production of this book,
no legal responsibility or liability is accepted, warranted or implied by the
authors, editors publishers or the Law Society in respect of any
errors, omissions or mis-statements.

OUTLINE CONTENTS

CONTENTS

CONTENTS

CONTENTS

CONTENTS

CONTENTS

PREFACE

This manual has been written as a basic text in Irish employment law for trainee solicitors attending the Law Society of Ireland's Law School. It is hoped that it will provide a foundation for their study of employment law whilst at the Law School but also assist them once their training period has ended and they enter the profession.

While every effort has been made to ensure that the text is accurate, the authors, the editor and the Law Society of Ireland do not accept legal liability for any errors, omissions or misstatements of law. Your comments or queries on the contents of this manual are welcomed and should be sent to the editor at the Law Society.

March 2006

AUTHORS

EDITOR

Jane Moffatt BA, HDE, LLB is a South African qualified attorney and conveyancer. She is the Course Manager for Employment Law in the Education Department at the Law Society of Ireland.

AUTHORS

Gary Byrne BCL UCD is a partner in BCM HanbyWallace, Solicitors where he is head of the employment law department. He qualified as a solicitor in 1977. Gary lectures extensively on employment law and is a regular speaker at, amongst others, the Irish Management Institute and the Institute of Personnel and Development. Gary is the author of *Transfer of Undertakings: Employment Aspects of Business Transfers in Irish and European Law*. He is a fellow of the Chartered Institute of Arbitrators.

Duncan Inverarity BComm LLB is a partner in the Employment Law Department of BCM HanbyWallace Solicitors. Duncan regularly lectures to students in the Law Society of Ireland Law School and legal practitioners on the Continuing Professional Development Programme. Duncan is also admitted in Australia, New Zealand and England and Wales.

Elaine Kelly LLB Trinity is an associate in the Employment Law Department of BCM HanbyWallace Solicitors. She also holds a diploma in business studies from the Michael Smurfit School of Business. She was admitted as a solicitor in 2002.

Michael Kennedy BCL UCD is a partner in BCM HanbyWallace, Solicitors. He qualified as a solicitor in 1987. Michael has been Secretary of the Irish Society for Labour Law, a member of the Dublin Solicitors Bar Association Litigation Committee and a member of the Law Society's Employment and Equality Committee. He has lectured widely on employment law issues and is a regular speaker on the Law Society's Continuing Professional Development Programme. He is a contributor to Practical Employment Law published by Thomson Professional Information.

Sandra Masterson Power MBE Dip Employment Law UCD is an associate in the Employment Law Department of BCM HanbyWallace Solicitors. Sandra was admitted as a solicitor in 2001. She is a member of the Dublin Solicitor's Bar Association and the Irish Society for Labour Law.

AUTHORS

Michelle Ní Longáin LLB (Hons) QUB is a partner in BCM HanbyWallace, Solicitors. Michelle is a member of the Council of the Law Society of Ireland. She regularly lectures to students in the Law Society of Ireland Law School and legal practitioners on the Continuing Professional Development Programme. Michelle specialises in employment, equality and administrative law matters. Michelle is also admitted in Northern Ireland and England and Wales.

Margaret Pilkington BA (Hons) UCD is an associate in the Employment Law Department of BCM HanbyWallace. She holds a Diploma in Business Studies specialising in human resources and industrial relations and a Diploma in Employment Law. She was admitted as a solicitor in 2000.

Geoffrey Shannon BComm LLB LLM is a solicitor and Deputy Director of Education in the Law Society of Ireland. Geoffrey lectures on the Professional Practice course and has written extensively in the field of health and safety in the workplace.

TABLE OF CASES

TABLE OF CASES

TABLE OF CASES

TABLE OF CASES

TABLE OF STATUTES

TABLE OF STATUTES

TABLE OF STATUTES

TABLE OF STATUTORY INSTRUMENTS

CHAPTER 1

CONTRACTS OF EMPLOYMENT

1.1 Introduction

The legal relationship between an employer and a person carrying out work comes mainly within the scope of the law of contract. Legislation has had a very considerable impact on employment relationships in recent times. To a lesser extent the law of tort will impinge on the relationship. Contracts of employment are no different from other contracts and require the four essential ingredients:

    (a)   offer;

    (b)   acceptance;

    (c)   consideration; and

    (d)   intention to create legal relations.

With the exception of merchant seamen under the Merchant Shipping Act, 1894 and articles of apprenticeship there is no requirement in law that an employment contract be wholly or partly in writing. Prudent employers will specify the essential terms of contracts of employment in writing and in many cases provide a comprehensive statement of the terms and conditions of a contract of employment. On 16 May 1994 the Terms of Employment (Information) Act, 1994 came into force. It requires employers to furnish employees with certain of the terms and conditions of an employment contract in writing. The Act does not have regard to contract law in a couple of respects. First it allows that the terms and conditions of employment be furnished after the employment relationship has been entered into—which could well give rise to difficulty if there is a dispute over the terms as the contract will have been entered into and any disputed term might be deemed to be an attempted unilateral variation. Secondly, reference is made to amendment and the notification of amendments to employees. No mention is made of the necessity to have consent to contractual amendments or variations.

While the modern employment relationship appears to be dominated by legislation it is still very much underpinned by the law of contract. Those charged with the implementation and enforcement of legislative remedies, such as unfair dismissal, frequently have regard to the terms agreed between the parties, particularly where a dispute might be resolved or helped to be resolved by reference to what was specifically agreed between the parties.

In providing a written statement of terms and conditions of employment employers and employees may use either a letter of appointment or a more comprehensive detailed document. The majority of employment situations may be accommodated by a comprehensive letter of appointment which should make things administratively easier for the employer and transparent and understandable for the employee. Over the years there has been an element of snobbery in the drafting of contracts. Senior executives tend to get more detailed contracts, many of which, however, fail to recognise the potential difficulties and cost of a parting of the ways with such a senior executive, frequently omitting terms such as a probationary period.

1.1.1 REQUIREMENTS OF WRITING

A contract will be made up of both express and implied terms. Legislation requires that certain terms be expressed in writing.

Prior to 1973 employers were not obliged to put terms and conditions of employment in writing. Prudent employers did and have always done so without there being any legal obligation. The Minimum Notice and Terms of Employment Act, 1973 provides that details of certain terms and conditions of employment are made available to employees on request. Under the terms of the Unfair Dismissals Act, 1977 an employer should make known to an employee, in writing, the procedure that would be adopted in the event of dismissal being proposed or taking place.

1.1.2 TERMS OF EMPLOYMENT (INFORMATION) ACT, 1994

The Council of the EC adopted Directive 91/533/EEC on 14 October 1991 obliging employers to inform employees of conditions applicable to a contract of employment or employment relationship. As a result of the Directive the Oireachtas enacted the Terms of Employment (Information) Act, 1994 in May 1994 which provides as follows:

(a) the legislation applies as between employers and employees. It also applies to persons employed through employment agencies who are deemed for the purposes of this legislation to be employed by the party paying the wages;

(b) the legislation only applies to those employees normally expected to work at least eight hours per week;

(c) the legislation does not apply to employees with less than one month's service;

(d) an employer is obliged to provide an employee with a statement in writing no later than two months after the commencement of employment containing the following particulars:

(i) the full names of both employer and employee;

(ii) the address of the employer;

(iii) the place of work or, alternatively, a statement specifying that the employee is required or permitted to work at various places;

(iv) the title of the job or nature of the work;

(v) the date of commencement of the contract of employment;

(vi) in the case of temporary contracts, the expected duration or in the case of a fixed-term contract the date on which the contract expires;

(vii) the rate or method of calculation of the employee's remuneration and details as to at what intervals the payment of remuneration will be made;

(viii) any terms or conditions relating to hours of work including overtime;

(ix) any terms or conditions relating to paid leave (other than paid sick leave);

(x) any terms or conditions relating to sick leave or for payment due to incapacity as a result of injury;

(xi) details of pensions or pension schemes;

(xii) the period of notice which the employee is required to give and entitled to receive whether by statute or contract. If a specified period of notice is not provided for then the method or manner by which notice is to be calculated is to be specified;

(xiii) reference must be made to any collective agreements which directly affect the terms and conditions of the employee's employment including, where the employer is not a party to such agreements, particulars of the bodies or institutions by whom they were made. This requirement only applies to contracts entered into after the commencement of the Act—May 1994;

(xiv) it is further provided that if after the commencement of the Act (May 1994) an employee is required to work outside the State for a minimum period of one month the following details are to be given to the employee or added to the above-mentioned statement:
— the period of employment outside the State;
— the currency in which the employee is to be remunerated in respect of that period;
— any benefits in cash or kind for the employee while working outside the State; and
— the terms and conditions applying to the employee's repatriation; and

(xv) employers are obliged to notify employees of any changes in their terms and conditions of employment as soon as possible after the change but no later than one month thereafter;

(e) where a contract has been entered into prior to the commencement of the Act an employee is entitled to ask for a statement such as is required above and the employer must furnish the statement within two months of the request; and

(f) any complaints by an employee of a contravention of the Act by employers may be referred to a rights commissioner. The rights commissioner may require the employer to provide the particulars and also, if appropriate, may order payment of compensation not to exceed a maximum four weeks' remuneration. Remuneration is to be calculated in accordance with the formula provided for under the Unfair Dismissals Acts. Reference must be made to a rights commissioner no later than six months after the date of termination of the contract of employment. Appeals from the rights commissioner are to the EAT within six weeks (42 days) of the date on which the recommendation was communicated to the party appealing.

None of the above legislation can or does affect the law of contract in so far as it applies to employment relationships.

All of the above legislative requirements are dealt with in more detail in the context of the contract of employment within this chapter.

The European Court of Justice considered the scope of Directive 91/533 in *Kampelmann v Landschaftsverband Westfalen-Lippe* [1998] IRLR 333.

1.2 Employees in Irish Law—Contract of Service/Contract for Services

1.2.1 INTRODUCTION

Tax and social welfare law and virtually all Irish employment statutes draw a distinction between an employee and an independent contractor. The employee works under a contract of service. The independent contractor provides services under a contract for services. Persons carrying out work for an employer not readily fitting into one of these two categories may be deemed to be employees of a third party or sub-contractor or contracted to an employment agency. Given that a person must establish 'employee' status in order to qualify to benefit under most employment statutes the status of persons carrying out work has frequently come under legal consideration. Status is a question of fact determined in light of the rules of legal interpretation as set out below. While the distinction should be relatively easy to draw it has proven in many instances to be extremely difficult to do so. It has been dubbed the 'elephant test': instantly recognisable when one sees it but difficult to describe accurately.

Regardless of what label parties seek to put on their relationship the courts will look at the factual situation and decide as a matter of law what type of contractual relationship exists.

The leading precedent cases on the approach to be applied to determine the correct status in law are the cases of:

- *Ready Mixed Concrete (South East) Ltd v Minister of Pensions and National Insurance* [1968] 2 QB 497;

- *Young and Woods Ltd v West* [1980] IRLR 201;

- *Mara (Inspector of Taxes) v Hummingbird* [1982] ILRM 421;

- *Re Sunday Tribune Ltd* [1984] IR 505;

- *McDermott (Inspector of Taxes) v Loy* 29 July 1982, High Ct (unreported);

- *O'Coindealbhain (Inspector of Taxes) v Mooney* [1990] 1 IR 422;

- *Henry Denny & Sons (Ireland) Ltd (t/a Kerry Foods) v Minister for Social Welfare* [1998] ELR 36;

- *Express and Echo Publications v Tanton* [1999] IRLR 367;

- *Castleisland Cattle Breeding Ltd v Minister for Social and Family Affairs* Supreme Court 15 July 2004 unreported.

1.2.2   WRITTEN EVIDENCE OF TERMS

In *O'Coindealbhain (Inspector of Taxes) v Mooney* [1990] 1 IR 422 the employment relationship was set out in a written contract. Blayney J was heavily influenced by the existence of the written contract and stated:

> 'Where the agreement creating the relationship between the parties is expressed in writing, . . . the entire agreement between the parties is to be found in the writing so it is the unique source of their relationship: it follows that it is from its terms alone that the nature of the relationship can be determined.'

That statement is questionable as to do literally as he suggests would be to remove the legal assessment of the status of the contract, possibly ignore facts of the relationship not dealt with in the written document and leave status as a matter of fact to be determined only by the parties in drawing up their agreement. The better approach was taken by Barron J (who was quoted and agreed with by Blayney J in *O'Coindealbhain*) in *McDermott (Inspector of Taxes) v Loy*. Barron J held that:

> 'The facts as found support the proposition that the respondent is in business on his own account.'

In *Re Sunday Tribune* [1984] IR 505 Carroll J stated:

> 'The court must look at the realities of the situation in order to determine whether the

relationship of employer and employee in fact exists regardless of how the parties describe themselves.'

In *Henry Denny & Sons (Ireland) Ltd (t/a Kerry Foods) v Minister for Social Welfare* [1998] ELR 36 the Supreme Court considered a situation where the contract between the parties provided inter alia as follows:

'*Independent Contractor*
'The demonstrator is and shall be deemed to be an independent contractor and nothing in this agreement shall be construed as creating the relationship of master and servant or principal and agent. It is further agreed that the provisions of the Unfair Dismissals Act, 1977 shall not apply to the contractual relationship that exists between Kerry Foods and the demonstrator.'

Keane J, in referring to that clause of the contract, held that the social welfare appeals officer was 'entirely correct in holding that he should not confine his consideration to what was contained in the written contract but should have regard to all the circumstances of Ms Mahon's employment'. He went on to hold that Ms Mahon, the demonstrator concerned, was an employee engaged under a contract of service contrary to what was specifically provided in the written agreement. In his concurring judgment Murphy J referred to the views of Blayney J in *O'Coindealbhain v Mooney* (above) and went on to state:

'[T]he terms and conditions governing the engagement of Ms Mahon were not "the unique source" of the relationship. . . . I am satisfied that the Appeals Officer was correct in his conclusion that he was required to consider "the facts or realities of the situation on the ground" to enable him to reach a decision . . . whether the respondent was an employee or an independent contractor. In seeking to ascertain the true bargain between the parties rather than rely on the labels ascribed by them to their relationship the Appeals Officer was expressly and correctly following the judgment of Carroll J in *Re Sunday Tribune*.'

The existence of a written document specifying the nature of the relationship will not alter the nature of the relationship but it may well influence the determination of a court or tribunal as to the status of the person carrying out the work, where such status is unclear or where there is a fine balance as to which category the relationship falls into. In *Young and Woods Ltd v West* [1980] IRLR 201 the UK Court of Appeal held:

'[T]he label which the parties choose to use to describe their relationship cannot alter or decide their true relationship although in deciding what that relationship is the expression by them of their true intention is relevant but not conclusive. The legal relationship between the parties must be classified not by appearance but by reality.'

1.2.3 TESTS TO BE APPLIED

The law has developed from setting out fixed tests to differentiate one type of contract from another into a broader approach.

In *Ready Mixed Concrete v Minister of Pensions and National Insurance* [1968] 2 QB 497 the court had to assess whether an owner/driver of a Ready Mixed Concrete truck was an employee or an independent contractor. The court held that a contract of service exists if:

(1) 'A worker provides his own work or skill for payment in performing some service for the employer.' *This element of personal service and the facility of assigning the duties to another person to perform is particularly inconsistent with the status of employee.*

(2) 'He agrees to be sufficiently subject to the other party's control to make that other party his employer.' *Clearly a genuine independent contractor has more control over how, what, where, when and why he does the work.*

(3) 'The other provisions of the contract are consistent with it being a contract of service.' *This aspect is the one that has particularly given rise to a widening of the test in modern times. The modern employee has more perks and benefits associated with his employment than was the case in the past and these will be assessed to see whether or not they are consistent with one status or another. Some of the matters that would be considered under this heading will be the right to paid holidays, sick leave, pension, trade union membership, staff concessions etc.*

1.2.4 A MATTER OF DEGREE

It should be noted that none of the above tests is ever likely to be conclusive. They are merely measurements by which the degree of control, personal service and other provisions are examined to see whether it is more likely that the contract falls into one category or another.

1.2.5 EMPLOYMENT APPEALS TRIBUNAL APPROACH

1.2.5.1 *Kirwan v Dart Industries*

While the Employment Appeals Tribunal (EAT) must apply the law as interpreted by the courts it has tended to take a more comprehensive and broader approach. One of the leading EAT determinations is that of *Kirwan v Dart Industries Ltd and Leahy* M1 UD 1/80. Dart Industries Ltd were an international organisation producing Tupperware. The Leahys were distributors in a certain part of Ireland. Mrs Kirwan worked for the Leahys selling Tupperware through an organised dealership. The dealers organised Tupperware parties at the homes of members of the public. The products were transported by the dealers to the home of the member of the public and displayed at the premises to persons who had been invited. When goods were purchased the dealer was paid and in turn paid the distributor, less a commission. In the case of the dealer therefore it was a case of no sale no pay. Dealers were trained by distributors and, in order to assist in the training and running of the business, successful dealers were appointed managers. Mrs Kirwan was a manager, and both acted as a dealer organising parties and assisted in the training and recruiting of dealers in respect of which she was paid an overriding commission arising from their efforts. She was provided with a car, taxed and insured, but she discharged the maintenance and running costs of the vehicle. She was under no continuing obligation to do any particular hours of work. PAYE tax was not deducted. Managers were at liberty to take whatever holidays they wished but to properly carry out their functions it was necessary to take one week's holiday out of season and two weeks in season. Paid holidays were not given.

The EAT considered the relationship between the claimant and both of the respondents under the following headings:

(a) control;

(b) was the claimant carrying out the job on her own behalf? Was she in business on her own account?

(c) was there a personal obligation to perform the work?

(d) was the relationship between the claimant and the respondent such as would allow her to do other work in her spare time which would be inconsistent with the status of employee?

Having considered these tests the EAT held that the claimant was an employee of the second-named respondent but not of the first-named respondent. See also *Mehigan v Dyflin Publications Ltd* UD 582/2001 and *Kirwan v TEEU* [2005] ELR 177.

1.2.6 THE DEEMED EMPLOYEE

1.2.6.1 The *Labour Force* case

Applying the above-mentioned tests persons carrying out work were classified as being either employees or self-employed persons until 1970 when judgment was issued in the British case of *Construction Industry Training Board v Labour Force Ltd* [1970] 3 All ER 220. Labour Force was engaged in supplying labour to the construction industry. When builders required labour the company agreed to supply workmen at certain rates which were payable by the builders to Labour Force. The workmen were then paid by Labour Force depending on the hours they worked. The relationship was a three-cornered one. The builders provided the work and controlled and directed how it was to be done. The workers carried out the work under the direction of the builders but without any contractual link to them and while holding a contractual link with Labour Force. Labour Force placed the workers, paid them when work was obtained and worked with them in order to ensure that they got work wherever it was available from time to time. Labour Force, however, had no control over the work carried out by the workmen. The builders had the right to terminate the workers' employment. The Construction Industry Training Board applied a levy to Labour Force. This levy was payable if Labour Force had employees engaged in the construction industry. Labour Force argued that they had no employees. They argued that their contracts with the workers were commercial contracts, not contracts of service. The court had to examine the three-cornered relationship and to determine whether or not Labour Force was subject to the levy. The court examined the nature of the relationships between the parties and held:

(a) no contract of any kind was made between the builders and the workmen;

(b) as no contractual relationship was formed between the builders and the workmen Labour Force contracted as principals with the workmen who were paid on agreed terms for the work carried out by them for the builders;

(c) in all the circumstances of the case the contracts into which the workers entered with Labour Force were not contracts of service; and

(d) the contracts entered into by the workers were not contracts of service or contracts for services but contracts sui generis, since the workers had agreed with Labour Force Limited to render services to third persons, the contractors. (See also *Meechan v Secretary of State for Employment* [1997] IRLR 353.)

1.2.6.2 *Minister for Labour v PMPA Insurance Co Ltd*

Labour Force was followed in Ireland in *Minister for Labour v PMPA Insurance Co Ltd* [1986] JISLL 151. The Minister prosecuted PMPA, which employed a temporary typist, for alleged breaches of the Holidays (Employees) Act, 1973. The temporary typist was engaged by PMPA under the terms of a written agreement with Alfred Marks Bureau (Ireland) Ltd. The contract provided that payment would be made to the Bureau and deemed the Bureau to be the employer of the temporary typist. The contract also provided that supervision, direction and control was assigned to and was the responsibility of PMPA. The question for the court was whether or not the temporary typist was an employee of PMPA at the time she carried out work for them. Barron J made reference to the *Labour Force* case and held:

'I do not regard the facts as establishing any contract express or implied between . . . [PMPA] . . . and the employee. In this view I am supported by the English decision to which I have referred.'

The High Court considered the effect of the *PMPA* and *Labour Force* decisions in *O'Rourke v Cauldwell (t/a Recruitment and Engineering Design Services)* [1998] ELR 287.

1.2.6.3   Employment Agencies

The Oireachtas sought to close this 'loophole' in the Unfair Dismissals (Amendment) Act, 1993, the Terms of Employment (Information) Act, 1994, the Maternity Protection Act, 1994, the Protection of Employment Order, 1996, SI 370/1996 and the Organisation of Working Time Act, 1997, by deeming persons working for an employer through another body or agency to be employees of the person for whom they are doing the work. The attempts to close the loophole are, however, crude. In order to bring the supplier of labour within the legislation they must be deemed to be an 'employment agency' within the meaning of the Employment Agency Act, 1971. The definition of an employment agency in the 1971 Act is, however, very wide. It does not require that the supplier of labour be actually trading as an employment agent or licensed as one. The definition appears to be sufficiently wide to encompass companies who carry out sub-contract work and in doing so use workers who may then be deemed to have a direct relationship with the client company. The definition is so wide that many employers may genuinely be sub-contracting work and services and not realise that the persons carrying out the work and providing the services are capable of being deemed to be employees. This is bound to give rise to particular problems in the area of unfair dismissal. It may also give rise to genuine and innocent breaches of the 1994 Act and substantial liabilities, financial and otherwise, under the 1997 Act.

Section 13 of the Unfair Dismissals (Amendment) Act, 1993 provides:

> *'Where, whether before, on or after the commencement of this Act, an individual agrees with another person, who is carrying on the business of an employment agency within the meaning of the Employment Agency Act 1971, and is acting in the course of that business, to do or perform personally any work or service for a third person (whether or not the third person is a party to the contract and whether or not the third person pays the wages or salary of the individual in respect of the work or service), then, for the purposes of the Principal Act, as respects a dismissal occurring after such commencement . . . the individual shall be deemed to be an employee employed by the third person under a contract of employment . . . and any redress under the Principal Act for unfair dismissal of the individual under the contract shall be awarded against the third person.'*

Similar definitions appear in the legislation referred to above. The definition of employment agency in the 1971 Act, section 1 provides as follows:

> *'[T]he business of an Employment Agency means the business of seeking, whether for reward or otherwise, on behalf of others, persons who will give or accept employment and includes the obtaining or supplying for reward of persons who will accept employment from or render services to others.'*

In *Bourton v Narcea Ltd and AIBP* UD186/94 the EAT, under the 1993 Act, took a decision on this particular point. AIBP is a large meat-processing company with a number of factories. The meat business is seasonal. An essential part of meat processing is the boning of sides of beef. Boning is largely seasonal work. As meat processors do not require boners all year round they tend to hire them in from specialist companies engaged in the sub-contracting of boning work such as Narcea Ltd. Boners are generally nomadic and may travel to other countries to ply their trade during quiet times in Ireland or when rates of pay are better in those countries. Narcea supplied boners to AIBP. The boners worked in AIBP plants under the supervision of AIBP's employees to ensure a high quality of work. They also, however, had their own Narcea supervisor. Bourton was an employee of Narcea engaged under a contract of service subject to PAYE and PRSI and worked in a number of meat plants, latterly an AIBP plant where he became involved in a row with an AIBP employee. The AIBP employee was disciplined. The management of the plant requested Narcea management not to deploy Bourton in that plant. Narcea management sought to place Bourton in another plant. He refused. He claimed constructive dismissal. He initially brought his claim against Narcea and during the hearing it was decided to adjourn to allow AIBP to be joined under the provisions of the 1993 Act, section 13. When AIBP was joined, the EAT examined the definition of employment agency in the 1971 Act and held that

Narcea, while contracting to do work itself for AIBP, was, in the course of seeking that business, 'supplying for reward . . . person who . . . render services'. The unfair dismissal claim then proceeded against the joint respondents, Narcea Ltd and AIBP. While Bourton failed in his actual claim against AIBP due to a service problem under the 1993 Act it was held that the relationship between Narcea and AIBP conferred on Bourton the status of an employee of AIBP pursuant to the provisions the Unfair Dismissals (Amendment) Act, 1993, section 13. See also *Diageo Global Supply v Rooney* [2004] ELR 133 and *Dacas v Brook Street Bureau (UK) Ltd* [2004] ELR 358.

Given that in many cases the so-called 'agency' will retain a degree of control and may well actually dismiss the 'employee' it may well prove to be a practical impossibility for the deemed 'employer' to justify such a dismissal as being fair. Section 13 is a clumsy attempt to remedy an injustice by implying a contractual relationship between parties who may never have considered making an agreement between them. An employment relationship created by section 13 will have no express terms. How then will it operate within the requirements of the statute?

1.2.6.4 Conclusion

It is possible that the deemed employer under section 13 will not know of their liability to the deemed employee until a problem arises. If the 'contractual' employer acts unlawfully towards the employee and the employee then claims against the 'deemed' employer, the 'deemed' employer will find it almost impossible to defend a dismissal in which he played no part and will more than likely lose such claim and be liable for the remedies available to the employee under the legislation. The concept of the deemed employee is a statutory creation for the purposes only of those statutes which specifically provide for the concept to apply. The concept does not create an employer/employee relationship but merely confers statutory obligations on a particular employer in particular circumstances.

This is dealt with in more detail in Chapter 4: Atypical Employees.

1.2.7 PARTNERSHIPS

Partners are not employed by or with each other but may, as a partnership, have employees. A partnership or the business of a partnership may constitute an undertaking for the purposes of the Transfer of Undertakings Directive 2001/23/EC and the European Communities (Protection of Employees on Transfer of Undertakings) Regulations, 2003, SI 131/2003. As between themselves partners are deemed to be self-employed and not to have contracts of service with each other as in *DPP v McLaughlin* [1986] IR 355, where the High Court examined an employment relationship where the crew of a ship engaged on a voyage basis were rewarded on the basis of varying shares depending on the size of the catch on each voyage less expenses of the trip. McLaughlin was the owner of the boat and he, in consultation with the crew, determined the precise proportions to be applied. The court held that the relationship between the members of the crew and the owner/skipper of the boat was not that of employer and employee but as self-employed partners engaged in a common enterprise. Where partners in their capacity as members of the partnership carry out work for clients they do so in the capacity of independent contractors. See also *Ellis v Ellis & Co* [1905] 1 KB 324 and *Cowell v Quilter Goodison* [1989] IRLR 392.

1.2.8 SHAREHOLDERS/DIRECTORS—EMPLOYEE STATUS

Difficulties may arise where a shareholder and/or director of a company is sought to be classified as an employee for the purposes of the contract or, more commonly, for statutory purposes. This is dealt with in more detail in Chapter 8: Unfair Dismissals. See also the following cases:

- *Buchan and Ivey v Secretary of State for Employment* [1997] IRLR 80;
- *Fleming v Secretary of State for Trade and Industry* [1997] IRLR 682;
- *Secretary of State for Trade and Industry v Bottrill* [1998] IRLR 120.

1.3 Pre-contractual Matters

There are three matters that will arise prior to a contract of employment being entered into and they may need to be examined closely in any dispute over the details of the contract itself.

1.3.1 ADVERTISEMENT

Jobs are frequently advertised and, as applicants rely on an advertisement, the wording is important as it will be deemed to form part of the overall contract. Regard should be had in advertisements to equality law. Employment equality legislation makes specific reference to advertisements. The UK Court of Appeal in *Pedersen v London Borough of Camden* [1981] IRLR 173 held that in construing the terms of an employee's contract as to his duties the UK EAT was entitled to look at surrounding circumstances and, in particular, to the advertisement which led him to apply for the job in question. See also *Financial Techniques (Planning Services) Ltd v Hughes* [1981] IRLR 32.

This is dealt with in more detail in Chapter 6: Equality and Discrimination in the Workplace.

1.3.2 INTERVIEWS

What is discussed at interview may be extremely important. Both parties may make representations to each other which could be deemed to form part of any subsequent contract. A misrepresentation may give rise to a cause of action. The parties should take careful note of what transpires at interview. Employers will normally do this but it is less easy for an interviewee to do so. Where interviewees ask questions about a job at interview they should carefully note the answers and, if necessary, confirm the answers they have received and upon which they are relying in accepting the position subsequently. *McNally v Welltrade International Ltd* [1978] IRLR 497. Anyone carrying out an interview will have to ensure compliance with the terms of the Employment Equality Acts, 1998–2004 and to avoid discriminatory or potentially discriminatory questions about marital status, disability, age and the other areas of discrimination covered by the Employment Equality Acts.

This is dealt with in more detail in Chapter 6: Equality and Discrimination in the Workplace.

1.3.3 CONDITIONS PRECEDENT

1.3.3.1 Generally

Employers frequently require that certain conditions be satisfied before a contract becomes effective. In practice, however, given the nature of these conditions precedent employers tend to make the offer and allow it to be accepted subject to these conditions being satisfied. The satisfaction of the conditions can give rise to difficulties. The usual conditions are set out below.

1.3.3.2   **References**

It would be unusual for a job applicant who is in employment to advise his employer that he is applying for another position. The proposed new employer will, however, require a reference. A reference cannot be sought or furnished until the candidate has made a commitment to the new employer. It is not unusual for a reference to be issued and when the new employer checks out the reference or speaks with the old employer to find that the recommendation is not possibly as fulsome as he might wish or that some element not dealt with in the reference arises, such as attendance record. If the prospective employer then decides not to proceed he is in a very difficult position. The employee might well be able to argue that the condition has in fact been satisfied. References may also give rise to liability in tort.

Is an employee or former employee entitled to a reference? There is no general requirement in law that an employer furnish a reference. The contract of employment is usually silent on the question. It has been argued that it is an implied term of a contract of employment that an employer will provide a reference at the employee's request. In *Lawton v BOC Transhield Ltd* [1987] IRLR 404 it was held that an employer was free to decline to give a reference. That places employees in a very difficult position. That position is likely to be compounded by recent decisions on an employer's liability where he does actually furnish a reference.

In *Hedley Byrne & Co Ltd v Heller & Partners Ltd* [1964] AC 465 it was held that a person who carelessly provides a reference (albeit not a job reference), which is misleading is liable if the person receiving the reference suffers loss in consequence of his reliance on that reference. In *Lawton* the judge held that a duty of care was owed in respect of a job reference to ensure that it was honest, accurate and not negligently written. Liability in respect of references was comprehensively dealt with by the House of Lords in *Spring v Guardian Assurance plc* [1994] IRLR 460.

In *Coote v Granada Hospitality Ltd* [1998] IRLR 656 the European Court of Justice (ECJ) considered an employee's entitlement to a reference where the employee was refused a reference and claimed that such refusal offended Article 6 of the Equal Treatment Directive 76/207/EEC. The Directive requires that there be no discrimination on grounds of sex in relation to a number of situations including selection criteria and access to all jobs or posts. Ms Coote was employed by Granada from December 1992 to September 1993. She brought a sex discrimination complaint alleging that she had been dismissed because of pregnancy. The complaint was settled. Subsequently Ms Coote encountered difficulties in finding employment and claimed that Granada had failed to provide an employment agency with a reference which she believed was a reaction to her complaint and was an action which in itself constituted unlawful victimisation contrary to the UK Sex Discrimination Act 1975. The UK EAT referred questions to the ECJ which held as follows:

- Article 6 of the Equal Treatment Directive provides that Member States introduce into their national legal system such measures as are necessary to enable all persons who consider themselves the victims of discrimination to pursue their claims by judicial process;

- this requires Member States to ensure judicial protection for workers whose employer, after the employment relationship has ended, refuses to provide references as a reaction to legal proceedings brought to enforce compliance with the principle of equal treatment;

- by virtue of Article 6 of the Directive all persons have the right to obtain an effective remedy in a competent court against measures which they consider interfere with the equal treatment provisions of the Directive;

- the principle of effective judicial control laid down in Article 6 would be deprived of an essential part of its effectiveness if the protection which it provides did not cover measures which an employer might take as a reaction to legal proceedings brought by an employee;

- fear of such measures where no legal remedy was available against them might deter workers who consider themselves victims of discrimination from pursuing their claims by judicial process which would be liable seriously to jeopardise implementation of the aim pursued by the Directive. Therefore protection against retaliatory measures by an employer taken after the employment relationship has ended falls within the scope of the Directive.

1.3.3.3 UK approach

The UK Court of Appeal has offered some clarification in *Bartholomew v London Borough of Hackney* [1999] IRLR 246. Mr Bartholomew was suspended pending investigations into alleged financial irregularities while employed by Hackney Council. Mr Bartholomew, in the meantime, had presented a complaint to an employment tribunal alleging racial discrimination by Hackney Council. During the course of the hearing of his complaints the parties reached a settlement under which Mr Bartholomew agreed to take voluntary severance and to withdraw his complaint. It was also agreed, as part of the settlement, that the disciplinary action would come to an end. The following year another prospective employer, who had offered a job to Mr Bartholomew, sought a reference for him from Hackney Council. The reference stated that he had taken voluntary severance following the deletion of his post, that at the time of leaving he was suspended from work due to a charge of gross misconduct, that disciplinary action had commenced and that the said disciplinary action automatically lapsed when he left Hackney Council. On receiving the reference the prospective employer withdrew the offer of employment given to Mr Bartholomew following on which he made a claim for damages against his former employers alleging that they were in breach of their duty of care in providing a reference which, though factually correct, was unfair. The UK Court of Appeal held against him stating:

> 'The defendants were not in breach of the duty of care owed to the plaintiff former employee in providing a reference for a prospective employer which referred to the fact that, at the time of plaintiff's voluntary severance, he was suspended from work because of a charge of gross misconduct and that the disciplinary action had lapsed automatically with the end of his employment, but which gave no details as to the nature of the gross misconduct, the fact that he strongly denied the charge and the terms of the voluntary severance. An employer is under a duty of care to provide a reference which is in substance, true, accurate and fair. The reference must not give an unfair or misleading impression overall, even if its discrete components are factually correct. However the duty of care owed by an ex-employer to an ex-employee in accordance with *Spring v Guardian Assurance plc* does not mean that a reference must in every case be full and comprehensive. In the present case though the form of the reference might have been improved upon in some respects it was not, as a whole, unfair, inaccurate and false. Had the defendants omitted all reference to the suspension they might have considered themselves as failing in their duty not to be unfair or misleading to the recipient of the reference.'

The law relating to references was dealt with in some detail in the UK case *Kidd v Axa Equity and Law Life Assurance Society* [2000] IRLR 301.

1.3.3.4 Medical evidence

In commercial life it is quite common for employers to require an employee only to submit to medical examination after the offer has been made and accepted. There is no reason why a prospective employee should not be asked to undergo a medical prior to an offer being made. The medical will be confidential and will not become known to the candidate's then employer. Disputes may arise as to whether or not a medical condition will impact on the employment relationship in the future. Employees may consider themselves fully fit to carry out duties, whereas the employer, having become aware of a medical condition, may take a different view. Employers can avoid such disputes by ensuring that medicals are carried out prior to the making of an offer of employment. The status of a pre-employment medical carried out by a medical adviser nominated by the employer is unclear in Ireland. In the UK the court of Appeal has held that a medical practitioner retained by an employer to carry out pre-employment medicals does not owe a duty of care to the job applicant even if it is reasonably foreseeable that negligence by the doctor might lead to the applicant losing the opportunity for employment.

In *Kapfunde v Abbey National plc* [1998] IRLR 583 Mrs Kapfunde applied to Abbey National for a permanent post in a branch where she was already employed on a temporary basis. She completed a standard confidential medical questionnaire disclosing a condition which had led to her being absent from work in the past. The questionnaire was then passed to a GP retained by Abbey National who gave, as his opinion, that Mrs Kapfunde's medical history indicated that she was likely to have a higher than average level of absence and assessed her as not suitable for employment. Acting on that advice the company rejected the application. Mrs Kapfunde brought negligence proceedings against Abbey National and the doctor claiming damages for the economic loss she suffered as a result of not getting the job. The UK Court of Appeal held:

(a) the medical practitioner did not owe a duty of care to the plaintiff;

(b) a medical practitioner retained by a company to carry out pre-employment medical assessments is not under a duty of care to a job applicant in assessing suitability for employment even though it is reasonably foreseeable that the applicant might suffer economic loss if a careless error in the doctor's assessment leads to the loss of the opportunity of employment. In order for a duty of care to exist there must be some relationship of sufficient proximity between the plaintiff and the person alleged to be subject to such duty from which the duty may be derived. The fact that a person's actions are likely to cause damage to the plaintiff if he fails to take due care is not sufficient by itself to create a duty of care;

(c) the existence of a duty not to make negligent misstatements and the identity of the person to whom the duty is owed depend upon the circumstances in which the statement is made. A duty of care will generally be owed to the person to whom the statement is made and who relies on it. In the case of a medical report this is normally the person who commissions the report, not the subject of it;

(d) in the present case there was no special relationship between the defendant doctor and the plaintiff such as to give rise to a duty of care. The plaintiff did not rely on the doctor—report; it was not a report to her and she never even saw it;

(e) the Court of Appeal distinguished this case from the House of Lords decision in *Spring v Guardian Assurance plc* [1994] IRLR 460 on the basis that the duty in *Spring* was derived from the pre-existing relationship between the employer and the former employee. There was no pre-existing relationship between the defendant doctor and the plaintiff from which duty of care to the plaintiff could be derived in *Kapfunde*.

In giving its decision the UK Court of Appeal overruled the UK High Court decision in *Baker v Kaye* [1997] IRLR 219 which had held that a doctor retained by a company to examine a potential employee owed a duty of care to the potential employee. See also *X (minors) v Bedfordshire County Council* [1995] 2 AC 633.

With the development of disability discrimination, employers who encounter what they believe to be a medical reason not to employ a potential candidate must now have regard to the body of law on disability discrimination in making such a decision. That body of law has complicated what was previously a straightforward decision, essentially at the discretion of the employer as to whether the employee was fit to do the job for which they were a candidate. This is dealt with in more detail in Chapter 6: Equality and Discrimination in the Workplace.

1.3.3.5 **Union membership**

The pre-contractual closed shop is lawful under the common law and under European law. Where an employer operates a closed shop it is essential that the closed shop provision is explained to candidates and forms part of the employment offer. Union membership should be documented either prior to the offer being made or the acceptance being deemed valid.

1.4 Implied Terms

There are four sub-categories of implied terms as follow.

1.4.1 TERMS IMPLIED BY STATUTE

Terms implied by statute include the right not to be unfairly dismissed, the right to redundancy payments in the event that employment is terminated in a situation of redundancy, equality, safety from sexual harassment etc.

1.4.2 TERMS IMPLIED BY CUSTOM OR PRACTICE

Terms may be implied by custom or practice (see *Spring v Guardian Assurance plc* [1994] IRLR 460). Such rights include the right to suspend, the right to sick pay, selection for redundancy etc. In *DP Refinery (Westernport) Pty Ltd v Shire Hastings* [1978] 52 AJLR 43 the court set out the test that will normally be applied before a term may be implied into a contract as follows:

(a)   the term must be reasonable and equitable;

(b)   it must be necessary to give business efficacy to the contract, so no term will be implied if the contract is effective without it;

(c)   it must be so obvious that it goes without saying;

(d)   it must be capable of clear expression; and

(e)   it must not contradict any express term of the contract.

1.4.3 COLLECTIVE AGREEMENTS

In unionised employment employers usually copy written collective agreements to new employees and make it clear to them that these agreements form part of their terms and conditions of employment. Subsequent variation of or addition to contractual terms by agreement between a trade union and an employer may be of particular relevance, particularly where the employee objects to the terms. A trade union cannot bind all of its members where some of those members make it quite clear that they do not wish to or intend to be bound (*Goulding Chemicals Ltd v Bolger* [1977] IR 211).

The position was somewhat altered by a Supreme Court decision arising from the provisions of the Postal and Telecommunications Act, 1983 which provided for the formation of An Post and Bord Telecom Éireann. The Act provided at section 45(2) that conditions of service could only be changed in accordance with a collective agreement negotiated with any recognised trade union or staff association.

In *O'Cearbhaill v Bord Telecom Éireann* [1994] ELR 54 the plaintiffs' terms and conditions were changed after the company had entered into a collective agreement with their representative trade union. The plaintiffs, however, had not consented to the change as constituting an alteration in their contractual terms and conditions. The Supreme Court held in favour of the defendant Bord Telecom Éireann, holding that where a collective agreement had been concluded with a representative trade union which had the effect of changing the plaintiffs' terms and conditions of employment the plaintiffs were bound by the change by virtue of the provisions of the subsection referred to.

This is dealt with in more detail at **1.8** below.

1.4.4 **TERMS IMPLIED BY LAW**

Terms will be implied where necessary to give commercial efficacy to a contract of employment. This arises usually in the context of courts analysing specific agreed terms which may not have been comprehensive enough to cover what was intended to be covered or where a dispute has arisen as to their meaning. The Supreme Court examined the circumstances in which a term might be implied into a contract of employment in *Sweeney v Duggan* [1997] 2 ILRM 211. The plaintiff had been injured but the company he worked for had been placed in voluntary liquidation and was unable to pay its debts. The plaintiff sought to sue the managing director personally and sought to imply into his contract of employment a duty on the employer to insure him for personal injury and then to hold the defendant liable for breach of that implied term. In its judgment the Supreme Court referred to the leading cases of *The Moorcock* [1889] 14 PD 64 and *Shirlaw v Southern Foundries [1926] Ltd* [1939] 2 KB 206, and held that there were two principal situations where the courts will independently of a statutory requirement imply a term which has not been expressly agreed by the parties:

(a) on the basis of the presumed intention of the parties; and

(b) as a matter of law independently of the intention of the parties as a necessary legal incident of a definable category of contract.

The court rejected the plaintiff's case that a term requiring insurance should be implied into the particular contract concerned.

Implied terms include the usual terms such as the employer's duty of care and an employee's duty to perform and conduct himself properly and to take reasonable care in the performance of his work. Employees have an implied duty of fidelity to their employer. This duty of fidelity is frequently pleaded in dismissal cases where employers seek to argue that the necessary 'trust and confidence' that must exist in order to properly underpin a contract of employment has been irreparably damaged by the actions of the employee.

The duty of fidelity was initially laid down in *Boston Deep Sea Fishing & Ice Co v Ansell* [1888] 39 Ch D 339. Ansell received a secret commission when placing contracts with ship-builders and this was deemed to be in breach of a duty of fidelity to his employer. The duty of fidelity frequently arises in the context of restrictive covenants dealt with in more detail at **1.5.17** below.

In *Soros and Soros v Davison and Davison* [1994] IRLR 264, Mr and Mrs Davison were employed by Mr and Mrs Soros as butler/chauffeur and cook/housekeeper. They were dismissed and an industrial tribunal found the dismissal to have been unfair. After the finding of unfair dismissal the Davisons sold information about their employment to a national newspaper. The Soros instituted proceedings to restrain them from disclosing information which was claimed to be in breach of an alleged implied term in their contracts of employment and of an alleged duty of confidence arising from the relationship of employer and employee. While much of the case was taken up with legal argument on the effect of post-dismissal conduct on an unfair dismissal claim, and available remedy, reference was made to the general duty of confidentiality and the fact that it survived termination of a contract whether the dismissal is fair or unfair.

In modern cases the duty of fidelity is more often referred to as the duty of 'trust and confidence'. This is a mutual duty on both the employer and the employee and if either party is in breach it entitles the other party to terminate and may entitle them to damages. This is dealt with in more detail at **1.5.18.7** below. The implied duty of mutual trust and confidence is outlined in detail in *TSB Bank plc v Harris* [2000] IRLR 157.

1.5 Express Terms

The principal express terms that should be contained in any document setting out the terms and conditions of a contract of employment are set out below.

1.5.1 PARTIES

While it may seem self-evident, confusion often arises as to who the employer actually is. It is particularly important to specify who the employer is where an individual might be trading as a limited company, a partnership, or a subsidiary company within a group of companies. It may happen that an employee is employed by one company or individual but is paid through the account of another. It is important for the employer to specify who the actual employer is in such circumstances.

In *Clifford v Union of Democratic Mineworkers* [1991] IRLR 518 the UK Court of Appeal held that the question as to by whom an employee is employed is a question of law which will often depend not only on construction of relevant documentary evidence but also on evaluation of the facts. In *O'Rourke v Cauldwell (t/a Recruitment and Engineering Design Services Ltd)* [1998] ELR 287 a dispute arose as to whether the plaintiff had entered into a contract of employment with a recruitment agency or the client of the recruitment agency.

1.5.2 DATE OF COMMENCEMENT

With most statutory entitlements being dependent on length of service, as would be a pension entitlement, it is most important to specify what the commencement date of the employment is deemed to be. It is particularly important where an employee is made an offer and cannot take up the employment for some time because of commitments to a previous employer or otherwise.

1.5.3 JOB FUNCTION

Employers normally seek to avoid disputes over what work an employee may be required to do. They therefore frame job specifications or job descriptions in as wide a manner as possible. That, however, may give rise to difficulties if a redundancy was later to be considered, in which event employees could argue that their job function obliged them to carry out duties different from those duties which had become redundant.

In *Haden v Cowen* [1982] IRLR 314 Cowen's contract included a provision that he was required 'to undertake at the direction of the company any and all duties which reasonably fall within the scope of [his] capabilities'. Cowen was subsequently made redundant. In justifying redundancy his employers focused on the duties he was carrying out at the time the decision was made. The UK EAT held that it was not sufficient to show merely that the requirements of the employer for employees to carry out work of the kind on which the employee was actually engaged had ceased or diminished. It was necessary for the employer to show that such diminution or cessation covered any work that the employee could have been required to do under the contract of employment. The UK Court of Appeal held, however, that there had been a diminution in work for persons carrying out the particular kind of work which Cowen was contracted to do and he was therefore redundant. Employers should also have regard to the possibility of requiring an employee to carry out work for a subsidiary or associated company.

In *Cresswell v Board of Inland Revenue* [1984] IRLR 190 staff of the Inland Revenue sought a declaration that a changeover to computerisation without their consent was breach of an implied term in their contract of employment that they could not be required to change the manner in which their stipulated tasks had been habitually performed either at all or in such a manner as to make these tasks different in nature from those previously performed. The court held that employees must adapt to new methods and techniques provided that the employer ensured that there was the necessary training or retraining to assist them in performing such methods or techniques. Employees had no implied right to remain in perpetuity doing one defined type of work even if this resulted in less job satisfaction. A loss of job satisfaction by itself provided no cause of action.

The general common law rule is that an employer is not contractually obliged to provide work for the employee. *Collier v Sunday Referee Publishing Co* [1940] 2 KB 647 and *Turner v Sawdon & Co* [1901] 2 KB 653. Exceptions to that general rule will be where the employee's remuneration depends on performance, e.g. commission *Re Rubel Bronze & Metal Co* [1918] 1 KB 315, and where performance of work is linked to reputation and ability to use and improve one's skills and talents *Marbe v George Edwards (Days Theatre) Ltd* [1928] 1 KB 269.

1.5.4 HOURS OF WORK

Apart from setting out the basic hours of work an employer should make reference to breaks, shifts and overtime, particularly where an employee may be required to work beyond the normal hours on a regular basis. A specific reference should be made to payment for overtime, whether payment is to be made or not to be made.

In *Green v Roberts* [1992] IRLR 499 reference was made to the manner in which hours of work should be calculated in the event of there not being a specific provision. This case followed *Deane v Eastbourne Fishermen's and Boatmen's Protection Society and Club Ltd* [1977] IRLR 143 and *Larkin v Cambos Enterprises (Stretford) Ltd* [1978] ICR 1247, where a simple averaging out of hours actually performed over a period that covered most variations in the contract was sufficient.

Where averaging out may not give a fair result see *Opie v John Gubbins Insurance Brokers Ltd* [1978] IRLR 540. Where salary is reduced by an employer for good commercial reason but possibly in breach of terms of a contract of employment see *Burdett-Coutts v Hertfordshire County Council* [1984] IRLR 91, *Millar v Hamworthy Engineering Ltd* [1986] IRLR 461 and *Rigby v Ferodo Ltd* [1987] IRLR 516.

Regard must also be had to hours of work set by statute such as:

- Protection of Young Persons (Employment) Act, 1977;

- Conditions of Employment Acts, 1936–1944;

- Shops (Hours of Trading) Act, 1938;

- Organisation of Working Time Act, 1997.

There is no right in law to lay off staff or place them on short time due to a temporary shortage or downturn in work and so it is best to provide for this right in the contract of employment (*Devonald v Rosser* [1906] 2 KB 728).

1.5.5 PLACE OF WORK

Place of work may give rise to difficulties both in respect of the department or area in which an employee works and geographical location, or as to working in different geographical locations. The first situation was dealt with in *White v Reflecting Roadstuds Ltd* [1991] IRLR 331. White originally worked in the rubber-mixing department of the company which attracted the highest level of pay but involved the hardest physical work and longest hours. White had difficulty with the work and asked to be moved to lighter work. He could not be moved and remained in the mixing department. His attendance, however, deteriorated and other staff complained about the effect his absence was having upon them in earning their entitlement to team bonuses. After warning White was transferred from the mixing department to the pressing department which resulted in a considerable drop in pay. He resigned and claimed constructive dismissal on the basis that the move from mixing to pressing constituted a fundamental breach of his contract. The contract included an express term covering job flexibility which provided that:

'[T]he company reserves the right when determined by requirements of operational efficiency to transfer employees to alternative work and it is a condition of employment that they are willing to do so when requested.'

The UK EAT held:

(a) where organisation and reorganisation are concerned it is for management to reach the decisions provided they do so responsibly and give effect to their decisions within the legal framework of a clear contractual term on mobility or job transfer. Even where there is an express clause a purely capricious decision would not be upheld. There must be reasonable or sufficient grounds for requiring the employee to move—otherwise the employer would be in breach of the specific term of the clause which had implied into it the obligation to act responsibly and reasonably;

(b) a reduction in pay as a result of a contractually allowed transfer is not a breach of a fundamental implied term that there would be no unilateral reduction in pay. There is clear binding authority that where an employer acts within the contract of employment the fact that thereby there is caused a loss of income to the employee does not render the employer's act a breach of contract.

On geographical mobility it may be taken that a similar onus lies on an employer to act reasonably and responsibly even where there is a geographical mobility clause in the contract. Geographical mobility was considered in *Parry v Holst & Co Ltd* [1968] ICR 317 where the employee's contract provided for mobility between different workplaces and he was refused a redundancy payment when his current workplace closed and he refused to transfer to another.

In *Wilson-Undy v Instrument & Control Ltd* [1976] ICR 508 an employee accepted a job as part of a mobile workforce but he stipulated at the time of his appointment that he was not prepared to work at any sites beyond daily travelling distance of his home. When work at his site finished he claimed a redundancy payment. He refused to transfer to another site which was not within daily travelling distance from his home. He was held to be entitled to his redundancy payment. The UK Court of Appeal refused to allow an employer to use the mobility provisions of a contract to establish that a place of work was in a particular location where that sought to defeat an entitlement of the employee—in this case a redundancy entitlement—in *High Table Ltd v Horst* [1997] IRLR 513.

In *Macari v Celtic Football and Athletic Co Ltd* [1999] IRLR 787 Lou Macari was appointed manager of Celtic Football Club in 1993. It was a term of his contract that he reside no further than 45 miles from the centre of Glasgow while carrying out his duties. Mr Macari did not do so. This was held to be a material breach of his contract in failing to comply with the lawful and legitimate instruction of his employers entitling the employers to terminate the contract.

1.5.6 EXCLUSIVE SERVICE

Employees have the right to work for another employer in their spare time provided this does not conflict with their duties, including fidelity and confidentiality, to their employers (*Nolan v Irish Snack Foods Ltd* UD 303/79, *Conroy v Travenol Laboratories* UD 47/81 and *Mulchrone v Feeney* UD 1023/82).

In *Fairbrother v Stiefel Laboratories* UD 665/85, the EAT reached an interesting decision. Dr Fairbrother held the position of Director of Research and Development. His wife, who had no link with Stiefel Laboratories, was a trained pharmacist who formed her own company and launched a product which competed with a product manufactured by Stiefel. Dr Fairbrother's employment contract contained clauses designed to protect confidentiality and trade secrets. There was no allegation that Dr Fairbrother had breached these provisions but, given his position of responsibility and control and his wife's activities, there was a conflict of interest which could have been resolved by Mrs Fairbrother ceasing her activities. Dr Fairbrother could not oblige her to do so. In those circumstances the company resolved the conflict by terminating Dr Fairbrother's employment. The EAT held the dismissal to be fair.

In *ECI European Chemical Industries Ltd v Bell* [1981] ILRM 345 an interlocutory injunction was granted to restrain a chemist from joining a competitor in breach of a restraint of trade clause in his contract.

1.5.7 PROBATION

Unfair dismissal legislation provides that a probationary period cannot exceed one year. Probationary periods are useful to employers in unionised employment as employees tend not to be deemed by unions to be 'permanent' until they have completed the probationary period. It is also useful to employers employing senior employees who might have a lengthy notice period, in the event of the employment continuing, to have a probationary period although it may be difficult to attract senior employees where they lack job security in the early stages of their employment. The wording of probationary periods may sometimes give rise to a possible construction that the probationary period is in itself a fixed term within the contract. If a contract were to state, for example, 'The first six months of this contract shall be a probationary period' this might give rise to a claim on early termination, e.g. after one month, that the employee is entitled to be paid the balance of five months' salary. There has in fact been a District Court finding to this effect. The position, however, at common law seems to be that the employer has an implied right to terminate during the probationary period on the giving of specified or reasonable notice (*Dalgleish v Kew House Farm Ltd* [1982] IRLR 251). A prudent employer will provide that during a probationary period the employment may be terminated on specified notice often shorter than the notice required to terminate the contract when employment has become permanent. In *Doyle v Grangeford Precast Concrete Ltd* [1998] ELR 260 the employer sought to impose a probationary period in a written document produced to the employee for his signature after he had commenced employment. The employee obtained an interlocutory injunction pending the outcome of his claim for damages.

1.5.8 TERM OF CONTRACT

The term or duration of a contract is relevant only in relation to fixed-term or specified-purpose contracts which are dealt with more specifically in Chapter 4: Atypical Employees.

1.5.9 SALARY/REMUNERATION

Precision is necessary in setting out the various components of a remuneration package. Basic salary tends not to cause difficulty. However, bonuses and commission do. Employers normally seek to have bonuses described as discretionary where employees will require first to establish that they have a right to a bonus and, secondly, that where there is a bonus or commission system in place its terms are specifically set out so that the employee can enforce payment in the event of any dispute arising. Reference should be made to what the entitlement will be in the event of either party terminating during the course of a bonus/commission period. The method in which remuneration may be paid is dealt with in the Payment of Wages Act, 1991 which is dealt with in Chapter 2: Payment of Wages. This legislation repealed the Truck Acts, 1743–1896.

1.5.10 COMPANY CAR

Again it is in an employer's interest to provide that a company car is furnished at the discretion of the employer either in terms of the basic entitlement or in terms of the make, model and renewal terms. The provision of a company car may give rise to consideration as to vicarious liability for the employer both in the normal use of the vehicle and for the employee outside the hours of work (*Smith v Stages* [1989] 1 All ER 833). For where employees may be entitled to car allowances and they are varied or withdrawn see *Keir and Williams v County Council of Hereford and Worcester* [1985] IRLR 505.

1.5.11 HOLIDAYS

Holidays are governed in Ireland by the contract and since the Organisation of Working Time Act, 1997 should make reference to the statutory entitlement and, if extra days' holidays are to be conferred, they should be deemed to be in addition to the statutory entitlement to annual leave and public holidays. As the legislation vests in the employer the right to determine when holidays are to be taken it will normally suffice for a contract of employment to refer to the mechanics of taking holidays as being governed by the legislation. Employers and employees cannot contract out of the terms of the 1997 Act. Leave entitlements are dealt with in more detail in Chapter 3: Working Time and Statutory Leave Entitlements.

1.5.12 SICK PAY

1.5.12.1 Generally

There is no general right in law to be paid while absent from work due to illness. An entitlement to sick pay may, however, be implied from the custom and practice of the employment. *Halsbury's Laws of England* (4th edn) vol 16, para 24 states in relation to non-statutory sick pay in the UK:

> 'Whether any such private sick pay is payable, its amount, its duration, and its relationship with statutory sick pay or any other benefit depends entirely on the terms of the individual employee's contract, since there is no rule of law that it either is or is not payable. The relevant term may be expressed in the contract and this is common; if not so expressed a term may be implied. In the absence of an expressed term there is however no presumption that a term is to be implied. It is rather a case of considering all the evidence in the particular case, including the normal method of remuneration, custom and practice, and any pronouncement by the employer.'

In *Howman & Son v Blyth* [1983] IRLR 139 the court considered whether or not an employee should have implied into his contract of employment an entitlement to sick pay. There had in the past been a term expressly provided for in all contracts of employment within the company that employees would be entitled to sick pay. The onus was on the employers to show that the respondent had either expressly or by implication agreed to vary his contract to lose this right and it was held that such variation was not proven. On the question of implication of terms the court stated:

> 'Where the relationship between the parties requires that there should be some agreed term which has not in fact been agreed but both parties would not have agreed what that term would be if they had been asked, the court is free to imply a reasonable term. In the present case there was undoubtedly a contractual obligation to pay sick pay but there was no agreed term as to the duration of the sick pay.'

As there had to be some contractual term regulating the duration it was legitimate to imply a reasonable term. See also *Marrison v Bell* [1939] 2 KB 187 and *Mears v Safecar Security Ltd* [1983] 1 QB 54.

1.5.12.2 Implied entitlement

The question of an implied entitlement to sick pay was raised in the context of an employee seeking injunctive relief to restrain a disciplinary hearing, and other reliefs in the case of *Charlton v HH The Aga Khan's Studs Société Civile* [1999] ELR 136. The disciplinary investigation was initiated against the plaintiff and she sought eight interlocutory injunctions restraining her employer from continuing the enquiry into the disciplinary matters and other reliefs. During the course of the disciplinary enquiry the plaintiff became ill. Her employers refused to make payments to her in respect of sick pay claiming they had no contractual obligation to do so and suggesting that she rely on social welfare entitlements. In the course of her judgment Laffoy J commented:

> 'It is common case that the terms of the plaintiff's employment with the defendant are not contained in a written contract. It is also common case that it is not an express term of the plaintiff's employment with the defendant that she is entitled to be paid her salary while absent from work due to illness or incapacity. The plaintiff's contention is that her entitlement to sick pay is an implied term of her contract of employment. Her case is that it has always been the position in the defendant's Studs that long-standing employees were paid their salary in full when they were absent through illness and that this custom is part of her terms of employment. This is disputed by the defendant.'

Laffoy J went on to state that the plaintiff had established a fair issue to be tried that there was an implied sick pay term in her contract of employment and ordered that her salary be paid pending the resolution of the matters in dispute and for so long as she remained ill provided that she furnished to the employer a weekly illness report. A similar decision was made by the High Court in *Mullarkey v Irish National Stud Co Ltd* [2004] ELR 172.

1.5.12.3 Drafting the sick pay clause

In drafting clauses relating to sick pay entitlement reference may well be made also to health care insurance entitlements and to income continuance plans which may cover payment to an employee after the employer's obligation to pay sick pay has ceased. In *Adin v Sedco Forex International Resources Ltd* [1997] IRLR 280 the court of Session in Scotland held against an employer who sought to dismiss an employee who was entitled to claim under short-term and long-term disability plans but by reason of the dismissal was prevented from obtaining the benefit of the plans. Even though the employer had no restrictions on the circumstances in which it could dismiss the employee the court refused to allow such a dismissal in the circumstances of the dismissal acting to defeat the entitlement under such policies. The Court of Session accepted that where an employee is off work due

to illness and in receipt of sick pay there was an implied term in the contract that the employee would not be dismissed on grounds of sickness or for an arbitrary reason since to do so would be to subvert the employee's entitlements to payments while sick.

In *Hill v General Accident Fire and Life Corporation* [1998] IRLR 641 the court did state, however, that the employer was not in breach of the employee's contract of employment in dismissing on grounds of redundancy while the employee was off work ill and in receipt of sickness benefit with a prospective entitlement to long-term sickness benefit under an ill-health policy. The court held that there was no implied term that the employers would not use their contractual powers of dismissal where that would frustrate an accruing or accrued entitlement to sickness benefit or ill health and early retirement. The court refused to accept that there was an implied term that gross misconduct was the only cause that would warrant dismissal of an employee who was in receipt of sick pay. The court examined the implied term of mutual trust and confidence and held that an employer would be prohibited from terminating a sick employee's employment:

> '. . . solely with a view to relieving themselves of the obligation to make such payment for a specious or arbitrary reason or for no cause at all. To do so would be to subvert the employee's entitlement to payment while sick.'

This decision is arguably only of use to an employee who can prove that the actual reason for dismissal was to deny him his entitlement to short-term or long-term sickness benefit and is unlikely to avail an employee where an employer dismisses for cause, e.g. misconduct or redundancy. The practice of courts in the UK has been to prevent employers from terminating employment due to incapacity if the effect of the termination would be to deny the employee rights to third-party benefits such as an insured permanent health scheme or income continuance.

Hill was reviewed and partly affirmed in *Villella v MFI Furniture Centres Ltd* [1999] IRLR 468 where the UK High Court held that termination of the plaintiff's employment in that case would have been a breach of an implied contractual term that the employers would not terminate employment except for cause 'in circumstances which would deprive the plaintiff of the continuing entitlement to disability benefit in the course of payment or due to him'. The court in that case felt that such an implied limit on the employer's power to dismiss was necessary in order to give 'business efficacy' to the contract which allowed for disability benefit to be made available to the employee. See also *Briscoe v Lubrizol Ltd* [2002] IRLR 607.

1.5.13   PENSION

Pension should always be referred to where it is part of the employment relationship. It may be best to simply refer to the pension entitlement being subject to the terms of the trust deed and rules and being dependent on the operation of the scheme by the trustees. Most schemes allow for the termination of the scheme or the suspension of payments by the principal employer which effectively allows an employer to discontinue pension entitlement under the contract. Schemes must in turn comply with the Pensions Act, 1990. Care must be taken to ensure that employees are not excluded from pension schemes in situations where they may be able to claim entitlement by virtue of direct or indirect discrimination. Employers may inadvertently create a situation of indirect discrimination fully believing that they have no obligation to provide a pension in line with the general common law position in that regard but where they provide pension to workers of a different type or class and are held to have indirectly discriminated against those excluded from the pension scheme, pension entitlement may follow. See the ECJ decision in *Magorrian and Cunningham v Eastern Health and Social Services Board and Department of Health and Social Services* [1998] IRLR 86 and *Hill and Stapleton v Revenue Commissioners* [1998] ELR 225.

1.5.14 RETIREMENT AGE

Many employers omit to make reference to retirement age because it is provided for in the pension scheme. Employers should specify the actual retirement age. That age may in turn be subject to variation within the terms of the pension scheme. The possibility of such variation should also be referred to by the employer. In *Buckley v Ceimici Teo* UD 528/80 at the time the claimant commenced employment, there was no contractual provision and the normal retirement age was 70 years. His employment was terminated when he reached 65 which was the pension age. The claimant maintained he was entitled to continue working until the normal retirement age of 70. The respondents, however, were in a position to produce documentary evidence that the normal retirement age had changed to 65 years and that the claimant was aware of this. The dismissal was held to be fair.

The issue of age, retirement age and fitness to work was considered by the High Court in *Donegal County Council v Porter* [1993] ELR 101. The respondents were employed by the county council as part-time firemen. When they commenced service the retirement age was 60. In the intervening years the policy of Donegal County Council, in common with other fire authorities in Ireland and Britain, had changed in favour of compulsory retirement at age 55 for firemen. Firemen engaged in the years subsequent to the respondents had a contractual provision to this effect. The reason for this was because the work had become more hazardous and stressful and required more agility and flexibility. In December 1985 the Department of the Environment issued a Directive recommending the introduction of a retirement age of 55 and a compulsory annual medical examination for all operational personnel.

The respondents' contracts provided for retirement at age 60 and they never at any time agreed to an alteration or variation in their contract. The county council subsequently retired them at age 55 which the court held was an attempt to unilaterally alter the contract and was in breach of contract unless it could be justified in some other lawful way which it was not.

The council put forward a strong plea, with expert evidence, that employees should retire at 55 and made reference to the Safety, Health and Welfare Act, 1989, section 61. The court held, in dismissing the claim of the county council to be entitled to compulsorily retire firemen at 55, that there was a statutory duty to observe but it could be observed:

> '. . . by a much less draconian measure than dismissal at the age of 55 and one which does not involve a blatant disregard for the Council's contractual obligations . . . they can comply with their statutory obligation in requiring . . . the respondents to undergo medical examination from such age and at such frequency as they consider necessary to assure all persons concerned of the physical fitness of the men in the fire-fighting services . . . this is consistent with the terms implicit in the men's contract of service—while fit and capable they have a contractual expectation of service to age 60—if not fit and capable there are "substantial grounds justifying dismissal".'

1.5.15 GRIEVANCE PROCEDURE

In the interest of good industrial relations and to avoid industrial action taking place without the employer at least having an opportunity to consider the matters at issue, employees should be bound to process any grievance they have in a specified manner. Grievance procedures may be constructed quite simply by proving an obligation on employees to raise their grievance at the next level supervisor, manager etc and, if the matter is not determined at that stage, appeal to a further higher level. For senior executives grievances should be referable to either the managing director or board of directors. Sexual harassment policies frequently make reference to grievance procedures and require that any problem in relation to alleged sexual harassment should be treated as a grievance although the nature of sexual harassment complaints may be required to be dealt with in somewhat different manner and will require particular undertakings of confidentiality. Employers must also apply the principles of both grievance and disciplinary procedures set out in the statutory Code of Practice Industrial Relations Act, 1990 (Code of Practice on Grievance and Disciplinary Procedures) (Declaration) Order, 2000, SI 146/2000.

1.5.16 DISCIPLINARY PROCEDURE

With a very heavy emphasis on the following of procedures in the processing of disciplinary action, and in particular dismissals, laid down by courts and tribunals over the years, employers should have a specified disciplinary procedure. There is no requirement to have an over-elaborate procedure, simply a procedure specifying the following:

(a) what will be done in the event of a complaint or allegation being made;

(b) how many stages are likely to be followed in each event;

(c) the right of the employer to choose the appropriate stage and/or penalty depending on the nature of the matter at issue;

(d) the right of representation; and

(e) whether there is a right to appeal against the imposition of disciplinary penalty—it should be kept in mind that the EAT does not have regard to appeals against dismissal in assessing whether the original dismissal was fair or unfair.

See also SI 146/2000.

1.5.17 RESTRICTIVE COVENANTS

1.5.17.1 Introduction

Restrictive covenants and the right of employees to compete with their employers after they leave employment, and the law relating to the proprietary interests of an employer in trade secrets and information imparted to an employee while in employment, all raise very considerable practical difficulties in the area of employment law and contract law. In order to understand how the respective parties' rights and entitlements are to be treated regard must be had both to the common law position and the changes effected by the provisions of the Competition Act, 1991. Both of these areas are dealt with below.

At common law an employer is entitled to expressly protect, and by terms and conditions implied in the contract to have the law protect, his trade secrets and confidential information and, in certain circumstances, to limit the ability of an employee to compete after employment has terminated. Traditionally the common law categorised such restrictions as restraints on trade and took the view that they were prima facie unlawful unless they could be shown to be reasonable in protecting an interest that is entitled to be protected, reasonable in intended duration and reasonable in respect of geographic scope or product scope.

1.5.17.2 Fidelity and loyalty

The common law courts will imply a duty of fidelity and obligations of loyalty in all contracts of employment. This duty is one of the most basic elements of the employment relationship. In 1888 it was held that a company's managing director who received a secret commission for the placing of contracts was in breach of an implied duty of good faith to his employer. He had the employing company make contracts with a third-party company in which he was a shareholder, thereby receiving benefit from the employing company, albeit indirectly, and was held to be liable to his employer to account for such money earned and, in failing to do so, to be in breach of contract (*Boston Deep Sea Fishing & Ice Co v*

Ansell [1888] 39 Ch D 339). In *Redding v Attorney-General* [1951] AC 507 a British Army sergeant turned a blind eye to a criminal practice which resulted in him making substantial money in respect of which the House of Lords, per the judgment of Lord Oaksey commented:

> 'I do not think that there is any difficulty in imputing to a servant an implied promise that he will account to his master for any moneys he may receive in the course of his master's business, or by the use of his master's property, or by the use of his position as his master's servant.'

This duty has been held to include an obligation not to compete with the employer while in his employment. In *Thomas Marshall (Exporters) Ltd v Guinle* [1978] 3WLR 116 the court considered a situation where, during working hours, the managing director was trading in competition with the employing company, and held his actions to be unlawful. The duty clearly applies to the normal hours of work but does it also apply to spare-time work?

In *Hivac Ltd v Park Royal Scientific Instruments Ltd* [1948] 1 Ch 169 the employer succeeded in preventing competing activity during the employee's free time as they were held to be entitled to protect confidential information. Contrasted with that is the case of *Nova Plastics Ltd v Froggatt* [1982] IRLR 146 where a manual worker was held not to be in breach of duty where he worked for a competitor of the employer in his spare time. This implied contractual duty of good faith was held to only apply during the currency of the contract of employment. The EAT has upheld dismissals as being fair where the employee has breached or threatened to breach the contractual duty of good faith and loyalty. In *Preece v Irish Helicopters Ltd* UD 236/84 the employee had a specific provision in his terms and conditions of employment not to compete with the employing company. In the course of its determination the EAT commented:

> 'An employer is entitled to insist that an employee does not interest himself in a company which will compete with the business of the employer. Failure of the claimant to commit himself not to do anything while in the respondent's employment in pursuit of his own interest which might conflict with the interest of his employer was reasonably construed as a breach of duty or loyalty.'

In *Mulchrone v Feeney* UD 1023/82 the EAT upheld a dismissal of an employee working for a direct competitor in her spare time. The EAT has taken contrasting positions in situations where an employer has dismissed an employee in fear of potential breach of the duty of fidelity. In *Goggin Carroll & Co v Dineen* UD 106/85 an employee, who had a relationship with a person working in a competing business, was offered an alternative position in another branch of the employing company but refused it as a result of which she was dismissed. The EAT held that the dismissal was unfair as 'the fear of an inadvertent slip is not grounds for dismissal'.

In *Coffey v Alcan Metal Centres (Dublin) Ltd* UD 603/90 the respondent was a substantial company with two main competitors in Dublin. The pricing or rebating of products was highly sensitive and if leaked to either competitor, it was submitted, could have caused considerable damage to the employing company. The respondent's brother and fiancé worked for the company. Both left within a short period of time to join one of the two competitors. The claimant subsequently married her fiancé. The company explained its concerns to the employee about the possibility of breach of confidence while not aware of any actual breach of confidence. Discussions were had about what could be done to avoid a dismissal. No suitable alternative position was available. The claimant was dismissed. The EAT held that where an employer had a real and significant concern bona fide derived from circumstances which could reasonably justify such concern, and the circumstances did not reasonably permit the adoption of an alternative solution to that of dismissal then dismissal was justified. See also *Fairbrother v Stiefel Laboratories (Ireland) Ltd* UD 665/85.

When the contract comes to an end the duty also comes to an end unless the contract contains a specific provision whereby the parties have agreed that restrictions will continue to apply. That is not the case, however, where the employer is seeking to protect confidential information or trade secrets. An employee working out his notice, or on 'garden leave' whereby he is still employed and still in receipt of remuneration but is not required to work, remains under the contractual duty of good faith (*J A Mont (UK) Ltd v Mills* [1993] IRLR 172).

1.5.17.3 Confidential information and trade secrets

While the common law duty and many restrictive covenants provide for the protection of an employer's confidential information and trade secrets, in determining the enforcement of these terms, the information sought to be protected must be examined to see if it has the necessary quality of confidentiality; if not it will not enjoy the protection sought to be conferred on it no matter how clear the duty or the terms of the restriction.

Faccenda Chicken Ltd v Fowler [1986] IRLR 69 set out the proposition that something which may properly be categorised as a trade secret and is known, or should be known to the former employee as being such, remains protected after the employment has ceased even in the absence of the employer pointing out to the employee the precise limits of what he seeks to protect as confidential or binding the employee on foot of a written agreement.

In *Lancashire Fires Ltd v S A Lyons & Co Ltd* [1997] IRLR 113 the second-named defendant had worked for the plaintiffs and had become familiar with trade secrets. He left and set up his own business. The UK Court of Appeal held that given his position in the plaintiff company the second defendant must have known that the information he exploited after he left their employment was properly a trade secret belonging to the plaintiff and therefore he was in breach of an obligation of confidence in using the process for his own benefit.

See also *Printers and Finishers Ltd v Holloway* [1965] 1 WLR 1, *Sun Printers Ltd v Westminster Press Ltd* [1982] IRLR 292 and *British Railways Board v Natarajan* [1979] ICR 326.

1.5.17.4 What is protected

It is not essential that an employer has a written or express term in a contract of employment to protect confidential information and trade secrets. The common law will protect confidential information and trade secrets if it can be shown that the information sought to be protected is of such a nature that confidentiality must apply to it or that it be treated as a trade secret. In *Faccenda Chicken Ltd v Fowler* the UK Court of Appeal examined various types of information and set out the principles that would apply in its protection and held as follows:

(a) in the absence of any express term in a contract of employment the obligations of an employee in respect of the use and disclosure of information are the subject of implied terms;

(b) while the employment subsists the obligations protecting the employer's information are included in the general implied common law term imposing a duty of good faith and fidelity on an employee;

(c) when the employment ceases the obligation not to use or disclose information covers only information that is of a sufficiently high degree of confidentiality as to amount to a trade secret. The obligation does not continue to cover all of the information covered prior to termination. In determining what constitutes a trade secret no hard and fast criteria can be laid down but the following will be taken into account:

   (i) the nature of the employment—as some employments may impose a higher obligation than others;

   (ii) the nature of the information itself—some matters clearly qualify as trade secrets, others may be less obviously so; and

(iii) whether the employer impressed on the employee the confidentiality of the information. While the employer cannot prevent use or disclosure merely by telling the employee that the information is confidential his attitude may provide evidence that is of use in determining the question as to how confidential the information actually is.

The distinction between trade secrets and what is merely confidential during the currency of the employment and usable by the employee when employment ends was also considered in *Roger Bullivant Ltd v Ellis* [1987] IRLR 491. See also *Cantor Fitzgerald (UK) Ltd v Wallace* [1992] IRLR 215 dealt with at **1.5.17.10** below.

In *SBJ Stephenson Ltd v Mandy* [2000] IRLR 233 the UK High Court drew a distinction between two types of knowledge that may be acquired by an employee in the course of employment, one of which is protected, the other which is not. Mr Mandy had been employed by a firm of insurance brokers (SBJ) and his contract contained a clause restricting him from disclosing or using information of which he became possessed while in the service of the company. Mr Mandy sought to take business from SBJ when he left and joined another insurance broker. The information used was the identity of SBJ clients and knowledge of their renewal dates, cover, premiums etc. The judge drew a distinction between 'objective knowledge' which is the property of the employer and 'subjective knowledge' which is the employee's own property. In this case, however, the judge stated that what the employee innocently remembered of SBJ's business:

'. . . may be objective knowledge or subjective knowledge. Therefore, whether the recollected identity of customers is capable of legitimate protection has to be decided on the evidence of the case. The fact that the employee could remember the customers and go to them to obtain information which the covenant purported to protect could not in itself make the covenant too wide and therefore invalid.'

The court granted SBJ an injunction against Mr Mandy in the particular circumstances of that case.

1.5.17.5 Whistle blowers

'Whistle blowers' are protected in law. It is not possible to prevent the disclosure of wrongdoing under a duty of confidence. Given the interest of the media in business, and the possibility of employees disclosing information to the media, as stated in *Faccenda Chicken* an employer cannot choose what to describe as 'confidential'. The information must have the necessary element of secrecy or confidentiality attaching to it in order to be protected. Even if the information has the necessary element of confidentiality attaching to it to qualify under the *Faccenda Chicken* test disclosure may be legitimate where it is in the public interest that such information should be disclosed.

In *National Irish Bank Ltd v RTE* [1998] 2 ILRM 196 the Supreme Court upheld the disclosure by RTE of confidential information in the public interest. The court balanced the public interest in the maintenance of confidentiality and the public interest in defeating wrongdoing and held that where the publication of confidential information could be of assistance in defeating wrongdoing then the public interest in such publication may outweigh the public interest in the maintenance of confidentiality. Keane J stated:

'The authorities . . . make it clear that where someone is in possession of confidential information establishing that serious misconduct has taken place or is contemplated the courts should not prevent disclosure to persons who have a proper interest in receiving information.'

Disclosure of such information will only be allowed to appropriate persons or authorities and whistle blowing will not be allowed indiscriminately. The dissemination of such information cannot be to the world at large. See *also Gartside v Outram* (1857) 26 LJCH 113 and *Initial Services Ltd v Putterill* [1968] 1 QB 396 and *Re A Company Application* [1989] ICR 44.

In *Camelot v Centaur Communications Ltd* [1998] IRLR 80 Camelot obtained a restraining order preventing Centaur from publishing certain financial information which had been made known to a journalist employed by Centaur. Camelot sought the return of documents in the possession of Centaur to its system, identifying the source of the leak whom they believed to be an employee of theirs. They wanted to identify the source and dismiss the employee as otherwise their activities would continue to suffer damage and in order to protect all of their confidential information from disclosure. In the UK the Contempt of Court Act 1981 restricts the entitlement to the return of information and/or the making of disclosure of a source. The UK Court of Appeal, however, held that it was proper to make an order requiring Centaur to return the confidential documents to enable Camelot to identify the employee responsible for leaking the information and dismiss him. The court stated inter alia:

> '[A]n employer has a legitimate and a continuing interest in enforcing an obligation of loyalty and confidentiality against an employee who has made unauthorised disclosure and use of documents acquired by him in his employment.'

1.5.17.6 Restrictions on competing with employer after termination of employment

There is no common law restriction on a former employee competing with his employer or soliciting the employer's clients and customers in the absence of a specific contractual restriction on doing so. However, if an employee breaches the employer's proprietary rights in confidential information or trade secrets in the course of competing with the former employer, the employer can prevent the unlawful use of such information or trade secrets thereby limiting the damage that might be done by such competition. While employees are entitled to retain information in their heads and to use their established personal contacts and relationships, copying customer lists or details is a breach of the employer's proprietary rights.

In *Robb v Green* [1895] 2 QB 315 Green copied the names and addresses of customers from his employer's books intending to solicit them after he left his employment. The court held that he had a duty not to breach the employer's proprietary rights in the information contained in its books and Green was restrained from using the information he had obtained. This may be contrasted with *Diamond Stylus Co Ltd v Bauden Precision Diamonds Ltd* [1973] RPC 675, where the employee left his employment and solicited his former employer's customers on the basis of information he had retained in his head. The number of customers was quite small and he was able to recall all of the necessary details. The employer failed to obtain an order restricting him.

In *Laughton v Bapp Industrial Supplies Ltd* [1986] ICR 634 two employees in their own time and on their own stationery wrote to their employer's customers advising them that they were setting up a business and, while not directly soliciting business, made it clear that they would be available to do business with them. It was held that there was no breach of the duty of fidelity.

The rights and entitlements of employers and employees must be distilled from the three sources of law on this topic: the common law, the law of contract and a relatively limited intervention of statute law.

1.5.17.7 Soliciting business

There is no common law restriction on former employees canvassing or soliciting business being done or previously done by their former employer. Restrictions on soliciting the business of a former employer may apply where the employer can show that protected confidential information or trade secrets have been violated or, alternatively, where there is a specific contractual commitment against soliciting business. Even where there is such a specific written provision it can be difficult to define what is meant by 'soliciting' or 'solicitation'. The parties may be clear what they mean but the use of such terminology can lead to difficulties and requires great care in draftsmanship. Where possible the use of such a term should be qualified by expressly stating what it means rather than leaving it to a court to define the term.

As to whether 'solicitation' means actively seeking business from customers of the former employer or whether ex-employees can be restrained when they are approached by the customers (i.e. when the customer makes the initial contact), see the contrasting decisions in *John Michael Design plc v Cooke* [1987] 2 All ER 332 and the unreported UK Court of Appeal decision in *Merrill Lynch Pierce Fenner v Besman* 5 December 1985.

The limits of the common law or implied protections of employers are set out in the UK Court of Appeal decision in *Wallace Bogan & Co v Cove* [1997] IRLR 453. The three defendants were solicitors who left the plaintiff firm, each giving four weeks' notice of termination and informing the plaintiffs that they intended setting up together on their own account. They were then placed on garden leave for the notice period by the plaintiffs. After leaving the employment of the plaintiffs the defendants wrote to clients with whom they had dealings while employed with the plaintiffs informing them of the existence of the new firm, the type of work undertaken and offering to act for them if they wished. A number of clients left the plaintiffs and transferred their instructions to the new firm. The contracts under which the defendants had been employed by the plaintiffs did not contain any express covenants restricting their dealings with former clients after their employment terminated. The plaintiffs sought to get such undertakings in writing after the defendants had given notice but the defendants refused to give them. The plaintiffs applied for an injunction in the UK High Court in order to prevent the defendants from canvassing or soliciting their clients. An interlocutory injunction was granted by the UK High Court on the basis that there was a serious issue to be tried as to whether there should be implied into the contracts of service between solicitors and the firms employing them an obligation after their contracts terminate not to canvass or solicit customers of the employing firm with whom they had dealt. The judge in the UK High Court went on to say that he believed 'solicitors are regarded by the law as having a more onerous obligation imposed on them because of the special position which they occupy in relation to the client'. On appeal the UK Court of Appeal reversed the decision, discharged the injunction and, in dismissing the plaintiff's claims, held:

> 'In the absence of an express covenant there is no general restriction on ex-employees canvassing or doing business with customers of their former employers. This rule applies to solicitors as much as to any other trade or profession. In the eye of the law all are equal. Although in canvassing their former employer's clients solicitors are taking advantage of a professional connection with those clients, that connection is no different in principle from the trade connection that, for instance, milk roundsmen may acquire with their employer's customers. Clients and customers alike represent the employer's goodwill which the employer is entitled to protect by an express covenant in reasonable restraint of trade but which is not protected for them by an implied term if they do not bother to extract an express covenant forbidding solicitation after employment has ended. In the present case there was no express covenant restricting the defendant solicitors' dealings with former clients after their employment terminated. Therefore after leaving the plaintiffs and together setting up a new firm they were not in breach of any contractual obligation in writing to the plaintiff's clients and canvassing their business.'

In *International Consulting Services (UK) Ltd v Hart* [2000] IRLR 227 Mr Hart had a restriction in his contract which provided that for a period of twelve months following the termination of his employment he would not 'canvass, solicit, approach, deal or contract with any company, firm or person who at any time during the 12 months immediately preceding the date of termination is or was' negotiating with ICS or was a client or customer or in the habit of dealing with ICS. ICS were dealing with a prospective customer during Mr Hart's employment and after he left he took up a course of dealing with that company. ICS sought to restrict him from doing so. Mr Hart argued that simply because ICS were negotiating with that company they did not have a legitimate interest to protect in restraining him and, further, that a restriction that stopped him dealing with third parties with whom ICS were simply 'negotiating' was too vague to be enforceable. The UK High Court rejected his claims and granted ICS an injunction. The court stated that 'negotiations' must mean more than a customer simply expressing an interest in dealing with a company and stated:

> 'What is required is a discussion between the parties about the terms of a contract which both parties have in view and which is a real possibility. In most cases, whether there have been negotiations will be clear on the facts. Where it is not the court has to make up its mind as part of the ordinary process of interpreting a contract.'

If solicitation arises from the abuse of documentation or information in respect of which the former employer can claim a proprietary interest, as in *Robb v Green* [1895] 2 QB 315, solicitation would be restricted if the use of the information upon which the solicitation was based was to be restricted.

See also *Brightwater v Allen and Robert Walters Ltd* High Court unreported per Laffoy J 12 May 2005.

Peart J gave judgment in *European Paint Importers Limited v O'Callaghan & Others*, 10 August 2005 where an interlocutory injunction had been sought to prevent the defendants competing with the plaintiffs on the basis of the terms of a restrictive covenant applicable to certain of the defendants who were former employees of the plaintiff. In summary, the particular covenant concerned read as follows:

> 'The employee covenants with the company that he will not for the period of one year after ceasing to be employed by the company, in the connection with the carrying of any business similar to or in competition with the business of . . . directly or indirectly seek to procure orders from, or do business with, any person, firm or company who has at any time during the one year immediately preceding such cessation of employment done business with the company.'

For the detailed reasons set out in the judgment the High Court granted an injunction restraining the defendants from doing business and seeking business from customers of the plaintiff. This judgment also distinguished the judgment of Finlay CJ in *Curust Financial Services Ltd v Loewe-Lack-Werk* [1994] 1IR 450, on the basis that damages would not be an adequate remedy for the plaintiff in the particular circumstances of this case and the manner in which the defendants had solicited the plaintiff's entire customer base.

1.5.17.8 Poaching staff

Not all staff of a business are liable to cause significant commercial damage if they leave the employment, but if such staff were to leave and join up with staff that are more obviously liable to cause difficulty, the problems for the transferee can be greatly compounded. Some employers seek to protect their business by the inclusion in contracts of employment of key staff of a restriction preventing such key staff from poaching or enticing away from the employer other staff whom the key people may need to assist them in the event that they leave the employment and become engaged in a competing enterprise. These clauses are not directed against the staff sought to be enticed away but rather are intended to be enforceable against the departing staff who need such people to assist them in their new enterprise. The validity of such clauses is unclear. In the context of non-solicitation clauses, the UK Court of Appeal has cast doubt upon the validity of clauses restraining employees from poaching their former employer's staff.

In *Hanover Insurance Brokers Ltd v Schapiro* [1994] IRLR 82 the court refused to enforce a restrictive covenant under which the employee agreed, for 12 months after termination of employment, not to 'solicit or entice any employees of the company to the intent or effect that such employee terminates that employment'. The court pointed out that 'the employee has the right to work for the employer he wants to work for, if that employer is willing to employ him'. While the court accepted that the goodwill of the employer's business depended upon its staff, it distinguished staff from assets of the company 'like apples or pears or other stock in trade'. The court held:

'[T]he restriction as drawn would apply to all employees of Hanover, irrespective of expertise or juniority and would apply to those who were employees at the time of the solicitation or enticement, even if they had only become employees after all the defendants had left Hanover's service.'

The *Hanover* case was a decision of the UK Court of Appeal at interlocutory stage. The UK Court of Appeal effectively reversed its finding in *Hanover Insurance Brokers* in the later case of *Dawnay Day & Co Ltd v De Braconier D'Alphen* [1997] IRLR 442 when the court held:

'The judge was also entitled to hold that the clause in the managers' service agreements prohibiting them for a year after their employment terminated from soliciting or enticing away anyone who, during the managers' employment, was a director or senior employee of the company, was not unreasonable. An employer's interest in maintaining a stable trained workforce is one which can properly be protected within the limits of reasonableness by means of a non-solicitation covenant, although it does not follow that it will always be so. The employer's need for protection arises because the ex-employee may seek to exploit the knowledge which he has gained of employees' qualifications, rates of pay and so on. In the present case the managers had acquired confidential information of that kind and, in the circumstances, the one-year restriction was justified. It could not be accepted the reference to "senior employee" was so uncertain that the covenant should be regarded as unenforceable on that ground alone. The broad classification was clear and there was no reason to suppose that applying it would present any undue difficulty to anyone with knowledge of the kind of business carried out by the company in the present case. Moreover it was not clear what other formula could be adopted if something more precise and detailed was required.'

See also *Alliance Paper Group plc v Prestwich* [1996] IRLR 25. In *SBJ Stephenson Ltd v Mandy* [2000] IRLR 233, referred to at **1.5.17.4** above, the UK High Court considered a clause restraining Mr Mandy from soliciting employees of the company and held that the stability of the workforce was a legitimate interest which the company was entitled to protect, having invested a great deal in training and because the staff were its prime asset. The clause in that case was upheld as being legitimate and necessary to protect that legitimate interest of the employer.

1.5.17.9 Restrictive covenants permitted in contract

The general common law principle at **1.5.17.1** above is that the law will not uphold restraints on normal trade. The law will, however, allow the restriction in specific contractual terms where the following circumstances exist.

1.5.17.10 Where employer has legitimate interest to protect

This is an area that gives rise to practical difficulty and may tend to be overlooked. Many employers believe that if there is a general prohibition on certain conduct then the former employee cannot engage in such conduct. That is not the case. The employer must isolate and define the interest that is being or may be damaged by the employee; restricting general competition will not be sufficient (*Herbert Morris Ltd v Saxelby* [1916] AC 688 and *Office Angels Ltd v Rainer-Thomas & O'Connor* [1991] IRLR 214).

While it is clear that, at common law, employers are entitled to protect, by way of restraint, a proprietary right such as a customer base, this does not mean that former employees can always be lawfully prevented from taking the company's customers with them when they leave. In *Cantor Fitzgerald (UK) Ltd v Wallace* [1992] IRLR 215, the UK High Court held that an employer could not claim a proprietary interest in, and protect for itself, the customer connection an employee builds up during the course of employment where, in truth, that client connection is a function of the employee's personal qualities, such as personality, temperament and ability to get on with people. In that case, the court declined to enforce a restrictive covenant restraining bond dealers from working in a competing business after their employment terminated, because the court found that the skills and art of the job of producing clients lie in the make-up of the person performing it. In that case the court found that 'there was no magic about the job [the former employees] were doing'. The court heard evidence to the effect that it would not take long to train replacements for the former employees, that replacements could master the technique in three months. The court accepted that it would take longer 'to build up a reputation; and in the end it is that reputation, the speed, ease of dealing with, manner of dealing, trustworthiness in the sense of giving confidence to [clients] . . . that matters'. The court took the view that 'once the technique and procedure have been learned, the rest of the maturity as a broker depended on the personality and character of the individual . . . consequently, some would be better brokers than others because their personality and particular qualities suited the job of broking'. The court held that there was no proprietary right in any of these matters which an employer could claim to protect for himself as part of his business. The plaintiff claimed a proprietary right by virtue of the customer connection, built up while the employee was in his employment and before. The court, however, held that this customer connection was nothing more than those personal qualities to which reference is made above. It is, however, of interest to note that the court distinguished other types of employee 'such as the milk roundsman or the hairdresser [as] a very different category from the defendants'. The court accepted that:

> '. . . just as the milk roundsman may endear himself to the housewives on his round, so an assistant in a ladies hairdressing establishment may well endear herself, either by her personality or by her skill, to the customers of the establishment who come there for service and that constitutes part of the goodwill of the employer's business which the employer is fully entitled to protect.'

However, the court stated that, in such cases, 'a goodwill is built up which attaches to the business and in addition, of course, when dealing with a milkman, for example, he is selling product also'. In that way, the court distinguished between brokers, relying solely on 'speed, ease of dealing with, manner of dealing, trustworthiness in the sense of giving confidence to [clients]' and ladies hairdressers, relying on 'personality or . . . skill'. The distinction is, to say the least, subtle. See *also Wallace Bogan & Co Ltd v Cove* [1997] IRLR 453.

In *Marshall v NM Financial Management Ltd* [1996] IRLR 20 Mr Marshall was employed as a commission agent under a contract which provided that he would only get renewal commissions after his employment terminated if he had at least five years' service at the date of termination, did not work in competition with the company or was aged 65 at termination. The court held that this provision was in reality a restriction on competition, was far broader than was necessary to protect any legitimate interest of the company in seeking to protect its existing clients, and was therefore void as being an unlawful restraint of trade. See also the linked case, involving the same parties, where one of the consequences of the striking down of the restraint was considered (*Marshall v NM Financial Management Ltd* [1997] IRLR 449 which is dealt with at **1.5.17.14** below).

See also *Scully UK Ltd v Lee* [1998] IRLR 259 where Mr Lee was subject to a restriction that he not work with a company involved in certain types of business in which the employing company was involved. The court held that the restriction was such that it was not limited to a business which was in competition with his employers. There was no intention to limit the restriction to competing businesses in the wording of the restriction and the court found no reason to imply such a restriction. The restrictive covenant was therefore too wide and was struck down. This was against the background that the employee wished to work with a company which was not competing with the previous employer but used certain equipment and carried out certain processes similar to those manufactured and sold by the previous employer, albeit not in competition with it. This, not surprisingly, was held to be too wide. In this case also the UK High Court judge, in striking down provisions of the restrictions, severed them from the balance of restrictions which were upheld against the employee.

The concept of 'legitimate interest' was also examined and applied in *International Consulting Services (UK) Ltd v Hart* [2000] IRLR 227 and *SBJ Stephenson Ltd v Mandy* [2000] IRLR 233.

1.5.17.11 Restraint must be reasonable in terms of conduct sought to be restricted

Such conduct or activity must relate to the conduct or activity the employee engaged in while working with the employer and not be any wider (*Stenhouse Ltd v Phillips* [1974] AC 391).

1.5.17.12 Duration of restriction must be reasonable

A thread running through all of the recent cases on restrictive covenants and their duration, is the assessment by the courts of the time it will take for the employer to take the necessary steps to protect the goodwill of the business and measuring the reasonableness of the restrictions sought to be imposed against such necessary time period or, alternatively, only allowing the restriction to continue for whatever time is determined to be, or have been, necessary to allow the employer to take steps to limit the damage done by the departure of the employee (*Cantor Fitzgerald (UK) Ltd v Wallace* [1992] IRLR 215 at **1.5.17.10** above). If, therefore, a restriction were to be stated to last for two years but the court held that only six months was necessary to adequately protect the goodwill, the restriction is likely to be struck down as being unreasonable. If an employee is prevented from working in a competitive area for even a short time after leaving the employer, the impact of the employee's departure will be greatly lessened. It is hard to conceive of a situation where an employer would need more than one year to minimise the effect of an employee's departure and, if the effect is to be long term, the employer can do a lot in that period to protect his interests into the future. In many cases six months or less might well suffice. See also *Dentmaster (UK) Ltd v Kent* [1997] IRLR 636.

1.5.17.13 Geographical extent of restriction must be reasonable

In *Commercial Plastics Ltd v Vincent* [1965] 1 QB 623 it was held that where an employer had a worldwide restrictive covenant, but only operated in the UK, the covenant was geographically too wide and was unenforceable. A restriction on competing within a 25-mile radius of the employer's business may be too wide if the employer's customers are all within a 20-mile radius.

In *Spencer v Marchington* [1988] IRLR 392 the court held that 'a restriction is too wide to be enforced if its area was more than was adequate to protect the employer's legitimate business interests'. In *Marley Tile Co v Johnson* [1982] IRLR 75 the employee was subject to a restrictive covenant covering more than 2,000 customers in the area of Devon and Cornwall. The restriction related to 'within any area in which you have been employed by the employer at any time during the 12 months before . . . termination'. It happened that Johnson was promoted during that 12-month period which meant that, in two separate periods within the 12 months, he had operated in two different areas. The court held that the combined area thereby restricted was too wide in that Johnson could not possibly have known of, or come into contact with, more than a small percentage of the company's customers in the area. Lord Denning stated in the course of the judgment:

> 'Taking the size of the area, the number of customers, the class of products—because Marley have many lines other than roofing and tiling—it seems to me that the covenant is too wide to be reasonable.'

The courts will look at geographical restrictions, not just as to their extent but also as to whether they are appropriate or necessary. *In Office Angels Ltd v Rainer-Thomas & O'Connor* [1991] IRLR 214 the court examined a restriction precluding the defendants from opening an office of an employment agency anywhere within an area of about 1.2 square miles, including most of the City of London, for a period of six months and held that it was not appropriate or necessary for the protection of the plaintiff's connection with their clients holding:

> 'The area restriction was not an appropriate form of covenant because it would do little to protect the plaintiff's connection with their clients. The client's orders were placed over the telephone and it was of no concern to them where the office was located. It was unlikely therefore that the restriction would serve to prevent the defendants from attracting the custom of clients with whom they had dealings during their employment with the plaintiffs.'

In *Howlis & Co v Stocks* [2000] IRLR 712 the UK Court of Appeal examined a restriction on an assistant solicitor restraining him from setting up a competing business within 10 miles of the firm's office. Taking into account the geographical extent of that 10 miles and the cities and towns covered by it the UK County Court judge and the UK Court of Appeal on appeal held that the ambit of the covenant covering a 10-mile radius was reasonable.

1.5.17.14 Blue pencil clauses

It is frequently provided in contracts that if any particular provision of the agreement is held to be unenforceable then first the unenforceable clause is to be severed from other covenants and, secondly, the court is called upon to substitute what it considers to be reasonable. These two elements must be considered in drafting or seeking to rely on restrictive covenants and supportive clauses.

The general principle is that severance will not be applied by the courts as enunciated in *Mason v Provident Clothing and Supply Co Ltd* [1913] AC 724, where it was held that there should only be severance if the enforceable part is clearly severable. This line was followed in *Living Design (Home Improvements) Ltd v Davidson* [1994] IRLR 69 where the Scottish Court of Session held, per Lord Coulsfield, that:

> '[T]here should be severance only if the enforceable part is clearly severable and even so, only where it is of trivial importance or technical and not part of the main import or substance of the clause. In the present case I think it very doubtful whether the offending part of the clause could be said not to be part of its main import and substance and it is certainly not trivial.'

See also *Attwood v Lamont* [1923] KB 571. In *J A Mont (UK) Ltd v Mills* [1993] IRLR 172, Simon Brown LJ indicated:

> '[A]s a matter of policy, . . . the court should not too urgently strive to find within restrictive covenants, ex facie too wide, implicit limitations such as alone could justify their imposition.'

Simon Brown LJ went on to state that, in the event that the courts proved too amenable to limiting restrictive covenants which were, on their face, too wide, 'what possible reason would employers ever have to impose restraints in appropriately limited terms?'

In *Marshall v NM Financial Management Ltd* [1997] IRLR 449 the UK Court of Appeal, having already held that a restriction within a clause was unreasonable and unenforceable, was then asked to consider whether the balance of the clause, which gave rise to a commission entitlement, should stand. The court held:

> '[T]he plaintiff . . . was entitled to enforce those parts of a contractual clause providing for payment of post-termination renewal commission which will not void an unreasonable restraint of trade. That part of the clause was excised did not mean the whole of the

clause should be struck out. A party who has been freed from an invalid restraint of trade can enforce the remainder of the contract without it unless the invalid restraint forms "the whole or substantially the whole consideration" for the promise. The contract will be upheld even if the consideration for the promise of the promisee includes an invalid restraint. It will be struck down in its entirety only if, in substance and regardless of its form, it is an agreement for an invalid restraint.'

In *Marshall* the court was anxious to avoid removing a clause and by what was left consequentially imposing on the parties a condition that was radically different from what was originally contemplated. In severing the restriction on being paid renewal commissions in certain circumstances the court was anxious that it not deprive Mr Marshall of the payment. The court held that he had earned the commissions and was entitled to them without the burden of the restrictions attaching.

In *Sadler v Imperial Life Assurance Co of Canada Ltd* [1988] IRLR 388 it was held that severance could be effected if the following conditions were met:

(a)   the unenforceable provision is capable of being removed without the necessity of adding to or modifying the wording of what remains;

(b)   the remaining terms continue to be supported by adequate consideration;

(c)   the removal of the unenforceable provision does not so change the character of the contract that it becomes 'not the sort of contract that the parties entered into at all'; and

(d)   that the severance must be consistent with the public policy underlying the avoidance of the offending term.

The courts have always had an understandable reluctance to rewrite a contract that at least one of the parties got wrong in the first place, but will allow severance where appropriate. In *Hinton and Higgs (UK) Ltd v Murphy* [1989] IRLR 519 Lord Dervaird observed:

'It has often been said that the courts will not make contracts for the parties. Here however as it seems to me the parties have agreed in advance they will accept as continuing to bind them such part of the arrangements which they have made as the court finds by deletion only to be alterations which permit the restriction to be regarded as reasonable . . . I do not see why the court should refuse to perform that role, not being one of rewriting the contract but of selecting that version of it which the parties have inter alia made with each other and enabling the bargain as so modified to stand.'

Many agreements contain a provision that by signing the document the employee accepts that the restrictions contained therein are reasonable. The courts have no difficulty in ignoring these provisions. The courts have been invited to defeat such provision by accepting the argument of economic duress but the simple answer was given in *Hinton and Higgs* where the court held such a clause to be an attempt to oust its jurisdiction and therefore unenforceable.

1.5.17.15   Employer's repudiation of contract

An employer who repudiates a contract or is involved in fundamental breach will normally be unable to rely on restrictive covenants in that contract which effectively crystallised as a result of the employer's breach.

In *Cantor Fitzgerald International v Callaghan* [1999] IRLR 234 the defendants were employed by the plaintiffs as dealer brokers. Their contracts contained restrictive covenants aimed at preventing them working for competitors for a specific period. As part of an improved salary package aimed at retaining their services, the plaintiffs made non-forgivable loans to the staff with an assurance that there would be no tax liability during the period of the loan. Due to an error by the company the Revenue was misinformed about the nature of the loans and raised a tax charge on the loans. One of the plaintiffs' directors tried to sort out matters and to make money available to the staff to deal with the tax liabilities. Another director, however, intervened and decided not to advance money to meet the tax liabilities as an incentive to the employees to work harder. The employees handed in a joint written notice of termination intending to go to work for a competitor. In defending a claim by the company to enforce the restrictive covenants in their contracts the employees contended that the company could not rely on the restrictions as they were in repudiatory breach of contract in refusing to pay them the money to meet their tax liabilities on the loans which they had been assured would be tax-free. The UK High Court held against them but, on appeal, the UK Court of Appeal held that the employer was in fundamental breach in refusing to pay the employees sums due under their salary packages in connection with assurances given to them about tax liabilities. The UK Court of Appeal held that this was a deliberate refusal by an employer and not a mere failure or delay in paying agreed remuneration. The court held that consequently the entire foundation of the contract of employment was undermined and the injunction was discharged.

1.5.17.16 'Springboard' injunctions

Injunctive relief may be granted to employers where a departing employee seeks to use or rely on trade secrets or confidential information belonging to the former employer as a springboard to allow a more immediate advantage in setting up the competing business than might otherwise be available if the employee were to act lawfully and only use information, the use of which is permitted in law. The UK Court of Appeal held in *Roger Bullivant Ltd v Ellis* [1987] IRLR 491 that it is unlawful for an employee setting up a business on his own account to use confidential information belonging to his former employers as a springboard to establish himself in competition with them and such use will be restrained by injunction—but any such injunction should be limited to the period during which the unfair advantage may be expected to continue. In many cases where injunctions are granted they are granted on an interlocutory basis which means that they remain in effect until the full trial of the action. Depending on how long the case takes to come to full hearing will therefore determine how long the restriction remains in force rather than, in line with normal legal principle, remaining in force only as long as it should.

In *Roger Bullivant* Mr Ellis set up a competing business and, on leaving the plaintiffs, took with him a large number of documents including a card index listing the company's trade contacts. The documents were recovered on the execution of an Anton Piller order and the employers then applied for and were granted an injunction restraining the former employee until after judgment in an action for damages, from entering into or fulfilling contracts made with or through any person whose name appeared on the card index. The injunction was granted by the UK High Court until the trial of the full action. The UK Court of Appeal was asked to decide whether the injunction ought to have been granted at all and if so whether it ought to have been granted until the trial of the action or for a more limited period. In its decision the UK Court of Appeal made the following statements:

(1) 'The principle established in *Robb v Green* [1895] 2 QB 315 that an employee's duty of fidelity would be broken if he makes or copies a list of the employer's customers for use after his employment ends or deliberately memorises such a list even though there is no general restriction on an ex-employee canvassing or doing business with customers of his former employer, should be steadfastly maintained. The principle is one of no more than fair and honourable dealings. The plaintiffs were entitled to an injunction restraining use of the information contained in the card index.'

(2) 'An injunction to prevent unfair advantage being taken of the springboard that may be gained by the misuse of confidential information should not normally extend beyond the period for which the unfair advantage may reasonably be expected to continue. The law does not restrain lawful competition and in restraining unlawful competition it seeks to protect the injured and not punish the

guilty. In the present case as the restrictive covenant contained in the contract was for a period of one year after termination they could not reasonably expect, and the law could not reasonably allow, a longer period and therefore regardless of when the full trial was to take place the restriction should only apply for that period of one year.'

See the High Court interlocutory injunction decision in *European Paint Importers Ltd v O'Callaghan & Others*, 10 August 2005 per Peart J unreported and *Curust Financial Services Ltd v Loewe-Lack-Werk* [1994] 1 IR 450.

1.5.17.17   Competition Act, 1991

The enforceability of restrictive covenants was altered by the provisions of the Competition Act, No 24 of 1991.

Section 4(1) of the Act provides inter alia, as follows:

> '... All agreements between undertakings, decisions by associations of undertakings and concerted practices which have as their object or effect, the prevention, restriction or distortion of competition in trade of any goods or services in the State or any part of the State are prohibited and void ...'

While not specifically aimed at employment contracts (and indeed, many commentators are of the view that the Act is an inappropriate means of controlling the employer/employee relationship), the Competition Authority has, in a number of cases, considered employment contracts which include restrictions placed on employees or former employees.

1.5.17.17.1   *Notice on employee agreements*

The Competition Authority, on 15 September 1992, issued a Notice on Employee Agreements and the Competition Act, which was published in Iris Oifigiúil on 18 September 1992. The Notice was issued on foot of a number of requests regarding the status of employee contracts or agreements under the Competition Act. The Authority indicated its position relating to such agreements as follows:

(a)   in general, employees are not deemed to be undertakings within the meaning of the Act, as employees normally act on behalf of an undertaking and do not therefore constitute an undertaking themselves;

(b)   accordingly, an agreement between an employer and an employee is not, in the Authority's view, an agreement between undertakings and therefore does not fall within the ambit of section 4(1) of the Competition Act. Such an agreement is not therefore notifiable to the Authority;

(c)   once an employee leaves an employer and establishes his/her own business, the Competition Authority then regards such an individual as an undertaking. In such circumstances an agreement with a former employer will be regarded as an agreement between undertakings, which is within the scope of section 4(1);

(d)   while a single agreement between an individual and a former employer containing a non-competition clause might not have a substantial impact on competition, the effect of a network of such agreements could greatly restrict competition by foreclosing the market and the Authority stated its view that it would be difficult for such an agreement to satisfy the requirements specified for the grant of a licence under the Act.

In issuing this notice, the Competition Authority acknowledged that it is adopting a similar position to that taken by the European Commission in *Suiker-Unie v Commission* [1975] ECR 1663 (Case 40/73) concerning Article 85.1 of the EC Treaty (upon which section 4(1) is based). The guiding principle adopted by the Commission in that case was that of economic unity—where an employee is in the employment of an employer, they are effectively deemed to operate as one economic unit. However, once the employee leaves that employment, the economic interests of the parties are no longer similar and the employee may be regarded as a separate and independent undertaking.

The further implications of the notice are that the Competition Act does not apply to employees who are competing during their employment, or employees who subsequently leave that employment and take up new employment with a new firm.

1.5.17.17.2 *Apex v Murtagh*

The leading decision of the Competition Authority on employer/employee agreements is *Apex Fire Protection v Murtagh* [1993] ELR 201. Mr Murtagh had been in the employment of Apex and left that employment to establish his own business. His contract of employment included a covenant which prevented him, for a period of two years after termination, from soliciting persons who were customers of Apex for two years prior to termination, and also included a confidentiality clause preventing him from disclosing information. Apex sought an injunction to prevent Mr Murtagh from breaching the terms of this contract, and notified the agreement to the Competition Authority requesting a certificate, or in the alternative, a licence.

Section 4 was used by Mr Murtagh as a defence in the Circuit Court. The injunction was granted on the basis that damages were not an adequate remedy, and pending the Competition Authority decision. It should be noted that this was a motion for an injunction only and was not a hearing of the case on its merits and cannot be taken to reflect judicial opinion on the interpretation of the Competition Act, 1991.

The Competition Authority, in its decision which issued in June 1993, refused a certificate or a licence in this case.

The Authority distinguished between a non-competition clause (which prevents an individual from entering the market on his own account) and a non-solicitation clause. In relation to the non-solicitation clause, Apex had argued that the restraints were justified because of the knowledge which their former employee had acquired during the course of his employment with the company and it further argued that the company was entitled to protect itself by virtue of the employment and training which it had provided to Mr Murtagh.

The non-solicitation clause was held to be overly restrictive and in the course of the hearing, Apex agreed to modify the clause to limit its applicability.

In relation to the confidentiality clause, Apex gave an assurance that the clause would only be used to protect confidential business information, and the Competition Authority accepted this, notwithstanding that the clause itself referred to 'any information'.

The Competition Authority held that the restrictions imposed went beyond what was required to protect the legitimate interests of the company and emphasised that any restrictions imposed should not exceed what was absolutely necessary to protect the interests of the company.

The clause was held to be in breach of section 4(1) because of the two-year time restraints which, the Competition Authority felt, were excessive. The Authority stated that while the European Commission had allowed a two-year period for the transfer of the goodwill of a business, the same period could not apply to employment contracts. The following conclusions can be drawn from the *Apex* decision:

    (a)   a business which is owned and controlled by an ex-employee can constitute an undertaking, bringing the contract with the former employer within the ambit of the Act;

    (b)   trade secrets and direct customer connections constitute legitimate proprietary interests of an employer which may warrant protection;

(c)   the legality of restraints in any agreement depends on the facts of each individual case and the position of the employee in the firm;

(d)   the decision in *Apex* implies that a one-year restraint is acceptable in order to allow the former employer to re-establish customer goodwill, following on the departure of the former employee;

(e)   with regard to confidentiality clauses, the decisions of the Competition Authority to date have shown no notable deviation from the common law position. The *Apex* case makes it clear that it is necessary that an employer should be able to entrust confidential information to employees and the employer should be able to rely on such information being used only on the terms on which it is disclosed.

In the subsequent case of *Cambridge v Imari*, Competition Authority Decision No 24, the Authority held a part-owner and managing director of Imari, who was also an employee of the company, to be an undertaking within the meaning of the Competition Act.

1.5.18   TERMINATION OF CONTRACT

1.5.18.1   Notice

Notice is probably one of, if not the, most important provisions in a contract of employment as far as an employer is concerned. In the absence of agreed notice an employer is obliged to give 'reasonable' notice. What is or is not reasonable may well be open to dispute allowing or obliging the parties to resort to the courts. An agreed or specified notice period will avoid litigation in this regard at least. Where a person is dismissed with notice paid for the notice period and not required to work it, the employment does not come to an end until the end of the period of notice (*Adams v GKN Sankey Ltd* [1980] IRLR 416).

1.5.18.2   Reason for termination

Prior to 1977 a dismissed employee had only one form of legal remedy available, the breach of contract action known as wrongful dismissal. In order for an employee to succeed in a claim of wrongful dismissal it is necessary to show that a term of the contract was breached by the employer. It is rare to find a term in a contract that prevents or limits an employer's right to terminate. The most notable exceptions are specified-purpose or fixed-term contracts. Most contracts of employment are of indefinite duration and will continue in force until terminated by either party. The rights of both parties to terminate at common law are similar. A contract may be terminated on the giving of the requisite notice provided for in the contract. If notice is not specifically provided for in the contract, the common law implies the right of either party to terminate on the giving of reasonable notice. Following the normal common law principle of endeavouring to place the parties in no better position than they would have been had the contract been properly terminated an employee's damages will be limited to what he would have earned if proper notice had been given in accordance with the terms of the contract (*Sanders v Ernest A Neale Ltd* [1974] ICR 565; *Ridge v Baldwin* [1964] AC 40; *Hill v C A Parsons & Co Ltd* [1972] Ch 305).

A prudent employer will provide a specific period of notice which will normally obviate any dispute and avoid a wrongful dismissal action unless the employer specifically refuses to honour the notice entitlement of the employee.

At common law an employer has the power to dismiss an employee for any reason, or for no reason, once appropriate notice is given—or where a notice period is not specified 'reasonable' notice is given. This long-standing principle was restated by the High Court in *Sheehy v Ryan and Moriarty* [2004] ELR 87 and *Carey v Independent Newspapers (Ireland) Ltd* [2004] ELR 45.

1.5.18.3   **Contract silent as to notice**

If a contract is silent as to notice entitlement it is a matter for the courts to assess what they consider to be reasonable notice in all the circumstances of the employment (see Dix and Crump, *Contracts of Employment* (6th edn) pp 137–38). In determining what notice would be reasonable in any particular case the courts will have regard to the following criteria:

(a)   job function—the more senior a person is in an organisation the more likely he is to be held to be entitled to a longer period of notice;

(b)   length of service;

(c)   age and experience of the employee; and

(d)   custom and practice in the particular employment if such exists (*Produce Brokers Co Ltd v Olympia Oil and Cake Co Ltd* [1916] 2 KB 296). It is sometimes thought that reasonable notice will relate to the frequency at which remuneration is paid, e.g. monthly or weekly. That is not the case. Neither, as stated above, will regard be had to statutory notice entitlement as provided for in the Minimum Notice and Terms of Employment Act, 1973 (as amended). If payment is made in lieu of notice this will normally suffice to cover an employee's entitlement as it would equate to the amount that he would expect to receive from a court in any event.

The absence of a notice provision in the contract will not be construed by the courts as granting employment for life (see *Salt v Power Plant Co Ltd* [1936] 3 All ER 322 and *McClelland v Northern Ireland General Hospital Services Board* [1957] 2 All ER 129). Even where the term 'permanent' is used or where a job is described as 'permanent and pensionable' this does not mean that it cannot be terminated by reasonable notice (*Walsh v Dublin Health Authority* [1998] ILTR 82 and *Grehan v North Eastern Health Board* [1989] IR 422).

1.5.18.4   **Length of notice period**

In *Lyons v M F Kent & Co (International) Ltd (in liquidation)* [1996] ELR 103 the High Court considered the length of notice to which an employee was entitled at common law. The court first held that the aged common law doctrine of 'general hiring', which implied employment for fixed periods of one year at a time, had fallen into disuse but that in any event it did not apply in the instant case. In considering what constituted 'reasonable' notice in all the circumstances of this particular case Costello J was of the view that he got little assistance from decided cases because each case must depend on its own facts. He held that the modern world is far different even from the world of twenty years ago. In considering what was reasonable the court took the following into account:

(a)   the plaintiff's status within a group of companies;

(b)   the fact that he was engaged in very substantial work abroad;

(c)   he carried very considerable responsibilities related to the size and nature of the contracts in which he was involved and the work took place in foreign countries;

(d)   he was a professionally qualified person; and

(e)   he was required to work abroad even though he was Irish and was based with his family in Ireland.

Costello J asked what would be said by the 'officious bystander' in the particular circumstances of this case and he considered it unlikely that a person would leave his profession in this country and travel abroad without at least a minimum of six months' notice and, in this case, considered 12 months' notice to be appropriate. In *Carey v Independent Newspapers (Ireland) Ltd* [2004] ELR 45 the High Court held that a notice period of six months was appropriate and reasonable notice for the employee in that case.

1.5.18.5 Clear and unequivocal

In order for notice to be valid it must be clear and unequivocal with a specific expiry date or be stated to occur on the happening of a specific event. Notice does not have to be in writing—unless specifically provided for in the contract (*Hughes v Gwynned County Council* [1977] ICR 436). Calculation of notice is the period starting on the day after notice is given. If therefore an employee is told during the course of a working day that his employment is to terminate the notice does not start to run until the following day (*West v Kneels Ltd* [1986] IRLR 430). Notice may be given at any time and during periods of illness or leave, but not maternity leave, as notice given during a period of maternity leave is deemed to be void under maternity legislation which is dealt with in more detail in Chapter 3: Working time and Statutory Leave Entitlements.

Regard must also be had to the provisions of the Minimum Notice and Terms of Employment Act, 1973 (as amended). Section 4 sets out specific notice that an employer is required to give to an employee who is covered by the legislation. The notice is based on a sliding scale starting with one week's notice for those employed for up to two years with a maximum entitlement of eight weeks' notice for those employed for 15 years or more. In all cases the notice required to be given by the employee is one week's notice. If the contractual notice is less than the statutory notice there would be a breach of the statute unless the statutory notice is given. If the contractual notice is longer than the statutory notice it will be deemed to include the statutory notice so two periods of notice do not have to be given and they can run concurrently rather than consecutively. The requirements of giving valid notice under the 1973 Act are dealt with by the Supreme Court in *Bollands Ltd (in receivership) v Ward* [1988] ILRM 382. See *also Waterford Multiport Ltd (in liquidation) v Fagan* [1999] ELR 185 and *Irish Leathers Ltd v Minister for Labour* [1986] IR 177. If an employee is dismissed by reason of misconduct he loses his entitlement to notice under the 1973 Act in terms of section 8 (*Leopard Security Ltd v Campbell* [1997] ELR 227).

1.5.18.6 Expiry of notice period

Where a person is dismissed with notice, paid for the notice period and not required to work it, the employment does not come to an end until the end of the period of notice (*Adams v GKN Sankey Ltd* [1980] IRLR 416). Regard should also be had to the statutory date of dismissal as defined under the Unfair Dismissals Acts, 1977–2001 which effectively provide that the date of dismissal shall be the date notice expires whether the notice is given or not and whether it is worked or whether payment in lieu is made (Unfair Dismissals Act, 1977, section 1). Where the employee is deemed to have lost his right to notice this provision would not have effect and the date of dismissal would be the last day worked. This is particularly relevant where long periods of notice, such as three months or more, are allowed for in a contract. This can cause difficulty in the transfer of an undertaking. A transferee might therefore take the view, mistakenly, that an employee with less than one year's continuous service would not have the right to claim unfair dismissal against the transferee in the event of his employment terminating and his seeking to initiate a claim under unfair dismissal legislation. Given that notice is added to the actual period of employment the notice period may carry the employee over the threshold of the one year's continuous service even though he may have only worked for the transferor for a relatively short period of time and not be an obvious employee covered by the Transfer of Undertakings Directive and Regulations at the time of transfer. With a six-month notice provision an employee is effectively covered by unfair dismissal legislation on the expiry of six months at work. An employer may place an employee on what is known as 'garden leave' during a notice period whether that notice is given by the employer or the employee.

In *Marshall (Cambridge) Ltd v Hamblin* [1994] IRLR 260 the employee had given notice and the employer cut it short but made payment in lieu of notice. The employee was entitled, as part of his contract, to commission on vehicles sold. The payment of commission was described by the contract as being 'at the absolute discretion of the company'. Commission at times constituted as much as 75 per cent of the employee's earnings. It was held that the employee had no right to work out his notice. Until such time as the notice period expired the contract of employment continued and the employer was entitled to utilise a term of that contract to bring the employment to an end at an earlier date and, where it was specified in the contract, make a payment in lieu of the remuneration that would have been earned during the notice period. The position was held not to be affected by the fact that the employee derived a major part of his remuneration from a discretionary commission payment. It was not accepted that it was an implied term of the employee's contract that the employers would not prevent the employee from placing himself in a position whereby the employer's discretion could be exercised and that the employers were in breach of that term in refusing to allow him to work out his notice.

It was held in *Marshall* that the nature of the payment in lieu fell within the category of what damages the employee might be entitled to for breach of contract. As there was no contractual entitlement to the commission there was no entitlement to be paid it during the notice period. The courts will not have regard to the provisions of the Minimum Notice and Terms of Employment Acts, 1973–1991 unless that legislation has been specifically incorporated into the contract. Notice provision might also cover a right to temporarily suspend the employment contract with or without pay due to shortage of work, during the currency of an investigation or because of a requirement for the employee to work for short time.

1.5.18.7 Punitive damages—termination and the duty of trust and confidence

The mutual duty of trust and confidence resting on both the employer and the employee has been outlined in a number of cases (see *TSB Bank plc v Harris* [2000] IRLR 157). If the employee is in breach this generally entitles the employer to terminate the contract but it would be rare that the employer would have the right to seek damages from the employee unless some specific and measurable damage was caused wilfully by the employee. If the employer is in breach the employee may leave and claim that he has been constructively dismissed. In some cases the actual reason for, or manner of, dismissal may be without foundation or substance, improper and consequently damaging to the employee. In general punitive damages or damages for distress or inconvenience are not available following a dismissal regardless of the manner in which the dismissal is carried out. Damages are limited to recoverable losses which cover all incidents of remuneration to which the employee was contractually entitled. It is well established that punitive damages cannot be awarded against the employer. The leading case *Addis v Gramophone Co Ltd* [1909] AC 488, was affirmed in *Bliss v South East Thames Regional Health Authority* [1987] ICR 700 and *O'Laoire v Jackel International Ltd* [1991] ICR 718.

A significant move away from the general principle was made, albeit in exceptional circumstances, in *Malik v Bank of Credit and Commerce International SA (in compulsory liquidation)* [1997] IRLR 462. The plaintiffs were bank managers dismissed on grounds of redundancy by the provisional liquidators of BCCI. They claimed that their mere association with BCCI at the moment of its liquidation and the fraudulent practices which subsequently came to light caused them considerable personal disadvantage and stigma in the marketplace. They contended that there was an implied term in their contracts of employment that the employer would not, without reasonable and proper cause, conduct itself in a manner calculated to be likely to destroy or seriously damage the relationship of confidence and trust that must exist between an employer and an employee and in their circumstances, in light of such a breach, they were entitled to punitive, or what were described as 'stigma', damages. The UK Court of Appeal held:

(a) the managers were not entitled to damages for breach of contract in respect of losses which allegedly resulted from the stigma attaching to them as former employees of BCCI and the adverse effect that had on their employment prospects; and

(b)   'stigma damages' cannot be recovered where an employee claims that his reputation has been damaged by the employer's breach of an implied term.

1.5.18.8   Principles of punitive damages awards

The UK Court of Appeal held that there were three well-established principles to be derived from the precedent cases as follows:

(a)   an employer has no obligation to employ or pay an employee for longer than the period of notice for which the contract provides;

(b)   damages are not recoverable for the manner of the breach, an award of exemplary damages being confined in practice to certain specific claims in tort; and

(c)   damages are not recoverable for damage to or loss of an existing reputation. However, this principle does not apply where loss is sustained as the foreseeable consequence of a breach of contract in specific contracts such as apprenticeships or the promotion or preservation of a reputation, e.g. advertising or the opportunity to appear in a prestigious place or part for an actor.

In so holding the UK Court of Appeal stated that the object of the employment contracts in *Malik v Bank of Credit and Commerce International* was to employ, not to promote or preserve existing reputations or to prepare for future employment. The House of Lords on appeal reversed the finding of the UK Court of Appeal in relation to stigma damages and held as follows.

(a)   The Court of Appeal had erred in holding the appellants could not bring claims for damages for financial losses allegedly suffered because the stigma attaching to their reputations as former employees of BCCI put them at a disadvantage in the labour market. The court had wrongly decided the case on the basis that there is a positive rule debarring recovery of damages for injury to an existing reputation.

(b)   Damages for loss of reputation caused by breach of contract may be awarded provided that a relevant breach of contract can be established and the requirements of causation, remoteness and mitigation can be satisfied. If conduct by the employer in breach of the implied term of trust and confidence prejudicially affects an employee's future prospects so as to give rise to continuing financial losses and it was reasonably foreseeable that such a loss was a serious possibility, in principle damages in respect of the loss should be recoverable.

(c)   The observations in *Addis v Gramophone Co Ltd* [1909] AC 488 could not be read as precluding the recovery of damages where the manner of dismissal involved a breach of the trust and confidence term and that caused financial loss. *Addis* was decided in the days before this implied term had been adumbrated. Now that the term exists, and is normally implied in every contract of employment, damages for its breach should be assessed in accordance with contractual principles. There is no basis for distinguishing in this respect between wrongful dismissal following a breach of the trust and confidence term, constructive dismissal following a breach of the trust and confidence term and a breach of the trust and confidence term which, as in the present case, only becomes known after the contract had ended for other reasons.

(d)   An employer which operates its business in a dishonest and corrupt manner is in breach of the implied contractual term of trust and confidence. In agreeing to work for the employer an employee, whatever his status, cannot be taken to have agreed to work in furtherance of a dishonest business.

(e)   In the present case therefore, on the assumption that BCCI had operated its business in a corrupt and dishonest manner, it was in breach of the implied term of trust and confidence. Since it was arguable that the employees might be able to establish as a matter of fact that the corruption associated with the bank under-mined their employment prospects causing them financial loss there was a good cause for action and the appeal would be allowed.

1.5.18.9 Employer's wrongdoing

In a follow-on case to *Malik v Bank of Credit and Commerce International* the UK High Court clarified an employer's obligations in relation to its own wrongdoing and stated that there is no duty on an employer to disclose its breaches of contract.

In *Bank of Credit and Commerce International SA v Ali* [1999] IRLR 226 the defendant and others were made redundant by BCCI as part of a restructuring. They received ex gratia payments which they accepted 'in full and final settlement of all or any claims whether under statute, common law, or in equity of whatsoever nature that exist or may exist'. Following *Malik* Ali and others wished to make claims against BCCI for stigma damages. The bank contended that they could not do so by virtue of the terms of the severance agreement they had signed. The employees argued that they were unaware of the bank's wrongdoing at the time they signed and that the agreement was invalid because the bank had failed to disclose that it was insolvent in carrying on a dishonest business and that had they known this they would not have signed the agreement. The UK High Court held that the agreement the employees signed 'was not invalidated by the employer's failure to disclose to the employees that, at the time the agreement was signed, it was carrying on a dishonest business and was insolvent'. The court went on to state:

> 'Since the agreement was a "compromise" rather than a "release" the employer did not owe the employees a duty to disclose its prior misconduct or breaches of contract before entering into the agreement. In the case of a release there is a duty of disclosure on the party obtaining the release of such claims against him but there is no such obligation in the case of a compromise. The essential difference between a compromise and a release is that in the case of a compromise there is a release of claims for valuable consideration and in the case of a release there is no such consideration. . . . [T]he employer was not under a duty by reason of the implied term of trust and confidence in an employment contract, to disclose, when it entered into the compromise agreement, that it had com-mitted breaches of the contract. . . . [T]hat the employees did not know at the time they signed the compromise agreement that they had common law claims against the bank did not amount to a unilateral mistake such as to entitle the employees to impugn the agreement. The agreement was designed to afford the employer protection against any further claims by the employees and the employer agreed to make an additional pay-ment for obtaining this protection. The fact that the employees did not focus on the claims covered by the agreement could not lead to any re-opening of the bargain. The real complaint of the employees was that, with the knowledge acquired since the col-lapse of the employer of the extent of its wrongdoing and, since the commencement of the proceedings in *Malik*, of the possibility of substantial claims and damages in respect of the loss occasioned to them by such wrongdoing they now repent of what they see as a bad bargain and wish to be free of it. Such a complaint cannot vitiate a contract or give grounds for relief.'

1.5.19 SEARCH CLAUSE

Any attempt to search employees without their consent would constitute assault and battery. It may also constitute false imprisonment and/or give rise to defamation claims. Employers frequently provide therefore in contracts of employment that they have the right to search employees, their baggage, locker, vehicles etc. Given that there would be a considerable practical problem if an employee refused to be searched the employer may seek to resolve that difficulty in advance by further providing in such a clause that in the event of the employee refusing to submit to search this will be treated as misconduct (or gross misconduct if that is the definition in common use within the employment) and process the refusal through the disciplinary procedure. Employers frequently emphasise that they take a very serious view of such a refusal and dismissal is a possibility in such events.

1.5.20   PATENTS, COPYRIGHTS AND INVENTIONS

The common law position on patents, copyrights and inventions is set out in *Sterling Engineering Co Ltd v Patchett* [1955] 1 All ER 369 and *British Syphon Co Ltd v Homewood* [1955] 2 All ER 897. The Copyright and Related Rights Act, 2000 provides at section 23(1) that the copyright in material made in the course of a person's employment belongs to the employer as first owner of the copyright and not to the author, subject to any agreement between the parties. In some instances it can be difficult to ascertain whether the material sought to be copyrighted, and which relates to business of the employer and the work done by the employee, was actually created or made in the course of the employment, such as when created or made in the employee's spare time (*Byrne v Statist Co* [1914] 1 KB 622 and *Stevenson Jordan and Harrison Ltd v Macdonald and Evans* [1952] ILTR 101). The exception contained in section 23(2) in respect of journalists allows for limited use of the material by the author (*Beloff v Pressdram Ltd* [1973] 1 All ER 241 and *Re Sunday Tribune Ltd* [1984] IR 505).

An employer is also entitled to protect inventions under the terms of the Patents Acts, 1964 and 1992. The position is less clear under the Patents Acts as there is no specific provision in the Acts determining when employees' inventions might be the property of their employers. Disputes can be decided by the Controller of Patents, Designs and Trademarks, originally under section 53 of the 1964 Act, and section 96 of the 1992 Act, subject to appeal to the High Court as provided in that section. If the employee is obliged to carry out research and development work resulting in an invention the employer is likely to be deemed to be the owner of the patent thereby arising and the employee is deemed to hold the patent on trust for the employer in such circumstances (*British Reinforced Concrete Ltd v Lind* (1917) 34 RPC 101; *Sterling Engineering Co Ltd v Patchett and Electrolux Ltd v Hudson* [1977] FSR 312).

A former employee can of course also be restrained from breaching an employer's rights in a registered design or a trademark as with any person who breaches such rights. Employers may have rights under the Trade Marks Act, 1996 and any attempt by a former employee to breach the employer's rights under that legislation or proprietary rights arising thereunder can be restrained as would be the case with any person. An employer or transferor is also entitled to have computer programs protected under the terms of the Copyright and Related Rights Act, 2000.

1.5.21   SHARE OPTIONS

Most employers who offer share options do so on foot of detailed share option schemes. The contract may therefore simply refer to the availability of share options at the discretion of the employer and subject to the employer's share option scheme. Reference should in particular be made to the position that will pertain in the event of the employee's job function or geographical location changing or otherwise providing that the option will be available during the currency of the contract. Provision should be made for the position that would pertain on termination.

In *Micklefield v SAC Technology Ltd* [1990] IRLR 218 the contract provided that the option holder must continue to be employed in order to exercise the option granted and the holder shall be deemed to have waived his right to damages for loss of option rights as part of any claim for compensation for loss of office. The court held that this was in the nature of an exclusion clause which applied to exempt the employers from liability to pay compensation for loss of rights under the option scheme in the event of termination of employment. Micklefield was held not to be entitled to recover damages for loss of his option rights even where he could show that he had been wrongfully or unfairly dismissed just prior to the date when the option became exercisable.

In contrast, the UK EAT awarded compensation based on loss of value in share options forgone as a result of a dismissal in *Leonard v Strathclyde Buses Ltd* [1998] IRLR 693. In *Levett v Biotrace International plc* [1999] IRLR 375, Mr Levett was entitled to participate in a share option scheme which provided that the options would lapse immediately if the option holder became 'subject to the company's disciplinary procedures' leading to the termination of his contract. Mr Levett's employment was subsequently terminated. Mr Levett claimed that the termination was in breach of his contract and this was conceded at hearing by the company. In those circumstances the UK Court of Appeal held that the strict interpretation of the rule disqualifying Mr Levett from share options only applied where employment was lawfully terminated and applied the general rule of construction of a contract that a party to a contract cannot rely on its own wrong.

Loss of value of share options consequent on termination of employment is dealt with in Chapter 11: Trade Union, Trade Disputes and Industrial Relations.

1.5.22 BULLYING AND HARASSMENT

It is well-established practice now that employers must meet their obligations to employees to create a work environment free of bullying and harassment by putting in place a policy or policies designed to prevent such bullying or harassment occurring in the first place and not just to deal with incidents when they arise. Failure to have such a policy can lead to liability being imposed on the employer the first time such an incident arises. Policies of this sort are rarely included in the text of a letter of appointment or contract but rather are contained in a separate document which is appended to or referred to and incorporated in the contract. See Chapter 6: Equality and Discrimination in the Workplace and Chapter 8: Unfair Dismissals.

1.5.23 E-MAIL, INTRANET AND INTERNET USE

Employers are conscious of the significant risks and legal liabilities that may arise where their employees use e-mail, intranet or internet facilities as part of their work. Employers have been held liable for defamation (*Western Provident Association v Norwich Union*, 1997 unreported) and a range of other possible legal liabilities such as sexual or racial harassment, copyright infringement, spreading of viruses, accessing of pornography and waste of computer capacity and employer's time. Increasingly employers are adopting policies setting out the rules and regulations relating to use of electronic information and equipment and again these policies are usually contained in a document separate from the actual letter of appointment or contract of service but referred to therein and incorporated as part of the contract or employment relationship.

1.5.24 RESIGNATION OF DIRECTORSHIPS OR OFFICES ON TERMINATION OF EMPLOYMENT

Resignation of directorships or other offices should be catered for in a contract of employment. In any event the Companies Act, 1963, section 182 provides that shareholders may by ordinary resolution remove any or all of the directors of a company from the board before their period of office expires. This provision takes effect notwithstanding anything in the articles of association or a contract of service. The power could be overwritten by the provisions of a shareholders' agreement governing how votes will be cast in respect of the removal of a director. Neither can a director for life be removed by this provision from a private company as per section 182(1).

1.5.25 PROPER LAW

The proper law of a contract is of particular importance where an employee may be required to work abroad. The employment by a foreign employer of a foreign citizen in Ireland is covered by unfair dismissal legislation (*Scheel v Kelly Engineering Ltd* UD 535/86 and *Roder v Liebig International Ltd* UD 144/79).

In *McIlwraith v Seitz Filtration (GB) Ltd* [1998] ELR 105 the claimant had a written contract of employment with the respondent company which was based in the UK. The contract provided that the area of work was the Republic of Ireland and Northern Ireland. The contract was stated to be subject to the laws of the United Kingdom. When the claimant claimed unfair dismissal in the Republic the respondent claimed that the contract provided that it be governed by the laws of the UK. The EAT held that such provision was void as being contrary to the Unfair Dismissals Act, 1977, section 13 and, as the UK was a party to the Convention on the Law Applicable to Contractual Obligations, 1980 which became law in Ireland through the Contractual Obligations (Applicable Law) Act, 1991, article 6 of the Convention allowed the employee to choose the applicable law and he was therefore entitled to claim under the Unfair Dismissals Acts in the Republic of Ireland.

1.5.26 MISCELLANEOUS

There is almost no limit to the number of provisions that may be included in a contract of employment. Where lawyers are asked to draft a 'standard' contract of employment great care should be taken to ensure that the contract meets the actual needs of the specific employer and with the specific work sought to be done. Provisions that might be included in this regard are:

— attendance and punctuality;

— particular safety regulations;

— responsibility for property, tools or machinery;

— deportment, wearing of uniforms;

— severance of obligations;

— survival of obligations;

— waiver (where certain conduct may be tolerated from time to time it should be deemed not to be a waiver of any specific provision of the contract);

— requirement to hold a driving licence;

— right of residence in employer's property (this, under the law of landlord and tenant, merely creates a licence and not a tenancy);

— return to employer of all property, notes, copies etc on termination of the contract;

— reconstruction in receivership or liquidation and any surviving rights;

— maternity leave entitlements particularly where these are over and above statutory entitlement;

— compassionate leave;

— parental leave (also subject to statutory entitlement);

— work standards;

— insider dealing; and

— holding of stocks and shares;

1.6 Company Directors

Under company law a service contract for a director, whether an employee or independent contractor, may not be longer than five years in duration. Any term longer than five years must be approved by the shareholders. In the case of the director of one or more companies in a group, the approval must come from the shareholders in the holding company. Before approval may be given a written note of the terms must be available for inspection for at least 15 days prior to the general meeting at which the vote would be taken. Terms of any contract which contravene these requirements are void and the contract may be terminated by the company at any time on giving reasonable notice. Similar provisions apply to termination payments to directors that might exceed the equivalent of five years' remuneration. The Companies Act, 1963, sections 187–189 and the Companies Act, 1990, section 28.

Section 50 of the Companies Act, 1990 requires that every shareholder is entitled to inspect copy of each director's service contract and that such a copy must be kept at the registered office, principal place of business or where the shareholders' register is kept. Similar provisions relate to subsidiaries of holding companies.

1.7 Contractual Provision or Work Practice?

1.7.1 GENERALLY

The distinction between what is a contractual entitlement, which may not be varied without consent, and what is a work practice, which may be changed by the employer, is unclear in Irish law. Despite the existence of a vast body of modern case law on employment law and an impressive number of textbooks now available there has been very little analysis of what exactly constitutes a contractual term or condition and what is merely at the discretion of the parties to give, take away or alter as they see fit. What is clear is that what is contractual may not be changed or varied unilaterally but only by agreement whether that is implied, by acquiescence, or otherwise (*Cowey v Liberian Operations Ltd* [1966] 2 Lloyd's Rep 45). What is actually written down by the parties, no matter how comprehensive, cannot cover all of the incidents or requirements of a contract of employment or employment relationship. In practice many employers use relatively simple and understandable letters of appointment and provide for the application of additional terms and conditions as may be contained in other documentation such as union management agreements. Issues will, however, arise on a regular basis which will fall to be determined on whether or not the employer or employee has a legal right, entitlement or obligation. If, for example, an employee were to be provided with a company car it might be described in a written document as being provided at the discretion of the employer which would normally allow the employer the right to remove the car from the employee. On the other hand, a contract might simply state that the employee will be provided with a vehicle, or make no reference to the vehicle and the employer simply makes it available, in which event it would be expected that the employee would be deemed to have an implied contractual right to be provided with the substantial benefit of a car. What then if the employer changed the make or model of the vehicle or provided the employee with a new but less luxurious vehicle? Is the employer in breach of contract? One would expect that it would be relatively easy to answer such a question. It is not. In order to answer the question it must be determined whether or not the point in issue relates to a term or condition of the contract of employment or otherwise.

Assistance in determining what is a term or condition and what is a work practice is afforded by the judgment of O'Hanlon J in *Kenny v An Post* [1988] IR 285. This case involved a claim by the plaintiffs to a contractual right to a 15-minute break paid at the ordinary overtime rate. There was a slight complicating factor in that the contracts of An Post staff carried certain guarantees in relation to conditions of service provided for in the Postal and Telecommunications Act, 1983, section 45 when An Post and Bord Telecom Éireann were created out of what was previously the one employing authority, the Department of Posts and Telegraphs.

Mr Kenny and his colleagues were employed as postal sorters. In 1969 they had agreed with their supervisor that on the 8.00 p.m. to 11.30 p.m. shift they would be allowed a 15-minute paid break. In 1983 An Post decided that the privilege of the paid break would be withdrawn and no payment was made thereafter in relation to the taking of the break. No issue was taken by the employees trade union but the plaintiffs instituted proceedings claiming that An Post was in breach of contract or, alternatively, had failed to continue in operation all conditions of service as required by the 1983 Act, section 45.

Evidence was given that the supervisor came up with the idea of allowing the staff a fixed break in order to lessen the disruption to work caused by small groups leaving at irregular intervals to deal with calls of nature. The supervisor's suggestion was discussed with staff representatives drawn from the union representing the men, was agreed, and was introduced as a work practice from that time. The matter was raised for discussion a number of years later and in or about 1983 a decision was taken by another supervisor to discontinue the practice of having the entire workforce cease work for a 15-minute period paid at overtime rates. O'Hanlon J said he had to consider whether An Post (a) were in breach of contract, or (b) in breach of the duties imposed upon them by the 1983 Act, in seeking to implement and enforce the change in working practices.

1.7.2   WRITTEN AGREEMENT

1.7.2.1   *Kenny v An Post*

O'Hanlon J referred in *Kenny v An Post* [1988] IR 285 to the fact that the 15-minute break:

'... was never made the subject of any formal written agreement or ... of any exchange of letters or other written communication between the employers and the employees or their representatives. Nor did it go any higher than the supervisors who did not seek formal sanction from the Department of Posts and Telegraphs.'

It was argued for the plaintiff that the decision had been implemented and continued over many years and must by implication be regarded as having become one of the terms of employment of the employees concerned. In reaching his decision on whether or not the term was contractually binding O'Hanlon J had regard to what he described as 'collective bargaining' which resulted in agreements not normally intended to create legal relations rather than contractually binding commitments and stated:

'Alteration of, and adjustment to, work practices may have to take place constantly in the sphere of employment where large numbers of people are working on the premises and it seems to me that where a particular change in the terms of employment is intended to be regarded as binding contractually the parties should take some positive steps to achieve this objective.'

He went on to state that he was not satisfied on the evidence that the supervisors had authority from the Department of Posts and Telegraphs to change the contract between the Department and their employees but at the same time he accepted that the supervisors 'must be regarded as having authority to adapt the work practices in the sorting office to the particular needs of the work situation'. He stated, however, that he 'would not be prepared to hold that they [the supervisors] had authority to bring about changes in the entitlement to remuneration for overtime on a contractual basis so that the employer was to be henceforth bound to pay for time not worked by the employee'.

Section 45 of the 1983 Act sought to preserve employees' 'conditions of service' when their employment contracts transferred from the Department of Posts and Telegraphs to An Post. O'Hanlon J was not satisfied that the right to the paid work break came within the meaning of the term 'conditions of service'. In this regard he stated:

> '[I]t is not clear to me that when the Act refers to "conditions of service" it includes within its ambit conditions of service which were not legally enforceable as terms of the contract of employment, but were merely customs and usages practised in a particular section. On the view I have taken of the arrangement . . . the work practice in question was one which the employer was entitled to terminate unilaterally at any time . . . without being involved in any breach of the contractual rights of the workers.'

See also *O'Cearbhaill v Bord Telecom* Éireann [1994] ELR 54.

1.7.2.2   *Cresswell v Board of Inland Revenue*

In *Cresswell v Board of Inland Revenue* [1984] 2 All ER 713, [1984] IRLR 190 the plaintiffs were employees of the UK Inland Revenue involved in the administration of the PAYE tax scheme. The case arose following the computerisation of the scheme, which had previously been operated by the plaintiffs on a manual basis. In the course of the change from manual to computerised systems a dispute arose, as a result of which the plaintiffs refused to operate the first phase of computerisation but indicated their willingness to continue the previous manual operation. The employers would not allow the use of the manual method of operation and indicated that they would not pay the plaintiffs while they refused to work the computerised system. The contracts were not brought to an end but payment was suspended until such time as the plaintiffs returned to operating the computerised system.

The employees took the position that their employers were acting in breach of contract in requiring them to operate the computerised system. They claimed the work which they were employed to perform involved dealing manually with files, records and correspondence, and maintained it was an implied term of their contracts of employment that they could not be required to perform tasks or carry out functions other than those expressly stipulated in their contracts or their terms and conditions of service and/or such as were habitually carried out by custom and practice. It fell to the UK High Court to determine what the contractual positions of the employer and the employees were and to determine whether the plaintiffs were entitled to refuse to follow the instruction given to them.

The court did not analyse in any detail what is meant by a term or condition of employment or how it might be possible to distinguish a contractual term or condition from a work practice but gave assistance in its judgment as follows:

> 'The defendants were not in breach of the plaintiffs' contracts of employment in requiring them to carry out their job duties associated with the administration of the PAYE scheme by means of a new computerised system instead of the traditional manual method of working. Although the content of some of the jobs in question had been considerably altered by computerisation the degree of such alteration was nothing like sufficient to fall outside the original description of the proper functions of the grade concerned.' *See also* O'Neill v Merseyside Plumbing Co Ltd *[1973] ICR 96.*
>
> 'An employee is expected to adapt himself to new methods and techniques introduced in the course of his employment. On his side, the employer must provide any

necessary training or retraining. It is a question of pure fact in each particular case whether the retraining involved the acquisition of such esoteric skills that it would not be reasonable to expect the employee to acquire them. Nowadays, however, it cannot be considered esoteric or unusual to ask an employee to acquire basic skills as to retrieving information from a computer or feeding information into one.' *See also* North Riding Garages v Butterwick *[1967] 2 QB 56.*

'In the present case after computerisation of the PAYE scheme each of the jobs in question was the same as it was before though in part done in a different way. Computerisation merely introduced up-to-date methods for dealing with bulk problems. Though there may have been some loss of job satisfaction on the part of the employees concerned that was regrettable but by itself provided no cause for action. Moreover, in the present case, there was no suggestion that the plaintiffs themselves or anybody else in any similar category affected by computerisation had found any real difficulty in accepting the necessary instruction in the use of the computerised system or putting it into practice.

'The defendants had not committed any act in breach of contract in refusing to allow the plaintiffs to continue working manually and in refusing to pay them as long as they refused to work the new computerised system.'

1.7.2.3 *Rafferty v Bus Éireann*

Kelly J delivered a useful High Court judgment on terms and conditions of employment and work practices in *Rafferty, Ward and the National Bus & Rail Union v Bus Éireann and Irish Bus* [1997] 2 IR 424. In the course of his judgment he stated:

'[T]hat in the totality of the relationship between employer and employee certain aspects of it may truly be described as conditions of service whereas other aspects are not. Even though these other aspects may have important implications for both employer and employee they are nonetheless not to be regarded as conditions of service. . . . Accordingly there is a difference in law between conditions of service and work practices.'

In *Rafferty* the court was asked to consider whether or not the respondents could change rostering arrangements, abolish certain duties and replace them with other duties. The plaintiffs took issue with the changes and complained that they were unilateral alterations in terms and conditions of employment. The respondents submitted that as a result of serious financial difficulties they had to achieve cost savings and that the changes they sought to impose were not contractual alterations but changes in work practices which are effectively at the discretion of the employer to order in the best interests of the business. Kelly J cited the *O'Cearbhaill* and *Cresswell* cases, the latter of which he appeared to feel was particularly apposite having regard to the facts in *Rafferty*. He accepted that the requirements to be imposed on Mr Rafferty and his colleagues required them to undertake duties which they had not formerly done, but took the view that after the proposed changes the principal occupation of Mr Rafferty and his colleagues, who were bus drivers, 'remains that of driving'. He concluded as follows:

'The position therefore is that in my view Irish Bus is correct in saying that the changes which it seeks to bring about are ones which involve work practices rather than changes in conditions of service. These alterations do not affect the rate of pay, hours of work, length of holidays, sick leave or pension rights. Neither do they in my view alter the basic or core work of a bus driver. These altered duties will only fall to be executed at times where drivers would otherwise be idle and yet remunerated. In each case these duties will constitute a small part of the overall work which will remain bus driving. I therefore conclude that the proposed alterations relate to work practices rather than conditions of service.'

See also *Fitzgerald v South Eastern Health Board* [2003] ELR 257.

1.7.3 VARIATION OF CONTRACT

Once it is established that a provision is a term or a condition of a contract of employment is it the case that the employer cannot then make any change or variation to the contract? It is a basic tenet of contract law that the terms of a contract cannot be varied except by agreement of the parties. A change or variation in the contract cannot be unilateral. Neither party can impose any change they desire. The change must occur by agreement whether that agreement is express or implied, tacit or by acquiescence.

1.7.3.1 Variation by the parties

The law of contract has had great difficulty with the scope of what constitutes variation by one of the parties. While the basic rule expressed above seems to be quite straightforward judges have come across many situations in commercial agreements where an element of unilateral variation or modification becomes necessary in order to give commercial efficacy to the contract. Their desire to see the bargain of the parties carried out can sometimes override specific terms of an agreement which may defeat that purpose, albeit unwittingly. Robert Clarke in *Contract Law in Ireland* (3rd edn), p 407 states:

'Post-contractual representations which purport to have the effect of abrogating or modifying contractual terms present acute difficulties, due in the main to a failure on the part of judges to use and define terms like . . . "variation" . . . with any degree of precision.'

In *Tradax (Ireland) Ltd v Irish Grain Board Ltd* [1984] IR 1 the Chief Justice stated that the power to imply terms must 'be exercised with care'.

The courts will not make a bargain that was badly made in the first place. In normal commercial contracts that doctrine is not difficult to adhere to. In employment contracts, however, the situation is different. The relationship between the parties is radically different from a normal commercial contract. The parties are bound together throughout their working day and, possibly for one or both, throughout their working lives. The consequences of any difficulty will tend to be considerably worse for the employee than for the employer which may be a firm or company.

If a term is so obvious that common sense would hold that it must be included in a contract then the courts are likely to hold that it is part of the contract. Clarke also refers to *Shirlaw v Southern Foundries [1926] Ltd* [1939] 2 KB 206 where it was stated:

'[W]here . . . that which in any contract is left to be implied and need not be expressed is something so obvious that it goes without saying; that, if while the parties were making their bargain, an officious bystander were to suggest some express provision for it in their agreement they would hastily suppress him with a common "oh of course".'

The Supreme Court had followed *Shirlaw* in *Sweeney v Duggan* [1997] 2 ILRM 211 in refusing to imply a term into a contract of employment that an employer should carry insurance against negligence of personal injury to an employee. See also *The Moorcock* (1889) 14 PD 64 and *Spring v National Amalgamated Stevedores and Dockers Society* [1956] 1 WLR 585.

In *Wandsworth London Borough Council v D'Silva* [1998] IRLR 193 the council had a code of practice on staff illness which included procedures for monitoring and reviewing absence. A review process was triggered when employees reached a certain level of absence. The council proposed changing the method of triggering such a review and the staff objected to such a change. The staff maintained that the code of practice formed part of their contractual terms and conditions and could not be changed by the employer unilaterally. The employers argued that the relevant provisions of the code were not contractually binding and that, even if they were, the contracts expressly allowed the employers to amend those provisions unilaterally. In making this latter argument the employer was relying on a clause which stated inter alia 'from time to time variations in your terms of employment may occur and these will be separately notified to you or otherwise incorporated in the documents to which you have reference'. The UK Court of Appeal held that the provisions in the employer's code of practice on staff sickness were not contractually binding and could be altered by the employers unilaterally. The court stated:

> 'Whether a particular provision in an employer's code of practice is contractually binding depends upon whether it should properly be regarded as conferring a right on employees or as setting out no more than good practice which managers were intended to follow.'

In the present case the language of the provisions in question did not provide an appropriate foundation on which to base contractual rights. They did no more than provide guidance for both supervisors and employees as to what was expected to happen in certain circumstances. They did not set out what was contractually required to happen. The whole procedure in its initial stages was designed to be flexible and informal in a way which was inconsistent with contractual rights being created. Therefore the employers were entitled to amend the provisions unilaterally.

See also *Doyle v Grangeford Precast Concrete Ltd* [1998] ELR 260 where the employer took on an employee and later gave him the letter of appointment which contained a probationary clause. Probation had not previously been discussed or agreed. The High Court held that this was a breach of trust and that the employer was not entitled to unilaterally impose a new contractual provision. Interlocutory relief was granted to the employee pending the outcome of his action for damages. The employee subsequently obtained damages measured at six months' remuneration in lieu of notice.

1.7.3.2 **Variation by third party or agent—trade unions**

The most common form of variation other than one expressly agreed between employer and employee is variation agreed with a trade union acting on behalf of specific employees or employees generally.

In unionised employment employers normally copy collective agreements to new employees and make it clear to them that these agreements form part of their terms and conditions of employment. Collective agreements may be varied by the main parties, being the employer and the trade union, from time to time and the question may arise as to how that variation affects the employees. In the main employees will in practice accept terms or conditions negotiated on their behalf by their trade union and, even where a vote may be taken on such changes, those voting against the changes are likely to accept them and to continue working under such changed terms and conditions. There is unlikely therefore to be any doubt as to whether or not the contract has been changed. If there is a doubt in most cases that doubt can be removed by the application of the common law doctrine of 'acquiescence' where a party will be estopped from denying a term if they have acquiesced in its application and, in particular, where they have benefited from the operation of the term. Variation of, or addition to, contractual terms by agreement between a trade union and an employer may be problematic, particularly where the employee objects to the change. A trade union cannot bind those of its members who have made it clear that they did not wish or intend to be bound.

In *Goulding Chemicals Ltd v Bolger* [1977] IR 211 the Supreme Court took a straightforward traditional common law line on the change or variation to a contract and the need for the consent of the contracting parties. Bolger and some of his workmates had made it quite clear that they did not intend to be bound by a change even where the majority of their colleagues in the trade union voted for a change. The Supreme Court in that case had no difficulty in construing each employee's individual contract as requiring the consent of that individual employee be it express, implied or by acquiescence. Bolger and his workmates had made it very clear that they were not to be bound in any of these ways and were held therefore not to be bound.

In *Gray Dunn & Co Ltd v Edwards* [1980] IRLR 23 it was held that where employers negotiate a detailed agreement with a recognised union they are entitled to assume that all unionised employees know of and are bound by its provisions, where the employees had not made it clear that they had no intention to be bound.

It was held in *Dal v A S Orr* [1980] IRLR 413 that an agreement between employer and union that employees' hours of work should be changed will effectively vary their contracts and will not amount to a fundamental breach of contract entitling the employees to claim constructive dismissal where the employers have reserved the right to alter the hours of work in the contract of employment.

In *Scott v Formica Ltd* [1970] IRLR 104 it was held that if there is to be an important variation in the contract of employment resulting from a collective agreement this variation must be brought to the employee's attention in some way such as the issue of an amended statement of terms and conditions, a slip in the employee's pay packet or an address by management or a union official; otherwise the variation will not become part of the contract.

The question of whether collective agreements are legally binding in themselves is dealt with at **1.8** below. In *Whent v T Cartledge Ltd* [1997] IRLR 153 rates of pay were linked to a collective agreement agreed between a transferor and trade unions. Following the transfer of the undertaking the question arose as to whether or not the transferee was obliged by rates of pay set under the terms of the collective agreement. In the course of its decision the UK EAT held:

> '[T]he terms of a collective agreement can be incorporated into and become legally binding terms of individual contracts of employment and that unilateral abrogation of or withdrawal from the collective agreement does not affect the latter.'

1.7.3.3 Custom and practice

In contracts of employment many terms are implied by operation of custom and practice of the employment. In order for a term to be implied by custom and practice it must be 'notorious' as in *O'Reilly v Irish Press* [1937] ILTR 194 where it was held that for a custom to be implied into a contract it must be:

> '. . . so notorious, well known and acquiesced in that in the absence of agreement in writing it is to be taken as one of the terms of the contract between the parties.'

In *DP Refinery (Westernport) Pty Ltd v Shire Hastings* (1978) 52 AJLR 43 the court set out the test that will normally be followed before a term may be implied into a contract as follows:

(a)   the term must be reasonable and equitable;

(b)   it must be necessary to give business efficacy to the contract, so no term will be implied if the contract is effective without it (see also *Whent v Cartledge* [1997] IRLR 153 at p 157);

(c)   it must be so obvious that it goes without saying;

(d)   it must be capable of clear expression; and

(e)   it must not contradict any express term of the contract.

1.7.3.4 Express contractual right to vary

It is possible to provide, within the terms of a contract that the employer reserves the right to alter or vary terms but courts and tribunals will not allow that right to be exercised in an unfettered manner. They will require both business efficacy and reasonableness to apply. In *BBC v Beckett* [1983] IRLR 43 it was held that the right to demote an employee for a disciplinary offence was limited by an implied term that the employers would not exercise such a right in other than a reasonable manner. Such a clause will also be construed strictly against the employer (*Lister v Fram Gerrard Ltd* [1973] ITR 610).

Express contractual right to vary, while not specifically provided for in the contract, may be implied by construction of one or other of the terms of the contract as in *Parry v Holst & Co Ltd* [1968] ITR 317 where it was held that where an employee's contract provides for mobility between different workplaces he cannot claim a redundancy payment when his current workplace closes and he refuses to transfer to another.

In *Simmonds v Dowty Seals Ltd* [1978] IRLR 211 it was held that whether there has been a consensual variation of the terms of the employment depends on the evidence in the particular case. An agreement to vary the terms of a contract is not required to be in writing to have legal effect. Where an employee stays silent and works on under changed terms without objecting, this may amount to an implied agreement to the variation in his terms. This view should be adopted with caution and mainly in respect of terms like pay changes of immediate effect. Changes of future import like workplace should be regarded even more circumspectly (*Jones v Associated Tunnel Link Co Ltd* [1981] IRLR 477, *Wandsworth London Borough Council v D'Silva* [1998] IRLR 193, *Clark v Bet plc* [1997] IRLR 348 and *Rank Xerox Ltd v Churchill* [1988] IRLR 280).

1.7.3.5 Time limits on variation

Courts and tribunals will be slow to bind a party to a particular term or variation in terms to that party's detriment where they are satisfied that on the facts of the case a change was agreed but it was not the purpose or intention of one of the parties, usually the employee, that the change be binding on him without any limit in time.

1.7.3.6 Co-operation not variation

Where a rearrangement of terms of work is based upon co-operation and not contract, the variation of contract so as to bind the employee to the new arrangement will not be inferred (*Turriff Construction Ltd v Bryant* [1967] ITR 292). In *Saxton v National Coal Board* [1970] ITR 196 it was held that where an employee with twenty years' service accepts a reduced working week for a short period of months while his workplace runs down prior to closure, consensual variation of his contract is not to be inferred. Courts will not allow employers to slip in change unknown to an employee as in *Stepney Cast Stone Co Ltd v MacArthur* [1979] IRLR 181, where the court held that an employer who wishes to make a fundamental change in an employee's terms and conditions it must bring it clearly to the employee's notice or it will not amount to consensual variation.

1.7.3.7 Continuing contract or new contract

In *Meek v Port of London Authority* [1918] 2 Ch 96 it was held that employees who accepted promotion to a higher grade of employment were held to have entered into a fresh contract of service. It is unlikely, given the modern authorities, that a court or tribunal would today hold that such a change within the scope of a contract of employment constituted the termination of one contract and the commencement of another, but even if a court or tribunal was to follow that line of reasoning the likelihood is that the court would find that the new 'contract' would be identical in all respects to the 'old' contract with the addition of the new term. The introduction, however, of such new terms is not merely a legal or contractual matter but it may well have practical implications for the parties' relationship into the future. Frequently disputes arise following a consensual variation in a contract in circumstances which might well have been anticipated at the time of the variation but to which the parties gave insufficient thought. If, for example, an employee was to be promoted from a post that he had held for a considerable period of time, for example, promotion from shop floor to management, little or no thought might be given to the consequences for the parties if the employee failed to perform in the new role. May the employee revert to the old job? If someone else has been recruited to fill the shop floor job that might well be a practical impossibility. Does the failure to perform in the new role lead to the destruction of the entire relationship? Such issues are relevant to variation in terms and conditions of employment and variation of contracts; however, the parties effecting the variation may not anticipate such difficulties arising and therefore find themselves embroiled in a dispute as to what should happen when the event occurs. Employers and employees should seek to anticipate what possible difficulties might arise and to cater for them at the time the variation is agreed and put into effect, otherwise disputes will almost inevitably arise.

1.7.3.8 Trade disputes

It should be kept in mind at all times that even where the employer is legally correct in taking action, or where the employees are seeking a change which they cannot enforce in law, employees may, where appropriate, engage in a trade dispute and use their industrial powers of persuasion to seek to bring about the changes they require or to prevent the employer from imposing changes the employer may require.

It is very important to be aware that even in so-called 'non-union' companies, a union representing the employees may be able to secure certain pay and conditions in the employer organisation. This possibility has come about as a result of a number of union representation cases brought under the Industrial Relations (Amendment) Act, 2001 as amended by the Industrial Relations (Miscellaneous Provisions) Act, 2004. Up to recently, there was an acceptance by the legislature and the judiciary that employers were not obliged to recognise trade unions for the purposes of engaging in collective bargaining negotiations in industrial relations. However, the above Acts now state that notwithstanding anything in the Industrial Relations Acts, 1946–1990, the Labour Court may, at the request of a union, investigate a trade dispute where it is not the practice of the employer to engage in collective bargaining in respect of that group, grade or category of worker and the ordinary internal dispute resolution procedures have failed to resolve the dispute.

The change in the legislation has recently been successfully utilised by trade unions in companies where unions are not recognised. In *United Airlines v Communicaton Workers Union* CD/05/707, the CWU referred a dispute between United Airlines and 100 staff represented by CWU to the Labour Relations Commission. The Labour Court awarded enhanced redundancy pay to the workers who were set to lose their jobs due the outsourcing of certain work.

1.8 Collective Agreements and Contracts of Employment

In practice many terms and conditions of employment are negotiated between employers and trade unions on a collective basis. Two issues arise in relation to collective agreements, the first of which is how they might be binding in respect of individual contracts and the incorporation, alteration or variation of terms or conditions of employment through a trade union. In *O'Rourke v Talbot (Ireland) Ltd* [1984] ILRM 587 the plaintiffs, through their trade union, had negotiated with the company on the redeployment of certain employees as a result of financial difficulties encountered by the company. In the course of the negotiations the employees sought a written assurance from the company in relation to job security for the future. The company produced a document which gave 'an assurance that compulsory redundancy' would not be introduced. A further document was sought by the employees giving guaranteed protection against compulsory redundancy up to a certain date. This 'guarantee' was given by management. Barrington J held that productivity agreements similar to the first agreement in this case, which contained the assurances that there would be no compulsory redundancies, were agreements of a sort that 'did not contemplate legal relations, at any rate so far as all their clauses were concerned, but were meant to be binding in honour on the management and the trade union'. He went on to hold, however, that given the circumstances of the second commitment wherein the word 'guarantee' was used and taking the view that 'the representatives of management did not think that they were entering into a legally binding arrangement' that he was 'satisfied however that not only were the men looking for something which was legally binding but that management knew this' and thereby held that the second commitment was legally binding.

In reaching his conclusion Barrington J considered the leading British and Irish precedents on the legal status of collective agreements, *Edwards v Skyways Ltd* [1964] 1 WLR 349, *Ford Motor Co Ltd v AEF* [1969] 2 QB 303 and *Goulding Chemicals Ltd v Bolger* [1977] IR 211, and went on to hold that the agreement sought to be upheld by the plaintiffs was a commercial agreement legally binding on the parties. The way in which collective agreements are incorporated in individual contracts of employment is referred to in *Becton Dickinson v Lee* [1973] IR 1.

It should also be kept in mind that the terms of the collective agreement may apply to employees who are not members of the trade union with which the agreement was concluded. This may arise in a number of ways. The employee may have commenced employment and been advised that his terms and conditions would be governed, at least in part, by the terms of the collective agreement (*Singh v British Steel Corporation* [1974] IRLR 131), or the employee may have left or been expelled from his trade union at a time when the collective agreement was in being. It should also be noted that a trade union cannot bind all of its members where some of those members have made it clear that they did not intend or wish to be bound (*Goulding Chemicals Ltd v Bolger*).

1.8.1 LEGALITY OF COLLECTIVE AGREEMENTS

The Supreme Court in *Goulding Chemicals Ltd v Bolger* [1977] IR 211 considered a situation where agreement was reached between the company and representative trade unions as to the manner in which a plant would be closed and the amounts of redundancy payments the employees were to be paid. The trade unions arranged for a vote to be taken on the proposals and a majority of the members of the various unions supported the company's proposals and accepted them. The company then acted on the acceptance by the majority and treated it as an acceptance by the entire workforce. The company had negotiated on a collective basis and then proceeded to act in relation to each individual employee's contract of service on the basis of what was collectively negotiated. The defendants were part of the minority of the workforce who had voted against the proposals. They made their objections clear to their employers. The agreement reached between the company and the trade unions restricted unions' and employees' rights to picket. The defendants engaged in a picket. The company sought to restrain them on a number of grounds, one of which was that they were bound by the collective agreement concluded with their trade union. Two issues had to be considered. The first was whether or not collective agreements of the sort concluded in this case were legally binding on the parties to the agreement and, secondly, whether a collective agreement binds the employees who are members of the unions involved in concluding the agreement. The judgments in *Goulding* refer extensively to *Edwards v Skyways* [1964] 1 WLR 349 and *Ford Motor Co Ltd v AEF* [1969] 2 QB 303.

In *Edwards* agreement was reached between the employer and the employees that an ex gratia payment would be paid in the event of redundancy. In that case the court held that the agreement was binding on the parties. As the subject matter was business relations there was an intention to agree and, further, that where there is a difference between the parties the onus of proof lies on the party who asserts that no legal effect was intended and this onus was not discharged in the *Edwards* case.

In the *Ford Motor Co* case it was held that collective agreements negotiated between a large industrial company and various trade unions were, due to the contents which were stated to be mainly aspirational, and the fact that the parties were seeking to order their day-to-day relations rather than impose legal obligations on each other, not legally binding as there was no intention to create legal relations. The court stated:

> 'Agreements such as these, composed largely of optimistic aspirations presenting grave practical problems of enforcement and reached against a background of opinion adverse to enforceability, are, in my judgment not contracts in the legal sense and are not enforceable at law.'

In *Goulding* the Supreme Court expressed reservations about the *Ford Motor Co* decision (per Kenny J at p 237). The Supreme Court analysed the nature of the particular agreement reached and held that it was 'a business-like document and had all the appearances of being intended to create legal relations'.

1.8.2 TESTS APPLIED

In *O'Rourke v Talbot (Ireland) Ltd* [1984] ILRM 587 Barrington J also referred to *Edwards v Skyways* and the reference at p 355 of that report to the leading textbooks on the law of contract, which maintain that the test of intention to create or not to create legal relations is an 'objective' test. The court held that the conditions of the objective test had been met: that Talbot could not rebut the presumption that the agreement they reached with the trade unions and the workforce was one intended to create legal relations; that the agreement was binding on the company and that they were in breach of agreement in making the plaintiffs redundant prior to the date after which employment had been guaranteed.

The conclusion reached by the Supreme Court in *Goulding Chemicals Ltd v Bolger* on the general issue of whether or not a collective agreement is legally binding was effectively that regard must be had to the circumstances in which the agreement was concluded and its contents which might suggest it was not intended to be legally binding but concluded on the first issue as per O'Higgins CJ:

> 'I would regard the agreement resulting from the acceptance of these proposals as being similar in effect to that dealt with in *Edwards v Skyways Ltd* and, there being nothing to suggest the contrary, in my view a valid contract is thereby created between these unions and the plaintiff.'

He went on to refer to 'this valid enforceable agreement'. Kenny J stated:

> 'An agreement between parties is enforceable by the law unless the agreement itself or the surrounding circumstances show that the parties did not intend to enter into legal relations.'

In reviewing the authorities Kenny J stated: 'I have considerable doubts about the correctness of the decision in the *Ford Motor Company* case'. In relation to the agreement concluded between the company and trade unions within Goulding Chemicals Ltd he said:

> 'It seems to me that the six-point agreement was intended to create legal relations and was intended to be a contract between the plaintiffs and the unions engaged in the negotiations ... when an apparent agreement in relation to business relations is entered into the onus on the party who asserts that it was not intended to have legal effect is a heavy one. In my opinion the six-point statement and its acceptance created a valid enforceable contract between the plaintiffs and the unions who took part in the negotiations.'

On the second issue, as to whether or not in the circumstances of this particular case, where the defendants rejected an agreement accepted by the majority membership of the trade unions concerned, and made this rejection clear to their employers, the Supreme

Court considered whether they were or should be bound by the terms of the agreement which in itself the court had found to be binding on the company and trade unions. In this regard O'Higgins CJ stated:

'I find it hard to accept . . . the defendants can be bound by an agreement which they have expressly repudiated and opposed. It seems to me that to hold them bound would be contrary to all principle.'

On this point Kenny J stated:

'Membership of a corporate body or of an association does not have the consequence that every agreement made by that corporate body or association binds every member of it. None of the defendants are parties to the agreement and as they consistently opposed it no question of their being bound by acquiescence can arise.'

See also *Holland v London Society of Compositors* (1924) 40 TLR 440 and *Young v Canadian Northern Railway Co* [1931] AC 83.

If a collective agreement is legally binding then in itself it constitutes a contract by which employer and employee, and in certain circumstances the trade union, will be legally bound to each other. Even if the collective agreement is not in itself legally binding it may be incorporated into the contract of employment as referred to in *Whent v Cartledge Ltd* [1997] IRLR 153 referred to at **1.7.3.2** above and the cases of *Robertson v British Gas Corporation* [1983] IRLR 302 and *National Coal Board v National Union of Mineworkers* [1986] IRLR 439.

1.8.3 TRANSFER OF UNDERTAKINGS

Whent v Cartledge was related to the transfer of an undertaking. Prior to the transfer the employees had their rates of pay determined under the terms of a collective agreement by a body known as the NJC. The individual contracts of employment provided that the employees' pay would be that set by the NJC. On 11 April 1994 the undertaking was transferred. On 21 April 1994 the transferee wrote to the trade union concerned withdrawing recognition and from the agreement stating that any collective agreements relating to employees transferred would no longer have effect. The employees were individually advised of the discontinuance of 'any formal or implied recognition arrangements or collective agreements or related arrangements' which were stated to no longer have any effect and to have ended with immediate effect. The employees claimed that despite these letters their pay was still to be ascertained by reference to the rates agreed and established from time to time by the NJC for their respective grades. The transferee contended that pay for the relevant employees was frozen at the level last fixed before the employers withdrew from the collective agreement.

The UK EAT held:

'The transferee employers were still bound by the NJC agreement so far as incorporated in individual contracts of employment notwithstanding their withdrawal from the collective agreement. Until the transfer it was undisputed that the appellants' contracts incorporated the result of the annual round of negotiations and there were no grounds for holding that the transfer caused any change in the meaning of the words.'

In *Whent v Cartledge* the industrial tribunal, whose decision was overturned by the UK EAT, had reasoned that 'it cannot be right that an employer is bound ad infinitum by the terms of the collective agreement negotiated by bodies other than themselves'. The UK EAT described that as a 'fallacious reasoning' and stated:

'The employer was not bound ad infinitum since it could at any time without breach of contract negotiate variations of contract with individual employees or terminate their contracts on due notice and offer fresh ones. In any event there was no reason why the parties should not if they choose agree that matters such as remuneration be fixed by processes in which they do not themselves participate.'

Transfer of undertakings is dealt with in more detail in Chapter 11: Transfer of Undertakings.

1.8.4 APPLYING CONTRACTUAL TERMS

Even where a contract is clear as to its provisions and an employer seeks to apply the provision to the letter, the courts may intervene to restrict the employer and require the employer to act 'reasonably' in all the circumstances of the employment relationship. In *Bass Leisure Ltd v Thomas* [1994] IRLR 104 Mrs Thomas had worked for Bass in their Coventry depot for more than 10 years. When the depot closed she was offered relocation in a depot some twenty miles away. She reluctantly agreed to try the new post but because of the disruption to her life she decided not to continue working there. She terminated her employment and sought a redundancy payment. Her employers rejected her claim and sought to rely on a paragraph in her contract which gave the employer the right to transfer any employee either temporarily or permanently to a suitable alternative place of work and went on to state that domestic circumstances would be taken into account in reaching a decision if relocation was involved. The UK EAT analysed the clause and, while holding that the actual wording of the clause favoured the employee, considered whether strict reliance on the terms of the contract would work an injustice on the employer. In *United Bank v Akhtar* [1989] IRLR 507 the UK Court of Appeal implied a term into the contract that the literal contractual rights of the employer would not be applied in an oppressive or unfair manner which is the line most likely to be followed by Irish courts.

1.8.5 REGISTERED EMPLOYMENT AGREEMENTS

Registered Employment Agreements are provided for in the Industrial Relations Act, 1946–2004 and will be binding and enforceable on the parties who have made the agreement. These agreements are negotiated by the relevant trade union and the employer in an industry or enterprise and are presented to the Labour Court for registration. Where the Labour Court is satisfied that the agreement presented satisfies the statutory requirements, it will register the agreement. The effect of this is to make the provisions of the agreement legally enforceable in respect of every worker of the class, type or group to which it is expressed to apply and to his or her employer, even if such worker or employer is not a party to the agreement. There are currently 45 registered employment agreements, dealing with issues of pay and conditions in various sectors of industry.

CHAPTER 2

PAYMENT OF WAGES

The Payment of Wages Act, 1991 ('the 1991 Act') came into operation on 1 January 1992.

2.1 Interpretation

The 1991 Act governs the payment of wages to an employee by an employer and, in that context, the meanings of 'contract of employment' and 'wages' are particularly important (section 1).

2.1.1 CONTRACT OF EMPLOYMENT

For the purposes of the 1991 Act, 'contract of employment' means:

'A contract of service or of apprenticeship, and any other contract whereby an individual agrees with another person to do or perform personally any work or service for a third person (whether or not the third person is a party to the contract) whose status, by virtue of the contract, is not that of a client or customer of any profession or business undertaking carried on by the individual, and the person who is liable to pay the wages of the individual in respect of the work or service shall be deemed, for the purposes of this Act, to be his employer, whether the contract is express or implied and if express, whether it is oral or in writing.'

2.1.2 EMPLOYEE

'Employee' means:

'A person who has entered into or works under (or, where the employment has ceased, entered into or worked under) a contract of employment and references in relation to an employer, to an employee shall be construed as references to an employee employed by that employer; and for the purpose of this definition, a person holding office, or in the service of, the State (including a member of the Garda Síochána or the Defence Forces) or otherwise as a civil servant, within the meaning of the Civil Service Regulation Act, 1956, shall be deemed to be an employee employed by the State or the Government, as the case may be and an officer or a servant of a local authority for the purposes of the Local Government Act, 1941, a harbour authority, a health board or a vocational education committee shall be deemed to be an employee employed by the authority, board or committee, as the case may be.'

2.1.3 EMPLOYER

'Employer' in relation to an employee means:

'The person with whom the employee has entered into or for whom the employee works under (or, where the employment has ceased, entered into or worked under) a contract of employment.'

In *Sullivan v Department of Education* [1998] ELR 217 the EAT held that the Department of Education employs teachers for the purposes of the 1991 Act. While it is generally accepted that teachers are employed by the manager or board of management of the schools in which they are employed, the EAT refused to accept that that is the case under the Payment of Wages Act. The EAT stated:

'When it comes to the question of remuneration, for the Department to say it is not the employer would effectively mean that as far as the question of remuneration would go the teacher would have no employer which is inconceivable. If a deduction is made from a teacher's salary the school is likely to say that it, having no role in the question of payment of remuneration, cannot be considered to have made such deduction and the Department may say that it is not the employer for the purposes of any aspect of the teacher's employment. It is inconceivable that all of the teachers in the country should not have the benefit of the Payment of Wages Act, 1991. It is difficult to see how the Board of Management could, short of ordering the Department to make a deduction, actually make a deduction from any particular teacher's remuneration.

'In all the circumstances we are satisfied there are sufficiently close ties and controls exercised by the Department in relation to individual teachers. We are satisfied that the Department is the employer for the purposes of the Payment of Wages Act, 1991.'

While the reasoning of the EAT is based on a certain attractive logic, it is difficult to view the Department as anything other than a 'paying agent', in circumstances where the EAT accepted that 'the board of management or other managing authority of a school may well have a role in the day-to-day running of the school and indeed in engaging teachers, interviewing etc'. Certainly, it is difficult to argue that the Department is the 'person with whom the [teacher] has entered into or for whom the [teacher] works under a contract of employment'. In reality, all of the incidents of the employment relationship pertain as between teacher and school, while the Department of Education funds that relationship. So, the Department could fund an award made against a school under the 1991 Act and removing the Department from the employment relationship need not give rise to a situation where 'all of the teachers in the country should not have the benefit of the . . . Act'.

2.1.4 WAGES

'Wages', in relation to an employee, means:

'Any sums payable to the employee by the employer in connection with his employment, including—

(a) any fee, bonus or commission, or any holiday, sick or maternity pay, or any other emolument, referable to his employment, whether payable under his contract of employment or otherwise, and

(b) any sum payable to the employee upon the termination by the employer of his contract of employment without his having given to the employee the appropriate prior notice of the termination, being a sum paid in lieu of the giving of such notice.'

In the UK, part (a) of this definition of wages (above) is reflected in the Employment Rights Act, 1996, at section 27(1)(a), where wages is defined as meaning any sums payable to a worker in connection with his employment, including:

'. . . any fee, bonus, commission, holiday pay or other emolument, whether payable under his contract or otherwise.'

In *Commissioners of Inland Revenue v Ainsworth* [2005] IRLR 465, the UK Court of Appeal addressed the issue of whether, in the context of a claim pertaining to holiday pay (and in circumstances where the UK Working Time Regulations embody a 'regime for the enforcement of . . . rights pertaining to holiday pay'), an employee might choose as between the Employment Rights Act and the Working Time Regulations. The UK Court was not prepared to consider that, 'in 1996 (when the Employment Rights Act came into operation), Parliament can have intended to refer to a subsequently created statutory right (the right to holiday pay) which comes with its own enforcement regime' and held that applications to enforce entitlement to holiday pay under the UK Working Time Regulations can only be pursued under those Regulations and not by way of 'unauthorised deduction' claim under the UK Employment Rights Act.

From an Irish perspective, it is to be noted that, in that context, the UK Court took the view that 'any doubt' was 'dispelled' by section 205(2) of the 1996 Act which provides that the remedy in respect of any contravention of that Act's section 13 (being the section which prohibits unauthorised deductions from wages) 'is by way of complaint under section 23 (of the said Act of 1996) and not otherwise'. The Irish Payment of Wages Act does not embody any provision similar to the said section 205(2) of the Employment Rights Act, 1996. Consequently and while it can be argued, that the Oireachtas cannot 'have intended to refer to a subsequently created statutory right' (the right to holiday pay under the Organisation of Working Time Act, 1997) 'which comes with its own enforcement regime', when enacting the Payment of Wages Act, it still remains to be seen whether rights commissioners and the EAT and the High Court will allow claims in respect of holiday pay to be processed pursuant to the provisions to the Payment of Wages Act in this jurisdiction. However and in the light of the judgment of the UK Court of Appeal in *Ainsworth*, it is submitted that practitioners should process such claims pursuant of the provisions of the Organisation of Working Time Act.

To the extent that 'wages' includes 'bonus', under the Irish Payment of Wages Act and the UK Employment Rights Act, the decision of the UK EAT in *Farrell Matthews & Weir v Hansen* [2005] IRLR 160 is interesting. In that case (and by reference to the elaborate provisions in the Employments Rights Act pertaining to 'non-contractual bonus'), the UK EAT held that a discretionary bonus which has been 'declared' is a wage which is properly payable to an employee in terms of section 13(3) of the Employment Rights Act (which subsection is very similar in terms to section 5(6) of Ireland's Payment of Wages Act—see **2.5.4.1** below). With regard to such discretionary bonuses, the UK EAT stated that 'until the discretion is exercised in favour of granting a bonus, provided that the discretion is exercised properly, no bonus is payable. Once, however, an employer tells an employee that he is going to receive bonus payments on certain terms, he is, or ought to be obliged to pay that bonus in accordance with those terms until the terms are altered and notice of the alteration is given. . . . This situation applies equally where a discretion to award a bonus is granted under contract . . . or by custom or by ad hoc decision.'

In the English case of *Saavadra v Aceground Ltd* [1995] IRLR 198 the UK EAT held that a restaurateur who retained part of the service charges for himself, was making unlawful deductions from the wages of his employees. The UK EAT stated that what is 'properly payable to those who give service' is 'that which is paid for service'.

The definition continues:

> *'Provided, however, that the following payments shall not be regarded as wages for the purposes of this definition:*
>
> *(a)   any payment in respect of expenses incurred by the employee in carrying out his employment,*
>
> *(b)   any payment by way of a pension, allowance or gratuity in connection with the death, or the retirement or resignation from his employment, of the employee or as compensation for loss of office,*
>
> *(c)   any payment referable to the employee's redundancy,*

(d) *any payment to the employee otherwise than in his capacity as an employee,*

(e) *any payment in kind or benefit in kind.'*

2.1.5 MISCELLANEOUS DEFINITIONS

'Cash', 'the Minister', 'strike', 'industrial action' and 'the Tribunal' are also defined for the purposes of the Act, in section 1.

2.2 Modes of Payment of Wages

Section 2 provides that *'wages may be paid by and only by one or more of the . . . modes'* set out in the section, including cheque, draft, postal order, credit transfer and cash.

The section makes special provision governing the mode of payment of wages, when, owing to a strike or other industrial action affecting a financial institution, cash is not readily available to the employee.

The section creates an offence and provides for a fine not exceeding €1,250.

2.3 Repeal of Truck Acts, 1831–1896 and Related Enactments

Apart from repealing the Truck Acts, section 3 also repealed the Payment of Wages Act, 1979 and contains transitional arrangements relating to cash and non-cash payment of wages under the 1979 Act.

2.4 Statements of Wages and Deductions from Wages

Section 4 requires employers to furnish employees with written statements of wages and deductions, *'at the time of the payment'* (except in the case of credit transfers, when the statement should be given to the employee *'as soon as may be thereafter'*). The employer is obliged to *'take such reasonable steps as are necessary to ensure'* confidentiality in this context.

The section creates an offence and provides for a fine not exceeding €1,250.

2.5 Regulation of Certain Deductions Made and Payments Received by Employers

2.5.1 DEDUCTIONS PERMITTED BY STATUTE AND CONTRACT

Section 5(1) prohibits an employer from making a deduction from the wages of an employee (or receiving any payment from an employee) unless:

'(a) *. . . required or authorised . . . by virtue of . . . statute or . . . instrument . . .*

(b) *. . . required or authorised . . . by virtue of a term of the employee's contract of employment included in the contract before, and in force at the time of, the deduction or payment, or*

(c) *in the case of a deduction, the employee has given his prior consent in writing, to it.'*

In *Curust Hardware Ltd v Elaine Dalton* [1993] ELR 10 the employee was contractually obliged to give one month's notice of termination of employment. She received an offer of a new job and was required to start work in two weeks. She gave notice to her employer on a Monday that she would be leaving the job on the following Friday week (less than two weeks' notice). On termination of her employment, she collected her P45 and wages and found that one month's pay, plus her bonus for the previous month, had been deducted. Her employer stated that the deduction was made because she failed to give one month's notice as was specified in her contract of employment but agreed that the contract did not specify the withholding of payment if notice was not given (although the employer claimed that the employee had been told this at her interview). The EAT held that while the contract of employment provided for one month's notice to be given by either party on the termination of the contract, there was no express provision in the contract that a deduction from wages could be made for failure to give notice. The EAT stated:

'[T]he remedy for default on a term of a contract lies in contract law and such a remedy would have its basis in compensation rather than penalty. In the Minimum Notice and Terms of Employment Acts, 1973–1991 there is no provision for a penalty to be imposed on either the employee or employer for failure to comply with the Act. There is, however, a provision for payment of compensation by an employer to an employee for any loss sustained by the employee as a result of the employer's failure to give notice.'

The EAT held that the deduction in this case contravened the 1991 Act and ordered Curust to pay Ms Dalton for the period worked by her and also to pay her bonus and holiday pay.

In similar vein, the UK EAT, in *Hill v Chapell* [2003] IRLR 19, held that, in circumstances where a worker's employment is terminated during the course of a leave year and at the date of termination, the worker has taken proportionately more leave in that leave year than the leave to which he or she was entitled, the employer cannot recover 'the excess holiday pay' in the absence of an agreement enabling the employer so to do.

In *International Packaging Corporation (UK) Ltd v Balfour* [2003] IRLR 11, the UK EAT held that a reduction in employees' pay following the unilateral introduction of short-time working by the employers amounted to an unauthorised deduction from wages. The UK EAT stated that '(r)eduction in working hours is plainly a variation of a contract of employment and, unless expressly catered for within that contract, or allowed by implication again within the terms of the contract, any actual deduction of wages, even if related to the hours worked, is not authorised by [the UK equivalent of our Payment of Wages Act] and can only be achieved by agreement'.

In *John Grimes v Iarnród Éireann/Irish Rail* PW3/95, the EAT stated that it:

'. . . is prepared to consider that the signature of an employee on the contract of employment might indicate that the employee is subscribing and indicating his consent to matters which are not referred to specifically in the contract of employment document proper but in a separate document, such as the booklet dealing with applicable grievance and disciplinary procedures and which is drawn to the employee's attention prior to his signing the actual contract of employment.'

2.5.2   ACTS OR OMISSIONS/SUPPLY OF GOODS AND SERVICES

2.5.2.1   Generally

Section 5(2) further restricts an employer from making deductions from wages in respect of:

'(a)   *any act or omission of the employee, or*

(b)   *any goods or services supplied to or provided for the employee, by the employer, the supply or provision of which is necessary to the employment.'*

Such deductions may only be made where:

'(i)   *. . . required or authorised . . . by. . . the contract of employment . . .*
(ii)   *. . . fair and reasonable.'*

In *Jerome Lynch v Clonlara Wholesalers* PW3/98 the employee was suspended, without pay, for a period of four weeks, in circumstances where, having previously received a final warning, he allegedly used foul and abusive language in a threatening manner in dealing with his store manager. The EAT determined that a four-week suspension without pay was too harsh and was not 'fair and reasonable' in all the circumstances, as required by the Act. The EAT found 'that the appellant did use foul and abusive language' and held 'that a reduced sanction of one week's suspension without pay would be fair and reasonable in all the circumstances'. It ordered the company to repay three of the four weeks' pay which had been deducted from Mr Lynch's wages.

2.5.2.2   Notice of contractual term

Under section 5(2)(iii) deductions may also be made where:

'. . . *before the time of the act or omission or the provision of the goods or services, the employee has been furnished with a copy of the contractual term, where it is in writing, or otherwise a notice in writing of the existence and effect of the term.'*

In *Murphy v Ryanair plc* [1993] ELR 215 the employee (Mr Murphy) was employed as a pilot by Ryanair plc. He gave evidence to the EAT of the duty requirements that he had to fulfil. These included the requirement that he have at least 14 hours' rest before he flew one of the company's planes. At 2.30 p.m. on a Saturday early in March 1992, he was asked to fly a scheduled flight, which would finish at 11.30 p.m. He refused to comply with this request on the grounds that it would prevent him from having the maximum 14 hours' rest between one flight and the next. He was told that if he did not fly the plane, he would be suspended. Following a meeting with his employer, he was suspended for one week, without pay. The EAT held that:

'[U]nder section 5(2)(iii) of the Payment of Wages Act, 1991, an employee must be furnished with a written copy of such a term, or written notice to that effect, before the act or omission if wages are to be deducted.'

The EAT went on to find that 'the deduction of pay in the circumstances outlined, was not in accordance with the provisions of the Payment of Wages Act, 1991 [and] that the employee [was] entitled to the payment in the normal way of the amount that was deducted'.

2.5.2.3   Notification requirements

Further requirements will arise, depending on the nature of the deduction. Section 5(2)(iv) provides:

'. . . *where the deduction is in respect of an act or omission of the employee, the employee must be furnished, at least one week before the making of the deduction, with particulars in writing, of the act, or omission and the amount of the deduction.'*

In *John Grimes v Iarnród Éireann/Irish Rail* PW3/95 the EAT stated as follows:

'The clear intendment behind the 1991 Act is to introduce certainty surrounding the making of deductions from the wages of employees so that employers and employees will know in advance the nature and amount of deductions. In those circumstances, it is important that section 5(2)(iv) be strictly construed and in those circumstances the EAT finds that any notice not specifying the amount of the deduction expressly and clearly is a defective notice.'

In that case, the EAT refused to accept that a letter, which made reference to 'one day's suspension', but made no reference whatever to a monetary amount, could constitute 'particulars in writing of . . . the amount of the deduction'. The EAT refused to 'place reliance' on evidence that Mr Grimes would have been aware of the amount that was to be deducted, in the context of the day's suspension from negotiations that took place prior to the suspension being effected, reiterating that:

> '[T]he intendment of the 1991 Act is to introduce certainty in and about the whole area of deductions from the wages of employees and clearly the Act intends that the most satisfactory way of doing this is to provide for the issuing of a notice at least one week in advance, containing certain prescribed details so as to remove any uncertainty.'

However, in *Lynch v Clonlara Wholesalers* PW3/98, the EAT stated that 'no binding case law that the statutory requirements [at sections (5)(2)(i) and (iv) of the Act] are strict was cited to the EAT'. In those circumstances, the EAT found that there had been 'compliance with the spirit, if not with the black letter of the Act', in circumstances where the employee had received a letter, informing him that he was going to be 'suspended without pay' for four weeks. The EAT found that 'while the amount of the deduction [was] not specified in figures, it [was] ascertainable. Accordingly . . . the spirit of the requirement [that the employee be furnished with particulars in writing of the amount of the deduction] [had] been complied with'.

2.5.2.4 Amount of deductions and time limits

Section 5(2)(v)–(vii) provide:

> '(v) where the deduction is in respect of compensation for loss or damage sustained by the employer as a result of an act or omission of the employee, the amount of the deduction cannot exceed the amount of the loss or the cost of the damage;
>
> (vi) where the deduction is in respect of necessary goods or services supplied to the employee by the employer, the amount deducted cannot exceed the cost to the employer of the goods or services;
>
> (vii) the deduction (or the first in a series of deductions) must be made not later than six months after the act or omission becomes known to the employer or after the provision of the goods or services.'

Payments can only be received by employers from employees in respect of an act or omission or the supply of necessary goods or services, in circumstances where all of the conditions set out above, in relation to such deductions, are satisfied in respect of such payment.

2.5.3 EXCLUDED DEDUCTIONS

2.5.3.1 Reimbursement for overpayments

Section 5(5)(a) provides that the section does not govern deductions made by an employer from the wages of an employee (or, where appropriate, payments received by an employer from an employee), in the following circumstances:

> '. . . reimbursement of overpayments of wages or expenses, where the amount of the deduction or payment does not exceed the amount of the overpayment.'

In *Department of Defence v Cathal O'Riordan* PW3/92, the EAT found that it had no jurisdiction to determine the case, when deductions were made from Mr O'Riordan's wages following a period of sick leave. Evidence was given to the effect that Mr O'Riordan had been removed from the Department's sick pay scheme for disciplinary reasons. However, while he was out sick the Department continued to pay his wages, by reason of an administrative error. It seems that he assumed that he was receiving sick pay. When he returned to work, the Department stopped his pay until the money received by him, while he was out sick, had been recouped. The EAT stated:

> 'The principal question that arises here, however, is did the payment of the wages to the respondent while out sick constitute an overpayment of wages, made for any reason by the employer to the employee? The word "overpayment" means "to pay too much". It follows then that where the employer has paid too much as in this case, the matter is caught by section 5(5) and the EAT has no jurisdiction to determine the case and the appeal is allowed.'

In the UK, in *Hill v Chapell* [2003] IRLR 19, the UK EAT refused to accept that there is an 'overpayment', for the purposes of the UK equivalent of our Payment of Wages Act where, on termination of employment, an employee has taken proportionately more leave, in the leave year during which the employment is terminated, than that to which the employee was entitled. The UK EAT held that such circumstances do not give rise to 'overpayments', in that context.

2.5.3.2 Disciplinary proceedings

Section 5(5)(b) provides that the section does not apply to deductions made:

> '. . . in consequence of any disciplinary proceedings held by virtue of a statutory provision.'

In *Grimes v Iarnród Éireann/Irish Rail* PW3/95 the employee was suspended for one day, without pay, as a result of disciplinary proceedings taken against him. Inter alia, it was submitted on behalf of Iarnród Éireann, that the day's pay constituted a deduction 'in consequence of . . . disciplinary proceedings . . . held by virtue of a statutory provision'. Iarnród Éireann argued that, because disciplinary proceedings are required to be conducted according to the rules of fairness of procedures, by the Unfair Dismissals Act, the disciplinary proceedings invoked in this case constituted disciplinary proceedings held pursuant to or by virtue of a statutory provision. The EAT had no hesitation in rejecting that argument and stated:

> 'They were ordinary disciplinary proceedings not held specifically under the aegis of any statute or statutory regulation such as the Garda Síochána Discipline Regulations and the connection that (Iarnród Éireann) sought to draw with the Unfair Dismissals Acts, 1977–1993 was not a direct connection and that part of the Act dealing with statutorily held disciplinary proceedings appears to the Tribunal to require a direct connection between the Act under which disciplinary proceedings are held and the proceedings themselves.'

In *Lynch v Clonlara Wholesalers* PW3/98 the EAT refused to accept that, where there are no disciplinary procedures agreed between employer and employee, the Code of Practice on Disciplinary Procedures set out in the schedule to the Industrial Relations Act, 1990 Code of Practice on Disciplinary Procedures (Declaration) Order, 1996, SI 117/1996 governs the employment relationship. Article 14(d) of the Code provides that disciplinary action 'may include, inter alia, suspension without pay'. The EAT stated that:

> '. . . taking into account the use of the word "may" in that article and the fact that the code is merely a guideline on disciplinary procedures, the Tribunal holds that Article 14(d) of the Code of Practice and the disciplinary action mentioned therein cannot be the "disciplinary proceedings pursuant to a statutory provision" referred to in section 5(5)(b) of the Payment of Wages Act, 1991.'

The EAT went on to state that to accept such argument:

> '. . . would be to allow a procedural guideline to supersede a statutory provision and to deny the employee in this case, and indeed, most, if not all, employees, the very protection which the Act sets out to provide for them. Where a deduction is to be made from the wages of an employee for "any act or omission of the employee", section 5(2) imposes a

firm duty on the employer to ensure that the employee has prior knowledge of the fact that a deduction can be made, that the amount of the deduction is fair and reasonable and that the employee has timely notice of the amount of the deduction and the reason(s) for it. To accept [the Code of Practice] argument would set these protections at nought.'

2.5.3.3 Other exclusions

Section 5(5) further provides that the section does not govern deductions made:

'(c) . . . in pursuance of a requirement imposed on the employer by virtue of any statutory provision to make deductions with a view to making payments to a public authority;

(d) . . . in pursuance of any arrangements whereby deductions are made by the employer with a view to making payments to a third person of amounts due to that third person by the employee, consequent on the employer receiving a notice in writing from the third person, to that effect and the payment is made to the third person, in compliance with the said notice and on condition that the employee has given his prior consent in writing, either to the embodiment of such arrangement in a contract with his employer or otherwise;

(e) . . . in consequence of the employee having taken part in a strike or other industrial action . . .'

In *Beaumont Hospital v McNally* PW29–33/96 the hospital refused to pay the employees in respect of hours during which they engaged in a protest. There was some disagreement between the parties as to whether there was a total cessation of work. Consequently, the EAT did not make a finding that there was a strike as defined. However, the EAT did determine that the employees had engaged in 'industrial action' as defined, and consequently determined that it had no jurisdiction 'to address the rights or wrongs of the dispute'.

Section 5(5) further provides that the section does not govern deductions made:

'(f) . . . for the purposes of satisfying an order of a court or tribunal requiring the payment of any amount by the employee to the employer;

(g) . . . for the purpose of satisfying an order of a court or tribunal requiring the payment of any amount by the employer to the court or tribunal or a third party out of the wages of the employee.'

2.5.3.4 Litigation and 'excluded' deductions

In the UK, the EAT has held that where a deduction falls within one of these categories, a tribunal has no jurisdiction to hear a complaint about such a deduction. 'In (these) cases . . . the restriction . . . against deductions . . . does not apply and, if it does not apply, it cannot be contravened, so as to entitle the worker to present a complaint . . . In (these) cases . . . the appropriate procedure is not to make a complaint about the deduction to an Industrial Tribunal, but to institute appropriate proceedings in the civil courts for alleged breach of contract and recovery of the sum deducted.' (*SIP (Industrial Products) Ltd v Swinn* [1994] IRLR 323)

That is not to say that, in cases pertaining to these 'excluded' deductions, a tribunal should not make findings of facts with a view to determining whether it has jurisdiction. In joined cases *Gill v Ford Motor Company Ltd and Wong v BAE Systems Operations Ltd* [2004] IRLR 840, the UK EAT held that a tribunal is not entitled to refuse to make such findings of fact. 'The carefully circumscribed limits to the jurisdiction of the tribunal (insofar as the 'excluded' deductions are concerned) would be avoided if a tribunal was entitled to determine that it had no jurisdiction without making findings as to the existence of the jurisdictional questions . . . [W]here the facts are disputed, to decline jurisdiction without making findings of fact would, in effect, allow a respondent to choose whether the employment tribunal or the (civil) court has jurisdiction by the form of its response to a claim. Where the jurisdictional question is a pure question of law, the tribunal will almost invariably be able to reach a decision on the basis of submissions. Where, however, the jurisdictional question at issue is factual and is contested, the tribunal will generally have to have evidence before it upon which it can make the necessary finding of fact, and to make that finding of fact'. The UK EAT '(did) not consider that investigating the jurisdictional facts . . . necessarily involves investigating the lawfulness of a deduction i.e. whether it is contractually authorised'. The cases before the UK EAT involved 'overpayments of wages' and 'having taken part in a strike' exclusions and in the context of the latter, the UK EAT expressed the view that '(d)etermining whether (employees) have done so need not involve any consideration of the lawfulness of the deduction. Although the distinction is less bright in the case of (overpayments of wages), we consider that the question whether an employee in fact received an overpayment can be considered separately from the question whether the employer may contractually, i.e. lawfully, deduct wages as a result of that overpayment'. The UK EAT held that, generally, tribunals should make findings of fact before concluding that they have no jurisdiction.

2.5.4   DEFICIENCY IN OR NON-PAYMENT OF WAGES

2.5.4.1   Statutory provisions

Section 5(6) provides as follows:

> 'Where—
> (a)   the total amount of any wages that are paid on any occasion by an employer to an employee is less than the total amount of wages that is properly payable by him to the employee on that occasion (after making any deductions therefrom that fall to be made and are in accordance with this Act), or
> (b)   none of the wages that are properly payable to an employee by an employer on any occasion (after making any such deductions as aforesaid) are paid to the employee,
> then, except insofar as the deficiency or non-payment is attributable to an error of computation, the amount of the deficiency or non-payment shall be treated as a deduction made by the employer from the wages of the employee on the occasion.'

2.5.4.2   Reduction in wages

In *Morgan v West Glamorgan County Council* [1995] IRLR 68, the UK EAT held that an employee whose salary was reduced consequent upon a demotion which was imposed in breach of contract, is entitled, under the UK Wages Act 1986, to the shortfall in pay, because a deduction in wages made as a result of an error of law is not an 'error of computation' so as to fall outside the protection provided by the Act. Mummery J stated that an 'error' is 'a mistake, something incorrectly done through ignorance or inadvertence'.

> 'Computation of wages [is] a matter of reckoning the amount, of ascertaining the total amount due by a process of counting and calculation. That does not cover a deliberate decision to demote an employee and reduce his salary and although that decision was itself the result of an erroneous or mistaken view of the legal and factual position, the reduction in salary and consequent deduction from the wages paid to the employee was attributable to that decision and not to any error of computation.'

The EAT has ruled that a reduction in wages does not constitute a 'deduction' for the purposes of the 1991 Act. In *Mary Redmond v South Eastern Health Board* PW47/96 TE6/96 ('*Redmond No 2*'), Mrs Redmond claimed that she had, 'at one time been paid £90 indicating that her wages had been reduced by £10 per week when she was furnished with her written contract of employment which cited her pay as £80'. While the determination is lacking in factual detail, it seems that the dispute arose by reason of confusion in relation to the appropriate hourly rate of pay. In 1995 the same Mrs Redmond had presented a complaint under the 1991 Act, in circumstances where she claimed that she was an employee of the South Eastern Health Board and, for that reason, refused to accept 'wages' from a third party. The circumstances of that case are outlined at **2.5.4.4** below and it will be noted that the EAT determined that Mrs Redmond was an employee of the health board. Bearing that fact in mind, it would appear that Mrs Redmond was then furnished with a written contract of employment by the health board and that that contract 'cited her pay as £80, i.e. £2 per hour'. Mrs Redmond claimed that she used to receive £90 per week, but she 'could not show that the £90 was a payment in excess of £2 per hour.' The health board claimed that 'the rate had always been £2 per hour and had not changed'. The EAT stated as follows:

> 'The Tribunal's jurisdiction under the Payment of Wages Act, 1991 arises from an appeal from the Rights Commissioner recommendation and is only under section 5 of the Act. This jurisdiction covers deductions from wages but not the situation when an employer reduces wages. A reduction in wages is not covered by the legislation. The EAT has no jurisdiction derived from this legislation then in what constitutes an alteration in the conditions of employment, i.e. a reduction in wages, but does not constitute a deduction in wages.'

With respect to the EAT, it is difficult to accept this reasoning. Section 5(6) clearly states that where the total amount of any wages that are paid on any occasion is less than the total amount of wages 'that is properly payable' then the amount of the deficiency shall be treated as a deduction. While Mrs Redmond might not have been able to establish that £90 was 'properly payable' to her each week, it does seem clear from section 5(6) that the EAT did have jurisdiction to decide on the issue of whether the 'reduction' constituted a lawful or unlawful deduction for the purposes of the 1991 Act. While it is clear that non-payment of wages constitutes a 'deduction' for the purposes of the 1991 Act, the position under the UK Wages Act was not so clear and was the subject of conflicting decisions, until 1991, when the court of Appeal held that the Act covered 'any claim by an employee that . . . his employer failed to pay him at the appropriate time, the full amount of the wages as defined . . . which he ought then to have been paid' (*Delaney v Staples* [1991] IRLR 112). However, the later case of *Bruce v Wiggins Teape Stationery Ltd* [1994] IRLR 536, is of more interest in this jurisdiction. In that case, the UK EAT ruled that a 'reduction' in wages is a 'deduction' in wages for the purposes of the UK Wages Act, in circumstances where the employer unilaterally reduced an overtime rate. It is clear from *Redmond No 2* that the EAT here has not followed the UK Tribunal, on this particular point, although it is submitted that the reasoning of the UK Tribunal is to be preferred.

In *Elizabeth Claire Care Management Ltd v Francis* [2005] IRLR 858, the UK EAT held that a failure by an employer to pay any or all of an employee's wages on time amounts to an unlawful deduction from wages.

Hussman Manufacturing v Weir [1998] IRLR 288 is also interesting in this context. Mr Weir was moved from a night shift to a day shift, pursuant to the provisions of his contract of employment. As a consequence, his weekly wages were reduced by £17, being the amount that he had been receiving by way of pay for unsocial hours. The UK EAT heard that a reduction in income, which is a consequence of a lawful act, does not in itself amount to an unauthorised deduction from wages. The wages 'properly payable' to the employee, once he was moved to the day shift, were those payable to all persons working on that shift.

2.5.4.3   **Reduced rate of pay from outset**

What is the position where an employee 'continues to receive the same amount (and the same composition) of wages from the outset'? In *Sullivan v Department of Education* [1998] ELR 217 the complaint concerned the amount that was properly payable to the claimant, a secondary school teacher. Ms Sullivan was a graduate of UCC and held a BA single honours degree in French and English. Part of her remuneration comprised a degree allowance. The level of such allowance was dependent on whether the recipient held an honours or a pass degree. Part of Ms Sullivan's degree course had been taken at honours level and part had been taken at pass level. The Department of Education only paid the higher level of allowance to teachers with degrees where all subjects were taken to honours level in the final examinations. The EAT was 'satisfied that the BA (single honours) programme was in all respects an honours degree programme and could not in any respect be considered to be a pass degree programme'. In those circumstances, the EAT was 'satisfied that there was no justification for the Department to have applied . . . the qualification allowance appropriate to the primary degree (pass)'. The EAT went on to hold that Ms Sullivan was entitled to compensation in respect of the 'non-payment' of the appropriate degree allowance. The EAT made some very interesting observations in this context:

> '[T]he Tribunal considers that if an employee does not receive what is properly payable to him or her from the outset then this can amount to a deduction within the meaning of the 1991 Act. We take "payable" [in the definition of 'wages'] to mean properly payable. The definition of "wages" goes on to give examples of types of payments which can amount to "wages" and states that the payments can amount to wages "whether payable under [his] contract of employment or otherwise. . . .". Although in our view it is not simply a matter of what may have been agreed or arranged or indeed paid from the outset but, in the view of the Tribunal, all sums to which the employee is properly entitled.
>
> 'An employee may not be aware of his or her full entitlements and an employer may have a greater awareness of the employee's entitlements in terms of pay etc and it would be highly unjust for an employee to lose a claim under the Payment of Wages Act, 1991 for an unlawful deduction simply because an employer, being aware of the employee's proper entitlement, chose, unknown to the employee, to pay less than that from the outset.'

While this argument is undeniably interesting, it is surely inconsistent with the basic principles of the law of contract. It suggests that an employer is not entitled to recruit an employee on terms as agreed between them and seeks to introduce a 'compulsory collective agreement' on parties, in circumstances where they may have voluntarily entered into an independent arrangement. If an employee is recruited, at a specific rate of pay, how can the employee unilaterally demand a higher rate and claim that a failure to pay that higher rate equates to an unlawful deduction from wages, under the Payment of Wages Act?

2.5.4.4   Indirect payments

In *Mary Redmond v South Eastern Health Board* PW14/95 ('*Redmond No 1*'), the EAT had to determine the nature of the relationship between Mrs Redmond and the health board. Mrs Redmond provided 'home help' to elderly patients on the instructions of the health board. She was not regarded by the health board as an employee. Health board payments were made directly to the individual patients and there was a dispute as to whether the patients always endorsed the cheques or whether Mrs Redmond lodged them directly to her own bank account. Either way, Mrs Redmond refused to accept the cheques in June 1994 and claimed that the health board had contravened the provisions of the 1991 Act. It was submitted on behalf of the health board that no unlawful deduction had been made from Mrs Redmond's wages, but that she had refused to accept payment. It was further submitted that the EAT did not have jurisdiction under the Act to consider whether or not she was an employee in the absence of such an unlawful deduction. The EAT determined that Mrs Redmond was employed by the health board and that:

> '. . . as an employee [she] was entitled to insist that she be paid directly. [She] was entitled to refuse to accept payment as it was not tendered to her in the correct form in the first instance. In the circumstances, this amounts to an unlawful deduction within the meaning of section 5 of the Payment of Wages Act, 1991 and [she] is entitled to payment in respect of all such deductions, to date, for work done.'

2.5.4.5   **Conditional payments**

In *Dominic Dineen v Mid Western Health Board* PW16/97 the board agreed to pay the employee an extra £5 per week, on condition that he sign an authorisation form (for Paypath) and on the understanding that it had been agreed with his union that the payment of the £5 per week would be discontinued in the case of individual staff members who failed to return the completed authorisation form by a specified date. Mr Dineen received the extra £5 per week for a period, but ultimately it was discontinued by reason of his failure to complete the authorisation form. He claimed that the board had contravened the provisions of the 1991 Act. The EAT stated as follows:

> 'The £5 was a pay increase negotiated on the appellant's behalf by his trade union, but conditional on his completing an authority for "Paypath". Admittedly the increase was paid in advance of completing the formalities for "Paypath" but the agreement expressly provided that it would be "discontinued" in respect of any employees who failed to sign the necessary authorisation. After the date provided by that agreement . . . the £5 was no longer "properly payable" to him because he had failed to complete his side of the bargain.
>
> 'If the £5 was not "properly payable" to him under the agreement, its non-payment to him cannot be said to be a deduction. That it was originally paid to him and later discontinued is a complication, but this complication arose following an agreement reached with the trade unions, which insisted upon that sequence. Having regard to the terms of the [union/management] agreement, this complication does not take from the essential point that the payment was subject to a condition with which the appellant did not comply.'

2.6   Complaints by Employees in Relation to Contraventions of Section 5 by their Employers

2.6.1   GENERALLY

Section 6 governs complaints in relation to unlawful deductions. Complaints are entertained by rights commissioners. Section 6(2) provides:

> '*Where a rights commissioner decides . . . that the complaint is well-founded . . . the commissioner shall order the employer to pay to the employee compensation of such amount . . . as he thinks reasonable in the circumstances, not exceeding—*
>
> (a)   *the net amount of the wages . . . that—*
>
>   (i)   *in case the complaint related to a deduction, would have been paid to the employee in respect of the week immediately preceding the date of the deduction if the deduction had not been made, or*
>
>   (ii)   *in case the complaint related to a payment, were paid to the employee, in respect of the week immediately preceding the date of payment, or*
>
> (b)   *if the amount of the deduction of payment is greater than the amount referred to in paragraph (a) twice the former amount.*'

This provision does not seem to have ever been specifically addressed by the EAT. It prevents a rights commissioner from awarding compensation amounting to more than twice the net amount of the wages that would have been paid to the employee in respect of the week immediately preceding the date of the deduction, if the deduction had not been made. Yet, in *Redmond No 1*, the EAT held that Mrs Redmond was 'entitled to payment in respect of all . . . deductions' made over a lengthy period. In *Sullivan v Department of Education* [1998] ELR 217 the EAT found that Ms Sullivan was 'entitled to compensation calculated by reference to the differential amounts between primary degree (pass) qualification allowance amount and primary degree (first and second honours) amount for the relevant period', where the relevant period ran from 1 September 1991 to 1 July 1994. A close reading of the relevant provision (section 6(2)) reveals that the EAT cannot make awards of such nature, as the level of such awards surely exceeds the maximum compensation that can be awarded under the Act.

A rights commissioner cannot give a decision under the 1991 Act at any time after the commencement of the hearing of proceedings in a court brought by the employee concerned in respect of the deduction or payment, while an employee cannot recover any amount in proceedings in a court in respect of such a deduction or payment at any time after a rights commissioner has given a decision in relation to the deduction or payment. Section 6(4) provides:

> 'A rights commissioner shall not entertain a complaint under this section, unless it is presented to him within the period of six months beginning on the date of the contravention to which the complaint relates or (in a case where the rights commissioner is satisfied that exceptional circumstances prevented the presentation of the complaint within the period aforesaid) such further period not exceeding six months as the rights commissioner considers reasonable.'

A complaint is presented by way of notice in writing to a rights commissioner. It is for the rights commissioner to pass the complaint to the employer.

2.6.2   TIME LIMITS

In *Dominic Dineen v Mid Western Health Board* PW16/97 the health board claimed that the complaint was not made within the requisite six-month period. The EAT rejected the argument, stating:

> 'The claim was dealt with by a rights commissioner and there is no record of the time limit being raised at that stage. The Tribunal, on appeal, cannot go behind the face of the recommendation before it and the respondent did not lodge an appeal on those grounds. Moreover, the "deduction" complained of . . . is of a continuing nature and the time limit does not arise.'

In *Byrne v P J Quigley Ltd* [1995] ELR 205 the EAT considered section 7(2) of the Unfair Dismissals (Amendment) Act, 1993, which also allows the rights commissioner (or the EAT) to extend the period for claiming unfair dismissal in circumstances where they are 'satisfied that exceptional circumstances prevented' the making of the claim during the requisite six-month period. In that case, the EAT stated as follows:

> 'In the view of the Tribunal, (subject to the reservations of Mr O'Donnell on 2(a) and 2(b) in his dissenting opinion . . .) there are two, if not three elements involved:
> (1)   the words "exceptional circumstances" are strong words and should be contrasted with the milder words "reasonably practicable" in the claimant's written submission or "reasonable cause" which permit the extension of time for lodging a redundancy claim under section 12(2)(b) of the Redundancy Payments Act, 1971. "Exceptional" means something out of the ordinary. At the least, the circumstances must be unusual, probably quite unusual, but not necessarily highly unusual.
> (2)   (a) In order to extend the time the EAT must be satisfied that the exceptional circumstances "prevented" lodging the claim within the general time limit. It is not sufficient if the exceptional circumstances caused or triggered the lodging of the claim.
> (3)   (b) It seems to follow that the exceptional circumstances involved must arise within the first six months, "the period aforesaid". If they arose later, they could not be said to "prevent" the claim being initiated within that period.'

The 'exceptional circumstances rule' has been considered by the EAT on a number of occasions, under the Unfair Dismissals Acts and the relevant determinations of the EAT are considered in Chapter 8: Unfair Dismissals.

In *Sullivan v Department of Education* [1998] ELR 217 the complaint related to Ms Sullivan's salary during the entirety of her teaching career, from 1 September 1991 to the date of the hearing. However, as a result of agreement reached in the context of the 'Revised Teachers' PCW Proposals', which were concluded, prior to the hearing, in PCW negotiations, the Department had committed to treating qualifications such as Ms Sullivan's, as a primary degree. In that context, the Department had agreed to backdate the primary degree allowance, in such cases, to 1 July 1994. Nonetheless, Ms Sullivan insisted on proceeding with her complaint, claiming that 'an unlawful deduction continues in respect of the period from which she commenced work until, at least, 1994'. The EAT acknowledged that 'that is the period we are concerned with and we have to consider the matter in that light'. It seems clear, from the record number of the case, that Ms Sullivan presented her complaint in early 1997. In those circumstances, it is difficult to understand how the EAT might have awarded compensation 'in respect of the period from which she commenced work until, at least, 1994'. It seems manifest that Ms Sullivan could not have made a complaint, in that context, within the requisite six- (or 12-) month period.

2.7 Appeal from Decision of Rights Commissioner

Section 7(2) provides for a right of appeal to the EAT:

> 'An appeal under this section shall be initiated by a party by his giving, within six weeks of the date on which the decision to which it relates was communicated to him—
> (a) a notice in writing to the EAT . . ., and
> (b) a copy of the notice to the other party concerned.'

In *Sahid Sultan Trading As Tandoori Nites v Nasem and Others* [2001] ELR 302, the EAT dismissed an appeal against a rights commissioner's recommendation by reason of the Appellant's failure to serve Notice of Appeal on the Respondents within the statutory six weeks' period (in circumstances where the Notice of Appeal was filed with the Tribunal on the last day of that six weeks' period and 'the Tribunal Secretariat, in writing to the Appellant to acknowledge receipt of the notice, stated that it had sent a copy of the notice to the Respondents'.

In terms of section 7(4) *'the Minister may, at the request of the EAT, refer a question of law to the High Court, (while) parties to proceedings before the EAT may appeal to the High Court on a point of law'.*

The decision of the High Court is *'final and conclusive'.*

The Payment of Wages (Appeals) Regulations, 1991, SI 351/1991 govern appeals under this section.

2.8 Enforcement of Decisions of Rights Commissioner and Determinations of the EAT

A decision of a rights commissioner or a determination of the EAT under this Act may be enforced as if it were an order of a Circuit Court, made in civil proceedings by the judge of the Circuit Court for the place where the person in whose favour the decision or determination was made ordinarily resides (section 8).

The rights commissioner or the EAT may provide that a decision/determination shall be carried out before a specified date. Otherwise, the decision/determination will be deemed to provide that it shall be carried out within six weeks from the date on which it is communicated to the parties concerned.

2.9 Powers of Authorised Officers

Section 9 empowers the Minister to appoint 'authorised officers' for the purpose of ensuring compliance with the Act and gives the officers power to enter premises, conduct inspections and make enquiries, demand information and copy documents.

The section creates an offence and provides for a fine not exceeding €1250.

2.10 Provisions in Relation to Offences

Section 10 empowers the Minister to prosecute offences arising under the Act.

2.11 Voidance of Certain Provisions in Agreements

Section 11 provides:

'A provision in an agreement (whether a contract of employment or not and whether made before or after the commencement of this Act) shall be void insofar as it purports to preclude or limit the application of, or is inconsistent with, any provisions of this Act.'

It is clear from decisions of the EAT, dealing with the Unfair Dismissals Act, 1977, section 13, which is almost identical to this section, that agreements reached in full and final settlement of a potential claim under the Act do not contravene the section. See *Gaffney v Fannin Ltd* UD 1/89 and *McGrane v Avery Label Ltd* UD 573/88 (both reproduced in Madden and Kerr, *Unfair Dismissal Cases and Commentary* (2nd edn, 1996) at pp 29 and 30 respectively.

2.12 Miscellaneous

Sections 12–14 deal with the laying of regulations before the houses of the Oireachtas, expenses of the Minister and the short title and commencement of the Act.

CHAPTER 3

WORKING TIME AND STATUTORY LEAVE ENTITLEMENTS

3.1 Introduction

The amount of time workers are required to spend at work and their entitlement to be absent from the workplace are regulated by a number of Acts and Regulations, both at the national and European Community levels. This chapter will deal with the hours workers are required to work, annual leave and public holidays, maternity leave, parental leave, adoptive leave and carer's leave entitlements.

3.2 Working Time

The Organisation of Working Time Act, 1997 ('the Act') implemented Directive 93/104/EC concerning certain aspects of the organisation of working time ('the Directive') which had been adopted by the Council of the European Union on 23 November 1993.

Significantly, the Directive was adopted pursuant to the provisions of the former Article 118a (now Article 138) of the EC Treaty, which provides for 'encouraging improvements, especially in the working environment, as regards the health and safety of workers'. Thus, working time and annual leave are to be viewed as health and safety issues. See *United Kingdom of Great Britain and Northern Ireland v Council of the European Union* [1997] IRLR 30, in which the UK unsuccessfully challenged the health and safety basis of the Directive.

The Act was signed by President Robinson on 7 May 1997 and in accordance with the provisions of SI 392/1997, came into operation on varying dates between 30 September 1997 and 1 March 1998.

3.2.1 INTERPRETATION

The start point in any analysis of the Act is the definitions of 'working time' and 'rest period'.

3.2.1.1 Working time

'Working time' is defined at Section 2 of the Act as meaning:

'(a) any time that the employee is at his or her place of work or at his or her employer's disposal, and

(b) carrying on or performing the activities or duties of his or her work, and "work" shall be construed accordingly.'

This definition does not quite mirror the Directive's definition of 'working time', being *'any period during which the worker is working, at the employer's disposal and carrying out his activity or duties, in accordance with national laws and/or practice'*. However, both of the definitions give rise to the same question—should their conditions be interpreted in conjunctive or disjunctive fashion? Is it only time during which an employee is actually working that constitutes 'working time' for the purposes of the Act/Directive? It was the conjunctive/ disjunctive nature of the conditions that gave rise to the first decision of the ECJ Justice relating to the Directive.

In *Sindicato de Medicos de Asistencia Publica (SIMAP) v Conselleria de Sanidad Y Consumo de la Generalidad Valenciana* [2000] IRLR 845 (hereafter *'SIMAP'*), the court was asked whether time spent 'on call' by Spanish doctors was to be regarded as 'working time', for the purposes of the Directive.

The doctors who worked in primary care teams in the public health sector were required to work 40 hours a week to which could be added, where appropriate, duty on call. Where duty on call or standby duty was worked which required the doctor to be contactable, only actual working hours were taken into account in determining the maximum working time. Against this background, the court was asked 'essentially to determine whether time spent on call . . . whether (the doctors were) required to be present in the health centre or merely contactable, must be regarded as working time or as overtime within the meaning of Directive 93/104/EC'.

The court held that the time spent on call by the doctors in primary care teams must be regarded in its entirety as working time, and where appropriate, as overtime, within the meaning of the Directive, if the doctors are required to be present at health centres. However, the court stated that, where the doctors must merely be contactable at all times when on call, only time linked to the actual provision of primary care services must be regarded as working time.

Significantly, the court pointed out that 'in the scheme of the Directive, working time is placed in opposition to rest periods, the two being mutually exclusive.' The following extract from the judgment of the court is instructive:

> 'In the . . . proceedings, the characteristic features of working time are present in the case of time spent on call by doctors in primary care teams where their presence at the health centre is required. It is not disputed that during periods of duty on call under those rules, the first two conditions are fulfilled. Moreover, even if the activity actually performed varies according to the circumstances, the fact that such doctors are obliged to be present and available at the workplace with a view to providing their professional services means that they are carrying out their duties in that instance. That interpret- ation is also in conformity with the objective of Directive 93/104/EC, which is to ensure the safety and health of workers by granting them minimum periods of rest and adequate breaks. . . . It is clear . . . that to exclude duty on call from working time if physical presence is required would seriously undermine that objective.'

However, the court stated that 'the situation is different where doctors in primary care teams are on call by being contactable at all times without having to be at the health centre. Even if they are at the disposal of their employer, in that it must be possible to contact them, in that situation doctors may manage their time with fewer constraints and pursue their own interests. In those circumstances, only time linked to the actual provision of primary care services must be regarded as working time within the meaning of Directive 93/104.'

It will be apparent from the above that it is the requirement to be at a particular place, a requirement for 'physical presence', that is the crucial factor in determining whether time spent on call or on standby is 'working time' for the purposes of the Directive. Thus, in *Landeshauptstadt Kiel v Jaeger* [2003] IRLR 804, the court held that time during which a German doctor was sleeping while on call constituted 'working time' for the purposes of the Directive. When the doctor was on call, he stayed at the hospital where he was employed and was called upon to carry out his professional duties as the need arose. He was allocated a room with a bed in the hospital, where he could sleep when his services were not required. The court was asked whether the Directive must be interpreted as meaning 'that a period of duty spent by a doctor on call . . . where presence in the hospital is required, must be regarded as constituting in its entirety working time for the purposes of (the) Directive, even though the person concerned is permitted to rest at his place of work during the periods when his services are not required. . . .'. In response, the court stated that, 'in contrast to a doctor on standby where the doctor is required to be permanently accessible but not present in the health centre, a doctor who is required to keep himself available to his employer at the place determined by him for the whole duration of periods of on-call duty is subject to appreciably greater constraints since he has to remain apart from his family and social environment and has less freedom to manage the time during which his professional services are not required. Under those conditions, an employee available at the place determined by the employer cannot be regarded as being at rest during the periods of his on-call duty when he is not actually carrying on any professional activity'.

Again, the court made reference to the health and safety 'objective' of the Directive and the requirement for minimum periods of rest, pointing out that 'the periods during which (the services of doctors on call) are not required in order to cope with emergencies may, depending on the case, be of short duration and/or subject to frequent interruptions' in circumstances where it could not be 'ruled out' that the doctors 'may be prompted to intervene, apart from any emergencies, to monitor the condition of patients placed under their care or to perform tasks of an administrative nature'.

In *Dellas and Others v Premier Ministre and Another* [2006] IRLR 225, the position of the court was reiterated, in the following terms:

> '. . . it is settled case law that on-call duty performed by a worker where he is required to be physically present on the employer's premises must be regarded in its entirety as working time . . . regardless of the work actually done by the person concerned during that on-call duty . . .'

The court made clear that '(t)he fact that on-call duty includes some periods of inactivity is thus completely irrelevant in this connection'. The court pointed out that 'although periods of professional inactivity are inherent in on-call duty performed by workers where they are required to be physically present on the employer's premises, given that, unlike during normal working hours, the need for urgent interventions during such duty cannot be planned in advance and the activity actually performed depends on the circumstances, the decisive factor in considering that the characteristic features of the concept of "working time" . . . are present in the case of such on-call duty performed by a worker at his actual workplace is that he is required to be physically present at the place determined by the employer and to be available to the employer in order to be able to provide the appropriate services immediately in case of need. Those obligations must therefore be regarded as coming within the ambit of the performance of that worker's duties . . .'

The court held that French working time law which provided that in certain situations, 'each period of night duty on call in a room provided is counted as three hours of actual work for the first nine hours and half an hour for each hour in excess of nine hours' contravened the provisions of the Directive.

3.2.1.2 Rest period

'Rest period' is defined at Section 2 of the Act as meaning:

> '. . .any time that is not working time.'

3.2.2   APPLICATION

While none of the Act's provisions govern those employees to whom reference is made at **3.2.2.1** below and those to whom reference is made at **3.2.2.2** below are not covered by Part II, it is open to the Minister for Enterprise, Trade and Employment to order that any provision or provisions of the Act shall apply to any of those employees. The Minister has already made such orders in respect of 'employees engaged in offshore work' (Organisation of Working Time (Inclusion of Offshore Work) Regulations, 2004, SI 819/2004) and employees who are 'engaged in the activities of a doctor in training' (European Communities (Organisation of Working Time) (Activities of Doctors in Training) Regulations, 2004, SI 494/2004).

3.2.2.1   Non-application

The Act governs all employees apart from members of the Garda Síochána and the Defence Forces (section 3(1)).

While it is only members of the Garda Síochána and Defence Forces who are not covered by the Act, large numbers of employees are exempt from the application of certain of the Act's provisions.

3.2.2.2   Non-application of certain provisions

3.2.2.2.1   *Section 3(3) regulated employees*

Specified provisions of the Act do not apply to employees who are covered by regulations made under section 3(3).

3.2.2.2.2   *Section 4(3) regulated employees*

Subject to a requirement that applicable regulations must include a provision requiring employers to ensure that employees have available such rest periods or breaks 'as the provision specifies to be equivalent to the rest period' provided for by sections 11 and/or 12 and/or 13, sections 11 and/or 12 and/or 13 and/or 16 and/or 17 do not apply to employees who are covered by regulations made under section 4(3) (see section 4(5) and (6) and section 6(1)).

3.2.2.2.3   *Employees who are covered by agreements*

Subject to a requirement that applicable collective agreements, registered employment agreements or employment regulation orders must include a provision requiring employers to ensure that employees have available such rest periods or breaks 'as the provision specifies to be equivalent to the rest period' provided for by sections 11 and/or 12 and/or 13 do not apply to employees who are covered by a collective agreement (which, 'for the time being stands approved of by the Labour Court') or a registered employment agreement, which agreement states that sections 11, 12 or 13 do not apply in relation to those employees and employees, to whom an employment regulation order relates, which order provides that section 11, 12 or 13 shall not apply in relation to those employees (see section 4(5) and (6) and section 6(1)).

3.2.2.2.4   *Employees who are working in exceptional circumstances or an emergency*

Subject to the employer's obligation to ensure that an 'equivalent' section 11, 12 or 13 rest period or break is made available to the employee or (where 'for reasons that can be objectively justified, it is not possible' for the employer to do so) 'otherwise make such arrangements as respects the employee's conditions of employment as will compensate the employee', in circumstances where 'compensation' must not be monetary or comprise of a 'material benefit', other than such benefit 'as will improve the physical conditions under which the employee works or the amenities or services available to the employee while . . . at work', sections 11 and/or 12 and/or 13 and/or 16 and/or 17 do not apply to a person employed by an employer who does not comply with any of those sections where 'due to exceptional circumstances or an emergency (including an accident or the imminent risk of an accident), the consequences of which could not have been avoided despite the exercise of all due care, or otherwise to the occurrence of unusual and unforeseeable circumstances beyond the employer's control, it would not be practicable for the employer to comply with the section concerned'

3.2.2.3   **Non-application of minimum rest and working time provisions**

Part II of the Act which governs daily and weekly rest, breaks during the working day, night work, Sunday work, weekly working hours, provision of information in relation to working time and 'zero-hours contracts' does not apply to the following employees. 'The excluded employees' are as follows:

(a)   a person engaged in sea fishing (section 3(2));

(b)   a person engaged in other work at sea (section 3(2)).

    However Part II of the Act applies to 'employees engaged in offshore work', by virtue of Regulation 4 of the Organisation of Working Time (Inclusion of Offshore Work) Regulations, 2004, SI 819/2004 and where 'offshore work' means 'work performed mainly on or from offshore installations (including drilling rigs), directly or indirectly in connection with the exploration, extraction or exploitation of mineral resources, including hydrocarbons, and diving in connection such activities, whether performed from an offshore installation or a vessel' (Article 2 of Directive 93/104/EC as amended by Article 1.2 of Directive 2000/34/EC);

(c)   a person engaged in the activities of a doctor in training (section 3(2)).

    However rights to daily and weekly rest and breaks during the working day are conferred on employees who are 'engaged in the activities of a doctor in training' by virtue of the European Communities (Organisation of Working Time) (Activities of Doctors in Training) Regulations, 2004, SI 494/2004, which regulations also govern night work, weekly working hours and provision of information in relation to working time insofar as those employees are concerned;

(d)   a person who is employed by a relative and is a member of that relative's household and whose place of employment is a private dwelling house or a farm in or on which he or she and the relative reside (section 3(2)).

    'Relative', in relation to a person, 'means his or her spouse, father, mother, grandfather, grandmother, step-father, step-mother, son, daughter, grandson, granddaughter, step-son, step-daughter, brother, sister, half-brother or half-sister';

(e)   a person the duration of whose working time (saving any minimum period of such time that is stipulated by the employer) is determined by himself or herself, whether or not provision for the making of such determination by that person is made by his or her contract of employment (section 3(2)).

3.2.2.4   **Non-application of sections 11 and 13**

Subject to the employer's obligation to ensure that an 'equivalent' rest period is made available to the employee or, where 'for reasons that can be objectively justified, it is not possible' for the employer to do so, 'otherwise make such arrangements as respects the employee's conditions of employment as will compensate the employee', in circumstances where 'compensation' must not be monetary or comprise of a 'material benefit', other than such benefit 'as will improve the physical conditions under which the employee works or the amenities or services available to the employee while . . . at work (see section 4(1) and (2) and section 6(2) and (3)) section 11, which provides for a daily rest period, or section 13, which provides for a weekly rest period, or, in the case of the shift workers and 'as appropriate', both those sections, do not apply to the following:

(a) a person employed in shift work, each time he or she changes shift and cannot avail himself or herself of the rest period to which the section refers (section 4(1))—'shift workers';

(b) a person employed in an activity consisting of periods of work spread out over the day (section 4(2))—'those doing spread work'.

3.2.3 MINIMUM REST PERIODS AND OTHER MATTERS RELATING TO WORKING TIME (PART II)

Part II of the Act governs daily and weekly rest, breaks during the working day, night work, Sunday work, weekly working hours, provision of information in relation to working time and 'zero-hours contracts', as follows.

3.2.3.1 Section 11—daily rest period

Section 11 of the Act confers an entitlement on employees to *a rest period of not less than 11 consecutive hours in each period of 24 hours*' during which they work for their employer.

Section 11 does not apply to (a) members of the Garda Síochána and the Defence Forces and (b) the excluded employees, subject to conditions embodied in those regulations, employees who are covered by the (c) Organisation of Working Time (Exemption of Civil Protection Services) Regulations, 1998, SI 52/1998, (d) Organisation of Working Time (Inclusion of Transport Activities) Regulations, 2004, SI 817/2004 and (e) Organisation of Working Time (General Exemptions) Regulations, 1998, SI 21/1998 and on terms as set out above, (f) shift workers, (g) those doing spread work, (h) exceptional circumstances/ emergency employees and (i) employees who are covered by agreements.

3.2.3.2 Section 12—rests and intervals at work

Section 12 prohibits employers from requiring employees to work for a period of more than four and a half hours without allowing the employee a break of at least 15 minutes, while employers are also prohibited from requiring employees to work for periods of more than six hours without allowing a break of at least 30 minutes.

The 15-minute break can be included in the 30-minute break. However in such circumstances, the 30-minute break would obviously have to commence no later than four hours and 30 minutes after the commencement of the period of work.

A break at the end of the working day does not satisfy the requirements for breaks of 15 minutes and/or 30 minutes, as set out above (*The Tribune Printing & Publishing Group v Graphical Print & Media Union* [2004] ELR 222).

Section 12 does not apply to (a) members of the Garda Síochána and the Defence Forces and (b) the excluded employees, subject to conditions embodied in those regulations, employees who are covered by the (c) Organisation of Working Time (Exemption of Civil Protection Services) Regulations, 1998, SI 52/1998, (d) Organisation of Working Time (Inclusion of Transport Activities) Regulations, 2004, SI 817/2004 and (e) Organisation of Working Time (General Exemptions) Regulations, 1998, SI 21/1998 and on terms as set out above, (f) exceptional circumstances/emergency employees and (g) employees who are covered by agreements.

3.2.3.3   **Section 13—weekly rest periods**

Section 13 confers an entitlement on employees to *'a rest period of at least 24 consecutive hours'* in each period of seven days and the 24-hour period must be immediately preceded by a section 11 *'daily rest period'* or, at the discretion of the employer, two rest periods each of which must be for at least 24 consecutive hours during a second seven-days period, i.e. during the period from day 8 to day 14 inclusive, and if the two rest periods are consecutive, they must be preceded by a section 11 'daily rest period' and if they are not consecutive, each one of them must be preceded by a section 11 *'daily rest period'*. However, where *'considerations of a technical nature or related to the conditions under which the work concerned is organised or otherwise of an objective nature would justify the making of such a decision'*, an employer may decide that the 24-hours rest period or the 48-hours rest period, to which reference is made above, shall not be preceded by a section 11 *'daily rest period'*.

Unless the contract of employment provides otherwise, the 24-hours rest period, or one such, where two such periods are granted, during the one period of seven days, *'shall be a Sunday or, if the rest period is of more than 24 hours' duration, shall include a Sunday'*.

Section 13(6) of the Act, logically, provides that a 24-hours break, or a 48-hours break, as the case may be, need not be preceded by a section 11 *'daily rest period'*, in the case of an employee who is not covered by or is excluded from the provisions of section 11.

Section 11 does not apply to (a) members of the Garda Síochána and the Defence Forces and (b) the excluded employees, subject to conditions embodied in those regulations, employees who are covered by the (c) Organisation of Working Time (Exemption of Civil Protection Services) Regulations, 1998, SI 52/1998, (d) Organisation of Working Time (Inclusion of Transport Activities) Regulations, 2004, SI 817/2004 and (e) Organisation of Working Time (General Exemptions) Regulations, 1998, SI 21/1998 and on terms as set out above, (f) shift workers, (g) those doing spread work, (h) exceptional circumstances/ emergency employees and (i) employees who are covered by agreements.

3.2.3.4   **Section 14—sunday work**

Section 14 confers an entitlement to compensation on employees who are required to work on a Sunday, where that fact 'has not otherwise been taken account of' in determining pay. Employees can be compensated by way of an allowance or pay increase or paid time off or a combination of these measures, all of which must be 'reasonable having regard to all the circumstances'.

In *Group 4 Securitas v SIPTU* [1999] DWT 996, the Labour Court rejected a claim for an increase in the Sunday premium payable to all employees in unionised employment in the security industry. SIPTU had claimed that the rate of premium was not 'reasonable in all the circumstances', but the Labour Court ruled that, as employees received an allowance for working on Sunday, no claim could arise under the Act. The court was of the view that section 14 could not be used to secure an increase in a rate that had already been agreed. See also *Campbell Catering Ltd v SIPTU* [2000] DWT 0035.

Section 14 introduces a unique mechanism whereby employees can, in certain circumstances, rely on agreements governing 'comparable employees', with a view to establishing appropriate levels of compensation for Sunday work. Thus, an employee who is not governed by a collective agreement which specifies 'the value or the minimum value of the compensation to be provided' in respect of Sunday work, can rely on the value(s) specified in that regard by a collective agreement governing 'a comparable employee', in the context of the making of a complaint of non-compliance with section 14, before a rights commissioner or the Labour Court.

At this juncture, it is important to note that, for the purposes of the Act, 'collective agreement' means 'an agreement by or on behalf of an employer on the one hand, and by or on behalf of a body or bodies representative of the employees to whom the agreement relates on the other hand'.

A 'comparable employee' in this context means, 'an employee who is employed to do, under similar circumstances, identical or similar work in the industry or sector of employment concerned' to that which the employee who presents the complaint is employed to do.

In cases where other relevant collective agreements have not 'come to the notice of the rights commissioner or the Labour Court', it is for the complainant employee to bring such collective agreements to their attention and where there are two or more relevant agreements, which specify different values for Sunday work, the lesser value shall be applied by the rights commissioner or the Labour Court to the particular case.

The Labour Relations Commission has prepared a Code of Practice for the purposes of Section 14: Organisation of Working Time (Code of Practice on Sunday Working in the Retail Trade and Related Matters) (Declaration) Order, 1998, SI 444/1998.

3.2.3.5   **Section 15—weekly working hours**

Section 15 introduced the concept of the '48-hours week' into Irish law. The section prohibits employers from permitting employees to work 'in each period of seven days, more than an average of 48 hours'. Sixty and 55-hour weeks were allowed up to 28 February 1999 and 29 February 2000 respectively, in circumstances as set out in transitional provisions embodied in the Fifth Schedule to the Act. However, that is not to say that an employee can never work for more than 48 hours in a given week. The section prohibits employers from permitting employees to work 'more than an average of 48 hours', in a week and provides that the 'average of 48 hours' is to be calculated over 'a reference period'.

3.2.3.5.1   *'Reference period'*

3.2.3.5.1.1   *Generally—four months*

Generally, the 'reference period' is a 'period that does not exceed four months'.

3.2.3.5.1.2   *Night workers—two months*

In the case of night workers, as defined by section 16 of the Act, a reference period is a period that does not exceed two months.

3.2.3.5.1.3   *Specific workers—six months*

A reference period may exceed four months but should not exceed six months:

(a)   in the case of an employee employed in an activity where the worker's place of work and his place of residence are distant from one another or where the worker's different places or work are distant from one another, involving security and surveillance, requiring a permanent presence in order to protect property and persons, particularly security guards and caretakers or security firms, or involving the need for continuity of service or production, particularly services relating to the reception, treatment and/or care provided by hospital or similar establishments, residential institutions and prisons, dock or airport workers, press, radio, television, cinematographic production, postal and telecommunications services, ambulance, fire and civil protection services, or gas, water and electricity production, transmission and distribution, household refuse collection and incineration plants, or industries in which work cannot be interrupted on technical grounds, or research and development activities, agriculture and where there is a foreseeable surge of activity, particularly in agriculture, tourism and postal services;

or

(b)   in the case of an employee employed in an activity as respects which it would not be practicable for the employer concerned to prohibit the employee from working, in each period of seven days, more than an average of 48 hours (if a reference period not exceeding four months were to apply in relation to the employee) 'because of considerations of a technical nature or related to the conditions under which the work concerned is organised or otherwise of an objective nature'[and possibly, in the case of 'an employee employed in an activity, the weekly working hours of which vary on a seasonal basis', although the Act is unclear in that regard—see section 15(1)(b)(ii) and 15(5)] and such employees, including those to whom reference is made at **3.2.3.5.1.3(a)** above can agree a reference period of up to 12 months in circumstances as set out at **3.2.3.5.1.4** below.

3.2.3.5.1.4   *Collective agreement—12 months*

A reference period may exceed four or six months, as the case may be, but should not exceed 12 months in the case of an employee, including an employee to whom reference is made at **3.2.3.5.1.3(a)** above, employed in an activity, the weekly working hours of which vary on a seasonal basis or an employee employed in an activity as respects which it would not be practicable for the employer concerned to prohibit the employee from working, in each period of seven days, more than an average of 48 hours (if a reference period not exceeding four or six months as the case may be, were to apply in relation to the employee) 'because of considerations of a technical nature or related to the conditions under which the work concerned is organised or otherwise of an objective nature'. Such reference periods may be agreed, as between employer and employee, by way of 'a collective agreement that for the time being has effect in relation to the employee and which stands approved of by the Labour Court under section 24'.

The days or months comprising a reference period must be consecutive days or months but such reference period does not include annual leave (being statutory minimum leave), parental leave, force majeure leave, carer's leave, absence from work which is authorised under the Maternity Protection Act, 1994 or the Adoptive Leave Act, 1995 or sick leave.

As will be seen below the Act provides for complaints to a rights commissioner in cases of alleged contraventions of certain sections of the Act, including section 15, and a rights commissioner has certain decision making powers as set out at section 27(3) of the Act. However, the UK High Court has held that the equivalent UK provision confers a contractual right on employees. Thus, in *Barber v RJB Mining (UK) Ltd* [1999] IRLR 308, Gage J took the view that 'Parliament intended that all contracts of employment should be read so as to provide that an employee should work no more than an average of 48 hours in any week during the reference period'. He went on to state that 'this is a mandatory requirement which must apply to all contracts of employment'. While he granted declaratory release to the plaintiffs, with the intention of 'making it clear that they are entitled, if they so choose, to refuse to continue working until the average working hours come within the specified limit'. While he refused to grant injunctive relief, on the facts of the particular case, it is clear from Gage J's judgment that he would not feel constrained from granting such relief, in appropriate circumstances.

Given that Irish courts have been far more willing than their UK counterparts to grant injunctions in an employment context, in recent years, the possibility of such relief being granted, in this jurisdiction, in circumstances where employees are being required to work for more than an average of 48 hours per week, must be borne in mind by practitioners. Further, if section 15 confers contractual rights on employees, it must surely follow that prohibitions on employers, such as those embodied in sections 12 and 16 also give rise to contractual rights and it is clear that if the Irish Courts follow *Barber*, the contractual position of employees will be greatly enhanced by virtue of the provisions of the Act.

Section 15 does not apply to (a) members of the Garda Síochána and the Defence Forces and (b) the excluded employees and subject to conditions embodied in those regulations, employees who are covered by the (c) Organisation of Working Time (Exemption of Civil Protection Services) Regulations, 1998, SI 52/1998.

It should be noted that section 33 of the Act prohibits employers from employing 'an employee to do any work in a relevant period during which the employee has done work for another employer, except where the aggregate of the periods for which such an employee does work for each of such employers respectively in that relevant period does not exceed the period for which the employee could, lawfully under (the) Act or the Activities of Doctors in Training Regulations, be employed to do work for one employer in that relevant period' (see section 33(2) with regard to the meaning of 'relevant period'). Where an employer employs an employee in contravention of this provision, the employer and the employee will each be guilty of an offence.

3.2.3.6   Section 16—nightly working hours

Section 16 confers additional statutory protections on those who work at night.

For the purposes of section 16 'night work' means work carried out during 'night-time' which means the period between midnight and 7.00 a.m. on the following day.

A 'night worker' is an employee 'who normally works at least three hours of his or her daily working time during night-time, and . . . the number of hours worked by whom during night-time, in each year, equals or exceeds 50% of the total number of hours worked by him or her during that year'.

Thus, in order to qualify as a 'night-worker' an employee's daily working hours would 'normally' have to include at least three post-midnight hours. The issue arises as to what is meant by 'normally' in that context. The Directive speaks in terms of working at least three hours during night-time 'as a normal course'. That phrase was examined by the Northern Ireland High Court in *R v Attorney General for Northern Ireland ex parte Burns* [1999] IRLR315 where the respondent claimed that the applicant was not a 'night-worker' because she only spent one week of each three-week shift cycle working during 'night-time'. It was submitted that this period of night-shift work was insufficient to qualify the applicant as a night-worker, that, for the purposes of the Directive, a 'night-worker' was a person who worked night-shift only. Alternatively, the respondent suggested, a 'night-worker' was a person who worked night-shifts predominantly and it was submitted that the proportion of the applicant's night-work was so small that she did not qualify for protection under the Directive. Kerr J did not accept those arguments and stated as follows:

> 'The requirement that a night-worker should be one who works at least three hours during night-time "as a normal course" involves no more, in my opinion, than that this should be a regular feature of her employment. The Directive contemplates that a night-worker may be someone who works as little as three hours during night-time. It is inconceivable, therefore, that the definition of night-worker should be confined to someone who works night-shifts exclusively or even predominantly. Moreover, Article 2(4)(d) explicitly recognises that a night-worker should include those who work only a proportion of their time during the night.'

Thus, insofar as Kerr J is concerned, an employee need only show that the requirement to work at least three hours during night-time is 'a regular feature of (the) employment' in order to qualify as a 'night-worker'.

Section 16 also introduces the concept of a 'special category night-worker' meaning 'a night-worker as respects whom an assessment carried out by his or her employer, pursuant to a requirement of regulations under section 28(1) of the Safety, Health and Welfare at Work Act, 1989, in relation to the risks attaching to the work that the night-worker is employed to do indicates that that work involves special hazards or a heavy physical or mental strain'.

(a) An employer is prohibited from permitting a 'special category night-worker' to work for more than eight hours in each period of 24 hours, in a case where the work done by the worker in that period includes night-work.

(b) An employer is prohibited from permitting a 'night-worker' to work for more than an average of eight hours in each period of 24 hours where the average of eight hours is calculated over a 'reference period' that does not exceed two months or 'such greater length of time as is specified in a collective agreement that for the time being has effect in relation to that night-worker and which stands approved of by the Labour Court under section 24. Approval of collective agreements by the Labour Court (for the purposes of the 1977 Act) pursuant to section 24 is addressed at **3.2.2.2.3** above.

It should be noted that the specific prohibition relating to special category night-workers only applies where the workers are doing work which includes night-work, which is not the case insofar as the prohibition which relates to night-workers generally is concerned.

The days or months comprising a reference period must be consecutive days or months but such reference period does not include any weekly rest periods granted pursuant to section 13, being statutory minimum entitlements, annual leave, being statutory minimum leave, parental leave, force majeure leave, carer's leave, absence from work which is authorised under the Maternity Protection Act, 1994 or the Adoptive Leave Act, 1995 or sick leave.

Section 11 does not apply to (a) members of the Garda Síochána and the Defence Forces and (b) the excluded employees, subject to conditions embodied in those regulations, employees who are covered by the (c) Organisation of Working Time (Exemption of Civil Protection Services) Regulations, 1998, SI 52/1998, (d) Organisation of Working Time (Inclusion of Transport Activities) Regulations, 2004, SI 817/2004 and (e) Organisation of Working Time (General Exemptions) Regulations, 1998, SI 21/1998 and on terms as set out above, (f) exceptional circumstances/emergency employees.

3.2.3.7   **Section 17—provision of information in relation to working time**

Section 17 provides that, where an employee does not have 'normal or regular starting and finishing times of work', as set out in the contract of employment or a relevant employment regulation order, registered employment agreement or collective agreement, the employer must give the employee at least 24 hours' notice of the relevant starting and finishing times, before the first day or, as the case may be, the day, in each week that the employer proposes to require the employee to work. Similarly, where an employee is required to work 'additional hours', being such hours as the employer may from time to time decide—typically 'overtime'—the employee is also entitled to such notice. Where the employee has not been required to work during the notice period, he must be furnished with notice 'not later than before the last period of 24 hours . . . in which he or she has been required to do work for the employer', preceding the day(s) to which the notice relates.

A notification to an employee, pursuant to section 17, does not prejudice the right of an employer to alter starting and finishing times of work 'if circumstances, which could not reasonably been foreseen, arise that justify the employer in so doing'.

The posting of a notice 'in a conspicuous position in the place of the employee's employment' constitutes 'sufficient notification' for the purposes of section 17 (see *Anglo Irish Beef Processors v SIPTU* [2000] DWT 0019).

Section 17 does not apply to (a) members of the Garda Síochána and the Defence Forces and (b) the excluded employees, and on terms as set out above, (c) exceptional circumstances/emergency employees.

3.2.3.8 Section 18—provision in relation to zero-hours working practices

Where an employee is contractually obliged to be *'available to work for the employer in a week—*

(a)   a certain number of hours . . . or

(b)   as and when the employer requires him or her to do so, or

(c)   both a certain number of hours and otherwise as and when the employer requires him or her to do so'

other than on *'a casual'* basis, section 18 operates to ensure that the employee receives remuneration, in circumstances where the employee is not required to work for the employer at all, in that week, alternatively, where the employee is only required to work in that week *'less than the percentage of hours referred to in paragraph (a) or (b) . . . and that percentage of hours is less than 15 hours'*.

Employees who would not have been available for work in the relevant week or were not required to work by reason of lay-off or short time or due to exceptional circumstances or an emergency (in circumstances as set out at section 18(3)(a)(ii)) are not entitled to such remuneration.

3.3   Annual Leave

3.3.1   INTRODUCTION

The Organisation of Working Time Act, 1997 (the 1997 Act) sets out statutory rights for employees in respect of holidays (as well as in respect of rest and maximum working time). It repealed the Holidays (Employees) Act, 1973. The purpose of the Act is to implement into Irish law Council Directive 93/104/EC concerning certain aspects of the organisation of working time.

3.3.2   ENTITLEMENT TO ANNUAL LEAVE

3.3.2.1   Who is entitled to annual leave?

Part III of the 1997 Act sets out the rights and obligations of employees and employers respectively with respect to annual leave. The 1997 Act applies to any person of any age working under a contract of employment or apprenticeship, any person employed through an employment agency, or any person in the service of the State, excluding members of the Garda Síochána and the Defence Forces but including civil servants and employees of any local authority, health board, harbour authority or vocational education committee. There is no qualifying period for holidays and all employees, regardless of status or service, qualify for paid holidays. All time worked qualifies for paid holiday time.

An employee is not limited to the annual leave provided for in the 1997 Act and is entitled to negotiate a more beneficial level of annual leave. The level provided for in the 1997 Act however is the minimum that an employee is entitled to receive.

3.3.2.2   **Full-time and part-time entitlements**

The entitlement of part-time employees is calculated in accordance with section 19 of the 1997 Act and the Protection of Employees (Part-time) Work Act, 2001, 'the Part-Time Work Act'. While the 1997 Act provides the minimum entitlement for full-time and part-time employees, the Part-Time Work Act is relevant in circumstances where employees receive in excess of the minimum holiday entitlement. Section 9 of the Part-Time Work Act provides that a part-time employee shall not, in respect of his or her conditions of employment be treated in a less favourable manner than a comparable full-time employee.

This prohibition does not apply if the difference between the full-time and part-time employee can be justified on 'objective grounds'. Such grounds must be based on considerations other than the status of the employee as a part-timer and the less favourable treatment must be for the purpose of achieving a legitimate objective of the employer and must be necessary for that purpose. Put simply, the most expeditious way to avoid offending the Part-Time Work Act is to provide the benefit to the part-time employee on a pro-rata basis to that enjoyed by the full-time employee.

3.3.3   **CALCULATING ENTITLEMENT**

Section 19 of the 1997 Act provides that an employee shall be entitled to paid annual leave equal to:

> '(a)   *Four working weeks in a leave year in which he or she works at least 1,365 hours (unless it is a leave year in which he or she changes employment),*
>
> (b)   *One-third of a working week for each month in the leave year in which he or she works at least 117 hours,*
>
> (c)   *Eight percent of the hours he or she works in a leave year (subject to a maximum of four working weeks.'*

If more than one of the above methods is applicable, the employee is entitled to whichever method provides the greater entitlement. However, the maximum statutory leave entitlement of an employee in a leave year is four of his or her normal working weeks. A common mistake in employment contracts is the provision of '20 days' holidays in accordance with the Organisation of Working Time Act'. When drafting contracts of employment it is important to remember that the legislation refers to four working weeks and a working week, in many cases is not the standard Monday to Friday five-day week.

For the purposes of annual leave, an employee will be regarded as having worked on a day of annual leave, the hours he or she would have worked on that day had it not been a day of annual leave. A working week is construed as the number of days that that employee would normally work in a particular week.

Working week is not defined by the 1997 Act but in *Irish Ferries v Seamen's Union of Ireland* [2001] DWT 0135, the Labour Court ruled that a working week can only be construed by referring to the number of days or hours encompassing each work cycle. In this particular case, the claimants worked under an annualised-hours contract by which they were required to work 2016 hours per year. They were rostered for work over a continuous seven-day period starting on a Wednesday in each week and ending on the Tuesday of the following week. They were then rostered off duty for the next following seven days. Their annual leave entitlement was calculated by the company as being 168 hours' paid leave (14 days × 12 hours) which was equivalent to 8.33% of the hours worked. The union, however, contended that they effectively only received two weeks' paid holidays per year. Both the rights commissioner and, on appeal, the Labour Court rejected the union's claim.

The court said that the entitlement to annual leave must correspond with the amount of time that the employee would normally be required to work in each work cycle. Here the claimants were required to work 14 12-hour days (168 hours) over each four-week period, hence their entitlement had been correctly calculated.

Section 19(3) of the 1997 Act provides that where an employee works eight or more months in a leave year, the annual leave shall, subject to the provisions of any employment regulation order, registered employment agreement, collective agreement or any agreement between the employee and his or her employer, include an unbroken period of two weeks.

Section 20 (2) of the Act provides that pay in respect of annual leave should be paid to the employee 'in advance' of the taking of the leave. Some employers have sought to construe this as entitling them to make a payment in respect of annual leave, not during the period of annual leave but at some point, perhaps many months, before the period of leave in question. This involves including an amount in an employee's weekly pay, over and above the agreed weekly rate, that is to be regarded by the employee as his/her holiday pay. When the employee actually takes annual leave he/she is not paid for the time they are absent. This practice of paying 'rolled-up' holiday pay is common in the UK and where employers in Ireland have sought to put in place such an arrangement, they have been found to be unlawful.

The matter has recently been considered by the ECJ in several joined cases: namely *CD Robinson-Steele v RD Retail Services Ltd; Michael Jason Clarke v Frank Staddon Ltd and JC Caulfield & Others v Hanson Clay Products Ltd* Joined Cases C–131/04 and C–257/04. The ECJ found that the term 'paid annual leave' means that remuneration must be maintained for the duration of the leave employees must receive their normal remuneration for that period of rest.

Whilst the decision is likely to have a bigger impact in the UK where 'rolled-up' holiday pay arrangements are widespread, it is interesting to note the observation submitted to the ECJ on behalf of Ireland in respect of the joined cases. The Chief State Solicitor in his observation put forward the view that it follows from the words 'paid annual leave' in Article 7(1) of the Directive that the employee must be paid during or immediately before the leave period and in the system of 'rolled-up' holiday pay, the employee is not paid during the period of leave. The purpose of the Directive is to protect the health and safety of employees and the employee is not only entitled to that leave but he/she must be in a position to actually take that leave. The Chief State Solicitor argued that 'rolled-up' holiday pay militates against employees taking leave, as they are required to take leave during a period when they are not paid, whereas if they work they are paid regularly every week or month.

3.3.4   EFFECT OF SICKNESS

If an employee becomes ill during a period of annual leave, the employee will not be regarded for the purposes of the 1997 Act, as being on annual leave, if that employee furnishes to his or her employer a medical certificate in respect of his or her illness (section 19(2)). This does not mean however that an employee will be paid for the absence if the employer's sick leave policy does not provide for paid sick leave.

3.3.5   TIMING OF LEAVE

The times at which annual leave may be taken by an employee are unclear. Section 20(1) of the 1997 Act vests the discretion with the employer as to when the annual leave will be taken having regard to work requirements and subject to the employer taking into account the need for the employee to reconcile work and any family responsibilities and the opportunities for rest and recreation available to the employee. The employer must consult with the employee or his or her trade union at least one month before the holidays are due to commence.

The holidays must be given to the employee within the leave year or, with the employee's consent, within six months of the following leave year. It is the responsibility of the employer to ensure that the employee takes his or her full statutory leave allocation within the appropriate period. Employees may, with the consent of the employer, carry over holidays in excess of statutory minimum leave to a following year.

In *Costello v Gerard F May Roofing Ltd* [1994] ELR 19, the company issued a circular about the times at which holidays could be taken. The claimants ignored the circulars and booked holidays at a time when the employer had prohibited holidays. Their employment was terminated upon taking the holidays in contravention of their employer's instruction. The EAT held that the claimants were aware of the employer's position with regard to the taking of the holidays and in disregarding the circulars were responsible for the resulting dismissals. Consequently, their claims failed.

3.3.6   PAYMENT FOR ANNUAL LEAVE

An employee is entitled to be paid in respect of the period of annual leave and such payment shall:

(a)   be paid to the employee in advance of his or her taking their leave; and

(b)   be at the normal weekly rate or as the case may be at a rate which is proportionate to the normal weekly rate; and

(c)   where the employer would normally receive board or lodging, include compensation for any such board or lodging as will not be received by the employee whilst on annual leave (section 20(2)).

The Organisation of Working Time (Determination of Pay for Holidays) Regulations, 1997 SI 475//1997 sets out the method of calculating the weekly rate of holiday pay.

If the employee's pay is calculated wholly by reference to a time rate or a fixed rate or salary, the amount paid to the employee for one week of paid annual leave is equal to the amount paid to him/her in respect of the normal weekly working hours last worked by the employee before the annual leave commences. This payment includes any regular bonus or allowance that does not vary in relation to work done, but excludes any pay for overtime (regulation 3(2)). Whilst overtime is excluded, the Labour Court has recommended that where 'regular rostered overtime' is worked it should be reflected in the holiday pay (*Banagher Concrete v SIPTU* LCR 18118, 28 February 2005).

If the employee's pay is not calculated wholly by reference to the matters referred to above (e.g. employees who earn commission or who work on piece or productivity rates), the amount paid to him or her for one week of paid annual leave is equal to the average weekly pay of the employee (excluding any pay for overtime) calculated over the period of 13 weeks ending immediately before the annual leave commences.

If no time was worked by the employee during that period, the average weekly pay is calculated over the period of 13 weeks ending on the day on which time was last worked by the employee before the annual leave commences.

In calculating how many days' holidays to which an employee may be entitled, an employer should include all hours worked including time spent on annual leave, time spent on maternity leave, parental leave, force majeure leave, or adoptive leave and time spent on the first 13 weeks of carers' leave. Employees do not accrue annual leave while on sick leave, occupational injury, temporary lay-off or career break.

It is interesting to note that the term 'Paid Annual Leave' is not defined in the 1997 Act. However, the Labour Court in *Royal Liver Assurance Ltd v Services Industrial Professional Technical Union* [2001] DWT 0141 ruled that it is:

> '. . .a term of common usage in industrial relations and is well understood as meaning a period of rest and relaxation during which a worker is paid his or her normal wages without any obligation to work or to provide any service to the employer.'

3.3.7   LEAVE NOT TAKEN AND ACCRUALS

The leave year is defined by section 2 of the 1997 Act to be a year beginning on any first day of April. Accordingly, the leave must be given and must be taken within the leave year save for the situation where the employee consents to the leave being taken within the six months following the leave year. Any leave not taken within that leave year will be forfeited by the employee and can only be accrued for the six months in the following leave year. An employee has no cause of action against an employer for compensation for any leave untaken in previous leave years. An employer may not pay an employee an allowance in lieu of the minimum statutory holiday entitlement of an employee unless the employment relationship is terminated. Section 20(2) provides that pay in respect of annual leave shall be paid to the employee in advance of him or her taking the leave. The only exception to this is contained in section 23(2) which provides that where an employee is leaving his job, then he or she is entitled, as compensation for the loss of the annual leave, to be paid for any outstanding holidays.

The 1997 Act provides at section 27 that a complaint to a rights commissioner regarding breach of the 1997 Act must be taken within a period of six months beginning on the date of contravention to which the complaint relates. In *Campbell Catering Ltd v SIPTU* [2000] DWT 0035 the Labour Court ruled that the limitation period should run from the last such contravention. The matter was further considered by the Labour Court in *Royal Liver Assurance v Services Industrial Professional Technical Union* where the complaint concerned, inter alia, the alleged failure of the company to provide any annual leave or public holiday entitlements in a particular leave year. In the court's view, an infringement of the 1997 Act could not occur while the opportunity to lawfully comply with the provision in question still subsisted. It followed that, where it was alleged that an employer had failed to make a determination pursuant to section 21(1) (relating to public holidays) an infringement of that provision would only occur six months after the end of the leave year if, by that time, the employee had not been granted an additional day's paid annual leave in respect of such public holiday.

In effect therefore an employee can only claim, at most, annual leave and public holiday entitlements for the 18 months preceding the date of complaint. The legislation does not prohibit, however, agreements between employees and employers regarding accruing annual leave. If however, the employer breaches the agreement the employee will not be entitled to seek redress pursuant to the 1997 Act (save for the preceding 18 months entitlement).

3.3.8   TERMINATION AND HOLIDAY PAY

Section 23(1) of the 1997 Act provides that where an employee ceases to be employed, and the whole or any portion of the annual leave in respect of the current leave year or, in the case where the termination of employment occurs during the first half of that year, in respect of that year, the previous year or both these years remains to be granted to the employee, the employee shall as compensation for the loss of that annual leave be paid by his or her employer an amount equal to the pay, calculated at the normal weekly rate or, as the case may be, at a rate proportionate to the normal weekly rate, that he or she would have received had he or she been granted that annual leave.

Put simply, if an employee ceases employment and they have not received their full entitlement to annual leave, they are entitled to be compensated for the loss of that leave. The maximum compensation that they are entitled to is an amount equivalent to untaken annual leave for the leave year and untaken annual leave for the previous leave year where they are terminated within the first six months of the current leave year. There is no entitlement to compensation for any other untaken leave. See the Labour Court determinations in *P R Reilly Ltd v Rob Stronge* [2004] DWT 0437 and *Grosvenor Cleaning Services Ltd v Services Industrial Professional Technical Union* [2004] DWT 0440.

If an employee ceases to be employed because they die, any compensation payable shall be paid to the personal representative of the employee. The compensation payable is by reference to the normal weekly rate.

3.3.9 PUBLIC HOLIDAYS

Public Holidays are defined in the Second Schedule of the 1997 Act as:

(a) Christmas Day (25 December);

(b) St Stephen's Day (26 December);

(c) St Patrick's Day (17 March);

(d) Easter Monday;

(e) the first Monday in May;

(f) the first Monday in June;

(g) the first Monday in August;

(h) the last Monday in October;

(i) New Year's Day (1 January).

In total there are nine public holidays in any particular leave year and employees, other than part-time employees, have an immediate entitlement to public holiday benefits. Part-time employees must have worked at least 40 hours in the five weeks ending on the day before the public holiday to qualify for the public holiday benefit.

The employee is entitled to whichever of the following the employer determines in respect of a public holiday:

(a) a paid day off on that day;

(b) a paid day off within a month of that day;

(c) an additional day of annual leave;

(d) an additional day's pay.

If the employee was otherwise entitled to a paid day off on the relevant public holiday, the first option above will not apply (section 21(1)).

Public holidays should not be confused with bank holidays. For instance Good Friday is a bank holiday and not a public holiday.

An employee is entitled not later than 21 days before the public holiday falls to request his or her employer to make a determination as to which option the employer will avail of. The employer is then obliged to notify the employee of that determination at least 14 days before that holiday. If an employer fails to comply with the request of an employee (or a request is not made), the default will be a paid day off for the public holiday (section 21(2)).

An employee will not be entitled to a public holiday where the employee is absent from work immediately before that public holiday where the absence is:

1. in excess of 52 consecutive weeks by reason of an injury sustained by an employee in an occupational accident;

2. in excess of 26 consecutive weeks by reason of an injury sustained by an employee in any accident or by reason of any disease from which the employee suffers or suffered;

3. in excess of 13 weeks caused by any reason not referred to above being an absence authorised by the employer, including a lay-off;

4. by reason of a strike in the business or industry in which the employee is employed (Schedule 3);

5. on carer's leave in excess of the first 13 weeks of the 65-week entitlement for each person being cared for (section 13(3) Carer's Leave Act, 2001).

Employees on maternity leave, additional maternity leave, parental leave, force majeure leave, or adoptive leave maintain their public holiday entitlement for the duration of their absence.

3.3.10 PAY FOR A PUBLIC HOLIDAY

The method for calculating the rate of pay for a public holiday is set out in the Organisation of Working Time (Determination of Pay for Holidays) Regulations, 1997, SI 475/1997 at regulation 5. The method for calculating the rate of pay is similar to that used to calculate the rate of pay applicable for annual leave.

Where the public holiday falls on a day on which the employee normally works, the employee is entitled to a day's pay for the public holiday. Where the public holiday falls on a day on which the employee does not normally work, the employee is entitled to one-fifth of his or her normal weekly wage for the public holiday. Where the employee is required to work on a public holiday, the employee is entitled to an additional day's pay for the public holiday (or to a paid day off within a month of the public holiday or to an additional day of annual leave).

In relation to the termination of employment, section 23(2) of the 1997 Act provides that where an employee ceases to be employed during the week ending on the day before a public holiday and the employee has worked for his or her employee during the four weeks preceding that week, the employee is entitled to receive pay for the public holiday.

In *Gazboro Ltd v Building and Allied Trades Union* [1999] DWT 9916, the Labour Court considered what period constitutes the week ending on the day before the public holidays in dispute for the purpose of section 23(2) and whether or not an employee who receives an additional day's pay under section 23(2) of the 1997 Act, is deemed to have worked on that day.

In that case, the claimants ceased to be employed on 18 December 1998 and claimed an entitlement to be paid in respect of 25 and 26 December. Such an entitlement would only arise if their employment ceased during the week ending on the day before the public holidays and they worked for the employer in the four weeks preceding that week. The court found that the week ending at midnight on 24 December commenced at midnight on 18 December and since the claimants worked for the employer during the four weeks preceding that week, they were entitled to compensation in an amount equal to an additional day's pay in respect of 25 December. However, the court found that since the week ending on 25 December commenced at midnight on 19 December and as the claimants ceased to be employed on 18 December, they had no entitlement under the 1997 Act in respect of 26 December.

The union however had argued that as they had received an extra day's pay in respect of 25 December, the claimants were deemed to have worked an extra day, thus bringing their termination date within the week ending on the day before 26 December. The court rejected this argument and found that section 22(2) of the 1997 Act provides that time off granted to an employee under section 21 in respect of the public holiday is to be regarded as time worked for the purpose of that section. In this case, the claims were not entitled to time off under section 21 in respect of 25 December but to compensation in an amount equal to an additional day's pay under section 23(2).

3.3.11 RECORD KEEPING

The Act requires employers to maintain employee records of holidays and public holidays for a period of three years (section 25). The manner in which records must be kept is prescribed by the Organisation of Working Time (Records) (Prescribed Form and Exemptions) Regulations, 2001, SI 473/2001 ('the OWT Regulations'). The OWT Regulations provide that an employer is required to keep records that contain the following particulars and documents in relation to each employee.

(a) The name and address of the employee, the employee's revenue and social insurance number, a brief statement (which may be by reference to any form of job description or classification used by the employer) of the employee's duties.

(b) A copy of the statement of terms and conditions of employment provided to each individual employee which complies with the provisions of the Terms of Employment (Information) Act, 1994.

(c) The days and total hours worked in each week by the employee, any days and hours of leave in each week granted by way of annual leave or in respect of a public holiday to the employee and the payment made to the employee in respect of that leave, any additional days paid to the employee where the employee worked on a public holiday.

(d) A copy of a written record of a notification issued to the employee in relation to any of the matters provided for in section 17 of the 1997 Act. Section 17 provides that an employee is entitled to be notified in advance of the hours which the employer will require the employee to work, subject to unforeseeable circumstances justifying a change in the notified times. For example, an employer must notify an employee at least 24 hours before overtime is required to be worked.

The records which contain the above information must be in a form that will enable an Inspector (within the meaning of section 8 of the 1997 Act), to understand the particulars contained without difficulty (regulation 3).

Appended to the Regulations is Form OWT1 to be completed by the employer to record the days and hours worked in each week by the employee. An employer can elect to complete an alternative document so long as it is substantially to like effect of Form OWT1. The requirement to complete Form OWT1 is only in circumstances where an employer has no clocking-in facilities at the place of work (regulation 4(1)). The obligation to keep the records resides with the employer. However, by agreement, the employee may be responsible for the completion of the form so long as the form is countersigned by the employer and retained by the employer (regulation 4(2)).

The only exception to the employer's obligation to comply with the requirements of the OWT Regulations is in relation to the requirement to keep records of rest breaks. This exemption only applies where employers utilise electronic record-keeping facilities and for employers who use manual records where those manual records are in accordance with the Form OWT1. In addition, the employer can only rely on the exemption with respect to the recording of rest breaks provided the employer has notified each employee of the rest periods that the employee is entitled to, pursuant to the 1997 Act. The employer must also put in place and notify in writing to each employee of a procedure whereby an employee may notify in writing to their employer the fact that they were unable to take a rest break that they would have been otherwise entitled to. The employer must keep a record of having notified the employee of their right to rest breaks and also keep record of having notified each employee of the procedure to notify the employer in the event that they do not take their rest break (regulation 3).

In the event that an employer fails to keep records pursuant to the 1997 Act and the OWT Regulations, they will be guilty of an offence under the 1997 Act and liable to a summary conviction and a fine, section 25(3) and regulation 7. However, from a practical perspective, employers who fail to keep proper records will find it very difficult to defend any claim brought against them. Many of the decisions issuing from rights commissioners and the Labour Court find for the claimant on the basis that the evidence of the claimant is not contradicted. In *Edward James Feeney v Milagros Baquiran* [2004] DWT 0427, the Labour Court found that the respondent had failed to maintain records in relation to the claimant's working time as is required by the Regulations and that:

> 'Section 25(4) of the 1997 Act provides, in effect, that where records are not kept in the prescribed form, the onus of proving in proceedings before this Court, that the provisions of the 1997 Act have been complied with in respect of the claimant, rests on the employer.'

3.3.12 ENFORCEMENT PROCEDURES

Any dispute between an employer and an employee can be dealt with by way of a complaint to the rights commissioner (section 27). Written notice of the complaint must be made within six months of the date of the alleged contravention and this time limit may be extended by a further 12 months if the rights commissioner is satisfied that the failure to present the complaint within the normal six-month period was due to reasonable cause.

The Labour Court, in the case of *Cementation Skanska (formerly Kvaerner Cementation Ltd) v A Worker* [2004] DWT 0426 addressed the 'reasonable cause' standard set out in section 27(5) of the 1997 Act. The worker had appealed the decision of the rights commissioner who held that his complaint was out of time. The Labour Court stated that the 'reasonable cause' standard is lower than the standard of 'exceptional circumstances preventing the making of the claim' set out in other employment-related statutes. The Labour Court went on to say that:

> '[I]n considering if reasonable cause exists, it is for the claimant to show that there are reasons, which both explain the delay and afford an excuse of the delay. The explanation must be reasonable, that is to say it must make sense, be agreeable to reason and not be irrational or absurd. In the context in which the expression reasonable cause appears in the statute it suggests an objective standard, but it must be applied to the facts and circumstances known to the claimant at the material time'.

A rights commissioner can do one or more of the following:

(a)   declare that the complaint was well founded or was not well founded;

(b)   require the employer to pay the employee compensation not exceeding two years' remuneration;

(c)   require the employer to comply with the relevant provision (section 27(3)).

The employer or employee may appeal the rights commissioner's recommendation to the Labour Court within six weeks from the date it was communicated to the parties.

Following the hearing of the appeal, the Labour Court will issue a determination and if that determination is not implemented within six weeks from the date on which the determination is communicated to the parties, the Circuit Court, on application, can make an order directing the employer to carry out the determination in accordance with its terms (section 28).

It should also be noted that holiday and public holiday entitlements may be claimed at the Employment Appeals Tribunal where the employee may also have a claim under minimum notice legislation, unfair dismissals legislation, adoptive, carer's leave and maternity leave legislation, payment of wages or minimum wage legislation, insolvency or redundancy legislation, protection of young persons legislation, employment information legislations or part-time and fixed-term workers legislation. The complete list is set out at the table to section 39(2) of the 1997 Act.

3.4 Maternity Rights of Employees

3.4.1 INTRODUCTION

The Maternity Protection Act, 1994 and the Maternity Protection (Amendment) Act, 2004 are the main legislative provisions on maternity leave in Ireland operating in conjunction with the Safety, Health and Welfare at Work (Pregnant Employees) Regulations, 1994, SI 446/1994. The 2004 Act amends the Maternity Protection Act, 1994 and further copper-fastens the rights of employees in this area. The 2004 Act implements the recommendations made by the Working Group on the Review and Improvement of the Maternity Protection Legislation and fulfils a statutory component of the Work/Life Balance Programmes to which the government is committed under the Programme for Sustaining Progress. Additional maternity benefits arose out of the 2006 Budget. The additional maternity leave benefits were given effect by the Maternity Protection Act, 1994 (Extension of Periods of Leave) Order, 2006 which came into operation on 1 March 2006.

3.4.2 ENTITLEMENT TO MATERNITY LEAVE

3.4.2.1 Generally

Section 8 of the 1994 Act as amended by the 2004 Act and the 2006 Order provides that a pregnant employee shall be entitled to 22 consecutive weeks as a minimum period of maternity leave. This will increase to 26 weeks on 1 March 2007. A 'pregnant employee' is defined in the Act as an employee who is pregnant and who has informed her employer of her condition.

Section 9 provides that to avail of this right, the employee must notify the employer in writing of her intention to take maternity leave and must have a medical certificate confirming the expected date of confinement. 'Confinement' is defined in section 41 of the Social Welfare (Consolidation) Act, 1993, as *labour resulting in the issue of a living child, or labour after 28 weeks of pregnancy resulting in the issue of a child whether alive or dead*.

3.4.2.2 Allocation of minimum period of leave

Section 10 deals with the allocation of the minimum period of maternity leave. It provides that the maternity leave shall commence when the employee decides but it must not be later than two weeks before the end of the expected week of confinement. The maternity leave will end when the employee decides but shall end no earlier than four weeks after the end of the expected week of confinement.

3.4.2.3   Variation in allocation of leave

Section 11 provides for a variation in the allocation of maternity leave. It states that maternity leave can commence at an earlier date if there are medical grounds. A medical practitioner must provide a medical certificate to that effect and the provision of those medical certificates to the employer constitutes a notification to the employer in accordance with section 9.

3.4.2.4   Extension of leave

Section 12 provides for the extension of maternity leave where the baby is born after the expected week of confinement. The common practice is that employees take two weeks before the baby is born and ten weeks afterwards. However, in the event that the baby arrives late and the employee has fewer than four weeks left to the end of her maternity leave, the Act provides for an extension of maternity leave by a maximum of four weeks. The section provides that the employee should notify her employer as soon as practicable of her intention to avail of the extension.

3.4.2.5   Additional leave

It should be noted that even if an employee has an extension of maternity leave under section 12, she is still entitled to take the 'additional maternity leave' provided for in section 14. Section 14 allows for an additional 12 weeks beginning immediately after the end of the maternity leave. This additional leave increases to 16 weeks with effect from 1 March 2007. This 'additional maternity leave' is unpaid and at the employee's own expense. The employee must notify the employer not later than four weeks before the expected date of return to work.

3.4.2.6   Unexpected early confinement

Section 13 provides for the commencement of maternity leave on unexpected early confinement. If the baby is born four weeks or more before the due date, the employee is still entitled to 22 (26 from 1 March 2007) weeks but the commencement date of the maternity leave will be the earlier of the date when she commenced maternity leave or the date of confinement. The employee must notify her employer within 14 days of the date of confinement so as to comply with section 9.

3.4.3   SICKNESS OF THE EMPLOYEE

Section 14A provides that in the event of the sickness of the employee (if this occurs during her last four weeks of maternity leave or if she is already on additional maternity leave) the employee may request her employer to terminate her period of additional maternity leave. The employee's absence from work due to sickness following such termination shall be treated in the same manner as any absence from work of the employee due to sickness. The employee shall not however be entitled to then avail of the untaken period of additional maternity leave. Section 16A applies similar provisions to fathers.

3.4.4   HOSPITALISATION OF THE CHILD

Section 14B provides that in the event of the hospitalisation of the child (in respect of whom the maternity leave is taken) an employee may request her employer to postpone her maternity leave/additional maternity leave and allow her to return to work on an agreed date. Maternity leave may only be postponed in the case of an employee who has taken at least 14 weeks' maternity leave, four of which are after the end of the week of confinement. The employee shall be entitled to take the postponed maternity leave/ additional maternity leave in one continuous block known as resumed leave commencing not later than seven days after the discharge of the child from hospital. Regulations made under this section provide for the maximum period of postponement of leave and the evidence to be furnished to the employer of the hospitalisation, and the discharge from hospital, of the child. Section 16B applies similar provisions to fathers (refer Maternity Protection (Postponement of Leave) Regulations, 2004, SI 655/2004).

3.4.5   PAYMENT DURING MATERNITY LEAVE

There is no provision in Irish law for maternity pay from employers to employees, unlike several other European countries. Employees on maternity leave are entitled to claim social welfare benefits, but not to receive any payment from their employers. The social welfare benefit is at the rate of 80 per cent of the employee's reckonable earnings provided that she has made the requisite PRSI contributions. The social welfare benefit is available for the 22 (26 from 1 March 2007) weeks' maternity leave but not for the 12 (16 from 1 March 2007) weeks of additional leave. As the social welfare benefit is subject to change the practitioner would be advised to always check the current rate with the Department. Parties may make their own contractual arrangements but are not compelled by law to do so. Many employees are contractually entitled to receive some form of payment from their employers during maternity leave.

3.4.6   PAID TIME OFF FOR ANTE-NATAL AND POST-NATAL CARE

Section 15 of the 1994 Act entitles pregnant employees to paid time off from work for ante-natal and post-natal care. Such a right existed under the 1981 Regulations, but the 1994 Act also entitles pregnant women to be paid for time off for medical appointments for examinations and tests.

Section 15 does not specifically state the period of post-natal care after the birth of the baby. Section 15(2) provides for the making of regulations in relation to the right to time off. Regulation 5 of the Maternity Protection (Time Off for Ante- and Post-Natal Care) Regulations, SI 18/1995 provides for a 14-week period.

If the employee is on maternity leave following the birth of the child, it is difficult to see how the entitlement to paid time off from work will arise. The entitlement will arise if the employee does not take the full 22 (26 from 1 March 2007) weeks' leave or if the baby arrives late and the employee returns to work while still receiving post-natal care.

Section 15A provides that a pregnant employee shall be entitled to paid time off from work for the purpose of attending one set of ante-natal classes (other than the last three classes in such a set) and that those classes may be attended during one or more pregnancies. Provision is also made for a once-off entitlement for an expectant father to time off work, without loss of pay, for the purpose of attending the last two ante-natal classes in a set of such classes attended by the expectant mother (refer to Maternity Protection (Time Off for Ante-Natal Classes) Regulations, 2004, SI 653/2004).

3.4.7   BREASTFEEDING BREAKS

Section 15B provides that an employee who is breastfeeding shall be entitled, without loss of pay, to either:

    (i)   breastfeeding breaks, where facilities for breastfeeding are provided in the work-place, or;

    (ii)   reduction of working hours.

The employer is not required to provide facilities for breastfeeding in the workplace if the provision of such facilities would give rise to more than a nominal cost. Regulations made under this section provide for: the amount of time off and the number and frequency of breastfeeding breaks to be allowed; the reduction of working hours to be allowed; the terms or conditions relating to breastfeeding breaks/reduction of working hours; the notification procedures; and the evidence to be furnished to the employer in relation to the date of confinement (Maternity Protection (Protection of Mothers who are Breastfeeding) Regulations, 2004, SI 654/2004). An employee who is breastfeeding is defined to be an employee whose date of confinement was not more than 26 weeks earlier and who is breastfeeding and who has informed her employer of her condition. The employee is entitled, without loss of pay, to take one hour from her work each working day as a breastfeeding break. This break may be taken in the form of:

— one break of 60 minutes;

— two breaks of 30 minutes each;

— three breaks of 20 minutes each; or

— such other manner as to number and duration of breaks as may be agreed by her and her employer.

An employee who chooses a reduction of working hours, without loss of pay, is entitled to identical periods.

3.4.8   DEATH OF MOTHER

Section 16 provides that if a woman who has delivered a living child dies at any time before the expiry of the 32nd (40th from 1 March 2007) week following the week of her confinement, the father of the child (provided he is employed under a contract of employment) shall be entitled to leave for a period ending as follows:

(a)   if the mother dies before the expiry of the 20th (24th from 1 March 2007) week following the week of her confinement, the period ends at the end of that 20th (24th from 1 March 2007) week; and

(b)   if the mother dies at any time after the expiry of that 20th (24th from 1 March 2007) week the period ends at the end of the 32nd (40th from 1 March 2007) week following the week of her confinement.

The father is also entitled, if he so wishes, to take further leave from his employment for a maximum period of 12 (16 from 1 March 2007) consecutive weeks commencing immediately after the end of the leave referred to in (a) above.

3.4.9   HEALTH AND SAFETY

The Safety, Health and Welfare at Work Act, 2005 and the Safety, Health and Welfare at Work (Pregnant Employees) Regulations, 2000, SI 218/2000 require employers to carry out risk assessments in respect of their employees. The Pregnant Workers Directive 92/85/EEC requires specific risk assessment for pregnant employees.

In Ireland, because of the broad framework of the health and safety legislation, such risk assessment was required in any event, although not specifically provided for in respect of pregnant workers as a separate group of workers. The 2000 Regulations require employers to carry out a specific risk assessment for pregnant women even if there are no pregnant employees in the firm. As soon as an employer is on notice of an employee's pregnancy or the fact that she has just given birth to a child or is breastfeeding, the employer must reassess the risk in the workplace for that employee without delay and ensure she is not exposed to anything which will damage either her health or that of her developing child. Until the risks are at an acceptable level pregnant workers and new mothers must not be exposed to these risks. The employer must move the employee to alternative work if a risk assessment shows unacceptable risks or if the employee cannot be required to perform night work. If this is not technically or objectively feasible or if the other work is not suitable or a move cannot reasonably be required on duly substantiated grounds, the employee must be granted health and safety leave and receive payment for the first three weeks of that leave. The entitlement to leave on health and safety grounds is provided for in section 18 of the 1994 Act. The employee is entitled to receive three times the normal weekly pay for the 21 days of health and safety leave as provided for in the Maternity Protection (Health and Safety Leave Remuneration) Regulations, 1995, SI 20/1995. For any period after the first 21 days, the employee will be entitled to social welfare benefits.

The health and safety leave can end when the risk no longer exists, as provided for in section 20 of the 1994 Act. Employers are not entitled to dismiss employees if they are unable to work during pregnancy, just after giving birth or while breastfeeding, if that inability to work arises for health and safety reasons.

3.4.10   EMPLOYMENT PROTECTION AND THE RIGHT TO RETURN TO WORK

3.4.10.1   Protective leave

Section 21 provides that protective leave includes maternity leave, additional maternity leave, fathers' leave and health and safety leave. Where leave is postponed in accordance with section 14B or 16B, the time on leave before the postponement and the time on leave after such postponement, shall also be regarded as protective leave. The employee's statutory and contractual rights remain in place while on protective leave. Any termination notice by an employer during that period is void.

Section 22 preserves or suspends certain rights while on protective leave. Section 22(4) provides that absence while on protective leave will not be treated as part of sick leave or annual leave and section 22(6) provides that when an employee is on health and safety leave she will not be entitled to payment for any public holidays falling during that period of absence.

3.4.10.2   Right to return to work

Section 26 of the 1994 Act provides for a general right to return to work. An employee has a general right to return to the position held before the maternity leave. Similarly, if there was a transfer of undertaking while the employee was on leave, she is still entitled to return to work.

3.4.10.3   Suitable alternative work

Alternatively, section 27 provides for a right to suitable alternative work. This means that an employer is not always required to offer an employee her original job back at the end of her maternity leave. Section 27 provides that where the employee is entitled to return to work but it is not reasonably practicable for the employer to permit her to return to work, she is entitled to be offered suitable alternative employment under a new contract of employment. Section 27(2) imposes two requirements in respect of the new contract of employment. It provides that the work required to be done shall be of a kind that is suitable in relation to the employee concerned and appropriate for her to do in the circumstances. It also provides that the terms and conditions relating to the place where the work is required to be done, the capacity in which the employee is to be employed and then the other terms and conditions of employment are not to be less favourable to the employee than those of her contract of employment immediately before the start of her period of absence from work while on maternity leave or additional maternity leave. In addition the terms and conditions need corresponding improvements to the terms and conditions that the employee would have been entitled to had she not been absent.

This means that the suitable alternative work is work that is suitable in relation to the particular employee concerned and appropriate for her to do in the circumstances. This requires a subjective analysis of the work done and the conditions of employment of the employee before she took maternity leave. In *Tighe v Travenol Laboratories (Ireland) Ltd* [1989] 8 JISLL 124 a woman claimed that she had been unfairly constructively dismissed when she returned from maternity leave to be given production work, having previously been employed as an office worker. The EAT took on board the subjective test and said that the nature of work involved in production is so very different from office work that they did not consider it appropriate from the employee's standpoint, although the management might and did argue that the production work was appropriate for the employee in the circumstances.

The employer must show that it was not reasonably practicable to permit the employee to return to work, in order for the employer to be able to rely upon the provisions of section 27 allowing it to offer the employee suitable alternative work. The employer must be able to establish that it made reasonable attempts to be in a position to allow the employee to return to her job, which may mean the employer having to show that it sought a temporary rather than a permanent replacement for the woman while she was on maternity leave. The EAT has twice held, in *Butler v Smurfit Ireland Ltd* UD 137/88 and *O'Brien v Harringtons & Goodlass Ltd* P5/81, that temporary replacements can often be found by employers. In both these cases, the employer was found to have unfairly dismissed the employee when a vacancy was filled on a permanent basis during maternity leave.

3.4.11 NOTIFICATION OF INTENTION TO RETURN TO WORK

An employee is not entitled to return to her job or suitable alternative work unless she has complied with the provisions of the 1994 Act in respect of notification of her intention to return to work. The employer is not obliged to make enquiry of the employee in respect of her intention to return or otherwise.

It is still the employee who must notify the employer of her intention to return to work as provided in section 28. The employee must do so not later than four weeks before the date in which she expects to return to work. She must provide written notification of her intention to return to work and the date on which she expects to do so. A rights commissioner or EAT may extend the time for an employee giving notification where there are reasonable grounds for her failure to give notification or for her giving notification other than as provided for in the Act. Section 28(2) of the 1994 Act governs this. If there are no reasonable grounds, the employee's failure to give the required notification may be taken into account by a rights commissioner, tribunal or the Circuit Court in determining her rights under the 1977 Unfair Dismissals Act, the 1994 Act and any other enactment as far as the remedies of reinstatement, re-engagement or compensation are concerned. Specific provision is also made for the notification requirements for the protective leave.

3.4.12 PREGNANCY-RELATED DISMISSALS

Section 23 of the Maternity Protection Act, 1994 provides that any purported termination, notice of termination or purported suspensions of an employee's employment while, inter alia, absent on protective leave will be void. This includes while the employee is absent to attend ante-natal classes or any period of absence attributable to breastfeeding.

Section 38(1) provides that dismissals are automatically unfair if connected with pregnancy or giving birth. This includes women made redundant during the maternity period and not offered suitable alternative employment if such is available. No qualifying period is necessary to bring a claim for unfair dismissal by reason of pregnancy or the taking of maternity leave.

The Unfair Dismissals Act, 1977 is amended by the Maternity Protection Act, 1994, section 38(4) provides that a dismissal of an employee will be deemed to be unfair dismissal if it results wholly or mainly from

(a) *'the employee's pregnancy, giving birth or breastfeeding or any matter connected therewith'*;

(b) *'the exercise or proposed exercise by the employee of a right under the Maternity Protection Act, 1994 to any form of protective leave or natal care absence . . . or time off from work to attend ante-natal classes or time off from work or a reduction in hours for breastfeeding'.*

3.4.13   PREGNANCY-RELATED ILLNESS

A substantial jurisprudence has developed in the European Court of Justice in respect of the rights of employees suffering from pregnancy-related illness, before and after the birth of their children and in the periods during and after the end of statutory maternity leave. An equality officer applied ECJ case law in deciding *McKenna v North Western Health Board* DEC-E2001. Margaret McKenna claimed that she suffered discrimination contrary to Article 119 of the EC Treaty (now Article 141 of the Treaty of Amsterdam) when her employer treated all of her sick leave in the same manner, despite the fact that some of her sick leave took place while she was pregnant and during her period of statutory maternity leave. The North Western Health Board's sick pay scheme provided for full pay for a period of six months and then half pay for a further six-month period. The way in which it applied its scheme meant that Ms McKenna lost salary because she was treated as having used her six months' full sick pay and therefore had her sick pay reduced to half pay. The equality officer held that her period of sickness during her pregnancy and during her statutory maternity leave could not be used to calculate the amount of sick leave she had incurred and therefore the amount of full sick pay she had received. The period of sickness during pregnancy and maternity leave was to be discounted for the purposes of calculating the six-month period of full pay.

The essence of the decision is that employers must not treat pregnancy-related illness as normal illness when applying the provisions of their sick leave schemes. This is consistent with many judgments of the ECJ in respect of pregnancy-related illness. The decision is, however, restricted to illness prior to the birth of a child and during the period of statutory maternity leave. Again, this is consistent with the jurisprudence of the ECJ and in particular the judgment in *Brown v Rentokil* [1998] ECR I–4185.

In that case the ECJ said that:

'[W]here a woman is absent owing to illness resulting from pregnancy or childbirth and that illness arose during pregnancy and persisted during and after maternity leave, her absence not only during maternity leave but also during the period extending from the start of pregnancy to the start of maternity leave cannot be taken into account for computation of the period justifying her dismissal under national law. As to her absence after maternity leave, this may be taken into account under the same conditions as a man's absence, of the same duration, through incapacity for work.'

The equality officer's decision in *McKenna v North Western Health Board* approves this ECJ judgment and states that the special protection cannot prevail for an indefinite period and ceases at a particular point in time. A female employee is protected from less favourable treatment that results from pregnancy throughout the pregnancy and all the way through to the end of the statutory period of maternity leave. The equality officer states that, in accordance with European jurisprudence, an employer can take full account, for the purposes of its sick leave scheme, of pregnancy-related absence occurring after the statutory period of maternity leave.

A pregnant employee, or an employee suffering from pregnancy-related illness during the period of her statutory maternity leave, can be compared to a sick man. An employee who was absent from work due to pregnancy-related illness may be compared with a sick man and treated as a sick man absent from work for a similar period would be treated.

3.4.14   RESOLUTION OF DISPUTES

Part V of the 1994 Act deals with disputes. Section 31 provides that disputes are to be referred to a rights commissioner within six months of the employer being informed of the initial circumstances of the dispute. The rights commissioner may, in exceptional circumstances, extend the six-month period to 12 months. Section 32(3) provides that the rights commissioner may award up to 20 weeks' remuneration. Section 33 provides for an appeal to the EAT within four weeks and section 34 provides for an appeal to the High Court on point of law only. The Maternity Protection (Disputes and Appeals) Regulations, 1995, SI 17/1995 set out the procedures to be followed and incidental matters, in relation to the hearing of disputes and appeals by a rights commissioner or the EAT under the 1994 Act.

3.4.15   SUMMARY OF MAIN MATERNITY LEAVE PROVISIONS AS AMENDED BY THE MATERNITY PROTECTION ACT, 1994 (EXTENSIONS OF PERIODS OF LEAVE) ORDER, 2006

Date	Entitlement to maternity leave (section 8)	Entitlement to additional maternity leave (section 14)	Entitlement to leave for fathers in the event of mother's death (section 16)	Entitlement to additional leave for fathers in the event of the death of the mother where leave in accordance with section 16(1)(a) leave is taken
Person who commences maternity leave not less than four weeks after 1/2/06	22 weeks	12 weeks	If mother dies at any time before expiry of the 32nd week following the week of her confinement then the father of the child shall be entitled to leave from his employment for a period ending as follows: (a) if the mother dies before the expiry of the 20th week following the week of her confinement then at the end of the 20th week; (b) if the mother dies after the 20th week at the end	12 weeks

			of her 32nd week following her week of confinement.	
Person who commences maternity leave not less than four weeks after 1/2/07	26 weeks	16 weeks	If mother dies at any time before expiry of the 40th week following the week of her confinement then the father of the child shall be entitled to leave from his employment for a period ending as follows: (a) if the mother dies before the expiry of the 24th week following the week of her confinement then at the end of the 24th week; (b) if the mother dies after the 24th week at the end of her 40th week following her week of confinement.	16 weeks

3.5   Parental Leave

3.5.1   INTRODUCTION

The Parental Leave Act, 1998 implemented EU Directive 96/34/EC.

The Act (as amended by the European Communities (Parental Leave) Regulations, 2000, SI 231/2000) confers an entitlement to parental leave and 'force majeure leave' on qualifying employees.

For the purposes of the Act the following definitions apply (section 2):

' *"Contract of employment" means—*
(a)   a contract of service or apprenticeship, or
(b)   any other contract whereby an individual agrees with another person, who is carrying on the business of an employment agency within the meaning of the Employment Agency Act, 1971, and is acting in the course of that business, to do or perform personally any work or service for a third person (whether or not the third person is a party to the contract),
(c)   whether the contract is express or implied and if express, whether it is oral or in writing.'

See *Bourton v Narcea Ltd and AIBP* UD 186/94.

'"Employee" means a person of any age who has entered into or works under (or where the employment has ceased, entered into or worked under) a contract of employment . . .
'"Employer" in relation to an employee—
(a)   means the person with whom the employee has entered into or for whom the employee works under (or, where the employment has ceased, entered into or worked under) a contract of employment, subject to the qualification that the person who under a contract of employment referred to in paragraph (b) of the definition of "contract of employment" is

105

liable to pay the remuneration of the individual concerned in respect of the work or service concerned shall be deemed to be the individual's employer, and

(b)   *includes, where appropriate, the successor or an associated employer of the employer.'*

3.5.2   ENTITLEMENT TO PARENTAL LEAVE

In terms of section 6 the natural or adoptive parent of a child is entitled to a period of 14 working weeks' parental leave to enable him or her to take care of the child.

The period of parental leave must end not later than the day on which the child reaches its fifth birthday, or in the case of an adopted child who had reached three years of age but not eight years of age on or before the date of the making of the adoption order, not later than the expiration of the period of two years beginning on that date.

Parental leave is only available to employees with one year's continuous service with the employer from whose employment the leave is taken (subject to one exception: see below).

An employee is entitled to parental leave in respect of each child of which he or she is the natural or adoptive parent.

Where a person is both a natural and adoptive parent of a particular child, that person is only entitled to parental leave as the natural parent.

Parental leave is non-transferable between the parents of a child.

Where the employee will not have completed the requisite one year's continuous service on the latest day for commencing a period of parental leave, but will have completed three months on the latest day for commencing pro rata leave, the person will be entitled to one week for each month of continuous employment completed at the time of commencement (section 6).

3.5.3   MANNER IN WHICH PARENTAL LEAVE MAY BE TAKEN

Parental leave may be taken as:

(a)   a continuous period of 14 weeks; or

(b)   any combination of days or hours with the agreement of the employer or an industry-wide collective agreement (section 7).

In *O'Neill v Dunnes Stores* [2000] ELR 306 the EAT, upholding the decision of a rights commissioner, determined that 'whilst a continuous period of 14 weeks is an absolute entitlement for an employee, in order for the employee to be entitled to take uncontinuous leave, it must be pursuant to an agreement between the employer and the employee'. Thus, an employee who wishes to avail of leave by way of 'a number of periods of days[and/or]hours' (pursuant to section 7(1) of the Act) may only do so with the permission of the employer.

In the context of the determination of the EAT (and notwithstanding the manner in which the case is reported in the Employment Law Reports), it is to be noted that the determination, when considered in isolation, is ambiguous and unclear. It sets out the respondent's argument and allows the reader to have some understanding of the appellant's argument. However, having failed to make any reference to the decision of the rights commissioner in the case, the findings of the EAT are articulated only to the extent that the determination states that 'the Tribunal upholds the decision of the rights commissioner'. The decision of the rights commissioner has never been reported. All of that said, it is clear that the appellant sought to rely on 'a spirit and intention of the Act which was other than the interpretation made by Mr Flemming, rights commissioner', while the EAT refused to 'go behind the expressed provisions of the Act', preferring to uphold Mr Flemming's decision.

Parental leave taken as days or hours should equate to the hours the employee worked in an agreed 14-week period before the parental leave period or in the absence of agreement, 14 times the average number of hours per week the employee worked in each of the periods of 14 weeks ending immediately before commencement of each week in which leave is taken.

Where an employee is entitled to parental leave in respect of more than one child (not being children of a multiple birth) the leave in total cannot exceed 14 weeks in any period of 12 months, without the employer's consent.

Holidays (apart from public holidays), if they fall within a period of parental leave, must be taken at such other time as determined by the employer pursuant to the Organisation of Working Time Act, 1997, section 20.

In respect of public holidays, where entitlement arises during a period of parental leave a day is added to the period of parental leave in respect of each such public holiday.

3.5.4   NOTICE PROVISIONS

A minimum of six weeks' notice in writing of intention to take parental leave must be given to the employer, specifying the date of commencement, the duration, the manner in which it is proposed to be taken and the notice shall be signed by the employee. Not less than four weeks before taking the leave the employer and the employee must sign 'a confirmation document'.

The employer and the employee are obliged to retain the notice and the confirmation document (or copies of the same, as the case may be) (section 8).

There are interesting provisions in relation to establishing proof of parenthood. In respect of an adopted child, the employer is entitled to call for evidence of the dates of birth of the child and of the making of the adoption order. In respect of any other child, the employer can call for 'evidence in relation . . . to the employee being a parent of the child and the date of birth of the child'. The employer is only entitled to evidence which is 'reasonably' required, but no detail is given as to what might be covered by such 'reasonable' requirements.

3.5.5   POSTPONEMENT, CURTAILMENT AND VARIATION OF LEAVE BY THE PARTIES

Once a confirmation document has been signed, the employee is not entitled to work during the agreed period of parental leave, but the parties may agree to postpone, curtail or vary the leave at any time. Curtailed leave may be taken at another time, by agreement (section 10).

3.5.6   POSTPONEMENT BY THE EMPLOYER

Employers may postpone parental leave entitlement for no more than six months, by notice in writing (to be retained by the parties) of not less than four weeks, following consultation with the employee, where the taking of parental leave would have a substantial adverse effect on the business, profession or occupation by reason of:

(a)   seasonal variations in the volume of the work concerned;

(b)   the unavailability of a person to carry out the duties of the employee in the employment;

(c)   the nature of those duties;

(d)   a number of employees in the employment

(e)   the number of employees in the employment whose periods, or part of whose periods, of parental leave will fall within the period specified by that employee in their notice; or

(f)   'any other relevant matters',

and on condition that no confirmation has been signed by the parties.

An employer may not postpone the commencement of parental leave more than once, unless a ground for the postponement is seasonal variation in the volume of work concerned, in which circumstances, the leave may be postponed twice—being leave in respect of a particular child.

Postponed leave will give rise to a deferred entitlement, beyond the normal expiry date (section 11).

3.5.7   CONDITION OF TAKING PARENTAL LEAVE

Entitlement to parental leave is subject to the condition that it must be used to take care of the child concerned.

Where an employer 'has reasonable grounds for believing that an employee . . . who is on parental leave is not using the leave for the purpose of taking care of the child concerned' he can terminate the leave by no less than seven days' notice in writing, whereupon the employee must return to work.

Where an employer 'has reasonable grounds for believing that the employee is not entitled to . . . parental leave', the employer may refuse the leave by notice in writing.

In both of the above cases, the employer must give the employee written notice of intent, advising the employee of the right to make representation, within seven days, which representation the employer must consider.

Notices must be retained by the parties (section 12).

3.5.8   FORCE MAJEURE LEAVE

3.5.8.1   Meaning

Section 13 of the Parental Leave Act, 1998 provides that, in certain circumstances, an employee will be entitled to force majeure leave. Force majeure leave arises where for urgent family reasons owing to an injury or illness the immediate presence of the employee 'at the place where the [injured or ill] person is, whether at his or her home or elsewhere is indispensable'.

3.5.8.2   Entitlement to force majeure leave

Force majeure leave may be taken in respect of the following people:

(a)   child;

(b)   spouse or person with whom the employee is living as husband or wife;

(c)   a person to whom the employee is in loco parentis;

(d)   a brother or sister; or

(e)   a parent or grandparent.

108

By its very nature notice cannot be given of force majeure leave but the employee is obliged 'as soon as reasonably practicable thereafter' to give a written notice to the employer of the date on which the leave was taken and giving a statement of facts as to why it was taken.

Force majeure leave may consist of one or more days but shall not exceed three days in any period of 12 consecutive months or five days in any period of 36 consecutive months.

Where an employee is absent on force majeure leave for part of a day it is deemed to be a full day.

3.5.8.3   Case law

3.5.8.3.1   Carey v Penn Racquet Sports Ltd

In *Carey v Penn Racquet Sports Ltd* [2001] ELR 27 the employee was 'a single mother caring for an eight-year-old child'. The determination of the EAT recites that:

> 'She did not come to work on 11th June 1999 as her eight-year-old child was sick. During the very early morning she noticed that she was sick and she did not know if she had a temperature. When she got up for work she noticed that the child had rash on her two legs and she decided to stay at home and observe her. The rash was getting worse and she took her to the doctor, 3 miles away. [The employee] lives alone, is a single parent and is 18–20 miles from Mullingar. The doctor advised her to get calamine lotion and to keep an eye on her daughter. She then had to travel 10 miles to a chemist in Ballymahon. She felt it was best to stay with her child that day and that her presence was indispensable.
>
>   'During cross-examination [the employee] said that between 12 am and 6 am she had been concerned about her child. She said she would not be in a position herself to diagnose whether her condition may be serious. She was due to start work at 8 am that day and sometimes she worked on the 4 am shift. She took the child to the doctor at around 10 am or 11 am and asked her sister to ring the respondent.'

The EAT determined:

> '. . .that the applicant was concerned about her child's health on 11th June 1999. She became aware very early in the morning that her daughter was sick. She did not know if she had a temperature. She did not call the doctor. When she got up she noticed a rash on the child's legs. She took the child to the doctor at around 10.30 am. According to her evidence she could not be sure of the time. Again, according to her own evidence she did not panic. The first mention of meningitis was at the hearing before the rights commissioner. There was conflicting evidence as to the time she had to start work. She had a child minder.'

The EAT, by a two to one majority, determined that 'the particulars of [the] case [did] not fall within the meaning of the Act, as urgent, immediate and indispensable'.

The matter came before the High Court on 24 January 2001. Carroll J stated that, '[w]hile it [was] not spelt out in the determination of the Tribunal, it [seemed] clear that the reason the force majeure leave was refused was that the rash turned out to be not serious'. The judge went on to state:

> '[T]he Tribunal should not have approached the matter on that basis. This was judging with hindsight the urgency of the family reasons and the question of whether the employee's presence with her child was indispensable. The matter should have been looked at from the plaintiff's point of view at the time the decision was made not to go to work. Also the plaintiff could not be assumed to have medical knowledge which she did not possess.'

109

It is to be noted that the defendant did not contest the matter and did not appear in court.

Carroll J held that it was a mistake of law to decide the issue on the basis of the ultimate outcome of the illness and, accordingly, she held that the plaintiff was entitled to one day of paid force majeure leave for Friday, 11 January 1999.

3.5.8.3.2 McGaley v Leibherr Container Crane

In *McGaley v Leibherr Container Crane* [2001] 12 ELR 350 the employee's wife 'became violently ill and vomited repeatedly'. The employee and his wife had a child who was under 12 months' old. The employee's wife submitted that she was unable to take proper care of the baby who was on a special diet. She did not call a doctor as she was convinced that she was suffering from a stomach bug. The employee was absent from work for a day by agreement with his employer. He then applied for paid force majeure leave and his employer refused. The matter came before a rights commissioner who refused the employee's application and then in turn to the EAT. The EAT held that 'that the appellant's claim for leave does not meet the requirements of force majeure leave. . . . He has failed to show that his immediate presence was indispensable'. The employee appealed to the High Court on a point of law. The matter was heard by McCracken J. who affirmed the decision of Carroll J in the *Carey v Penn Racket Sports Ltd* and in doing so held:

> 'This is clear authority that the Tribunal must judge whether the facts of the particular case come within section 13 but that such judgment must be based on the facts as they existed at the time of the circumstances which it is alleged gave rise to the implementation of the section.'

However, while conceding that the facts were similar in the case before him to that before Carroll J, he held:

> 'I must emphasise that the only appeal to the court under the Act is on a question of law. I am quite satisfied that it is a question of fact as to whether the appellant's immediate presence was or was not indispensable, although the Tribunal must determine that fact only by looking at the circumstances that were known at the time the appellant decided to stay at home. It is not open to this Court to look at those circumstances and decide that this Court would have reached a different decision, provided the Tribunal did not err in law in the manner determined in the *Carey* case.
>
> 'I do not think I can take the same inference from the facts of this case or the decision of the Tribunal that Carroll J took in the *Carey* case. The evidence in this case is that the illness was not considered by the appellant or his wife to be a serious illness or indeed one which required the attention of a doctor. Thus the seriousness or otherwise of the illness was not determined by the Tribunal with hindsight, but had been determined by the parties themselves at the time of the illness. . .[T]he Tribunal is the sole arbiter of fact, and heard evidence from witnesses who were cross-examined, and on that evidence it made the determination that the appellant's presence was not indispensable. In my view that is a pure question of fact decided on the evidence, and there is nothing to suggest or from which I would draw the inference that the Tribunal applied wrong principles in making their decision. Accordingly, I do not feel there is a question of law involved which would warrant an appeal under section 20 of the Act I must refuse the order sought.'

In affirming the decision of Carroll J in *Carey*, McCracken J was clearly of the view that the appellant's case failed on the basis that he was being asked to determine a question of fact and not a question of law.

3.5.8.3.3   Murphy v Celtic Linen Ltd—*EAT—18 September 2003*

In *Murphy v Celtic Linen Ltd* the employee's 22-month-old child became ill with an ear throat and chest infection. The employee's child was diagnosed with an infection and was prescribed antibiotics. The child was very ill for the following two days and the employee argued that she had to remain at home with her child because the child was very 'clingy'. The employee applied for force majeure leave for two days but was refused. The employer argued that the employee's absence was a 'routine absence' and it was incumbent on parents to have arrangements in place for routine illnesses. Such routine absence was not an absence to be covered by force majeure leave.

The EAT considered the facts in the *Carey* case and in granting the employee's application held 'in the present case the child is younger [than the child in the *Carey* case] and would be more likely to cling to its mother. In the final analysis we think it is for the parent to decide whether his or her immediate presence is necessary at his or her home or elsewhere is indispensable.'

In effect what the EAT has concluded is that the decision as to whether or not the relevant person is indispensable, for the purposes of the force majeure leave provisions of the Parental Leave Act, is subjective.

3.5.8.3.4   Foley v Dunnes Stores—*Rights Commissioner—July 2005*

In *Foley v Dunnes Stores*, the employee's husband became suddenly ill with appendicitis. The employee was at work when she was notified that her husband had taken ill and her employer paid her force majeure leave for that day. The employee was subsequently notified that her husband would be discharged from hospital some days later and during this period the employee informed the employer that she intended to take force majeure leave when her husband was discharged from hospital. Ms Foley was informed that she was not entitled to force majeure leave. Ms Foley took the leave and subsequently made an application to the rights commission for payment for two days' force majeure leave being the date her husband was discharged and the day following. The rights commissioner in finding against the claimant said the claimant did not provide the respondent employer with the notice in either the scheduled form or a form to like effect containing the information and declaration. In addition she held that on the basis of the evidence presented the claimant failed to show that her immediate presence was indispensable on the days in question.

3.5.9   EMPLOYMENT PROTECTION AND THE RIGHT TO RETURN TO WORK

While on parental leave employees have to be treated as benefiting from all of their employment rights and entitlements other than remuneration and pension benefits, and absence cannot be treated as part of any other type of leave including sick leave, annual leave, maternity leave and force majeure leave (section 14).

In the context of the above, the decision of the ECJ in *Lewen v Denda* [2000] IRLR 67 is of interest. In that case, the court held that Article 119 of the EC Treaty precludes an employer from entirely excluding women on parental leave from the benefit of a Christmas bonus without taking account of the work done in the year in which the bonus is paid, or of periods of maternity leave during which they were prohibited from working, where that bonus is awarded retroactively as pay for work performed in the course of that year (and the case turned primarily on the differentiation as between payments which might be regarded as 'retroactive pay' and payments which might be regarded as incentives to work hard in the future/rewards for future loyalty). The court stated that a worker who exercises a statutory right to take parental leave is in a special situation, which cannot be compared to that of a man or woman at work, since such leave involves suspension of the contract of employment and, therefore, of the respective obligations of the employer and the worker. Therefore, community law does not preclude a refusal to pay a Christmas bonus to a woman on parental leave where the award of such a bonus is subject to the sole condition that the worker must be in active employment when it is awarded. Article 119 of the EC Treaty precludes an employer, when granting a Christmas bonus, from taking periods during which mothers are prohibited from working into account, so as to reduce the benefit pro rata. However, community law does not preclude an employer, when granting a Christmas bonus to a female worker who is on parental leave, from taking periods of parental leave into account, so as to reduce the benefit pro rata.

Probation, training or apprenticeship may be suspended during parental leave.

An employee on force majeure leave retains all entitlements including remuneration and pension and again such absence cannot be treated as part of any other leave.

There is a general right to return to work, for the same employer (or the employer's successor) in the same job, under the same contract, but if it is not 'reasonably practicable for the employer to permit the employee to return to work . . . the employee shall be entitled to be offered . . . suitable alternative employment' (section 15).

3.5.10 RESOLUTION OF DISPUTES

Disputes are dealt with at first instance by a rights commissioner and, on appeal, to the EAT with appeal to the High Court on a point of law thereafter.

The rights commissioner or EAT may order 'appropriate' redress including the grant of leave or an award of compensation, not exceeding 20 weeks' remuneration.

Decisions/determinations of a rights commissioner or the EAT are enforced by the Circuit Court.

It should be noted that the Act does not oblige an employer to pay an employee while on parental leave although it leaves it open for employers to do so. Many believed that the EU Directive would lead to paid parental leave but this has not happened.

3.5.11 REGULATIONS

The following regulations have been made under the Parental Leave Act:

(a) Parental Leave (Disputes and Appeals) Regulations, 1999, SI 6/1999;

(b) Parental Leave (Maximum Compensation) Regulations, 1999, SI 34/1999;

(c) Parental Leave (Notice of Force Majeure Leaver) Regulations, 1998, SI 454/1998.

3.6 Adoptive Leave

3.6.1 INTRODUCTION

The Adoptive Leave Act, 1995 gave effect to one of the recommendations in the *Report of the Second Commission on the Status of Women*, January 1993. The Adoptive Leave Act, 2005 which came into operation on 28 November 2005 (with the exception of sections 9 and 10) amends the 1995 Act and revokes the Adoptive Leave Act, 1995 (Extension of Periods of Leave) Order, 2001 and the Adoptive Leave Act, 1995 (Extension of Periods of Leave) Order, 2004. Additional adoptive leave benefits arose out of the 2006 Budget. The additional adoptive leave benefits were given effect by the Adoptive Leave Act, 1995 (Extension to Periods of Leave) Order, 2006 and came into operation on 1 March 2006.

The Act entitles female employees, and in certain circumstances male employees to leave from their employment for the purpose of child adoption, and to extend to them the protection against unfair dismissal conferred by the Unfair Dismissals Acts, 1977–2001. The definition of 'contract of employment' is identical to that in the Parental Leave Act, 1998 (refer **3.5.1**). The definitions of 'employee' and 'employer' are similar to those contained in the Parental Leave Act. Additionally, and relevant to the Adoptive Leave Act, the following definitions apply:

> '*"adopting father" means a male employee in whose care a child has been placed or is to be placed with a view to making of an adoption order, or to the effecting of a foreign adoption or following any such adoption where the adopting mother has died.*
>
> *"adopting mother" means a woman, including an employed adopting mother, in whose care a child (of whom she is not the natural mother) has been placed or is to be placed with a view to the making of an adoption order to the effecting of a foreign adoption or following any such adoption.*
>
> *"adopting parent" means employed adopting mother, adopting father or sole male adopter.*
>
> *"day of placement" means*
>
> *(a)   the day on which the child is placed physically in the care of the adopting parent with a view to the making of an adoption order, or*
>
> *(b)   the day on which the child is placed physically in the care of the adopting parent with the view to the effecting of a foreign adoption, or*
>
> *(c)   in the case of a foreign adoption, where the child has not previously been placed in the care of the adopting parent, the day on which the child has been so placed following the adoption.*
>
> *"employed adopting mother" means a female employee in whose care a child (of whom she is not the natural mother) has been placed or is to be placed with a view to the making of an adoption order, or to the effecting of a foreign adoption or following any such adoption.*
>
> *"sole male adopter" means a male employee who is not an adopting father within the meaning of this Act and whose sole care of child has been placed or is to be placed with a view to the making of an adoption order, or to the effecting of a foreign adoption or following any such adoption.'*

3.6.2   ENTITLEMENT TO ADOPTIVE LEAVE

Part II of the Acts set out the entitlement of employees to adoptive leave. An employed adopting mother (or sole male adopter) shall be entitled to adoptive leave from his or her employment for a period beginning on the day of placement of not less than 20 (24 from 1 March 2007) consecutive weeks (or such other period as the Minister may prescribe) (section 6).

An employed adopting mother (or sole male adopter) who is entitled to, or is on adoptive leave shall, if on request, be entitled to further leave known as additional adoptive leave for a maximum period of 12 (16 from 1 March 2007) consecutive weeks (or such other period as the Minister may prescribe) commencing immediately after the end of his or her adoptive leave (section 8(1)).

The 2005 Act makes provision for the termination of additional adoptive leave, on written request, in circumstances of the sickness of the adoptive parent (section 11B(1)). The effect of the termination of additional adoptive leave is that absence from work owing to sickness after the termination will be treated in the same way as any other absence owing to illness. The employee loses the right to any leave not taken by then.

In the case of a foreign adoption, the employed adopting mother (or sole male adopter) is entitled to some or all of the adoptive leave before the day of placement, for the purposes of familiarisation with the child who is to be adopted (section 8(5)). A period of additional adoptive leave in respect of foreign adoptions shall expire immediately before the day of placement (section 8(8)).

3.6.3   DEATH OF MOTHER

The Adoptive Leave Acts, 1995 and 2005 only extends adoptive leave to adopting fathers in certain circumstances. Where an adopting mother dies, the adopting father shall be entitled to adoptive leave for one of the following periods:

(a)   12 (16 from 1 March 2007) weeks; or

(b)   in a case where the adopting mother dies on or after the day of placement, 20 (24 from 1 March 2007) weeks less a period equivalent to the period between the date of placement and the date of her death; or

(c)   such other period as the Minister may prescribe (section 9(1)).

Similarly, in respect of additional adoptive leave, where an adopting mother dies, the adopting father can request the additional adoptive leave for one of the following periods:

(a)   12 (16 from 1 March 2007) weeks; or

(b)   in a case where the adopting mother dies on or after the expiration of the 20 (24 from 1 March 2007) weeks from the day of placement, 12 (16 from 1 March 2007) weeks less the period between the date of that expiration and the date of her death; or

(c)   such other period as the Minister may prescribe (section 10(1)).

The Act also provides for the entitlement of an adopting father in the case of a foreign adoption for additional adoptive leave for the purposes of familiarisation with the child in circumstances where the adopting mother dies (section 11).

The right of an adopting father to adoptive leave is secondary to the rights of the adopting mother and only available in circumstances where the adopting mother dies.

3.6.4   TIME OFF TO ATTEND PRE-ADOPTION CLASSES

In terms of section 11A (inserted by the 2005 Act) an employee is entitled to time off without loss of pay to attend pre-adoption classes and meetings.

3.6.5   POSTPONEMENT OF LEAVE ON HOSPITALISATION OF CHILD

The 2005 Act introduces provisions for the postponement on written request to the employer of the whole or part of adoptive or additional adoptive leave where the adopted child is hospitalised (section 11C).

Subject to the agreement of the employer the employee is entitled to continue or return to work, as the case may be and the leave is postponed until it is taken as a continuous period beginning not later than seven days after the child is discharged from hospital or such other time as agreed.

3.6.6   ABSENCE OWING TO SICKNESS WHILST LEAVE POSTPONED

Where an employee, whose request to postpone leave has been granted by the employer continues or returns to work and then is absent due to sickness, the employee is deemed to have begun the postponed leave on the first day of absence unless the employer is given written notice that the employee does not wish to begin the postponed leave.

The effect of the notification is that the absence is treated in the same way as any other absence owing to sickness and the employee ceases to be entitled to the postponed leave (section 11D).

3.6.7 PAYMENT FOR ADOPTIVE LEAVE

Like maternity leave there is no provision in Irish law for payment of adoptive leave from employers to employees. Employees are however entitled to claim social welfare benefits, but not to receive any payment from their employers. The social welfare benefit is at the rate of 70 per cent of the employee's reckonable earnings provided the employee has made the requisite PRSI contributions. The social welfare benefit is available for the adoptive leave but not for the additional leave. Parties are entitled to make their own contractual arrangements or their own bargains with their employers.

3.6.8 NOTICE PROVISIONS

Like all statutory leave an employee wishing to avail of adoptive leave must provide their employer with notice of their intention to take such leave.

In the case of an adoption other than a foreign adoption, an employed adopting mother or sole male adopter will not be entitled to the minimum period of adoptive leave unless:

(a) having, as soon as is reasonably practicable but not later than four weeks before the expected day of placement, notified the employer in writing of his or her intention to take adoptive leave; and

(b) having, as soon as is reasonably practicable, caused his or her employment to be notified in writing of the expected day of placement; and

(c) causing his or her employer to be supplied with a certificate of placement as soon as is reasonably practicable but not later than four weeks after the day of placement (section 7(1)).

Similar provisions apply in the case of foreign adoption with the added requirement that the employee provide a copy of the declaration made pursuant to the Adoption Act 1991 which relates specifically to foreign adoptions (section 7(2)).

Where the day of placement is postponed, the commencement of the period of adoptive leave shall also be postponed subject to the employed adopting mother (or sole male adopter) notifying the employer of the expected new day of placement as soon as is reasonably practicable (section 7(4)).

When an employed adopting mother (or sole male adopter) intends to avail of additional adoptive leave, they must notify their employer at the same time they notify them of their adoptive leave or alternatively not later than four weeks before the date which would have been the expected date of his or her return to work had they not taken the additional adoptive leave (section 8(2) and (3)).

In the case of a foreign adoption, where the employed adopting mother (or sole male adopter) intends to take a period of additional adoptive leave before the day of placement, for the purposes of familiarisation with the child, the employed adopting mother (or sole male adopter):

(a) must notify his or her employer in writing not later than four weeks before the date on which he or she intends to take such leave, of the intended date of commencement of such additional adoptive leave; and

(b) must supply his or her employer to be supplied with a copy of the declaration made pursuant to the Adoption Act, 1991.

In the event that an adopting father is entitled to take adoptive leave he is required to notify his employer. Having regard to the circumstances in which the adopting father is entitled to adoptive leave and additional adoptive leave i.e. on the death of the adopting mother, the notification requirements are not as onerous as those applying to adopting employed mothers or sole male adopters. Refer to sections 9(2), 10(3) and 11(2).

If placement of the child with the adopting parent terminates before the expiry of the leave to which the adopting parent is entitled (other than as a result of the death of the child) the adopting parent shall notify his or her employer in writing of the date of termination of placement as soon as is reasonably practicable but not later than seven days after the termination of placement (section 12(1)).

The adopting parent shall then be required to return to work on such a date as is convenient to his or her employer but not later than the date on which the period of adoptive leave or additional adoptive leave expires (section 12(2)). The employer is required to give one week's notice of the day on which he or she is required to return to work (section 12(4)).

In the case of a foreign adoption where the adopting parent takes additional leave before the day of placement and no placement takes place, he or she shall return to work on the day on which the notified period of such leave was to expire at the latest. In any event, he or she should notify his or her employer of the intended date or return to work as soon as is reasonably practicable (section 12(3)).

The entitlement to time off to attend pre-adoption meetings and classes is subject to the employee having notified the employer in writing of the times and dates of the classes as soon as practicable but not later than two weeks before the first class and produced documentary proof of the dates and times of such classes on request. In certain circumstances the notification period is reduced to one week (section 11A(3)).

The employee is only entitled to time off without loss of pay to attend pre-adoption classes or meetings held within the State (section 11A(4)).

3.6.9 EMPLOYMENT PROTECTION AND THE RIGHT TO RETURN TO WORK

Part III of the Adoptive Leave Act provides protection to employees who avail of adoptive leave in respect of their employment. While absent from work on adoptive leave an employee shall be deemed to have been in the employment of the employer and shall be treated as if he or she had not been absent and the absence shall not effect any right related to his or her employment (other than his or her right to remuneration during the absence) (section 15(1)).

This blanket protection however does not apply to employees:

- on probation;
- undergoing training in relation to that employment; or,
- who are apprentices.

In those circumstances the probation, training or apprenticeship shall be suspended during any absence from work and must be completed by him or her on his or her return to work. Similar provisions apply for additional adoptive leave. The adopting parent, while on adoptive leave, will have their employment treated as continuous for employment entitlements (section 15(2)). A period of absence while on adoptive leave or additional adoptive leave shall not be treated as part of any other leave (section15 (5)). Likewise adopting parents attending pre-adoption classes or meetings will have their employment rights protected (section 15(3)).

The Act also prohibits certain purported terminations of employment (section 16). Specifically, each of the following shall be void:

(a) any purported termination or suspension from employment of an adopting parent while he or she is absent from work on adoptive leave or additional adoptive leave, or attending pre-adoption classes or meetings;

(b) any notice of termination of the employment of an adopting parent given while he or she is absent from work on adoptive leave or additional adoptive leave or attending pre-adoption classes or meetings and expiring subsequent to such absence (section 16).

This would include termination for any reason including redundancy.

If an employer has given an employee notice of termination or notice of any suspension from his or her employment before the adopting parent begins a period of leave under the Act, which is due to expire during his or her absence from work on that leave, such notice shall be extended by the period of his or her absence from work on adoptive leave or additional adoptive leave or whilst attending pre-adoption classes or meetings (section 17).

An adopting parent who is absent from work while on adoptive leave or additional adoptive leave, the adopting parent shall be entitled to return to work with the employer with whom he or she was working immediately before absence (or their successor) (section 18(1)(a)) in a job which he or she held immediately before the absence began (section 18(1)(b)) and under the contract of employment under which he or she was employed immediately before the absence began (or with the employer's successor) under terms or conditions not less favourable than those that would have been applicable to and that incorporates any improvements in the terms and conditions of employment to which he or she would have been entitled (section 18(c)).

In circumstances where an employee is entitled to return to work but it is not reasonably practicable to allow the employee to return to work, the employee shall be entitled to be offered suitable alternative employment in accordance with a new contract of employment (section 19(1)). Work under a new contract of employment will only constitute suitable alternative work if it is of a kind that is suitable to the employee and appropriate for the employee to do in the circumstances and where the terms or conditions of the contract are not substantially less favourable to the employee than those of his or her contract of employment immediately before the employee went on adoptive leave or additional adoptive leave and incorporates any improvements in the terms and conditions of employment to which he or she would have been entitled if he or she had not been absent (section 19(2)).

3.6.10   NOTIFICATION OF INTENTION TO RETURN TO WORK

An adopting parent who is entitled to, or is on adoptive leave or additional adoptive leave shall notify his or her employer, in writing, of his or her intention to return to work not later than four weeks before the date on which he or she expects to return to work, however, where the period of leave is four weeks or less the notification must be given at the same time as the notification of the intention to take leave. Where the leave is for more than four weeks and the leave is postponed leave, the notification must be given at the same time as the notification of intention to take the leave or at least four weeks before the date of expected return to work whichever is the latest. Where he or she is absent from work owing to sickness while on postponed leave the notification must be given as soon as reasonable after the beginning of absence due to sickness but not later than the date on which he or she expects to return to work (section 20).

3.6.11   RESOLUTION OF DISPUTES

Generally, a dispute between an adopting parent and his or her employer relating to the adopting parent's entitlements under the Adoptive Leave Acts (or to any matter arising out of or related to such entitlements) may be referred by either party to the dispute to a rights commissioner (section 32(2)). Disputes relating to an unfair dismissal, a claim under the Redundancy Payments Act, or a claim under the Minimum Notice and Terms of Employment Act are dealt with pursuant to the provisions of the relevant statutes. Either party is entitled to appeal the decision of a rights commissioner to the EAT within four weeks of the date on which the rights commissioner's decision was communicated to the parties.

On the hearing of a dispute a rights commissioner or the tribunal shall:

(a)   in the case of a rights commissioner, make a decision in relation to the dispute; or

(b)   in the case of the tribunal, make a determination in relation to the dispute;

and may give such directions as the rights commissioner or the tribunal, as the case may be, considers necessary or expedient for the resolution of the dispute (section 33(1)).

A rights commissioner or a tribunal may if considered it appropriate, make an award of compensation in favour of the adopting parent to be paid by the employer. The amount of compensation shall be of such amount as the rights commissioner or tribunal deems just and equitable having regard to all the circumstances of the case but shall not exceed 20 weeks' remuneration (section 33 (2) and (3)).

A dispute must be lodged with the rights commissioner within six months from either the day of placement or where no placement has taken place, within six months from the date the employer is first notified of the employee's intention to take either adoptive leave or additional adoptive leave. An adopting father must refer a dispute within six months of the adopting mother's death. The time limit can be extended to 12 months if the rights commissioner is satisfied there were exceptional circumstances that prevented the referral within the six-month period (section 34 (1)).

3.6.12   SUMMARY OF MAIN ADOPTIVE LEAVE PROVISIONS AS AMENDED BY THE ADOPTIVE LEAVE ACT, 1995 (EXTENSIONS OF PERIODS OF LEAVE) ORDER, 2006

Date	Entitlement to adoptive leave (section 6)	Entitlement to additional adoptive leave (section 8)	Entitlement to leave for fathers in the event of adopting mother's death (section 9)	Entitlement to additional leave for fathers in the event of the death of the adopting mother (section 10)
Person who commences adoptive leave not less than four weeks after 1/2/06	20 weeks	12 weeks	If adopting mother dies, the adopting father shall be entitled to leave from his employment for: (a) where the adopting mother dies on or after the day of placement, 20 weeks less the period between the date of placement and the date of her death; (b) in any other case, 20 weeks.	Where an adopting mother dies, the adopting father can request additional adoptive leave for one of the following periods: (a) 12 weeks; or (b) in a case where the adopting mother dies on or after the expiration of 20 weeks from the day of placement, 12 weeks less the

				period between the date of that expiration and the date of her death.
Person who com- mences adoptive leave not less than four weeks after 1/2/07	24 weeks	16 weeks	If adopting mother dies, the adopting father shall be entitled to leave from his employment for: (a) where the adopting mother dies on or after the day of placement, 24 weeks less the period between the date of placement and the date of her death; (b) in any other case, 24 weeks.	Where an adopting mother dies, the adopting father can request additional adoptive leave for one of the following periods: (c) 16 weeks; or (d) in a case where the adopting mother dies on or after the expiration of 24 weeks from the day of placement, 16 weeks less the period between the date of that expiration and the date of her death.

3.7 Carer's Leave

3.7.1 INTRODUCTION

The Carer's Leave Act was signed by the President on 2 July 2001 and came into immediate effect. The Carer's Leave Act does not specifically implement an EU Directive but it follows on from the Parental Leave Act, 1998 which implements EU Directive 96/34/EC. The Act fulfilled a Government promise in both 2000 and in the Programme for Prosperity and Fairness that legislation would be introduced to give effect to a carer's benefit and a parallel right to carer's leave.

The Act:

(a) provides for the temporary absence from employment of employees for the purpose of the provision of full-time care and attention to a person requiring it; and

(b) to protect the employment rights of those employees during such absence.

The definitions of 'contract of employment', 'employee' and 'employer' are the same as the Parental Leave Act, 1998 (3.5.1 above). Additionally, and relevant to the Carer's Leave Act, the following definitions apply:

(a) *'full time care and attention'* has the meaning attributed to it in section 82A of Chapter 11A of Part II of the Social Welfare (Consolidation) Act, 1993.

Although the section does not refer to 'full-time care and attention' it does provide a definition at Part III of the 1993 Act states that 'the Minister may make regulations specifying the circumstances and conditions under which a person is to be regarded as providing full-time care and attention to a relevant person'. It is also stipulated that a relevant person shall be regarded as requiring full-time care and attention where:

(i) he or she has such a disability that he or she requires from another person—

— continual supervision and frequent assistance throughout the day in connection with normal bodily functions; or
— continual supervision in order to avoid danger to himself or herself; and

(ii) the nature and extent of his or her disability has been certified in the prescribed manner by a medical practitioner;

(b) *'relevant person'* is defined in section 82A(1) of Chapter 11A of Part II of the above Act as person (other than a person in receipt of an increase of disablement pension under section 57 in respect of constant attendance) who has such a disability that he or she requires full-time care and attention and who:

(i) has attained the age of 18 years; or

(ii) is under the age of 18 years and is a person in respect of whom an allowance is paid for domiciliary care of handicapped children under section 61 of the Health Act, 1970.

3.7.2   ENTITLEMENT TO CARER'S LEAVE

An employee who has been employed for a period of a months' continuous employment (as defined by the First Schedule to the Minimum Notice and Terms of Employment Act, 1973) by the employer from whose employment the carer's leave is proposed to be taken shall be entitled to leave for the purpose of providing full-time care and attention to a relevant person for a period not exceeding 65 weeks for each relevant person if:

(a) the person to whom the employee proposes to provide full-time care and attention is a relevant person;

(b) the employee provides the employer concerned with a decision from the Minister for Social, Community and Family Affairs by a deciding officer that the person in respect of whom the employee proposed to avail of carer's leave in order to provide full-time care and attention is a relevant person (refer section 6(5) and on appeal subsection (6));

(c) during the period of carer's leave the employee provides full-time care and attention to the relevant person; and

(d) during the period of carer's leave the employee does not engage in employment or self-employment other than employment or self-employment (defines the parameters as prescribed under section 82B(3) of Chapter 11A of Part II of the Act of 1993, section 6(1)).

All the above criteria must be satisfied before an employee is entitled to undertake carer's leave.

An employee is not be entitled to carer's leave during the same period in which another employee is absent from employment on carer's leave for the purpose of providing full-time care and attention to the same relevant person (section 6(3)).

An employee is be entitled to a period of carer's leave for one relevant person at any one time (section 6(4)). Notwithstanding this provision of the Act, an employee may while on carer's leave in respect of a relevant person, apply for carer's leave for another person if that person resides with the relevant person (section 7(2)). In the event that a person undertakes carer's leave for two relevant persons, the period of carer's leave for the first mentioned relevant person shall not exceed 65 weeks from its commencement and the period of carer's leave for the second mentioned relevant person shall commence on the date of the decision of the deciding officer under section 6(5) or section 6(6) and shall not exceed 65 weeks from its commencement and the total amount of weeks of such carer's leave shall not exceed 130 weeks.

3.7.3 MANNER IN WHICH CARER'S LEAVE MAY BE TAKEN

An employee is entitled to 65 weeks for each relevant person. Carer's leave may be taken in the form of:

(a) one continuous period of 65 weeks for each relevant person (section 8(1)(a)); or

(b) a number of periods, the aggregate duration of which does not exceed a total of 65 weeks from the date of commencement of carer's leave.

Notwithstanding the manner in which the leave may be taken by an employee, an employer may refuse, on reasonable grounds, to permit an employee to take a period of carer's leave which is less than 13 weeks. Where the employer refuses the employee, he or she must specify in writing to the employee the grounds for such refusal (section 8(2)). Also, an employee who has taken periods of carer's leave pursuant to section 8(1)(b) i.e. a number of periods whose aggregate duration does not exceed 65 weeks, is not be entitled to commence a further period of carer's leave in respect of the same relevant person until a period of six weeks has elapsed since the termination of the previous period of carer's leave (section 8(3)).

Where an employee has taken carer's leave and that period of carer's leave has terminated, the employee can not commence carer's leave in respect of another person until a period of six months has elapsed since the end of the previous period of carer's leave (section 8(4)).

An employee is entitled to come to an arrangement with their employer on terms which are more favourable to the employee than the entitlements provided for under the Act (section 8(5)).

3.7.4 NOTICE PROVISIONS

Section 9 prescribes the notice required to be given by an employee. A minimum of six weeks' notice before the proposed commencement of carer's leave must be given to the employer in writing (section 9(1)). In exceptional emergency circumstances where it is not practicable to give the required notice, the employee shall given a notice as soon as is reasonably practical (section 9(2)).

An employee who is on carer's leave and intending to return to work must give not less than four weeks' written notice before the date on which that employee is due to return to work (section 9(6)). Where the employee has informed the employer of the decision of the deciding officer regarding the relevant person the employee and the employer must not less than two weeks before the commencement of the carer's leave prepare and sign a document referred to as a confirmation document (section 10(1)).

3.7.5 POSTPONEMENT, CURTAILMENT AND VARIATION OF CARER'S LEAVE BY THE PARTIES

Section 12 of the Act allows for the postponement, curtailment and variation of carer's leave by the employer and employee if they so agree, to the following effect:

(a) the carer's leave, or part of it, may be postponed to such time as may be so agreed between the parties;

(b)   the period of carer's leave may be curtailed in a manner and to an extent as may be so agreed between the parties; or

(c)   the form of carer's leave may be varied in a manner as may be so agreed between the parties.

In these circumstances the confirmation document must be amended to reflect the parties' agreement.

3.7.6   EMPLOYMENT PROTECTION AND THE RIGHT TO RETURN TO WORK

The effect of the Act is to protect the employment rights of employees during periods of carer's leave (Part III, section 13). Accordingly, an employee who is absent from work on carer's leave must be regarded as still working for all purposes relating to his or her employment and none of his or her rights or obligations related to the employment must be affected by the taking of carer's leave. This general protection of employment rights does not apply to:

(i)   remuneration;

(ii)   annual leave with the exception of section 19 of the Organisation of Working Time Act, 1997 for the first 13 weeks of absence;

(iii)   public holidays with the exception of section 21(1) of the Organisation of Working Time Act, 1997 for the first 13 weeks of absence; and

(iv)   superannuation benefits.

Employees who are absent from employment on carer's leave must not be treated as being on any other leave from employment (including sick leave, annual leave, adoptive leave, maternity leave, parental leave and force majeure leave) (section 13(4)).

On termination of the carer's leave the employee is be entitled to return to work in the job that the employee held before the commencement of the leave (section 14(1)(b)), and under the contract of employment in respect of which the employee was employed immediately before the commencement of the leave (section 14(1)(c)). The right to return to work also applies to any successor of the employer who during the employee's absence from work on carer's leave there was a change of ownership (section 14(1)(a)).

In circumstances where an employee is entitled to return to work but it is not reasonably practicable to allow the employee to return to work, the employee is entitled to be offered suitable alternative employment under a new contract of employment (section 15(1)). Work under a new contract of employment will only constitute suitable alternative work if it is of a kind that is suitable to the employee and appropriate for the employee to do in the circumstances and where the terms or conditions of contract are not substantially less favourable to the employee than those of his or her contract of employment immediately before he or she went on carer's leave and the continuity of service of the employee is preserved (section 15(2)).

An employer may not penalise an employee for proposes to exercise of having exercised his or her entitlement to carer's leave (section 16). The Act defines penalisation of an employee to include: dismissal; unfair treatment of the employee, including selection for redundancy; and an unfavourable change in the conditions of employment of the employee.

An employee who is entitled to return to work but is not permitted by his or her employer to do so shall be deemed to have been dismissed on the date his or her was entitled to so return to work and the dismissal shall be deemed for the purposes of the Unfair Dismissal Acts, 1977–2001 to have been an unfair dismissal unless, having regard to all the circumstances there were substantial grounds justifying dismissal (section 15(4)). In addition, where the employee is not permitted to return to work the employee shall be deemed for the purposes of the Redundancy Payments Act, 1967–1991 to have had his or her contract of employment terminated on the date on which he or she was entitled to return to work.

3.7.7 TERMINATION OF CARER'S LEAVE

Section 11 of the Act prescribes the circumstances in which the period of carer's leave will terminate. Those are:

(a) the date specified in the confirmation document;

(b) on a date agreed between the employer and employee;

(c) where the person whom the employee is looking after no longer satisfies the conditions for a relevant person;

(d) where the employee ceases to satisfy the conditions for the provision of full-time care and attention;

(e) where a deciding officer of the Minister for Social, Community and Family Affairs (or an appeals officer) determines that the person who the employee is looking after is not a relevant person; the employee does not satisfy the conditions for providing full-time care and attention; or, the employee is engaging or has engaged in employment or self-employment;

(f) where the relevant person dies during the leave on the earliest of the following dates: the date that is six weeks after the date of death; or the date of termination of the period specified in the confirmation document.

3.7.8 RESOLUTION OF DISPUTES

Any dispute between an employee and the employer relating to any entitlement of the employee under the Carer's Leave Act (or any matter arising out of or related to such an entitlement) may be referred to a rights commissioner (sections 17 and 19). An employee referring a dispute to a rights commissioner must do so within six months of the date of the contravention giving rise to the dispute (section 19(3)). This time limit may be extended by a rights commissioner (not exceeding a further period of six months) if he or she considers it reasonable to do so having regard to all the circumstances. An appeal lies from the decision of the rights commissioner to the EAT. The appeal must be taken within four weeks of the date that the decision of the rights commissioner was communicated to the parties.

The rights commissioner or the tribunal may order such redress for the party concerned as the rights commissioner or the tribunal considers appropriate, having regard to all the circumstances. They may specify (section 21):

(a) the grant of carer's leave of such length to be taken at such time or times and in such manner as may be so specified;

(b) an award of compensation in favour of the employee concerned to be paid by the employer concerned; or

(c) a combination of (a) and (b).

In terms of compensation, the rights commissioner or the tribunal may award an amount as is deemed just and equitable having regard to all the circumstances but shall not exceed 26 weeks' remuneration. The award of compensation is not necessarily based on any financial loss suffered by the employee (unlike the compensation awarded in a claim for unfair dismissal) giving the rights commissioner or the tribunal, as the case may be, a far-reaching and wide-ranging discretion.

	Female employees	Male employees
Annual leave *Organisation of Working Time Act, 1997*	20 days (if work 1,365+ hours) Part-time employee: 8 per cent of the hours worked in a leave year OR 1/3 of a working week for each month in which employee worked 117+ hours	20 days (if work 1,365+ hours) Part-time employee: 8 per cent of the hours worked in a leave year OR 1/3 of a working week for each month in which employee worked 117+ hours
Public holidays *Organisation of Working Time Act, 1997*	Nine public holidays: — paid day off on the holiday — paid day off that month — extra day's annual leave — extra day's pay provided they have worked 40 hours in previous five weeks.	Nine public holidays: — paid day off on the holiday — paid day off that month — extra day's annual leave — extra day's pay provided they have worked 40 hours in previous five weeks
Maternity leave *Maternity Leave Act, 1994 and Maternity Protection (Amendment) Act, 2004*	22 (26 from 1 March 2007) weeks unpaid (two weeks to be taken before birth) and 12 (16 from 1 March 2007) weeks' additional unpaid leave. Also entitled to reasonable time off for medical visits connected with pregnancy.	No entitlement to leave bar once-off right to paid time off work to attend the two antenatal classes immediately prior to the birth. In event of mother's death, entitled to the following: — if she dies before the 20th (24th from 1 March 2007) week of confinement, may take leave until expiry of that 20th (24th from 1 March 2007) week. Also entitled to 12 (16 from 1 March 2007) additional weeks. — if she dies after 20th (24th from 1 March 2007) week, may take leave until expiry of 32nd (40th from 1 March 2007) week.
Adoptive leave *Adoptive Leave Acts, 1995–2005*	20 (24 from 1 March 2007) consecutive weeks' unpaid leave and additional adoptive leave of 12 (16 from 1 March 2007) consecutive weeks unpaid.	Sole male adopter: 20 (24 from 1 March 2007) consecutive weeks' unpaid leave and additional adoptive leave of 12 (16 from 1 March 2007) consecutive weeks unpaid.

		Leave only available to father in event of mother's death for entire period or balance of period if mother dies on or after the date of placement. Father also entitled to entire period of additional adoptive leave or balance of period if mother dies on or after the commencement of additional adoptive leave.
Carer's leave *Carer's Leave Act, 2001*	13–65 weeks if continuously employed by that employer for 12 months	13–65 weeks if continuously employed by that employer for 12 months
Parental leave *Parental Leave Act, 1998*	14 weeks per child under five if continuously employed by that employer for 12 months. In cases of adoption, leave available for child between ages of three and eight.	14 weeks per child under five if continuously employed by that employer for 12 months. In cases of adoption, leave available for child between ages of three and eight.
Force majeur leave *Parental Leave Act, 1998*	three days in any 12-month period or five days in 36-month period	three days in any 12-month period or five days in 36-month period

CHAPTER 4

ATYPICAL EMPLOYEES

4.1 Introduction

The past two decades have seen a marked increase in Ireland in the number of employees whose working arrangements are atypical in that they work part time, are employed on fixed-term contracts or are employed through agencies. Many of these employees found themselves outside the scope of a regulatory framework, with no dedicated employment protection legislation. This problem was recognised at a European level and in order to address the deficiency in protection, the European Social Partners were consulted and cross-industry agreements were concluded on part-time workers in 1997 and on fixed-term workers in 1999. This resulted in a major leap of reform at national level with the Protection of Employees (Fixed-Term Work) Act 2003 and the Protection of Employees (Part-Time Work) Act 2001, while a Directive to protect agency workers is in the pipeline. This chapter deals with the legislation and case law affecting such employees.

4.2 Agency Workers

4.2.1 THE EMPLOYMENT AGENCY ACT, 1971

For the purposes of the Employment Agency Act, 1971, *the business of an employment agency* means *the business of seeking, whether for reward or otherwise, on behalf of others, persons who will give or accept employment, and includes the obtaining or supplying for reward of persons who will accept employment from or render services to others*.

However, while the Employment Agency Act, 1971 addresses the regulation of employment agencies, it does not deal with the responsibilities of the agencies to the workers and there is currently no dedicated legislation in Ireland dealing with agency workers.

4.2.2 STATUTORY PROTECTION

Since the 1990s, Irish employment legislation has tended to define 'contract of employment' as meaning 'a contract of service or apprenticeship' and 'any other contract whereby an individual agrees with another person, who is carrying on the business of an employment agency within the meaning of the Employment Agency Act, 1971 and is acting in the course of that business, to do or perform personally any work or service for a third person (whether or not the third person is a party to the contract), whether the contract is express or implied and if express, whether it is oral or in writing'.

Just as modern Irish employment legislation tends to define 'contract of employment', in terms as set out above, so that legislation tends to define 'employee' and 'employer' by reference to that broad definition of 'contract of employment'.

'Employer' will normally be defined as 'the person with whom the employee has entered into or for whom the employee works under (or, where the employment has ceased, entered into or worked under) a contract of employment, subject to the qualification that the person who under (an employment agency contract) . . . is liable to pay the wages of the individual concerned in respect of the work or service concerned shall be deemed to be the individual's employer'.

These definitions of 'contract of employment', and 'employer' while broadly reflecting the range of modern employment statutes, will vary (more in language than in effect), from one statute to another.

Agency workers who work for and are paid by a third party are deemed to be employed by that third party, for the purposes of the Redundancy Payments Acts, 1967–2003, Payment of Wages Act, 1991, Terms of Employment (Information) Act, 1994, Maternity Protection Act, 1994, Adoptive Leave Act, 1995, Protection of Young Persons (Employment) Act, 1996, Organisation of Working Time Act, 1997, Employment Equality Acts, 1998 and 2004, Carer's Leave Act, 2001 and the Protection of Employees (Part-Time Work) Act, 2001.

While no employment relationship will be deemed to be in place insofar as agency workers and those for whom they work ('the end-users') are concerned, in the typical situation in which the worker is remunerated by the agency which agency in turn receives payment of a fee from the end user, the situation is different insofar as the Unfair Dismissals Acts are concerned.

Section 13 of the Unfair Dismissals (Amendment) Act, 1993 provides as follows:

> 'Where . . . an individual agrees with another person, who is carrying on the business of an employment agency within the meaning of the Employment Agency Act 1971, and is acting in the course of that business, to do or perform personally any work or service for a third person (whether or not the third person is a party to the contract and whether or not the third person pays the wages or salary of the individual in respect of the work or service), then, for the purposes of the (Unfair Dismissals Act, 1977), as respects a dismissal . . . the individual shall be deemed to be an employee employed by the third person under a contract of employment . . . and . . . any redress under the (Unfair Dismissals Act, 1977) for unfair dismissal of the individual under the contract shall be awarded against the third person.'

This provision governs the 'typical' agency worker/end user relationship. There is no requirement for remuneration to pass directly from the end user to the agency worker and an employment relationship is deemed to have been in place, merely by reason of the agency worker having agreed (with the agency) to work for the end user and irrespective of who remunerates the agency worker in respect of the work.

4.2.3   THE IMPLIED CONTRACT OF SERVICE

While modern employment legislation endeavours to protect agency workers, in the manner described above, for all practical purposes and in most cases (apart from unfair dismissal cases), the statutory protections that are conferred on agency workers pertain only to the relationship with the employment agency (in circumstances where the employment agency will normally be 'liable to pay the wages'). However, recent developments on both sides of the Irish Sea have served to confer employment rights on agency workers in the context of their relationship with the end users, by means of 'implied contracts of service'. Relying on the *Ready-Mixed Concrete* test, as set out in Chapter 1: Contracts of Employment, the UK Court of Appeal and our Labour Court have seen fit to imply contractual relationships as between agency workers and end users, where those relationships satisfied the *Ready-Mixed Concrete* conditions.

In *Diageo Global Supply v Mary Rooney* (2004) ELR 133 Ms Rooney was a nurse and had worked part-time at Diageo's Occupational Health Department at the Guinness Brewery in Dublin since 1991. The evidence which was before the court was to the effect during April 1991, when Ms Rooney became aware of a vacancy for a nurse to work part-time with Diageo she submitted a letter of application to Ms Mary Ryan the sister in charge of Diageo's Occupational Health Centre. Ms Rooney was subsequently contacted by Ms Ryan and was interviewed by her for the post. Ms Ryan later offered her the post and her hours of work, rate of pay and other particulars of her duties and benefits were agreed with Ms Ryan. On being initially employed Ms Rooney was told by Ms Ryan that her wages would be paid through a licensed employment agency, Irish Recruitment Consultants (IRC). Throughout the continuance of her employment Ms Rooney's wages were paid by IRC and her P60 tax form was issued by IRC. However, she never met with any person representing IRC and did not negotiate with them in relation to her conditions of employment.

The Labour Court, in its determination, made reference to the 'variety of tests' which have been 'developed' with a view to facilitating determinations on the status of working relationships. Cognisant of *Denny* the court stated that '[i]n many cases the question for determination is whether a person is engaged as an employee or is self-employed on a contract for service'. The court stated that '[i]n such cases the modern approach is to apply an enterprise test. This essentially asks if the person is in business on their own account or are they an integral part of the business of the other party'. The court then went on to state that that test was 'not appropriate in the [*Diageo*] case, as it was not suggested that the claimant was self-employed'. Against that background, the court turned to the *Ready-Mixed Concrete* test. Satisfied that 'there was an offer of employment made by Ms Ryan which was accepted by [Ms Rooney] . . . and there was valuable consideration' and 'mutuality of obligations in the sense that [Diageo] undertook to provide work and [Ms Rooney] undertook to perform that work' the court concluded that the first condition of the *Ready-Mixed Concrete* test had been satisfied. With regard to the wage arrangement, the court simply stated that '[w]hilst it was agreed that the . . . wages . . . would be paid through IRC, this does not mean that consideration did not pass from [Diageo]. The court is satisfied that IRC were acting on behalf of [Diageo] in paying [Ms Rooney's] wages from funds provided by [Diageo]'.

Turning to the second limb of the *Ready-Mixed Concrete* test, the court noted that '(t)he control test has diminished in importance in some modern employment relationships or in some occupations where employees have a significant degree of autonomy in carrying out their work'. However, the court went on to state that the control test 'nonetheless remains as a highly relevant factor in defining a contract of service'. Dealing with that 'control' aspect, the court noted that Diageo's director of medical services 'directed [Ms Rooney] in her employment at all material times. From time to time [Ms Rooney] sought increases in pay and this was negotiated and agreed with [Diageo]. [Ms Rooney] was required by [Diageo] to be a member of a trade union and they paid the union contribution on her behalf. [Diageo] determined [Ms Rooney's] hours of work and when she was required for work [Diageo] would contact her'. The court was 'satisfied that she was contractually bound to attend for work when so contacted. The reduction in [her] hours of work, which gave rise to [the] claim, was decided upon by [Diageo] and was conveyed to her by [Diageo]. She worked exclusively at [Diageo's] Occupational Health Centre. She had never been assigned to other locations during periods in which [Diageo did] not require her services'.

'Against that background', the court was satisfied that 'the contract between the parties [allowed Diageo] to exercise control over [Ms Rooney] in the performance of her work to such a degree as to make them her employer'.

Bearing the third limb of the *Ready-Mixed Concrete* test in mind, the court briefly considered whether 'other aspects of the contract are consistent with it being one of service'. It was noted that Ms Rooney's wages 'were paid through IRC' and that 'this might not seem consistent with [Diageo] being her employer'. However and in that context, the court stated that they were 'satisfied that IRC was at all times acting on behalf of [Diageo] as its paymaster', while 'the contract between the parties provided that [Diageo] would make work available to Ms Rooney which she would personally perform. [Ms Rooney] worked exclusively for [Diageo] and did so over a period of 11 years. Her work was integral to the medical service provided by [Diageo] and she [appeared] to have been accepted as part of the staff of the Medical Centre in that she always attended the staff Christmas party'. In all of those circumstances, the court was satisfied 'that the other aspects of [Ms Rooney's] contract with [Diageo were] consistent with it being a contract of service'.

In *Dacas v Brook Street Bureau (UK) Ltd* [2004] IRLR 358 Patricia Dacas worked as a cleaner. She was registered with Brook Street Bureau, an employment agency, under a 'temporary worker agreement'. The agreement made clear that its provisions 'shall not give rise to a contract of employment between Brook Street and the temporary worker, or the temporary worker and the client'. Brook Street had a contract with Wandsworth Borough Council for the provision of agency staff at various of the council's establishments. The contract set out Brook Street's responsibilities, including ensuring that they had a policy and procedure for investigating complaints against staff which they had provided, and made provision for the council to pay Brook Street on being given invoices, which were calculated from time sheets completed by the staff supplied to the council by the agency. For a number of years, Mrs Dacas had been assigned by the agency to work exclusively at a hostel ('West Drive') for the long-term care of people with mental health problems run by the council. The council, through the management at the hostel, exercised day-to-day control over her and supplied her with cleaning materials, equipment and an overall. She worked prescribed hours, from 8.30 a.m. to 5.30 p.m. five days a week on a two-week rota. The agency set her rate of pay and paid her wages out of the payments made to them by the council for supplying her services. The agency was responsible for deducting PAYE and national insurance contributions, issuing payslips and for the performance of statutory obligations in relation to holiday and sick pay. Mrs Dacas booked her holidays and notified any sickness absence through the agency. In April 2001, the council asked that she be withdrawn from the contract and the agency informed her that it would no longer be finding work for her. Mrs Dacas presented a complaint of unfair dismissal on the basis that she was an employee either of the agency or of the council.

By reference to the *Ready-Mixed Concrete* test, Mummery LJ spoke of 'an "irreducible minimum of mutual obligation necessary for a contract of service", i.e. an obligation to provide work and an obligation to perform it, coupled with the presence of control'. He then went on to speak of the 'problem' of applying 'the basic legal requirements to the case where an employment agency is interposed between the "worker" and the end-user and where the functions normally found in a single employing entity are redistributed between two entities, each of which denies that it is the employer'. In this case, the employment agency was denying any employment relationship with Mrs Dacas. The agency was under no obligation to provide her with work. She was under no obligation to accept any work offered by the agency to her. The agency did not exercise any relevant day-to-day control over her or her work. That control was exercised by the council. In all of those circumstances and notwithstanding '[t]he fact that Brook Street agreed to do some things that an employer would normally do [payment]', Mummery LJ made clear that that did 'not make it the employer . . . The role of Brook Street was not that of an employer of Mrs Dacas. Rather it was that of an agency finding suitable work assignments for her and, so far as the council was concerned, performing the task of staff supplier and administrator of staff services'.

With regard to Mrs Dacas' relationship with the end-user/council, he stated as follows:

> '. . . while the end-user is the real and immediate recipient of the work done by

[Mrs Dacas], the employment agency is made responsible for paying remuneration to [her] and for arranging other benefits usually associated with employment, such as sick leave and holiday pay. If there were no interposed employment agency there would be no doubt that, even in the absence of an express contract, Mrs Dacas worked under a contract of service with the council: it was managing and controlling work done by her in the mutual expectation that she would be paid for what she was told to do and had in fact done. So what difference does the presence of the employment agency really make to the status of Mrs Dacas? Does it mean that, although working under the daily control of the council, she was an employee of Brook Street, who supplied her services to the council? Or does it mean that she was not an employee of anyone?'

With regard to how the UK Employment Tribunal should have set about 'ascertaining the overall legal effect of the triangular arrangements on the status of Mrs Dacas', Mummery LJ stated as follows:

'. . . the Employment Tribunal should not focus so intently on the express terms of the written contracts entered into by Brook Street with Mrs Dacas and the council that it is deflected from considering finding facts relevant to a possible implied contract of service between Mrs Dacas and the council in respect of the work actually done by her exclusively for the council at its premises and under its control, until it took the initiative in terminating that arrangement. The formal written contracts between Mrs Dacas and Brook Street and between Brook Street and the council relating to the work to be done by her for the council may not tell the whole of the story about the legal relationships affecting the work situation. They do not, as a matter of law, necessarily preclude the implication of a contract of service between Mrs Dacas and the council. There may be evidence of a pattern of regular mutual contact of a transactional character between Mrs Dacas and the council, from which a contract of service may be implied by the Tribunal. I see no insuperable objection in law to a combination of transactions in the triangular arrangements, embracing an express contract for services between Mrs Dacas and Brook Street, an express contract between Brook Street and the council and an implied contract of service between Mrs Dacas and the council, with Brook Street acting in certain agreed respects as an agent for Mrs Dacas and as an agent for the council under the terms of the express written agreement.

'I approach the question posed by this kind of case on the basis that the outcome, which would accord with practical reality and common sense, would be that, if it is legally factually permissible to do so, [Mrs Dacas] has a contract, which is not a contract of service, with the employment agency, and that [she] works under an implied contract, which is a contract of service, with the end-user and is therefore an employee of the end-user . . . The objective fact and degree of control over the work done by Mrs Dacas at West Drive over the years is crucial. The council in fact exercised the relevant control over her work and over her. As for mutuality of obligation, (a) the council was under an obligation to pay for the work that she did for it and she received payment in respect of such work from Brook Street, and (b) Mrs Dacas while at West Drive, was under an obligation to do what she was told and to attend punctually at stated times. As for dismissal, it was the council which was entitled to take and in fact took the initiative in bringing to an end work done by her at West Drive. But for the council's action she would have continued to work there as previously. It is true that the obligations and the power to dismiss were not contained in an express contract between Mrs Dacas and the council. The fact that the obligations were contained in express contracts made between Mrs Dacas and Brook Street and between Brook Street and the council does not prevent them from being read across the triangular arrangements into an implied contract and taking effect as implied mutual obligations as between Mrs Dacas and the council.'

The decisions in *Diageo* and *Dacas* clearly have very far-reaching implications for agency workers. In the many, many cases where employment agencies simply place people with third-party end-users, in circumstances where mutuality of obligation and control arise only in the context of the relationship as between the agency worker and the end-user, it is to be presumed that the end-user will be considered to be the agency worker's employer, regardless of any contractual terms to the contrary.

4.2.4   DRAFT DIRECTIVE

On 20 March 2002, the EU Commission adopted a draft EU Directive designed to afford particular protection to temporary agency workers. The draft Directive aims at striking a balance between flexibility and job security. The European Council held a policy debate on the draft Directive in October 2004, where the discussion focused mainly on the outstanding issue of equal pay and conditions for temporary workers. It was recognised that further efforts would be needed to enable the Council to reach an acceptable compromise for all delegations. It is expected that the Directive will be implemented at EU level in the not-too-distant future.

4.3   Fixed-term Employees

Traditionally, much confusion has surrounded the use and operation of fixed-term and specified-purpose contracts. They may be classified as one type of contract. In a fixed-term contract the actual period of employment is specified. A specified-purpose contract is identical except that the exact period of the contract is not necessarily measured but its life is measured by reference to the occurrence of an event or the cessor of a purpose.

Fixed-term employees have always been protected to some extent in Irish law. Prior to the Protection of Employees (Fixed-term Work) Act, 2003, this protection was available under the Unfair Dismissals Acts, 1977–2001 and the Employment Equality Acts, 1998–2004.

4.3.1   THE EMPLOYMENT EQUALITY ACTS, 1998–2004

The Employment Equality Acts, 1998–2004 apply to all employees regardless of their length of service. Prior to 2003, fixed-term employees who considered that they were being discriminated against by virtue of their fixed-term status could claim indirect discrimination if the reason for their working on a fixed-term basis fell within one of the nine discriminatory grounds provided for in the Acts. The principle of indirect discrimination is addressed in detail in Chapter 6: Equality and Discrimination in the Workplace.

4.3.2   THE UNFAIR DISMISSALS ACTS, 1977–2001

Section 2 of the Unfair Dismissals Act, 1977 provides that the Act shall not apply to a dismissal which consists only of the expiry of the term of a fixed-term contract or the cesser of the purpose of a specified-purpose contract without its being renewed provided the following conditions are adhered to:

(a)   the contract is in writing;

(b)   the contract specifies that the Act will not apply to a dismissal which consists only of the expiry of the term of the contract without its being renewed or the cesser of the purpose; and

(c)   the contract is signed by the employer and the employee.

Many employers have taken it as automatic that if they draw up a fixed-term or specified-purpose contract and comply with the above-mentioned conditions the employee has no right to claim unfair dismissal when the contract comes to an end. That may not be the case. If, on the ending of such a contract, an employee claims unfair dismissal a rights commissioner or the EAT will determine whether the contract was genuinely a fixed-term or a specified-purpose contract or was in reality open-ended employment dressed up as being for a fixed term or specified purpose. The leading EAT case on this point is *Fitzgerald v St Patrick's College, Maynooth* UD 244/78 reported in Kerr and Madden, *Cases and Commentary on Unfair Dismissals*, p 86. A vacancy for a permanent junior lecturer arose in St Patrick's College. Before a permanent appointment could be made certain procedures had to be followed. While these procedures were being followed Ms Fitzgerald was appointed on a temporary basis by way of a fixed-term contract for one academic year. The first attempt to secure a permanent appointment failed and the permanent appointment was deferred. Ms Fitzgerald was reappointed for a further academic year as a temporary lecturer on foot of a further fixed-term contract for that academic year containing the necessary terms to provide for the exclusion of the Act. On the expiry of the contract and its non-renewal Ms Fitzgerald claimed unfair dismissal.

The College claimed that this was a case of a fixed-term contract complying with the conditions of the 1977 Act and Ms Fitzgerald, therefore, had no right to claim unfair dismissal.

The EAT held that there had been a dismissal on the expiry and non-renewal of the fixed-term contract. The EAT further held that the mere fact that the appointment was temporary could not of itself, regardless of other factors, constitute substantial grounds for or justifying the non-renewal. The EAT looked at the employer's reasoning for entering into the temporary contract in the first place. The EAT also looked at what was happening at the time the contract expired and the reasons as to why it was not renewed. In cases of genuine fixed-term or specified-purpose contracts an employer should have no difficulty in showing how circumstances had changed or that the temporary need catered for at the time of entering into the contract had in some way been satisfied.

In *Fitzgerald* the EAT found that the reasons offered, which were in essence, the deemed temporary nature of the contract, did not constitute substantial grounds to justify dismissal under the 1977 Act and held:

> 'If the mere expiry of a fixed-term contract of employment were to be regarded as a substantial ground for the non-renewal of the employment, the Unfair Dismissals Act could be rendered abortive in many cases. An employer could side-step its provisions by employing his employees on fixed-term contracts only. Then to get rid of an employee on whatever grounds, be they trivial or substantial, fanciful or solid, fair or unfair, he need only wait until that employee's fixed-term contract expired and then refuse to renew it. The threat of non-renewal of his contract might well be enough to make many an employee submit to oppressive conditions or treatment at the hands of an employer.'

4.3.3   UNFAIR DISMISSALS (AMENDMENT) ACT, 1993

The Unfair Dismissals (Amendment) Act, 1993 does not in any way affect the EAT's interpretation referred to above or the status of fixed-term or specified-purpose contracts. It merely deals with continuity of service between successive fixed-term or specified-purpose contracts. It attempted to prevent employers getting around the provisions of the legislation by employing people on what may appear to be genuine fixed-term contracts, waiting a period of time, and then re-employing such persons on further fixed-term contracts. In the absence of the Unfair Dismissals (Amendment) Act, 1993, the break in continuity would mean that until at least one year of the renewed period had elapsed the employee would not have unfair dismissal protection. The 1993 Act confirms continuity for the purpose of ascertaining the service of the employee where the gap is three months or less between successive contracts, provided that the nature of the employment, the subject of the contracts, is the same or similar and, in the opinion of the rights commissioner, EAT or the Circuit Court, the entry by the employer into the subsequent contract(s) was wholly or partly for or connected with the avoidance of liability under the Act.

It should be borne in mind that if an employer terminates a fixed-term or specified-purpose contract in advance of the expiry of the term of the contract or the cesser of the purpose, either with notice as provided for in the contract or without notice, the employee will have the right to claim unfair dismissal provided he or she has the requisite one-year continuous service. This is whether or not the conditions mentioned at **4.3.2** above are met. These conditions are only applicable to a dismissal which consists of the expiry of the term of a fixed-term contract without it being renewed or the cesser of the purpose of a specified-purpose contract.

If a fixed-term contract does not contain a notice provision and the employer wishes to terminate the contract in advance of the expiry of its term or the cesser of its purpose, the employee will, arguably, be entitled to receive the remuneration the employee would have received had the contract been performed to the expiry of its term or the cesser of its purpose.

4.3.4 THE PROTECTION OF EMPLOYEES (FIXED-TERM WORK) ACT, 2003

With the passing of the Protection of Employees (Fixed-Term Work) Act, 2003 (the 2003 Act'), on July 14 2003, comprehensive protection was afforded to all fixed-term employees.

The 2003 Act implements Council Directive 1999/70/EC concerning the framework agreement on fixed-term work concluded by ETUC, UNICE and CEEP. Reflecting the objectives of that Directive, the purpose of the 2003 Act is to:

(a) improve the quality of fixed-term work by ensuring the application of the principle of non-discrimination;

(b) establish a framework to prevent abuse arising from the use of successive fixed-term contracts.

4.3.4.1 Fixed-term employee

The 2003 Act applies to all fixed-term employees. A fixed-term employee is defined as '*a person having a contract of employment entered into directly with an employer where the end of the contract of employment concerned is determined by an objective condition such as arriving at a specific date, completing a specific task or the occurrence of a specific event*'.

The following employees are specifically excluded from the scope of the 2003 Act:

(1) members of the Defence Forces;

(2) trainee Gardai within the meaning of the Garda Síochána (Admissions and Appointments) Regulations, 1998, SI 164/1998;

(3) nurses in training within the meaning of the Nurses Act, 1985;

(4) employees in vocational training or apprenticeship schemes;

(5) employees with a contract of employment that has been concluded within the framework of a specific public or publicly supported training, integration or vocational retraining programme e.g. job initiative or community employment schemes.

Given that the definition of fixed-term employee covers only those employees whose contract of employment is entered into directly with an employer, agency workers are also excluded. While this is a significant exclusion which will, no doubt, lead some employers to seek to avoid the protection offered by the 2003 Act by using agency workers, it should be remembered that a separate Directive on agency workers is in the pipeline. Of course, agency workers who are employed under a contract of employment with the employment agency are covered by the 2003 Act as the agency is the employer.

4.3.4.2   No less favourable treatment

One of the dual aims of the 2003 Act is to ensure that fixed-term employees are given parity of treatment in respect of their conditions of employment as comparable permanent employees. Consequently, the Act expressly provides that a fixed-term employee must not be treated less favourably in respect of his or her conditions of employment than a comparable permanent employee. The 2003 Act defines both 'conditions of employment' and 'comparable permanent employee'. If less favourable treatment is established, the employer must justify the less favourable treatment on objective grounds. The 2003 Act also provides guidance on what constitutes 'objective grounds'.

4.3.4.3   Comparable permanent employee

A permanent employee is defined as '*an employee who is not a fixed-term employee*' and so it is clear that an employee cannot be both a fixed-term and permanent employee in respect of the same employer.

With regard to what constitutes a comparable permanent employee, section 5 of the Act sets out three situations in which fixed and permanent employees are comparable.

(1) The permanent employee and the fixed-term employee are employed by the same employer or associated employers. The nexus between associated employers is control. Employers are deemed to be associated if one is a body corporate over which the other has control, or, both are bodies corporate of which a third person (whether directly or indirectly) has control.

(2) The permanent employee is specified in a collective agreement to be a type of employee who is to be regarded as a comparable permanent employee.

(3) Where neither (1) or (2) apply, the permanent employee is employed in the same industry or sector of employment as the relevant fixed-term employee.

And, insofar as (1) and (3) above are concerned, one of the following conditions is met:

(i) both employees perform the same work on the same or similar conditions, or the employees are interchangeable with each other;

(ii) the work performed by the two employees is the same or of a similar nature and any differences in the work or the working conditions are minor or so irregular as to be insignificant;

(iii) the relevant fixed-term employee performs work of equal or greater value than the work performed by the permanent employee. In determining the value of the work performed, matters such as skill, physical or mental requirements, responsibility or working conditions are considered relevant.

Recourse to the third situation above is only available where a comparator cannot be found under 1 and 2. However, this is a significant departure from other equality legislation and has potentially serious ramifications for an employer. A similar provision in the Employment Equality Bill was removed before its enactment as the Employment Equality Act, 1998.

Pursuant to 3 above, a fixed-term worker is allowed to choose a comparator employed by another employer with no nexus whatsoever between the two employers. This is likely to give rise to serious difficulties for employers who could potentially be held responsible for a difference in treatment of which they are not aware. Employers could be made to objectively justify differences in treatment where they are not aware of the underlying reasons for such treatment. With no reported cases concerning this provision as of yet, it will be interesting to see how it is interpreted.

While it is preferable to be in a position to actually name a comparator, the absence of so doing will not defeat a claim under the 2003 Act. In *Aer Lingus v A Group of Workers*, Labour Court 10 April 2005, the respondent contended that the claimants had failed to name a comparator or comparators whom they claimed to be comparable permanent employees and that this omission was fatal to their claim for relief. The Labour Court noted that it was not denied that the permanent cabin crew who were engaged in identical work to that of the claimants, received the benefits the subject of the claim. The Labour Court determined that the court should be concerned with the substance of a complaint, rather than with the form in which it is presented and in so doing said 'in these circumstances, the claimant could not be defeated by a failure to formalistically name an individual comparator'.

4.3.4.4   **Conditions of employment**

Conditions of employment are defined as '*conditions in respect of remuneration and matters relating thereto (and in relation to any pension scheme or arrangement, includes conditions for membership of the scheme or arrangement and entitlement to rights thereunder and conditions relating to the making of contributions to the scheme or arrangement)*'.

Remuneration, in relation to an employee, means:

(a)   any consideration, whether in cash or in kind, which the employee receives directly or indirectly from the employer in respect of the employment; and

(b)   any amounts the employee will be entitled to receive on foot of any pension scheme or arrangement.

The definition of employment conditions is very broad and clearly includes pay, bonus, company car, stock options, entitlement to sick pay, etc. Interestingly, while the 2003 Act expressly includes remuneration among conditions of employment, the Directive does not.

Insofar as pensions are concerned, it should be noted that since 15 September 2003 employers are obliged to provide access to a Standard Personal Retirement Savings Account (PRSA) for all employees. While there is no obligation on an employer to provide a pension scheme to a fixed-term employee, if one is provided to a comparable permanent employee, then the fixed-term employee must be able to access it on the same basis unless a different pension scheme can be objectively justified. The requirement for equal treatment in respect of pension schemes/arrangements is not absolute. It does not apply where the normal hours of work of the fixed-term employee constitute less than 20 per cent of the normal hours of work of the comparable permanent employee.

It is likely that problems will arise where the rules of a particular pension scheme state that no more employees are to be allowed entry to the scheme and the employer is required to provide an equivalent scheme to a fixed-term employee. In *Eircom v McDermott*, Labour Court 16 February 2005, the respondent operated two types of pensions schemes: a direct-benefit scheme and a direct-contribution scheme. The direct-benefit scheme applied to graded staff whose terms and conditions were subject to collective bargaining agreements and who were permanent staff (this scheme had applied to non-graded staff prior to 14 July 2003). The direct-contribution scheme applied to non-graded staff whose terms and conditions were negotiated on a personal contract basis and who were on fixed-term contracts or contracts of indefinite duration. The claimant, who was employed on a fixed-term contract in respect of a non-graded position, was not transferred from the defined-contribution scheme into the defined-benefit scheme on the passing of the Act and it was contended that this constituted less favourable treatment of the claimant from the 14 July 2003 until she obtained a permanent non-graded position some months later.

The Labour Court determined that, while there was a difference in the treatment of the fixed-term claimant and the named comparators—the former being in a direct-contribution scheme while the latter were in a direct-benefit scheme—it was not possible for the court to predict whether the claimant's treatment during the specified period was less favourable than that which applied to the named comparators as any potential loss of benefit would only crystallise when the claimant's employment ended or she retired. Both sides provided actuarial predictions, however, both sides also agreed that it would be impossible to say with certainty whether the claimant's treatment under the direct-contribution scheme would have been more or less favourable than the defined-benefit scheme. The Court held that any contingent detriment could only be measured when the benefit became payable at retirement and that at the point in time of the hearing, the claimant did not prove on the balance of probabilities that placing her in the defined-contribution scheme constituted unfavourable treatment.

This case highlights the difficulty in comparing pension schemes for the purposes of establishing less favourable treatment in breach of the 2003 Act. It should be noted, however, that in this case the level of both employer and employee contributions under the defined-contribution scheme was more beneficial than the norm and equalled the level of contribution under the defined-benefit scheme.

4.3.4.5 Length-of-service qualification

A period-of-service qualification relating to a particular condition of employment must be the same for the fixed-term employee as for the comparable permanent employee unless there are objective grounds justifying different periods. For example, if an employer requires a permanent employee to have completed six months' service in order to qualify for sick pay under the company scheme, the employer cannot require the fixed-term employee to have a longer period of service to access the scheme. Clearly, any requirements for *continuous* service are in breach of the 2003 Act.

4.3.4.6 Proportionality

The pro-rata principle applies in relation to any benefit, the amount or scope of which is dependent on the number of hours worked by an employee. In advance of applying the pro-rata principle to a benefit, employers must be certain that the benefit in question is dependent on the number of hours worked by an employee. This may not always be clear-cut, especially if the benefit concerned is a bonus. While many employers automatically assume that they can halve the bonus of a fixed-term employee who has only worked for six months of the year in which the bonus is payable, this may not be the case if the bonus is, for example, based on the achievement of certain objectives either personal or organisational and the employee in question has achieved these objectives.

An employee's entitlement to annual leave and public holidays pursuant to the Organisation of Working Time Act, 1997 is not affected by the 2003 Act.

4.3.4.7 Successive fixed-term contracts

While the amendments introduced by the Unfair Dismissals (Amendment) Act, 1993 placed significant barriers on the use of successive fixed-term contracts, the provisions in section 9 of the 2003 Act further hamper their use.

Section 9 distinguishes between employees who commenced fixed-term contracts prior to 14 July 2003 and those who commenced fixed-term contracts post that date.

In the case of the former, '*where the fixed-term employee completes or has completed his or her third year of continuous employment with his or her employer or associated employer, his or her fixed-term contract may only be renewed on one occasion for a term of no longer than one year*' (section 9(1)).

In the case of the latter, *'where the fixed-term employee is employed by his or her employer or associated employer on two or more continuous fixed-term contracts and the date of the first such contract is subsequent to the date on which this Act is passed, the aggregate duration of the contracts cannot exceed four years'* (section 9(2)).

Where any term of a fixed-term contract purports to contravene these provisions, the term of the contract will have no effect and the contract concerned is deemed to be a contract of indefinite duration (section 9(3)).

As the provisions refer to the 'contract concerned' being deemed to be a contract of indefinite duration, it would appear that, aside from tenure, the terms and conditions of the contract of indefinite duration should be the same as the terms and conditions of the fixed-term contract that the employee is employed on at the time of the breach which gives rise to the contract of indefinite duration.

This issue was addressed in *Northern Area Health Board v Christina Hughes*, Labour Court 15 March 2005. The claim concerned a worker who commenced employment with the Health Board in May 1999. Initially she was employed in residential services and community services. In January 2000, she was employed as a temporary social care manager at Carrickbeag Children's Residential Home. She was assigned to the position of temporary alternative care manager in September 2002 for a two-month period pending the filling of the post in a permanent capacity through open competition. On 31 December 2002, a decision was made to extend her appointment in this position to 28 February 2003, or until alternative arrangements were made, whichever was earlier. The record of this decision, which was furnished to her, stated that the claimant '[would] revert to her position of temporary manager, Carrickbeag Children's Residential Home when her assignment as temporary alternative care manager [ceased]'. In December 2003, the claimant was advised that the full-time vacancy was being advertised, she applied for the position but was unsuccessful. The claimant was offered the post of manager of the Carrickbeag Children's Residential Home. The claimant claimed that she was entitled to a contract of employment of indefinite duration as alternative care manager on the basis this was the post she held at the date on which her contract of employment became one of indefinite duration by operation of law.

The Labour Court did not accept this contention. The court stated that whilst the terms of the contract were not reduced to writing, the court was satisfied that the records of the various discussions surrounding her appointment to the post of alternative care manager showed that a term of that contract was that the claimant would revert to her original post if and when the post of alternative care manager was permanently filled. The court stated that it '[was] satisfied that the respondent was entitled to redeploy the complainant into the post which she was offered'.

It appears that the claimant in this case was, what is commonly referred to as 'acting up', in the position of alternative care manager and so when her contract was deemed to be a contract of indefinite duration, the 'contract concerned' included a term that she would revert to the position of manager.

An employer may justify a renewal in breach of section 9(1)–(2), where there are objective grounds justifying such a renewal (section 9(4)).

Some commentators have extracted a rule of thumb from these provisions that, in the absence of objective grounds, there is now an overall limit of four years on successive fixed-term contracts with the same employer or associated employer. This is not the case in respect of fixed-term employees who were employed on fixed-term contracts prior to the passing of the Act. For example, a fixed-term employee employed on an eight-year fixed-term contract might only have completed three years of the contract on the passing of the Act. The fixed-term contract will not expire for another five years, while the employer may renew it on its expiry for a further period of one year. The fixed-term employee will have been employed on successive fixed-term contracts for six years after the passing of the Act.

Although these provisions do seem quite restrictive, they are much tempered by the proviso that they do not apply where there are objective grounds. The prevention of the abuse of successive fixed-term contracts will depend solely on how difficult it is to objectively justify a renewal.

Clearly, these provisions only apply to successive fixed-term contracts and so there is no restriction on the duration of a first fixed-term contract.

4.3.4.8   Objective justification

Section 7(2) of the Act specifically provides that where a fixed-term employee is treated in a less favourable manner than a comparable permanent employee with regard to any one term of his/her contract, the difference can be justified on objective grounds, if, taken as a whole, the terms of the fixed-term employee's contract of employment are as favourable as the terms of the comparable permanent employee's contract of employment.

Therefore, it is permissible to compare the overall benefits afforded to a fixed-term employee with the overall benefits afforded to a comparable permanent employee for the purposes of justifying a difference in treatment in respect of one particular benefit. It is very difficult to see how an employer will avail of this provision. If, for example, a permanent employee is entitled to sick pay and access to a pension scheme and the fixed-term employee is not entitled to sick pay or to a pension but has a higher annual bonus and is given access to a company car, which set of benefits is worth more? Clearly, persuasive arguments could only be made by way of actuarial and other expert evidence, which could be costly. Where the monetary value of the benefit may change over time, the problems are even more acute.

Section 7(1) of the Act also provides that '*a ground shall not be regarded as an objective ground . . . unless it is based on considerations other than the status of the employee concerned as a fixed-term employee and the less favourable treatment which it involves for that employee (which treatment may include the renewal of a fixed-term employee's contract for a further fixed term) is where the purpose of achieving a legitimate objective of the employer and such treatment is appropriate and necessary for that purpose.*'

In order to objectively justify less favourable treatment an employer must show that the difference in treatment is attributable to a reason other than the fact that one employee is a fixed-term employee and the other is a permanent employee and that the less favourable treatment is for the purpose of achieving a legitimate aim on the part of the employer and the treatment is appropriate and necessary to achieve that aim.

The concept of objective justification is, however, not new to European employment equality law. It is the long-established defence to claims of indirect discrimination and in the context of such discrimination cases, it has been examined by the courts. The classic analysis of the concept was articulated by the ECJ in 1986 in *Bilka–Kaufhaus GHmb v Weber Von Hartz* [1986] IRLR 317. The Labour Court undertook a helpful analysis of the concept in *NBK Designs Ltd v Mary Inoue*, Labour Court 25 November 2002. It should be borne in mind that the Labour Court's analysis of the concept issued in the context of an indirect discrimination claim and that different issues may arise when the concept is analysed for the purposes of the 2003 Act, particularly because the 2003 Act adds the further criterion of 'achieving a legitimate objective of the employer'. Nonetheless, the Labour Court's analysis is instructive.

In order for measures to be objectively justifiable, the court stated that measures should:

(a)   correspond to a real need on the part of the employer;

(b)   be appropriate with a view to achieving the objective pursued;

(c)   be necessary to that end.

138

These criteria mirror the 2003 Act with the exception of the additional 'legitimate objective' criterion. The Labour Court elaborated on their meaning. For the purposes of determining whether there is 'a real need' the court held that 'it is insufficient to conclude that a requirement is reasonable', the accepted test is that it be 'essential'. Insofar as measuring whether the measure is appropriate, the court spoke of the need for proportionality and expressed the view that 'the value of the benefit which accrued to the employer, when balanced against the discriminatory effect of the method by which it was achieved, must be proportionate'. Finally, with regard to the requirement of necessity, the court stated that the requirement in this context is for the employer to demonstrate that 'there were no alternative means having a less discriminatory effect by which the objective could have been achieved'.

It is clear that these are the type of steps that the Labour Court will go through to ascertain whether a measure is objectively justified. The jurisprudence of the ECJ has made it clear that economic factors will not justify discrimination. There is no reason to think that this approach will not be taken in relation to the equal treatment of fixed-term employees.

4.3.4.9   Written notification by the employer

The 2003 Act gives fixed-term employees a host of other rights with concomitant obligations on employers. One such right is that a fixed-term employee must be informed in writing as soon as practicable by the employer of the objective condition determining the contract whether it is:

(a)   arriving at a specific date;

(b)   completing a specific task; or

(c)   the occurrence of a specific event.

Where an employer proposes to renew a fixed-term contract, the fixed-term employee must be informed in writing by the employer of the objective grounds justifying the renewal of the fixed-term contract, and the failure to offer a contract of indefinite duration at the latest by the date of the renewal. This statement is admissible as evidence in proceedings under the 2003 Act. These provisions are found in section 8.

Presumably, it is not sufficient for the employer to simply inform the fixed-term employee in writing of the grounds which the employer considers to be objective grounds justifying the renewal of the fixed-term contract. These grounds must fall within the definition of objective grounds in the 2003 Act to meet this requirement.

In *Irish Rail v Malcom Stead*, Labour Court 1 March 2005, the Labour Court considered a number of issues, one of which was the failure by the employer to provide a written statement. The court noted that it was entitled to draw an inference from the employer's failure to provide this statement. The court noted that the day after the expiry of the contract, the employer supplied a written statement indicating that the contract would not be renewed and that the employee would be entitled to a statutory redundancy payment but this was subsequently rescinded after union intervention and a four-month contract was issued. The court stated that the failure to provide a written statement to the claimant 'as if the Act did not exist' was, in the court's view, 'an indication of the company's lack of compliance of their statutory obligation, which obviously required to be addressed and rectified'.

4.3.4.10   Training opportunities and vacancies

Section 10 provides that an employer must inform a fixed-term employee of vacancies which arise so that the fixed-term employee has the same opportunity as other employees to secure a permanent job.

There is no requirement to specifically and individually inform each employee on a fixed-term contract and it is sufficient if the information in respect of vacancies is provided by way of a general announcement at a suitable place in the company. In *Scoil Iosagain v Martin Henderson*, Labour Court 18 April 2005, a complaint was made by a teacher against the Board of Management of Scoil Iosagain that the Board had contravened this provision of the 2003 Act, or in the alternative contravened the Directive on foot of which the national legislation was implemented.

The claimant was employed on a fixed-term contract from August 2002 until August 2003. In May 2003 the respondent placed an advertisement in a national newspaper seeking applicants for six permanent teaching posts. The claimant contended that he had not been advised of the vacancies and that he did not see the advertisement. The court noted that the 2003 Act had become law on 14 July 2003, but that the latest date on which the State was obliged to implement the EU Directive was 10 July 2002. The court held that by the application of direct effect, the complainant was entitled to rely on the provision of the Directive, as his complaint related to a date prior to the enactment of the national legislation. The rights commissioner had held that he lacked jurisdiction to deal with the claim on the basis that the 2003 Act had not been implemented at the time of the alleged contravention but the Labour Court held that by the application of direct effect, and on the basis that the school was an emanation of the State, the claimant was entitled to rely on the provisions of the Directive.

The Labour Court went on to say that placing an advertisement in a newspaper did not meet the requirements of the Directive or the Act (which are almost identical in terms of the obligation placed on employers to make fixed-term workers aware of vacancies). The court held that what was clearly required was that information on relevant vacancies be imparted personally to fixed-term employees or that a notice be placed in the workplace. The court noted that the Directive and the 2003 Act both state that information can be given about vacancies by way of a general announcement suitably placed in the employer's premises and the employer had not met this obligation. While the court noted that the usual form of redress would be an instruction that the employer make the fixed-term worker aware of vacancies within the employer organisation in the future, on the basis that this individual was no longer employed by the school, compensation of €2,000 was deemed to be the appropriate remedy.

In *Aer Lingus v A Group of Workers,* the Labour Court stated that it is noteworthy that this obligation is not simply to inform fixed-term employees of the existence of vacancies for permanent positions, but of vacancies which may enable them to obtain permanent positions. This would apply to a position which may initially be temporary but will subsequently be made permanent.

An employer must also, as far as practicable, facilitate access by a fixed-term employee to appropriate training opportunities to enhance his or her skills, career development and occupational mobility. The success of this measure in helping fixed-term employees to keep apace with their permanent counterparts will depend entirely on the interpretation that is given to the proviso 'as far as practicable'.

4.3.4.11   Voidance of certain provisions

Pursuant to section 12 of the Act, any provision in an agreement is void if it purports to exclude or limit the application of, or is inconsistent with, any provision of the Act. In other words, employees cannot contract out of their rights under the Act. This means that even if an agreement is concluded between an employer and a trade union, this will not prevent an employee who is covered by the agreement from availing of the protection afforded by the Act if the agreement seeks to exclude or limit the application of or is inconsistent with the Act.

4.3.4.12   Prohibition on penalisation

Section 13 of the Act provides that an employer is prohibited from penalising an employee for:

(a)   invoking any right of the employee to be treated in respect of the employee's conditions of employment in the manner provided for in the Act or giving notice of an intention to do so;

(b)   having in good faith opposed by lawful means an act which is unlawful under the Act or giving notice of an intention to do so;

(c)   giving evidence in any proceedings under the 2003 Act or giving notice of an intention to do so.

An employee is penalised if he or she suffers any unfavourable change in his or her conditions of employment or any unfair treatment (including selection for redundancy) or is the subject of any other action prejudicial to his or her employment. A dismissal may also constitute penalisation if the dismissal is wholly or partly for or connected with the avoidance of a fixed-term contract being deemed to be a contract of indefinite duration under section 9(3) of the Act.

The early termination or expiry and non-renewal of an employee's fixed-term contract will not give rise to a cause of action under the Act unless it constitutes penalisation. If an employee's fixed-term contract is allowed to expire and is not renewed or is terminated early to avoid the fixed-term contract being deemed to be a contract of indefinite duration, that amounts to penalisation.

If the penalisation of an employee constitutes a dismissal under the Unfair Dismissals Acts, 1977–2001, relief may not be granted to the employee in respect of the penalisation under both the Unfair Dismissals Acts and the Act. This does not prevent an employee from actually lodging a claim under each Act but does prevent them from obtaining redress under both. It should be noted that an employee whose dismissal constitutes penalisation who does not have one year of continuous service will not have the right to claim unfair dismissal before a rights commissioner or the EAT but may present a complaint to a rights commissioner under the Act as there is no service requirement for a penalisation complaint.

4.3.4.13   Redress

Sections 14–16 govern enforcement and draw upon existing labour law enforcement mechanisms.

Under section 14, either an employee or a trade union may make a complaint to a rights commissioner. The complaint must be made in writing and must be made within six months from the date of the contravention of the Act or the date of termination of the contract of employment, whichever is the earlier. The time limit may be extended by a further 12 months if the rights commissioner is satisfied that the failure to present the complaint within the six-month period was due to a reasonable cause. This is to be contrasted with other employment legislation, e.g. the Unfair Dismissals Acts, 1977–2001, which require an employee to establish exceptional circumstances to extend the six-month time limit. It should be noted that proceedings before a rights commissioner are not conducted in public.

A decision of the rights commissioner can do one or more of the following:

(a)   declare that the complaint was or was not well founded;

(b)   require the employer to comply with the relevant provision;

(c)   require the employer to reinstate or re-engage the employee, including on a contract of indefinite duration;

(d) require the employer to pay compensation in an amount as is just and equitable having regard to all the circumstances but not exceeding two years' remuneration.

Similar to the redress provisions of the Employment Equality Acts, 1998–2004 and unlike the redress provisions of the Unfair Dismissals Acts, 1977–2001, compensation is not linked to actual financial loss and there is no duty on the employee to mitigate loss. Thus it would appear that the current employment status of an employee whose dismissal constitutes penalisation should dictate whether the employee brings an unfair dismissal or a penalisation claim in the event that the employee is seeking compensation by way of redress. If the employee obtains alternative employment immediately following his dismissal and has little financial loss, the employee would be foolhardy to bring an unfair dismissals claim in place of a penalisation claim.

Section 15 provides that an appeal to the Labour Court may be made from a decision of a rights commissioner within six weeks of the decision being communicated to the parties and from there to the High Court on a point of law.

Where a decision of a rights commissioner is not carried out by the employer and no appeal has been brought within the time limit, the employee may, no later than six weeks after the expiry of the appeal time limit, bring the complaint before the Labour Court and the Labour Court may make a determination in the same terms as the decision without hearing the employer or any evidence other than evidence in respect of the terms of the decision.

Section 16 provides that if an employer does not carry out a determination of the Labour Court, the employee or trade union may, within six weeks from the date on which the determination is communicated to the parties, make an application to the Circuit Court and the Circuit Court may make an order directing the employer to carry out the determination in accordance with its terms without hearing the employer or any evidence. Interest may be payable by the employer where the order relates to payment of compensation.

4.3.5 REDUNDANCY

A fixed-term employee may be redundant within the meaning of the Redundancy Payments Acts, 1967–2003 on the expiry and non-renewal of his or her fixed-term contract. This will depend on whether the circumstances giving rise to the expiry of the fixed-term contract fall within the definition of redundancy in the Redundancy Payments Acts, 1967–2003. If they do, and providing that the employee has the requisite two years' service under the Redundancy Payments Acts, 1967–2003, the fixed-term employee will be entitled to a statutory redundancy payment and, of course, an ex gratia payment if applicable.

4.4 Part-time Employees

4.4.1 INTRODUCTION

The Social Policy Agreement attached to the Treaty of the European Union came into force within the Member States in 1992. The Social Partners agreed at European level to conclude a formal agreement amongst themselves on one type of atypical work, part-time work. This agreement was then adopted as a Directive on 20 January 1998. Ireland had until 20 January 2000 to implement this Directive. That date passed without any implementation and the Protection of Employees (Part-Time Work) Act, 2001, was not enacted until 20 December 2001.

The purpose of the Directive is to remove discrimination against part-time workers and to improve the quality of part-time work. Prior to the passing of the 2001 Act, part-time and casual workers were in a somewhat precarious position. Although most statutory employment rights had been successfully extended to part-time employees in advance of the 2001 Act, this did nothing to protect part-time workers against discrimination concerning contractual benefits and other entitlements. The 2001 Act achieved this.

It should be noted that there is no statutory entitlement to work part-time. However, a refusal to facilitate an employee in respect of part-time working, may give rise to a claim of indirect discrimination under the Employment Equality Acts, 1998–2004 unless it can be objectively justified. It should also be noted that in March 2003, the Minister requested the Labour Relations Commission under section 42(1) of the Industrial Relations Act 1990 and section 13 of the 2001 Act to prepare a Code of Practice on access to part-time working and this was introduced by the Labour Relations Commission on 12 January 2006. See para **4.4.2.10** below.

In *Weir v St. Patricks Hospital,* Equality Officer 26 February 2001, the hospital adopted a blanket policy of refusing to allow job sharing at supervisory grade and failed to examine the various supervisory posts to ascertain whether any of them were suitable for job sharing. The equality officer concluded that the general policy of not allowing staff at supervisory level to job share adversely impacted on females rather than males and had not been objectively justified by the respondent.

In *Burke v NUI Galway,* Labour Court 12 August 2002, the Labour Court held that each case concerning a request to work part-time must be considered on its merits. The determination highlights the danger for employers in failing to reasonably consider a request to transfer to working on a part-time basis or not having a proper policy in place for dealing with such requests.

4.4.2   THE PROTECTION OF EMPLOYEES (PART-TIME WORK) ACT, 2001

The 2001 Act repealed the Worker Protection (Regular Part-Time Employees) Act, 1991 and amended several other pieces of legislation to ensure that the rights and entitlements of full-time employees are applied to part-time employees on a pro rata basis.

4.4.2.1   Part-time employee

The 2001 Act applies to all part-time employees. The following definitions are set out in Section 7(1).

A *'part-time employee'* means *'an employee whose normal hours of work are less than the normal hours of work of an employee who is a comparable employee in relation to him or her'.*

The term *'normal hours of work'* means *'the average number of hours worked by the employee each day during a reference period'.*

A *'reference period'* means *'a period which complies with the following conditions:*

(a)   the period is not less than seven days or more than 12 months' duration;

(b)   the period is the same period by reference to which the normal hours of work of the other employee referred to in the definition of 'part-time employee' in this section is determined; and

(c)   the number of hours worked by the employee concerned in this period constitutes the normal number of hours worked by the employee in a period of that duration.'

A permanent *'full-time employee'* is defined as *'an employee who is not a part-time employee'.*

4.4.2.2 Comparable full-time employee

While the definition of comparable full-time employee in section 7(2) mirrors the definition of comparable permanent employee in the Fixed-term Work Act, it differs substantially from the definition in the Framework Agreement. The Framework Agreement defines a comparable full-time worker as a full-time worker in the same establishment, whereas the Act allows for an external comparator.

In *Cahill May Roberts v Rachel O'Leary*, Labour Court 4 May 2004, the Labour Court carried out a work inspection to determine if the claimant and the named comparator performed like work.

The 2001 Act clarifies that the gender of the comparator is irrelevant.

A part-time agency worker can only compare himself or herself to a comparable full-time employee who is also an agency worker. Likewise, a part-time employee, who is not an agency worker, cannot compare himself to a full-time agency worker. Section 7(4).

4.4.2.3 Definition of conditions of employment

The definition of conditions of employment in section 9 is identical to the definition found in section 6 of the Fixed-term Work Act.

The annual leave and public holiday entitlement of part-time employees is set out in Chapter 3: Working Time and Statutory Leave Entitlements.

4.4.2.4 No less favourable treatment

The main aim of the 2001 Act is to ensure that part-time employees are given parity of treatment in respect of their conditions of employment as comparable full-time employees. Similar to the Fixed-term Work Act, if less favourable treatment is established it may be justified on objective grounds (section 9(3)). The saver in respect of pensions schemes and arrangements in the Fixed-term Work Act is also found in this Act (section 9(4)).

In *Boxmore Plastics Ltd v Roisin Curry*, Labour Court 19 December 2003, the Labour Court dealt with the issue of overtime in the context of part-time employees. In the company, weekend workers were not entitled to receive any overtime payments until they had completed 40 hours in any one week. The company argued that overtime was only paid after the equivalent of full-time hours were worked. Both parties referred to the ECJ decision of *Stadt Lengerich v Helmig* (Case C-399/92) [1996] ICR 35. The court stated that this judgment is quite clear: 'A provision whether in a collective agreement or in terms and conditions of employment whereby part-time workers do not receive overtime until they have completed the standard number of hours under which a comparable full-time worker would be entitled to claim overtime is not unfavourable treatment and is not discriminatory.' The court found that the decision of the company not to pay overtime to the claimants until they had worked the same number of hours as the comparable full-time workers did not constitute unfavourable treatment in breach of the 2001 Act.

In *Abbott Ireland Ltd v SIPTU*, Labour Court 28 January 2004, part of the claim before the Labour Court was that part-time employees who worked four-hour shifts between 4 p.m. and 8 p.m. and 8 p.m. and midnight were not paid the shift premium which was paid to full-time employees working from 4 p.m. to midnight. It was accepted that both the claimants and the full-time comparators performed like work. The company argued that the decision to pay the full-time workers a shift premium arose from the fact that the hours between 4 p.m. and midnight had historically, within the industry, been regarded as unsociable hours and that it was the practice to pay a premium to full-time workers who work this shift and that therefore the decision to treat the part-time workers less favourably could be objectively justified. In addition the company argued that there were full-time employees who worked the shift between 12 noon and 8 p.m. who were not paid a premium, that the hours between 4 p.m. and midnight are both unsocial and family unfriendly and the workers working an eight-hour shift miss the whole of this period with their families whereas the part-time workers miss only a couple of hours.

The court found that the company's failure to pay part-time workers who worked between 4 p.m. and midnight shift premium payments was not proportionate and held that the claimants must be paid a shift premium.

4.4.2.5   **Proportionality**

The 2001 Act embodies the principle of pro rata temporis in the Framework Agreement. Section 10(1) provides that the extent to which a condition of employment should be provided to a part-time employee must be related to the proportion which the normal hours of work of that employee bears to the normal hours of work of the comparable full-time employee concerned.

Similar to the Fixed-term Work Act, the 2001 Act clarifies that this provision only relates to conditions of employment which are dependent on the number of hours worked and employers must be aware that when applying entitlements to part-time employees on a pro rata basis, the entitlement in question must be capable of being applied in such a manner.

In *Department of Justice, Equality and Law Reform v Margaret Ennis*, Labour Court 14 January 2004, the employer paid Ms Ennis and her colleagues a lower rate of travel allowance than that paid to her full-time colleagues. In this case, part-time workers worked 19.5 hours per week, while the full-time comparator worked a 39-hour week. The amount of travelling allowance paid to the part-time worker was half that paid to the full-time worker.

The complaint was dealt with by a rights commissioner in the first instance who found that the Department relied on the pro rata principle embodied in the 2001 Act to justify the treatment in question. The rights commissioner found that the travel allowance was not dependent on the number of hours worked but rather was dependent on the distance from the GPO to the place of work and held that the complaint was well founded. The Department appealed the decision to the Labour Court on the basis that the allowance was an intrinsic part of the basic pay and it was therefore consistent with the provisions of the 2001 Act to pay the allowance on a pro rata basis. The court held that regardless of its interpretation prior to February, 2002, when the nature of the allowance changed to a radial distance-based system; it could not be regarded as 'an allowance in the nature of pay which forms part of the weekly remuneration package' but must be seen as compensation for the time and expense involved in the distance travelled. The court upheld the rights commissioner's decision.

4.4.2.6   **Casual part-time employees**

Casual part-time employees are also afforded protection under the 2001 Act and employers are prohibited from treating casual part-time employees in a less favourable manner than their full-time comparators (section 11). A casual part-time employee is a part-time employee who works on a casual basis. A part-time employee is considered to work on a casual basis if:

    (a)   he or she has been in the continuous service of the employer for a period of less than 13 weeks, and that period of service and any previous period of service by him or her with the employer could not reasonably be regarded as regular or seasonal employment; or

    (b)   he or she fulfils the conditions specified in a collective agreement which has effect in relation to him or her and regards him or her for the purposes of that agreement as working on a casual basis (section 11(5)).

An employee's service is continuous unless that service is terminated by dismissal or the employee voluntarily resigning from his or her employment (section 11(6)).

The Schedule to the 2001 Act provides for the approval of collective agreements for the purpose of this provision and a register of collective agreements that have been approved under this Schedule is maintained by the Labour Court.

4.4.2.7 Objective justification

Like the Fixed-term Work Act, the 2001 Act provides that a ground will not be regarded as an objective ground unless it is based on considerations other than the status of the employee concerned as a part-time employee and the less favourable treatment which it involves for that employee is for the purpose of achieving a legitimate objective of the employer and such treatment is appropriate and necessary for that purpose (section 12).

In *Louth VEC (Department of Education and Science) v A Worker*, Labour Court 13 January 2005, the Labour Court considered what exactly constitutes objective justification under the 2001 Act.

The case before the Labour Court was an appeal from a right commissioner's decision concerning the awarding of incremental credit in respect of the claimant's previous unqualified service. The claimant contended that she was treated less favourably in respect of her years of service for incremental purposes. The Department argued that incremental credit was only awarded to teachers who were fully qualified and therefore the less favourable treatment was not based solely on the fact that the claimant was a part-time teacher and was objectively justified. The court stated that the issue was not whether qualified or unqualified teachers were entitled to incremental credit for their years of service but whether part-time teachers performing the same functions as full-time teachers were entitled to the same pro rata benefits, including being placed on the incremental scale and if they were, was the fact that they did not have the same qualifications as the comparable full-time teachers sufficient objective justification. In this regard, the court looked at the test set out by the ECJ in *Bilka–Kaufhaus GHmb v Weber Von Hartz*:

(a)   does the measure correspond to a real need on the part of the employer?

(b)   is it appropriate with a view to achieving the objective pursued (i.e. is it proportionate)?

(c)   is it necessary to achieve that end?

The Labour Court held that the treatment of teachers who were not fully qualified did correspond to a real need on the part of the employer, this was to ensure that all teachers have the appropriate academic qualifications. With regard to the appropriateness of the measure, the court said that this aspect of the test requires that the means chosen be proportionate to the objective which they are intended to achieve and in this case it was. In relation to the third step, as to whether or not the means were necessary to achieve the end in view, the Labour Court said there must be no alternative means which would have a less discriminatory effect by which the objective in view could have been achieved. The court accepted that there were no alternative means having a less discriminatory effect. In the circumstances, the court held that the different treatment of the part-time teacher was objectively justified.

The 2001 Act provides that a ground which does not constitute an objective ground for the purpose of justifying less favourable treatment in respect of part-time employees may be capable of constituting an objective ground for the purpose of justifying less favourable treatment of *casual* part-time employees. Thus it is clear that it will be easier to justify less favourable treatment of part-time employees who work on a casual basis than part-time employees who do not. It remains to be seen how this wider definition of objective justification in respect of part-time casual workers will be interpreted by rights commissioners and the Labour Court.

4.4.2.8 Voidance of certain provisions

Section 14 of the Act provides for the voidance of certain provisions in agreements that are inconsistent with or purport to exclude or limit the application of the Act.

4.4.2.9 Prohibition on penalisation

The prohibition on penalisation contained in section 15 of the 2001 Act is identical to that found in the Fixed-term Work Act save that an employer is also prohibited from penalising a part-time employee on the grounds of the employee's refusal to accede to a request by the employer to transfer from performing full-time work to performing part-time work or vice versa.

In addition, employers will not be considered to have penalised part-time employees in certain circumstances. For example, a request by the employer that the employee transfers from full-time to part-time work (or vice versa) will not constitute penalisation if both of the following conditions are complied with:

(i) there were substantial grounds both to justify the employer making the request concerned and the employer taking that action following the employee's refusal; and

(ii) the taking of that action is in accordance with the employee's contract of employment.

4.4.2.10 Opportunities for part-time work

The 2001 Act does nothing to fully implement the provisions contained in clause 5 of the Framework Agreement in respect of opportunities for part-time work. It envisages the implementation of these provisions, in that it provides that the Labour Relations Commission may, and, at the request of the Minister for Enterprise, Trade & Employment, shall study every industry and sector of employment for the purpose of identifying any obstacles to people being able to work part-time and make recommendations as to how any such obstacle could be eliminated.

There are other provisions which relate to how the Labour Relations Commission will carry out this task if it chooses to carry it out or is requested by the Minister to carry it out, and relate to how it shall report and publish such a study.

In March 2003, the Minister requested the Labour Relations Commission under section 42(1) of the Industrial Relations Act 1990 and section 13 of the 2001 Act to prepare a Code of Practice on access to part-time working and this was introduced by the Labour Relations Commission on 12 January 2006.

The Preamble to the Code of Practice sets out the benefits of part-time working to both the employer and the employee. It emphasises the importance of part-time work and its positive social and economic effects.

The Code minimises the potential for indirect discrimination in relation to part-time work. It introduces positive measures to encourage greater participation in employment.

The purpose of the Code is:

- to encourage best practice and conformity with the Employment Equality Acts, 1998–2004;

- to promote policies and procedures to facilitate part-time work;

- to promote discussion between employers, employees and their representatives and to encourage these parties to consider, where appropriate, part-time work;

- to stimulate employers to provide more access to part-time work;

- to provide a framework and practical guidance to assist employers and employees in accessing part-time work; and

- to inform those interested in part-time work.

The Code is admissible as evidence before the Civil Courts, the Labour Court, the LRC, the EAT, Rights Commissioners and the Equality Tribunal and any relevant provisions of the Code may be taken into account in the determinations of claims before such fora.

4.4.2.11   Collective agreements

The Labour Court has the power to approve a collective agreement under section 11(5) of the 2001 Act. If the court receives an application for approval of a collective agreement, it must consult with representative of employees and employers that the court considers to have an interest in the matter.

The Labour Court will not approve a collective agreement unless the following provisions are fulfilled:

(a)   it is satisfied that it is appropriate to approve of the agreement having regard to clause 2.2 of the Framework Agreement, which relates to employees who work on a casual basis;

(b)   the agreement has been concluded in a manner usually employed in determining the pay or other conditions of employees in the employment concerned;

(c)   the body which negotiated the agreement on behalf of the employees is the holder of a negotiation licence under the Trade Union Act, 1941, or is an excepted body within the meaning of that Act;

(d)   the agreement is in a suitable form.

The Labour Court can request the parties to the collective agreement to vary it if the court is not satisfied that the conditions in (a) or (d) above are fulfilled. If the parties agree to vary it, the court will approve it.

The 2001 Act permits the Labour Court to withdraw its approval of collective agreements and sets out the procedure to be followed in making applications for their approval or variation. The Labour Court must publish, in any way it sees fit, details of these procedures. It must also establish and maintain a register of collective agreements approved by it under the 2001 Act.

4.4.2.12   Redress

The provisions in respect of obtaining redress which are found in sections 16–18 of the Act differ substantially from the directive and legislation on equal pay for men and women. The 2001 Act contains no provisions empowering rights commissioners to investigate complaints, merely to hear such complaints. Nor does it contain provisions authorising rights commissioners to carry out preliminary investigations into claims in respect of equal remuneration, but again only to hear complaints in respect of conditions of employment which include remuneration.

Save that rights commissioners do not have the power to order an employer to reinstate or re-engage an employee, the redress provisions in the 2001 Act are the same as the redress provisions in the Fixed-term Work Act. These provisions do not apply to members of the Defence Forces.

4.5   Young Persons

The Protection of Young Persons (Employment) Act, 1996 consolidated the law on young workers and gives effect to Council Directive 94/33/EC on the Protection of Young People at Work (other than Articles 6 and 7) and repeals the Protection of Young Persons (Employment) Act, 1997 and certain provisions of the Conditions of Employment Act, 1936.

Generally speaking, the Act aims to protect the health of young workers and to ensure that a young person's education is not put at risk by working during the school year.

The Act sets minimum age limits for employment, rest intervals and maximum working hours. It prohibits the employment of under 18s on late-night work. The Act defines a 'child' as meaning any person under the age of 16, while 'young person' is defined as meaning a person who has reached the age of 16 years but has not reached the age of 18 years.

Section 15 of the Act provides that employers must keep specific records in respect of their employees who are under 18 years of age.

The following Regulations have been made under the Act:

- SI 1/1997 Protection of Young Persons (Employment) (Exclusion of Workers in the Fishing or Shipping Sectors) Regulations, 1997;
- SI 2/1997 Protection of Young Persons (Employment of Close Relatives) Regulations, 1997;
- SI 3/1997 Protection of Young Persons (Employment) (Prescribed Abstract) Regulations, 1997;
- SI 350/2001 Protection of Young Persons (Employment) Act, 1996 (Employment in Licensed Premises) Regulations, 2001;
- SI 351/2001 Protection of Young Persons (Employment) Act, 1996 (Bar Apprentices) Regulations, 2001.

4.6   Migrant Workers

'*Migrant worker*' is defined in Article 2 of the International Convention on the Protection of the Rights of all Migrant Workers and Members of the Families 1990 as a person who is, or has been, '*engaged in a remunerated activity in a state of which he or she is not a national*'.

Migrant workers include those who have moved voluntarily in search of economic opportunities, refugees and asylum-seekers who are in paid employment in countries other than their own and people who have been trafficked for the purpose of labour exploitation. The Convention protects all migrant workers and members of their families regardless of whether they are registered with authorities or are undocumented.

The Convention, which entered into force in July 2003, sets out the minimum obligations and responsibilities of countries of origin, host states and states through which migrant workers transit. Ireland has not signed the Convention which is one of the seven core UN Human Rights Treaties. Ireland has ratified the other six UN Human Rights Treaties.

4.6.1   THE EMPLOYMENT PERMITS ACT, 2003

Non-EEA nationals generally require permission to work in Ireland depending on their individual circumstances. Details of the different types of permission which are required to work in Ireland can be found on the Department of Enterprise, Trade and Employment's website www.entemp.ie. The granting of work permits is currently governed by the Employment Permits Act, 2003 which came into effect on 10 April 2003.

A non-national is defined in the Act as *'a person who is not a citizen of the State'*. The Act provides that non-nationals must not enter the service of an employer in the State or be in employment in the State except in accordance with an employment permit granted by the Minister for Enterprise, Trade and Employment. The Act also provides that a person must not employ a non-national in the State except in accordance with an employment permit. The Act sets out certain categories of non-nationals who do not require work permits.

It is a criminal offence for an employer to employ someone who requires a work permit and does not have one. Similarly it is a criminal offence for the individual in question to enter into employment without a work permit.

4.6.2 THE EMPLOYMENT PERMITS BILL, 2005

In June 2005, the Employment Permits Bill was published. The Bill aims at codifying the procedures governing the application, granting, renewal and revocation of work permits/visas etc. At the time of writing the Bill was still at the Committee stage.

The Bill codifies the current employment permits administrative procedures including the work permits and working visa/work authorisation schemes. It provides for the application, grant, renewal, refusal and revocation of work permits and introduces a 'green card' scheme for skilled migrant workers. The Bill provides for the issue of permits to the employee rather than to the employer.

While applications by employers on behalf of employees will continue, individuals will be permitted to apply for a work permit once they have received a written offer of employment prior to making their application. Work permits will be issued initially for a period of two years and then on renewal for a further period of three years.

Employers who breach the legislation will face tougher fines of up to €50,000 and a potential prison term of up to five years.

CHAPTER 5

HEALTH AND SAFETY LAW

5.1 Introduction

The focus of this chapter is on the legislative and common law positions relating to health and safety and the consequent implications for employers and employees. It reviews in particular the recent Safety, Health and Welfare at Work Act, 2005 ('the 2005 Act') that repeals and replaces the Safety, Health and Welfare at Work Act, 1989 ('the 1989 Act').

The burden or liability placed upon employers has significantly altered in the past two hundred years most notably in the 2005 Act. It is clear from any examination of this area that the process must be viewed as a continuum, with all developments broadly moving in one direction, generally favouring employees. The regime of protection established may be classified under two general headings: obligations imposed by the legislature and obligations imposed by the judiciary under the common law.

5.2 Statutory Regulation

Until the nineteenth century there was little or no statutory intervention by the legislature which was composed, in the main, of property owners and employers, to afford protection to employees. However, in the early nineteenth century specific limited intervention was demanded to remedy glaring injustices. One of the earliest examples of legislative intervention to stem this clamour for reform was the Act of 1802 entitled 'An Act for the Preservation of the Health and Morals of Apprentices and Others Employed in Cotton and Other Mills and Cotton and Other Factories' 42 Geo III c 73. This first Act to regulate the operation of factories provided, inter alia, that the rooms in mills or factories to which the Act applied should be washed with quicklime and water twice a year and that care should be taken to admit fresh air. It also provided that no apprentice should be employed or compelled to work for more than 12 hours (excluding meal times) in any one day, as well as requiring that no more than two apprentices should sleep in the one bed. Progress continued apace with further reforming legislation which, in the main, sought to improve the safety and working conditions of employees.

Major reform, so far as factories were concerned, was introduced in the Factories and Workshop Act, 1878. This Act consolidated and amended all earlier statute law governing factories and introduced additional sanitary and safety provisions. It limited the hours that might be worked by children, young persons and women and it prohibited children under the age of 10 years from being employed in a factory or workshop (Factories and Workshop Act, 1878, section 20). This Act, and subsequent amending measures, were repealed by the Factories and Workshop Act, 1901. Following the now-established practice, the 1901 Act brought all previous legislation in the area within the ambit of the one enactment. Further, it expanded both in substance and application, the provisions relating to health and safety. It still, however, continued only to apply to factories and workshops. Importantly, section 79 of the 1901 Act provided the Secretary of State with the power to make special regulations for health and safety in respect of factories, workshops, building operations, operations at docks, quays and warehouses. The importance of this procedure will be evidenced later as it is under this procedure that all modern regulations are introduced.

The next significant enactment was the Factories Act, 1955. This repealed and replaced the 1901 Act in Ireland. Unlike previous legislation it did not seek to ameliorate or eliminate specific hazards. Rather, it provided a code to ensure the safety, health and welfare of factory employees. Section 3(1) of the Factories Act, 1955 provided a primary definition of the term 'factory':

> *'Subject to the provisions of this section, in this Act "factory" means any premises in which, or within the close or curtilage or precincts of which, persons are employed in manual labour in any process for or incidental to any of the following purposes:*
> *(a)   the making of any article or part of any article;*
> *(b)   the altering, repairing, ornamenting, finishing, washing, or the breaking up or demolition, of any article;*
> *(c)   the adapting for sale of any article,*
> *being premises in which, or within the close or curtilage or precincts of which, the work is carried on by way of trade or for purposes of gain and to or over which the employer of the persons employed therein has the right of access or control.'*

If a place of work fell within the ambit of the primary definition, then it was deemed a 'factory' within the meaning of the Act. Further, section 3(1) also provided for and extended the definition of factory to include places which would not otherwise have fallen within that definition. In addition, the Act contained the proviso that its provisions would also apply to places not otherwise falling within section 3(1). These 'notional factories' included, inter alia, docks, warehouses, building operations and electrical stations.

There were further Acts, including the Office Premises Act, 1958, the Mines and Quarries Act, 1965, the Safety in Industry Act, 1980 and the Safety, Health and Welfare at Work (Offshore Installations) Act, 1987 as well as various regulations made under these Acts. All these legislative interventions went a long way towards improving the safety, health and welfare of employees. However, three major difficulties remained. First, the piecemeal approach to legislation, with each new Act superseding and amending prior legislation, rendered the law both inaccessible and confusing. Secondly, despite the volume of legislation many premises and places of work were entirely excluded from regulation. Consequently, those employees were deprived of protection granted as a matter of course to others. Finally, the myriad of statutory provisions had entirely failed in the preceding years to reduce the level of accidents. Allied to the realisation of the foregoing considerations was the requirement to introduce into domestic law the terms of the 1989 Framework Directive on Safety and Health, 89/391/EEC. A central feature of this directive was the setting down of a minimum level of protection for all employees throughout the Member States. It established general rules on occupational health and safety that employers were required to conform to and set out worker obligations and responsibilities. The Framework Directive was followed by six further directives, all of which were required to be implemented by 1 January 1993.

5.3   Common Law

5.3.1   GENERALLY

As well as obligations under statute law, employers have a common-law duty of care to their employees. For example, employers owe a specific duty to their employees to provide them with a safe premises, independently of any duty they may owe to them under the health and safety legislation. The common law rules are laws extracted from several hundred years of judicial experience and decisions. Over the centuries remedies and, more importantly, compensation were available to an injured employee. However, the grounds for recovery in the eighteenth and nineteenth centuries were extremely circumscribed. In the nineteenth century 'fault' or negligence fell to be the main basis upon which liability was to be decided. To recover against an employer an injured employee had to prove that his employer failed to act in the same manner as a reasonable employer would have in the circumstances. He also had to demonstrate that this failure caused the loss or damage of which he complained. Further, even were he to so demonstrate, he still had to surmount the infamous triumvirate of defences created by the judiciary and relied upon by employers: volenti non fit injuria (voluntary assumption of risk), the doctrine of common employment and the preclusion from recovery of a finding of contributory negligence on the part of the employee. These defences have now been considerably relaxed as a result of legislative intervention.

5.3.2   VOLENTI NON FIT INJURIA

The defence of volenti non fit injuria equated knowledge on the part of the employee of the risk of harm with the consent of the employee to accept that risk. As Hawkins J in *Thrausser v Handyside* [1880] 20 QBD 359 at p 364 commented, the employee's 'poverty, not his will, consented to incur the danger'. This defence was only finally emasculated in this jurisdiction by virtue of section 34(1)(b) of the Civil Liability Act, 1961. It is important to note, however, that this defence was never accepted in actions for breach of statutory duty. This obviously increased the importance of statutory duties being imposed on employers.

5.3.3   DOCTRINE OF COMMON EMPLOYMENT

The doctrine of common employment operated to oust the doctrine of vicarious liability in circumstances where an employee was injured through the negligence of a fellow employee (*Priestly v Fowler* [1837] 3 M & W 1). Vicarious liability arises where an employer is liable for the wrongs of his employees. In summary, the doctrine of common employment provided that where one employee was injured through the negligence or wrongdoing of another employee, and where both employees were employed by the same employer, the employer could not be held liable for that wrong. This doctrine was curtailed over the years, surviving, albeit in a limited form, until the enactment of the Law Reform Personal Injuries Act, 1958.

5.3.4   CONTRIBUTORY NEGLIGENCE

Until the enactment of the Civil Liability Act, 1961 contributory negligence was a complete bar to recovery. Section 34 of the 1961 Act provided that contributory negligence could only operate to reduce the amount of damages awarded, having regard to the respective degrees of fault of both the plaintiff and defendant.

5.3.5 **EVOLUTION OF MODERN DUTY OF CARE OWED BY EMPLOYER TO EMPLOYEE**

It was not until 1937, with the decision of the House of Lords in England in *Wilson and Clyde Coal Co Ltd v English* [1937] 3 All ER 628, that the modern duty of care owed by an employer to an employee was established. In summary, an employer was deemed to owe a duty of care to his employees, which was personal to the employer and was not capable of being discharged merely by delegating its performance to another apparently competent person. This duty included the provision of a safe place of work, a safe system of work, the provision of competent staff and proper equipment. These particular duties, in expanded form, were finally enacted into legislation in Part II of the Safety, Health and Welfare at Work Act, 1989.

McGuinness J considered the modern duty of care alluded to above in the High Court in *Bradley v An Post*, 7 July 1998, High Court unreported. The case concerned an employee of the defendant company, who sustained back injury while delivering letters to low-level letterboxes in June 1993. He reported the matter to his supervisor and subsequently attended the company doctor. The injury resulted in an absence of two months by the plaintiff from the defendant's employment. His injury and consequent vulnerability were well known to his employers, yet in October 1993 he was dispatched on non-emergency overtime to deliver mail to a development where some 350 houses had low-level letterboxes. During the course of this delivery the plaintiff again suffered back injury. McGuinness J held that the defendant company's duty of care towards the plaintiff included a duty to ensure that, at least in the short term after his illness, he did not assume duties which would place undue and extraordinary strain on his back. Consequently, the defendant company was held liable as it did not properly discharge the employer's duty of care in the case of the plaintiff's second injury.

McGuinness J's approach to the employer's duty of care is consistent with the approach adopted in previous cases. These cases decided that an employer discharges his duty of care 'if he does what a reasonable or prudent employer would have done in the circumstances'. The employer's duty is therefore not an unlimited one and varies according to the employee's circumstances.

5.4 Safety, Health and Welfare at Work Act, 1989

The Safety, Health and Welfare at Work Act, 2005 re-enacts an expanded version of many of the provisions contained in the 1989 Act, and the subsequent Safety, Health and Welfare at Work (General Application) Regulations, 1993 with some significant additions. The 2005 Act is framework in nature and focuses on broad general duties and the organisational arrangements necessary to achieve better safety and health. It sets out the duties of employers, employees and other parties such as the designers of workplaces and work equipment and the suppliers of goods for use in the workplace. As with its predecessor, the general ethos of the Act is that of prevention of accidents and illnesses. The failure to observe the new more onerous responsibilities is therefore likely to be pleaded in personal injuries actions taken in the courts. There is increased emphasis on deterrence by strengthening of the enforcement provisions.

The 2005 Act reflects and accommodates many of the radical changes that have occurred since the 1989 Act was introduced. While the 2005 Act could not be described as a radical departure from its predecessor, some of the more striking features in the Act include:

— a definition of 'competent person' and 'reasonably practicable';

— an increase in the explicit duties and responsibilities of both employees and employers;

— provision for testing employees for intoxicants;

— specific provision regarding the responsibilities of designers, manufacturers and importers;

— new duties for persons who commission, procure, design or construct places of work;

— a reduction in the onus on small business and the farming sector regarding safety statements;

— joint safety and health agreements;

— a new dispute resolution mechanism for dealing with disputes between employers and employees concerning health and safety matters;

— expanded provisions concerning responsibilities of directors and managers;

— evidentiary changes for the prosecution of directors and persons significantly influencing the management of a company;

and

— a strengthening of the enforcement powers for non-compliance (increased penalties and also on-the-spot fines).

It is organised in eight parts and seven schedules.

5.5   General Duties Imposed by the 2005 Act

Part 2 of the 2005 Act, sections 8–11, sets out a number of general duties owed by various stakeholders. Each of these duties will be considered in turn.

5.5.1   GENERAL DUTIES OF EMPLOYERS

Chapter 1 of Part 2 of the 2005 Act sets out a range of general duties of employers. Many of the duties provided for in the 1989 Act and the Safety, Health and Welfare at Work (General Application) Regulations, 1993 ('the 1993 Regulations') are reiterated in the 2005 Act. The significance of the 2005 Act arises from the fact that many of the employer's obligations contained in the 1993 Regulations are now placed on a statutory footing. The ease of assessing rights that are now consolidated in one statute is significant. Section 8(1) of the 2005 Act addresses the general duty on employers and provides that it shall be the duty of every employer to do everything he or she can, as far as is reasonably practicable, to ensure the safety, health and welfare of his or her employees.

Some of the new duties identified in section 8(2) of the 2005 Act include:

> '(a)   *managing and conducting work activities in such a way as to ensure, so far as is reasonably practicable, the safety, health and welfare at work of his or her employees;*
>
> (b)   *managing and conducting work activities in such a way as to prevent, so far as is reasonably practicable, any improper conduct or behaviour likely to put the safety, health or welfare at work of his or her employees at risk . . .'*

These new provisions underline the importance of an employer having an integrated safety management system and are particularly relevant when addressing the identification of bullying, harassment and stress in the workplace. In particular the sections relate to the following duties:

● section 8(2)(b) protects employees against the exposure to noise, vibration or ionising or other radiations or any other physical agent;

- section 8(2)(e) expands the duty to provide safe systems of work by obliging the employer to revise and update as appropriate;

- section 8(2)(h) is a broad new provision which may impose new obligations on employers to address stress in the workplace arising from the carrying out of a risk assessment under section 19 of the 2005 Act or when preparing a safety statement under section 20 of the 2005 Act;

- section 8(2)(i) consolidates into one provision the employer's duty to provide protective clothing or equipment, where risks cannot be eliminated or adequately controlled;

- section 8(2)(j) extends provisions of section 6(2)(g) of the 1989 Act in relation to preparation and revision, as appropriate, of adequate plans and procedures, to be followed in emergencies and in cases of serious and imminent danger. The inclusion of '*procedures*' in the section requires the employer to set down the procedures for carrying out any emergency plans. The addition of '*circumstances of imminent danger*' suggests that plans and procedures must be in place not only in respect of the case of an actual emergency but also in respect of a situation where there is an immediate threat of an emergency. Furthermore, the 1989 Act required that plans be revised '*as necessary*', whereas the 2005 Act provides that the revision of such plans and procedures must take place '*as appropriate*';

- section 8(2)(l) reiterates the duty to obtain, as necessary, the services of a competent person as per section 6(2)(j) of the 1989 Act;

- section 8(2)(c) provides that an employer's duty extends, as regards the place of work concerned, to ensuring, so far as is reasonably practicable—
  '*(i) the design, provision and maintenance of it in a condition that is safe and without risk to health,*
  (ii) the design, provision and maintenance of safe means of access to and egress from it, and
  (iii) the design, provision and maintenance of plant and machinery or any other articles that are safe and without risk to health; . . .'
  Previously sections 6(2)(a) to (c) of the 1989 Act, applied to '*any place of work*' which was '*under the employer's control*'. Significantly, these words have been deleted from the 2005 Act so that an employer is now required to ensure, so far as is reasonably practicable, compliance with the duties detailed in section 8(2)(c) of the 2005 Act, even if the place of work is not under his or her control. This subsection imposes an increased burden on an employer with respect to employees who carry out their work otherwise than at the employer's place of work e.g. an electrician or haulier;

- section 8(3) of the 2005 Act specifically extends the duties of the employer to temporary or fixed-term employees;

- section 8(4) obliges the employer to ensure that the working conditions for the duration of an assignment of any fixed-term or temporary employee will protect the safety, health and welfare of such an employee;

- section 8(5) mirrors article 7 of the 1993 Regulations and obliges an employer to ensure that any measures taken by him or her in relation to the safety, health and welfare at work, do not involve financial cost to his or her employees. In considering the concept of employee section 2(1) of the 2005 Act should also be noted in that it defines an employer in relation to an employee as:
  '*(a) the employer under the terms of a contract of employment;*
  (b) includes a person (other than an employee of that person) under whose control and direction an employee works; and
  (c) includes, where appropriate, the successor of the employer or an associated employer of the employer.'
  It is clear from the foregoing definition that an employer/employee relationship, for the purposes of the 2005 Act, arises where an employee is working in the capacity of an

employee (regardless of whose employee he or she is) and is under an employer's direction and control.

Any breach of section 8 of the 2005 Act attracts criminal liability.

5.5.1.1 Information for employees

Section 9(1) of the 2005 Act includes an additional requirement that the employer, when furnishing information to employees, regarding health and safety matters, do so in a manner, form and as appropriate, language that is reasonably likely to be understood by his or her employees.

5.5.1.2 Instruction, training and supervision of employees

Section 10 of the 2005 Act mirrors many of the provisions in article 13 of the 1993 Regulations in respect of providing training and instruction on matters of safety and health to employees. Section 10(1)(a) of the 2005 Act requires an employer, when furnishing instruction, training and supervision to employees regarding health and safety matters, to do so in a manner, form and as appropriate, language, that is reasonably likely to be understood by his or her employees. Employers are also obliged to give employees time off work with no loss of pay to receive instruction on emergency measures. Further, where appropriate, if an employee requires competency for a certain task, to release an employee from work, without loss of pay, where appropriate, so to allow for the training of the employee in safety and health matters regarding that activity.

It is important to note that this list is not exhaustive and is merely an expanded statement of the existing common law position. (The common law duty owed by employers to employees is broadly stated as to provide a safe place of work, a safe system of work, proper equipment and competent staff.) In *Donegal County Council v Porter and others* [1993] ELR 101, the county council sought to implement a December 1985 Department of Environment circular which recommended, inter alia, the introduction of a retirement age of 55 for all fire fighters and a compulsory annual medical examination 'on a uniform basis for all operational personnel'. Due to an industrial dispute, Porter and the other respondents refused to undergo a medical examination requested by the council. They were dismissed after refusing to undergo the medical examination for three years.

The council relied for its defence, in part, on *Maureen Heeney v Dublin Corporation*, 16 May 1991, High Court unreported. In this case the widow of a fire officer successfully sued Dublin Corporation for damages in negligence arising from her husband's death on 12 October 1987. Mr Heeney, a fire fighter, collapsed and died from a heart attack after entering a burning building on a number of occasions without breathing apparatus. On 12 March 1985 the Labour Court recommended the retirement of fire fighters for ill health at the age of 55 as well as annual medical examinations for all fire fighters over the age of 55. No such medical examinations were in place at the time of Mr Heeney's death. Mr Heeney suffered from hypertension and was aged in excess of 55 at his death.

Donegal County Council, in its case against Porter and others, claimed that the *Heeney* case demonstrated a clear risk to the safety, health and welfare of Porter and his fellow respondents that the council was seeking to avoid by requiring a medical examination. The council, relying on section 6 as aforesaid, in furtherance of complying with its duty to ensure the safety, health and welfare of the respondents, so far as it was reasonably practicable, argued that their dismissal was permitted under the Unfair Dismissals Act, 1977. Flood J, however, held that the respondents' dismissal was unfair:

> 'Dismissal, as I see it, would be a blanket performance [of] the said statutory duty under section 6 of the Safety, Health and Welfare at Work Act, 1989. In my view there is

undoubtedly a statutory duty to observe. The council can observe it by a much less draconian measure than dismissal at the age of 55 and one which does not involve a blatant disregard for the council's contractual obligations to the respondents and others in their category.'

It is clear, therefore, that an employer, in endeavouring to comply with the general duty imposed upon him by virtue of section 6(1), must take into account all the circumstances of each case and act accordingly. See also *Scally v Westmeath County Council* [1996] ELR 96. If an employee's conditions and terms of employment are to be affected, only the minimum intrusion possible will be countenanced. See *Deborah Timmons v Oglesby & Butler Ltd* [1999] ELR 119.

5.5.2   GENERAL DUTIES OF EMPLOYERS AND SELF-EMPLOYED TO PERSONS OTHER THAN THEIR EMPLOYEES

Section 12 of the 2005 Act now provides that every employer must manage and conduct his or her undertaking in such a way as to ensure, so far as is reasonably practicable, that in the course of work being carried on, others at the place of work, not being employees, are not exposed to risks to their safety, health or welfare. This was previously dealt with under section 7 of the 1989 Act and was seen to to have particular relevance to construction sites where many of the skilled craftsmen and artisans would be independent contractors and thus self-employed. However, the use of the words '*manage and conduct his or her undertaking*' in section 12 of the 2005 Act is significant in that it underlines the new emphasis in the 2005 Act on safety management. This section applies, for example, to members of the public that have access to a place of work, while work is in progress. The reference to '*in the course of the work being carried on*' seems to limit the liability of an employer in respect of injuries suffered by members of the public at his or her place of work. The definition of '*place of work*' in section 2 of the 2005 Act should, however, be noted in interpreting section 12 of the 2005 Act in that it refers to '*a place of work*' as being '*a location at, in, upon or near which work is carried on*'.

5.5.3   GENERAL DUTIES OF EMPLOYEES

Many of the duties of employees provided for in section 9 of the 1989 Act and article 14 of the 1993 Regulations are re-enacted in the 2005 Act, including the employee's duty to take reasonable care for their own and others' safety, health and welfare. There is also a duty on an employee to co-operate with his employer, to use the protective equipment and clothing provided to him and to report dangerous risks of which he becomes aware. A number of new employee obligations are created in section 13 of the 2005 Act. These include an obligation:

- to comply with the relevant statutory provisions, as appropriate;

- not to be under the influence of an intoxicant at the place of work to the extent that the state he or she is in, is likely to endanger his or her own safety, health or welfare at work or that of any other person;

- if reasonably required by his or her employer, to submit to any appropriate, reasonable and proportionate tests for intoxicants by, or under the supervision of, a registered medical practitioner who is a competent person, as may be prescribed;

- not to engage in improper conduct or behaviour that is likely to endanger his or her own safety or that of any other person;

- to attend such training and, as appropriate, undergo such assessment as may reasonably be required by his or her employer or as may be prescribed relating to safety, health and welfare at work or relating to the work carried out by the employee;

- to report to his or her employer or any other appropriate person as soon as practicable any work being carried on, or likely to be carried on, in a manner which may endanger the safety, health or welfare at work of an employee or that of any other person, of which he or she is aware;

- to report to his or her employer or any other appropriate person as soon as practicable any contravention of the relevant statutory provisions which may endanger the safety, health and welfare at work of the employee or that of any other person, of which he or she is aware; and

- not, on entering into a contract of employment, to misrepresent himself or herself to an employer with regard to the level of training he or she may have.

One of the most significant additions to the duties of employees is to submit to any appropriate testing for intoxicants. An *'intoxicant'* is defined in section 2(1) of the 2005 Act as *'alcohol and drugs and any combination of drugs or of drugs and alcohol'*. This is a significant addition to the duties of an employee and it is short on detail, although it will not come into force in the absence of regulations, which are expected to be introduced in mid-2006. Section 13(1)(c) of the 2005 Act prescribes three preconditions that must be satisfied before such testing may be carried out. These preconditions are that the test must be:

(1) appropriate;

(2) reasonable; and

(3) proportionate.

In light of the possible violation of an employee's constitutional right to liberty, the above preconditions must be strictly construed. Certain parts of this section would also appear to strengthen the position of employers defending cases before the EAT in the instances of employees dismissed for serious breaches of safety rules. In *Michael Kellegher v Power Supermarkets Ltd* UD 720/89 the dismissed employee lifted the forks on a forklift some seventeen to twenty feet in the air, while another employee was perched on them. He then drove back and forth, stopping quickly, thereby causing the forks to rattle. The night manager observed the claimant's actions and he was dismissed. Subsequently the EAT unanimously held the applicant's dismissal for a breach of the safety procedure to have been justified in the circumstances.

Mr Eamon Leahy, Chairman of the EAT, summarised the position in the following terms:

'[H]aving regard to the seriousness of the incident which brought about the dismissal, it is the unanimous view of the Tribunal that the respondent acted reasonably in dismissing the appellant.'

Section 14(a) of the 2005 Act mirrors section 9(2) of the 1989 Act. It imposes a duty on a person (whether an employee or not) not to interfere with, damage or misuse any items provided for securing safety, welfare or health at work. Section 14(b) introduces an additional duty which requires a person (whether an employee or not) not to endanger other persons, in connection with his or her work activities.

A breach of any of the duties prescribed in sections 13 or 14 of the 2005 Act attracts criminal liability.

5.5.4 GENERAL DUTIES OF DESIGNERS, MANUFACTURERS, IMPORTERS AND SUPPLIERS OF ARTICLES AND SUBSTANCES FOR USE AT WORK

Section 16(1) of the 2005 Act sets down duties of designers, manufacturers, importers and suppliers of articles and substances. It provides that it is the duty of *'a person who designs, manufactures, imports or supplies any article for use at work'* to ensure, so far as is reasonably practicable, that the article is designed and constructed so as:

'(i)   *to be safe and without risk to health when properly used by a person at a place of work, and*

(ii)   *to comply with the relevant statutory provisions and with the provisions of any relevant enactment implementing any relevant directive of the European Communities . . .'*

Significantly, this section places on a statutory basis, the obligations on designers, manufacturers, importers and suppliers of articles and substances to comply with any relevant legislation implementing an EU directive. The expanded definition of *'article'* in section 2 of the 2005 Act should also be noted. The definition of *'article'* now includes machine, appliance and tool, any article designed for use as a component part of or to control any such plant, machine, machinery, and appliance or any other product used by a person at work. The 2005 Act does not amend the definition of *'substance'*.

Section 16(1)(c) of the 2005 Act imposes a duty on a person who designs, manufactures, imports or supplies any article to provide adequate information about any such article to the persons to whom it is supplied to ensure that it is used safely. Some guidance as to what amounts to *'adequate information'* is to be found in section 16(2) which provides that adequate information includes information relating to:

'(a)   *the use for which the article has been designed, manufactured or tested, as the case may be, and*

(b)   *any conditions necessary to ensure its safe installation, use, maintenance, cleaning, dismantling or disposal without risk to safety or health.'*

Any breach of sections 16 of the 2005 Act attracts criminal liability.

5.5.5   GENERAL DUTIES OF PERSONS WHO DESIGN AND CONSTRUCT PLACES OF WORK

Section 17 of the 2005 Act combines duties imposed on designers under the 1989 Act and the duties imposed on clients, designers, contractors, project supervisors for the design stage, and project supervisors for the construction stage, under the Safety, Health and Welfare at Work (Construction) Regulations, 2001 and 2003 ('Construction Regulations'). It creates new obligations for persons who commission or procure a project for construction work. The 2005 Act does not define either *'commission'* or *'procure'* and gives no guidance as to when a project is commissioned or procured, i.e. whether it occurs when you buy the site, when you apply for planning permission or when you commence building. These new obligations include the appointment of a competent person or persons to ensure, so far as is reasonably practicable, that the project:

- is designed and is capable of being constructed to be safe and without risk to health (section 17(1)(a));

- is constructed to be safe and without risk to health;

- can be maintained safely and without risk to health during subsequent use; and

- complies in all respects, as appropriate, with all the relevant statutory provisions.

The appointment of a competent person or persons must be *'in writing'*.

Section 17 of the 2005 Act increases considerably the standard of care to be exercised by all involved in the construction process, and, in particular, clients and consultants. The use of the word *'ensuring'* in section 17 of the 2005 Act has increased the duties of clients, designers, contractors and project supervisors.

Section 17(2) of the 2005 Act expands the duties of a person who designs a project for construction work. Pursuant to the 2005 Act, such a person must ensure, so far as is reasonably practicable, that the construction project can be maintained safely and complies in all respects with the relevant legislation.

Section 17(3) sets down duties in respect of persons who carry out construction work and is similarly phrased to its counterpart in the 1989 Act, (see section 11(2)). Section 17(4) of the 2005 Act defines 'project' for the purposes of the section. It states:

> 'For the purposes of this section, "project" means any development which includes or is intended to include construction work.'

It is interesting to note that the draft new Safety, Health and Welfare at Work (Construction) Regulations require employers to provide employees with site-specific safety induction before commencing work on a construction site. These regulations are likely to be introduced in the early part of 2006.

Any breach of section 17 of the 2005 Act attracts criminal liability.

5.6 General Overview of the 2005 Act

Throughout sections 8–17 reference is made to what is 'reasonably practicable'. The 2005 Act contains the first ever statutory definition of the words 'reasonably practicable'. Section 2(6) of the 2005 Act states:

> 'For the purposes of the relevant statutory provisions, "reasonably practicable", in relation to the duties of an employer, means that an employer has exercised all due care by putting in place the necessary protective and preventive measures, having identified the hazards and assessed the risks to safety and health likely to result in accidents or injury to health at the place of work concerned and where the putting in place of any further measures is grossly disproportionate having regard to the unusual, unforeseeable and exceptional nature of any circumstance or occurrence that may result in an accident at work or injury to health at that place of work.'

The foregoing definition imposes a high standard on employers by obliging them to show that they have taken all reasonably foreseeable steps against risk. That said this definition appears to only apply to 'the duties of an employer' and self-employed persons. What then do the words 'reasonably practicable' mean and how are the courts likely to interpret the new statutory definition accorded to such words? Section 2(1) of the 2005 Act attempts to incorporate the terms of Article 5(1) of the Framework Directive, which imposes an absolute duty on employers 'to ensure the safety and health of workers in every aspect related to work'. Article 5(4) of the Framework Directive, which is also reflected in the statutory definition, states:

> 'The Directive shall not restrict the option of a Member State to provide for the exclusion or the limitation of the employers' responsibility where occurrences are due to unusual and unforeseeable circumstances beyond the employers' control, or to exceptional events, the consequences of which could not have been avoided despite the exercise of all due care.'

The Framework Directive exception to the general duty alludes 'to unusual and unforeseeable circumstances beyond the employer's control, or to exceptional events', while section 2(6) of the 2005 Act refers 'to the unusual, unforeseeable and exceptional nature of any circumstance or occurrence'.

It is important to distinguish the concept of negligence from that of 'reasonably practicable'. A defendant may avoid liability in negligence for failing to fulfil certain duties merely by demonstrating that the burden imposed upon him (time and/or cost) by taking those precautions outweighs the scale of the loss, taking into account the chance of that loss occurring. It is clear from section 2(2)(6) of the 2005 Act that reasonable practicability is an altogether different creature. For reasonable practicability there must be a gross disproportion. An employer must be in a position to establish that any further measures would have been *'grossly disproportionate having regard to the unusual, unforeseeable and exceptional nature of any circumstance or occurrence that may result in an accident at work or injury to health at that place of work'*. It is evident from the foregoing that the burden imposed by what is *'reasonably practicable'* in section 2(2)(6) of the 2005 Act is set at a higher standard than that imposed by the general principle of negligence. It would appear, therefore, that in monetary terms the monies required to be expended would have to be very significant before it would not be *'reasonably practicable'* to take the precautions. That said, it would seem that what could be construed as being *'reasonably practicable'* for a multinational corporation might not necessarily pertain in a small corner shop.

For other duty-holders under the 2005 Act, such as manufacturers, suppliers and designers, the common law definition is likely to continue to apply. That said, the 2005 Act lacks clarity on this issue in that the interpretation section of the Act, (see section 2(1)), does not expressly confine the statutory definition to the duties of an employer and states:

> *'. . . reasonably practicable has the meaning assigned by subsection (6).'*

If a court were to apply the statutory definition of *'reasonably practicable'* in section 2(6) of the 2005 Act to other duty-holders, a higher standard would apply than if the common law definition were to be followed.

The common law definition of *'reasonably practicable'* has been elaborated upon in a number of cases. Asquith LJ classically defined the *'reasonably practicable'* standard in *Edwards v National Coal Board*, in the following manner:

> ' "[R]easonably practicable" is a narrower term than "physically possible" and seems to me to imply that a computation must be made by the owner in which the quantum of risk is placed on one scale and the sacrifice involved in the measures necessary for averting the risk (whether in money, time or trouble) is placed in the other, and that, if it be shown that there is a gross disproportion between them—the risk being insignificant in relation to the sacrifice—the defendants discharge the onus on them. Moreover, this computation falls to be made by the owner at a point of time anterior to the accident . . .'

In *Daly v Avonmore Creameries Ltd* [1984] IR 131, McCarthy J, in the Supreme Court, considered 'reasonably practicable' at p 131:

> 'I am not to be taken as supporting a view that, where lives are at stake, considerations of expense are any more than vaguely material.'

The Supreme Court reinforced this view in *Boyle v Marathon Petroleum Ireland Ltd*, 12 January 1999, Supreme Court unreported. In that case, O'Flaherty J made reference to what 'reasonably practicable' meant. He stated:

> 'I am . . . of the opinion that this duty is more extensive than the common law duty which devolves on employers to exercise reasonable care in various aspects as regards their employees. It is an obligation to take all practical steps. That seems to me to involve more than that they should respond that they, as employers, did all that was reasonably to be expected of them in a particular situation. An employer might sometimes be able to say that what he did by way of exercising reasonable care was done in the "agony of the moment", for example, but that might not be enough to discharge his statutory duty under the section in question.'

It is a matter for each individual employer to determine, however, what is *'reasonably practicable'* as pursuant to section 81 of the 2005 Act, in any prosecution for an offence consisting of a failure to comply with a duty to do something, so far as it was practicable or *'reasonably practicable'*, it is for the accused to prove that it was not practicable or was not *'reasonably practicable'* to do more than was in fact done to satisfy this duty or requirement.

5.7   Safety Statements

Section 20 is probably the most important provision in the 2005 Act in terms of the implementation and application of health and safety measures. Under section 20 every employer must prepare or cause to be prepared a statement in writing which is known as a safety statement. This statement is to be based on the hazards identified and the risk assessment carried out under section 19 of the 2005 Act. It must set out how the safety, health and welfare of employees are to be secured and managed in the workplace. The safety statement must specify the risks assessed and identify the hazards to safety, health and welfare at the place of work, which is a new requirement introduced under section 20(2)(a) of the 2005 Act. It must also set out the protective and preventive measures taken and the resources provided for safeguarding safety, health and welfare at the place of work to which the safety statement relates. The safety statement must specify the plans and procedures to be followed and the measures to be taken in the event of an emergency or serious and imminent danger. In addition, a safety statement must identify the co-operation required from employees and include the names and job titles of persons responsible for the safety tasks assigned to them under the 2005 Act and under the safety statement.

A copy of a safety statement or relevant extract must be kept available for inspection in or near every place of work to which it relates while work is being carried out there. This provision attempts to ensure that the safety statement is a living document to be used as necessary. Another new provision in section 20(2)(f) of the 2005 Act is that a safety statement must specify the arrangements made regarding the appointment of safety representatives and safety consultation in the place of work and the names of the safety representatives and the members of the safety committee, if appointed, must also be included in the safety statement. Employers must also bring the safety statement to the attention of new employees upon commencement of employment and other persons at the place of work who may be exposed to any specific risk to which the safety statement refers. Section 20(5) of the 2005 Act now requires an employer to review the safety statement where there has been a significant change in the matters to which a safety statement refers or when there is reason to believe that the safety statement is no longer valid.

This must be done in a form, manner and, as appropriate, language that is reasonably likely to be understood by the employees. This requirement should prompt employers to examine the profile of their workforce in order to decide whether the safety statement should be made available in one or more languages. A similar requirement applies in respect of a safety plan.

Employers conducting activities as may be prescribed in regulations or rules and who contract for services with another employer must check that the service supplier has an up-to-date safety statement. This provision adopts a holistic and joined-up approach to the management of safety and health. In particular, section 20(6) of the 2005 Act attempts to target large organisations, including those in the public sector, which buy in services extensively. It will require all employers who engage sub-contractors to ensure that the sub-contractor has an up-to-date safety statement.

Section 20(8) of the 2005 Act adopts a more streamlined approach to complying with the requirement to prepare a safety statement by removing the requirement on an employer with three or fewer employees to have an up-to-date safety statement. It provides that such an employer can satisfy the safety statement requirement by observing the terms of a special code of practice. The farming sector and small businesses in the maintenance and service sectors are the likely beneficiaries of the relief available under this provision.

An employer is obliged to engage one or more competent persons to enable him or her to perform functions to be specified by the employer in order to ensure the prevention of risks to safety, health and welfare at work. Unlike the 1989 Act, section 18 of the 2005 Act requires an employer to appoint a *'competent person'* as the organisation's safety officer. Section 2(2)(a) of the 2005 Act introduces a definition of *'competent person'* and places on a statutory basis an expanded definition of *'competent person'* previously contained in the Safety, Health and Welfare at Work (General Application) (Amendment No 2) Regulations, 2003. It states:

> *'For the purposes of the relevant statutory provisions, a person is deemed to be a competent person where, having regard to the task he or she is required to perform and taking account of the size or hazards (or both of them) of the undertaking or establishment in which he or she undertakes work, the person possesses sufficient training, experience and knowledge appropriate to the nature of the work to be undertaken.'*

Failure to comply with the section 20 safety statement requirement is a criminal offence and civil liability may also attach. Where there has been loss or damage suffered by an employee the mere failure of an employer to prepare a safety statement does not automatically impose liability on the employer for that loss or damage. In *Matthews v Irish Society of Autism*, 18 April 1997, High Court, unreported Laffoy J held that the defendant's failure to prepare a safety statement was irrelevant in that case as the risk in question was not one that would have been averred to in the safety statement, had one been prepared.

5.8   Consultation

Part 4 of the 2005 Act places a special emphasis on safety representatives and re-enacts the provisions in the 1989 Act on the consultation of workers. This part of the 2005 Act includes an important new provision whereby an employer cannot penalise an employee for acting in good faith in the interests of health and safety.

Section 25 of the 2005 Act enhances the rights of worker safety representatives. This section confers the right on employees to elect a safety representative, or more than one, if the employer agrees, from among their number, to represent them in consultations with the employer on matters of safety, health and welfare. This safety representative has wide powers to inspect, investigate accidents or dangerous occurrences, accompany an inspector who is carrying out an inspection and make oral and written submissions.

Section 25(2)(a) of the 2005 Act provides that the safety representative has the right to inspect the place of work after giving reasonable notice to the employer. The safety representative, however, may inspect immediately if there is an accident, dangerous occurrence or imminent danger or risk to safety, health and welfare. Section 25(2)(b) enables a safety representative to investigate accidents and dangerous occurrences provided this does not interfere with another person carrying out duties under health and safety laws.

Section 26 of the 2005 Act places a duty on employers to consult with their employees, so as to make and maintain arrangements to enable employers and employees to co-operate to promote and develop safety, health and welfare and to monitor the effectiveness of those arrangements. As part of the aforementioned arrangements, employers must consult employees, their safety representatives or both, *'as appropriate'*, on any measure *'proposed to be taken in the place of work which may substantially affect the safety, health and welfare'* of employees. It is clear from the use of the words *'as appropriate'* in section 26(1)(b) that there is no obligation on employers to consult with both their employees and a safety representative. In some cases the employer may deem it sufficient and more efficient to consult only with the safety representatives. The extent of the information and consultation requirement was recently clarified by the ECJ in *Irmtraud Junk v Wolfgang Kühnel*, Case C–188/03, 27 January 2005, a case that dealt with consultation and information in the context of collective redundancies. The ECJ referred, with approval, to Article 2 of Council Directive 98/59/EC of 20 July 1998, which establishes the *'obligation to negotiate'* and seemed to impose a standard or requirement of *'meaningful consultation'*. An even more onerous obligation is likely to be imposed by the ECJ on employers in respect of information and consultation in the safety and health context.

Section 27 of the 2005 Act includes an important new provision that employees should not be penalised for acting in good faith in the interests of health and safety. This section prohibits an employer from penalising an employee for:

- being a safety representative;

- complying with health and safety legislation;

- making a complaint or a representation about health and safety to the safety representative, or to the employer, or to an inspector;

- giving evidence in enforcement proceedings; and

- leaving, or while the danger persisted, refusing to return to his or her work in the face of serious or imminent danger, (see section 27(3)).

The dismissal of an employee following such penalisation will be deemed to be unfair under the Unfair Dismissal Acts, 1977–2001.

5.8.1 HEALTH SURVEILLANCE AND MEDICAL FITNESS TO WORK

Section 22 of the 2005 Act mirrors article 15 of the 1993 Regulations. It imposes specific duties in respect of health surveillance on every employer. Section 22(1) provides that:

> *'[e]very employer shall ensure that health surveillance appropriate to the risks to safety, health and welfare that may be incurred at the place of work identified by the risk assessment . . . is made available to his or her employees.'*

Section 23 of the 2005 Act is a new provision. It provides that where an employee is working in a safety critical situation, he or she, subject to such regulations as may be prescribed (i.e. in accordance with the regulations that have yet to be introduced by the Minister), may be required to undergo a periodic medical assessment of fitness for work to be carried out *'by a registered medical practitioner, nominated by'* his or her employer.

5.8.2 JOINT SAFETY AND HEALTH AGREEMENTS

Section 24 of the 2005 Act includes an innovative new provision which has its origins in a number of the northern Member States of the European Union. In summary, it enables the social partners (i.e. trade unions and bodies representing employers) to enter into agreements setting out practical guidance on safety, health and welfare, and the requirements of health and safety laws. Such an agreement is known as a *'joint safety and health agreement'*. The parties can apply to the Authority for approval of a joint safety and health agreement or to amend it.

5.9 Implementation of Regulations under the 2005 Act

Section 58 of the 2005 Act empowers the Minister for Enterprise, Trade and Employment to make regulations relating to any matter referred to in the 2005 Act or prescribed or to be prescribed for the purposes of giving full effect to the Act or in respect of any of the matters in Schedule 7 of the 2005 Act. Crucially, the nature of the duties imposed under certain regulations currently in force appear to be absolute in nature. That is to say they require the result imposed by virtue of the statutory provision to be achieved by the person or body upon whom the duty is imposed. It is not a defence to state that reasonable care was taken or, alternatively, that it was not *'reasonably practicable'* or practicable to achieve the required result. At best this absolute standard of care might be considered unfair and, at worst, ultra vires the Act. The expanded list of matters identified in Schedule 7 in respect of which the Minister for Enterprise, Trade and Employment can introduce regulations pursuant to section 58 of the 2005 Act, should be noted. Of particular significance is article 4 of Schedule 7 which states that the Minister may introduce regulations on the:

> *'. . . requirements to be imposed on an employee in relation to conduct or behaviour likely to endanger his or her own safety, health and welfare at work or that of any other person including as regards intoxication and submission to reasonable and proportionate tests . . .'*

This provision is broadly drawn and could be invoked to address the growing problem of bullying and stress in the workplace. Section 58(8) should be noted in that it ensures that existing regulations introduced under section 28 of the 1989 Act (i.e. the 1993 Regulations) remain in force until regulations under the 2005 Act have been introduced.

The Safety, Health and Welfare at Work (General Application) Regulations, 1993, SI 44/1993 supplanted many provisions found in or made under the Factories Act, 1955 and related legislation. Any remaining overlap between the Factories Act, 1955 and the Safety, Health and Welfare at Work (General Application) Regulations, 1993 was addressed in the Safety, Health and Welfare at Work Act, 1989 (Repeals and Revocations) Order, 1995, SI 357/1995.

The main regulations are the Safety, Health and Welfare at Work (General Application) Regulations, 1993 and the Safety, Health and Welfare at Work (Construction) Regulations, 1995, SI 138/1995 that were implemented under the 1989 Act.

5.10 Safety, Health and Welfare at Work (General Application) Regulations, 1993

Prior to the 2005 Act the 1993 Regulations were probably the most important legal development relating to safety, health and welfare at work for the past forty years. The Safety, Health and Welfare at Work (General Application) Regulations 1993, SI 44/1993 ('the 1993 Regulations') impose certain absolute duties and are divided into ten parts, each of which now falls to be considered. At the time of writing it is anticipated that further regulations will be implemented shortly by the Oireachtas.

5.10.1 PART I: INTERPRETATION AND APPLICABILITY

The duties imposed under the 1993 Regulations are placed on employers and employees for the benefit of employees. The term *'employee'*, however, is not defined in the regulations. It seems clear that *'employee'* in the regulations bears the same meaning as in the 1989 Act under which the regulations were enacted. Section 2(1) of the 1989 Act defined an employee as a person under a contract of service or apprenticeship. Part I of the regulations provides that they shall *'also apply in respect of the use by [the employer] of the services of a fixed-term employee or a temporary employee'* (see regulation 4(2)). *'Fixed-term employee'* and *'temporary employee'* are defined in the regulations. The former is defined as an *'employee whose employment is governed by a contract of employment for a fixed term or for a specified purpose (being a purpose of a kind that the duration of the contract was limited but was, at the time of its making, incapable of precise ascertainment)'* (see regulation 2(1)). The latter is defined as an '*employee in a temporary employment business which is the employer of that employee and where the employee is assigned to work for and under the control of another undertaking making use of his services*' (see regulation 2(1)).

It has been suggested that certain independent contractors, for example, an electrician employed to rewire a factory (and thus a fixed-term employee), would be governed by the regulations. However, the workman employed by the electrician performing identical work to the electrician is not entitled to the protection afforded such fixed-term employees, as his contract is a contract for services (White, JPM, *Civil Liability for Industrial Accidents* (Dublin: Oak Tree Press, 1993), vol 1, p 1021). This would not leave the employee of the electrician without protection as a duty of care would still be owed to him by the electrician as a deemed occupier under the Occupiers' Liability Act, 1995 as well as an employer at common law. It would, however, be fair to say that the level of protection afforded under the 1993 Regulations is greater. A further point to be made is that a person casually borrowed from another employer would not fall within the definition of temporary employee for the purpose of the regulations, even though he may qualify as an employee under the borrowing employer's liability insurance policy (MacNamee, M, 'Employers' Liability; Recent Legislative and Common Law Developments' (1997) *Irish Insurance Law Review*, vol 1, no 1, p 15).

5.10.2   PART II: GENERAL SAFETY AND HEALTH PROVISIONS

5.10.2.1   Generally

Part II of the 1993 Regulations, and in particular regulation 5, obliges every employer, in taking measures for the safety, health and welfare of his employees, to take into account '*the general principles of prevention*' which are outlined in Schedule 1 to the regulations. Broadly, these relate to the evaluation and avoidance of risk, the adaptation of the workplace, system of work and the provision of safe equipment to the employee. Part II of the regulations imposes specific duties in respect of training, health surveillance, protective and preventative services, emergency duties, risk assessment, provision of information to employees and consultation with employees where safety measures are concerned. This part has been criticised as presenting 'a problem of interpretation' due mainly to 'an appalling want of specificity' (White, *Civil Liability for Industrial Accidents*, p 1024). The regulations must be read in conjunction with the 2005 Act particularly in light of the extended and expanded duties contained in section 19 dealing with risk assessments and section 20 dealing with safety statements. Furthermore, the significance of the 2005 Act arises from the fact that many of the employer's obligations contained in the 1993 Regulations are now placed on a statutory footing.

5.10.2.2   Bullying and stress as a health and safety issue

The duties imposed on every employer to provide safe systems of work are greatly extended in the 2005 Act. There is a greater concentration on safety management and an obligation to manage the workplace to ensure health and safety. The new provisions contained in sections 8(2)(b) and 8(2)(d) in particular underline the importance of an employer having an integrated safety management system and are particularly relevant when addressing the identification of bullying, harassment and stress in the workplace. The enforcement mechanisms available under the 2005 Act could be invoked, for example, where the Authority considered that an employer was exposing his or her employees to unacceptable levels of stress. In such circumstances, the Authority could issue directions for an improvement plan.

Section 8(2)(h) of the 2005 Act is a broad new provision which may impose new obligations on employers to address stress in the workplace. It requires the employer to determine and implement the safety measures necessary for the protection of the safety, health and welfare of his or her employees when identifying hazards and carrying out a risk assessment under section 19 of the 2005 Act or when preparing a safety statement under section 20 of the 2005 Act. These safety measures must have regard to the general principles contained in Schedule 3 of the 2005 Act. This subsection emphasises that the duty is not merely confined to formulating health and safety procedures but also extends to implementing such procedures.

An employer's duty of care to look after the health and safety of employees includes the reasonable prevention of bullying and stress-related injuries in the workplace. Breach of this duty may be treated as a breach of the contract of employment, enabling the employee to claim constructive dismissal (see Chapter 9: Unfair Dismissal Law). Constructive dismissal should only be availed of where an employee is left with no option other than to resign. Consequently, it is important that the employee exhausts any grievance procedure before adopting this course of action. In *Liz Allen v Independent Newspapers (Ireland) Ltd*, UD 641/2000, the EAT awarded the claimant £70,500 compensation. Significantly, the EAT included compensation for stress suffered as a result of constructive dismissal.

5.10.2.3 Bullying

The 2005 Act provides that employers shall carry out a risk assessment at their place of work in the preparation of a safety statement. Such an assessment should include the risks associated with bullying. Procedures or preventative measures should follow this risk assessment in order to eliminate the risk or reduce the level of risk to an acceptable level. Regulation 10 of the 1993 Regulations requires employers to document the result of these risk assessments. Section 19 of the 2005 Act also requires that every employer be in possession of a written assessment documenting the risks presented by the identified hazards in the place of work.

A relevant and instructive case is that of *Michael Shanley v Sligo County Council*, 10 October 2001, High Court unreported. In this case the plaintiff was 'systematically abused, bullied, and belittled' over a protracted period of time (i.e. eight years) by a superior officer. The abuse had been so severe that the plaintiff had contemplated suicide. It was noted that the plaintiff had filed complaints with senior management, who failed to act. Butler J assessed damages at £65,000, the defendant council having admitted liability.

5.10.2.4 Stress

The Health and Safety Authority ('HSA') defines workplace stress as arising 'when the demands of the job and the working environment on a person exceed their capacity to meet them'. The Authority identifies the following as situations that can cause stress in the workplace:

- poor communication at work;
- poor working relationships;
- poorly organised shiftwork;
- faulty work organisation;
- ill-defined work roles;
- lack of personal control over work;
- machine-paced work;
- highly demanding tasks;
- dull repetitive work;
- dealing directly with the public.

The HSA notes that stress can affect the individual at the emotional level (fatigue), the cognitive level (making mistakes), the behavioural level (excess drinking or over-eating) and the physiological level (heart disease, reduced resistance to infection and skin problems). At the macro level, a company/organisation may be affected by someone who is suffering from stress through poor industrial relations, increased absenteeism, faulty decision-making and reduced productivity. An employer's duty is not to provide a stress-free environment but to take reasonably practicable steps to shield employees from exposure to stress and from the consequences of unreasonably stressful working conditions. The new provisions in section 8(2) of the 2005 Act go even further requiring employers and managers to prevent 'improper conduct' likely to put the safety, health or welfare at work of his or her employees at risk.

'Improper conduct', is not defined in the 2005 Act. It is, however, likely to cover 'horseplay', which did not, as such, come within the scope of the 1989 Act. In addition, it might cover the inappropriate use of work equipment or unsafe work practices. These new provisions underline the importance of an employer having an integrated safety management system and are particularly relevant when addressing the identification of bullying, harassment and stress in the workplace. The enforcement mechanisms available under the 2005 Act could be invoked, for example, where the Authority considered that an employer was exposing his or her employees to unacceptable levels of stress. In such circumstances, the Authority could issue directions for an improvement plan.

Employers have both a statutory and common law duty of care to protect their staff against stress. Whilst there have been few cases decided on this point, the potential for litigation in this area is growing. This can be seen from the case of *Saehan Media Ireland Ltd v A Worker* [1999] ELR 41, where the Labour Court acknowledged work-related stress as a health and safety issue and held that 'employers have an obligation to deal with instances of its occurrence which may be brought to their attention'. The issue of foreseeability has therefore been to the forefront in the evolution of the stress at work case law. Once an employer is on notice that a particular employee has a greater susceptibility to stress than others, the employer is under a higher duty as a work-related stress injury is more likely to occur. This implies work activities and environments that minimise stress. However, it should be noted that some work is regarded as intrinsically containing certain stressors and the voluntary assumption of such jobs creates a degree of defence for the employer in civil law.

Health and safety law requires risks to be eliminated or reduced so far as is reasonably practicable, a concept previously discussed at length. The 2005 Act also requires employers to conduct risk assessments. Any such risk assessments should include assessments of activities that could potentially cause unreasonable stress to workers. Section 19 of the 2005 Act provides that the results of these assessments and the risks presented by the identified hazards should be documented. Regulation 17 of and Schedule 2 to the 1993 Regulations cover a number of workplace standards on ventilation, room temperature, natural and artificial room lighting, space allocation and sanitary facilities that must be in place, and failure to do so could amount to contributing to stress at work.

The distinction between physical and psychiatric injury is no longer either medically or legally defensible. Section 2 of the 2005 Act defines 'personal injury' as including:

'(a)   any injury, disease, disability, occupational illness or any impairment of physical or mental condition, or

(b)   any death.'

In the Circuit Court decision of *Curran v Cadbury (Ireland) Ltd* [2000] 18 ILT 140, McMahon J held that the duty of the employer towards his employee extends to protecting the employee from non-physical injury such as psychiatric illness or the mental illness that might result from negligence or from harassment or bullying in the workplace. He referred to *Walker v Northumberland County Council* [1995] 1 All ER 737, a case in which the English courts imposed liability where the plaintiff foreseeably suffered a nervous breakdown because of unreasonably stressful working conditions imposed on him by his employer, and stated that there was no reason to suspect that courts in Ireland would not adopt this approach. The learned judge held that the plaintiff could recover since her employer owed her a duty of care not to expose her to reasonably foreseeable psychiatric illness caused by the employer's negligence.

McMahon J also found that the defendant company had breached paragraph 13 of Schedule 5 to the 1993 Regulations, which states as follows:

> '(a) Where possible, maintenance operations shall be carried out when equipment is shut down.
> (b) Where this is not possible, it shall be necessary to take appropriate protection measures for the carrying out of such operations or for such operations to be carried out outside the area of danger.'

The judge held that since the defendant company should have foreseen that the plaintiff might have suffered psychiatric illness as a result of its breach of the foregoing provision, the plaintiff was also entitled to recover on the ground of breach of statutory duty. Significantly, McMahon J held that in defining 'personal injury', section 2 of the 1989 Act included 'any disease and any impairment of a person's physical or mental condition'.

A relevant and instructive decision on stress at work from the Scottish Court of Session is *Cross v Highlands and Islands Enterprise* [2001] IRLR 336 wherein Lord Macfadyen stated that the duty on an employer to take reasonable care for an employee's safety and health, and to provide and maintain a safe system of work, includes a duty not to subject the employee to work conditions which are reasonably foreseeably likely to cause him or her psychiatric illness or injury. See also *Ingram v Worcester County Council* (Health and Safety Review, March 2000, p 26) and *Howell v Newport County Borough Council* (The Times, 5 December 2000).

5.10.2.5 Increased liability for work-related bullying and stress claims

There is a definite obligation on employers to manage health and safety issues, and more importantly to implement health and safety measures, and this is particularly pertinent when addressing the identification of bullying and stress in the workplace. Such an approach involves inter alia the employer carrying out a risk assessment on an ongoing basis. The risk assessment should form part of the safety statement. This statement should aver not merely to the physical hazards but also to the potential damages of stress and bullying.

Section 80 of the 2005 Act introduced new liabilities for directors, employers and senior managers who, for the first time, could be personally liable for breaches of health and safety legislation, and could face either two years' imprisonment or a maximum fine of up to €3 million, or both, on conviction on indictment.

Section 80(2) of the 2005 Act is a significant provision. It is likely to be very useful to the Authority and the DPP in initiating prosecutions under the Act. It is presumed, until the contrary is proven, that at the material time, the acts resulting in the offence were authorised, consented to, or were attributable to connivance or neglect on the part of a director or a person significantly influencing the management of a company.

In the Scottish case of *Cross v Highlands and Islands Enterprise* [2001] IRLR 336 Lord Macfadyen alluded to the many publications and guidelines on stress at work which emphasise that 'stress should be treated like any other health hazard'. Consequently he held that it is 'strongly arguable that today a reasonable employer would carry out assessments of the risk of injury to their employees of stress at work'.

Bullying policies are essential in the defence of a bullying and stress claim by an employee arising out of alleged bullying. For example, the sanctions to be taken against those found to be in breach of the anti-bullying policy should be clearly stated. Indeed, the HSA's booklet recommends that a bullying policy be incorporated into the company's safety statement. To be effective, bullying policies should be brought to the attention of every employee before he enters into a contract with the employer.

Formal grievance procedures should be put in place to ensure access to management. Such procedures are central to the avoidance of bullying and stress-related claims in that they impose an obligation on the employee to alert the employer of the existence of a bullying and stress-related problem. Each complaint must be comprehensively investigated.

Where an employer becomes aware that an employee is exposed to work-related stress, the employer should relieve the employee of his or her duties on full salary and obtain advice from health professionals. Such an approach will enable the employer to investigate the matter and discharge his/her duty to take reasonable care for his or her employees' health and safety. The foregoing procedure was adopted in *Nolan v Ryan Hotels plc (t/a The Gresham Hotel)* [1999] ELR 214, where the EAT held that 'the employer acted in a proper manner in investigating the matter'.

5.10.3 PART III: WORKPLACE

5.10.3.1 Meaning of workplace

Regulation 16 defines a place of work in the following manner:

> ' "[p]lace of work" means a place of work intended to house workstations on the premises of the undertaking and any other place within the area of the undertaking to which an employee has access in the course of his employment but does not include:
> (a) means of transport used outside the undertaking or a place of work inside a means of transport;
> (b) construction sites;
> (c) extractive industries;
> (d) fishing boats;
> (e) fields, woods and land forming part of an agricultural or forestry undertaking but situated away from the undertaking's buildings.'

It is clear from the foregoing that certain areas are excluded. Workplaces such as schools and colleges are, however, regulated. Regulation 17 confines the scope of applicability by limiting the duty of an employer only to 'any place of work within his control'. The protection provided under these provisions has been criticised as being seriously deficient (White, *Civil Liability for Industrial Accidents*, p 1026). Part III of the 1993 Regulations and the attending schedules err principally in omission. In particular, the writer refers to the former duty imposed by the Factories Act, 1955, section 37, as amended by the Safety in Industry Act, 1980, section 12 with regard to access to and egress from the workplace. (Section 37 of the Factories Act, 1955, as amended by the Safety in Industry Act, 1980, section 12 was repealed by the Safety, Health and Welfare at Work Act, 1989 (Repeals and Revocations) Order, 1995.) An employee, injured accessing or egressing the workplace, will now have to rely on the common law duty of care which imposes a lower standard of care upon the employer, the 1989 Act which attracts criminal, but not civil sanctions and the Occupiers' Liability Act, 1995.

As in the 1989 Act 'place of work' is broadly defined in section 2 of the 2005 Act but now includes 'any, or any part of any, place (whether or not within or forming part of a building or structure) land or other location at, in, upon or near which, work is carried on'. The reference to a 'trailer' in subsection (b) is new and was not included in subsection (c) of the 1989 definition. In addition it is worth mentioning section 8(2)(c) of the 2005 Act provides that an employer's duty extends, as regards the place of work concerned, to ensuring, so far as is reasonably practicable:

> '(i) the design, provision and maintenance of it in a condition that is safe and without risk to health,

(ii)   *the design, provision and maintenance of safe means of access to and egress from it, and*

(iii) *the design, provision and maintenance of plant and machinery or any other articles that are safe and without risk to health . . .'*

While the foregoing duties correspond to the duties previously contained in subsections 6(2)(a) to (c) of the 1989 Act, they only applied to *'any place of work'* which was *'under the employer's control'*. Significantly, these words have been deleted from the 2005 Act so that an employer is now required to ensure, so far as is reasonably practicable, compliance with the duties detailed in section 8(2)(c) of the 2005 Act, even if the place of work is not under his or her control. This subsection imposes an increased burden on an employer with respect to employees who carry out their work otherwise than at the employer's place of work e.g. an electrician or haulier.

Section 8(3) of the 2005 Act specifically extends the duties of the employer to temporary or fixed-term employees.

5.10.3.2   Passive smoking claims

The employer's responsibility in respect of smoking arises both under the 2005 Act and Part III of the 1993 Regulations. In particular, section 8 of the 2005 Act requires all employers to provide safe places of work, which includes a working environment free from tobacco smoke. Part III and paragraph 10(3) of Schedule 3 to the 1993 Regulations offer further protection to the non-smoker employee in the following terms:

> *'In rest rooms appropriate measures shall be introduced for the protection of non-smokers against discomfort caused by tobacco smoke.'*

See also *Working Together for Cleaner Air* (Department of Health, 1997).

While there is a deficit of case law on this topic in Ireland, the matter has been considered on a number of occasions in the neighbouring jurisdiction. A relevant and instructive case is *Rae v Strathclyde Joint Police Board* (OH) 1999 SCLR 793, where Lord Bonomy stated that:

> '[S]moking is a non-industrial activity, indeed, a social activity indulged in by workers and tolerated by employers which has got absolutely nothing to do with the industrial process. If to the knowledge of an employer smoking in the workplace gives rise to the risk that an employee will contract illness through working regularly in close proximity to smokers, then it may well, depending on the circumstances, be very easy to regard the employer as under a duty to stamp out smoking, or at the very least mitigate the effects of smoking since there may well in the circumstances be no difficult issues of practicability or expense to be weighed against the risk.'

See also *Dryden v Greater Glasgow Health Board* [1992] IRLR 669, *Bland v Stockport Borough Council* [1993] New Law Journal, 13 February and *Waltons & Morse v Dorrington* [1997] IRLR 488.

5.10.4   PART IV: USE OF WORK EQUIPMENT

5.10.4.1   Statutory regulation

Part IV of the 1993 Regulations addresses the issue and use of work equipment. Regulation 18 defines the use of work equipment as 'any activity involving work equipment'. Significantly, regulation 19 outlines the duties of employers, which cover responsibilities such as risk assessment (regulation 19(b)) and the provision of training relating to the proper use of the work equipment (regulation 19(e)). All work equipment acquired before 31 December 1992, for use by employees, at a place of work, must comply with certain minimum standards set out in Schedule 5 to the Regulations (see regulation 20). Schedule 5 details the minimum design standards, conditions of use and maintenance of all work equipment regardless of type, provided for use before 31 December 1992. Equipment provided after that date must comply with both the minimum requirements and any relevant and applicable EU directive (see regulation 20). An example of a regulation implementing a directive that would take precedence over the Schedule 5 requirements is the European Communities (Electricity Hydraulically or Oil-Electricity Operated Lifts) Regulations, 1991, SI 41/1991. Accordingly, work equipment brought into use after 31 December 1992, and relating to electrically-operated lifts, must satisfy the minimum design standards set out in the above regulations and not Schedule 5.

The Safety, Health and Welfare at Work (General Application) (Amendment) Regulations, 2001, SI 2001/188, which came into force in May 2001, set down new requirements, such as ergonomic risk assessments, in respect of all work equipment. Schedule 3 is also to be amended to outline the minimum requirements for mobile work equipment.

5.10.4.2   Case law

All equipment supplied must be maintained to the requisite standard throughout its life. In *Doherty v Bowaters Irish Wallboard Mills Ltd* [1968] IR 277 a load suspended from a travelling crane fell, injuring the plaintiff. The cause of the accident was a latent defect in the hook of which the defendant correctly protested he could not have been aware. The Supreme Court held that the requirement in section 34(1) of the Factories Act, 1955, that the hook be of adequate strength, was an absolute duty. The mere fact that the hook broke and caused injury was sufficient of itself to impose liability for the accident upon the employer. It can be seen from *Everitt v Thorsman (Irl) Ltd and Jumbo Bins and Sludge Disposals Ltd*, 23 June 1999, High Court unreported that this absolute standard has been maintained in regulations 19 and 20 and paragraph 8 of Schedule 5 to the 1993 Regulations. In that case Kearns J stated:

> '[W]hile there is no blameworthiness in any meaningful sense of the word on the part of the employers in this case, these Regulations do exist for sound policy reasons at least, namely, to ensure that an employee who suffers an injury at work through no fault of his own by using defective equipment should not be left without a remedy. . . . [A]n employer in such a situation may usually, though not always, be in a position to seek indemnity from the third party who supplied the work equipment.'

The handling, preparation and use of dangerous machinery which is a product of the workplace, as provided for in the Factories Act, 1955, section 23 has not been included in the fencing provision in Part IV of and Schedule 5 to the regulations. It should be noted that sections 21–23 of the Factories Act, 1955 have not been repealed by the Safety, Health and Welfare at Work Act, 1989 (Repeals and Revocations) Order, 1995. Regrettably, this means that the objective of consolidating all health and safety legislation into one statute has not been achieved.

The onerous duty imposed upon employers in relation to work equipment was addressed in *Eamon Stakelum v Governor and Company of the Bank of Ireland*, 5 July 1999, High Court unreported. In summary, the High Court held that employers have a duty to ensure that any equipment used by an employee in the course of his work is free from defects and suitable for the purposes for which it is used. O'Donovan J placed particular emphasis on the employer's duty to submit equipment used by an employee in the course of his employment to risk/safety assessment. In *Gilna v Maguire and 3M Ireland Ltd*, 19 May 1999, High Court unreported, the plaintiff, a 25-year-old radiographer employed at Beaumont Hospital, experienced a shock from a laser image processor, supplied by the second-named defendant, 3M Ireland Ltd. The shock catapulted Ms Gilna across the room causing her personal injury. Her injuries endured for some time notwithstanding extensive physical treatment. The High Court (Johnson J) held that the first-named defendant, who was the representative of Beaumont Hospital in the proceedings, had failed to provide safe equipment to the plaintiff. The court also held that the manufacturer had been negligent in selling a machine in a condition that caused the plaintiff to experience an electrostatic shock. Damages of £664,203 were awarded. See also *Everitt v Thorsman (Irl) Ltd and Jumbo Bins and Sludge Disposals Ltd*, 23 June 1999, High Court unreported discussed above.

173

5.10.5 PART V: PERSONAL PROTECTIVE EQUIPMENT

Part V of the 1993 Regulations requires employers, where risk to health and safety cannot be avoided by technical measures and procedures, to provide personal protective equipment for use by their employees. Prior to the supply and use of personal protective equipment, the employer must ensure that the equipment is effective and compatible with other equipment. Further, every employer must also ensure that the personal protective equipment supplied by him is maintained at all times in good working order. The employer must also give information, training and instruction to the employee in the use of the personal protective equipment (see *Joseph P Magee v Ideal Cleaning Services Ltd* [1999] ELR 218). Section 8(2)(i) of the 2005 Act consolidates into one provision the employer's duty to provide protective clothing or equipment, where risks cannot be eliminated or adequately controlled as per section 6(2)(f) of the 1989 Act, and the precondition that an employer evaluate a risk as one not avoidable by other means before the use of protective equipment as per article 22 of the 1993 Regulations. These duties are absolute in nature. It would appear that the regulations do not impose a duty on an employer to enforce the use of the personal safety equipment that he is obliged to provide to his employees. A common law duty is imposed on an employer in this regard, however, through the tort of negligence.

5.10.6 PART VI: MANUAL HANDLING OF LOADS

5.10.6.1 Statutory provisions

Lifting manual loads in the workplace was formerly regulated by the Factories Act, 1955 (Manual Labour)(Maximum Weights and Transport) Regulations, 1972, SI 283/1972. By virtue of the Safety, Health and Welfare at Work Act, 1989 (Repeals and Revocations) Order, 1995, which came into force on 21 December 1995, Part VI and Schedules 8 and 9 of the 1993 Regulations now replace the 1972 Regulations. Regulation 27 defines what constitutes the manual handling of loads:

> ' "Manual handling of loads" means any transporting or supporting of a load by one or more employees, and includes lifting, putting down, pushing, pulling, carrying or moving a load, which, by reason of its characteristics or of unfavourable ergonomic conditions, involves risk, particularly of back injury, to employees.'

Part VI envisages the manual handling of loads by employees as a last resort. Where such handling is required an employer is obliged to minimise the risk involved and provide, where possible, information concerning the weight and centre of gravity of a load to the employee (see regulation 28). Schedule 8 details the four factors that must be taken into account by an employer for the manual handling of loads:

(a) the characteristics of the load;

(b) the physical effort required;

(c) the characteristics of the working environment; and

(d) the requirements of the activity.

Schedule 9 identifies individual risk factors in the manual handling of loads. This schedule provides that an employee may be at risk if he is physically unsuited to perform the task in question, is wearing unsuitable clothing and does not have the adequate or appropriate knowledge or training. Schedule 9 provides that wearing unsuitable footwear or other personal effects may also put an employee at risk.

On a literal interpretation of the regulation an employer would be under an absolute duty to eliminate all manual handling of goods. The logical consequence of such an interpretation would be to mechanise a system and remove the need for employees altogether. Perhaps the greatest defect in this part is one of omission. Whereas the 1972 Regulations included a list of maximum weights, broken down by age and sex, the new regulations are silent on this point. (The 1972 Regulations were abolished by the Safety, Health and Welfare at Work Act, 1989 (Repeals and Revocations) Order, 1995.) This has resulted in considerable uncertainty, which will ultimately benefit neither employees nor employers.

5.10.6.2 Training

Regular manual handling training will reduce the exposure of an employer to a claim under this part of the Act. In *Gorry v British Midland Airways Ltd* (1999) 17 ILT 224, Dunne J, citing Part VI of the 1993 Regulations, noted that all reasonable precautions were required. The learned judge held that, even where employees were performing a task on a daily basis, they acquired bad habits and needed to be provided with regular training so as to carry out their tasks safely. For manual handling training prior to the 1993 Regulations, see *Catherine Firth v South Eastern Health Board*, 27 July 1993, High Court unreported. The 2005 Act has introduced a greater emphasis on safety training generally in the workplace section 10(1)(a) of the 2005 Act requires an employer, when furnishing instruction, training and supervision to employees regarding health and safety matters, to do so in a manner, form and as appropriate, language, that is reasonably likely to be understood by his or her employees. Section 10(1)(b) of the 2005 Act imposes an additional obligation on employers to give employees time off work with no loss of pay to receive instruction on emergency measures.

Section 10(4) of the 2005 Act imposes a further obligation on an employer, if an employee requires competency for a certain task, to release an employee from work, without loss of pay, where appropriate, so as to allow for the training of the employee in safety and health matters regarding that activity. The phrase *'where appropriate'* has been added in relation to these sections and arguably qualifies the obligations under these sections.

5.10.6.3 Repetitive strain injury

It is worth noting that this part, considering the characteristics specified in Part IV and Schedule 8, which refers, inter alia, to *'over-frequent or over-prolonged physical effort involving in particular the spine'*, could be pleaded in claims involving repetitive strain injury (RSI). RSI is a term covering all kinds of work-related injuries to the muscles, nerves and tendons of the upper limbs. While its recognition as a medical disorder has been slow, there is ample authority to conclude that its existence has been acknowledged at Circuit Court and High Court level in this jurisdiction. In *Sammon v Flemming GMBH*, 23 November 1993, High Ct unreported the plaintiff alleged that she was suffering tennis elbow as a result of her employment. Her work involved screwing caps by hand onto phials on a production line. Barron J accepted on the evidence that the repetitive nature of the work required of her was the probable cause of her condition. He dismissed the claim, however, on the basis that:

> '[T]he Defendant acted reasonably and could not reasonably be expected to have anticipated that the particular work which the Plaintiff was doing would lead to such an abuse of the muscles of her forearm that she would sustain an injury.'

See, however, *Paul Bolger v Queally Pig Slaughtering Ltd*, 8 March 1996, High Court, Barron J unreported.

As the *Sammon* case pre-dated the 1993 Regulations they were not considered. The 1993 Regulations now oblige employers to evaluate the potential risk to their employees and review their safety policies. In the above case, the plaintiff first complained in 1987, six years prior to the enactment of the 1993 Regulations. Knowledge of RSI is now widely publicised. (This was a key factor in the decision of the judge in the English case of *McSherry and Lodge v British Telecommunications plc*, 1991, UK High Court unreported in holding for the plaintiffs.) It may thus be said to be a known risk factor which should fall to be considered by an employer. It is contended that it would now be open to an employee in a similar situation to *Sammon* to claim and to utilise the higher standard imposed by statute (see regulations 5, 10, 11, 13 and 15 of the 1993 Regulations).

In *Brennan v Telemecanique Ltd* [1997] ILLW 254, RSI sustained during assembly work fell to be considered. Lynch J held that the overuse by the plaintiff of the middle finger caused the injury, the subject matter of the proceedings. Further, he held that the overuse of the finger was foreseeable by the defendant. Consequently, the employer was held to be in breach of his duty to provide a safe system of work. It is unclear whether the regulations and/or breach of statutory duty were pleaded or relied upon in this case.

In May 1999 a typist was awarded record damages (£100,000) by the English county court in a landmark case (*McPherson v Camden Council* 19 May 1999 unreported). Thornton J, in the course of his judgment, stated that the council should have provided a wrist rest and a flat keyboard to prevent the onset of the plaintiff's condition and criticised it for its failure to ensure regular breaks from typing.

McPherson v Camden Council, while only of persuasive authority in this jurisdiction, shows that employers can now ill afford to ignore RSI. Indeed, in the short term and the medium term it is widely believed that the number of RSI claims will continue to rise.

In RSI cases much depends upon evidence of the system of work operated by an employer. It would be difficult for a judge, faced with evidence of repetitive work, few breaks and inadequate rotation (see Organisation of Working Time Act, 1997), to find, on the balance of probabilities, that work practices were not to blame. Employers must be proactive in risk prevention and control. Indeed, the 1989 Act and the 1993 Regulations firmly placed the onus on the employer for analysis and prevention of RSI risks. The issue of RSI is not one that is likely to disappear and employers must take care in advising their staff. This is borne out by the UK Court of Appeal decision in *Pickford v ICI* [1998] 3 All ER 462, where it was held that a typist who worked a seven-hour day could claim against her employer for injury caused by excessive typing for lengthy periods without proper breaks or rest periods because the employer had not given her the same instructions as he had other typists to take regular breaks.

From an insurance perspective it is the employer's liability insurance that will pay for any successful RSI claims. A policy will generally cover the compensation awarded by a court, all costs and expenses of litigation incurred by both the defendant and plaintiff and all other costs.

In line with the more onerous duties imposed upon employers by the 1989 Act and the regulations implemented thereunder, the future will undoubtedly result in a wider duty of care on the employer coupled with a more burdensome standard of care—an employer will be required to consider even more contingencies to an even greater depth. This is likely to impact upon the legal position of RSI and will necessitate the determination of a general date of knowledge. This is the date that the employer should have known that there was a danger to his or her employees and done something to protect them. Causation will, however, continue to be a significant obstacle to the employee asserting RSI. In short, the employee must not only establish a breach of duty on the part of his employer but must also satisfy the court that he is suffering from a clinically recognised condition caused by his employment.

5.10.7   PART VII: DISPLAY SCREEN EQUIPMENT

Part VII of and Schedules 10 and 11 to the 1993 Regulations impose new duties on an employer to protect an employee '*who habitually uses display screen equipment as a significant part of his normal work*'. Regulation 30 excludes the following:

'(a)   drivers' cabs or control cabs for vehicles or machinery;

(b)   computer systems on board a means of transport;

(c)   computer systems mainly intended for public use;

(d)   portable display equipment not in prolonged use at a work-station;

(e)   calculators, cash registers and any equipment having a small data or measurement display required for direct use of the equipment; and

(f)   typewriters of traditional design, of the type known as "typewriter with window".'

It is obvious from the foregoing that portable or laptop computers as well as conventional typewriters are excluded from the remit of this section. Regulation 31 imposes specific duties on employers to, inter alia, assess the risk presented by display equipment, plan employees' activities to provide breaks and provide training, information and advice to employees on the proper use of the equipment. The provision of eye tests at regular intervals before, during and after work, and the provision of special corrective appliances, where necessary, are dealt with in regulation 32.

5.10.8   PART VIII: ELECTRICITY

Part VIII of the 1993 Regulations applies, inter alia, to the generation, storage, transmission and provision of electrical energy in most places of work. Regulation 36 is worthy of particular note in that it imposes absolute duties:

'All electrical equipment and electrical installations shall at all times be so—

(a)   constructed,

(b)   installed,

(c)   maintained,

(d)   protected, and

(e)   used so as to prevent danger.'

5.10.9   PART IX: FIRST AID

Part IX of the 1993 Regulations imposes a duty on an employer in respect of first aid.

5.10.10   PART X: NOTIFICATION OF ACCIDENTS AND DANGEROUS OCCURRENCES

Part X of and Schedule 12 to the 1993 Regulations impose requirements with respect to the notification of accidents, the maintenance of records relating to accidents and the examination and tests to be effected in their investigation. It is a defence, however, to any proceedings under this section, for a person to prove that he has taken all reasonable steps to have all incidence of accidents and dangerous occurrences brought to his notice and that he was not aware of the accident or dangerous occurrence the subject matter of the prosecution. *'Dangerous occurrence'* is now defined in section 2(1) of the 2005 Act as:

'an occurrence arising from work activities in a place of work that causes or results in—

(a)   the collapse, overturning, failure, explosion, bursting, electrical short circuit discharge or overload, or malfunction of any work equipment,

(b)   the collapse or partial collapse of any building or structure under construction or in use as a place of work,

(c)   the uncontrolled or accidental release, the escape or the ignition of any substance,

(d)   a fire involving any substance, or

(e)   any unintentional ignition or explosion of explosives,

as may be prescribed . . .'

5.11   Maternity Protection Act, 1994

The Maternity Protection Act, 1994 provides that all employers shall carry out risk assessments taking particular account of risks to new and expectant mothers. It came into effect on 30 January 1995 (see SI 16/1995). The Act specifically provides for a reduction of risks where practicable, changes in working arrangements, the offer of suitable alternative employment or, if that is not possible, paid leave for the employee concerned for as long as is necessary to protect her health and safety or that of her child. It should be noted that regulation 17 of and Schedule 3 to the 1993 Regulations impose an obligation upon employers to provide suitable facilities for pregnant and nursing mothers. In summary, this involves the provision of a quiet and private area where rests may be taken during the working day, and where a breastfeeding mother may feed her baby during such a break.

5.12   Safety, Health and Welfare at Work (Construction) Regulations, 1995

The Safety, Health and Welfare at Work (Construction) Regulations, 1995, SI 138/1995 were introduced to regulate and protect the safety, health and welfare of persons on construction sites and building projects. Construction work is very broadly defined in the regulations. It includes site clearance, excavation and the erection of a new structure, the demolition and removal of structures as well as extensions to and the maintenance of existing buildings. Window cleaning, painting and decorating projects as well as routine maintenance works are all, to some degree, affected by these regulations. The erection of a single private dwelling, a development akin to the development of the Docklands area in Dublin, and all construction sites in between fall within the parameters of the regulations.

Regulation 3 requires the appointment of a project supervisor for the design stage and construction stage of every project. The one person may hold both positions if suitably qualified. Specific duties are imposed on both the design and project supervisors. Regulation 8 of and Schedules 4 and 5 to the 1995 Regulations impose general duties on contractors. The regulations provide for the co-operation and supply of information to the project supervisor. Any contractor who normally has more than 20 persons under his direct control at any one time on any one site is obliged under the regulations to appoint a qualified safety officer. (This figure includes sub-contractors, the self-employed and direct employees.) Particular provision is made in the regulations in respect of the erection, installation and modification of plant and equipment, and in particular scaffolding. Employees under these regulations must co-operate with the employer on matters affecting health and safety, report defects in plant and equipment and make proper use of the protective equipment provided.

In common with all regulations made pursuant to the 1989 Act, section 28, unless the regulations specifically provide otherwise, civil as well as criminal sanctions attach. Obviously in respect of civil actions, there must be a causal connection between the breach of the duty alleged and the loss or injury sustained.

It should be noted that the Safety, Health and Welfare at Work (Construction) Regulations 2001, which came into force on 1 January 2002, revoke the Safety, Health and Welfare at Work (Construction) Regulations, 1995. The 2001 Regulations impose a mandatory requirement that each construction worker receive a basic health and safety course under the FAS Safe Pass training programme and is in possession of a registration card. In addition, workers who are obliged to carry out specified safety critical duties are required to be in possession of a Construction Skills Certification Scheme registration card indicating they have successfully completed training approved by FAS under the Construction Skills Certification Scheme.

5.13 Occupiers' Liability Act, 1995

The occupier of a premises is obliged to take reasonable precautions in terms of the general condition of the premises. This is termed occupiers' liability and is largely governed by the Occupiers' Liability Act, 1995. Section 8(b) of this Act explicitly provides for the retention of the common law duty of care that an employer owes to an employee. For example, employers owe a specific duty to their employees to provide them with a safe premises, independently of any duty they may owe to them as occupiers. Section 8 of the 1995 Act makes it clear that the statutory prescription of occupiers' liability does not affect this type of duty. A relevant and instructive case is *McCarthy v Southern Health Board*, 1995, High Court unreported. The defendant employed the plaintiff. She slipped and fell on an icy patch while walking along a concrete footpath that formed part of the roadway leading to a hospital building controlled by the defendant. The plaintiff suffered personal injury and sued the defendant health board claiming, inter alia, that it was in breach of its duty of care to her as an employer and/or occupier. The court dismissed the claim holding that the most careful employer/occupier could never ensure that there would not be an occasional accumulation of water in such weather conditions.

5.14 Safety, Health and Welfare at Work (Miscellaneous Welfare Provisions) Regulations, 1995

The Safety, Health and Welfare at Work (Miscellaneous Welfare Provisions) Regulations, 1995, SI 358/1995 provide for a number of employer duties and repeal pertinent sections of the Office Premises Act, 1958 and the Safety in Industry Act, 1980. This statutory instrument, along with regulation 17 of and Schedule 2 to the 1993 Regulations, imposes an obligation on employers to provide a safe and comfortable place of work. The employer duties include, inter alia, the provision of adequate and suitable facilities for taking meals, facilities for sitting where practicable and an adequate supply of drinking water.

5.15 Protection of Young Persons (Employment) Act, 1996

The 2005 Act provides that employers must provide safe places and systems of work for all staff, including young persons. The Protection of Young Persons (Employment) Act, 1996 in effect limits the employment of young persons under the age of 18 but over 16 and restricts the employment of children under 16. In general, no child under the age of 13 is permitted to work without a licence from the Minister who must take cognisance of such matters as the safety, health, welfare and education of the child in granting such a licence. Likewise, a 13-year-old can only work under licence or by regulation. The Act requires the employer to receive a copy of the person's birth certificate and, in the case of children, written permission from the parent or guardian of the child, prior to the commencement of employment. The employer must maintain a register of employed young persons (including children) which outlines the times of attendance at work for each day, the rate of pay and the total amount paid in wages. Section 35 of the Organisation of Working Time Act, 1997 amends the Protection of Young Persons (Employment) Act, 1996 to extend to situations where a young person has more than one job.

5.16 Safety, Health and Welfare at Work (Children and Young Persons) Regulations, 1998

The Safety, Health and Welfare at Work (Children and Young Persons) Regulations, 1998, SI 504/1998, elaborate on the basic requirements detailed in the 2005 Act and the 1993 Regulations. These regulations require the employer to carry out a risk assessment that takes cognisance of the particular risks to young persons or children if they are employed by the employer. The risk assessment is to include an assessment of the exposure to certain physical, chemical and biological agents as well as particular work activities, which are detailed in the schedule to the regulations. The assessment must not only take cognisance of the safety and health of the child or young person but should also take account of their physical and mental development. The employer is to provide protective and preventative measures and consult any child or young person employed of these measures and of the risks that they are being protected from. The parent or guardian is also to be informed of these risks and preventative measures taken if the person employed is a child. Where the results of a risk assessment confirm that particular work activities may cause harm to a child or young person, they shall not be employed in any such activity (regulation 3(d)). Further, where an assessment shows that a child or young person may be exposed to a risk to their physical or mental development, then health surveillance must be made available to them without charge.

If the work involves night work, the employer must provide health assessment without charge prior to the commencement on night work and at regular intervals thereafter. (However, under the Protection of Young Persons (Employment) Act, 1996, young persons are expressly precluded from being employed after 11 p.m. or before 7 a.m.. Similarly, children cannot be employed after 8 p.m. or before 8 a.m. the next morning.) The parents or guardians of children must be informed of the results of health surveillances or assessments.

5.17 Safety, Health and Welfare at Work (Night Work and Shift Work) Regulations, 2000

The principal elements of the 1993 EC Working Time Directive, 93/104/EC, were implemented by the Organisation of Working Time Act, 1997. Articles 9 and 13 of the 1993 Directive were implemented by the Safety, Health and Welfare at Work (Night Work and Shift Work) Regulations, 1998, SI 485/1998, which became operative on 1 February 1999. The Safety, Health and Welfare at Work (Night Work and Shift Work) Regulations, 2000, SI 11/2000 revoke and replace the 1998 Regulations. Their purpose was to avoid any ambiguity as regards the application of the provisions of regulation 6 of the 1998 Regulations to night workers. The 2000 Regulations do not impose new obligations or conditions not intended in the 1998 Regulations.

In summary, the 2000 Regulations oblige employers to take such steps as, having regard to the nature of the work, are appropriate for the protection of the health and safety of night workers and shift workers. Regulation 6 of the 2000 Regulations requires an employer to carry out a risk assessment to determine if any night workers are exposed to special hazards or a heavy physical strain (see also the Organisation of Working Time Act, 1997, section 16(2)(a), (b)). The risk assessment must take account of the specific effects and hazards of night work and have regard to the risk assessment requirements detailed in the 1989 Act, section 12 (see **5.7** above).

Regulation 7(1) of the 2000 Regulations obliges employers before an employee is employed to do night work and at regular intervals thereafter to make available to the employee, free of charge, an assessment of the effects, if any, on the employee's health. Regulation 7(2) states that the health assessment must be conducted by a registered medical practitioner or a person acting under his or her supervision. The employer and employee are to be advised by the person carrying out the assessment of his or her opinion as to whether the employee is fit or unfit to perform the night work concerned (regulation 7(3)(b)). If of the opinion that the employee is unfit for night work by virtue only of the particular conditions under which it is performed, the employer and employee are to be informed of the person's opinion of what changes could be made which would result in his or her being able to consider the employee fit to perform that work (regulation 7(3)(b)).

Regulation 7(4) makes clear that the health assessment must comply with requirements of medical confidentiality. Regulation 7(5) requires employers, whose night workers become ill or otherwise exhibit symptoms of ill-health which are recognised as being connected with the fact that they perform night work, to reassign such workers to day work suited to them whenever possible.

5.18 European Communities (Protection of Workers) (Exposure to Asbestos) (Amendment) Regulations, 2000

The European Communities (Protection of Workers) (Exposure to Asbestos) (Amendment) Regulations, 2000, SI 74/2000 implement Article 7 of Council Directive 87/217/EEC on the prevention and protection of environmental pollution by asbestos by amending the requirements of the plan provided for in Article 12 of Directive 83/477/EEC which must be prepared prior to any demolition work involving asbestos. Regulation 4 of the 2000 Regulations also amends the length of time that medical records and the occupational health register must be maintained.

5.19 Safety, Health and Welfare at Work (Pregnant Employees etc) Regulations, 2000

The Safety, Health and Welfare at Work (Pregnant Employees etc) Regulations, 2000, SI 218/2000, implement the occupational health and safety provisions of Council Directive 92/85/EEC of 19 October 1992 by the introduction of measures to promote improvement in the health and safety at work of pregnant workers and workers who have recently given birth. These regulations revoke and replace the Safety, Health and Welfare at Work (Pregnant Employees etc) Regulations, 1994, SI 446/1994. They require employers to take such steps as, having regard to the nature of the work, are necessary for the protection of the health and safety at work of pregnant workers and workers who have recently given birth or are breastfeeding. Regulation 4 requires an employer to carry out a risk assessment to determine any possible effects on the pregnancy of, or breastfeeding by, employees resulting from any activity at the employer's place of work. Regulation 5 states that if a pregnant employee is certified by a medical practitioner as not being able to perform night work during pregnancy or for 14 weeks after childbirth, the employer shall find day employment for her. If this is not possible the employer must grant the employee leave or extend the period of maternity leave (see **3.4.9**). The introduction of the Safety, Health and Welfare at Work (Pregnant Employees etc) Regulations, 2000 has, however, had no material impact on the practical obligations previously imposed at the workplace under the 1994 Regulations.

5.20 Enforcement Under the 1989 Regime

5.20.1 HEALTH AND SAFETY AUTHORITY

The sanctions provided under the 2005 Act are primarily criminal. Given the fact that breaches would be technical in nature, it was logical to vest responsibility for enforcement in a new administrative body, namely the National Authority for Occupational Safety and Health, better known as the Health and Safety Authority. Part III of the 1989 Act established the Authority, while Parts V, VI, VII and VIII provided that body with its metaphorical teeth.

Part 5 of the 2005 Act deals with the Authority. Section 34(1) of the 2005 Act states that the general functions of the Authority are:

'(a) to promote, encourage and foster the prevention of accidents, dangerous occurrences and personal injury at work in accordance with the relevant statutory provisions,

(b) to promote, encourage, foster and provide education and training in the safety, health and welfare of persons at work,

(c) to encourage and foster measures promoting the safety, health and welfare of persons at work,

(d) subject to [section 34](2) and section 33 [of the 2005 Act], to make adequate arrangements for the enforcement of the relevant statutory provisions,

(e) to monitor, evaluate and make recommendations to the Minister regarding implementation of and compliance with—
   (i) the relevant statutory provisions, and
   (ii) best practice relating to safety, health and welfare at work, and the review and maintenance of relevant records by employers,

(f) to promote, encourage and foster co-operation with and between persons or bodies of persons that represent employees and employers and any other persons or bodies of persons, as appropriate, as regards the prevention of risks to safety, health and welfare at work in accordance with the relevant statutory provisions,

(g) to make any arrangements that it considers appropriate for providing information and advice on matters relating to safety, health and welfare at work,

(h) to make any arrangements that it considers appropriate to conduct, commission, promote, support and evaluate research, surveys and studies on matters relating to the functions of the Authority and for this purpose—
   (i) to foster and promote contacts and the exchange of information with other persons or bodies of persons involved in safety, health and welfare at work in and outside the State, and
   (ii) as it considers appropriate, to publish in the form and manner that the Authority thinks fit, results arising out of such research, studies and surveys,

(i) in accordance with section 43 [of the 2005 Act], to prepare and adopt a strategy statement and to monitor its implementation,

(j) in accordance with section 44 [of the 2005 Act], to prepare and adopt a work programme,

(k) to comply with any directions in writing, whether general or particular, relating to its functions, that the Minister may from time to time give to the Authority,

(l) to give to the Minister any information relating to the performance of its functions that the Minister may from time to time require, and

(m) to perform any additional functions conferred on the Authority by order under section 35 [of the 2005 Act].'

The matters detailed in subsections (1)(e), (1)(g)–(k) and (1)(m) above are new functions of the Authority. Section 34(1)(k) of the 2005 Act is to be regretted in that it undermines the independence of the Authority in that it requires the Authority to comply with any 'directions' that the Minister may give to the Authority.

Part 6 of the 2005 Act is devoted to the making of regulations and codes of practice, and enforcement. These codes serve primarily as aids to understanding the purpose and desired result of the regulations, though they are not legally binding. Part V of the Act enables the Minister to prescribe persons, including local authorities, to be enforcement agents in lieu of the Authority.

5.20.1.1 Regulations

Section 58 of the 2005 Act empowers the Minister for Enterprise, Trade and Employment to make regulations relating to any matter referred to in the 2005 Act or prescribed or to be prescribed for the purposes of giving full effect to the Act or in respect of any of the matters in Schedule 7 of the 2005 Act. The expanded list of matters identified in Schedule 7 in respect of which the Minister for Enterprise, Trade and Employment can introduce regulations pursuant to section 58 of the 2005 Act, should be noted. Of particular significance is Article 4 of Schedule 7 which states that the Minister may introduce regulations on the:

> '. . . requirements to be imposed on an employee in relation to conduct or behaviour likely to endanger his or her own safety, health and welfare at work or that of any other person including as regards intoxication and submission to reasonable and proportionate tests . . .'

This provision is broadly drawn and could be invoked to address the growing problem of bullying and stress in the workplace. Section 58(8) should be noted in that it ensures that existing regulations introduced under section 28 of the 1989 Act (i.e. the 1993 Regulations) remain in force until regulations under the 2005 Act have been introduced.

5.20.1.2 Codes of Practice

Section 60 of the 2005 Act empowers the Authority, with the consent of the Minister for Enterprise, Trade and Employment, to prepare or approve technical specifications in the guise of Approved Codes of Practice to support the detailed statutory provisions. The requirement that the Authority obtain the consent of the Minister before publishing or approving a code of practice is a new provision in the 2005 Act. The Authority may publish, in such a manner as the Authority considers appropriate, a draft of the code of practice, in full or in part, and must give persons one month from the date of publication to make written representations. Following the consultation and, where relevant, having considered the representations, if any, made, the Authority must submit the draft code to the Minister for his or her consent, with or without modification.

Section 31 of the 1989 Act provided that a failure to observe any part of a code of practice would not, of itself, render a person liable to criminal proceedings. No corresponding provision appears in the 2005 Act. That said, failure to observe a code of practice does not, as such, render a person liable under the 2005 Act. Section 61 of the 2005 Act, however, provides that a code of practice is admissible in evidence in criminal proceedings.

5.20.1.3 Enforcement

As under the 1989 Act, the responsibility for enforcement is entrusted to the Authority and certain other persons prescribed by the Minister for Enterprise, Trade and Employment. Under the 1989 Act, such other persons were described as 'enforcing agencies' and were appointed by the Minister under section 33 of the 1989 Act. Such terminology is not retained in the 2005 Act, with section 33(1) of the 2005 Act providing that the Minister 'may prescribe persons to perform such functions in lieu of the Authority in respect of the implementation of any of the relevant statutory provisions, and to the extent as may be prescribed'.

Inspectors are appointed under section 62 of the 2005 Act. As under the 1989 Act, the Authority or person prescribed may appoint persons as inspectors by issuing such persons with a certificate of authorisation. Inspectors appointed under the 1989 Act continue to act as such, despite the repeal of such enactment.

The powers of the inspector are set out in section 64 of the 2005 Act, which enlarges and refines many of the powers under the 1989 Act. Some comparison can be made with the powers of inspectors under statutory regimes who can enter places of work. These may include the inspectors under the Companies Act, 1990 and inspectors under the Competition Act, 2002. Although the role of such inspectors is somewhat different, there are certain similarities in the scope of their powers.

The powers of the inspectors are augmented by criminal sanctions, with section 77 creating certain offences in relation to the exercise of powers by inspectors. These include an offence where a person *'prevents, obstructs, impedes or delays an inspector from exercising any functions conferred on him or her by [the 2005 Act]'* or where a person *'fails to comply with a bona fide request, instruction or directions from an inspector in the exercise of his or her statutory functions'*.

Section 64 provides for very wide powers of entry, inspection, examination, search, seizure and analysis to be entrusted to the appointed inspectors. Among the particular powers of the inspector is the authority to issue improvement directions and plans (1989 Act, section 65), improvement notices (1989 Act, section 66) and prohibition notices (1989 Act, section 67). Under section 71 of the 2005 Act (previously section 39(1) of the 1989 Act) the Authority may apply ex parte to the High Court for an order when it *'considers that the risk to the safety and health of persons is so serious that the use of the place of work or part thereof should be restricted or should be immediately prohibited until specified measures have been taken to reduce the risk to a reasonable level'*. The High Court may make an interim or interlocutory order as it sees fit. In 1996, the Health and Safety Authority obtained, for the first time, a High Court order under this section. Two High Court orders were obtained in 1997, two again in 1998, four in 1999 and two in 2000.

It appears that the procedure under section 71 should only be invoked in exceptional circumstances in cases of urgency. A court order obtained without notices interferes with the constitutional right to earn a livelihood and the constitutional right to the enjoyment of property. The service of a prohibition notice at least provides some form of notice and opportunity for compliance, which is absent from the section 71 procedure. It will therefore be a necessary proof in any such application to demonstrate that the service of a prohibition notice was not appropriate.

The powers of the inspectors must be read subject to rights of persons affected by the search. These may include rights deriving from the Constitution and rights under the European Convention on Human Rights (ECHR). Relevant privileges may include legal professional privilege and the privilege against self-incrimination. Since the enactment of the 1989 Act, the ECHR has gained some force in domestic law by means of the European Convention on Human Rights Act, 2003. The case law of the European Court of Human Rights (ECtHR) has developed the notion of privilege under Article 6 of the ECHR. Other areas of uncertainty include whether there is a constitutional right to have a lawyer present when an inspection is being carried out.

5.20.1.4   Power of entry

As regards the power of entry, section 64(1)(a) of the 2005 Act enlarges the circumstances in which an inspector may enter by adding two other circumstances. In addition to the power to enter where the inspector has reasonable grounds for believing a place is used as a place of work, the inspector may also enter any place:

> *'(ii)   in which he or she has reasonable grounds for believing that articles or substances or records are kept, or*
>
> *(iii)   to which the relevant statutory provisions apply . . .'*

5.20.1.5   On-the-spot fines

Section 79 of the 2005 Act, which at the time of writing was not yet in force, introduces a new procedure for the imposition of on-the-spot fines by an inspector in lieu of a prosecution. Section 79(1) provides that where an inspector has reasonable grounds for believing that a person is committing or has committed a prescribed offence under the relevant statutory provision, he or she may serve the person with a notice in the prescribed form. The maximum on-the-spot fine which can be imposed is €1000, which is to be paid *'during the period of 21 days beginning on the day of the notice'*.

The level of the on-the-spot fine will be detailed in regulations along with the offences and employment sectors to which this fine will apply. A necessary precondition for the exercise of the on-the-spot fine is that the inspector must:

(a) have reasonable grounds to believe a prescribed offence is being committed; and

(b) serve a valid prescribed notice.

As previously stated, a person has 21 days from the service of the notice to pay the fine. If the fine is not paid during the 21-day period, the Authority can proceed to a prosecution.

The advantages of such a scheme include administrative convenience by removing the cost, risk and delay of bringing a prosecution in the District Court. The advantage for the perpetrator in paying the fine include a reduced level of fine compared to a fine which may be imposed in the District Court if the charge is contested. In any prosecution for non-payment under the 2005 Act, the onus is on the accused to prove that the payment has been made.

5.20.1.6 Naming and shaming

Section 85 of the 2005 Act provides that the Authority can compile a list of persons upon whom a fine or penalty has been imposed, upon whom a prohibition notice has been served or in respect of whom an interim or interlocutory order has been made by a court. The concept of naming and shaming is not new to the Irish legal system. It already exists in company and revenue law. For example, the Companies Registration Office publicises the names of defaulters in the submission of annual returns under the Companies Acts and the Revenue Commissioners publish the names of certain tax defaulters with whom they have made settlements.

5.20.2 PROSECUTION OF OFFENCES

Part 7 of the 2005 Act deals with offences and penalties.

Section 78 of the 2005 act creates three categories of offences. They are:

(1) summary offences for which a fine (not exceeding €3,000) only can be imposed;

(2) summary offences for which a fine (not exceeding €3,000) and/or imprisonment (not exceeding six months) can be imposed;

(3) indictable offences punishable by the imposition of a fine (not exceeding €3 million) and/or imprisonment (not exceeding two years).

In summary, the first category applies to less serious matters and the second and third categories cover the more serious offences. In addition, the person convicted can be ordered to pay the Authority's costs and expenses. The main changes under the 2005 Act include a significant increase in the level of fines and also the fact that certain summary offences can attract a prison sentence of up to six months. Any of the summary offences set out above which can attract a fine and/or imprisonment can also be prosecuted on indictment. It is a matter for the DPP to decide whether such contraventions are serious enough to justify a prosecution on indictment.

The largest fine imposed to date in Ireland was in a prosecution against Smurfit News Press Ltd on October 29, 2004. It was fined €1million following two serious accidents at its premises. In the *Oran Pre-Cast* case, where a man was killed when he fell 11 metres in the middle of repairing guttering in a factory in County Galway, Hardiman J in the Supreme Court in an extempore judgment delivered on 16 December 2003 reduced the fine of half a million euros imposed at first instance to €100,000. The learned judge stated:

> *'I would repeat what [the Supreme Court] said before in a case where there is no limit on the power of the Court, the court has to weigh all the aggravating factors but it has to also balance them with questions as to the actual degree of fault and not yield to a purely emotional reaction to the fact that there has been a fatality. The principal factor in assessing a penalty in this case is the degree of fault. The second factor is the context of the Company itself, that is to say its record and how it behaved since these events. And the third factor, which may not be a factor at all in some certain cases, is the ability of the company to pay any particular fine.'*

Significantly, section 60(1)(a) of the 1989 Act has been omitted from the 2005 Act in what is a fundamental departure from the approach adopted under the 1989 Act. This section provided that a failure to comply with the general duties of employers and self-employed persons did not give rise to a cause of action in civil proceedings. Contravention of these general duties merely attracted criminal sanctions.

The removal of the civil liability exemption in respect of a failure by an employer to comply with his or her general duties will necessitate increased vigilance on the part of employers to ensure compliance with the expanded list of general duties imposed on employers under the 2005 Act.

Section 77 of the 2005 Act contains an enlarged list of offences, which were formerly contained in section 48 of the 1989 Act. Many of the offences are the same although a different layout is provided in the section. Section 77(1)(a) creates certain additional offences in respect of the duties of the safety representative and also regarding consultation and participation of employees in safety committees.

The other offences in section 77(1) of the 2005 Act were also offences under the 1989 Act and arise where a person:

> *'(b) prevents or attempts to prevent any person from answering any question to which an inspector may require an answer under section 64,*
>
> *(c) fails to submit an improvement plan to an inspector within the time specified in a direction under section 65,*
>
> *(d) fails to implement an improvement plan, the adequacy of which has been confirmed in accordance with section 65,*
>
> *(e) contravenes any requirement imposed by a notice requiring information under section 72, or*
>
> *(f) prevents, obstructs, impedes, or delays an officer of customs and excise in the exercise of any of the powers conferred on him or her by section 87.'*

In relation to section 77(1)(d) and (e) above, the former defence to such offences contained in section 48(4), '*if it can be shown that other measures providing at least equal protection were taken*', is omitted.

Section 77(2) (a) criminalises:

— a failure to discharge a duty by employers, employees and persons in control of work;

— a failure to discharge a duty by designers, manufacturers, importers and suppliers;

— a failure to discharge duties relating to construction work; and

— a failure to discharge certain protective and preventive measures.

As Part 2 of the 2005 Act sets out an expanded list of responsibilities and duties of employers, there is a corresponding expanded set of offences.

There is little possibility of escaping responsibility for breaches of the 2005 Act as employers, the self-employed, employees and manufacturers, designers and builders may all be prosecuted for breaches of the Act. Both individuals and bodies corporate may be prosecuted. In most cases the company itself will be prosecuted. However, section 80 of the 2005 Act specifically provides for the prosecution of the officers and management of a company or other body. Where an offence has been committed by a 'body corporate', and that offence is shown to 'have been committed with the consent or connivance of, or to have been attributable to any neglect on the part of any director', or other officer, that person may be prosecuted in addition to the corporate body. This approach has been taken in England since the introduction in that jurisdiction of a similar provision in 1974 (Health and Safety at Work Act, 1974, section 37).

In *R v Boal* [1992] QB 591, for example, an inspection of a bookshop identified serious breaches of the Fire Precautions Act, 1971. That Act contained a provision similar to section 48(19) of the 1989 Act in this jurisdiction. Mr Boal held the position of assistant manager in the bookshop and was only in charge when the manager was absent. The manager was absent on the particular day of the inspection. However, the case against Mr Boal was dismissed, as it was held that, although he was in charge of the store on the particular day of the inspection, he had no control over the fire safety policy of the shop. That said, the owners were successfully prosecuted (see also *Armour v Skeen* [1977] IRLR 310). It would appear, therefore, that, for the imposition of personal liability on an officer or manager of a company, some element of control over corporate policy is required. The application of section 48(19) in this jurisdiction can be seen in the November 1998 case of *National Authority for Occupational Safety and Health v Noel Frisby Construction Ltd and Noel Frisby* (see Health and Safety Authority Annual Report 1998, p 17).

5.20.3 TIME LIMITS

Section 82(3) of the 2005 Act provides that summary proceedings must be brought '*within 12 months from the date on which the offence was committed*'. Section 82(4) provides that where a statutory report on foot of an investigation is required or where an inquest is held, summary proceedings must be brought within six months of the making of the report or the conclusion of the inquest. Prosecutions must be brought, pursuant to the 1989 Act, section 51(3), within one year from the date of the offence. Section 51(4) provides that where a statutory report on foot of an investigation is required or where an inquest is held, summary proceedings must be brought within six months of the making of the report or the conclusion of the inquest.

5.21 Future of Health and Safety Legislation and Management Standards

5.21.1 GENERALLY

There has been a powerful movement towards greater protection of the safety, health and welfare of employees at work. The general provisions of the 2005 Act, which include on-the-spot fines, increased sentences and fines, the naming and shaming by the Authority, testing for intoxicants, employers' duties, safety statements, increased personal liability for directors and managers, safety representatives, codes of practice and joint safety and health agreements, will improve the safety and health standards which employees enjoy in the workplace. Many more regulations affecting all aspects of the workplace and all those persons connected with it will be introduced. However, the success of the 2005 Act is dependent not only on ensuring compliance with the new statutory provisions but will also depend on changing existing mindsets.

5.21.2   DUTY OF CARE

With the introduction of the 2005 Act there is a higher threshold in relation to the duty of care owed by employers to employees.

The leading question that remains to be addressed is what duty of care will be imposed on employers in the future. Currently, the protection afforded by statute is in excess of that presently afforded by the common law. Several provisions of the 2005 Act require the high standard of reasonable practicability from employers. Surprisingly, very few references are made to this standard of reasonable practicability in the 1993 Regulations. In fact, the 1993 Regulations impose certain absolute duties (see regulations 19, 20 and 36). Is it likely, therefore, that future regulations will impose a higher standard of care on employers than the 2005 Act?

It has been argued that the duty of care imposed under future regulations should be one of absolute liability. Strict liability is not to be equated with absolute liability. Defences may be pleaded in respect of a strict liability standard whereas no defence is available to a standard of absolute liability. This standard is higher than that of reasonable practicability under the 2005 Act. A number of reasons for this approach are proffered. Most regulations commence life as directives from Europe, which this State is obliged, pursuant to its Treaty obligations, to implement. Directives set down minimum standards not maximum ones and do not preclude the imposition of a higher duty of care. Accordingly, it is always open to a court to hold that the regulations impose a higher standard than that provided for under the 2005 Act.

In addition, in some cases, absolute duties have already been in existence in Irish law since the Factories Act, 1955 and to withdraw or recoil from that now would be to reduce the level of protection available to employees under the 2005 Act. This would be totally contrary to the intention of the legislature and the spirit of the legislation. Further, many of the regulations are general in nature and, indeed, vague in parts. This would and should militate against too strict an interpretation of the regulations by the courts.

5.21.3   INCREASED EXPECTATIONS

The increased protection afforded by the 2005 Act may raise the expectations of society as a whole in so far as safety, health and welfare at work are concerned. It may serve in time to impact upon the common law duty of care. In other words, what is reasonable now may not be deemed reasonable in the future. In summary, the greater protection afforded by statute may become no more than merely declaratory of the common law position.

Society and the courts are already reflecting this increased awareness of health and safety. In *DPP v Cullagh* Irish Times Law Reports, 31 May 1999, the operator of a funfair was prosecuted for and convicted of criminal negligence arising out of the death of a member of the public. This case was not taken under the health and safety legislation but rather under the common law. The initiation of manslaughter charges by the Director of Public Prosecutions against the managing director of a company (arising from the death of two employees at work) in a case in 1999 should be noted by employers as it signposts the fact that workplace deaths can no longer be discounted as a minor matter for the District Court.

5.21.4   CORPORATE RESPONSIBILITY

In the future it is likely that individual members of management will face criminal charges arising out of deaths and injuries at work where it is possible to connect the individual failures of senior executives with the corporate body. A safety management system must be in place for directors to avoid conviction. There is now a strong case for express statutory provision for the offence of corporate manslaughter. Where someone loses his or her life through employer negligence, the offence of corporate manslaughter is likely to apply if such an offence is introduced in this jurisdiction.

In October 2005 the Law Reform Commission published its final report on corporate killing, *Consultation Paper on Corporate Killing* LRC CP 26–2005 October 2005. It recommended in that report that corporations should be subject to criminal liability for corporate killing. The Law Reform Commission's report identified the Stardust nightclub fire, the Whiddy Island disaster and the train crashes at Buttevant and Cherryville as instances where organisational failures in Ireland resulted in death. It also made reference to the Blood Transfusion Service Board, which breached its own rules when it neglected to investigate complaints adequately and to recall contaminated batches of blood produce, leading to the infection of large numbers of people.

The Law Reform Commission has therefore recommended the introduction of a new statutory offence of 'corporate manslaughter . . . which would make an organisation responsible for a death arising from its gross recklessness'. This offence would facilitate the prosecution of company directors and individual managers found to have acted with gross negligence. Significantly, it would render them liable for unlimited fines and imprisonment for up to 12 years ('as well as possible disqualification from acting as a manager in an undertaking') in circumstances where they are found to have neglected the health and safety of those affected by their activities. The offence of corporate manslaughter, as outlined in the draft Bill appended to the Law Reform Commission's report, requires gross negligence, which means recklessness as to the danger involved in an act or omission when the danger would have been obvious to any reasonable person.

CHAPTER 6

EQUALITY AND DISCRIMINATION IN THE WORKPLACE

6.1 Evolution of Irish Employment Equality Law

6.1.1 SOURCES OF IRISH EMPLOYMENT EQUALITY LAW

The sources of Irish employment equality law are:

- the Constitution;
- Article 119 (now Article 141) of the EC Treaty;
- Council Directive 75/117/EEC;
- Council Directive 76/207/EEC;
- Anti-Discrimination (Pay) Act, 1974;
- Employment Equality Acts, 1998 and 2004;
- Social Welfare (Miscellaneous Provisions) Act, 2004.

The Employment Equality Acts, 1998–2004 (the 'Equality Acts') add to the scope of equality legislation and replace both the 1974 Act and the 1977 Act.

6.1.2 THE CONSTITUTION

The 1937 Irish Constitution allowed an aggrieved employee to seek redress under the terms of the Constitution in addition to any relevant statutory or common law rights (Curtin, *Irish Employment Equality Law* (1989)). The Constitution does not contain any general prohibition on sex discrimination but article 40.3 provides for certain personal rights as follows:

> '(i) The State guarantees in its laws to respect and, as far as practicable, by its laws to defend and vindicate the personal rights of the citizen.
>
> (ii) The State shall, in particular, by its laws protect as best it may from unjust attack and, in the case of the injustice done, vindicate the life, person, good name, and property rights of every citizen.'

The first significant case dealing with this sub-article of the Constitution was *Ryan v Attorney General* [1965] IR 294 in which Kenny J held that there existed a number of unspecified rights in addition to those specifically mentioned in article 40.3. Kenny J found, which decision was upheld by the Supreme Court on appeal, that there existed a right to bodily integrity.

In *Murtagh Properties v Cleary* [1972] IR 330 the plaintiff publicans applied for an interlocutory injunction restraining the picketing of their premises by members of a trade union

190

who objected to the employment of female staff as part-time bar waitresses. The trade union contended that such employment was a breach of an agreement between an employer's association and a trade union. None of the women in question was a member of the union. It emerged that while there were some female members of the union, who were employed in the grocery and provision business, employment in licensed premises was confined to males. The plaintiffs contended (inter alia) that the Constitution recognised a right to earn a livelihood without discrimination on the grounds of sex and that that right was infringed when an employer who was willing to employ a woman was prevented from doing so by persons objecting solely on the grounds of sex. Kenny J concluded that the framers of the Constitution intended that in so far as the right to adequate means of livelihood was involved, men and women were to be regarded as equal. It followed that a policy or internal rule under which anyone sought to prevent an employer from employing men or women on the ground of sex only was prohibited by the Constitution. Kenny J confined his decision to finding that the women had the right to have an 'opportunity' to earn a livelihood. Such a personal right did not extend to the right to receive pay equal to that of their male colleagues.

6.1.3 THE EC TREATY

6.1.3.1 Introduction

The EC Treaty was signed in Rome on 25 March 1957 by six European countries in order to create the Common Market. The Preamble of the Treaty made it clear that the objective of the Community was to foster the development of an even closer union through a co-operative effort devoted to economic and social progress. The social aims of the Treaty were to a large extent merely regarded as a consequence of the economic aims, rather than as an end in itself (Curtin, *Irish Employment Equality Law*). Article 119 of the Treaty contains the only specific obligation which was created by the chapter of the Treaty dealing with social provisions and gives expression to the principle that men and women should receive equal pay. The practical position was that at the time of the negotiation of the Treaty, there were substantial differences in the scope of labour and social legislation in the Member States. In particular, France had enacted domestic provisions more favourable to female workers and which were more costly for employers. It was feared by France that the ability of other countries to compete in its market once the Common Market had been established would make its products uncompetitive having regard to this extra cost. In order to protect French industry against unfair competition from those Member States who had not enacted provisions dealing with equal pay, Article 119 was included. The article was seen for many years as aspirational, rather than conferring any rights.

6.1.3.2 Article 119

Article 119 provides as follows:

> *'Each Member State shall, during the first stage ensure and subsequently maintain the application of the principle that men and women should receive equal pay for equal work.'*

For the purposes of this article, 'pay' means the ordinary, basic or minimum wage or salary and any other consideration, whether in cash or in kind, which the worker receives, directly or indirectly in respect of his employment from his employer.

'Equal pay without discrimination based on sex' means that:

> *'(a) pay for the same work at piece rates shall be calculated on the basis of the same unit of measurement; and*
>
> *(b) pay for work at time rates shall be the same for the same job.'*

6.1.3.3   **The *Defrenne* case**

It was only during the 1970s that the equal pay guarantee in Article 119 was developed and its legal effect recognised. In *Defrenne v Sabena* [1976] ECR 455 the ECJ gave teeth to the provisions of Article 119. The court stated that:

> 'The aim of Article 119 is to avoid a situation in which undertakings established in States which have actually implemented the principle of equal pay suffer a competitive disadvantage in intra-Community competition as compared with undertakings established in States which have not yet eliminated discrimination against women workers as regards pay. Secondly, this provision forms part of the social objectives of the Community which was not merely an Economic Union, but is at the same time intended, by common action, to ensure social progress and see the constant improvement of the living and working conditions of their peoples, as emphasised by the Preamble to the Treaty.'

Ms Defrenne had been an air hostess with the Belgian airline, Sabena, and had lodged a series of claims with the Belgian courts claiming backdated equal pay and equal pension entitlements. She failed before the relevant national courts on all her claims before the reference to the European Court of Justice. Ms Defrenne was successful and the court of Justice not only held that the right contained at Article 119 was partly directly effective, but also that it was a right enforceable against private as well as public employers in so far as it was directly effective in the Member State. The provisions of Article 119 in the Treaty of Rome are now contained in Article 141 of the Treaty of Amsterdam, which incorporated equal treatment measures into the EC Treaty.

6.1.3.4   **The Treaty of Amsterdam**

The Treaty of Amsterdam adds to the Article 119 provisions. Article 141(3) adds a requirement that the Community adopt measures to provide equal treatment and opportunity in occupation and employment. Article 141(4) permits positive action by Member States. It does not require positive action.

6.1.4   **THE EQUAL PAY DIRECTIVE**

It was contended that the terms of Article 119 only provided that equal pay should be paid in circumstances where equal work was carried out. It was contended that this did not extend to giving a right to equal pay in situations where a woman carried out work equal in value to the work carried out by a male employee. The Equal Pay Directive 75/117/EEC resolved this interpretation problem and Article 1 of the Directive explains that the concept of 'same work' contained in the first paragraph of Article 119 includes cases of work to which equal value is attributed. The courts have decided that the Directive in no way affects the concept of 'pay' contained in the second paragraph of Article 119, but simply restates the principle of equal pay. It was stated that the Directive did no more than explain in greater detail the concept of equal work already used in Article 119. In *Jenkins v Kingsgate (Clothing Productions) Ltd* [1981] ECR 911 the court declared that Article 1 of the Directive was 'principally designed to facilitate the practical application of the principle of equal pay outlined in Article 119 of the Treaty' and that it 'in no way alters the scope of the content of that principle as defined in the Treaty'. The Directive identifies both equal work and work of equal value on an equal basis to a claim for equal pay and gives an equal and independent right to found such a claim on either basis.

6.1.5   **THE EQUAL TREATMENT DIRECTIVE**

The object of the Equal Treatment Directive 76/207/EEC is to implement in the Member States the principle of equal treatment for men and women in relation to access to employment, vocational training, promotion and working conditions. The purpose of the 1998 Act is articulated in Article 1, and Article 2 defines the principle of equal treatment and its limits. Article 3 provides that in relation to access to employment, no discrimination whatsoever on grounds of sex is permitted and Member States are also required to take active measures necessary to abolish laws, regulations or administrative practices contrary to the principle of equal treatment. Provisions contrary to this principle which appear in collective agreements, individual contracts of employment, company rules or the articles of professional associations must either be void or be declared void or amended. Article 6 of the Directive obliges Member States to introduce judicial remedies under their national legislation so all persons who consider themselves wronged may pursue their claims by judicial process.

6.1.6 GENERAL FRAMEWORK DIRECTIVE

6.1.6.1 Introduction

The Council adopted Directive 2000/78/EC establishing a general framework for equal treatment in employment and occupation on 27 November 2000. The Directive arises out of Article 13 of the EC Treaty as modified by the Amsterdam Treaty. Its purpose is to combat discrimination based on religion or belief, disability, age or sexual orientation.

The Employment Equality Act, 1998, which came into force in Ireland on 18 October 1999, prohibits discrimination on all but one of those grounds. It does not make particular reference to belief as a separate category to religious belief. The Act also prohibits discrimination on other grounds, to a total of nine. The grounds are gender, marital status, family status, sexual orientation, religion, age, disability, race and membership of the traveller community.

This Directive is part of a three-pronged Article 13 anti-discrimination package. A directive on race discrimination has also been adopted, Directive 2000/43/EC of 29 June 2000, together with an action programme to support the efforts of Member States to combat discrimination across the EU.

6.1.6.2 Areas covered by the Directive

The areas covered by Directive 2000/78/EC are access to employment, self-employment and occupation, promotion, vocational training, employment and working conditions and membership of certain bodies. The areas covered by the Irish Employment Equality Act are access to employment, conditions of employment, training or experience for or in relation to employment, promotion or regrading, classification of posts and membership of certain bodies. Discrimination on the ground of pay is also unlawful.

The Directive does not cover discrimination on the grounds of gender, which has been covered in earlier European Directives, 76/207/EEC and 86/613/EEC. The provisions cover self-employment and membership of professional bodies as well as salaried employment.

Paragraph 22 of the Preamble to the Directive provides that the Directive is without prejudice to national laws or marital status and the benefits dependent on marital status.

The Irish Employment Equality Bill, 1997 was referred to in the Commission's proposal for the Directive in respect of the provisions in respect of disability. In respect of harassment in the workplace the proposal referred to the Employment Equality Act rather than the Bill. This is interesting because the provisions of the Bill in respect of disability were overturned by the Supreme Court in a material respect, which was to provide that employers were only required to provide reasonable accommodation for persons with disabilities if same had a 'nominal cost'. No such provision was contained in the Directive.

The nominal cost provision was superseded by the Directive on its implementation by the Equality Act, 2004, in July 2004.

6.1.6.3 Measures to be taken to accommodate disability

Article 5 of the Directive provides that employers shall take appropriate measures, where needed in a particular case, to enable a person with a disability to have access to, participate or advance in employment, or to undergo training, unless such measures would impose a disproportionate burden on the employer. This burden shall not be disproportionate when it is sufficiently remedied by measures existing within the framework of disability policy in the Member State concerned.

The Preamble qualifies this provision as follows.

Paragraph 7 of the Preamble states that the Directive does not require the recruitment, promotion, maintenance in employment or training of an individual who is not competent, capable and available to perform the essential functions of the post concerned or to undergo the relevant training, without prejudice to the obligation to provide reasonable accommodation for persons with disabilities.

Paragraph 20 of the Preamble states that appropriate measures should be provided, i.e. effective and practical measures to adapt the workplace to the disability, for example, adapting premises and equipment, patterns of working time, the distribution of tasks or the provision of training or integration resources.

Paragraph 21 provides that, to determine whether the measures in question give rise to a disproportionate burden on the employer, account should be taken in particular of the financial and other costs entailed, the scale and financial resources of the organisation or undertaking, and the possibility of obtaining public funding or any other assistance.

This is quite different from the nominal cost test that was contained in the Employment Equality Act, 1998. As amended in 2004, the reasonable accommodation provisions in the Employment Equality Acts now incorporate the Directive provisions on appropriate measures and disproportionate burden.

6.1.6.4 Right of redress

Article 9 of the Directive specifically provides that persons who consider themselves wronged may pursue their claims through an administrative and/or judicial procedure to enforce their right to equal treatment even after an employment relationship has ended.

This reflects the ECJ's decision in *Coote v Granada Hospitality Ltd* [1998] IRLR 656, where it was held that there was an obligation on Member States to introduce into national law measures necessary to ensure protection for workers from retaliatory action taken by employers after the employment relationship had ceased. No such provision has yet been enacted in Ireland.

6.1.6.5 Burden of proof

Article 10 of the Directive provides that the burden of proof reverts to the defendant once the plaintiff has established facts from which it may be presumed that there has been direct or indirect discrimination. This does not apply to criminal proceedings. European Communities (Burden of Proof in Gender Discrimination Cases) Regulations, 2001, SI 337/2001 provided for a shift in the burden of proof in gender discrimination cases only.

The Employment Equality Act, 1998 has been amended by the Equality Act, 2004, inserting a new section 85A shifting the burden of proof in implementation of Article 10. The 2001 Regulations were repealed by the Equality Act 2004.

6.1.6.6 Victimisation

Article 11 of the Directive prohibits victimisation, which is prohibited in the Irish Employment Equality Act, 1998–2004. The definitions of victimisation and the categories of persons protected were amended by the 2004 Act.

6.1.6.7 Implementation

The Directive provides that Member States are required to transpose the Directive into national law by 31 December 2003. A further three-year period may be taken by Member States to implement the provisions on age and disability discrimination in order to take account of particular conditions.

6.1.6.8 Harassment

Article 2(3) of the Directive provides that harassment shall be deemed to be a form of discrimination within the meaning of Article 2(1), when unwanted conduct related to any of the grounds takes place with the purpose or effect of creating an intimidating, hostile, degrading, humiliating or offensive environment. This differs from the Irish Employment Equality Act, 1998 provisions in respect of harassment and sexual harassment. Part of those definitions provided that any act or conduct of a person including, without prejudice to the generality, spoken words, gestures or the production, display or circulation of written words, pictures or other material constitutes harassment of a person by another person if the action or conduct was unwelcome to the person and could reasonably be regarded, in relation to the relevant characteristics of the person, as offensive, humiliating or intimidating to the person. It incorporated both an objective and a subjective element. It did not, unlike the Directive, make reference to the environment created by the conduct, but rather to the effect on the person. The 2004 Act has amended the definitions of harassment and sexual harrasment inserting a new section 14A into the 1998 and 2004 Acts, in implementation of Article 2(3).

6.1.6.9 Age discrimination

The Directive contains provisions in respect of age discrimination which substantially mirror the provisions contained in the Irish Employment Equality Acts. No significant amendments to those provisions were required to implement the Directive. The 2004 Act removed the upper and lower thresholds for claiming age discrimination with some qualifying provisions for those under 18 and for normal retirement age for the employment.

6.1.6.10 Racial discrimination Directive

The Council adopted Directive 2000/43/EC on 29 June 2000, implementing the principle of equal treatment between persons irrespective of racial or ethnic origin.

The Directive's purpose is to lay down a framework for combating discrimination on the grounds of racial or ethnic origin, but not national origin, with a view to putting into effect in the Member States the principle of equal treatment. This is provided for in Article 1. Article 3(2) provides for the exception in respect of difference of treatment based on nationality.

The Directive provides at Article 3(2) for definitions of direct and indirect discrimination. The definition of direct discrimination is consistent with that in the 1998 Act, as amended by the 2004 Act, which contains the relevant provisions on direct discrimination on the grounds of race in Ireland.

Section 6(1) and (2)(a), of the 1998 Act, when read together, provide that for the purposes of that Act, discrimination shall be taken to occur where one person is treated less favourably than another is, has been or would be treated, on the ground that the persons are of different race, colour, nationality or ethnic or national origins. The 2004 Act amendments altered this definition to include discrimination in respect of a ground which exists, which existed in the past, discrimination by association (such as marriage or friendship) and where a ground is imputed to a person, such as where a person is mistakenly believed to be of a particular nationality and is treated less favourably than others because of this mistaken belief.

As stated above, the ground of nationality is not contained within the Directive but it is contained in the definition of the race ground in the 1998 and 2004 Acts, which defines race as race, colour, nationality, ethnic or national origins.

6.1.6.11   Indirect discrimination

The definition of indirect discrimination in Article 2(2)(b) differs from and is more favourable to complainants than the 1998 Act definition. The Equality Act 2004 has amended the indirect discrimination definitions on all grounds in implementation of the Directive.

Article 2(2)(b) of the Directive provides:

> '... *indirect discrimination shall be taken to occur when an apparently neutral provision, criterion or practice would put persons of a racial or ethnic origin at a particular disadvantage compared with other persons, unless that provision, criterion or practice is objectively justified by a legitimate aim and the means of achieving that aim are appropriate and necessary.*'

This definition is similar to that previously contained in the 1998 Act in respect of discrimination on the ground of gender only. The 1998 Act was amended by the European Communities (Burden of Proof in Gender Discrimination Cases) Regulations, 2001, SI 337/2001. These regulations gave effect to Council Directive 97/80/EC of 15 December 1997 on the burden of proof in cases of discrimination based on sex. They not only addressed the question of burden of proof but, at regulation 4, amended the definition of indirect discrimination on the grounds of gender as provided in section 22(1) of the 1998 Act. The Regulations were repealed on the enactment of the 2004 act and replaced with its provisions on burden of proof and indirect discrimination.

Prior to the 2004 Act, the indirect discrimination provision on all grounds other than gender, was contained in the 1998 Act, section 31(1).

Indirect discrimination on the grounds of race and all non-gender grounds could be justified where it was reasonable in all the circumstances of the case.

On implementation of the Directive by the 2004 Act, the Directive definition of indirect discrimination replaced the 1998 Act definition. Indirect discrimination is now defined as follows:

> '1.(a)   *Indirect discrimination occurs where an apparently neutral provision puts persons of a particular gender ... [or to whom a discriminatory ground applies] at a particular disadvantage in respect of any matter other than remuneration compared with other employees of their employer.*
>
> (b)   *Where paragraph (a) applies, the employer shall be treated for the purposes of this Act as discriminating against each of the persons referred to ..., unless the provision is objectively justified by a legitimate aim and the means of achieving that aim are appropriate and necessary.*'

The 2004 Act contains similar provisions on equal remuneration and indirect discrimination.

Indirect discrimination on the grounds of race and all other grounds contained in the 2004 Act can now only be justified where it can be shown that the indirectly discriminating provision, criterion or practice is objectively justified by a legitimate aim and the means of achieving that aim are appropriate and necessary. This is a more rigorous test than that contained in the repealed gender regulations and much more difficult to satisfy than the 1998 Act test for the non-gender grounds.

6.1.7 EQUAL PAY

6.1.7.1 Introduction

The Anti-Discrimination (Pay) Act, 1974 ('the 1974 Act') came into operation on 31 December 1975 and introduced the principle of equal pay for like work into Irish law. It was repealed when the Employment Equality Act, 1998 came into effect on 18 October 1999. The 1974 Act complied with the terms of the Equal Pay Directive and Article 119 of the EC Treaty. It established a legal right to equal pay for men and women employed on 'like' work by the same employer (or an associated one). The device used to achieve the aim of the 1974 Act was to insert into the contract of the person employed a term conferring an entitlement to equal pay.

6.1.7.2 Employment Equality Act, 1998–2004—remuneration provisions between women and men

Where 'A' and 'B' are persons of opposite sex, the Acts provide at section 19(1):

> '[I]t shall be a term of the contract under which A is employed that, subject to this Act, A shall at any time be entitled to the same rate of remuneration for the work which A is employed to do as B who, at that or any other relevant time, is employed to do like work by the same or an associated employer.'

At section 19(3) the Act provides:

> '[W]here B's employer is an associated employer of A's employer, A and B shall not be regarded as employed to do like work unless they both have the same or reasonably comparable terms and conditions of employment.'

Men and women employed to do like work at the same place by the same employer, or in the same area by two associated employers, are entitled to the same remuneration. Remuneration means any consideration in cash or kind received directly or indirectly by an employee from the employer in respect of his employment, excluding pension rights. Pension rights are governed by the Pensions Act, 1990 amended by the Social Welfare (Miscellanous Provisions) Act, 2004.

6.1.7.3 Case law

The Labour Court in *Linson Ltd v ASTMS* DEP 2/77 held that remuneration covered all benefits based on the wage or salary received by an employee. The definition must also be taken to include bonus payments, marriage gratuities, house purchase loans, and benefits in kind such as company cars and medical insurance cover. Prior to the 1998 legislation it also included pension rights, which are expressly excluded in the definitions section of that Act. This has not been changed by the 2004 Act, although it should be noted that the Social Welfare (Miscellaneous Provisions) Act, 2004 inserts a new Part VII into the Pensions Act, 1990 which prohibits direct or indirect discrimination on any of the nine grounds specified in the employment equality legislation in all occupational pension schemes.

In *Garland v British Rail Engineering Ltd* [1982] ICR 420 the ECJ held that the provision of travel concessions for retired male employees constituted discrimination against retired female employees who did not receive the same facilities. The travel concession was not a legal obligation forming part of the contract between the employer and employee (pensioner) but as a concessionary right which nonetheless was held to constitute remuneration within the meaning of Article 119 of the EC Treaty. In Ireland the Labour Court held, before the 1998 Act, that the provision of pension benefits came within the scope of the 1974 Act (*Clery & Co [1941] Ltd v O'Brien* EP17/84).

The full scope of the necessity for equal treatment is well illustrated in *Meyers v Adjudication*

Officer [1995] IRLR 498 where the ECJ considered the availability of what is known as 'family credit' under the UK Social Security Act 1986. Family credit is an income-related benefit awarded to supplement the income of low-paid workers who are responsible for a child. Ms Meyers' application for family credit was rejected on the grounds that her income was greater than the level conferring the entitlement. Ms Meyers argued, however, that in order to be able to work she had to incur childcare costs and that, in failing to permit her to deduct such childcare costs for the purposes of calculating her income to qualify for the benefit, she had been discriminated against as a single parent since it is easier for couples to arrange their working hours so that children may be looked after by one of them. She claimed that this constituted indirect discrimination on grounds of sex since most single parents are women. While the ECJ did not comment on whether there was discrimination—which was referred back to the national court—it did hold that a benefit such as family credit, which is concerned with both access to employment and working conditions, is not excluded from the scope of the Directive even though it is a State social security measure, and to confine the concept of an employment benefit or working condition solely to those working conditions which are set out in the contract of employment or applied by the employer in respect of a worker's employment, is not sufficiently wide to meet the terms of the Directive which cover the wider concept of an 'employment relationship'.

Under the 1974 Act it was not necessary for a person seeking to establish a comparison of like work to compare themselves to a male or female in a contemporaneous employment. The position remains unchanged by the 1998 and 2004 Acts. In *McCarthy's v Smith* [1980] IRLR 210 Mrs Smith was paid less per week than a man who had, until some four months before she took up the job, held the same position. The ECJ held that she could claim equal pay to that of her predecessor but left it to be decided as a question of fact in every case whether or not a pay differential was due to sex discrimination or whether it could be explained by the operation of other facts unconnected with sex.

6.1.7.4 Red circling

An employer may pay different rates of pay to male and female employees justified by objective criteria where these can be factors unrelated to sex. Red circling may be allowed in circumstances where an employee's rate of pay could be said to be above the normal rate for the job. Such a person could be red circled, thereby disallowing comparisons. This may happen, for example, if a long-serving male employee were to suffer a partially incapacitating illness and then be moved to a less demanding job. If he is allowed to retain his higher rate of pay on humanitarian grounds, then it is possible to red circle him for comparison purposes (*Minister for Transport v Campbell* [1996] ELR 106 and *Department of Tourism v 4 Workers* [1997] ELR 1).

6.1.7.5 Reference of disputes

Under the 1998 and 2004 Acts, a dispute over entitlements to equal pay may be referred by either party to the Equality Tribunal, who may refer the case for mediation to an equality mediation officer or investigate the case and hear evidence in private. Once the case has been investigated and a decision issued any party to the dispute may then appeal to the Labour Court for a full hearing if dissatisfied with the decision, or if the Equality Tribunal's decision has not been implemented. An appeal to the High Court may be brought on a point of law only.

6.1.7.6 Time limits

Even though action under the 1998 and 2004 Acts is based on contract, the ordinary limitation period of six years under the Statute of Limitations, 1957 does not apply. Section 8(4) and (5) of the Acts provide that arrears of remuneration may only be backdated three years from the date on which the relevant dispute was referred to an equality officer. A maximum of six years' remuneration can be awarded.

The 1974 Act was repealed by and replaced with the 1998 Act, which was amended by the 2004 Act.

6.1.8 EMPLOYMENT EQUALITY ACT, 1977

The Employment Equality Act, 1977 ('the 1977 Act') derived from the Equal Treatment Directive. The Act provided for equal treatment as regards access to employment, conditions of employment other than remuneration or conditions relating to occupational pension schemes, training, promotion and regrading. The Act also made unlawful certain discriminatory practices in relation to employment committed by bodies such as employment agencies, vocational training organisations, employers' organisations, trade unions and professional bodies. The Act also provided for a prohibition on the display or publication of discriminatory advertisements.

Discrimination was defined in section 2 of the Act as occurring in any of the following cases:

(a)   where by reason of his sex, a person is treated less favourably than a person of the other sex;

(b)   where because of his marital status a person is treated less favourably than another person of the same sex;

(c)   where because of his sex or marital status a person is obliged to comply with a requirement relating to employment or membership of a body referred to in section 5 which is not an essential requirement for such employment or membership and in respect of which the proportion of persons of the other sex or (as the case may be) of a different marital status but of the same sex able to comply is substantially higher; or

(d)   where a person is penalised for having in good faith, made a reference under the 1977 Act or the 1974 Act.

6.2 Employment Equality Acts, 1998 and 2004

6.2.1 CONSTITUTIONALLY REPUGNANT PROVISIONS

The Employment Equality Bill, 1996, passed all stages in both houses of the Oireachtas on 26 March 1997. The President referred the Bill in its entirety to the Supreme Court under article 26 of the Constitution on 3 April 1997, to determine whether or not any provisions of the Bill were inconsistent with the Constitution. The Supreme Court held that three aspects of the Employment Equality Bill, 1996 were so repugnant.

In December 1997 a revised version was published which essentially amended the 1996 Bill only to the extent necessary to take account of the Supreme Court's objections. The Act was finally passed into law in early 1998 and came into effect on 18 October 1999.

In the 1998 Act, the provisions found to be unconstitutional in the Employment Equality Bill, 1996 was replaced as follows:

(a)   sections 16(3) and 35 have been drafted so that the employer is obliged to bear the cost of special treatment or facilities, arising from the employment of a person with a disability, only in so far as these costs are nominal in nature. The term 'nominal' was not defined but case law of the equality officers and the Labour Court under the 1998 Act interpreted it as a relative test in relation to the resources of the employer on a case-by-case basis. The 1996 Bill had required an employer, in certain circumstances, to provide special treatment or facilities to a person with a disability unless the employer could show undue hardship. The Supreme Court held that the costs associated with the provision of such treatment or facilities constituted an unjust attack on the property rights of the employer. The 1998 Act provisions have been significantly amended by the 2004 Act, which replaces 'nominal cost' with 'disproportionate burden' as referred to at **6.1.6.3** above;

(b)   section 15 and the definition of 'proceedings' have been redrafted so that vicarious liability is applied only in respect of civil proceedings. The 1996 Bill applied the principle of vicarious liability in both civil and criminal proceedings which was found to be unconstitutional. Section 15 was not changed by the 2004 Act;

(c)   section 63(3) of the 1996 Bill, which had allowed for the use of a certificate as evidence of an offence, was also found to be unconstitutional, contrary to article 38.1 of the Constitution. No similar provision appears in the 1998 or 2004 Acts.

6.2.2   PROVISIONS OF THE 1998 AND 2004 ACTS

The 1998 Act replaced the Anti-Discrimination (Pay) Act, 1974 and the Employment Equality Act, 1977. The substantial body of case law which had developed under the earlier legislation remains binding in so far as the legislative provisions they interpret are consistent with the 1998 and 2004 Acts. New grounds of discrimination were created, new areas of discrimination were identified and, for the first time, statutory definitions of sexual harassment and indirect discrimination were created.

The Act prohibits discrimination in relation to:

(a)   access to employment;

(b)   conditions of employment;

(c)   training or experience for or in relation to employment;

(d)   promotion or regrading; or

(e)   classification of posts.

The legislation prohibits discrimination on the following grounds:

(i)   gender;

(ii)   marital status;

(iii) family status;

(iv) sexual orientation;

(v)   religion;

(vi) age;

(vii) disability;

(viii) race/colour/nationality/ethnic or national origins; and

(ix) membership of the traveller community.

6.2.3   GENDER

In *A Worker v Mid Western Health Board* [1996] ELR 1 the Labour Court determined:

(a)   to establish discrimination on gender grounds, a complainant must show both less favourable treatment and that such treatment arises from the sex of the complainant;

(b)   there is no discrimination if nurses are assigned to different tasks because of their gender. The legislation is only contravened if the assignments are less favourable treatment because of gender; and

(c)   a decision to assign a particular task to a nurse of a particular sex is not less favourable treatment if the task is within the range of responsibilities for which the nurse was employed.

See also *Martin Smyth v Eastern Health Board* [1996] ELR 72 and *Rodmell v University of Dublin, Trinity College*, DEC-E–201/016 where it was held that the secretary to an interview panel discriminated on the gender ground by addressing the only female candidate for a post as a 'lady electrician'.

In *Field v Irish Carton Printers* [1994] ELR 129 a free taxi service was provided to female employees on shift work when public transport was not available. The male claimant sought to be included in the taxi arrangement but this was refused. He brought a claim under the employment equality legislation seeking to prove that he was engaged on like work to a female comparator and for the purposes of the 1974 Act was denied remuneration in the form of provision of a free taxi service. He also claimed he was discriminated against because he was male in relation to a condition of employment under the 1977 Act.

The equality officer held:

(1)   the claim was admissible under the Anti-Discrimination (Pay) Act, 1974 as provision of a taxi service is a benefit in kind and consequently remuneration;

(2)   the company had not established a 'real need' for the agreement negotiated with the trade union representing the female employees;

(3)   the taxi service was provided for the protection of female staff and there were no legitimate 'grounds other than sex' to justify the provision of taxis;

(4)   the taxi facility should be made available to the claimant.

6.2.4   MARITAL STATUS

Section 2 of the 1998 and the 2004 Acts defines marital status as meaning single, married, separated, divorced or widowed persons. The inclusion of single persons for the first time in the definition of marital status would preclude employers from making certain benefits available to employees because they are married. If, for example, health benefits are provided for single employees only but is extended to the spouse and possibly also the children of married employees, this would constitute discrimination on grounds of marital status but for section 34(1)(b) of the Act, which is set out below.

In *Eagle Star Insurance Co (Ireland) Ltd v A Worker* [1998] ELR 306 the company operated a staff discount scheme whereby staff and their spouses were entitled to discounted motor policies for themselves. The worker concerned was a single man with a female partner who was a named driver on his policy. Because of the terms of the company scheme the discount was not available in respect of his female partner. He claimed that this was discrimination on grounds of his marital status under the Employment Equality Act, 1977. The company argued inter alia that a single person does not have a 'marital status' and that there was no discrimination under the 1977 Act. The equality officer at first instance found in favour of the employee on the basis that the company treated married persons more favourably than single persons by providing them with discounted policies in respect of their spouses. If the claimant was married he would have benefited from the company scheme; however, as he was single he was denied the benefit and this constituted discrimination under the 1977 Act. A sum of £1,000 by way of compensation for stress was awarded. On appeal the Labour Court found that the 'advantage of the married employee amounts to less favourable treatment of the single, or non-married employee, including the claimant'. The court upheld the recommendation of the equality officer including the award of £1,000 for stress. See also *Ormiston v Gypsum Industries* [1993] ELR 1 which dealt with VHI benefit.

In examining such benefits and the extension of the benefits to members of an employee's family, section 34(1)(b) of the 1998 Act states:

'(1)   *In relation to the discriminatory grounds . . . nothing in this Part . . . shall make it unlaw-ful for an employer to provide . . .*
(b)   *a benefit to or in respect of a person as a member of an employee's family.'*

'*A member of an employee's family*' is defined in section 2, the interpretation section, as a person's spouse or a brother, sister, uncle, aunt, nephew, niece, lineal ancestor or lineal descendent of that person or that person's spouse.

An employer can be found to have discriminated against an employee on a combination of grounds, and such discrimination may be inferred from the facts. In *Marie Inoue v NBK Designs Ltd* ED/02/34 Ms Inoue had been employed to job share as a part-time secretary/personal assistant. She was a lone parent. Due to an increased volume of work, her employer decided that it needed a full-time person to fill the role. Ms Inoue was offered this position, which she refused due to her childcare responsibilities. Ms Inoue was consequently dismissed. The Labour Court found that Ms Inoue had been indirectly discriminated against on a combination of the gender, marital status and family status grounds. The Court accepted statistics that significantly more women than men work part time and inferred from this (without the need for further statistical evidence) that the abolition of a part-time post would impact disproportionately on a woman and in particular, on a woman who was a lone parent.

6.2.5   FAMILY STATUS

Family status is defined as meaning responsibility as a parent or in locos parentis in relation to a person under the age of 18 or as a parent or the resident primary carer in relation to a person over 18 with a disability which is of such a nature as to give rise to the need for care or support on a continuing, regular or frequent basis. Employers must examine recruitment practices in light of the various discriminatory grounds created by the 1998 and 2004 Acts and this is one particular area that requires examination. If a person who has a child fails to secure a job at interview, that person may now claim discrimination and the employer may have to, in its defence, explain the reasons why the applicant failed to get the job, which previously an employer was not normally in law required to do. It is, however, the usual result of equality claims even under previous legislation.

In *An Employee v An Employer* [1995] ELR 139 the female employee concerned had been employed by the employer until she resigned on marriage in 1972. She had subsequently worked with the employer from time to time on a temporary basis. She applied for a permanent job but was unsuccessful. She claimed that the recruitment manager had told her that the reason for her failure to obtain a permanent position was because of her inflexibility due to her domestic background, the employee being separated and having two children. She claimed that she had been discriminated against on the basis of her employer's perception that she was inflexible and not transferable due to her childcare responsibilities and was discriminated against on the grounds of her sex and/or marital status. The employer contested the grounds of non-selection stating that it related to her overall suitability and not as alleged by the claimant. The equality officer held in favour of the claimant stating:

> 'The status of male candidates or female candidates who did not have the same child-care responsibilities would not have been similarly perceived by the employer as irreconcilable with the capacity to give a commitment to a permanent career position. The claimant was discriminated against within the meaning of section 2 of the Employment Equality Act, 1977 and contrary to section 3 thereof.'

The importance of the employer retaining detailed interview notes made by each interviewer and the allocation of marks cannot be overstated. It is clear from equality officer decisions and Labour Court determinations that, it is particularly difficult, if not impossible, to defend an equality action, in the absence of such notes (*South Eastern Health Board v Bridget Burke* DECE2003/014, *Carroll v Monaghan VEC* ADE/04/6, Determination No 0415 and *Allerdyce v Donegal County Council* DEC-E2005–052).

6.2.6   SEXUAL ORIENTATION

6.2.6.1   European Court of Justice

Protection against discrimination on grounds of sexual orientation does not expressly exist in European law. However, Article 13 of the Treaty of the European Community allows the Community to proscribe discrimination on the sexual orientation ground but it does not, in itself, ban such discrimination. The protection is, however, available under the 1998 and 2004 Acts. The ECJ considered the issue of sexual orientation in *Grant v South-West Trains Ltd* [1998] IRLR 206. Lisa Grant was a clerical worker, employed by South-West Trains who lived in a stable relationship with a same-sex partner. Staff of SWT were provided with free and reduced-rate travel concessions which extended to 'your spouse and dependants'. Privilege tickets were also granted to 'a married member of staff for one legal spouse . . . and . . . for one common law spouse (of the opposite sex) subject to a statutory declaration being made that a meaningful relationship has existed for period of two or more years'.

Ms Grant requested travel concessions for her female partner but this was turned down because her partner was not of the opposite sex. Ms Grant claimed that the rejection of her request was contrary to the principle of equal pay for men and women established by Article 119 of the EC Treaty and Article 1 of the Equal Pay Directive.

The ECJ held as follows:

> 'A refusal by an employer to grant travel concessions to a person of the same sex with whom a worker has a stable relationship does not constitute discrimination based directly on the sex of the worker prohibited by Article 119 of the EC Treaty or the Equal Pay Directive. Even where such concessions are allowed to the person of the opposite sex with whom a worker has a stable relationship outside marriage.
>
> 'A condition which applies in the same way to female and male workers cannot be regarded as constituting discrimination directly based on sex. In the present case the travel concessions are refused to a male worker living with a person of the same sex just as they are to a female worker if she is living with a person of the same sex.
>
> 'Discrimination based on sexual orientation does not constitute discrimination based on the sex of the worker within the meaning of Article 119. European Community law does not cover discrimination based on sexual orientation. The reasoning of the court in *P v S and Cornwall County Council* [1996] IRLR 347 that discrimination based on a worker's gender reassignment is based essentially on the sex of the person concerned and is therefore prohibited, is limited to the case of a worker's gender reassignment and does not apply to differences of treatment based on a person's sexual orientation.

'European Community law does not regard stable relationships between two persons of the same sex as the equivalent of marriages or stable relationships outside marriage between two persons of the opposite sex. Consequently Community law does not require an employer to treat the situation of a person who has a stable relationship with a partner of the same sex as equivalent to that of a person who is married or has a stable relationship outside marriage with a partner of the opposite sex.'

6.2.6.2   UK and Irish case law

Grant v South-West Trains Ltd was followed by the UK High Court in *R v Secretary of State for Defence, ex parte Perkins* [1998] IRLR 508. In that case the UK High Court stated that the decision of the ECJ in *Grant* was 'that Community law does not cover or render unlawful discrimination based on sexual orientation'. In this particular case Mr Perkins was discharged by the Royal Navy because of his homosexual orientation. His claim that this breached UK and European law on discrimination was rejected in light of the Grant decision.

See also *Smith v Gardner Merchant Ltd* [1998] IRLR 510 which was a sexual harassment case where the applicant claimed that the harassment occurred because of his sexual orientation. While following the Grant decision the UK Court of Appeal also held that Mr Smith was entitled to pursue a sexual harassment case albeit on other grounds, ie because he was male not because he was a male with a particular sexual orientation.

In *A Worker v Brookfield Leisure Ltd* [1994] ELR 79 the claimant was dismissed from her job in a leisure centre after it was claimed that she had been seen kissing another woman in the changing rooms of the leisure centre. The claimant denied the allegation. Following her dismissal the claimant claimed against her employer under the Employment Equality Act, 1977 and argued that she was dismissed by the respondent because of her sexual orientation on the basis that the respondent was aware that she was a lesbian and that this did not adversely affect her until such time as the allegations, which she denied, were made. The claimant argued that if she had not been homosexual or if she had been a male employee she would not have been dismissed, and argued that discrimination on the grounds of sexual orientation was prohibited by the 1977 Act. She further argued that lesbianism was a characteristic unique to females and thus any action against such females was a breach of the 1977 Act. The Labour Court, however, dismissed the claim on the basis that the unfair treatment she did suffer did not arise from any attribute of her sex but of her sexual orientation and, in all probability, a man would have suffered the same treatment for a similar display of his sexual orientation. That decision is now overruled.

A very similar decision was made by the House of Lords in *Pearce v Mayfield Secondary School* [2003] IRLR 669 and *MacDonald v Advocate General for Scotland* IRLR 512 where it was held that discrimination and harassment on the grounds of sexual orientation were not discrimination contrary to the UK's Sex Discrimination Act 1975. It was held that a homosexual person of the opposite sex would have received similar treatment to that meted out to Ms Pearce, and to Mr McDonald in their respective employments.

Such a decision could not now be made in Ireland, as discrimination on the grounds of sexual orientation is expressly prohibited. Section 2 of the 1998 and 2004 Acts defines 'sexual orientation' as meaning:

'*Heterosexual, homosexual or bisexual orientation.*'

In order to prove such discrimination, the alleged victim must prove that a comparator (a person of a different or perceived different sexual orientation) would not have been treated in the same way as alleged the victim (*Fernandez v Cable & Wireless* DEC-E–2002/052). The 2004 Act shifts the burden of proof if facts are established by the person from which discrimination may be presumed.

6.2.6.3   Transsexuals

It should be noted that, unlike the UK where specific regulations have been enacted, transsexuals are not specifically covered by the Irish legislation, however it appears likely that the legislation can be used to protect such persons. Those persons who undergo gender reassignment may, depending on the nature of the work and the possible requirement for a person of a particular sex, have difficulty if their employment is terminated because of their change of status from male to female, or female to male as the case may be. The ECJ in *P v S and Cornwall County Council* [1996] IRLR 347 suggests that transsexuals must in fact be protected under domestic law on gender discrimination, although the case arose in the context of the UK Sex Discrimination Act 1975. The effect of this ruling was that it applied immediately in the UK public sector, as a directly enforceable European directive. The private sector position was less clear. In *Chessington World of Adventures Ltd v Reed* [1998] IRLR 56 the UK EAT held that discrimination against transsexuals was to be regarded as unlawful discrimination on the grounds of sex contrary to the UK sex discrimination legislation. By analogy with sexual harassment and pregnancy discrimination a new category of discrimination was created. It is very likely that this decision will be followed in Ireland, in interpreting the Employment Equality Acts.

The ECJ held that where Mr P was hired as a male employee in 1991, subsequently had a gender reassignment and became a woman, her consequential dismissal was a breach of the Equal Treatment Directive. The court held:

> 'Where such discrimination arises . . . from the gender reassignment of the person concerned, he or she is treated unfavourably by comparisons with persons of the sex to which he or she was deemed to belong before undergoing gender reassignment.'

The Advocate General's opinion in this case is very helpful in clarifying the concepts of discrimination.

6.2.7   RELIGIOUS BELIEF

The Equality Act 2004 has amended the 1998 Act considerably in the context of religion and it has included within its scope people who are discriminated against on the ground of religion because of their association with another person, or because of their perceived religious belief or none, as with all the discrimination grounds.

Religious belief includes having no religious belief. The Department of Education pays salaries of chaplains employed in community schools. Such payment was challenged as being in breach of article 44.2.2 of the Constitution by which the State guarantees 'not to endow any religion' in *Campaign to Separate Church and State Ltd and Murphy v Minister for Education* [1996] ELR 164. Costello J held in that case:

(1)   the purpose of the payment is to recompense the recipient for the service which is rendered and not to endow religion and as such is constitutionally licit;

(2)   a further purpose of the payment is to fulfil the State's obligation to respect the parental rights and facilitate their exercise and it therefore does not infringe the Constitution;

(3)   the prohibition against endowment of religion must be construed as permitting State aid to assist in the religious formation of children in accordance with their parents' wishes and accordingly the payment of chaplains in schools is not unconstitutional;

(4)   the payment to hospital chaplains does not infringe article 44 because the purpose of the payment is to assist in caring for the spiritual and religious needs of hospital patients (which the State acknowledges that as human persons they possess) and not for the purpose of endowing any religion and is accordingly constitutionally valid.

6.2.8 AGE

The 1998 Act provided that, for persons aged between 18 and 65 no discrimination was permitted on grounds of age. The upper and lower age thresholds were removed by the 2004 Act. Older people who fail to secure jobs as against younger competition may bring discrimination claims. Unlike US law the 1998 and 2004 Acts do not simply protect workers over the age of 40; they prohibit discrimination between employees/applicants who are of different ages. Young employees/applicants, who are not promoted/appointed because they are assumed to be immature or too young for responsibility, may also bring discrimination claims. Claims have succeeded against employers in respect of 'youth' and 'age' discrimination under the 1998 Act.

The EAT held that selection for redundancy on the grounds of age constituted unfair dismissal in *Kerrigan v Peter Owens Advertising and Marketing Ltd* UD 31/97 where the claimant gave evidence to the EAT that the grounds for his redundancy included his age. The EAT rejected the company's claim that a redundancy situation existed and stated 'from the evidence produced we determine that the claimant's dismissal arose wholly or mainly from his age in contravention of section 6(2) of the Unfair Dismissals Act, 1977 as amended'.

An equality officer held against Ryanair in proceedings brought by the Equality Authority under the 1998 Act, section 85 at the end of 2000—*Equality Authority v Ryanair* DEC-E/2000/14. Ryanair advertised for a 'young and dynamic professional' in the *Irish Times*. It was held that they breached the age discrimination provisions of the Act. This provision does not require the employer to intend to discriminate. The question for the equality officer is whether or not the advertisement could be reasonably understood to indicate an intention to discriminate. The equality officer held that the advertisement could be reasonably understood to indicate that intention. The proceedings were brought by the Equality Authority. It had not sought an injunction, nor had it brought proceedings against the publisher of the advertisement, the newspaper. The equality officer recommended that the Equality Authority should, in further cases, consider making use of its powers under the Act to seek an injunction preventing a recruitment process going ahead where it appears to be discriminatory, and take action against both the publisher and the employer, as appropriate.

In *Perry v The Garda Commissioner* DEC-E–2001/029, the Equality Tribunal held that employers must ensure equal pay in ex gratia payments, regardless of the different amounts of pensions payable to employees of different ages. This situation has been ameliorated by section 34 of the 2004 Act which provides that in certain circumstances, there can be different treatment of employees on the age ground in severance payments.

6.2.9 DISABILITY

6.2.9.1 Generally

The ground of disability does not apply where the person is not willing to do, or fully capable of doing, the job in question. However, the Acts provide that a person who has a disability is fully competent and capable of duties if he or she would be so on provision of reasonable accommodation. An employer may, however, where the amount of work done by the employee with the disability is less than that done or reasonably expected to be done by a person without the disability, pay a different rate of pay to that person for that reason. The employer is allowed and obliged to provide reasonable accommodation, defined as 'appropriate measures' to a person with a disability. In relation to the provision of facilities or special treatment, the 1998 Act required only 'costs of a nominal value'. The 2004 Act amendments now require appropriate measures unless there is a 'disproportionate burden' on the employer. The Act identifies factors to assess the question of 'disproportionate burden'. Section 2 of the 1998 and 2004 Acts contains a comprehensive definition of disability as meaning:

'(a) the total or partial absence of a person's bodily or mental functions, including the absence of a part of a person's body;

(b) the presence in the body of organisms causing, or likely to cause, chronic disease or illness;

(c) the malfunction, malformation or disfigurement of a part of a person's body;

(d) a condition or malfunction which results in a person learning differently from a person without the condition or malfunction; or

(e) a condition, illness or disease which affects a person's thought processes, perception of reality, emotions or judgment or which results in disturbed behaviour.'

This is a very wide-ranging medical definition and has been held to cover almost all temporary and permanent physical and mental conditions, both of job applicants and existing employees, including a whiplash injury of three months' duration, a respiratory tract and lung infection resulting in five days' absence from work and stress.

There have been many decisions under the 1998 Act in respect of discrimination on the ground of disability.

Decisions are awaited under the 2004 Act's amending provision on 'appropriate measures'.

In *Niamh Humphries v Westwood Fitness Centre* (2004) 15 ELR 296 the Labour Court, in a determination approved by the Circuit Court, set out the approach to be followed by employers in considering dismissal on the grounds of incapacity due to disability.

The Labour Court stated:

'The nature and extent of the enquiries which an employer should make will depend on the circumstances of each case. At a minimum, an employer should ensure that he or she is in full possession of all the material facts concerning the employee's condition and that the employee has given fair notice that the question of his/her dismissal for incapacity is being considered. The employee must also be allowed an opportunity to influence the employer's decision.

'In practical terms this would normally require a two-stage enquiry, which looks firstly at the factual position concerning the employee's capability including the degree of impairment arising from the disability and its likely duration. This would involve looking at the medical evidence available to the employer from the employee's doctors or obtained independently.

'Secondly, if it is apparent that the employee is not fully capable, section 16(3) of the Act requires the employer to consider what, if any, special treatment or facilities may be available by which the employee can become fully capable. The section requires that the cost of such special treatment or facilities must also be considered.

'Finally, such an enquiry could only be regarded as adequate if the employee concerned is allowed a full opportunity to participate at each level and is allowed to present relevant medical evidence.'

This test must now be adapted to comply with the 2004 Act provisions.

In the case of *An Employee v A Worker (Mr O) No 1*, EED0410 the Labour Court held that an employer must make adequate enquiries so as to be in possession of all material information concerning the needs of an employee with a disability before taking decisions which are to the employee's detriment. In the case of *A Government Department v An Employee (Ms B)* ADE/05/16, Determination No 061, the Labour Court held that the duty to reasonably accommodate an employee with a disability is a proactive duty and a means to an end and that end is achieved when the person with a disability is placed in a position where they have access to our advance in employment. The Labour Court further held that were an employer fails to fulfil its reasonable accommodation duties it cannot defend a disability discrimination claim on the basis that the employee is not fully capable of his duties.

In *An Employer v A Worker (Mr O)* January 2005, it was made clear that an employer has an obligation to consider what possible adjustments can be made to the workplace to 'ameliorate' the employee's difficulties caused by their disability. Medical evidence should address the issue of modifications to the workplace/ work regime.

The Irish case law demonstrates a very broad interpretation of the term 'disability'. In *Customer Perception Limited v Gemma Leydon*, ED/02/1 Determination No 0317, the Labour Court held that a whiplash-type injury fell within the definition of disability as the definition includes a disability which has occurred in the past or which is imputed to a person, thereby including a disability which is temporary in nature. Similarly alcoholism, whether in recovery or not, has been held to be a disability (*A Complainant v Café Kylemore* DEC-S2002–024 and *An Employee v a Government Department* DEC E2005/034).

6.2.10 RACE

6.2.10.1 Ethnic origins

The full definition of the term 'race' is contained in section 6(2) of the 1998 Act and defines the ground of race as being differences 'in . . . race, colour, nationality or ethnic or national origins'. The question of 'ethnic' origins was considered in some detail in *Mandla v Lee* [1983] IRLR 209 by the UK House of Lords. The Lords stated that a group may be defined by reference to its 'ethnic origins' if it constitutes a separate and distinct community by virtue of characteristics which are commonly associated with common racial origin and is a term 'appreciably wider than strictly racial or biological'. In defining an ethnic group the Lords stated that a group must regard itself, and be regarded by others, as a distinct community by virtue of certain characteristics and went on to state that it was essential in order to constitute an ethnic group that there be the following:

(a) a long shared history of which the group is conscious as distinguishing it from other groups and the memory of which it keeps alive;

(b) a cultural tradition of its own including family and social customs and manners often but not necessarily associated with religious observance. In addition there are other relevant characteristics, one or more of which will commonly be found and will help to distinguish the group from the secondary community;

(c) either a common geographical origin or descent from a small number of common ancestors;

(d) a common language, not necessarily peculiar to the group;

(e) a common literature peculiar to the group;

(f) a common religion different from that of the neighbouring groups or from the general community surrounding it; and

(g) a sense of being a minority or being an oppressed or a dominant group within a larger community.

6.2.10.2 Application of ethnic origins test

As an example of how the test in *Mandla* may be used, it was held in *Dawkins v Department of the Environment* [1993] IRLR 284 by the UK Court of Appeal that Rastafarians are not a separate 'racial group' within the ethnic group of the Afro-Caribbean community. The court held that, although they are a separate group with identifiable characteristics, they have not established some separate identity by reference to their ethnic origins, and that comparing Rastafarians with the rest of the Jamaican community in England or with the rest of the Afro-Caribbean community there was nothing to set them aside as a separate ethnic group. Rastafarians are likely to be protected by the religious discrimination provisions of the 1998 Act. It is likely that Mr Dawkins would have brought his claim on the grounds of religious discrimination had religious discrimination been prohibited in England, which it was not.

On the matter of nationality the UK Court of Appeal held in *Dhatt v McDonald's Hamburgers Ltd* [1991] ICR 226 that an application form which distinguished between British citizens and EU nationals, on the one hand, and those who were neither British citizens nor EU nationals on the other hand, did not discriminate on grounds of nationality.

In *Northern Joint Police Board v Power* [1997] IRLR 610 Mr Power applied for the post of Chief Constable of the Northern Constabulary but was not shortlisted. He claimed this was because he was English rather than Scottish. The UK EAT held that discrimination against an English person or a Scot based on their 'national origin' was discrimination on 'racial grounds' within the meaning of the Race Relations Act 1976. It held that the Scots and the English are separate racial groups defined by reference to national origin. Mr Power had also claimed that he had been discriminated against on grounds of his 'ethnic origins'. This argument was rejected on the grounds that the Scots and the English do not have different 'ethnic origins'.

In *Bryans v Northumberland College of Arts and Technology* [1995] COIT in England an Irish employee was a special needs lecturer at a technical college. One of his colleagues called him an 'Irish prat'. He regarded this as racial harassment and raised a grievance under the college's grievance procedure. The colleague who made the remark refused to offer an apology and the employee's manager delayed in taking action over the grievance. The employee was subsequently denied a place on a shortlist for promotion because he had persisted in pursuing his grievance. He suffered stress as a result of the remark and the delay in investigating and addressing the matter, and was absent from work through illness as a result. He brought a claim of race discrimination to a tribunal. He was awarded a total sum of £29,900 compensation for racial discrimination, having fully succeeded in his claim. The tribunal broke down the elements of the compensation between individuals and the employer. A sum of £15,000 was awarded for injury to feelings and £5,000 for aggravated damages because of the way in which the matter was dealt with. £2,000 was awarded against the college principal, £6,500 against the line manager, £1,500 against the curriculum director and £5,000 against the colleague who made the offensive remark.

In a recent case of alleged race discrimination, *Dr Munck v National University of Ireland, Maynooth* DEC E2005/030, the Labour Court noted that it is recognised the direct evidence of discrimination on the grounds of race is very often allusive and that a decision must be made whether or not an inference of discrimination on the grounds of race can be determined on the facts.

There are a number of exceptions provided for in the Employment Equality Acts, 1998 and 2004 on the race ground. In *Irish Society of Chartered Physiotherapists v Venera Ilieva and Tsvetko Mitov* ADE/04/25 and ADE /04/26 Determination No 0519, the Labour Court held that exceptions to the general prohibition of discrimination on the grounds of age or race must be construed strictly and should be given no wider scope in the words used actually suggest. In the particular case a rule/practice allowing augmentation of qualifications for EU nationals but not of non-EU nationals was found not to fall within the exception contained in section 12(7) of the Employment Equality Acts. That section provides for different treatment in relation to course fees and the allocation of places on courses for persons who are citizens of Ireland or nationals of another EU Member State. It was therefore found that the Irish Society of Chartered Physiotherapists had discriminated against the complainants when it rejected their applications for membership without offering them the opportunity to undergo a period of adaptation, which was allowed for nationals of an EU Member State who lacked qualifications in a particular subject.

6.2.11 MEMBERSHIP OF THE TRAVELLER COMMUNITY

There have been numerous cases brought by members of the traveller community under the Equal Status Act, 2000 which provides for non-discrimination in the provision of goods and services. In those cases the concept of membership of the traveller community has been broadly interpreted to counteract prejudice against members of the traveller community, whether settled or otherwise. Fewer cases have been heard under the Employment Equality Acts.

In *Sweeney v McHale Ltd* DEC-E–2001/033, the complainant, who was a member of the traveller community applied for a job in a saw mill. His application was rejected. The equality officer agreed that the remark made by the respondent that the complainant was one of the 'Sweeneys from Sligo' and was not suitable to work with the respondent indicated that the complainant did not get the job on the ground of his membership of the traveller community and was therefore discriminated against.

6.3   Employer Policies

The Supreme Court in the United States, in two decisions handed down in June 1998, *Burlington Industries v Ellerth* [1997] and *Faragher v Boca Raton* [1997] held that in claims of sexual harassment an employer who does not have a policy against sexual harassment in place, notified to staff and operational, while not being devoid of the opportunity to defend a claim of sexual harassment, would have considerable difficulty and it would make it much easier for employees to succeed in claims of sexual harassment in the absence of the existence and promulgation of such a policy. US courts have followed *Ellerth* and *Faragher* to the extent of applying the principle to race discrimination cases. Irish employers would be well advised therefore in light of the provisions of the 1998 Act to either redraft their existing sexual harassment policies to include the other grounds prohibited by the 1998 Act or bring into existence similar type policies to cover the new grounds to ensure that these policies are implemented and that their employees are trained in respect of the policies. The Labour Court held in *A Hospital v An Appellant* AEE/ 02/06 Determination No 029, that the mere existence of policies is insufficient without further proactive steps to make out a defence of having done what is reasonably practicable; the defense to vicarious liability.

6.4   Forms of Discrimination

In seeking to deal with all areas of employment, the 1998 and 2004 Acts outlaw discrimination that may be perpetrated as follows.

- *Discrimination by employers* includes access to employment, conditions of employment, training and promotion.

- *Discrimination in collective agreements* with regard to access to, and conditions of, employment and equal pay for like work.

- *Discriminatory advertising* which includes advertising that might reasonably be understood as indicating an intention to discriminate. The Equality Authority may apply to the courts to injunct any proposed appointment of a person to be made on foot of a discriminatory advertisement until such time as the Equality Tribunal has made a decision in the matter or the court otherwise orders.

- *Discrimination by employment agencies*: employment agencies have become a popular target of the legislators in recent years. Under the provisions of the Unfair Dismissals (Amendment) Act, 1993, persons retained through a third-party company are deemed to be employees of the employer as is also provided for in the terms of the Employment (Information) Act, 1994. This has proven problematic for employers. While it may appear easy to identify an employment agency, the 1998 Act and the other legislation referred to defines an employment agency as per the provisions of the Employment

Agency Act, 1971. The definition of an employment agency in the 1971 Act is very wide and is not limited to licensed employment agencies. The 1971 Act provides:

> '. . . the business of an Employment Agency means the business of seeking, whether for reward or otherwise, on behalf of others, persons who will give or accept employment and includes the obtaining or supplying for reward of persons who will accept employment from or render services to others.'

To paraphrase, it can cover:

> 'The business of . . . supplying for reward . . . persons who . . . render services to others.'

The EAT *Bourton v Narcea Ltd and AIBP* M318 UD 186/94, held that the employees of a sub-contractor carrying out sub-contract work on a company's premises may, by virtue of the provisions of the 1993 Act, section 13, be deemed to be employees of that company. See also *Harrods Ltd v Remick* [1997] IRLR 9.

- *Discrimination in vocational training* to include the giving of instruction to carry on any occupational activity. Section 12 of the Act prohibits education and training bodies, and what it describes as 'any person' (which must include the employer), from refusing or omitting to afford access to training courses to any person. This requires careful planning by employers who make education and training available to staff to ensure that the offer is made on an open, transparent and across-the-board way to all relevant employees.

- *Discrimination by trade unions, professional and trade associations* as regards membership and other benefits falls within the ambit of the 1998 and 2004 Acts.

6.5 Indirect Discrimination

6.5.1 TEST FOR INDIRECT DISCRIMINATION

Discrimination may arise in an indirect way where an employer requires or applies a condition equally to all but the condition is one with which fewer of one gender than the other can comply. This may arise in situations where discrimination, even inadvertently, may be institutionalised as part of structures, practices or requirements.

The test under the 1998 Act, before the 2004 amendments were made was whether or not a substantially higher proportion of persons of one sex/marital status or other ground was able to comply with a requirement, practice, etc. This is no longer the case. In seeking to avoid an allegation of indirect discrimination on the gender ground, an employer must show that the practice complained of is based on objectively verifiable factors which have no relation to the ground in question. This is provided for on the gender ground under the 1998 Act, section 22, as amended. This concept existed in Irish law pre-October 1999 for gender and marital status only. Section 31 of the 1999 Act extends indirect discrimination to all categories of persons covered by the new discrimination grounds. An employer must be able to justify indirect discrimination on the gender ground by objective factors unrelated to the employee's sex. The 1998 Act was amended by the European Communities (Burden of Proof in Gender Discrimination Cases) Regulations, 2001 repealed by the 2004 Act. These regulations gave effect to Council Directive 97/80/EC of 15 December 1997 on the burden of proof in cases of discrimination based on sex. They not only addressed the question of burden of proof, but, at regulation 4, amended the definition of indirect discrimination on the grounds of gender as provided in the 1998 Act, section 22(1).

Prior to the amending regulations, indirect discrimination on the gender ground occurred:

> '. . . where a provision (whether in the nature of a requirement, practice or otherwise) which relates to any of [the grounds] or to membership of a regulatory body

> (a) applies to both A and B,
>
> (b) is such that the proportion of persons who are disadvantaged by the provision is substantially higher in the case of those of the same sex as A than in the case of those of the same sex as B, and
>
> (c) cannot be justified by objective factors unrelated to A's sex, then, for the purposes of this Act, A's employer or, as the case may be, the regulatory body shall be regarded as discriminating against A on the gender ground contrary to Sections 8 and 13 of the Act which prohibit discrimination in access to employment, conditions of employment, training or experience for or in relation to employment, promotion or regrading, classification of posts and membership of certain bodies.'

Subsection (c) is amended to 'is not appropriate and necessary and cannot be justified by objective factors unrelated to A's sex'.

No amendment was made by the 2001 Regulations to the provision in respect of indirect discrimination on all grounds other than gender, contained in the 1998 Act, section 31.

The 1998 Act provided that indirect discrimination on the other grounds could be justified by the employer as being reasonable in all the circumstances of the case. 'Reasonable' is of course less difficult for an employer to prove than 'appropriate and necessary and justified by objective factors' as provided in the amended section 22 for indirect discrimination between men and women. In the case of *Dr Eng v St James's Hospital* ADE/02/04 No 23, the Labour Court held that it was a question of fact to be decided in each case by applying ordinary objective standards of reasonableness.

The 2004 Act repealed the 2001 Regulations and amended the indirect discrimination provisions so that on all grounds indirect discrimination can only be justified on objective factors unrelated to a discriminatory ground, and where the impugned provision is appropriate and necessary to achieve a legitimate aim.

The 2004 Act amended the 1998 Act indirect discrimination provisions on each of the nine grounds with the following:

> '1. (a) Indirect discrimination occurs where an apparently neutral provision puts persons of a particular gender . . . [or to whom a discriminatory ground applies] at a particular disadvantage in respect of any matter other than remuneration compared with other employees of their employer.
>
> . . . (c) Where paragraph (a) applies, the employer shall be treated for the purposes of this Act as discriminating against each of the persons referred to . . ., unless the provision is objectively justified by a legitimate aim and the means of achieving that aim are appropriate and necessary.'

The 2004 Act contains similar provisions on equal remuneration and indirect discrimination.

These provisions equalise the law on indirect discrimination on all nine grounds, making it easier for a candidate for employment or an employee to show that he/she has been disadvantaged by a provision applied to all, and putting a strict onus on the employer to justify any such provision.

6.5.2   *NATHAN v BAILEY GIBSON*

6.5.2.1   Background

In *Nathan v Bailey Gibson, The Irish Print Union and the Minister for Labour*, Ms Nathan was employed by Bailey Gibson in the manufacture of cartons. She applied for a post which became vacant following the retirement of a man who had operated a folder/gluer machine. Ms Nathan had assisted him on the machine for the 10 years prior to his retirement. The man was a member of the IPU. In the printing industry craft workers are organised into specific unions, such as the IPU, while male non-craft employees are organised by the ITGWU and female non-craft workers by the Irish Women Workers Branch of the FWUI.

Bailey Gibson had a closed shop agreement with the IPU in relation to the machine in question, giving IPU members first call on the job when the man retired. If IPU members were unavailable a non-union member could be recruited but would be required to join the IPU and would be granted membership without any distinction whatsoever on the basis of sex.

Bailey Gibson was anxious to appoint Ms Nathan but the IPU would not agree to her appointment. A male IPU member was appointed to the vacant post. Ms Nathan claimed there had been a breach of the Employment Equality Act, 1977 by denying her access to the job and thereby indirectly discriminating against her on the grounds of her sex by making it a requirement that access to the vacant position be confined to members of the IPU which was traditionally male.

6.5.2.2 The Labour Court

The equality officer held that the company had indirectly discriminated against Ms Nathan by making it a requirement that access to the vacant position be confined to persons who held membership of the IPU. The matter was appealed to the Labour Court. The Labour Court, in dealing with the issue of indirect discrimination, ruled that in order for Ms Nathan to succeed in that argument she would have to show that there was a *causal link* between the requirement to have a union card and her sex and only then would it become a relevant consideration as to whether the proportion of men able to comply with the requirement was substantially higher. The Labour Court held that there were no conditions for membership of the IPU which discriminate against women, and while it was factually correct that more men than women have IPU membership, this was because historically males occupied the craft positions in the Irish printing industry. The agreement between the company and the IPU was craft-based and when it was imposed on Ms Nathan bore no relationship to her sex. The IPU was indifferent to whether a male or a female was recruited for the job, but given the imbalance (82 per cent male membership, 18 per cent female membership) against females, the likelihood of a female being appointed was far less once the restriction of IPU membership was imposed.

The Labour Court held that the disproportionate impact on women was not causally linked to sex but historic. It was not because she was a woman that she could not become a member of the IPU; it was because she was a non-craft worker in a non-craft union and there were existing IPU members available for employment. Reference was made to *Revenue Commissioners v Kelly* EE9/87 where a requirement of a driving licence was imposed on applicants for a job. The equality officer was unable to establish any attribute of sex which would result in a lower proportion of females than males being able to comply with that requirement. The Labour Court held here that unless the IPU was discriminating between men and women the worker could not claim that the requirement to have an IPU card discriminated against her. As the employee had failed to make a causal link between the requirement and her sex, her claim failed.

The matter was appealed to the High Court, where Murphy J held that the Labour Court was correct in requiring a causal link between sex and the job requirement being established by the applicant.

The matter was appealed to the Supreme Court which took a different view from the Labour Court and the High Court.

6.5.2.3 The Supreme Court

The Supreme Court [1996] ELR 114 on the issue of indirect discrimination held:

(a) the discrimination referred to in Directive 76/207/EEC and the 1977 Act covers both direct and indirect discrimination;

(b) the worker in this case was not required to prove a causal connection between the practice complained of and the sex of the complainant;

(c) it is sufficient for the worker to show that the practice complained of bears significantly more heavily on members of the complainant's sex than on members of the other sex;

(d) once the claimant has established a prima facie case of discrimination, the onus of proof shifts to the employer to show that the practice complained of is based on objectively verifiable factors which have no relation to the plaintiff's sex.

6.5.2.4 Remittance to the Labour Court

Following the Supreme Court decision in her favour Ms Nathan's case was remitted to the Labour Court which reheard the claim in light of the Supreme Court ruling and a decision was issued on 14 August 1997 rejecting Ms Nathan's claim of discrimination (reported at [1998] ELR 52). The Labour Court based its decision on the following.

(1) The practice engaged in by the company, which was sought to be impugned by Ms Nathan, was the recruitment of only IPU card-holding members to certain jobs. The requirement was to be a member of the IPU in order to be eligible for the job to which Ms Nathan sought access.

(2) It was not contradicted that the company, had it not had the obligation in relation to IPU membership, would have sought candidates for the position from its entire workforce including Ms Nathan.

(3) The workforce consisted of 89 persons of whom 61 were men and 28 were women. Twenty-one of the male employees were members of the IPU who would have been able to satisfy the requirement of IPU membership. The practice therefore affected 28 women and 40 men who were employees of the company but did not hold IPU membership. If a male worker who was not a member of the IPU applied for the post to which Ms Nathan sought access, the same requirement would have applied to him with the same result as complained of by Ms Nathan.

(4) Whereas the equality officer concluded that the impugned requirement affected more women than men because no women held an IPU card, the court found that statistically the requirement affected more men than women. Given the undisputed figures for the workforce and their respective sexes and the undisputed fact that normal recruitment at the time was from within the existing workforce 45 per cent of those who were affected by the impugned practice were male and 31.5 per cent of those affected were females. Those who could comply comprised 23.6 per cent of the workforce.

(5) The practice of requiring a worker to be an IPU member did discriminate against the women employees, including the worker in this case, but not in such numbers as to amount to discrimination within the meaning of the 1977 Act, section 3 since it was male employees who were more significantly affected.

(6) The court referred to the fact that the position referred to was eventually filled by a male non-IPU member who, at the time Ms Nathan complained of being discriminated against, was himself also 'equally disadvantaged'.

(7) The court concluded from the statistics referred to above that the practice complained of did not bear significantly more heavily on members of the female sex but rather bore more heavily on members of the male sex. The court held that there was no evidence that the obtaining of an IPU card was made more

difficult by the company for the women employees than it was for the male employees.

(8)   In light of the above the court held that there were no sex-based criteria operated by the company which resulted in the non-selection of Ms Nathan for the position she sought and the claim failed.

(9)   The court did hold that the company was responsible for accepting the constraints of a 'closed shop' arrangement and therefore was also responsible for the effect that practice had on its employees. The practice was, however, held not to be discriminatory of females.

6.5.3   BURDEN OF PROOF

The Employment Equality Act, 1998 did not make general provision concerning the burden of proof to be applied to cases of alleged discrimination contrary to the Act on any of the nine discriminatory grounds, with the exception of a number of specific and limited provisions.

Direct discrimination is governed by section 6 of the Act. It defines discrimination as one person being treated less favourably than another on one of the nine grounds, whether past or present, imputed or by association. Section 8 of the Act contains provisions in respect of discrimination in specific areas, subject to the general prohibition on discrimination contained in section 6. These are the direct discrimination provisions. The 1998 Act did not specify the burden of proof to be adopted. The Employment Equality Act, 1998 (Burden of Proof in Gender Discrimination Cases) Regulations, 1998, SI 337/2001 implemented the burden of proof directive in gender discrimination cases where an employee established a prima facie case. It was then for the employer to rebut a presumption of discrimination.

No such provisions were enacted in respect of the remaining eight grounds prior to the 2004 Act. The Equality Tribunal and Labour Court issued many decisions on the other grounds under the 1998 Act in which they took the view that the burden of proof shifts upon the making out of a prima facie case on any of the grounds provided for in the Employment Equality Act. The rationale adopted by the Equality Tribunal and Labour Court was essentially that they had already established a practice of shifting the burden of proof where a prima facie case was established on the grounds of gender and marital status pursuant to the Employment Equality Act, 1977 and that this practice could therefore continue, as it is a jurisprudence of the Equality Tribunal and Labour Court which was approved by the High Court and which they can follow in deciding cases under the Employment Equality Act, 1998.

Section 85A of the 1998 Act, as inserted by the 2004 Act, expressly shifts the burden of proof in cases on all grounds where facts are established by or on behalf of a complainant from which it may be presumed that there has been discrimination. It is then for the respondent to prove the contrary. Section 85A repeals the relevant provisions of the 2001 regulations, which applied to gender discrimination cases only.

Employers must now examine all work practices carefully to ensure that they do not give rise to discrimination as a result of some inadvertent ingrained or institutionalised practice which disproportionally affects one person as against another on one of the discriminatory grounds as set out in the 1998 and 2004 Acts, section 6. The practice of requiring telephonists to accept transfers and assignments throughout the country at short notice was held to be discriminatory in that it was unnecessarily onerous on married persons in *Department of Posts and Telegraphs v Mullins* EE1/78 DEE2/78.

In dealing with the proportion of persons able to comply or not comply with a requirement, use of statistics has become very prevalent. The 2004 Act amendments are likely to reduce their importance. A decision of McCracken J on a claim of indirect discrimination prior to the 1998 and 2004 Acts focused on the approach to be taken to such cases and, in particular, the approach taken by the Labour Court in the wake of the Supreme Court decision in *Nathan v Bailey Gibson* [1996] ELR 114.

In *Conlan v University of Limerick* [1999] ELR 155 the plaintiff was a lecturer in law in the University of Limerick. The defendant advertised the position of Professor of Law, a portion of the advertisement for which read as follows:

> 'Applications are invited from suitably qualified candidates holding a higher law degree, preferably at doctorate level. The successful candidate will have several years' experience at a senior academic level and be a leading published researcher in a specialised field of law.'

The plaintiff applied for the position but was not shortlisted on the grounds that there were other candidates whose qualifications and experience more closely matched the requirements of the defendants. The plaintiff claimed inter alia that in requiring that an applicant should have several years' experience at a senior academic level the defendant was indirectly discriminating against her on grounds of her sex in that this requirement meant that there would be very few females qualified for the post because there were very few females at a senior academic level. Her claims were rejected by the equality officer and the Labour Court. In referring to *Nathan v Bailey Gibson* [1996] ELR 114 McCracken J followed the principle set down in that case that initially it is for the worker to show that the practice complained of bears more heavily on one sex than on the other. Once this is established it is then for the employer to show that, notwithstanding this fact, the practice complained of is in fact based on factors which are unconnected with the sex of the worker. In this regard the onus of proof is clearly on the employer. He went on to quote Hamilton J at p 128 of that judgment where he said:

> 'In such a case the worker is not required, in the first instance, to prove a causal connection between the practice complained of and the sex of the complainant. It is sufficient for the worker to show that the practice complained of bears significantly more heavily on members of the complainant's sex than on members of the other sex. At that stage the complainant has established a prima facie case of discrimination and the onus of proof shifts to the employer to show that the practice complained of is based on objectively verifiable factors which have no relation to the plaintiff's sex.'

The type of analysis required to prove objectively verifiable factors was explained by McCracken J in referring to the pensions equality case, *Bilka-Kaufhaus GmbH v Weber Von Hartz* [1986] 2 CMLR 701, where it was stated at p 721:

> 'It falls to the national court which alone is competent to assess the facts, to decide whether, and if so, to what extent, the grounds put forward by an employer to explain the adoption of a pay practice which applies irrespective of the employee's sex, but which in fact affects more women than men can be considered to be objectively justified for economic reasons. If the national court finds that the means chosen by Bilka meet a genuine need of the enterprise, that they are suitable for attaining the objective pursued by the enterprise and are necessary for that purpose, the fact that the measures in question affect a much greater number of women than men is not sufficient to conclude that they involve a breach of Article 119.'

McCracken J had a difficulty with the manner in which the Labour Court approached the plaintiff's complaint of indirect discrimination but came to the view that, despite the apparent flaws in the approach and type of reasoning adopted, the right result was reached and he held that the Labour Court had taken an objective view of the factors relating to the requirements of the defendant and found as a fact that the defendant believed its requirements to be essential. McCracken J also quoted the decision of the ECJ in examining what are objectively justifiable and essential criteria in *Kording v Senator Fur Finanzen* [1997] ECR 5289 where the court stated:

'In . . . *Nimz* [*v Freie ünd Hansestadt Hamburg* [1991] IRLR 221] the court took the view that it is impossible to identify objective criteria unrelated to any discrimination on grounds of sex on the basis of an alleged special link between length of service and acquisition of a certain level of knowledge or experience since such a claim amounts to no more than a generalisation concerning certain categories of workers. Although experience goes hand in hand with length of service and experience enables the worker in principle to improve performance of the tasks allotted to him, the objectivity of such a criterion depends on all the circumstances in each individual case, and in particular on the relationship between the nature of the work performed and the experience gained from the performance of that work upon completion of a certain number of working hours.'

The plaintiff's claim was dismissed on the grounds that the university had discharged the onus of proof on it in justifying the reasons put forward for setting out the requirements of the job and that the Labour Court considered those reasons objectively and reached the conclusion that they were essential requirements which had no connection with the sex of the plaintiff.

The Labour Court addressed the question of indirect discrimination on the gender ground under the 1998 Act in *NBK Designs Ltd v Marie Inoue* ED/ 02/34 Determination No 0212. It found that a provision which would have required Ms Inoue to work full time amounted prima facie to indirect discrimination. It then considered objective justification, where it held that the onus rests on the respondent. It approved the decision of the ECJ in *Bilka Kaufhaus v Weber Von Hartz* [1986] ECR 1607. It held that the court must be satisfied that the impugned measures:

(a) correspond to a real need on the part of the undertaking;

(b) are appropriate with a view to achieving the objective pursued; and

(c) are necessary to that end.

The questions the Labour Court formulated were as follows.

(a) Does a requirement to work full time correspond to a real need on the part of the respondent? The court was far from convinced that the exigencies of the respondent's business made it essential that the complainant work full time. It held that this was the test to be satisfied.

(b) Were the means chosen appropriate? The court held that this meant that the means must be proportionate to the objective which they are attempting to achieve and that the value of the benefit accruing to the employer must be balanced against the discriminatory effect of the method by which it was achieved. In this case it held that the employer could not satisfy the requirement of proportionality.

(c) Was the method appropriate to achieve the end in view? The Labour Court held that it was for the employer to demonstrate that there were no alternative means, having a less discriminatory effect, by which the objective in view could have been achieved. It held that the respondent did not consider alternative ways of achieving its objective and that it could not therefore say that there were no alternative less discriminatory means by which this objective could have been achieved. The court therefore held that the impugned requirement was not necessary and appropriate and could not be justified by objective factors unrelated to the complainant's sex.

6.5.4 JOB SHARING

Indirect discrimination also arose in *Hill and Stapleton v Revenue Commissioners and Department of Finance* [1998] IRLR 466, [1998] ELR 225. Ms Hill and Ms Stapleton were employed as clerical assistants in the Civil Service where they worked with the Revenue

Commissioners. Ms Hill started as a full-time employee in 1981 and began job sharing in 1988. Ms Stapleton was recruited in a job-sharing capacity in 1986. Each worked half the time that a full-time employee worked on a week-on/week-off basis. The Civil Service job-sharing scheme provided that while on job share each employee moved one point up the incremental pay scale with each year of service and they were paid 50 per cent of the salary applicable to the point they had reached on the scale.

After two years both employees took up full-time employment but as the scheme treated each year's job share as only equivalent to six months' full-time service they were placed on a lower point of the full-time scale than they otherwise would have been. They claimed that equating two years' job-sharing service with one year's full-time service constituted indirect sex discrimination contrary to the Anti-Discrimination (Pay) Act, 1974 and Article 119 of the EC Treaty on the basis that far more female workers than male workers spent part of their working lives in a job-sharing capacity. The following questions were raised before the ECJ:

(1) is the principle of equal pay contravened if employees who convert from job sharing to full-time work regress on the incremental scale due to the application by the employer of the criterion of service calculated by time worked in the job?

(2) if so does the employer have to provide special justification for recourse to the criterion of service defined as actual time worked?

(3) if so can a practice of incremental progression by reference to actual time worked be objectively justified by reference to factors other than the acquisition of a particular level of skill and experience over time?

The ECJ held:

'A system for classifying workers converting from job sharing to full-time employment comes within the concept of "pay" for the purposes of Article 119 of the EC Treaty since it determines the progression of pay due to those workers. Rules which treat full-time workers who previously job shared at a disadvantage compared with other full-time workers by applying a criterion of service calculated by length of time actually worked in a post and therefore placing them on the full-time pay scale at a level lower than that which they occupied on the pay scale applicable to job sharing must, in principle, be treated as contrary to Article 119 and the Equal Pay Directive where 98 per cent of those employed under job-sharing contracts are women. When workers convert from job sharing, where they worked 50 per cent of full-time hours and received 50 per cent of the salary for full-time work, they should expect both their hours of work and the level of their pay to increase by 50 per cent in the same way as workers converting from full-time work to job sharing would expect those factors to be reduced by 50 per cent unless a difference in treatment can be justified. The onus was on the respondents to establish before the national court that the reference to the criterion of service defined as the length of time actually worked in the assessment and the incremental credit to be granted to workers who convert from job sharing to full-time work, is justified by objective factors unrelated to any discrimination on grounds of sex. However, an employer cannot justify discrimination arising from a job-sharing scheme solely on the ground that avoidance of such discrimination would involve increased costs. Nor was it relevant that there was an established practice within the Civil Service of crediting only actual service or that the practice was said to establish a reward system which maintained staff motivation, commitment and morale.'

6.5.5   PROPORTIONALITY

In *Irish Press Newspapers v Mandate* DEP 5/95, the Labour Court was faced with a claim relating to the exclusion of part-time workers from the company pension scheme. The proportion of male employees who could comply with the requirement was 56 per cent compared with the proportion of females which was 38 per cent. The Labour Court found that the difference between the proportion of female workers and the proportion of male workers who could comply with the requirement was 'not substantial'. The court said it did not regard a difference of 18 per cent as considerable. It should be noted that 62 per cent of women could not comply with the requirement as against 44 per cent of men who could not comply with the requirement.

The ECJ dealt with the question of indirect sex discrimination in *R v Secretary of State for Employment, ex parte Seymour-Smith and Perez* [1999] IRLR 253. Ms Seymour-Smith sought to claim unfair dismissal but did not have the necessary two years' continuous service required under UK unfair dismissal legislation. She sought to challenge the relevant UK legislative provision on the basis that the proportion of women who could comply with the two-year qualifying period is considerably smaller than the proportion of men so as to amount to prima facie indirect sex discrimination against women and that therefore the two-year qualifying period was contrary to the EC Equal Treatment Directive. Over the period from 1985 to 1991 the proportion of men who had two or more years of service with their current employer ranged from 72 per cent to 77.4 per cent. The proportion of women ranged between 63.8 per cent and 68.9 per cent. The female percentage as a percentage of the male percentage averaged 89.1 per cent. In 1991 it was 90.5 per cent. It was accepted that the differences found in the impact of the requirement on the sexes were statistically significant in that it could be said with confidence that they were due to social facts rather than to chance.

The ECJ held:

'In order to establish whether a measure adopted by a Member State has disparate effect as between men and women to such a degree as to amount to indirect sex discrimination the national courts must verify whether the statistics available indicate that a considerably smaller percentage of women than men is able to fulfil the requirement imposed by that measure. The best approach for determining whether a rule has a more unfavourable impact on women than on men is to consider the respective proportions of men in the workforce able to satisfy the requirement and those unable to do so and to compare those proportions as regards women in the workforce. It must be ascertained whether the statistics indicate that a considerably smaller percentage of women than men is able to satisfy the condition required, in this case two years' employment. That would be evidence of apparent sex discrimination. That could also be the case if the statistical evidence revealed a lesser but persistent and relatively constant disparity over a long period between men and women who satisfied the requirement of two years' employment. It is for the national court to determine the conclusions to be drawn from such statistics. It is also for the national court to assess whether the statistics are valid and appear to be significant or whether they illustrate purely fortuitous or short-term phenomena.'

In *Seymour-Smith* the ECJ went on to give some assistance as to the actual percentages that might be considered significant and stated:

'In the present case in 1985, the year in which the requirement of two years' service was introduced, 77.4 per cent of men and 68.9 per cent of women fulfilled that condition. Such statistics did not appear, on the face of it, to show that a considerably smaller percentage of women than men was able to fulfil the requirement imposed by the disputed rule.'

6.6   Equal Pay

6.6.1   EUROPEAN COMMISSION CODE OF PRACTICE

To avoid both direct and indirect discrimination in pay and conditions employers should review their terms and conditions of employment in light of the recommendations set out in the European Commission Code of Practice on the implementation of equal pay issued in July 1996.

The code is aimed at employers, whether from the public or private sector, and states that it seeks to help the parties in wage negotiations to remove all direct or indirect discrimination from collective agreements and further states that it:

> 'Also aims to assist women and men who believe their work is under-valued because of sexual discrimination to obtain the necessary information to resolve their problem through negotiation or, as a last resort, to bring the matter to the National Courts.'

6.6.2   THE 1998 AND 2004 ACTS

The 1998 Act repeats the definition of 'like work' as in the 1974 Act but broadens it to allow that a comparator employee need not be employed in the same place as the claimant. As regards the time of employment the comparator must be employed at the same time as the claimant or during the previous or following three years.

In relation to work which a person employed through an employment agency is required to do, comparison as regards like work may only be made with another agency worker. A comparison may not be made with non-agency workers.

In relation to like work, the old discrepancy where it was found that work was not like work but actually superior in value, is ruled out now and work greater in value deemed to be within the definition of 'like work'.

Sections 19 and 20 of the 1998 Act as amended by the 2004 Act insert an equal pay clause into every employment contract and, for the first time, expressly provide for indirect discrimination in equal pay. The definitions of equal pay in the 1974 Act are preserved, but the need for the claimant and the comparator employed in the same place is abolished. The notion of 'associated employer' is also preserved which has the effect of narrowing the potential pool of comparators.

Section 19(1) provides as follows:

> 'It shall be a term of the contract under which A is employed that, subject to this Act, A shall at anytime be entitled to the same rate of remuneration for the work which A is employed to do as B who, at that or any other relevant time, is employed to do like work by the same or an associated employer.'

Section 19(2) as amended by the 2004 Act provides that 'a relevant time' is any time (including a time before the commencement of the Act) during the three years which precede, or the three years which follow, the time in question.

Section 19(4) contained a prohibition on indirect discrimination in relation to equal pay and provides:

> 'Where a term of a contract or a criterion applies to employees (including A and B)—
> (a)   it applies to all the employees of a particular employer or to a particular class of such employees (including A and B);
> (b)   is such that the remuneration of those employees who fulfil the term or criterion is different from that of those who do not;
> (c)   is such that the proportion of employees who are disadvantaged by the term or criterion is

substantially higher in the case of those of the same sex as A than in the case of those of the same case as B; and(d) cannot be justified by objective factors unrelated to A's sex, then, for the purpose of subsection (1), A and B shall be treated as fulfilling or, as the case may be, as not fulfilling the term or criterion, whichever results in the higher remuneration.'

Section 29 of the Act provided a similar entitlement to equal pay for members of protected groups, on non-gender grounds.

The 1998 and 2004 Acts are firmly based on a system of comparisons between a person who is a member of the protected group and one who is not. The need for a comparator presents particular problems for claimants seeking to attack the notion of a lesser value being placed on work that is traditionally seen as women's work. Statistics show that there is still a significant differential between male and female earnings in Ireland and one of the main reasons for this is historically to be occupational sex segregation. There are industries where women are still clustered in particular jobs, and it may be difficult for a claimant in such circumstances to provide a male comparator.

The 2004 Act amended the indirect discrimination provisions on remuneration as with the non-remuneration provisions referred to at **6.5.1**. Statistics and comparisons may be of lesser importance in bringing claims under these amended provisions. Decisions are awaited at the time of writing.

6.6.3 ASSOCIATED EMPLOYER

Section 2(2) of the Act provides that two employers shall be taken to be associated if one is a body corporate of which the other (whether directly or indirectly) has control, or if both are bodies corporate of which a third person (whether directly or indirectly) has control. The nexus between two associated employers is that of 'control', a term which is not defined. Section 115 of the Companies Act, 1963 sets out relevant criteria determining whether a company is a subsidiary of another company and presumably such criteria apply in this context. It was found, for example, that where two hospitals were run by the same health board, that they rank as associated employers for the purposes of the 1974 Act.

6.6.4 LIKE WORK

6.6.4.1 Statutory definition

Section 7 of the 1998 Act provides that two people shall be regarded as being employed to do like work if:

'(a) *both perform the same work under the same or similar conditions, or each is interchangeable with the other in relation to the work;*

(b) *the work performed by one is of a similar nature to that performed by the other and any differences between the work performed or the conditions under which it is performed by each either are of small importance in relation to the work as a whole or occur with such irregularity as not to be significant to the work as a whole; or*

(c) *the work performed by one is equal in value to the work performed by the other, having regard to such matters as skill, physical or mental requirements, responsibility and working conditions.'*

6.6.4.2 Case law

Most of the cases which were brought under the 1974 Act were claims (under the similar provision of that Act) that the work performed by the claimant is equal in value to the work performed by the comparator. In practice, the equality officer carries out a detailed investigation (including interviews and work inspections at the place of work) in order to assess the demands placed on claimants and comparators in terms of skill, physical and mental effort, responsibility, and working conditions. In examining the work conditions, the equality officer will have regard to such matters as working times and the work environment. The decision of the equality officer in *550 Sales and Clerical Assistants (Mandate) v Penneys Ltd* EP06/94 where clerical and sales assistants (who were predominantly female) brought an equal claim against the respondent company is a useful example of the methodology employed by an equality officer. They named as comparators storemen who were all male. The equality officer (and on appeal the Labour Court) examined the very dissimilar jobs carried out by the claimants and comparators and found that the work was of equal value.

The equality officer carried out such a detailed investigation in *24 Female Employees v Spring Grove Services* EP01/96 and found that the work of the claimants was not equal in value to the work of the comparators. The female claimants worked in the finishing area of the respondent's linen services supply factory and sought remuneration with eight named male comparators who worked in the wash-house area of the same venture. The equality officer found that the demands made on the comparator, under the headings referred to above, were greater in each case. The equality officer also found that the fact that no female staff worked in the wash-house area, despite it being open to female members of staff to work there, was not an issue for consideration.

The equality officer in *8 Male Employees v Eastern Health Board* EP06/96 emphasised the greater volume of work being performed by the comparators in finding that their work was of greater value than that of the claimants. The claimants were employed by the health board as porters whose duties included answering the telephones one night every six weeks. The claimants argued that during that time they were doing like work to the female day telephonists and were therefore entitled to the same rate of remuneration. The volume of calls handled by the comparators was not comparable with the volume handled by the claimants.

The decision of the equality officer in *Rita O'Leary v Minister for Transport, Energy and Communications* 3 February 1998, Supreme Court unreported was appealed to the Labour Court, the High Court on a point of law, and then to the Supreme Court. The claimant was a communications assistant employed by the respondent at Dublin Airport. She alleged discrimination on grounds of sex as between her grade and that of radio officers. Her claim was rejected by the equality officer who found that she and her comparators did not carry out like work since the work of the comparators required additional qualifications, skills and responsibilities. Although it was not necessary to his decision, the equality officer indicated that he considered that the higher qualifications required by radio officers would have constituted valid grounds other than sex for the higher rate of remuneration associated with their grade. The claimant appealed and argued that the higher qualifications were unnecessary for the work which the comparators carried out. The Labour Court dismissed Ms O'Leary's appeal on the ground that the higher qualifications required of the comparators were necessary to comply with international broadcasting conventions. On appeal to the High Court, Barron J held that once the question of like work was decided against the applicants, their claim under the 1974 Act failed; it was not then necessary to determine the question of qualifications. On appeal, the Supreme Court determined that the essential finding of fact that the work of the comparators and the claimants was not 'like work' was made by reference to the skills and responsibilities demanded by the work rather than by reference to the qualification stipulated by others. Such qualifications might provide evidence of additional skills, but could not be evidence of the demands made by work.

The ECJ in *Angestektenbetriebszrat der Weiner Gebietskrankenkasse v Wiener Gebierskenkase* [1999] IRLR 481 held that the term 'the same work' does not apply where the same activities are performed over a considerable length of time by persons the basis of whose qualification to exercise their profession is different. The case concerned psychotherapy being carried out by medical doctors and psychologists. The doctors were paid 50 per cent more than the psychologists, most of whom were women. They unsuccessfully claimed equal pay.

6.6.5 GROUNDS OTHER THAN GENDER

Grounds other than gender are referred to in cases prior to the 1998 Act as grounds other than sex. In interpreting the 1998 Act similar principles apply with some exceptions so that the wider range of discriminatory grounds provided for in the 1998 and 2004 Acts are treated in similar fashion to the 'sex' ground.

Section 19(5) in relation to the gender ground, and section 29(5) in relation to non-gender grounds of the 1998 Act, provide that nothing shall prevent an employer from paying, on grounds other than a discriminatory ground, different rates of remuneration to different employees.

The ECJ in *Nimz v Freie und Hansestadt Hamburg* [1991] IRLR 221 established the principle that the reasons for which some employees are paid more than others must be based on 'objective criteria unrelated to any discrimination based on sex' and that 'the objectivity of such a criterion depends on all the circumstances in each case'. The court held here that the arguments that full-time workers acquired skills necessary for their employment more quickly and that they have greater experience, were generalisations and could not amount to objective criteria unrelated to any discrimination based on sex.

An example of where certain criteria for differential wage levels was held by the Labour Court to be objective and therefore lawful, occurred in *550 Sales and Clerical Assistants (Mandate) v Penneys Ltd* [1998] ELR 94 which is referred to at **6.6.4.2** above. The rates of pay were held to be unisex and reached through different negotiating routes, one via direct negotiations with the employer and one via an industry-wide basis. It was held by the quality officer and by the Labour Court in 1996 that although the claimants were performing work of equal value to that of the comparators, there were reasons other than sex for the differences in their remuneration, i.e. claimants' and comparators' rates of pay had been achieved by different industrial routes. On appeal, Barron J held that the correct principle to apply is whether the difference in remuneration between the claimants and the comparators is objectively justified on economic grounds. The Labour Court found, at the rehearing, that the employer was justified in paying different rates of pay to the claimants and comparators and that the justification was objectively based on economic grounds since the increase in pay which the comparators achieved was in return for a productivity agreement which generated economic and industrial benefit to the respondent. The court held that there was no sex-based ingredient in the negotiating process but that determination has again been appealed and would appear to conflict with the ECJ decision in *Enderby v Frenchay Health Authority* [1993] IRLR 591.

The fact that a person of the opposite sex to the claimant is paid the same remuneration does not prevent a claimant from bringing an equal pay claim. In an UK Court of Appeal decision, *Pickstone v Freemans plc* [1987] ICR 867, which was upheld by the House of Lords, it was held that Article 119 of the EC Treaty permitted a woman to bring an equal value complaint even though she was employed on like work or work rated as equivalent to that of a man other than her comparator.

In *C & D Food Ltd v Cunnion*, 30 July 1996, High Court unreported the situation was considered where both men and women were represented in the two pay grades in question. Employees in grade A were paid more highly than those in grade B. Female employees claimed that they were being discriminated against on grounds of sex as there were male employees engaged in occupations covered by grade A which were of no greater value than the employment of the claimants. The equality officer held that some of the claimants were employed on work of equal value to that of the comparators and that they should be paid equally. Both parties appealed to the Labour Court which rejected both appeals. The employer appealed the determination of the Labour Court claiming that as a matter of law, a finding that the difference in pay was not on grounds other than sex was not permissible when the evidence was that both men and women were recruited for and carried on the same occupations as the claimants and at the same wage. Barron J rejected the employer's appeal and held that in this case the comparator received more remuneration than the claimant because the employer had evaluated the male comparator's work more highly than that of the claimant. This was not a ground other than sex and the work was not more valuable. The decision as to what constituted 'like work' was for the tribunal, not the employer. If the employer's evaluation was incorrect, then unless there were grounds other than sex, the employer could not rely on it. The fact that men and women were recruited for the same job at the same wage was a matter which would be taken into account in determining the relative values of different occupations. It was relevant that the work of one of the male comparators was also done by a woman, as it was relevant that men and women did the same work as the applicants, but these factors went only to the issue of genuine belief.

In the light of the judgment of Barron J in *C & D Foods*, the determination of the Labour Court in *Mandate v Dunnes Stores* DEP 98/12 must be questioned. The equality officer found that certain of the claimants were performing like work with that of the comparators. The equality officer in *Dunnes* found that there were grounds other than sex for the differential in their remuneration. This finding was on the grounds that the comparators were six males out of a group of 24 sales assistants and that the remaining 18 sales assistants were all female. All canteen workers (the applicants) were female. On appeal, the court stated that it could find nothing in the claimants' claim to show that they were being paid less than the comparators by reason of their sex. This is not the test set out in the legislation or applied by the High Court, which prohibits not only direct, but also indirect discrimination in equal pay.

6.6.6   RED CIRCLING

Where an employee's rate of pay can be said to be above the normal rate for the job, due to purely personal factors related to the individual only, such a person may be red circled, thereby disallowing comparisons. It may arise where a long-serving male employee has suffered a partially incapacitating illness and has been moved to a less demanding job, but retained a higher rate of pay on humanitarian grounds. Such red circling is regarded as a genuine ground other than sex, for a difference in remuneration.

In *Department of Tourism, Transport and Communications v 4 Workers* [1997] ELR 1 female claimants, who were employed as communications assistants in the accounts section of the Irish Aviation Authority, sought equal pay with that of male comparators employed in the same section at a higher rate of pay. The equality officer found the claimants and comparators were employed on like work and recommended the same rate of remuneration. On appeal, the Labour Court upheld the equality officer's finding of like work and went on to consider a defence of red circling which had not been raised before the equality officer. It was argued by the employer that the comparators had been red circled as they were the subject of a special agreement to protect their pay while they were unfit for the duties of radio officers. The Labour Court held that red circling was to be recognised, factual and acknowledged if it is to serve as a defence.

The claimants appealed to the High Court [1996] ELR 106 where Keane J held that the Labour Court had misconstrued the relevant section of the 1998 Act. Keane J held that where it was established that the discrimination was based on grounds other than sex, that the employer could not be prevented from relying on the defence even if all parties to the red circling arrangement were not aware of the circumstances which brought it into operation. He remitted the matter to the Labour Court for reconsideration which found as a matter of fact that the positions of radio officers in the accounts section had not been red circled. Any male radio officer could be transferred into that section and retain his rate of pay.

6.7   Sexual Harassment

6.7.1   DEFINITION

One of the main historical difficulties with sexual harassment was finding an acceptable definition. Unless an offence is properly defined it is difficult, if not impossible, to prevent. There was no statutory definition prior to the 1998 Act. There were a number of acceptable definitions in use. Before examining the changes brought about by the 1998 Act it is worth looking at the development of the offence of sexual harassment. The early definitions ranged over the following:

— the creation of a hostile working environment by statements or conduct with a gender-based or sexual connotation;

— subjecting a person of the opposite sex to a detriment or less favourable treatment on grounds of sex may constitute sexual harassment;

— a single incident of sexual harassment, while it seems to contradict the dictionary definition of harassment which of itself suggests a continuing course of conduct, may amount to unlawful sexual harassment;

— for sexual harassment to be actionable, it must be sufficiently severe or pervasive to alter the conditions of the victim's employment and to create an abusive working environment.

The most frequently quoted definition in this jurisdiction was the decision of the Scottish Court of Session in *Strathclyde Regional Council v Porcelli* [1986] IRLR 134 in which the court stated:

'If the form of unfavourable treatment or any material part of it which is meted out included a significant element of a sexual character to which a man would not be vulnerable, the treatment is on grounds of sex.'

Some courts and tribunals favoured more direct and less subtle definitions such as:

— unnecessary touching or unwanted physical contact;

— suggestive remarks or other verbal abuse;

— leering at a person's body;

— compromising invitations or comments;

— demands for sexual favours; and

— physical assault.

A High Court judgment on sexual harassment, *Health Board v B C and the Labour Court* [1994] ELR 27 Costello J stated that sexual harassment is a term which, while it is in general use, 'has no well-established legal definition'. He then quoted the definition of sexual harassment adopted by the employers in that case in their staff handbook and commented that the definition appeared to him to 'reflect well the connotation of the phrase as it is used in everyday life in this country today'. The definition was:

' "Sexual harassment" is defined as unsolicited, unreciprocated behaviour of a sexual nature to which the recipient objects or could not reasonably be expected to consent and may include:

— unwanted physical contact;

— lewd or suggestive behaviour whether verbal or physical;

— sexually derogatory statements or sexually discriminatory remarks;

— the display of pornographic or sexually explicit material in the workplace.'

The European Commission drew up a code of practice on sexual harassment which defined sexual harassment as follows:

'Sexual harassment means unwanted conduct of a sexual nature, or other conduct based on sex affecting the dignity of women and men at work. This can include unwelcome physical, verbal or non-verbal conduct.

'A range of behaviour may be considered to constitute sexual harassment. The essential characteristic of sexual harassment is that it is unwanted by the recipient, that it is for each individual to determine what behaviour is acceptable to them and what they regard as offensive.'

The Commission definition did not include the requirement related to reasonableness as referred to by Costello J and which is relevant in the context of the definition that was contained in the 1998 Act referred to at **6.7.6.1** below.

6.7.2 EMPLOYMENT EQUALITY ACT, 1977

The Employment Equality Act, 1977, which set out to outlaw discrimination (other than in matters related to remuneration) on grounds of sex or marital status, provided at section 2(a) that for the purposes of the Act, discrimination shall be taken to occur:

'Where by reason of his sex, a person is treated less favourably than a person of the other sex.'

Section 3 of the Act provided that an employer:

'. . . shall not discriminate against an employee . . . in relation to . . . conditions of employment . . .

'A person shall be taken to discriminate against an employee . . . in relation to conditions of employment if he does not offer or afford to a person or class of person the same terms of employment, the same working conditions and the same treatment . . . as he offers or affords to another person or class of persons.'

The 1977 Act was repealed by the 1998 Act, which expressly defined sexual harassment. The 1998 definition was replaced by the 2004 Act.

6.7.3 LABOUR COURT APPROACH

The approach of the Labour Court prior to the 1998 Act was clear.

In Ireland's first reported case in 1985, *A Garage Proprietor v A Worker* EE02/85, the court held:

'Freedom from sexual harassment is a condition of work which an employee of either sex is entitled to expect. The court will accordingly treat any denial of that freedom as discrimination within the terms of the Employment Equality Act 1977.'

In a later decision in 1988, *A Company v A Worker* EE02/88, the court stated:

'Freedom from sexual harassment is a condition of work which an employee of either sex is entitled to expect. The court considers that employers have a duty to ensure their employees enjoy such working conditions.'

The EAT also held in *Allen v Dunnes Stores Ltd* [1996] ELR 203 that there was an onus on an employer to inform, educate and instruct its employees on sexual harassment and in that particular case the employer's failure to do so was fatal to the case which was actually brought by the alleged harasser. This case is dealt with in more detail at **6.7.5.2** below.

In *British Telecommunications plc v Williams* [1997] IRLR 668 a female employee claimed sexual harassment by a male manager who conducted an appraisal interview in what she claimed was an atmosphere she found sexually intimidating and claimed that the male manager was sexually aroused during the interview. The industrial tribunal rejected the claim that the manager was aroused but concluded that the absence of a third party, the proximity of the parties in the meeting, and the excessive length of the interview contributed to an atmosphere which the female employee was entitled to find sexually intimidating and held that there had been sexual harassment. On appeal the UK EAT overturned the tribunal decision on the basis that having found on the evidence that the manager was not sexually aroused, the only conclusion which the tribunal was entitled to reach was that the complaint was not proved. Either the manager was behaving inappropriately towards the applicant for sexual reasons or he was not. The UK EAT went on to state: 'if the reason why the Tribunal concluded that the interview was sexually intimidating was because there was no woman present and the interview took place in a confined space, their conclusion had to be rejected'. It is neither required by law nor desirable in practice that employers should see that male managers are chaperoned when dealing with female staff.

6.7.4 LEGAL ACTION

Victims of sexual harassment may seek legal remedy against either the harasser or the employer if they are different parties. They may also seek their remedy against both of them. The reality is that the harasser is unlikely to be a good 'mark' for a claim and the employer then becomes the focus of any such claim. That has given rise to problems, the main problem being one of vicarious liability which was not referred to at all in the Irish legislation until the 1998 Act came into force, is reasonably well defined at common law, and gives rise to all sorts of practical and policy considerations.

6.7.5 VICARIOUS LIABILITY

6.7.5.1 *Health Board v B C and the Labour Court*

The relevant provision of the 1998 Act relating to vicarious liability is covered at **6.9** below. The Labour Court approach is well set out in the case later dealt with by the High Court *Health Board v B C and the Labour Court* [1994] ELR 27, EE10/92. The facts of the case were that a female employee had been subjected to lewd and coarse comments from two male colleagues. One of the two was the prime mover in such conduct. She asked them on a number of occasions to stop or she would report them to a superior. Shortly after this, and before she reported anything, she found herself in a working area alone with the two men. One of the men physically restrained her while the other interfered with her. After a moment she was released. Later in the day she mentioned the incident to a colleague who advised her to tell a member of the supervisory staff. This she did the following morning and an immediate investigation of the incident was then held by the employer, which resulted in the suspension of one employee without pay for five weeks with a final warning regarding his future conduct, and the dismissal of the other.

The employer had issued policy guidelines to supervisory staff for dealing with sexual harassment. The claimant, through her trade union, made a claim against her employers under the provisions of the Employment Equality Act, 1977 on the basis that the single incident referred to constituted discrimination within the meaning of the Act. The union maintained that the issuing of guidelines solely to supervisory staff was insufficient. Staff generally were unaware of the procedure to follow if they were victims of sexual harassment. Employees were unaware of what is or is not acceptable in the working environment. As the employer had failed to take proactive steps to avert sexual harassment generally and the particular act of sexual harassment complained of, liability should lie on the employer and compensation was sought.

The employers responded that they had not discriminated against the employee within the meaning of the 1977 Act. The incident which occurred was not the responsibility of the employers. The perpetrators of the incident acted outside their duties and the employer could not and should not be held liable in those circumstances. The employer took every action possible when made aware of the complaint and felt it should not be blamed for something it was not aware of and did not condone. The Labour Court held against the employer. There was no dispute that the act complained of was a most serious case of sexual harassment, 'the persons responsible being two male employees'. The main issue the court addressed was the responsibility or liability of the employer for the actions of those two male employees. The court stated:

> 'The court wishes to state that in dealing with cases of sexual harassment it does and will take into account steps taken by employers to eliminate and prevent sexual harassment in the workplace. Whilst accepting that an employer cannot guarantee total prevention of harassment the court will look for and take note of what steps have been taken. The adoption of a code of practice, the adoption of a policy statement on the prevention of sexual harassment, the existence of guidelines as to how all staff should behave and the establishment of clear grievance procedures all constitute the kind of "reasonable steps" which employers should adopt and which will be accepted by the court as evidence of the employer's bona fides in this type of dispute. Clearly information about steps must be widely circulated in the place of work and information on the employer's attitude to acts of sexual harassment made available to all staff.
>
> 'In this case, the court does not consider that the action of the board in instructing supervisors and top management as to how complaints of this nature should be dealt with constituted "reasonable steps".'

The court stated its view that employers:

> '. . . have a duty to ensure that employees enjoy working conditions free from sexual harassment.'

The court held that in this particular case, as the employer had not taken reasonable steps to avoid sexual harassment, the employer was liable for the actions of the two employees concerned.

The health board appealed the Labour Court decision to the High Court on the grounds that the Labour Court had applied an incorrect test as to its liability for the actions of its employees. Costello J held that the Labour Court had not applied the correct test of employer liability. Costello J referred to the provisions of the Employment Equality Act, 1977 and noted that there was no express or implied provision in the Act that an employer should be automatically vicariously liable for the acts of employees and stated:

> 'I cannot envisage any employment . . . in respect of which a sexual assault could be regarded as so connected with it as to amount to an act within its scope.'

6.7.5.2   *Allen v Dunnes Stores Ltd*

In *Allen v Dunnes Stores Ltd* [1996] ELR 203 the claimant was employed as a security manager. His employment was terminated on grounds of gross misconduct. It was alleged that while carrying out a security check on staff bags he commented on the perfume worn by a shop assistant and attempted to kiss her. After an investigation the claimant was dismissed. The employers treated the actions of the claimant as sexual harassment. In the course of its judgment the EAT stated:

'Whether behaviour amounts to sexual harassment in a particular instance is determined from the point of view of the victim and what she/he regards as acceptable behaviour. Behaviour regarded as acceptable and innocent by the perpetrator, his colleagues and others may nonetheless be unacceptable to the victim and so could constitute sexual harassment. The Tribunal, by majority on this point, holds that this puts an onus on the employer to put in place a programme to inform, educate and instruct its employees on the issue of sexual harassment. The failure of the respondent to discharge that onus in this case was fatal.'

The tribunal went on to state:

'Sexual harassment is a broad category of offence and comprises conduct of varying degrees of seriousness. There should be a range of penalties commensurate with the seriousness of the offence which can be imposed with a particular instance.'

The EAT accepted the female employee's version of events but went on to hold that the ultimate sanction of dismissal of the claimant was disproportionate to the behaviour complained of and held the dismissal to be unfair and ordered the re-engagement of the claimant. Not only must an employer have a policy in place but must actively discourage sexual harassment, take firm but fair steps to deal with any allegation of sexual harassment and process such complaints in a structured, sympathetic and confidential manner. See also *An Employee v An Employer* [1993] ELR 75 where the employee claimed she was suffering ongoing harassment but that the employer took inadequate steps to prevent what was happening, was unsympathetic towards her and acted in an ineffective manner in respect of her.

6.7.5.3   *Reed v Stedman*

In *Reed and Bull Information Systems Ltd v Stedman* [1999] IRLR 299 Mr Reed and his employers appealed a decision of an industrial tribunal which held in favour of Ms Stedman arising from complaints she brought under the Sex Discrimination Act, 1975, claiming that she found working with Mr Reed to be intolerable. Ms Stedman had given evidence of comments, remarks and behaviour on the part of Mr Reed with sexual connotations which she found unacceptable. The industrial tribunal held that although no single incident was serious enough to be capable of constituting sexual harassment, there had been a series of events with a pervading sexual innuendo and sexist stance. While Ms Stedman had made no formal complaint she had complained to other members of staff and the personnel department was aware of a deterioration in her health. The tribunal took the view that there should have been an investigation into the cause of the illness and the complaints that had been made, even though the complaints were not made directly to the employer through its personnel department. The tribunal went on to hold that by failing to investigate, the employers were in breach of contract. That decision was appealed to the UK EAT which dismissed the appeal. The UK EAT was satisfied that there was a course of conduct which amounted to sexual harassment, which in turn forced Ms Stedman to leave her employment which amounted to a constructive dismissal and accordingly was an act of discrimination within the meaning of the Sex Discrimination Act.

In its judgment the UK EAT commented on the behaviour of Mr Reed as follows:

'There was a course of conduct which amounted to sexual harassment. The manager knew his actions which contained a sexual overtone were unwanted, yet he continued to make comments which contained sexual innuendo and to tell sexual jokes in the applicant's presence.'

On the employer's conduct or reaction to what was going on in its employment the UK EAT stated:

'Since the applicant had made complaints to other colleagues at work it was incumbent on the employers to investigate the matter and their failure to investigate was enough to justify a finding of breach of trust and confidence.'

6.7.6 SEXUAL HARASSMENT IN THE 1998 AND 2004 ACTS

6.7.6.1 Definition

Sexual harassment was defined at length in section 23 of the 1998 Act which prohibited harassment by fellow employees, the employer or a client, customer or other business contact of the employer. Sexual harassment was defined in part in section 23(3) of the 1998 Act as being:

(a)   any act of physical intimacy;

(b)   any express request for sexual favours;

(c)   any other act or conduct including spoken words, gestures or the production, display or circulation of written words, pictures or other material.

If the act, request or conduct is unwelcome and could reasonably be regarded as sexually, or otherwise on the gender ground, offensive, humiliating or intimidating it will constitute sexual harassment.

The 2004 Act replaced this part of the definition with a new section 14A defining harassment and sexual harassment as:

'*[A]ny form of unwanted conduct related to any of the discriminatory grounds, and. . . . references to sexual harassment are to any form of unwanted verbal, non-verbal or physical conduct of a sexual nature, being conduct which in either case has the purpose or effect of violating a person's dignity and creating an intimidating, hostile, degrading, humiliating or offensive environment for the person.*'

The Act further states that '*such unwanted conduct may consist of acts, requests, spoken words, gestures or the production, display or circulation of written words, pictures or other material*'.

The 2004 Act amendments do not alter the provisions of the definition that include non-employees. Under the 1998 and 2004 Acts harassment may occur in the workplace, otherwise in the course of employment or outside the workplace and the course of employment where the employee may reasonably anticipate being treated differently in the workplace or in the course of employment as a result of accepting or rejecting the harassment.

6.7.6.2 Defences

The 1998 and 2004 Acts provide a defence for employers if they can prove that they took such steps as were reasonably practicable to prevent the harassment and 'if and so far as any such treatment has occurred to reverse the effects of it' and to prevent fellow employees or others from sexually harassing the complainant.

In relation to the defence of taking 'such steps as were reasonably practicable' provided in section 15(3) of the 1998 Act the UK EAT held in *Balgobin v London Borough of Tower Hamlets* [1987] IRLR 401 that the employers had proved a defence to acts of sexual harassment committed by their employee where they had shown that the allegations had not been made known to management, that there was proper and adequate staff supervision, and that the employers had made known their policy of equal opportunities.

The Labour Court considered the issue in the case of *A Hospital v An Appellant* AEE/02/6 (No 29). The Labour Court divided the case into stages—

(a)   the period before the employer knew of the alleged harassment;

(b) the period after the victim informed her employer of the alleged harassment but would not name her alleged harasser; and

(c) the period after she named her harasser.

The Labour Court found against the employer ultimately in respect of stage (2) but, in respect of period at (1) above, the fact that the employer both had a policy on sexual harassment in place and had sent the alleged harasser on the course constituted sufficient steps to allow the employer to avail of the defence that it had taken such steps as were reasonably practicable. The Labour Court held that the mere existence of a policy without further proactive steps would be insufficient to make out the defence.

6.7.6.3 Who may commit an act of sexual harassment

It may be seen from the statutory provisions that the harassment may be carried out by a number of persons and not just fellow employees. It may include non-employees, as in *2 Female Claimants v Boys' Secondary School* DEC-E 2001–005, where an equality officer held that a board of management of a school may be vicariously liable for sexual harassment of teachers by pupils. That is an express statement which is supportive of the position taken by the Labour Court under the 1977 Act which was silent on the specific issue of sexual harassment and obviously silent on the extent of the employer's liability for various parties. Despite these shortcomings of the 1977 Act the Labour Court had held in *A Worker v A Company* [1992] ELR 40, in circumstances where it was claimed that an outsider who was not an employee of the company but had been granted permission to use the company premises and facilities for his own business purposes, had subjected a female employee to offensive conduct of a sexual nature. In holding for the claimant and awarding her compensation the Labour Court held inter alia:

'The worker was objected to sexual harassment while in the employment of the company. It was irrelevant that the perpetrator of the harassment was not an employee of the company since he was on the company premises with the agreement of the employer who was in a position to protect the worker. In failing to protect the worker against the harassment the employer had, in effect imposed discriminatory conditions of employment on the worker.'

In *2 Female Claimants v Boys' Secondary School* it was held that the board of management of a secondary school was clearly responsible for the disciplinary and working environment at the school and therefore in a position to exercise control over the behaviour of the pupils—in this case, the sexual harassment of teachers by pupils. The quality officer considered the disciplinary action taken by management against the perpetrators of the acts of sexual harassment and, in this particular case, found that the disciplinary action was what might reasonably be expected in the circumstances of the individual cases. However, the equality officer held that the school had victimised the two teachers because they had complained about the sexual harassment to the Labour Court. He recommended that the school make compensatory payments of £7,000 and £12,000, respectively, to the teachers.

As referred to at **7.3** above the US Supreme Court in two similar decisions *Burlington Industries Inc v Ellerth* [1997] and *Faragher v Boca Raton* confirmed that an employer effectively must have a policy against sexual harassment in order to show that it meets the present-day standards of provision of a safe system of work and place of work free of sexual harassment.

6.7.6.4 Code of Practice

The 1998 and 2004 Act do not define the concept of 'reasonably practicable'. SI 78/2002 introduced the Code of Practice on sexual harassment and harassment at work, an Equality Authority Code of Practice. Section 56 of the 1998 Act, amended by section 39 of the Equal Status Act, provides that the Code of Practice may be taken into account in deciding legal proceedings under the Acts. The Code is relevant to determining vicarious liability and reasonable practicability and has been taken into account in many decisions of equality officers and the Labour Court on sexual harassment. This Code of Practice is available on the Equality Authority's website, www.equality.ie.

The introduction to the Code sets outs the aims, status, application and adaptation of a code and refers to equality of opportunity. It notes that policies on sexual harassment and harassment at work would be more effective when operated in conjunction with similar policies on equal opportunities and health and safety. There are two relevant codes on bullying, which falls within the remit of health and safety and not equality law, one from the Labour Relations Commission and one from the Health and Safety Authority.

The definition of sexual harassment and harassment in the Code of Practice are those contained in the 1998 Act, which have since been amended by the 2004 Act. The Code of Practice has not been amended to reflect the changes, but can be used, substituting the 2004 definitions.

6.8 Harassment other than Sexual Harassment

The 1998 Act also seeks to outlaw harassment which occurs by reason of or as a result of the relevant characteristics which form the basis of the 1998 Act as detailed below. Harassment as defined may be carried on by a fellow employee, the employer, client, customer or other business contact and the circumstances of the harassment are such that the employer ought reasonably to have taken steps to prevent it. Harassment, other than sexual harassment, was defined in section 32 of the 1998 Act as being:

'. . . any act or conduct . . . including spoken words, gestures or the production, display or circulation of written words, pictures or other material, constitutes harassment . . . if the action or other conduct is unwelcome . . . and could reasonably be regarded in relation to the relevant characteristic [of the person harassed] as offensive, humiliating or intimidating.'

The new section 14A of the 1998 and 2004 Acts, inserted by the 2004 Act, deals with harassment other than sexual harassment and defines it at **6.7.6.1** above

6.9 Vicarious Liability under the 1998 Act

Section 15 of the 1998 Act deals with vicarious liability of the employer as follows:

'(1) *Anything done by a person in the course of his/her employment shall . . . be treated for the purposes of the Act as done also by that person's employer, whether or not it was done with the employer's knowledge or approval.*

(2) *Anything done by a person as agent for another person with the authority (whether express or implied and whether precedent or subsequent) of that other person shall be treated for the purposes of this Act as done also by that other person.*

(3) *In proceedings brought under this Act against an employer in respect of an act alleged to have been done by an employee of the employer it shall be a defence for the employer to prove that the employer took such steps as were reasonably practicable to prevent the employee—*

(a) *from doing that act; or*

(b) *from doing in the course of his employment acts of that description.'*

It is instructive to look at the case law which existed prior to 18 October 1999, when the 1998 Act took effect.

232

In *Health Board v B C* [1994] ELR 27, referred to at **6.7.5.1** above, Costello J was faced with a sexual assault that was in itself one of the more extreme forms of sexual harassment one may encounter. It was so extreme that Costello J had no difficulty in drawing a dividing line between the employer and the employee over which liability did not pass. The 1998 Act does not impose automatic vicarious liability given that there is a saver in section 15(3) as referred to above. That saver, however, requires the employer to show that he took such steps 'as were reasonably practicable'. In the *Health Board* case no steps were needed by the employer. The act spoke for itself. It was so serious and savage as to be totally unconnected with the employment. It appears now, however, that it is a matter for employers to specify that the act, no matter how extreme, must not occur before the saver referred to can be effective.

Vicarious liability is inferred where the conduct complained of was done by a person 'in the course of his or her employment'. The leading UK case on vicarious liability in sex or racial discrimination is *Jones v Tower Boot Co* [1997] IRLR 168. In that case the UK Court of Appeal stated that the words 'in the course of employment' should be interpreted in the sense in which they are employed in everyday speech and not restrictively by reference to the principles laid down by case law for establishing an employer's vicarious liability for the torts committed by an employee. The court held the employer to be vicariously liable for harassment of a black employee by his white colleagues, despite the fact that the harassment culminated in the branding of the black employee with hot metal, which was clearly a criminal act. The UK Court of Appeal held that to find otherwise would defeat the purpose of anti-discrimination laws by finding that the more serious the harassment the less likely an employer was to be held liable and an employee was to succeed in a discrimination claim. This contrasts with Costello J's finding in the *Health Board* case.

The UK Court of Appeal went on to state in *Waters v Commissioner of Police of the Metropolis* [1997]IRLR 589 that in applying the *Tower Boot* test no tribunal could find that an alleged sexual assault by a male police constable on a female police constable was committed in the 'course of employment' where both parties were off duty at the time of the alleged offence and the man was a visitor to the woman's room at a time and in circumstances which placed them in no different position from that which would have applied if they had been social acquaintances only with no working connections.

A later UK police case of *Chief Constable of Lincolnshire Police v Stubbs* [1999] IRLR 81 clarified the 'course of employment'.

It was held that where events or circumstances may be described as 'extensions of the workplace' they may come within the definition of course of employment. A distinction was drawn between chance meetings and circumstances closely related to work. The Chief Constable was held liable for two acts of harassment of one employee by another, one of which occurred during a routine visit to a pub after work and one of which occurred during a leaving party for a fellow employee. A social setting does not therefore mean that an employer is not liable for the actions of employees.

The Labour Court approach to vicarious liability under the 1998 Act can be seen in the case of *A Hospital v An Appellant* cited above at **6.7.6.2** and could be interpreted as demonstrating a willingness to find employers vicariously liable for the acts of their employees.

However, in *Ms ON v An Insurance Company* DEC-E2004/052, the Equality Tribunal found that the complainant was sexually harassed by a colleague in the nightclub after a pub quiz held by her employer's social club but that she was not sexually harassed in the course of her employment. The equality officer gave detailed consideration to the circumstances leading to the presence of the employee and the harasser in the nightclub. The equality officer noted that the complainant did not attend the nightclub for the purpose of her work. The equality officer did not consider the financial sponsorship by an employer at a social event where sexual harassment occurs sufficient in itself, and in the absence of other factors, to bring an act of sexual harassment within the course of employment.

The employer could still have been liable for the harassment within the statutory definition if it could reasonably have been anticipated that the complainant would be treated differently in the workplace or otherwise in the course of her employment because she rejected the harassment, even though the harassment itself was not in the workplace or in the course of employment. The equality officer considered this issue and noted that a colleague tried to deal with the matter helpfully on the night of the incident. The equality officer further noted that the company took the complaint seriously and made every effort to investigate the matter and dealt with within the confines of the informal procedures selected by the complainant. The equality officer noted that an apology from the harasser and a cover letter from the employer had been put on the complainant's file. In view of these facts, the equality officer did not consider that it could be reasonably be anticipated that the complainant would be treated differently as a result of having rejected the harassment.

The Equality Tribunal's decision shows the importance of employers acting promptly and properly in investigating complaints of harassment, even where the behaviour alleged did not take place in the workplace or in the course of employment. Failure to act is likely to result in a finding of harassment against the employer, despite the lack of connection between the harassment and the employment of the parties.

6.10 Positive Action

6.10.1 ACTION PERMITTED BY 1998 AND 2004 ACTS

Section 24(1) of the 1998 Act, amended, provides that the provisions of the Act are without prejudice to measures:

'(a) *maintained or adopted with a view to ensuring full equality in practice between men and women in their employments, and*

(b) *providing for specific advantages so as—*
   (i) *to make it easier for an under-represented sex to pursue a vocational activity, or*
   (ii) *to prevent or compensate for disadvantages in professional careers.'*

This 1998 Act version of section 24(1) was a very general provision and the amended provision above is more specific and encompasses all of the grounds. Furthermore, the 2004 Act allows for specific advantages for an under-represented sex, which could for example include men in vocational activities such as secretarial work and nursing. The provisions in respect of positive action on the non-gender grounds are contained in the section 33 of the 2004 Act.

Section 33 allows for measures maintained or adopted with a view to ensuring full equality in practice between employees, being measures:

(a) to prevent or compensate for disadvantages linked to any of the discriminatory grounds (other than the gender ground);

(b) to protect the health or safety at work of persons with a disability; or

(c) to create or maintain facilities for safeguarding or promoting the integration.

In *A Complainant v A Company* DEC-E2002–014, an equality officer held against a company in a claim of discrimination on the grounds of gender and age arising from harassment of the complainant by a colleague and the respondent's failure to act on her complaints and failure to provide her with a workplace free from harassment. The complainant, a young woman, alleged that an older male colleague who reported to her was hostile and extremely aggressive in his manner towards her. She alleged that he told her on many occasions that it would be wise for her to leave him alone and not interfere with his work, but that she could not do this because of the nature of her job. She said that he repeatedly told her that she was only a young foolish girl, more inexperienced than he. The equality officer found that the treatment to which the complainant was subjected constituted harassment on both the gender and age grounds. The equality officer held that the nature of the verbal abuse was intended to intimidate the complainant, and that it was offensive and humiliating to her. On that basis the equality officer found that it constituted harassment. The equality officer found that the company failed to adequately investigate the complaints made by the complainant and that they failed to put in place adequate systems to deal with possible future complaints of that nature. The equality officer ordered the respondent to pay monetary compensation for the stress suffered as a result of the harassment, to draft an equality policy and to draft a Code of Practice on harassment (including sexual harassment), which should be made available to all staff members.

6.10.2 ACTION PERMITTED BY EQUAL TREATMENT DIRECTIVE

The status of positive discrimination under the Equal Treatment Directive 76/207 was considered by the ECJ in *Marschall v Land Nordrhein-Westfalen* [1998] IRLR 39, where the civil service law of the region in question provided that where 'there are fewer women than men in the particular higher grade post in the career bracket, women are to be given priority for promotion in the event of equal suitability, competence and professional performance, unless reasons specific to an individual [male] candidate tilt the balance in his favour'.

Mr Marschall applied for a promotion but failed on the basis that fewer women than men were employed in the relevant post for which he had applied and that an equally qualified woman was to be appointed to the position. The ECJ was asked to consider whether Directive 76/207 allowed for positive discrimination. The court in its judgment held inter alia:

'A national rule which, in a case where there are fewer women than men at the level of the relevant post in sectors of the public service and both female and male candidates for the post are equally qualified in terms of their suitability, competence and professional performance, requires that priority be given to the promotion of female candidates unless reasons specific to an individual male candidate tilt the balance in his favour is not precluded by . . . Directive 76/207 . . . on the implementation of the principle of equal treatment for men and women as regards access to employment, vocational training and promotion and working conditions provided that:
— in each individual case the rule provides for male candidates who are as equally qualified as the female candidates a guarantee that the candidatures will be the subject of an objective assessment which will take account of all criteria specific to the candidates and will override the priority accorded to female candidates where one or more of those criteria tilts the balance in favour of the male candidate and;
— such criteria are not such as to discriminate against the female candidates.'

The court held therefore in favour of the rule under consideration and added that such a rule, since it does not guarantee absolute and unconditional priority to women, does not go beyond the limits of Article 2(4) of the Directive. The court distinguished an apparently contradictory decision in an earlier case, *Kalanke v Freie Hansestadt Bremen* [1995] IRLR 660.

Article 2(1) of the Directive provides:

'For the purposes of the following provisions the principle of equal treatment shall mean that there shall be no discrimination whatsoever on grounds of sex either directly or indirectly by reference in particular to marital or family status.'

Article 2(4) provides:

> 'This Directive shall be without prejudice to measures to promote equal opportunity for men and women in particular by removing existing inequalities which affect women's opportunities in the areas referred to in Article 1(1).'

In *Kalanke v Freie Hansestadt Bremen* the rule at issue provided that women who had the same qualifications as men, applying for the same post were to be given priority in sectors where they were under-represented and that there was under-representation if women did not make up at least half of the staff in the relevant pay bracket in the relevant personnel group within a department. There was no exception built into the provision.

Mr Kalanke and a female colleague were shortlisted for promotion. It was accepted that they were equally qualified for the post and that women were under-represented in the relevant sector. The national rule accordingly required the post to be offered to the female. Mr Kalanke challenged the operation of the rule. In its decision the ECJ stated that the rule was contrary to Article 2(1). It went on to examine whether the rule was permissible under Article 2(4). The court concluded that national rules which guaranteed women absolute and unconditional priority for appointment or promotion went beyond promoting equal opportunities and overstepped the limits of the exception allowed for in Article 2(4) of the Directive.

In *Marschall*, however, the court very much fine-tuned its decision in *Kalanke* and reached an apparently different conclusion to the effect that the rule which defeated Mr Marschall's entitlement to the post was not precluded either by Article 2(1) or 2(4).

6.11 Exemptions

6.11.1 INTRODUCTION

Employers may lawfully discriminate in certain circumstances as set out in the 1998 and 2004 Acts.

Many of the new grounds of non-discrimination listed in the 1998 Act, section 6 were already unfair grounds for dismissing an employee under the Unfair Dismissals (Amendment) Act, 1993. The 1998 Act represented the first attempt to prohibit such types of discrimination in relation to access to and conditions of employment. The prohibitions on discrimination have many specific exemptions throughout the Acts and some of the prohibitions have been watered down.

6.11.2 SEXUAL ORIENTATION

Section 16(5) provides as follows:

> 'Nothing in this Act shall be construed as requiring an employer to recruit, retain in employ mentor promote an individual if the employer is aware, on the basis of a criminal conviction of the individual or other reliable information, that the individual engages, or has a propensity to engage, in any form of sexual behaviour which is unlawful.'

Section 16(6) goes on to say that subsection (5) applies in particular where the employment concerned involves access to minors or to other persons who are vulnerable. Although drafted with the laudable aim of protecting children against paedophilia, section 16(4) may be used to avoid the prohibition on discrimination on grounds of sexual orientation, particularly as no definition of 'reliable information' is given. It is, however, a drastic improvement on the provisions of section 16(4) of the 1996 Bill which provided that an employer should not be obliged to recruit or retain in employment an individual if the employer was aware:

'On the basis of a criminal conviction of the individual or other reliable information, that the individual engages, or has a propensity to engage in any form of sexual behaviour to which the employer's clients, customers or any other business contact (a) might be at risk of exposure; or (b) might reasonably object.'

6.11.3 EXCEPTIONS RELATED TO THE FAMILY, AGE OR DISABILITY

Section 34(1) provides that nothing in Part II or IV of the 1998 Acts shall, in relation to the discriminatory grounds other than gender, make it unlawful for an employer to provide:

(a) a benefit to an employee in respect of events related to members of the employee's family or any description of those members;

(b) a benefit to or in respect of a person as a member of an employee's family;

(c) a benefit to an employee on or by reference to an event occasioning a change in the marital status of the employee; or

(d) to an employee who has family status a benefit intended directly to provide or assist in the provision, during working hours, of care for a person for whom the employee has responsibility as in the definition of family status.

Certain benefits are expressly protected from being unlawful, such as benefits for members of an employee's family or a benefit to an employee upon his or her marriage. Such benefit should not, however, be conferred in a way that would discriminate between persons whose circumstances are not materially different on the basis of one of the prohibited grounds of discrimination.

Section 34(3), as amended by the 2004 Act, provides that, in an occupational benefits scheme, it shall not constitute discrimination on the age ground for an employer:

(a) to fix ages for admission to such a scheme or for entitlement to benefits under it;

(b) to fix different such ages for all employees or a category of employees;

(c) to use, in the context of such a scheme, age criteria in actuarial calculations; or

(d) to provide different rates of severance payment for different employees or groups or categories of employees, being rates based on or taking into account the period between the age of an employee on leaving the employment and his or her compulsory retirement age, provided that that does not constitute discrimination on the gender ground.

Maximum ages for recruitment are expressly allowed by section 34(5) and again the cost implications are cited as a justification for permitting what would otherwise be unlawful discrimination.

Section 34(5)(b) allows an employer to take into account (in setting a maximum age for recruitment) the fact that there may need to be a reasonable period of time prior to retirement age during which the recruit will be effective in that job. Section 34(5)(a) also allows the employer to take into account any period of time involved in training a recruit to a standard at which the recruit will be effective in that job. This may be interpreted as implying that older people will take longer to train; however, it is unlikely that an employer would succeed in such an argument and more likely to be interpreted by reference to the normal training period for the job in question. Section 34(7) also provides that it shall not constitute discrimination on grounds of age for an employer to provide different rates of remuneration, or different terms and conditions of employment if the difference is based on the relevant seniority of the staff in question. Section 34(7A), inserted by the 2004 Act, allows for a term in a collective agreement determining seniority by reference to the relative ages of employees on their entry to the post or employment in question.

6.11.4 SPECIAL PROVISIONS FOR EMPLOYEES WITH DISABILITIES

Section 16(3), as amended by the 2004 Act, provides that an employee is fully capable of undertaking employment duties if they would be so fully capable of undertaking those duties upon the employer providing reasonable accommodation (now referred to 'appropriate measures'). Appropriate measures must be taken by the employer unless the measures would impose a disproportionate burden on the employer, having regard to (i) the financial and other costs entailed, (ii) the scale and financial resources of the employer's business, and (iii) the possibility of obtaining public funding or other assistance.

Section 35(1), as amended, allows for a particular rate of remuneration for work of a particular description to be paid to a person with a disability if, by reason of the disability, the amount of that work done by the employee during a particular period is less than the amount of similar work done, or which could reasonably be expected to be done, during that period by an employee without the disability.

6.11.5 SPECIAL EXEMPTIONS FOR STATE EMPLOYEES

Section 36 allows for a series of exemptions for many State employees in relation to residence, citizenship or proficiency in the Irish language. Section 37, as amended by the 2004 Act, provides an extremely broad exemption (on the age or disability grounds) to the Army, Gardaí or the prison services as a whole.

6.11.6 RELIGIOUS ETHOS

Section 37(1) permits discrimination by a religious, educational or medical institution established for a religious purpose, where it is reasonable to do so in order to maintain the religious ethos of the institution or is reasonably necessary in order to avoid the undermining of that ethos. While section 37(1)(a) appears to indicate that discrimination may only take place on the religion ground, paragraph (b) of that subsection also provides that it shall not be discriminatory for such a religious, educational or medical institution to take action which is reasonably necessary to prevent an employee or prospective employee from undermining the religious ethos of the institution.

6.12 Institutions

6.12.1 EQUALITY AUTHORITY

The 1998 Act established new institutions. It established the Office of the Director of Equality Investigations, now the Equality Tribunal. The Director carries out a quasi-judicial function and investigates and decides claims under Acts personally or by delegation to equality officers. Claims may be mediated on a voluntary basis. The Director may assist the Circuit Court at the court's request.

The 1998 Act replaced the Employment Equality Agency with the Equality Tribunal, which continued the agency's functions.

6.12.2   INFORMATION

The 1998 Act states that any person who considers he has been discriminated against must be provided with certain information material to the proposed claim. The Employment Equality Act, 1998 (Section 76 Right to Information) Regulations, 1999, SI 321/1999 came into effect on the same day as the Act. They prescribe a questionnaire form to be used to obtain material information to decide whether to bring a claim or to assist in formulating and presenting a case. The reply form is also prescribed. There is no obligation on an employer to reply to the questionnaire. No time is laid down for replying to the questionnaire. Inferences may be drawn from a failure to reply, to reply adequately or for a false or misleading reply.

There are provisions within section 76 to protect confidential information and to ensure that references and testimonials can be kept confidential.

6.12.3   ENFORCEMENT AND REMEDIES

6.12.3.1   Routes for seeking redress

The equality officers and the Labour Court continue their existing roles under the 1998 Act. Prior to the 2004 Act, all claims except those brought directly to the Circuit Court began at Equality Tribunal, other than those involving dismissals. Dismissal cases were heard by the Labour Court at first instance. The 2004 Act amendments provide for all cases, including dismissals, to commence before the Equality Tribunal, with an appeal for a full rehearing to the Labour Court, subject to the gender provisions referred to below.

The Equality Tribunal investigates complaints which are not resolved by mediation and gives a decision. The decision may be appealed to the Labour Court within 42 days of its issue. The Act provides quite extensive investigation powers for the Director and the Labour Court to secure information, interview relevant people and secure documentary evidence.

In cases of gender discrimination only, a claimant may bypass the Director and Labour Court and refer the matter directly to the Circuit Court. It seems that this provision, at section 77(3), follows the ECJ decision in *Marshall v Southampton Area Health Authority (No 2)* [1993] ECR I–4367. In that case the court held that a cap on the potential award for sex discrimination was inconsistent with the right to an effective judicial process pursuant to Article 6 of the Equal Treatment Directive. When gender discrimination cases are referred directly to the Circuit Court there is now no ceiling on the award that may be made by the court and section 82(3) allows that the award may exceed the normal civil jurisdiction of the Circuit Court. In cases not referred directly to the Circuit Court the compensation available under the legislation is as follows:

(a)   in an equal pay case the ordering of equal pay and maximum arrears up to equal pay for the preceding three years; and

(b)   in other cases the ordering of equal treatment or ending of the discrimination and compensation of a sum up to a maximum of two years' pay or, where the person was not in receipt of remuneration of up to €12,700.

Not many cases on the grounds of gender or sexual harassment have been referred directly to the Circuit Court, perhaps due to an uncertainty as to how such matters will be treated by the courts, in comparison to the Equality Tribunal and Labour Court, who deal with such matters on a daily basis. Judgment was given by the Circuit Court in *Barbara Atkins v Hugh Carty and others* [2005] 16 ELR 1, a sexual harassment matter referred directly to the Circuit Court. In that matter, the plaintiff was sexually harassed by an independent contractor, who provided an accountancy services, to the firm where she was employed as a legal accountant. The court held that the plaintiff had suffered a serious case of sexual harassment and that the defendant could not plead immunity from their failure to fulfil their statutory obligation to provide a safe place of work, a safe system of work and a safe working environment simply because the plaintiff failed to make a complaint. The court held that there were no adequate procedures in place and this rendered the defendant liable. The court further held that the defendant was correctly before the court as they were responsible for the actions of the independent contractor, and further that their purported investigation of a complaint was so flawed that it significantly exacerbated the problems for the plaintiff. The judge reduced the substantial award of damages made to the plaintiff by 25 per cent on the basis of a finding of contributory negligence, on account of the plaintiff being aware for a two-year period prior to making a complaint that she was being sexually harassed in the legal sense.

This is an interesting finding in circumstances where the defendant had no policy in place in respect of sexual harassment and the plaintiff's knowledge in respect of this matter arose only from information supplied to her by her husband about the sexual harassment policy that applied in his employment.

6.12.3.2 Awards of compensation

Equality officers and the Labour Court took it upon themselves under the 1977 Act in particular to award compensation for hurt feelings even though there was no specific provision in the legislation for them to do so. Section 82 of the 1998 and 2004 Acts provides for full redress referred to above. The section provides that the Director of the Equality Tribunal and the Labour Court may make:

> '... an Order for compensation for the effects of acts of discrimination or victimisation which occurred not earlier than six years before the date of the referral of the case.'

The ceiling on such an award of compensation is, for an employed person, the maximum of two years' remuneration referred to above, or for a person not in remuneration, €12,700. No guidance is given as to the level at which compensation might be ordered. Existing case law gives some indication as to what type of awards might be expected.

Some guidance was given by the UK EAT in *Armitage, Marsden and HM Prison Service v Johnson* [1997] IRLR 162. The awards for discrimination in the UK have traditionally been higher than in Ireland. Mr Johnson had been subjected to an ongoing campaign of racial discrimination described by the industrial tribunal as 'appalling treatment'. His complaint of race discrimination against two prison officers and the prison service was upheld and he was awarded £28,500 compensation including £20,000 for injury to feelings reflecting the fact that the campaign had gone on for some 18 months, and £7,500 aggravated damages against his employers for failure to properly deal with his complaints. £500 for injury to feelings was also awarded against both of the two prison officers personally for their victimisation and aiding the employer to discriminate.

6.12.3.3 Assessing injury to feelings

The EAT in upholding the award set out what it considered were the relevant principles for assessing awards for injury to feelings for unlawful discrimination as follows.

(1) Awards for injury to feelings are compensatory. They should be just to both parties. They should compensate fully without punishing the tortfeasor. Feelings of indignation of the tortfeasor's conduct should not be allowed to inflate the award.

(2) Awards should not be too low as that would diminish respect for the policy of the anti-discrimination legislation. Society has condemned discrimination and awards must ensure that it is seen to be wrong. On the other hand awards should be restrained, as excessive awards could be seen as the way of untaxed riches.

(3)   Awards should bear some broad general similarity to the range of awards in personal injury cases. This should be done by reference to the whole range of such awards, rather than to any particular type of award.

(4)   In exercising their discretion in assessing a sum, tribunals should remind themselves of the value in everyday life of the sum they have in mind. This may be done by reference to purchasing power or by reference to earnings.

(5)   Tribunals should bear in mind the need for public respect for the level of awards made.

In *Rotunda Hospital and the Mater Hospital v Gleeson* BC9/99, DEE003, where a female doctor was not appointed to the position of consultant obstetrician/gynaecologist, an award of £50,000 was made in favour of the claimant. The claimant had been asked discriminatory questions which had not been asked of the male candidates and an offensive comment of 'sink the sisters' had been made to her. The Labour Court made reference to the fact that only two of the eight interviewers were female, as one of the matters which had led them to make a finding of discrimination on the grounds of gender. The claimant had been unsuccessful before an equality officer.

6.12.4   BURDEN OF PROOF

Section 85A of the 1998 and 2004 Acts provides that where, in any proceedings, facts are established by or on behalf of a complainant from which it may be presumed that there has been discrimination against him or her, it is for the respondent to prove the contrary.

This provision explains the test usually described as a 'prima facie' case, the test de facto adopted by equality officers and the Labour Court prior to the enactment of the 2004 Act.

6.13   Impact of the 1998 and 2004 Acts

6.13.1   INTRODUCTION

The main impact of the 1998 Act since its commencement has been to increase awareness and to seek to eliminate wider areas of discrimination than had hitherto been the case. Indirect discrimination must now come into sharper focus not just because there is now a statutory definition but because the grounds upon which discrimination may now occur are considerably wider than they were.

6.13.2   RECRUITMENT AND PROMOTION

Practice in relation to the profile of a successful candidate, advertising the job and conducting interviews has had to change radically. Who is considered to be the 'best' candidate? The youngest, physically fittest individual with no family responsibilities? Not any longer. Focusing on the person who performed best at interview and is the most likely candidate is no longer sufficient. Each candidate rejected must be given thought. What is the reason for the rejection? Rejection at different stages, e.g. application, shortlisting, first, second or subsequent interviews, will all have to be considered in detail and non-discriminatory reasons relied on by the employer in rejecting each candidate.

6.13.3 TERMS, CONDITIONS AND BENEFITS

Terms, conditions and benefits will have to be examined to ensure that they do not directly or indirectly discriminate.

6.13.4 HARASSMENT POLICIES

Are policies on harassment and sexual harassment in place and enforced, given prominence and included in job offers? If a problem arises is the employer's paperwork in order and sufficiently well operated to ensure that the available defences under the Acts can be relied on? Are employees trained in respect of the policies?

6.13.5 DISCRIMINATION POLICIES

Are policies against discrimination or unequal treatment in place covering gender, marital status, family status, sexual orientation, religion, age, disability, race and membership of the traveller community? Are these policies enforced, communicated and part of employee training?

6.13.6 POSITIVE ACTION

What positive action has the employer taken to carry out an equality audit in regard to the EU code of practice on equal pay and what steps has the employer taken to ensure that pay and other discrimination has not arisen?

CHAPTER 7

RESTRAINING DISMISSALS: INJUNCTIONS AND THE CONTRACT OF EMPLOYMENT

7.1   Introduction

An injunction is an order restraining the person to whom it is directed from carrying out a specified act or requiring him to perform such an act. At common law the usual remedy where a plaintiff succeeded in his action was an award of damages. This form of relief was often inadequate or inappropriate and equity supplemented the legal remedies available by developing alternative types of remedy such as the injunction. The Rules of the Superior Courts provide at Order 50 Rule 6 (1) that:

> '. . . the court may grant an injunction . . . by an interlocutory order in all cases in which it appears to the court to be just or convenient so to do.'

Rule 6(2) provides that:

> 'Any such order may be made either unconditionally or upon such terms and conditions as the court thinks just.'

In the area of employment law the application of the injunction has increased and developed since the granting of the first Irish labour law injunction just over twenty years ago—*Fennelly v Assicurazioni Generali Spa & Another* [1985] 3 ILT 73. Since the *Fennelly* decision, the courts have on many occasions been requested to grant injunctive relief where a plaintiff employee claims to have been wrongfully dismissed.

Its application is not however confined to instances where there is a threatened or actual dismissal. The courts have granted injunctive relief to employees in a range of circumstances that are distinguishable from the anti-dismissal injunctive relief which is generally sought. By way of example, Kelly J ordered the employer to pay sick pay in *Mullarkey v Irish National Stud Company Ltd* [2004] ELR 172; see also *Rooney v Kilkenny* [2001] ELR 129. O'Sullivan J granted an order prohibiting the advertising of a position which the plaintiff claimed overlapped with his position in *Harkins v Shannon Foynes Port Company* [2001] ELR 75; see also *Garrahy v Bord na gCon* [2003] ELR 274. Macken J granted an order bringing to an end a suspension in *Martin v The Nationwide Building Society* [1999] ELR 241.

The development of the employment injunction must be reviewed against the general rule that a court will not order specific performance of a contract of personal service. The rationale of the rule has its basis in the principle that equity will not make an order the performance of which it cannot effectively supervise or where performance would require constant supervision. In order to appreciate the significance of the development of the employment injunction it is essential to have an understanding of the classification and the general rules governing the granting of injunctions.

7.2   Classification of Injunctions

The most common form of injunction is the one that seeks to restrain a party from doing a particular act. This is known as a prohibitory injunction. Another type is a mandatory injunction which imposes obligations on a party to take certain actions.

Injunctions can also be classified according to when they are sought. An interim or interlocutory injunction is sought to preserve the status quo in a dispute until such time as the action can be tried. An interim injunction is obtained for a limited period, usually a matter of days, and will have effect only until a further order is made. It is often, although not invariably, sought on an ex parte basis. An ex parte application will be made where a matter is particularly urgent. A plaintiff may apply for an order without the other side being present and/or having received notice of the application. The interim order will generally continue until the next motion day when the defendant will have the opportunity of putting forward his or her side of the case. Where injunctive relief is granted on an ex parte basis, it is purely on an interim basis and the successful applicant is then obliged to seek an interlocutory injunction on notice to the defendant.

An interlocutory injunction will have effect until the final hearing of the action takes place. Its purpose is to maintain the status quo between the parties as far as possible until the final determination of the issues in dispute by the court.

A perpetual injunction will be awarded or refused at the hearing of the action. It represents a final determination of the rights of the parties and permanently prevents an infringement of those rights.

7.3   Principles Governing the Granting of an Injunction

The court intervenes by way of an injunction where the injury is irreparable and where it is continuous. Irreparable injury means substantial or serious injury which cannot be adequately remedied by an award for damages. Generally a court will not grant an injunction in circumstances where damages are an adequate remedy.

As stated above an interlocutory injunction preserves the status quo between the parties until trial and will have effect until the final determination is made by the court. O'Higgins CJ summarised the principles governing the granting of an interlocutory injunction in *Campus Oil Ltd v Minister for Industry and Energy (No 2)* [1983] IR 88 at p 105. He said:

> 'Interlocutory relief is granted to an Applicant where what he complains of is continuing and is causing him harm or injury which may be irreparable in the sense that it may not be possible to compensate him fairly or properly by an award of damages. Such relief is given because a period must necessarily elapse before the action can come for trial and for the purpose of keeping matters in status quo until the hearing.'

The principles as outlined in *Campus Oil (No 2)* represented for the first time an approval, in Ireland, of the principles enunciated by Lord Diplock in *American Cyanamid Co v Ethicon Ltd* [1975] AC 396. Lord Diplock found that the plaintiff in an application for interlocutory relief must establish:

(i)   that there is a 'serious' question to be tried;

(ii)   that damages would not be an adequate remedy; and

(iii)   that the balance of convenience favours the granting of the injunction, rather that its refusal.

7.3.1   SERIOUS QUESTION TO BE TRIED

Lord Diplock said in *American Cyanamid* [1975] 1 All ER 504, 509e and 510c–d:

> '. . . the evidence available to the court at the hearing of the application for an interlocutory injunction is incomplete. It is given on affidavit and has not been tested by oral cross-examination. The purpose sought to be achieved by giving to the court discretion to grant such injunctions would be stultified if the discretion were clogged by a technical rule forbidding its exercise if on that incomplete untested evidence the court evaluated the chances of the plaintiff's ultimate success in the action at 50 per cent or less, but permitting its exercise if the court evaluated his chances at more than 50 per cent . . . there is no such rule. . . . The court no doubt must be satisfied that the claim is not frivolous or vexations: in other words, that there is a serious question to be tried.'

The use of the word 'serious' created difficulties for plaintiffs over the years as it tended to give the impression that the plaintiff case had to be very strong. It is now accepted that the plaintiff must establish that there is a fair or bona fide issue to be tried. See the comments of Macken J in *Lonergan v George Salter-Townshend and Others* [2000] ELR 15.

7.3.2   DAMAGES AN ADEQUATE REMEDY

Having considered whether or not there is a fair or bona fide issue to be tried the court will go on to consider the adequacy of damages. The court must consider whether the plaintiff would be adequately compensated by an award of damages if, at the interlocutory stage, no injunction was granted but that at the trial stage he succeeded in establishing an entitlement to a permanent or perpetual injunction. Equally, the court must consider whether the defendant would be adequately compensated by damages if an injunction was granted to the plaintiff at the interlocutory stage but lifted at the trial stage.

Lord Diplock said in *American Cyanamid:*

> '[T]he governing principle is that the court should first consider whether, if the plaintiff were to succeed at the trial in establishing his right to a permanent injunction, he would be adequately compensated by an award of damages for the loss he would have sustained as a result of the defendant's continuing to do what was sought to be enjoined between the time of the application and the time of the trial. If damages in the measure recoverable at common law would be adequate remedy and the defendant would be in a financial position to pay them, no interlocutory injunction should normally be granted, however strong the plaintiffs claim appeared to be at that stage. If, on the other hand, damages would not provide an adequate remedy for the plaintiff in the event of his succeeding at the trial the court should then consider whether, on the contrary hypothesis that the defendant were to succeed at the trial in establishing his right to do that which was sought to be enjoined, he would be adequately compensated under the plaintiff's undertaking as to damages for the loss he would have sustained by being prevented from doing so between the time of the application and the time of the trial. If damages in the measure recoverable under such an undertaking would be an adequate remedy and the plaintiff would be in a financial position to pay them, there would be no reason upon this ground to refuse an interlocutory injunction. It is where there is doubt as to the adequacy of the respective remedies in damages available to either party or to both that the question of balance of convenience arises. It would be unwise to attempt even to list all the various matters which may need to be taken into consideration in deciding where the balance lies, let alone to suggest the relative weight to be attached to them. These will vary from case to case.'

These views have been adopted by the Irish courts on numerous occasions (see *Campus Oil v Minister for Industry and Energy (No 2)* [1983] IR 88 at p 107 and *Irish Shell v Elm Motors Ltd* [1984] ILRM 595).

The plaintiff will be required to give an undertaking as to damages, that is, an undertaking that in the event of an injunction being awarded and it subsequently appearing to the court that such injunction should not have been granted, the plaintiff will pay damages to the person injuncted. It is critical that solicitors advise clients of the requirement of the undertaking as to damages and of the consequences of such undertaking, including the potential scale of the commitment. Ideally this advice should be in writing to the client beforehand or, where that is not possible in very urgent cases, confirmed in writing at the first opportunity. The undertaking is that of the plaintiff himself and is confirmed to the court by counsel or the plaintiff's solicitor. It is not an undertaking from the solicitor or counsel.

7.3.3   BALANCE OF CONVENIENCE

In addressing what was the purpose of an interlocutory injunction, Lord Diplock said in *American Cyanamid* [1975] 1 All ER 504, 509c–d:

> 'The object of the interlocutory injunction is to protect the plaintiff against injury by violation of this right for which he could not be adequately compensated in damages recoverable in the action if the uncertainty were resolved in his favour at the trial; but the plaintiff's need for such protection must be weighed against the corresponding need of the defendant to be protected against injury resulting from his having been prevented from exercising his own legal rights for which he could not be adequately compensated under the plaintiff's undertaking in damages if the uncertainty were resolved in the defendant's favour at the trial. The court must weigh one need against another and determine where "the balance of convenience" lies.'

Having decided that there is a fair issue to be tried and that damages would not be an adequate remedy, the court then has to decide whether the balance of convenience lies with the granting or the refusal of the injunction. The grant or refusal of the injunction should be determined according to the balance of convenience and not the substantive merits of each party's case as presented to the court at the interlocutory stage. Again in *American Cyanamid* Lord Diplock set out the approach:

> '[U]nless the material available to the court at the hearing of the application for an interlocutory injunction fails to disclose that the plaintiff has any real prospect of succeeding in his claim for a permanent injunction at the trial, the court should go on to consider whether the balance of convenience lies in favour of the granting or refusing the interlocutory relief that is sought.'

O'Higgins CJ in *Campus Oil Ltd v Minister for Industry and Energy (No 2)* [1983] IR 88 having reviewed the authorities including *Educational Company of Ireland v Fitzpatrick* [1961] IR 345 confirmed his agreement with the views expressed by Lord Diplock. Quirke J set out a helpful summary of the *Cyanamid* principles as they have developed in Ireland in *Clane Hospital Ltd v Voluntary Health Insurance Board* The High Court 1998 No 3740P 22 May 1998, unreported. Quirke J stated that

> 'when considering applications for interlocutory relief, the court should adopt the following sequence of consideration:
> 1   Whether or not the applicant has raised a fair, substantial bona fide question for determination.
> 2   Whether, if the applicant where to succeed at the trial in establishing his right to a permanent injunction, he could be adequately compensated by an award of damages.
> 3   Whether, if the respondent where to be successful at the trial, he could be adequately compensated under the applicant's undertaking as to damages for any loss which he would have sustained by reason of the grant of interlocutory relief.

4   If either party or both have by way of evidence raised a real and substantial doubt as to the adequacy of the respective remedies in damages available to either party, then where does the "balance of convenience" lie?

5   In some instances are there "special factors" (usually technical in nature) which may influence the exercise of discretion and the grant of the relief sought?'

The above considerations apply in any application for injunctive relief.

In conclusion, the principles that evolved from the *American Cyanamid* case are guidelines which the court will be mindful of in the exercise of its discretion and consequently, they may not be strictly adhered to. There will, more often that not and particularly in an employment context, be special factors that a judge will take into account in individual cases. It is not simply a matter of satisfying the Diplock criteria and getting an injunction: satisfying the criteria does not automatically guarantee success. In addition, as an equitable remedy it is governed by the maxims of equity e.g. laches and acquiescence and so it is incumbent on potential plaintiffs to move as quickly as possible where there has been an alleged infringement.

7.4   Injunctions in an Employment Context

Having considered the principles applicable to injunctions generally, an analysis of how those principles operate in the context of an employment relationship is called for. It is well established that generally the courts will refuse to order the specific performance of a contract of employment. The courts are loathe to compel an employer and employee to continue to work together in circumstances where one or other no longer wishes to maintain the relationship and where it would not be possible for the courts to supervise the relationship.

The traditional objections to the specific performance of an employment contract were, first, that it would be wrong to enforce a contract requiring personal services and, secondly, that damages could provide an adequate remedy to an employee seeking to enforce their contract.

In 1998 Kelly J speaking with regard to the *American Cyanamid* principles stated that:

'[T]hese principles have a wide but not a universal application. In a small number of cases special rules which are not encompassed by these principles apply. One such type case arises in the field of contracts of employment. Normally courts will not grant an injunction to restrain breaches of covenant in a contract of employment if that would amount to indirect specific performance of such a contract or would perpetuate a relationship based on mutual trust which no longer exists.'

(See *Reynolds v Malocco and Others* [1999] 1 ILRM 289).

7.5   Restraint of Trade

The first indication that the courts would be prepared to force people to remain in an employment relationship arose in restraint of trade cases. As early as 1853 in *Lumley v Wagner* [1852] 1 De GM 2 G 604 Ms Wagner was restrained by injunction from singing for a third party. Ms Wagner had been contracted to sing exclusively for Mr Lumley for a specified period. She repudiated her contract by entering into an arrangement to sing for someone else at a higher fee and Mr Lumley successfully applied for an injunction preventing her from doing so.

Lord Denning used this authority in the historic decision of the UK Court of Appeal in *Hill v C & A Parsons & Co Ltd* [1972] Ch 305. Mr Hill was a senior engineer in the employment of the defendant. In May 1970 a closed shop arrangement was put in place whereby all of the defendant's employees were obliged to become members of a particular trade union. Mr Hill refused to join the union and received one month's notice of dismissal. He successfully obtained an interlocutory injunction restraining the termination of his contract employment. Lord Denning made reference to the general rule that an employee cannot claim specific performance of the contract of employment.

However he then stated:

'The rule is not inflexible. It permits exceptions. The court can in the proper case, grant a declaration that the relationship still subsists and an injunction to stop the master treating it as at an end.'

And went onto state:

'It may be said that, by granting an injunction in such a case, the court is indirectly enforcing specifically a contract for personal services. So be it. Lord St Glenards LC did something like it in *Lumley v Wagner* and I see no reason why we should not do it here.'

In granting the injunction to Mr Hill, Lord Denning accepted that to award such a remedy, the court would have to be satisfied that trust and confidence still existed between the parties and that damages would not be an adequate remedy.

7.6 Mutual Trust and Confidence

The circumstances in *Hill* were special. Mutual confidence still existed between the employer and employee and the attempt to dismiss Mr Hill was made only by reason of the intervention of a third party, the trade union. Further, damages would not have been an adequate remedy. The court stated that as personal confidence between the parties continued to exist, one of the main grounds for refusing an injunction (that it was wrong to enforce a contract based on a confidential relationship in the absence of personal confidence) was not applicable.

The mutual trust and confidence issue was central to the development of the employment injunction. The courts were prepared to set aside the general rule that an employee could not claim specific performance of his contract of employment and grant an injunction under very special circumstances where it was satisfied that mutual trust and confidence still existed between the employer and the employee.

7.7 Development of the Injunction Restraining a Dismissal

The principles in *Hill* laid down the initial parameters for the granting of an injunction to restrain a dismissal. They were applied narrowly in *Irani v Southampton and South West Hampshire Health Authority* [1985] IRLR 203, where the UK Court of Appeal accepted that the court could order a specific performance of a contract of employment, on condition that the employer retains trust and confidence in the employee. In this case the defendants purported to dismiss Mr Irani, arguably in breach of contractual procedures, from his post as a part-time ophthalmologist, by reason of irreconcilable differences which had arisen as between Mr Irani and the consultant in charge of the clinic in which he worked. The court pointed out that the decision to dismiss was based on incompatibility with the consultant and that there was no criticism of the plaintiff's conduct or professional competence. In fact the court was satisfied 'that the defendant in authority [had] perfect faith in the honesty, integrity and loyalty of Mr Irani'.

7.7.1   IRISH DEVELOPMENTS: *FENNELLY*

Within months of the UK High Court granting the *Irani* injunction, the Irish High Court followed suit. In *Fennelly v Assicurazioni Generali Spa & Another* [1985] 3 ILT 73 the defendant purported to dismiss the plaintiff by reason of redundancy on the grounds of a massive downturn in business. The plaintiff claimed that he was employed under a fixed-term contract for a period of 12 years and, in that context, Costello J held that there was a fair question for trial. Turning to the issue of the balance of convenience, as between the parties he stated that, pending a hearing 'the plaintiff [would] be left without a salary and nothing to live on' and that his situation 'would be little short of disastrous'. Costello J held that the balance of convenience was in Mr Fennelly's favour and stated that it would be 'unjust' to leave him in a situation where he would 'be virtually destitute with the prospect of damages', pending a trial of the action. The judge stated that in view of the 'very special circumstances' pertaining, he would order the defendant to pay the plaintiff's salary and bonus until the trial of the action and went onto state:

> 'I accept that the court should not require an employer to take on an employee where serious difficulties have risen between them or where there is no work for the employee but in this case the parties have obviously the highest for regard for one another. I will take an undertaking that the plaintiff will be prepared to carry out such duties as the defendant will ask of him until the trial. If they could make use of him until the trial of the action, the plaintiff should attend and carry out such duties as they give him. They might prefer not to give him any duties and put him on leave of absence. That is for the defendant but they must continue to pay his salary until the trial.'

7.7.2   DEVELOPMENTS POST-*FENNELLY*

Fennelly stood alone as the sole example in Ireland of an exception to the rule against specific performance of contracts of employment for a further nine years. Then, in January 1994, Mr Terence Shortt, the managing director of Data Packaging Ltd, was informed by telephone, by the chairman of the company, that owing to a restructuring of the company, he was to be made redundant. Later that same day, he received a letter confirming that his employment was being terminated with immediate effect and he was directed to vacate his office that evening. Mr Shortt claimed that only the directors of the company had the power to dismiss him, that the directors had made no decision to that effect, given that he was a director and would have been aware of such decision. He claimed that his removal from office was ineffective in that it was in breach of the principles of natural justice and that his purported removal was by virtue of an alleged redundancy which he said was spurious and unsubstantiated. He claimed that the real reason for his dismissal lay in 'differences between himself and his employers'. Keane J was satisfied that 'in accordance with the tests required for the granting of an interlocutory injunction', Mr Shortt had made out 'a fair issue to be tried as to the legality of the purported termination' and that damages would not constitute an adequate remedy, 'where the plaintiff [would] have to await the trial of the action in circumstances where he [was] totally without remuneration and where a trial [would] inevitably, be some time away'. It was held that the balance of convenience was in favour of the granting of an injunction (*Shortt v Data Packaging Ltd* [1994] ELR 251).

The issue of continuing trust and confidence was not even addressed in *Shortt*. While it should have been possible for the plaintiff to contend that he continued to enjoy the defendant's trust and confidence, given that Data Packaging Ltd had purported to terminate his employment on grounds of redundancy, the issue was not addressed by

Keane J and an injunction was granted, in circumstances where the plaintiff spoke of 'differences between himself and his employers'.

In *Phelan v BIC (Ireland) Ltd* [1997] ELR 208 Mr Phelan, the managing director of BIC (Ireland) Ltd, like Terence Shortt, was summarily dismissed, purportedly on grounds of redundancy. He claimed that the termination of his office was in breach of the rules of natural justice and in breach of contract, that the decision to remove him was ultra vires the powers of a company and contravened the provisions of the Redundancy Payments Acts.

Costello J, making reference to the 'old rule' that the court should not grant specific performance of a contract of employment, set out the modified position:

> 'There is a general principle that the courts do not grant injunctions in cases of termin-ation of contracts of employment on the principle in the old law reports and text books that a contract of employment is a contract of personal service. But there has been a strong body of judgments and authorities that this old rule should be subject to qualifi-cations and in a number of cases, the courts have granted interlocutory relief where it was in the interests of justice to do so.'

7.7.3   CURRENT STATUS: 2006—20 YEARS POST-*FENNELLY*

There is no doubt that in recent years, there has been a shift back to old principles govern-ing the granting of employment injunctions in situations where there has been a pur-ported or actual termination of the contract of employment. O'Higgins J in *Garrahy v Bord na gCon* [2003] ELR 274 noted that the great majority of cases involving applications for interlocutory relief concern wrongful dismissal. Applications for injunctive relief had become extremely common and plaintiff employees were undeterred by the financial cost in making such an application. In the majority of cases, they were successful. It seemed that interlocutory injunctive relief was granted simply for the asking. The late Ms Justice Carroll however made her view very clear in the case of *Orr v Zomax* [2004] ELR 161 where referring to the *Hill* and *Fennelly* cases she said that both these cases emphasised that there were either special or exceptional circumstances entitling the plaintiffs to the relief sought. In addition, she said, in both these cases there was no loss of trust in the employee. Carroll J then referred to the judgments of Laffoy J in *Harte v Kelly* [1997] ELR 125 and McCracken J in *Gee v Irish Times* [2001] ELR 249 commenting that 'the position had apparently moved from being appropriate in either special or exceptional circumstances' to being a 'well-established practice'.

In *Orr* the plaintiff claimed that he was unfairly dismissed because there was no valid redundancy. He claimed he was actually dismissed because of criticisms made about him by Microsoft, who were a client of the defendant company. The plaintiff also claimed that there was an implied term in his contract of employment that his employer must act fairly and reasonably. The defendants countered this argument by submitting that that was not a fair issue to be tried as unfair dismissal is governed by the Unfair Dismissals Acts, which provide a statutory remedy mutually exclusive to the common law remedy for damages. Carroll J agreed with this argument finding that the common law claim for damages for wrongful dismissal and the statutory claim for unfair dismissal are mutually exclusive. She refused the relief sought on the basis that the plaintiff was attempting to introduce a new obligation under the common law on the employer to act reasonably and fairly in the case of dismissal. She stated that at common law an employer can terminate employment for any reason or for no reason provided the notice was adequate.

Some weeks earlier, Carroll J giving judgment in *Sheehy v Ryan* [2004] ELR 87 had adopted the same approach. The plaintiff in this case had refused to accept the termination of her contract of employment on the grounds of redundancy and claimed that she was entitled to remain on in her position as Diocesan Secretary until she attained 65 years of age. She sought various orders and declarations and an injunction restraining the purported termination of her employment. It was necessary to determine the conditions of employment of the plaintiff and in particular whether the plaintiff was entitled to be kept on in her job until she was 65 in the absence of misconduct or inability. Carroll J dismissed the plaintiff's action and held that in the absence of a special condition in the plaintiff's contract of employment entitling her to a job until she was 65, the plaintiff could be dismissed on getting reasonable notice. She held that there was no special condition in this case and no case was made by the plaintiff that the notice given was unreasonable. In her judgment, Carroll J stated:

> 'The plaintiff has chosen to sue at common law. There were other possibilities open to her. She could have initiated proceedings under the Unfair Dismissals Act, 1967 claiming unfair dismissal or under the Redundancy Payments Act claming that there was no valid redundancy or that she was unfairly chosen to be redundant. If successful she would have been awarded statutory compensation.
>
> 'The position at common law is that an employer is entitled to dismiss an employee for any reason or no reason, on giving reasonable notice.'

In *Mahalingham v The Health Service Executive* High Court unreported 11 May 2005 [2005] IEHC 186 Carroll J in refusing the relief sought stated that the issues raised were ones to be dealt with at the trial and were not issues which would prevent the defendant from terminating the plaintiff's employment. She stated that the general principle of not granting an interlocutory injunction in the case of termination of employment applied and the issues raised by the plaintiff in this interlocutory application were not such that the requirements of justice would constrain the court at its discretion to prevent termination on an interlocutory basis. She held that the plaintiff had a remedy in damages at common law. Alternatively, he could apply under the statutory scheme to the EAT for relief. In an appropriate case the tribunal could order reinstatement, but it was not for the court to interfere with the legislature's intention to provide a statutory remedy under the Unfair Dismissals Acts. The issue in relation to damages was not relevant to an injunction. She stated:

> 'He has been given three months' notice and the question of whether it is reasonable is the question to be determined at the trial, and if not reasonable, will attract damages. If there is an implied term of mutual trust and confidence in Irish law, and assuming that there is, this does not extend to ousting the statutory scheme under the Unfair Dismissals Acts. If the termination of the plaintiff's employment is wrongful, his remedy is before an Employment Appeals Tribunal and not at common law. If there was an attempt at interference by the consultants with the plaintiff's employment and if there was racial and ethnic discrimination by the consultants, it was not by the defendant. These are issues to be dealt with at the trial and are not issues which would prevent the defendant from terminating the plaintiff's employment.
>
> 'The last issue relates to damages which is not relevant to an injunction. I am of opinion that the general principle of not granting an interlocutory injunction in the case of termination of employment applies. The issues raised by the plaintiff in this interlocutory appeal are not such that the requirements of justice would constrain the court at its discretion to prevent termination on an interlocutory basis. The plaintiff has a remedy in damages at common law. Alternatively, he can apply under the statutory scheme to the Employment Tribunal for relief. In an appropriate case the Tribunal can order reinstatement, but it is not for this court to interfere with the legislature's intention to provide a statutory remedy under the Unfair Dismissals Acts.
>
> 'I refuse the injunction to restrain the defendant from terminating the plaintiff's employment and as all other interlocutory reliefs are consequential on the granting of that, they are also refused.'

Notwithstanding Carroll J's strong affirmation of the traditional position that damages are an adequate remedy in cases of a purported wrongful dismissal, this does not save the plaintiff employee from the sometimes serious financial consequences of such a dismissal, particularly where there will undoubtedly be a lengthy delay between the dismissal and the hearing; nor does it assist the plaintiff employee in securing alternative employment where perhaps his professional standing has been tainted.

It remains to be seen whether it is a view that is shared by other High Court judges and whilst, at the time of writing, there have been no reported judgments since *Mahalingham* dealing with wrongful dismissal it seems unlikely that the courts will shy away from exercising the discretion granted to it to award injunctive relief where it is 'just and convenient' to do so. In August 2005, Peart J granted an interlocutory injunction to the plaintiff in *Gannon v The Minister for Defence, Ireland and the Attorney General* High Court unreported 15 August 2005 [2005] IEHC 293 in circumstances where even though he believed that damages were an adequate remedy, the plaintiff was in a 'perilous position pending the hearing of [the] case, and whilst there can be no doubt as to the capacity of the defendants to meet any award of damages which may be made at any later stage of this case, the fact is that the plaintiff in my view comes within the principles of the judgment in the *Fennelly* case'.

Certainly, a significant part of the reluctance of the courts to grant orders in wrongful dismissal cases concerns the inability of a court to supervise what would amount to a specific performance of a contract of employment. These difficulties do not arise in other circumstances such as restraining the appointment of a person to a post where such appointment might have the effect of breaching an existing employee's contract of employment. This was the situation in *Garrahy v Bord na gCon* and also in *Evans v IRFB Services (Ireland) Ltd* [2005] 2 ILRM 358, where the plaintiff had held the position of head of rugby development with the defendant since 2001. In 2004, the defendant, as part of a reorganising of its structures, proposed the amalgamation of the plaintiff's department with another department to form a new rugby department. The plaintiff claimed he had a fixed-term contract for five years in the position of head of rugby development, that he was entitled to carry out duties similar to those set out in his initial job description for the remainder of the five-year period and sought an order restraining the appointment of anybody to the proposed new position. Clarke J granted an interlocutory injunction pending the trial of the action, preventing the defendant from making any appointment to the proposed new post save on terms that preserved, in the event of the plaintiff being successful, his contractual entitlements. Clarke J stated that whilst courts would not normally grant injunctions to restrain breaches of a covenant in a contract of employment if that would amount to indirect specific performance of such contract, no such difficulty arose in relation to restraining the appointment of a person to a post where such an appointment might have the effect of breaching an existing employee's contract. No question would arise of the court having to supervise the specific performance of a contract of employment in this instance.

7.8 When will the courts Grant an Injunction?

It is possible to distinguish between applications that concern the termination or purported termination of a contract of employment and those that do not involve a termination but involve the assertion of some other right, either express or implied under the contract of employment. The body of case law that has amassed over the past twenty years would suggest that injunctions may potentially be granted in the following situations.

7.8.1 WHERE THE DISMISSAL IS IN BREACH OF CONTRACT

Where the employee is dismissed in the absence of contractual notice or a contractual disciplinary process an injunction may be granted. An injunction may also arise where there is a substantive impediment to the employer's entitlement to dismiss. *Fennelly* is a good example of this as he was contending for a 12-year fixed-term contract. Similarly in *Keane v Irish Amateur Swimming* [2004] 15 ELR 6 the plaintiff left her job as a solicitor to take up a position with the defendants. Subsequently it became apparent that the defendants were seeking to resile from their appointment of the plaintiff. The court granted an interlocutory injunction restraining the defendants from embarking upon the termination of the plaintiff's employment, an injunction restraining the defendant from appointing any other person to the plaintiff's position, an injunction restraining the defendant from treating the plaintiff as other than continuing to be employed by the defendant and an injunction directing the defendant to pay the plaintiff's salary. In granting the reliefs above Gilligan J said:

> '[T]he facts of this case clearly place the plaintiff in a paticularly difficult situation. She does not appear in any way to be to blame for the events which have unfolded and I am satisfied on the evidence before me that she is entitled to have her position protected.'

Gilligan J declined to make an order to permit the plaintiff to perform her contract as chief executive officer.

7.8.2 WHERE THE DISMISSAL IS ULTRA VIRES

In *Shortt v Data Packaging* Ltd [1994] ELR 251, the plaintiff claimed that his dismissal as managing director was ultra vires and not in accordance with the defendant company's articles of association. Keane J was satisfied that there was a fair issue to be tried on this basis.

In *O'Donnell v Chief State Solicitor* [2003] ELR 268, the plaintiff claimed that the statutory power to terminate his employment vested in the Attorney General and the Minister for Justice. The court held that the Chief State Solicitor was not so empowered and an interlocutory injunction was granted.

7.8.3 WHERE THE DISMISSAL IS IN BREACH OF FAIR PROCEDURES

Laffoy J made an order in *Maher v Irish Permanent plc* [1998] 4 IR 302, [1998] ELR 77 restraining the defendant from taking any further steps to terminate the plaintiff's employment with the defendant save in accordance with the defendant's disciplinary procedure and the principles of natural justice. Laffoy J found that the decision to dismiss was based on a hearing which contravened the most elementary requirement of fair procedures, in that it was conducted in the absence of the person against whom the allegations were made.

7.8.4 ABSENCE OF GROUNDS JUSTIFYING DISMISSAL

This has arisen mainly in dismissals purporting to be by reason of redundancy. In *Moore v Xnet Information Services Ltd* [2002] 4 IR 362, [2002] 2 ILRM 278, [2002] ELR 65 it was contended that the plaintiff's position had been terminated by reason of redundancy. O'Sullivan J granted an order directing that the plaintiff's salary be paid pending the trial of the action, subject to a number of undertakings.

Interlocutory relief was refused in *Sheehy v Ryan* and in *Orr v Zomax* both of which related to dismissal on the grounds of redundancy. It is evident from Carroll J's judgments in these cases that if the contract is terminated by reason of redundancy and pursuant to the notice requirements in the contract, the High Court is not the place to challenge such a termination. Employees are better advised to pursue a claim in the EAT under unfair dismissal or redundancy legislation.

7.8.5 **WHERE THE DISMISSAL IS IN BREACH OF A CONSTITUTIONAL RIGHT**

This arose in *Maher v Irish Permanent* and also in *Meskell v Coras Iompair Éireann* [1973] IR 121 where the plaintiff was granted a declaration that his dismissal was a denial and violation of and an unlawful interference with his constitutional right of dissociation from a trade union.

7.8.6 **NON-DISMISSAL INJUNCTIONS**

Kelly J ordered the employer to pay sick pay in the case of *Mullarkey v Irish National Stud Company Ltd* [2004] ELR 172; see also *Rooney v Kilkenny* [2001] ELR 129.

O'Sullivan J granted an order prohibiting the advertising of a position which the plaintiff claimed overlapped with his position in *Harkins v Shannon Foynes Port Company* [2001] ELR 75 and Macken J granted an order bringing to an end a suspension in *Martin v The Nationwide Building Society* [1999] ELR 241.

The court prevented the appointment of new postholders in *Garrahy v Bord na gCon* [2003] ELR 274 and also in *Evans v IRFB Services (Ireland) Ltd* [2005] 2 ILRM 358.

Clarke J in *Becker v The Board of Management St Dominics Secondary School, Cabra* High Court unreported 15 April 2005 [2005] IEHC 122 despite finding that there was a fair issue to be tried and that damages would not be an adequate remedy refused the interlocutory relief sought finding that the balance of convenience favoured the defendant being entitled to continue to require the plaintiff to absent herself from work until a medical report was received. This case did not involve a purported dismissal. The plaintiff sought injunctive relief relating to her suspension from duties. She was a teacher in a school run by the defendant board of management and she instituted three sets of proceedings relating to her employment. The defendant attempted to have the plaintiff assessed by a psychiatrist but the plaintiff failed to attend her appointment and proffered a sick certificate. The defendant suspended the plaintiff on full pay pending her independent medical assessment.

7.9 **The Future?**

Roderick Horan SC in an article entitled 'Employment Injunction: Current Status and Future Developments' [2005] 1 ELRI 8 at p. 9 stated that:

> '. . . whilst it is verging on the trite to say that there is a scepticism amongst certain lawyers as to the legal basis for the granting of an order maintaining the employment relationship in the teeth of an apparent dismissal, the anti-dismissal injunction is no more than an affirmation of the guiding principle that a wrongdoer should not profit from his or her wrong rather than an attempt to shore up or create a dubious jurisprudence.'

Recent decisions certainly represent a forceful restatement of the original principles governing the granting of injunctions. It is not generally felt that these decisions signal the demise of the injunction as a remedy in circumstances where a plaintiff employee can establish a fair issue to be tried, that his employment has been lawfully terminated and where he will suffer immediate financial detriment which cannot be compensated by an award of damages at trial.

7.10 Wrongful Dismissal at Common Law and Statutory Unfair Dismissal Distinguished

Section 15(3) of the Unfair Dismissals Act, 1977 (as amended) provides as follows:

> 'Where the hearing by a Court of proceedings for damages at common law for wrongful dismissal of an employee has commenced, the employee shall not be entitled to redress under this Act in respect of the dismissal to which the proceedings relate.'

In *Parsons v Iarnród Éireann* [1997] IR 523, [1997] ELR 203, the Supreme Court considered the issue as to whether the plaintiff was precluded, by virtue of the provisions of section 15 of the 1977 Act, from bringing an action at common law in respect of a dismissal which had previously been the subject of a claim to a rights commissioner under the 1977 Act. Explaining the relationship of the statutory code to the common law jurisdiction, in delivering judgment in the Supreme Court, Barrington J stated as follows (at p 207):

> 'What the Unfair Dismissals Act 1977 does is to give the worker who feels that he has been unfairly dismissed an additional remedy which may carry with it the very far-reaching relief of reinstatement in his previous employment. It does not limit the worker's rights, it extends them. At the same time, s[ection]15 of the Unfair Dismissals Act provides that the worker must choose between suing for damages at common law and claiming relief under the new Act. Subsection (2) accordingly provides that if he claims relief under the Act he is not entitled to recover damages at common law; while subs[ection]. (3) provides that where proceedings for damages at common law for wrongful dismissal are initiated by or on behalf of an employee the employee shall not be entitled to redress under the Unfair Dismissals Act in respect of the same dismissal.
> 'The traditional relief at common law for unfair dismissal was a claim for damages. The plaintiff may also have been entitled to declarations in certain circumstances such as, for instance, that there was an implied term in his contract entitling him to fair procedures before he was dismissed. But such declarations were in aid of the common law remedy and had no independent existence apart from it. If the plaintiff loses his right to sue for damages at common law the heart has gone out of his claim and there is no other free-standing relief which he can claim at law or in equity.'

This issue arises time and time again in proceedings for wrongful dismissal and counsel will normally be extremely careful in framing proceedings for injunctive relief, so as to ensure that a plaintiff might not be considered to have taken part in a 'hearing by a court of proceedings for damages at common law'. To that end, proceedings in cases of this nature invariably seek declarations and injunctions, but rarely embody a claim for damages for breach of contract. In this way, it is intended to keep open the door to the EAT under the Unfair Dismissals Acts.

There are conflicting High Court judgments in this regard. In *Philpott v Ogilvy & Mather Ltd* [2000] 3 IR 206, [2000] ELR 225 Murphy J refused to grant declaratory and/or interlocutory relief to the plaintiff because the plaintiff had not claimed damages for wrongful dismissal. He stated as follows:

> 'If the traditional relief at common law for unfair dismissal was a claim for damages then the plaintiff may also have been entitled to declarations and injunctions in aid of his common law remedy. But if such equitable relief has no independent existence apart from the claim for damages for wrongful dismissal then, it seems to me, that there is no other free-standing relief which can be claimed at law or in equity.'

In coming to this conclusion, Murphy J relied on the judgment of the Supreme Court in *Parsons v Iarnrod Éireann* [1997] ELR 203 and, while such interpretation of *Parsons* would almost certainly reduce the popularity of the application for declaratory/injunctive relief in employment cases, Murphy J's judgment must be viewed beside that of Budd J in *Cassidy v Shannon Castle Banquets and Heritage Ltd* [2000] ELR 248, which was delivered less than nine months previously and illustrates an entirely different interpretation of *Parsons*.

Budd J took the view that *Parsons* 'is authority for the proposition that declaratory relief is available unless precluded by the option having been taken of making a claim under the Unfair Dismissals Act'. He pointed out that in *Parsons* the plaintiff, having claimed unfair dismissal, had 'forfeited his right to bring an action for damages for wrongful dismissal' and he went on to point out that it was in those circumstances that the declaratory relief sought could avail him nothing and was 'quite properly refused'.

Thus, while Murphy J is of the view that declaratory/injunctive relief may only be sought in conjunction with a claim for damages for wrongful dismissal, Budd J appears to be of the view that a plaintiff is only prohibited from seeking such declaratory/injunctive relief in circumstances where a recommendation has been made by a rights commissioner in respect of a claim by the employee for redress under the Unfair Dismissals Acts or the hearing of a claim by the EAT has commenced.

Practitioners should carefully advise their clients with regard to the ramifications of the Unfair Dismissals Act, 1977, section 15(3) while the choice of remedy in employment cases will have to be carefully considered, for fear of exposing a client to an order for High Court costs, alternatively depriving the client of the possibility of securing a substantial award for compensation under the Unfair Dismissals Acts.

As stated, proceedings claiming injunctive relief rarely include a claim for damages at common law, given that the Unfair Dismissals Act, 1977, section 15, as amended, prohibits an employee from claiming a statutory remedy for unfair dismissal, in circumstances where the hearing by a court of proceedings for damages at common law for wrongful dismissal has commenced. As the levels of compensation which are awarded under the Unfair Dismissals Acts will almost invariably exceed the levels of compensation that might be awarded by way of damages at common law, a dismissed employee will always be loath to 'close the door' on an unfair dismissal claim.

7.11 Procedure to Obtain an Injunction

Generally, in employment matters, injunctions are sought on an ex parte basis i.e. the application is made without notice to the other side. The initial application to the High Court on an ex parte basis will involve the drafting of a plenary summons, a notice of motion and a grounding affidavit. Where possible, the plenary summons should be stamped and filed in the High Court Central Office where the Registrar will allocate a record number to the action. The grounding affidavit will be sworn by the plaintiff and ought to contain clear and concise statements of facts giving rise to the claim in the proceedings, of facts giving rise to the claim for interlocutory relief, of the facts relied on as justifying an ex parte application to include details of any notice given to the defendant and, if not, why not. In addition, the affidavit should include details of any answer asserted by defendant (or likely to be so asserted) either to the claim in the action or to the claim for interlocutory relief, details of any facts known to applicant which might lead the court not to grant relief and details of the precise relief sought.

It is prudent to have the plaintiff present when the injunction application is being made in the event that the judge requires additional information or clarification. As the application is being made without the other party present, it is essential that a complete and honest disclosure of all the facts is made in order to avoid any suggestion whatsoever that a judge has been misled. The court will look to see when the plaintiff first had notice of the matters complained of in order to prevent an injunction order being made against a party in his absence. If the plaintiff has acquiesced for some time the order sought will not be granted.

The period for which the injunction will be awarded will normally be the shortest possible period and particularly where the application is on an ex parte basis, the period of time is only just sufficient to enable the plaintiff to issue and serve the notice of motion on the defendant. The judge will often order the injunction to continue until the next motion day. It is important to obtain an order abridging the time for service of the notice of motion, if, this is necessary. Unless abridged by order of the court, four clear days' notice must be served on the defendant (or two days if there is a solicitor already on record for the defendant).

It is likely that there will be some delay between the granting of the order and the drawing up of the written order and as such it will be necessary to give the defendant notice of the making of the order and the judge will usually direct how such notice is to be given to the defendant either by way of fax, telephone or other suitable means, depending on the circumstances.

Once the written order has been obtained from the Registrar, the notice of motion should be issued and served on the defendant together with a copy of the plenary summons and a copy of the affidavit grounding the application for the injunction together with any additional affidavits.

On the return date for the notice of motion, the plaintiff should have booklets available for the court to include copies of the plenary summons, notice of motion, grounding affidavit and affidavit of service of those documents on the plaintiff. The defendant may at that stage already have filed a replying affidavit and if so, this should be included in the booklet also. It is more likely that the defendant will seek a short adjournment to enable them prepare and file a replying affidavit. Ultimately, the court on hearing the argument of both sides will decide whether or not to grant an injunction pending the trial of action.

7.12   Implications of Unsuccessful Application

An unsuccessful injunction application may have extremely serious implications for a plaintiff employee. Injunction applications, by their very nature, often embody a claim that the purported termination of the employment relationship was unlawful and without effect and that the relationship continues to subsist. Thus, where a plaintiff fails to secure an injunction on, say, the grounds that the balance of convenience did not favour the granting of the injunction, the employee will probably be in a situation where he is a plaintiff in a High Court action in which it is claimed that the employment relationship subsists. Consequently, he may have difficulty in claiming unfair dismissal before the EAT while the efficacy of the dismissal is the subject of a 'live' High Court action. If the employee decides to abandon the High Court action, he will have a substantial exposure to costs. In this way, an employee who makes an unsuccessful application for an injunction may find that he is 'trapped' in the High Court and cannot gain access to the potentially more lucrative forum, that is the EAT, without incurring considerable cost.

CHAPTER 8

UNFAIR DISMISSALS

8.1   Introduction

In 1977 the Unfair Dismissals Act ('the 1977 Act') was enacted creating a new form of remedy for dismissed employees. The legislation brought about major changes in employment law and practice. The Act was substantially amended in 1993, and in 2001 the requirement for an employee to work a minimum number of hours per week in order to be covered by the legislation was removed by the Protection of Employment (Part-time Work) Act, 2001. For this reason the legislation on unfair dismissal law is referred to as 'the Unfair Dismissals Acts, 1977–2001'.

The legislation is based on two fundamental principles:

(a) substantial grounds must exist to justify the termination of a contract of employment; and

(b) fair procedures must be followed in effecting the termination.

8.2   Who is Covered by Unfair Dismissal Legislation?

Not all employees are covered by the legislation. Those who are covered are those who satisfy the basic requirements of having:

(a) one year's continuous service with the employer. This means 52 weeks' continuous service as defined by the rules of continuity contained in the Minimum Notice and Terms of Employment Act, 1973, Schedule 1. One year's continuous service is not required where employees can show that they were dismissed by reason of trade union membership or activity, pregnancy, breastfeeding or related matters, or because they exercised their statutory rights to maternity leave (*Maxwell v English Language Institute* [1990] ELR 226), additional maternity leave or time off for ante- and post-natal care. One year's service is also not necessary where an employee is dismissed for seeking to exercise his or her rights to adoptive leave (Adoptive Leave Act, 1995, section 25) or parental leave (Parental Leave Act, 1998) or carer's leave (Carer's Leave Act 2001). Holiday leave is not included in the calculation of service under unfair dismissal legislation and, in particular, in establishing whether the employee has the necessary one year's service to bring a claim (*Twomey v O'Leary Office Supplies Ltd* [1997] ELR 42);

(b) employees who have not reached the normal retirement age for the employment in question. Difficulty may arise in determining what the contractual pension age is if the contract is silent. Nowadays, with pension ages dropping, it is important for employers to specify what the actual retirement age is rather than seek to imply the retirement age because it is provided for in a pension scheme (*Buckley v Ceimici Teo* UD 528/80). See also the judgment of Flood J in *Donegal County Council v Porter* [1993] ELR 101 where the county council sought to unilaterally reduce the retirement age for firemen from 60 to 55 but failed in their attempt to do so.

In *Tipperary North Riding County Council v Doyle* [1996] ELR 93 the EAT stated that it had received clear documentary evidence from the council of the policy in practice of compulsory retirement for part-time firemen going back some four decades, and therefore the retirement age of 55 was a condition of the employment of Mr Doyle at all times and distinguished the case on that basis from *Donegal County Council v Porter*. In contrast, in *Scally v Westmeath County Council* [1996] ELR 96 the EAT held that, on the evidence, the fireman in that case came within the ambit of *Donegal County Council v Porter* and that his compulsory retirement on reaching the age of 55 was an unfair dismissal.

The 1977 Act also provided that employees were excluded from claiming unfair dismissal once they had reached the social welfare pension age. That exclusion was removed by section 4(d) of the Employment Equality Act, 2004. If therefore an employer does not have a normal retirement age, the fallback position originally provided in the 1977 Act does not apply. An employee can therefore continue to work indefinitely. If the employer seeks to dismiss them because of age, they will be entitled to claim unfair dismissal provided they satisfy the other requirements for claimants under the legislation.

8.3 Who is Excluded?

There are certain categories of persons excluded from the legislation. The full list of exclusions is contained in the 1977 Act, section 2, as amended by the Unfair Dismissals (Amendment) Act, 1993 ('the 1993 Act'), section 3. The main excluded categories are:

(a)   persons employed in the Defence Forces and Gardaí;

(b)   FAS trainees who are not employed (*Fallon v Athlone Bowl & Leisure Ltd* [1997] ELR 67 and *Morey v Rock Foundation* [1997] ELR 236);

(c)   civil servants (*Central Bank of Ireland v Gildea* [1997] ELR 238, *McLoughlin v Minister for Social Welfare* [1958] IR 1 and *Murphy v Minister for Social Welfare* [1987] IR 295);

(d)   officers of VECs (*O'Callaghan v Cork Corporation* in Kerr and Madden, *Unfair Dismissals Cases and Commentary*, p 182); and

(e)   officers of health boards, but temporary officers are not excluded by virtue of the 1993 Act amendment.

8.4 Definitions

There are some fundamental definitions provided for in unfair dismissal legislation of particular importance in understanding the application of the legislation.

8.4.1 EMPLOYEE

As may be seen in reference to **8.2** above only employees may claim under unfair dismissal legislation. The distinction between a contract of service and a contract for services is fundamental to most areas of employment law.

8.4.2 EMPLOYEE/INDEPENDENT CONTRACTOR

It is well established that regardless of what label parties seek to put on their relationship the courts will look at the factual situation and decide as a matter of law whether a contract was a contract of service or a contract for services (*Macken v Midland Community Radio Services Ltd* [1992] ELR 143 and *Phelan v Coillte Teoranta* [1993] ELR 56). In *Duncan v O'Driscoll* [1997] ELR 38 a 'share fisherman' was held to be a partner and not an employee. It can also be difficult to establish if a controlling shareholder is an employee of the company he owns. Ownership does not disqualify the person from being held to be an employee but is a factor, and sometimes a very relevant factor, to be taken into account (*Lee v Lee's Air Farming Ltd* [1961] AC 12, *Secretary of State for Trade and Industry v Bottrill* [1998] IRLR 120, *Buchan and Ivey v Secretary of State for Employment* [1997] IRLR 80, and *Fleming v Secretary of State for Trade and Industry* [1997] IRLR 682). This subject is dealt with in more detail in Chapter 1: Contracts of Employment.

8.4.3 AGENCY-SUPPLIED STAFF

8.4.3.1 Statutory provisions

Section 13 of the Unfair Dismissals (Amendment) Act, 1993 was enacted in order to provide that staff placed in a business by a third party usually, but not always, an employment agency are deemed to be the staff of the business in which they are placed for the purposes of unfair dismissal legislation. The section provides as follows:

> *'Where, whether before, on or after the commencement of this Act, an individual agrees with another person, who is carrying on the business of an employment agency within the meaning of the Employment Agency Act, 1971, and is acting in the course of that business, to do or perform personally any work or service for a third person (whether or not the third person is a party to the contract and whether or not the third person pays the wages or salary of the individual in respect of the work or service), then, for the purposes of the Principal Act, as respects a dismissal occurring after such commencement . . . the individual shall be deemed to be an employee employed by the third person under a contract of employment . . . and any redress under the Principal Act for unfair dismissal of the individual under the contract shall be awarded against the third person.'*

The definition of employment agency in the Employment Agency Act, 1971, section 1 provides as follows:

> *'[T]he business of an Employment Agency means the business of seeking, whether for reward or otherwise, on behalf of others, persons who will give or accept employment and includes the obtaining or supplying for reward of persons who will accept employment from or render services to others.'*

The Terms of Employment (Information) Act, 1994 contains a similar provision relating to agency-supplied employees. It confers a liability to provide details of basic terms and conditions of employment. This legislation causes considerable knock-on effects. If the employer were to comply with the legislation, the employer would in effect be accepting that the person is an employee and that the terms and conditions in place were a matter over which the employer had control. Compliance with the legislation effectively puts employers in a position that they would have enormous difficulty arguing under this legislation and, indeed, in other respects that the person is other than an employee.

8.4.3.2 Case law

In the first case heard by the EAT dealing with the 1993 Act, section 13, *Bourton v Narcea Ltd and AIBP* M318 UD186/94, Mr Bourton was a full-time employee of Narcea Ltd. Narcea provided boning services to the meat industry. Bourton was a boner working for Narcea. Narcea entered into commercial contracts with meat companies to bone meat at a piece rate. The money was paid to Narcea and Narcea in turn paid wages to its staff, including Bourton, subject to PAYE and PRSI. Narcea had the right to, and in practice did, move its employees from one meat plant to another as the work required. While working in a meat plant owned by AIBP Bourton became involved in a skirmish with an AIBP employee. Disciplinary action was taken against the AIBP employee and Narcea was requested not to allow Bourton to return to the particular factory. Bourton had a disagreement with Narcea and claimed unfair dismissal. During the course of the first hearing of his claim it was decided to adjourn the matter in order to join AIBP as a possible deemed employer under section 13. Bourton actually settled his dispute with Narcea and continued with his case against AIBP who at all times denied that he was an employee. AIBP made the case that they would not apply disciplinary procedures to a person who was not their employee. This raises practical and procedural problems with deemed employees under section 13. In the event, given the particular wording of the 1993 Act, Bourton did not have the necessary one year's service with AIBP and on that ground his claim failed. The EAT's comments indicated, however, that in all other respects Bourton came within the definition of a deemed employee in section 13.

There is a similar provision contained in the UK Race Relations Act, 1976 at section 7(1) which provides that for the purposes of that legislation the section:

> '. . . applies to any work for a person ("the principal") which is available for doing by individuals ("contract workers") who are employed not by the principal himself but by another person who supplies them under a contract made with the principal.'

In *Harrods Ltd v Remick* [1997] IRLR 9 Ms Remick was employed as a consultant by Shaeffer Pens (UK) Ltd who have a sales counter in Harrods. Employees require to be approved by Harrods for working in the store. Ms Remick's store approval was withdrawn by Harrods because she was considered to have failed to adhere to the store's dress code, as a consequence of which she was dismissed by Shaeffer Pens (UK) Ltd. She claimed discrimination on grounds of race. The UK EAT held that staff employed by concessionaires at Harrods were contract workers who worked 'for' Harrods within the meaning of section 7 of the Race Relations Act. The case hinged on the meaning of the word 'for' as Ms Remick had to prove that she was working 'for' Harrods, even though not employed 'by' them. Harrods claimed that Ms Remick did not work for them within the meaning of the Act. In holding for Ms Remick the UK EAT asked for whose benefit the work was carried out and held that it was a question of fact and degree in each case whether the particular work which was available for doing was work 'for' a principal. The UK EAT stated:

> '[I]n the present case the work in question was work "for" Harrods in that it was work done in the store for the benefit of Harrods and ultimately under Harrods' control as Harrods could grant, refuse or withdraw store approval for the worker to do the work available. The fact that the applicants as employees also worked for their employer did not prevent the work which they did from being work "for" Harrods within the meaning of section 7.'

8.5   Fixed-Term and Specified-Purpose Contracts

The legislation allows for the exclusion of dismissals resulting from the ending of a fixed-term contract at its expiry and the conclusion of a specified purpose contract on the cesser of the purpose. In order for these exclusions to apply the following conditions must exist:

(a)   the contract must be in writing;

(b)   the contract must specifically exclude the legislation; and

(c)   the contract must be signed by both parties.

In *Sheehan v Dublin Tribune Ltd* [1992] ELR 239 the employer had failed to specify in a fixed-term contract the exclusion of the Unfair Dismissals Act and the EAT held that, in the absence of such specific exclusion as required by the legislation, the exclusion of fixed-term contracts provided for in the legislation cannot be relied upon by the employer. Further, as no substantial ground had been shown to justify the dismissal the dismissal was held to be unfair.

Many employers use fixed-term contracts in the mistaken belief that they are under no obligation to renew on the expiry of the term. Non-renewal will amount to dismissal. The employer can only rely on justification for the non-renewal or dismissal where it can be shown that the contract was a genuine fixed-term or specified-purpose contract. The employer must be able to show that there was a commercial justification for using such a contract in the first place.

At common law these contracts do not cause particular difficulty. If an employer agrees to employ a person for a specified period of time then, in the absence of a fundamental breach of contract, the employer cannot be absolved from that obligation except by the agreement of the employee. If A agrees to hire B for five years and after two years decides to terminate the contract, B must be paid the balance of the contract. B has, of course, the normal common law duty to mitigate his loss but, in the absence of mitigation, his loss must be measured at the full value to him of the balance of the contract. A prudent employer will therefore seek to put into such a contract a provision allowing for early termination. This may seem to be a contradiction in terms but the UK Court of Appeal held in *Dixon and Constanti v BBC* [1979] IRLR 114 that the words 'fixed-term contract' referred to a contract for a specified term even though the contract is determinable by notice within that term.

An employer may enter into a fixed-term or specified-purpose contract in order to grant security of tenure to an employee which should tempt him to remain in the employment. While the contractual theory is all very well, if an employee were to abandon his employment under such a contract, there is little or nothing the employer can do to remedy the problems thereby caused. While the employer could claim that there was a cost in having to seek a replacement that cost would have been, in theory at least, incurred on the normal ending of the contract anyway. The cost of hiring a replacement will be met in the main by the money saved in not having to pay the departed employee. If, however, an employer were to be engaged in a special project which was in some way delayed or put in jeopardy the employer may well be able to seek compensation from the employee who has breached the agreement to remain for the fixed term or until the cesser of the purpose. In practice, however, employers' prospects of actually recovering compensation are minimal.

Highly skilled employees may well seek fixed-term or specified-purpose contracts to give themselves security of tenure. Employers must be aware of the risks of using such contracts if they do not reserve unto themselves the right to terminate on notice within the life of the contract.

Most of the difficulty of using fixed-term or specified-purpose contracts has arisen under unfair dismissal legislation (*Orren v Western Health Board* UD 268/96 and *Buckley v Southern Health Board* UD 110/96).

Substantial changes were made to the law applicable to fixed-term contracts and the manner in which employers may use or resort to such contracts by the Protection of Employees (Fixed-Term Work) Act, 2003, which is dealt with in more detail in Chapter 4: Atypical Workers.

8.6 Dismissal

8.6.1 GENERALLY

In order to succeed with a claim under the legislation, the employee must be able to show that he was actually dismissed. A person who has voluntarily resigned his position, or whose contract has come to an end by reason of frustration, could not establish a dismissal and cannot proceed with an unfair dismissal claim. The leading cases on frustration are *Marshall v Harland and Wolff* [1972] IRLR 90, *Egg Stores (Stamford Hill) Ltd v Leibovici* [1976] IRLR 376, and *Nolan v Brooks Thomas Ltd* UD 179/79.

In order for there to be an actual dismissal the employer must have evinced an intention to terminate the contract of employment. Where an employer has used unclear language or ambiguous terminology, an objective test is applied to the words used to see if they were capable of being construed by a reasonable person as indicating a dismissal (*Tanner v D T Kean Ltd* [1978] IRLR 110). In some cases employers have used crude or abusive language (*Maher v Walsh* UD 683/83). In *Futty v D & D Brekkes Ltd* [1974] IRLR 130 Futty had a reputation for turning 'banter into acrimony'. One day his foreman got fed up with him and said 'If you do not like the job, f . . . off'. Futty maintained his interpretation of those words was 'you are dismissed'. The company thought he had left in a 'huff' and would come back. He did not. The UK EAT considered the words actually spoken and also interpreted them 'not in isolation—but against a background of the fish dock'. They held that bad language was not uncommon and 'once the question of dismissal becomes imminent bad language tends to disappear and an unexpected formality seems to descend upon the parties'. The foreman's words were held to be no more than 'a general exhortation to get on with his job'. (See also *Wallace-Hayes v Skolars Hairdressing School Ltd* [1991] ELR 108.) Establishing that notice was actually given, and the length of the period of notice, whether summary or otherwise, can be of paramount importance to the bringing of a claim where there may be doubt as to whether the employee has the one year's continuous service requirement referred to at **8.2** above. This is dealt with in more detail in **8.8** below.

8.6.2 INDEFINITE SUSPENSION

In *Deegan v Dunnes Stores Ltd* [1992] ELR 184 the claimants had been placed on indefinite suspension for refusing to sign undertakings in relation to certain management requirements. The EAT held that:

> '. . . [i]ndefinite suspension amounted to dismissal and that the dismissal in this case was unfair as it was too severe a penalty but that the claimants had contributed to their dismissal through their lack of co-operation which gave rise to the undertaking requirement in the first place.'

On suspension generally, see the High Court decision in *Morgan v Trinity College* [2004] ELR 235.

8.6.3 APPEALS

Dismissal subject to an appeal will still be a dismissal. In *Michelle Kenny v Warner Music (Ireland) Ltd* UD 389/92 the employee was dismissed for misconduct and was written to advising her of her proposed dismissal subject to a right of appeal against the decision. She was advised that if she invoked her right of appeal she would be suspended on full pay until such time as the outcome of the appeal was known. The employee initiated her right of appeal, the appeal was heard and her dismissal was set aside. She refused to resume work and claimed unfair dismissal based on the original decision which had not been effected by the employer following the outcome of the appeal. The EAT held that she was dismissed and that the dismissal was unfair.

This may be contrasted with *Martin v Yeomen Aggregates Ltd* [1983] ICR 314 where there was an angry exchange between a director and the employee who refused to carry out an instruction. In the course of the exchange the director dismissed the employee. A few minutes later the director realised that he had acted improperly and revoked the dismissal advising the employee that he was suspended without pay for two days. The employee, however, treated himself as having been dismissed and claimed unfair dismissal. The UK EAT held, following *Tanner v Kean* [1978] IRLR 110, that there had been no dismissal, adding that it was a matter of common sense vital to industrial relations that either an employer or an employee should be given an opportunity of recanting from words spoken in the heat of the moment.

The *Kenny* case seems also to have taken the opposite line to that taken by the House of Lords in *West Midlands Co-operative Society Ltd v Tipton* [1986] IRLR 112 which in turn approved *Savage v J Sainsbury Ltd* [1980] IRLR 109.

The Industrial Relations Act, 1990 (Code of Practice on Grievance and Disciplinary Procedures) (Declaration) Order, 2000, SI 146/2000, while not legally binding, recommends that disciplinary procedures include a right of appeal against a dismissal decision. In *O'Leary v Eagle Star Life Assurance Company of Ireland Ltd* UD 99/2002 the EAT held that failure to provide an appeal for a dismissed employee can be a factor in determining the fairness or otherwise of the dismissal.

8.6.4 TERMINATION

In order for a contract to properly terminate where notice is given the notice must specify the date of termination, or be given in such a way that the date is ascertainable. A warning of dismissal at some time may not amount to a dismissal (*Morton Sundour Fabrics Ltd v Shaw* [1967] 2 ITR 84).

Issuing a P45 does not of itself terminate employment, as it is a separate statutory requirement governed by tax law and while it is an action that commonly follows the termination of employment, it does not of itself constitute termination but from an evidential perspective may be indicative of an intention to terminate. See *P J O'Flanagan v Houlihan (t/a Anner Hotel)* UD 579/1983, *McKenna v Bursey Peppard Ltd* [1997] ELR 87, and *Ennis v Carroll, David Carroll and Scale Force Ltd* UD 586/99 where the employee was offered and sought her P45 but this was held not to have been an indication of dismissal. Failure to allow an adopting parent to return to work is a deemed unfair dismissal by virtue of the provisions of section 26 of the Adoptive Leave Act, 1995.

8.6.5 NON-RENEWAL OF FIXED-TERM CONTRACT

The expiration of a contract of employment for a fixed term without its being renewed constitutes a dismissal. The dismissal by virtue of non-renewal may not be automatically unfair. In *Hade v Brunswick Press Ltd* 291 UD 377/84 the non-renewal of a fixed-term contract was held to be dismissal but the dismissal was held to be by reason of redundancy. See also Chapter 4: Atypical Employees which deals with fixed-term contracts in more detail.

8.6.6   CONSTRUCTIVE DISMISSAL

8.6.6.1   Generally

Constructive dismissal is defined in section 2 of the 1977 Act as:

> 'The termination by the employee of his contract of employment with his employer, whether prior notice of the termination was or was not given to the employer, in circumstances in which, because of the conduct of the employer the employee was or would have been entitled, or it was or would have been reasonable for the employee to terminate the contract of employment without giving prior notice of termination to the employer.'

Where an employee terminates his or her employment because of an employer's conduct towards the employee, and that conduct is deemed sufficiently serious, the employee may be entitled to claim constructive dismissal. The equivalent UK provision is more restrictive as far as employees are concerned and does not provide that it might be 'reasonable for the employee to terminate the contract of employment'. The UK cases tend therefore to focus on constructive dismissal more akin to fundamental breach at common law.

The Irish cases are broader and more wide-ranging in the types of conduct dealt with. The leading Irish case is *Byrne v RHM Foods (Ireland) Ltd* UD 69/79. Following the termination of employment of the manager for whom the claimant worked, the claimant noticed a considerable deterioration in her working conditions and particularly her relationship with the managing director, who had assumed the duties of her former boss. She was given no work to do and was effectively isolated. While she had her own office, her telephone was cut off and later her filing cabinets were removed. As a result of the stress she suffered, the claimant had to receive medical treatment and subsequently claimed constructive dismissal. The EAT in its determination in her favour stated:

> 'We appreciate that following an upset in the upper management level in any company difficulties can arise but no explanation or contact was made with the claimant who was left in her office for a period of approximately three weeks' continuous isolation without knowledge of what was going on or contact by any person and in our view it is reasonable and understandable that her confidence and trust in her employer should be undermined to the extent that she could tolerate it no longer. We are of the opinion that the managing director should have communicated in person or otherwise with the claimant so as to reassure her during this period concerning her position and thereby maintain reasonable confidence and trust which an employee is entitled to have in an employer.'

The employer's failure to pay tax and PRSI contributions on behalf of the employee was held to be sufficient grounds to entitle the employee to succeed with a claim of constructive dismissal in *Branigan v Collins* UD 28/77.

8.6.6.2   Reduction in pay

A unilateral reduction in pay, even for good reasons and to a relatively small extent, may be a material breach of a fundamental element in the contract of employment (*Industrial Rubber Products v Gillon* [1977] IRLR 389). The employer may, however, have a contractual right to vary the employee's income (*White v Reflecting Roadstuds Ltd* [1991] IRLR 331). A refusal to pay overtime payments for overtime hours worked was held to be a breach going to the root of the contract of employment entitling the employee to claim constructive dismissal in *Stokes v Hampstead Wine Company Ltd* [1979] IRLR 298.

8.6.6.3   Working environment

In *Waltons & Morse v Dorrington* [1997] IRLR 488 a secretary employed by a firm of solicitors claimed constructive dismissal as a result of the problems she encountered with smokers in the office. A limited smoking policy was adopted by the firm but this did not lead to a sufficient improvement for Mrs Dorrington. She succeeded with a constructive dismissal claim. The UK EAT held that the employer was in breach of an implied term in her contract of employment that the employer would 'provide and monitor for employees, so far as is reasonably practicable, a working environment which is reasonably suitable for the performance by them of their contractual duties'.

8.6.6.4 Lack of pay rise

A lack of pay rises may not entitle an employee to claim constructive dismissal depending on the circumstances (*Murco Petroleum Ltd v Forge* [1987] IRLR 50). In *Riddell v Mid-West Metals Ltd* M962 UD 687/80 the employee's terms and conditions were changed in that he received a lesser bonus than he had been led to believe he would receive and he was required to carry his own motoring expenses which he had not previously been required to do. The EAT noted, however, the remuneration was reviewable under the terms of the contract and, given the fact that the claimant did not seek to engage in negotiations on the issues causing him concern, took the position that he could not accept the proposal and terminated his employment. His claim failed. See also *Conway v Ulster Bank* UD 474/81 referred to at **8.6.6.10** below.

8.6.6.5 Change in job functions

Removal of job functions or changes imposed by the employer may give rise to an entitlement to claim constructive dismissal (*Coleman v S & W Baldwin* [1977] IRLR 342). If, however, an employer for good commercial reason directs an employee to transfer to other suitable work on a purely temporary basis at no diminution in salary and it is made clear that it is only a temporary arrangement, the employee may not be entitled to claim constructive dismissal.

8.6.6.6 Change of location

An imposed change of location, where the employee is not contractually obliged to work at the new location, may give rise to a constructive dismissal claim (*Bass Leisure Ltd v Thomas* [1994] IRLR 104 and *Rank Xerox Ltd v Churchill* [1988] IRLR 280).

8.6.6.7 Change in working hours

Where an employer has the contractual right to alter hours of work and shift systems, doing so did not constitute a breach of contract and did not give rise to a constructive dismissal claim (*Dal v A S Orr* [1980] IRLR 413).

8.6.6.8 Unmerited warnings

In *Walker v Josiah Wedgewood & Sons Ltd* [1978] IRLR 105 it was held that the giving of an unjustified warning or series of warnings can give rise to a legitimate complaint of constructive dismissal if the employee makes a case that the warnings were given, not with a view to improving his conduct and performance, but with a view to disheartening him and driving him out. A tribunal in such a case would have to fully investigate the merits of the warnings complained of.

8.6.6.9 Sexual harassment or abuse in workplace

In *O'Doherty v John Paul Hennessy Junior and Harrow Holdings Ltd* [1993] ELR 161 the claimant alleged that she had been subjected to sexual harassment by a member of the first-named respondent's family. She stated that she had complained to her manager. Nothing was done about her allegations. She left her employment and claimed constructive dismissal. The EAT held that the actions complained of by the claimant amounted to sexual harassment, which justified her in terminating her employment, amounting to constructive dismissal. This case ties in with the Labour Court requirement of employers that they have in place a procedure for dealing with claims of sexual harassment. The absence of such a procedure has, on a number of occasions, been used by the Labour Court to confer liability on an employer for an allegation of sexual harassment even where the employer may have been unaware of the allegations. Had the employer in *O'Doherty* had a procedure in place for dealing with claims of sexual harassment one must presume that this claim would have been dealt with and the outcome might have been considerably different. Such procedures are a requirement of the Codes of Practice on Bullying and Harassment.

In *Kennedy v Foxfield Inns Ltd* [1995] ELR 216 the claimant gave evidence of reporting her manager for rudeness and name-calling in front of customers, standing on her foot and slapping her on the back, as a result of which she decided she could no longer work with the company. She handed in a letter of resignation giving her reasons for leaving. The manager called her to his office and apologised for any offence claiming he had 'only been messing'. In evidence to the EAT, however, the manager denied any verbal or physical abuse and denied apologising. The general manager of the employer gave evidence that he was shocked on reading the claimant's letter of resignation and had instructed the manager in question to conduct an investigation. The EAT held in all the circumstances the claimant's decision to terminate her employment was reasonable and that she had been constructively dismissed.

In *Holmes v O'Driscoll* [1991] ELR 80 the claimant was a trainee machinist. The employer had poked her in the arm with clippers and warned her to get on with her work, an action he allegedly repeated later in the day. The claimant became upset, left work and claimed that she had been constructively dismissed. The EAT held she was entitled to treat herself as constructively dismissed and that her dismissal was unfair.

The mutual bond of trust and confidence is dealt with quite comprehensively in *Woods v WM Car Services (Peterborough) Ltd* [1981] IRLR 347 and *United Bank v Akhtar* [1989] IRLR 507.

8.6.6.10   Conduct of employee

Where an employee has a difficulty with his employer he will be required to act reasonably himself and seek to resolve the matter internally before resorting to a claim of constructive dismissal. In *Conway v Ulster Bank Ltd* UD 474/81 the claimant was employed at the Sligo branch of the bank. After she became engaged to an account-holder she was given two weeks' notice of proposed transfer to Ballina. In that notice period she submitted her resignation and claimed constructive dismissal. The employer had in place a detailed grievance procedure which had not been invoked by the claimant. In holding against the claimant the EAT stated:

> 'By majority the Tribunal considered that the claimant did not act reasonably in resigning without first having substantially utilised the grievance procedure to attempt to remedy her complaints. An elaborate grievance procedure existed but the claimant did not use it. It is not for the Tribunal to say whether using this procedure would have produced a decision more favourable to her but it is possible.'

See also *Beatty v Bayside Supermarket* UD 142/87, *Harrington v Julias Ltd* UD 140/82 and *Corcoran v Amusements Eden Quay Ltd* UD 681/80.

In *Olsson v John Quinn & Co* [1992] ELR 91 the claimant alleged assault by the head barman and continuing difficulties with him. When the difficulties were not resolved the claimant left his employment and claimed unfair dismissal. The EAT dismissed his claim, holding that it was not reasonable for him to leave his employment in the manner in which he did since his employer did not know of the incident which triggered his walk-out.

The EAT took an apparently different view in *Gallery v Blarney Woollen Mills Ltd* [1990] ELR 143. Following the takeover of the shop managed by the claimant she was unhappy with a lack of clarity about her position and felt she was being undermined in a number of ways. She sought written confirmation of the terms and conditions of her employment and confirmation that the company had full confidence in her. She was unhappy with the response and demanded a written response. She was asked to attend a meeting but refused to do so. She claimed the company's conduct amounted to constructive dismissal and she resigned. She succeeded in her claim despite the EAT considering the *Conway* and *Beatty* cases. In *Gallery* the EAT held that 'the respondent company acted unreasonably in its dealings with the claimant and she became frustrated leaving her with no option but to resign'.

In *Madden v Western Regional Fisheries Board* M1356 UD 857/82 the claimant was suspended without pay, and his solicitor wrote to state that it was being treated as a constructive dismissal. The EAT noted that there were procedures in existence for dealing with staff problems but that the claimant did not avail of them and that the employee's conditions of service allowed for suspension without pay pending an investigation. The EAT stated that it would have sympathy for the claimant if he had no alternative under his contract, but as he had the right to appeal the suspension and have the matter resolved in accordance with the terms of the contract or availing of the rights commissioner services under the Industrial Relations Acts, in not doing so he had not made out a case that he was constructively dismissed.

It has been established that a constructive dismissal is not automatically unfair but it will obviously be very difficult for an employer who claims he did not dismiss a person to then argue, once dismissal has been established, that substantial grounds existed to justify doing what he claimed he did not do (*Savoia v Chiltern Herb Farms Ltd* [1982] IRLR 166). There may, however, be certain circumstances in which the employer may wish to make that argument. In *Cawley v South Wales Electricity Board* [1985] IRLR 89 the UK EAT said that the considerations of fairness under the legislation and the concept of constructive dismissal are effectively 'two sides of the same coin'. If the employer's behaviour is unreasonable enough to amount to constructive dismissal it would normally almost automatically follow that the dismissal has to be unfair.

Grievance procedures are a requirement of the Code of Practice on Grievance and Disciplinary Procedures, section 1.

8.7 Resignations

The common law rule regarding notice given by either party is that once notice is given it cannot unilaterally be withdrawn. The giving of notice is itself not a dismissal because it may be withdrawn by agreement and the dismissal does not come about until notice has expired. If, however, one party seeks to withdraw notice and the other party does not agree, a dismissal will occur and difficulties may be caused for employees where they have resigned and they seek to overturn their resignation. A leading common law case is *Riordan v War Office* [1959] 1 WLR 1046 where Diplock J stated:

'This was sufficient notice given by the plaintiff terminating his employment . . . once given it could not be withdrawn save by mutual consent.'

Even where an employer claims that an employee has resigned, some steps should be taken to ascertain why the employee resigned, some effort made to get the employee to stay, as otherwise the employer's actions might be construed as either a constructive dismissal or an actual dismissal.

In *Maxwell v Coruscate Ltd (t/a Glenview Hotel)* [1992] ELR 122 the claimant had a dispute with the head chef about being told to 'get out of the kitchen'. He then asked for his P45 and entitlements and was again told to 'get out'. He then packed up and was leaving the hotel when the chef told him he had not sacked him, that he had walked out and was therefore entitled to nothing. Some days later the claimant went back to see the owner of the hotel, who was unaware that he had been dismissed, and when the claimant told him the story said that there was nothing he could do about it and referred him back to the head chef. The claimant sought out the head chef and offered him a sick note for his absence but the head chef was not interested in dealing with him any further. The EAT held that on the evidence the claimant had been dismissed. See also *Dodd and Murphy v Houston and Morrow* UD 257/259/78.

Not all apparent resignations will be held to be effective. In *Barclay v City of Glasgow District Court* [1983] IRLR 313 it was held that Barclay had resigned but was known to have an intellectual disability and his employers were not therefore entitled to treat his words of resignation as notice of termination. In *Sothern v Franks Charlesly & Co* [1981] IRLR 278 it was held that there may be exceptions to the resignation rules as in the case of an immature employee or a decision taken in the heat of the moment which may not in fact be an effective resignation at all. A refusal by the employer to allow the employee to retract or revoke or remain in employment may in those circumstances be deemed to be a dismissal.

8.8 Date of Dismissal

The date of dismissal is of particular relevance to an employee's entitlement to bring a claim and possibly also to the time at which a claim should be brought. Unlike in Britain, the date of dismissal in Ireland may be artificial, being a date other than the date on which the actual employment terminated. Section 1 of the 1977 Act provides that the statutory date of dismissal shall be the later of:

'(i)   the earliest date that would be in compliance with the provisions of the contract; or

(ii)   the earliest date that would be in compliance with the provisions of the Minimum Notice and Terms of Employment Act, 1973 (as amended).'

See Chapter 1: Contracts of Employment.

The statutory date of dismissal is therefore the date upon which notice expires, being the longer of either the statutory or the contractual notice entitlement. This is the case even where the employee does not actually work out the notice period. The situation might be altered if the contract specifically allowed for payment in lieu of giving notice as opposed to an accommodation reached between the parties where the payment is made in lieu of the employee actually working out the notice (*Ogden v Harp Textiles* UD 112/79 and *O'Reilly v Pullman Kellog Ltd* UD 340/79) Holiday entitlements are not added to a period of service to determine length of service *Maher v B & I Line* UD 271/78 and *Twomey v O'Leary Office Supplies* [1997] ELR 42.

In constructive dismissal cases an employee may opt to give notice or not as the case may be. The date of dismissal will be the date notice expires and not a deemed date where, for example, the employee gives no notice or gives lesser notice than he might be obliged to give under the contract or the 1973 Act (*Stamp v McGrath* UD 1243/83).

8.9 Remuneration

8.9.1 CALCULATION OF REMUNERATION

The calculation of remuneration is important in the assessment of the maximum value of a claim, being actual loss attributable to a dismissal. The ability to make these calculations is of vital importance in negotiating the possible resolution of claims.

Section 7(1)(c) of the 1977 Act allows for the award of compensation to an employee held to have been unfairly dismissed and caps the amount awarded at the equivalent of 104 weeks' remuneration. The subsection further provides that the compensation is awardable *'in respect of any financial loss incurred . . . and attributable to the dismissal as is just and equitable having regard to all the circumstances'*.

Section 7 defines 'remuneration' as including *'allowances in the nature of pay and benefits in lieu of or in addition to pay'*. Remuneration has been held to include not only basic payments to an employee but the value of the loss of benefits in kind. Remuneration has been held to include such diverse items as:

(a)   basic pay or salary;

(b)   overtime payments;

(c)   bonuses;

(d)   commission;

(e)   tips;

(f)   benefits in kind such as:

  (i)   clothing allowances;

  (ii)   subsidised telephone costs;

  (iii)   private use of company car;

  (iv)   professional and social subscriptions;

  (v)   health insurance; and

  (vi)   pension contributions—it is the employer's pension cost only that is calculated.

Tribunals do not allow for loss of benefits such as preferential loans or mortgages. These are facilities made available to employees that they may or may not avail of. Employees doing identical work, one of whom avails of a maximum mortgage entitlement and the other who avails of a nil mortgage entitlement, could not be deemed to have different rates of remuneration for unfair dismissal purposes (*Bunyan v United Dominions Trust (Ireland) Ltd* UD 66/80).

When assessing remuneration for the purposes of calculating the maximum award allowable under the legislation regard is had to the gross amount of such payment.

8.9.2   ASSESSMENT OF LOSS

For the purposes of compensation loss is a matter for assessment. The 1977 Act defined financial loss in section 7 as including:

> *'. . . any actual loss and any estimated prospective loss of income attributable to the dismissal and the value of any loss or diminution attributable to the dismissal of the rights of the employee under the Redundancy Payments Acts or in relation to superannuation.'*

In case of share options the share option scheme under which the employee gets the entitlement to the shares may provide that there is no compensation for loss of share options when employment terminates as in *Micklefield v SAC Technology Ltd* [1990] IRLR 218. However, in calculating unfair dismissal compensation under the UK legislation, the UK EAT awarded compensation where employees lost the value of share options as a result of being dismissed at a particular time in *Leonard v Strathclyde Buses Ltd* [1998] IRLR 693. The UK EAT interpreted the words 'actual loss' to mean precisely that. Any benefit gained by the employee following dismissal, including unemployment benefit, was deducted from the loss of income arising from the dismissal in order to arrive at 'actual loss'.

If an employee successfully mitigated his loss immediately following a dismissal he was liable to receive a nil compensation award in the event of succeeding with an unfair dismissal claim until the enactment of the 1993 Act, section 6.

The reason why an employee might not have a loss is usually related to the fact that he was successful in mitigating the loss, but could arise for other reasons such as illness and an inability to earn at the time of and after the dismissal. In *Coyle v Tipper House Trust Ltd* UD 904/93 the EAT held that the dismissal of the claimant was unfair but made no compensatory award under the 1977 Act as the claimant had been unfit for work since his dismissal and it could not be said when, if ever, he would be fit for work in the future and he therefore had no loss. That was made prior to the enactment of the 1993 Act which allowed for the awarding of up to one month's remuneration in cases where there is no loss. See also *Cadbury Ltd v Doddington* [1977] ICR 982.

The 1993 Act made two important changes in respect of actual loss. The changes are contained in section 6. The first change was to provide that if an employee incurred no financial loss he could in any event be awarded compensation up to a maximum equivalent of four weeks' remuneration. The second substantial change made by section 6 was to provide that in calculating actual financial loss regard should not be had to social welfare benefits or income tax rebates.

8.10   Continuity of Service

As has been seen at **8.2** above, one year's continuous service is necessary in order to establish the right to claim under the Act. The year is reckoned from the date of dismissal working backwards until one reaches a break in continuity. It is possible under the rules of continuity to work during a period which is not recognisable but which does not actually break service.

Service under the age of 16 years is not computable. Probationary service is computable. Once a person is established as an employee it does not matter what designation he carries such as casual, permanent, semi-permanent, temporary etc once he satisfies the rules of continuity of service. The rules for calculation of continuity are set out in the Minimum Notice and Terms of Employment Act, 1973, Schedule 1. Service is deemed to be continuous unless otherwise broken. Continuity is not broken by normal periods of absence such as illness, holidays, maternity leave or even strikes or lockouts. All of these periods may, however, not be actually recognisable as periods of service.

The rules provide that continuity is not broken where an employee is dismissed and 'immediately' re-employed. There is no definition of immediate but in *Howard v Breton Ltd* UD 486/84 re-employment a week after dismissal was sufficiently immediate to preserve continuity but a different decision had been arrived at in the earlier case of *Mulhall & Sons v Dunphy* UD 710/81. A break of three months between periods of employment was deemed not to be sufficient to come within the expression 'immediate' re-employment contained in the Minimum Notice and Terms of Employment Act, 1973, Schedule 1, paragraph 6 in *Myles v O'Kane* [1991] ELR 217.

It is sometimes thought that the issue of a P45 constitutes the termination of an employee's employment. That is not the case—see **8.6.4** above. The issue of a form P45 or termination papers of any other sort is merely indicative, but if other facts show that the employment was not brought to an end within the normal rules of notice of termination then the employment will be deemed continuous. *Allison v Incorporated Law Society and Cullen* UD 492/86 and *O'Flanagan v Houlihan* UD 579/83. In *McKenna v Bursey Peppard Ltd* [1997] ELR 87 the claimant was absent from work due to illness and when he furnished a fitness certificate from his doctor it was refused by the employer, who sought a more detailed form of certification. Pending that issue being sorted out the employee sought and obtained his P45 in order to claim social welfare entitlements. Dismissal as a fact was in dispute and the EAT held, by a majority, that the claimant was entitled to seek his P45 to claim social welfare benefit but there had been no dismissal, or constructive dismissal, by the employer.

Lay-off does not break continuity but where a lay-off exceeds 26 weeks, the period in excess of 26 weeks is not computable as a period of service. What actually constitutes a lay-off is a question of fact. It may be argued on behalf of an employee, who has been absent from the place of work for some time or who is seeking to link two apparently separate periods of service with one employer, that there was actually a lay-off covering the gap. In some of the more traditional industries the term 'lay-off' or 'laid off' is used and the word 'terminate' would be more appropriate.

8.11   Employees Working Outside Ireland

The legislation does not apply to the dismissal of an employee who ordinarily works outside the State unless (section 2(3) of the Unfair Dismissals Act, 1977):

> '(i)   he was ordinarily resident in the State during the term of the contract, or
>
> (ii)   he was domiciled in the State during the term of the contract, and the employer—
>
> > (I)   in case the employee was an individual, was ordinarily resident in the State during the term of the contract, or
> >
> > (II)   in case the employer was a body corporate or an unincorporated body of persons had, its principal place of business in the State during the term of the contract.'

The first part of the definition excludes from the legislation employees working outside Ireland and not ordinarily resident here during the term of the contract. What constitutes residence in the State will effectively be determined by the employee's base during the performance of the contractual obligations. If an employee lives and works outside the State during the currency of a contract of employment he will not be in a position to claim unfair dismissal on the termination of his contract.

In *Dignam v Sisk Nigeria Ltd* UD 125/83 and *D'arcy v General Electric Technical Services Company Inc* UD 542/86 both claimants were Irish nationals working outside the State and, in both cases, the employer's principal place of business was outside the State and the claimants were held not to be entitled to claim under the legislation.

Non-nationals are entitled to claim under the legislation if they work for Irish companies. Non-nationals working for foreign companies in Ireland are also covered by the legislation (*Roder v Liebig International Ltd* UD 144/79 and *Kay v Nobrac Carbon Ltd* Circuit Court No 63, 18 December 1985—Kerr and Madden, *Unfair Dismissals Cases and Commentary*, p 116).

A comprehensive assessment of entitlement to claim in respect of work carried on outside the State is set out in the British case of *Wilson v Maynard Shipbuilding Consultants* [1977] IRLR 419, albeit in the context of somewhat different British legislation. In determining the practice to be taken into account the UK Court of Appeal laid down the following tests.

(a)   An employee either works in Great Britain or outside it. He only does one or the other and not both. If he carries out some of his work in Great Britain that appears to be sufficient to entitle him to claim.

(b)   The key factor is what is envisaged under the contract and not what happens in practice.

(c)   It is necessary to look at the whole period contemplated by the contract at the time it was made. It is not sufficient to look at what happened the short time before the contract was terminated which may not be representative of what the parties had in mind at the time the contract was formed.

(d)   In the absence of special factors an employee's base is to be his ordinary workplace.

(e) An employee's base may be determined by looking at his headquarters, where he starts and finishes his travels, where he lives, where he is paid and in what currency and where he makes his tax and social security payments.

It is only necessary to use the base test if the ordinary workplace cannot be established otherwise from the terms of the employment contract (*Carver v Saudi Arabian Airlines* [1999] IRLR 991).

In *Zimmerman v Der Deutsche Schuliverein Ltd* [1999] ELR 211 the claimant, a German civil servant, had been appointed as principal of a German school in Dublin. The claimant brought a claim against the school for unfair dismissal and the EAT had to consider the question of its jurisdiction holding that the terms of the Rome Convention on the Law Applicable to Contractual Obligations, 1980 and section 13 of the 1977 Act, which renders void any contractual provision seeking to limit or exclude the effect of that Act, applied so that it had jurisdiction to hear the claim.

In *Murphy v NIPPA* UD 833/2004 the EAT heard evidence from the claimant as to the carrying out of her work in Northern Ireland and the Republic of Ireland, the fact that her job was part-funded by the Irish Department of Justice, Equality and Law Reform, that she was originally paid in Irish currency, and a number of other factors, in coming to its finding that it was entitled to hear the claimant's unfair dismissal claim.

See also **1.5.25** on proper law in Chapter 1: Contracts of Employment.

8.12 Diplomatic Immunity

Employees of embassies and foreign governments in Ireland cannot bring dismissal claims against their employers where the employer is entitled generally to diplomatic immunity—which is not provided for or referred to in the unfair dismissal legislation (*Government of Canada v Employment Appeals Tribunal* [1991] ELR 57).

8.13 Probation

There are complicated provisions relating to probation and training in the legislation. The 1977 Act allows for the exclusion of persons on probation or training but only where the period of such is less than one year, in which case all of the distinctions appear to be largely academic. The fact that employees are on probation or undergoing training has therefore no effect on continuity or status and is entirely recognisable. Employers should at all times have regard to the statutory date of dismissal where employees are being trained or are undergoing probationary assessment in order to ensure that the employment does not extend to or beyond the one-year period in which event, if they were to terminate the employment, they may find themselves having to show that substantial grounds existed to justify the termination in circumstances where they believed otherwise.

8.14 Apprentices

A contract of apprenticeship may be defined as one in which the apprentice agrees to serve the employer and to learn from him and the employer agrees to instruct the apprentice in his trade, profession or business and to maintain him during the continuance of that relationship. The general view is that an employer may terminate an apprenticeship if the apprentice's conduct is such that the employer can no longer instruct him. Certain apprenticeship agreements are capable of being construed as fixed-term or specified-purpose contracts and both parties should have regard to the specific terms of an apprenticeship or training contract which is something that is frequently overlooked.

Apprentices' rights are curtailed under the 1977 Act, section 4 which provides that '*the Act shall not apply in relation to the dismissal of a person who is or was employed under a statutory apprenticeship if the dismissal takes place within six months after the commencement of the apprenticeship or within one month after the completion of the apprenticeship*'.

What is the meaning of a 'statutory apprenticeship'? Section 1 of the 1977 Act defines statutory apprenticeship as being apprenticeship '*in a designated industrial activity within the meaning of the Industrial Training Act, 1967*'.

The effect of section 4 of the 1977 Act is that apprentices are not protected for the first six months of their employment and for a period of one month following completion of the apprenticeship. This means that once an apprentice has completed six months of an apprenticeship he is covered by the legislation where otherwise he might be thought to require the one year's continuous service (*MacNamara v Castlelock Construction & Development Ltd* UD 808/84). It must be stressed, however, that this relates only to statutory apprentices.

It appears that the employers of non-statutory apprentices, e.g. solicitors, are not in a position to allow a period of one month to elapse after the apprenticeship has ended. Non-statutory apprenticeships should be treated as specified purpose contracts where the employer wishes to be adequately protected from unfair dismissal claims.

In *Boal v IMED Ireland Ltd* [1995] ELR 178 the employee was employed under a statutory apprenticeship for six years. His contract was terminated one month after the completion of the apprenticeship. The employers claimed that they had informed the claimant on a number of occasions during the six years of his apprenticeship that they would not be retaining him on the ending of his apprenticeship. The EAT held that the claimant was employed under a contract of statutory apprenticeship and was therefore excluded from cover of the Unfair Dismissals Acts and his claim was dismissed.

In *O'Callaghan v Denis Mahony Ltd* UD 177/79 the claimant worked as an apprentice from 1974 to 1978 when his apprenticeship came to an end. When given notice of expiration of the apprenticeship the claimant requested a month's extension of time and this was granted. He planned on emigrating to Australia but encountered some delays as a result of which a further extension of time was granted to him. Eventually the respondent company dismissed the claimant on the basis that it maintained it could not longer afford to retain him as an employee. The EAT took the view that the respondent company could not rely on section 4 of the 1977 Act. The dismissal was in any event held to be fair. It should not be taken therefore that because the one-month period has elapsed the employer is under any obligation to give permanent employment to the former apprentice. Tribunals will look sympathetically on a situation where an apprentice ceases to hold that status and becomes a different type of individual and where the employer may reach temporary accommodation with him. Employers should, however, make their position very clear in this regard.

See also *Rooney and Byrne v Abbey Homesteads Ltd* UD 712/80 and UD 2/81 heard as one case and also *Farrell v J D Brian Motors Ltd* UD 341/87.

8.15   Unfair Dismissals

8.15.1   CATEGORIES

For the purpose of the legislation dismissals are divided into two categories:

(a)   dismissals deemed to be automatically unfair; or

(b)   dismissals deemed to be not unfair.

Section 6(2) of the 1977 Act as amended by the 1993 Act, section 5 sets out the categories of 'automatically' unfair dismissal which are:

(a)   an employee's membership (or proposed membership) or activity on behalf of a trade union where the times in which he engages in such activities are outside his hours of work or are at permitted times during his hours of work.

In *White v Betson* [1992] ELR 120 the EAT held that the coincidence of the employer having received correspondence from a trade union prior to the termination of the claimant's employment and the making of the decision to dismiss was such that the claimant was dismissed because of his trade union membership and, accordingly, the dismissal was unfair.

In *O'Riordan v Killine Eyewear Ltd* [1991] ELR 89 the EAT held that the coincidence of a clear intention by the claimants to join a trade union, the fact that this was known to the respondent and the making of the decision to terminate their contracts of employment were such that the dismissal was held to be by reason of trade union membership and held to be unfair;

(b)   the employee's religious or political opinions;

(c)   because the employee is engaged in civil or criminal proceedings against the employer or is a party or a witness to such proceedings whether they are actual, threatened or proposed, or where the employee has made any complaint or statement to the prosecuting authority connected with the case;

(d)   the race, colour or sexual orientation of the employee;

(e)   because the employee exercised or attempted to exercise the right to parental leave or force majeure leave under the Parental Leave Act, 1998, or carer's leave under the Carer's Leave Act, 2001;

(f)   the age of the employee.

In *Kerrigan v Peter Owens Advertising and Marketing Ltd* UD 31/97 the claimant was declared redundant by the company for a number of reasons, one of which was his age. While the EAT held that there was no redundancy situation at the time of dismissal it determined that the claimant's dismissal arose wholly or mainly from his age in contravention of the 1977 Act, section 6(2), as amended, and awarded compensation;

(g)   the employee's membership of the travelling community;

(h)   the pregnancy of the employee or matters connected therewith.

This provision must be cross-referenced to maternity legislation. Reasons connected with pregnancy have been held to include miscarriages and hypertension. *George v Beecham Group* [1977] IRLR 43 and *Elegbede v The Wellcome Foundation* [1977] IRLR 383.

Section 6(2)(f) of the 1977 Act provides however that the dismissal of a pregnant employee will not be unfair if the employee was unable by reason of the pregnancy or matters connected therewith:

'(I) to do adequately the work for which she was employed, or

(II) to continue to do such work without contravention by her or her employer of a provision of a statute or instrument made under statute, and

(ii) (I) there was not, at the time of the dismissal, any other employment with her employer that was suitable for her and in relation to which there was a vacancy, or

(II) she refused an offer by her employer of alternative employment on terms and conditions corresponding to those of the employment to which the dismissal related, being an offer made so as to enable her to be retained in the employment notwithstanding her pregnancy.'

An employer may therefore dismiss a pregnant employee who is incapable of doing her work provided the employer has sought out a suitable alternative vacancy and there is not one, or she refuses a reasonable offer of one (*Matthews v Ophardt Products Ltd* UD 550/83, *Hallissey v Pretty Polly (Killarney) Ltd* UD 362/84 and *McCarthy v Sunbeam Ltd* [1991] ELR 38). Regard must be had in all such cases to the provisions of the Maternity Protection Act, 1994, which makes provision in section 18 for health and safety leave for a pregnant employee in certain circumstances, and the Safety, Health and Welfare at Work (Pregnant Employees etc) Regulations, 2000 which place a duty on every employer to carry out a risk assessment and to make the employee aware of the results of that risk assessment (*Coffey v Byrne* [1997] ELR 230).

8.15.2   ENGAGING IN INDUSTRIAL ACTION

Section 5(2) of the 1977 Act as amended provides:

'The dismissal of an employee for taking part in a strike or other industrial action shall be deemed for the purposes of this Act to be an unfair dismissal if:

(a) one or more employees of the same employer who took part in the strike or other industrial action were not dismissed for so taking part, or;

(b) one or more of such employees who were dismissed for so taking part were subsequently permitted to resume their employment on terms and conditions at least as favourable to the employees as those specified in the said paragraph (a) or (b) and the employee was not.'

In *Tuke v Coillte Teoranta* [1998] ELR 324 the claimants engaged in industrial action together with a number of colleagues. The dispute was resolved with some of their colleagues but the claimants became subject to disciplinary procedures ultimately leading to their dismissal. The dismissal was held to be unfair on the following grounds:

(a) even though the claimants' actions were unreasonable they did constitute industrial action within the meaning of the Unfair Dismissals Act, 1977;

(b) the claimants were dismissed because of their industrial action;

(c) two employees who took part in the industrial action had been allowed to resume their employment while the claimants who also took part remained dismissed. Accordingly section 5(2) of the 1977 Act meant that the claimants had been unfairly dismissed;

(d) reinstatement was not the appropriate form of redress because the claimants' behaviour had been unreasonable and they were the authors of their own misfortune; and

(e) the claimants were to be re-engaged. Remuneration was not to commence until the date of the re-engagement and the respondent was not to be penalised with any claim for back pay.

8.16   Unfair Dismissal and Redundancy

The 1977 Act provides, at section 6(4)(c), that a dismissal is deemed not to be an unfair dismissal if it resulted wholly or mainly from the redundancy of the employee. Redundancy is therefore an absolute defence to a claim of unfair dismissal, provided the employee has been fairly selected for redundancy. Strict adherence to the definition of redundancy is required from employers if an employee is to be held to be dismissed by reason of redundancy. Redundancy defences are closely scrutinised. An example of a failure, on the part of an employer, to strictly adhere to the definition is to be found in *Keenan v Gresham Hotel Company Ltd* UD 478/88 where the EAT stated, in the context of section 7(2)(g) of the Redundancy Payments Act, 1967 that an employer, who dismisses employees on the grounds that his workforce requirements 'are expected to cease or diminish', must establish that the cesser or diminution was 'expected to occur at or within a very short time after the time of the alleged redundancy'. It is not enough for an employer to claim that his workforce requirements are expected to cease or diminish 'at some distant time in the future'.

Redundancy is dealt with in more detail in Chapter 10: Redundancy.

8.17   Strikes and Lock-outs

Where an employee participated in a strike or lock-out and one or more other participants were not similarly dismissed or were subsequently offered reinstatement or re-engagement and the claimant was not, the dismissal will be deemed to be unfair. Section 4 of the 1993 Act has amended the 1977 Act in relation to strikes and lock-outs. It extends the provisions of the Act to situations where the employee may have been taken back but on terms not as favourable as employees who did not take part in the strike or lock-out.

The original 1977 provision simply protected employees against victimisation of being the only one to be dismissed or the only one not to be taken back following a strike or lock-out. The 1993 amendment extended this to a situation where they were taken back but after return were treated less favourably than people who remained throughout. The 1993 Act provided not only that better terms and conditions should apply to employees taken back after a strike or lock-out if they had been afforded to others but also that reinstatement or re-engagement should be deemed to have commenced on the earliest date on which reinstatement or re-engagement was offered to the majority of other employees who are the subject of the lock-out or took part in the strike or other industrial action (*Tuke v Coillte Teoranta* [1998] ELR 324).

In *Butler v MB Ireland* UD 1058/82 the company maintained that the claimant was dismissed because of misconduct surrounding the taking of official action. The EAT, however, held on the evidence that 'the paramount reason for the termination was the action taken by the claimant . . . i.e. the strikes'. The EAT then referred to the 1977 Act, section 5 and found that the dismissal was unfair. Compensation was awarded and reduced by 33 per cent due to the contribution of the claimant to his own dismissal. This case also shows that section 5 will apply to unofficial action as well as official action.

8.18   Procedural Fairness

8.18.1   GENERAL

The 1977 Act made no reference to procedures that might or might not be followed by an employer prior to effecting a dismissal. Courts and tribunals, however, implied into the concept of 'fairness' under the 1977 Act the requirement that an employer not only have substantial grounds as is required by the legislation but also carry out the dismissal in a manner that was procedurally fair. This is a reflection of the constitutional right to fair procedures.

The 1993 Act enshrines procedural requirements in the legislation by providing at section 5(b) that in determining fairness the decision-maker shall have regard to:

'(a)   the reasonableness or otherwise of the conduct (whether by act or omission) of the employer in relation to the dismissal, and

(b)   the extent (if any) of the compliance or failure to comply by the employer, in relation to the employee, with the procedure referred to in section 14(1) of the 1977 Act.'

The 1977 Act provides for furnishing employees with the disciplinary procedure that will be followed in the event of dismissal being contemplated. Regard must also be had to an employer's failure to comply with any code of practice drawn up under the terms of the 1993 Act itself.

8.18.2   CASE LAW

8.18.2.1   Employment Appeals Tribunal

The EAT has always taken the view that if an employer acts in a manner that is procedurally unfair the dismissal itself will be held to be unfair. In *Caulfield v Verbatim Ltd* UD 938/93 the claimant was dismissed by reason of excessive absence from work. While the dismissal was held to be fair, the trade union representative gave a dissenting opinion stating:

'Regardless of the guilt or otherwise of the claimant ... the procedures used by the company to effect the decision to dismiss must, in my view, be open and transparent, and the company's behaviour must be seen to be reasonable. ... In this case those criteria were not met ... the procedures used by the company in dismissing the claimant were seriously flawed. Where the behaviour of the employer is seen as being unreasonable in this context I believe the Tribunal must find the dismissal to be unfair whether the employee is guilty or not of the offence for which the employer seeks to dismiss her.'

Whilst the EAT prefers to stick with the basic importance of fair procedure where an employer's procedural default arises in a case where a dismissal was in any event clearly justified the EAT tends to award compensation and reduce the amount of compensation by a significant percentage measure of the employee's contribution to his own dismissal. This is in some cases as high as 100 per cent (*Sheehan v HM Keating & Sons Ltd* [1993] ELR 12, *Murray v Meath County Council* UD 43/78 and *Condron v Rowntree Mackintosh Ltd* UD 195/79).

In *Gearon v Dunnes Stores Ltd* UD 367/88 the EAT held that fair procedures had not been followed and concluded:

'The right to defend herself and have her arguments and submissions listened to and evaluated by the respondent in relation to the threat to her employment is a right of the claimant and is not the gift of the respondent or this Tribunal ... the right is a fundamental one under natural and constitutional justice, it is not open to this Tribunal to forgive its breach.'

In *White v Cadbury (Ireland) Ltd* UD 44/79 the claimant was dismissed for failing to refuse to submit to a search properly requested in accordance with his conditions of employment. In essence the facts of what occurred were not in dispute. The evidence, however, showed that the decision to dismiss was taken following reports of the incident of refusal and not after any further investigation had been carried out involving White himself and the hearing with him. The EAT held:

> 'The denial to the appellant of the opportunity to make or present his counter-arguments prior to . . . [the] decision to dismiss him was, in our opinion, a breach of his fundamental right to be confronted with the evidence against him and to make counter-arguments, explanations, pleas etc as may be relevant. We are accordingly of the opinion that the denial of this fundamental right to the appellant had the inevitable result of rendering this dismissal an unfair dismissal and we determine accordingly.'

Given the accepted conduct of Mr White the EAT determined to award him compensation but reduced his compensation by 100 per cent attributable to his contribution to his own loss.

The EAT carried out an extensive review of the law on investigation, fair procedures and decision-making, in cases of alleged misconduct in its decision in the case of *Pacelli v Irish Distillers Ltd* [2004] ELR 25.

8.18.2.2   Supreme Court

In *Gallagher v Revenue Commissioners* [1995] ELR 108 the Supreme Court held that the requirements of fair procedures encompassed the following.

(a)   Given the consequences for the applicant in the event of a decision adverse to him the employer was obliged to act judicially and adopt procedures which were fair and reasonable. While tribunals exercising quasi-judicial functions are given a certain latitude in the exercise of their functions and in determining the requirements of natural justice and fair procedures in the circumstances of the case they may not act in such a way as to imperil a fair hearing or a fair result.

(b)   Mere administrative difficulties in securing the attendance of witnesses before a tribunal or inquiry are not a sufficient ground for depriving a person charged before the tribunal of the right to cross-examine witnesses as to facts which are essential to the establishment of the charges against him.

(c)   As far as the applicant was concerned the charges against him were substantial. The failure of the employer to require direct evidence . . . deprived the applicant of the opportunity of hearing this evidence, or challenging it by means of cross-examination. This was contrary to the requirements of natural justice and the requirements of fair procedures.

In a preliminary application in *Gallagher* the High Court, per Blayney J had held that having regard to the nature of the charges which could result in the respondent's dismissal in the event of an adverse decision he was entitled to legal representation at the disciplinary hearing. Against that Barr J had held in the case of *Aziz v Midland Health Board* [1995] ELR 48 that a doctor who was under investigation for an alleged failure to attend for duty had no general right to legal representation at a quasi-judicial disciplinary hearing. The Supreme Court judgment in *Georgopoulus v Beaumont Hospital Board*, 4 June 1997 unreported indicates that the courts are likely to require that if an employee seeks to be legally represented in a case where his employment is in jeopardy refusal by the employer rendered the procedure unfair.

8.18.3 EMPLOYEE SUBJECT TO CRIMINAL CHARGES

The making of criminal charges against an employee and the processing of such criminal charges may complicate an employer's disciplinary procedure. Frequently such disciplinary procedures are delayed or suspended while the criminal charges are being processed. This is often done at the behest of the employee, usually on the grounds that as he has the right to remain silent in the criminal case this right may be compromised if he is required to defend himself in a disciplinary case. Given that the criminal case would involve the individual losing his liberty it will take precedence.

What then happens to the disciplinary process if the employee is acquitted of the criminal charges? In the High Court decision in *Mooney v An Post* [1994] ELR 103 Keane J stated that the 'acquittal of criminal charges does not preclude employers from considering whether an employee should or should not be dismissed because of circumstances which gave rise to the charges'. (*McGrath v Commissioner of An Garda Síochána* [1991] 1 IR 69 was considered.)

See also **8.23.2** below.

8.18.4 IMPORTANCE OF PARTICULAR CIRCUMSTANCES

The requirements of procedural justice may vary depending on the particular circumstances of each case. In *A Worker v Hospital* [1997] ELR 214 Shanley J considered the procedural requirements of a disciplinary investigation where a hospital employee was accused by a patient, suffering from a schizophrenic condition and said to be mentally fragile, of sexually abusing her. The employee sought to cross-examine the patient in the course of the investigation but medical experts on behalf of the hospital advised that a validation interview take place and that she only be interviewed about the allegations by a person specially trained in interviewing mentally handicapped people. The plaintiff had the facility of nominating a suitable expert to assess the complainant in the presence of the hospital's experts but the complainant herself would not be produced for questioning by the plaintiff in the course of the investigation. The allegations of the complainant would therefore be conveyed by experts and would of necessity contain hearsay. The plaintiff sought an interlocutory injunction restraining the defendant from commencing and determining a disciplinary charge against him without him being afforded the opportunity to hear and test, by cross-examination, the evidence of the complainant. Shanley J refused to grant an injunction holding:

'1. The requirements of natural justice must depend on the circumstances of each case and the nature of each particular inquiry. In considering the question of the admissibility of hearsay evidence all the facts must be examined and the rights and interests of all the parties must, as far as it is practicable, be safeguarded.' [*Southern Health Board v CH* 11 March 1996, Supreme Court unreported followed.]

2. In determining the question as to the admissibility of hearsay evidence in the present case the court would seek to balance the risk of serious damage to the complainant's health if she were forced to give evidence against the risk that a serious injustice would be done to the plaintiff if she did not.

3. Injustice to the plaintiff could be avoided by directing that further validation of the complainant's complaints be carried out in the presence of the complainant's doctor by an expert nominated by the plaintiff. Such validation to be carried out in advance of the hearing and any report produced to be the property of the plaintiff.

4. Where as normally applications for interlocutory injunctions should be decided by reference to the principles of whether or not a serious issue was to be tried, the balance of convenience and the adequacy of damages, there are exceptional cases where those principles would have no application and the instant case was such a case.'

In *Pritchard v Oracle Ireland Ltd* [1992] ELR 24 the EAT's requirement for fair procedures focused on sales, budgets and forecasts and the employee's failure to meet his sales targets. The absence of adequate warnings rendered the dismissal unfair.

The EAT also places very considerable importance on the following of agreed procedures within an employment (*Mellett v Tara Mines Ltd* [1997] ELR 79). Such procedures are usually disciplinary procedures but may include grievance procedures—see **8.19** below.

8.19   Grievance Procedures

The Industrial Relations Act, 1990 empowers the Labour Relations Commission to prepare codes of practice on matters of relevance under that legislation and to industrial relations generally. The LRC drafted a Code of Practice on Grievance and Disciplinary Procedures which was given a statutory basis on the enactment of SI 2000/146 and the Industrial Relations Act, 1990 (Code of Practice on Grievance and Disciplinary Procedures), (Declarations) Order, 2000. The main features of the Order are as follows.

(a)   All employers should have specified or agreed procedures in place to deal with discipline and grievance issues which should be in writing and given to all employees at the commencement of employment.

(b)   All members of management, including supervisory personnel, should be fully conversant with such procedures and follow them when applicable.

(c)   The Code of Practice provides that employee representatives may and should assist employees in dealing with issues under such procedures. The Code of Practice however defines employee representatives as either being a colleague of the employee's choice, or a registered trade union. It excludes any other person or body 'unconnected with the enterprise'. This would seem to exclude legal representation, which while it may not be desirable from industrial relations perspective to have lawyers involved in internal employment disputes, particularly grievances, runs contrary to employees' entitlements in law—see Clause 4.4.

(d)   Procedures dealing with grievances and disciplinary issues require that the issues be fairly examined and processed with all allegations or complaints being put forward to be addressed with an opportunity to the employee to respond with the right of representation and to have fair and impartial determination of the issues concerned, taking into account any representations made by or on behalf of the employee and any other relevant or appropriate evidence, factors or circumstances.

(e)   A number of disciplinary sanctions are allowed for ranging from oral warning to dismissal and including 'demotion'. This also runs contrary to the common law which will only allow demotion where contractually provided for, or on foot of a contractual variation agreed between the parties, both of which would be unusual. It must be noted that at common law the Code of Practice does not confer the right on an employer to demote an employee as a disciplinary sanction.

(f)   The Code allows for suspension on full pay pending the outcome of an investigation into an alleged breach of discipline.

(g)   The Code provides that warnings should be removed from an employee's record after a specified period and the employee advised accordingly.

Grievance procedures are commonly contained in contracts of service or union/ management agreements or works rules books and may be very relevant to dismissal cases which may focus on the manner of operation of the grievance procedure by either the employer or the employee (*Conway v Ulster Bank* referred to in **8.6.6.10** above on constructive dismissal). Even where a formal grievance procedure is not in place one may be implied as in *W A Goold (Pearmak) Ltd v McConnell* [1995] IRLR 516 and *Waltons & Morse v Dorrington* [1997] IRLR 488 where the UK EAT held in considering an appeal from the industrial tribunal:

> 'The industrial tribunal was also entitled to find that the employers had failed properly to address the employee's grievance and therefore were in breach of the implied contractual term enunciated by the EAT in *W A Goold (Pearmak) Ltd v McConnell* that the employer will reasonably and promptly afford employees a reasonable opportunity to obtain redress of any grievance.'

8.20 Warnings

8.20.1 GENERALLY

In cases other than fundamental breach, such as dishonesty, gross misconduct, etc warnings are a necessity in order to show that fair procedures were followed. An employee is entitled to know that his job is in jeopardy. Many employments provide for detailed disciplinary procedures with variation dependent on the nature of the 'offence'. There is no particular format set out for a warning but it should be clear and unequivocal and the employee should be made fully aware of the cause of the complaint whether it be his conduct, lack of competence or other reason with the consequences clearly spelt out to the employee in the event that the warning is not heeded. The employee must also be given reasonable time and opportunity to improve. The EAT laid down principles relating to warning in *Richardson v H Williams Ltd* UD 17/79 where it stated:

> 'Where an employee has been given a justified warning that unless his work improved in a specific area and that his job would be in jeopardy otherwise then it follows that he must be given:
> (1) a reasonable work situation within which to concentrate on such defects;
> (2) a reasonable time in which to effect such an improvement; and
> (3) the employer must in a fair and reasonable way monitor his progress and reaction in relation to such warning.
> 'If an employee improves in the complained-of area to the reasonable satisfaction of the employer and such defect is not repeated then such a warning cannot be solely relied upon for dismissal for other reasons.'

Warnings must be clear and unequivocal and not simply hints or broad statements (see *O'Donoghue v Emerson Electric (Ireland) Ltd* UD 177/86). The claimant was the managing director of an American multi-national. His superiors had indicated on a number of occasions their dissatisfaction with the performance of the company. However, he did not receive a clear and unequivocal warning of possible dismissal. His dismissal was held to be unfair.

In *Evode Industrial Ltd v Hearst and O'Shea* UD 396/397/79 the EAT held that in cases of dishonesty no warning is necessary.

Tribunals will not allow a situation where warnings remain effective for an indefinite period. This will depend greatly on the nature of the warning but, in the main, tribunals will allow the clearing of an employee's record after a lapse of a period of time without the employer having any further cause for complaint. Some employments allow that warnings will lapse or be expunged after a specified period of time. In *Gibbons v Donnolly Mirrors Ltd* UD 196/82 the claimant was dismissed following warnings. However, the company grievance procedure allowed, in certain circumstances, that warnings would be expunged after a period of six weeks. The company felt, however, that although warnings were expunged they should remain on file and could not be ignored in the event of subsequent misconduct.

The EAT held that this was not made clear to the claimant or his union who were entitled to believe that the warnings had been expunged and the dismissal was held to be unfair.

There have been cases, where senior management were involved, in which the courts and tribunals have held that the need for warnings and opportunities to improve was less apparent or necessary than in relation to less senior employees. There have also been cases where inadequacy of performance was so extreme as to be irredeemable. In such cases warnings would not be effective (*Grant v Ampex Great Britain Ltd* [1980] IRLR 461, *James v Waltham Holy Cross UDC* [1973] IRLR 202 and *Cooke v Thomas Linnell & Sons Ltd* [1977] IRLR 132).

8.20.2   PERFORMANCE-RELATED PROBLEMS

For employers seeking to justify a dismissal for a performance-related problem the employer should be in a position to explain the problem and how they dealt with it under the following headings.

(a)   They must be able to give an explanation as to how the problem came to light. It is not safe to presume that the problem suddenly materialised, particularly where an employee has service of any appreciable length.

(b)   The employer must be able to show that they carried out a thorough investigation as to the reasons why performance fell short of what was normally required. Again it is not sufficient simply to show that there was a failure of performance and that disciplinary action resulted. It may later transpire that there was an obvious reason for the shortfall in performance. A thorough investigation will, or should, unearth such a difficulty at an early stage.

(c)   There must be a clear warning to the employee that he is falling short of the employer's requirements. Emphasis on what is required of him should be made at this stage. Employers should avoid vagueness and, while a blunt warning may appear harsh, it is in both parties' interests that there be no misunderstanding as to what was actually meant.

(d)   The employer must be able to show that the employee was counselled as to the need to improve and that assistance was offered to help the employee to improve.

(e)   The employer must be able to show that they monitored the response to the warning, not simply that the employee was left to his own devices until the employer came back at a later stage and expressed further dissatisfaction and imposed further disciplinary sanction.

(f)   If there is no improvement the employer must be able to show that they investigated as to why the warning, counselling and assistance had not given rise to the required improvement.

(g)   There must at some stage, if a dismissal was the result, have been a final warning that is clear and unequivocal as to:

(i)   what the problem was;

(ii)   what was required of the employee;

(iii)   the consequences of failing to meet the required standards; and

(iv)   when those consequences could be expected to result. An employer should not simply demand that the standards be met by a specific date but rather that the standards be met on an ongoing basis and maintained into the future.

(h)   The employer must have available evidence of the failure to meet the requirements of the final warning, that that evidence was put to the employee and the employee was allowed the facility of responding and making a case against dismissal before the final decision to dismiss was made.

8.21 Targets

As to employments where targets are set for the measurement of work and performance, see *Nagle v Mulcahy Group West Ltd* UD 621/81 where the employee was not given sufficient opportunity to improve. The EAT held that the claimant should have been clearly instructed as to the targets expected and warned of the consequences of not reaching those targets. Where an employee reaches a required target and then proceeds to deteriorate in respect of subsequent targets the EAT may well require the employer to revert to the first stage of a warning procedure.

In *Sweeney v Canada Life Assurance Ireland Ltd* UD 1994 the employee was warned of the consequences of failure to meet targets, met the targets and, in the next year for which targets were set, fell below target. The EAT held that once the claimant had reached the target following warning the employer should have recommenced from the initial stage of the disciplinary process in the event of further shortcomings.

Where employers encounter persistent highs and lows on target or budget achievement, warnings might be worded in such a way as to make it clear to the employee that reaching targets on an inconsistent basis is unsatisfactory and be advised as to the consequences of future failures which may not require the employer to revert to the first stage of a procedure. In *Murphy v Kilkenny Marble Works Ltd* UD 608/83 the claimant was dismissed for failure to reach specified sales targets. In examining the facts of the situation the EAT held that the targets themselves were unreasonable and the dismissal was unfair for that and for other specified procedural reasons.

In *Hanlon v Smith Dolphins Barn Ltd* UD 883/82 the EAT held that increases in targets, which the claimant subsequently failed to meet, were not reasonable and the dismissal was held to be unfair. See also *Pritchard v Oracle Ireland Ltd* [1992] ELR 24.

8.22 Suspension

Suspension may arise in the context of removing an employee from the workplace during the course of an investigation or, alternatively, as a disciplinary sanction. Suspension without pay may not be resorted to unless the employer has a contractual right to do so. In the context of suspension pending investigation, suspension without pay might well be deemed to be prejudgment of the outcome of the investigation. Suspension should only be for a limited time. Indefinite suspension will not be tolerated by the courts. In *Flynn v An Post* [1987] IR 68 the Supreme Court held that prolonged suspension was unfair and that the power of suspension must be construed as permitting suspension to continue only for the period of time in which it was not reasonably practicable to hold a full hearing or investigation.

In *Morgan v Trinity College* [2004] ELR 235 the court considered the legal principles governing suspensions generally and drew a distinction between punitive suspensions, being a disciplinary sanction in themselves, and suspensions effected in order that the employer can carry out an inquiry as to what occurred and what action or sanction, if any, should follow. The court held that suspension cannot be open-ended but may only continue for that period of time during which it would be reasonably practicable to hold a full hearing appropriate to the circumstances of what was under investigation.

In *D & J McKenzie Ltd v Smith* [1976] IRLR 345 it was held that an employer is not entitled unilaterally to suspend an employee unless there is some provision, express or implied, in the contract of employment permitting him to do so.

In *Deegan v Dunnes Stores Ltd* [1992] ELR 184 the claimants had been placed on indefinite suspension for refusing to sign undertakings in relation to certain management requirements. The EAT held that:

'. . . indefinite suspension amounted to dismissal and that the dismissal in this case was unfair as it was too severe a penalty but that the claimants had contributed to their dismissal through their lack of co-operation which gives rise to the undertaking requirement in the first place.'

8.23 Disciplinary Hearing

8.23.1 GENERAL REQUIREMENTS

The requirements to be followed in a disciplinary hearing were set out by the Supreme Court in *Connolly v McConnell* [1983] IR 172. It was held:

'When a person holds a full-time pensionable office from which he may be removed, and thus be deprived of his means of livelihood and of his pension rights the domestic tribunal or body having the power to remove him are exercising quasi-judicial functions. Therefore they may not remove him without first according to him natural justice. He must be given the reasons for his proposed dismissal and an adequate opportunity of making his defence to the allegations made against him—audi alteram partem. The members of the Tribunal must be impartial and not be judges in their own cause—nemo iudex in causa sua. They must ensure that the proceedings are conducted fairly. In determining whether the Tribunal is impartial a member is not to be regarded as impartial if his own interest might be affected by the decision: and this interest is not necessarily to be confined to pecuniary interest.'

While *McConnell* dealt with an officer of a trade union the quotation referred to encapsulates the thinking of the EAT. In *Ryan v CIE* UD 27/84 the EAT held:

'Whatever the seriousness of the allegations made against an employee there is a duty on the employer to:
(1) Fully investigate the circumstances surrounding the alleged offence.
(2) Complete such an investigation prior to taking disciplinary action.
(3) Offer the employee and his union or legal advisor the opportunity of defending the charge.
(4) Create an environment of parity between the employee and his accusers at any oral hearing of inquiry/appeal.'

8.23.2 CRIMINAL INVESTIGATIONS

In *Ryan v CIE* UD 27/84 the EAT also dealt with a situation where an employer wished to investigate at the same time as the Gardaí had become involved in a criminal investigation of the same or similar facts. The EAT stated:

'In addition it has been established in a previous unfair dismissal claim involving the same employer, *Kelly v CIE* UD 28/78, that involvement of the Gardaí in a criminal investigation should properly have resulted in the suspension of the company's internal investigations in so far as they required the appellant/accused person to comment on the allegations the subject of the criminal charge unless the accused person consents with the knowledge and agreement of his legal representative where such a representative has been instructed.'

In *Burlington Sportswear Fabrics Ltd v O'Connor* UD 103/83 the dismissal involved allegations of fighting. A number of statements had been taken by the employer in the course of investigation but not all of these statements were put to the claimant and he did not therefore have an opportunity to comment on them regardless of what his comment might have been. The dismissal was held to be unfair.

Even if an employee is convicted of a criminal offence arising from the facts which are of concern to his employer, the employer cannot dismiss without carrying out an investigation and having a disciplinary hearing (*Cranston v Independent Newspapers Ltd* UD 90/84). While this dismissal was held to be unfair because there was no separate management investigation and hearing the claimant was held to have contributed 100 per cent to his dismissal.

In *Redmond v Lever Brothers (Ireland) Ltd* UD 655/82 a criminal prosecution against the claimant was dropped when the prosecution entered a 'nolle prosequi'. The company, however, carried out its own investigation and dismissed the claimant. The EAT held that the respondent had good grounds to find the claimant's explanations unsatisfactory and that accordingly the bond of mutual trust had been broken and the dismissal was held to be fair.

8.23.3 DISHONESTY

Dishonesty during the course of a disciplinary hearing or investigation may itself constitute a breach of trust. In *Cody v Marlowe Cleaners Ltd* UD 120/83 the company was in the course of investigating allegations against the claimant when he sought to have other employees make false statements to protect him. The EAT held that this exacerbated the situation and, while expressing reservations about the original set of facts under investigation, the EAT held 'the attempt to conceal the matter by deceit constituted substantial grounds justifying the dismissal'.

8.23.4 EFFECT OF DELAY

Delay in carrying out an investigation may render the ultimate decision unfair if the delay prejudices the employee. In *Marley Homecare Ltd v Dutton* [1981] IRLR 380 Mrs Dutton was a part-time cashier at one of the company's stores. The employers regularly carried out test purchases. On 20 December 1979 a report was made that there were suspected irregularities regarding Mrs Dutton's operation of the till. Certain purchases did not show up on the till roll and yet Mrs Dutton's cash did not exceed the total shown on the till roll. Further test purchases were carried out on 16 January 1980. It was alleged that one of these tests was not registered on the till roll and, again, the cash did not exceed the amount recorded as taken. Mrs Dutton was interviewed on 23 January 1980. She was unable to put forward any explanations as to what had happened in relation to the test purchases and stated that she could not remember what had happened on the occasions in question. She was summarily dismissed for gross misconduct and not complying with the company's cash-handling procedures. Dismissal was held to be unfair on the basis that a seven-day delay between the date of the last test purchase and the date on which the employee was confronted by the employers was such as to be unreasonable in the circumstances of the case because, at that stage, the employee could not identify the matters at issue and was unable to properly defend herself. Had she been confronted at a time when she might have identified the purchases in question it was impossible to say that the employee could have had no explanation. In the course of this decision it was suggested that if the employer had matters to investigate other than the alleged offending test purchases the employer could have suspended the employee on full pay while carrying out that investigation. The employee then would be in no doubt as to the occasion on which the alleged misconduct occurred and would have some chance of recalling what had happened and properly defending herself.

8.24 Representation—Legal Representation

The EAT put a very substantial emphasis on an employee's right to be represented at a disciplinary hearing. Employers should always commence a disciplinary hearing by first advising the employee of the seriousness of the matter at issue and, secondly, the right to representation. There does not exist any right to legal representation. In *State (Smullen) v Duffy* [1980] ILRM 46, a case involving the expulsion of a child from a school and not a dimissal, the Supreme Court held that there was no automatic right to legal representation even though the consequences for the person of the decision affecting him were particularly serious. It is unlikely that the courts would follow that view in a dismissal case. However, it could prove difficult in a hearing before the EAT if an employer refused to allow legal representation and the employee was not a member of a trade union and had no competent available representation other than a lawyer, for example a work colleague.

See *Flanagan v University College Dublin* [1988] IR 724, [1989] ILRM 469, the High Court decision in *Gallagher v Revenue Commissioners* [1991] ILRM 632 and the Supreme Court appeal in that case ([1995] 1 ILRM 241). See also the comments of Laffoy J in *Maher v Irish Permanent plc* [1998] ELR 77 at p 89 which stand in contrast to the High Court decision in *Aziz v Midland Health Board* [1995] ELR 48 at p 50 where Barr J held 'there is no general right to legal representation at a quasi-judicial disciplinary hearing' and refused an order to the applicant where he had claimed inter alia that unfair procedures had been followed by the respondent in a number of respects, one of which was the refusal to afford him the right to legal representation at a domestic enquiry which resulted in his suspension and subsequent dismissal. The Supreme Court seemed to accept a right of legal representation in *Georgopolous v Beaumont Hospital Board* 4 June 1997 unreported.

8.25 Standard of Proof

8.25.1 GENERALLY

Where an employer has carried out a comprehensive investigation having regard to fair procedures how far does he have to go in establishing the guilt or innocence of the employee in order to justify a decision to dismiss?

Dismissals related to dishonesty or procedural irregularities provide a good illustration of the standard of proof required of an employer in establishing substantial grounds justifying dismissal. Every dismissal case is approached under two headings.

(a) How was the dismissal effected? The procedures adopted in effecting dismissal are extremely important, and even with the existence of a substantial reason justifying dismissal, improper procedures may render such dismissal unfair. In the case of dishonesty dismissals warnings will rarely be required and the procedural focus will be on the manner of investigation carried out prior to making the decision to dismiss and the preservation of the dismissed employee's position.

(b) Why was the dismissal effected? In dishonesty cases the employee will normally take it that he is being dismissed for theft and very often challenges his dismissal on that basis. As will be seen below tribunals and courts are not concerned with right and wrong or fact and fiction. Such would be an objective view. Tribunals take a subjective view in that they must place themselves in the shoes of the employer at the time the decision was made and consider whether, in all the circumstances of the case, the employer had reasonable grounds for believing what he believed prior to making his decision to dismiss.

8.25.2   UK CASE LAW

The seminal precedent case on dismissals of this nature is the British case *British Home Stores Ltd v Burchell* [1978] IRLR 379.

Miss Burchell was dismissed for allegedly being involved with a number of other employees in acts of dishonesty relating to staff purchases. The acts concerned counter-signing each other's staff purchases when this should have been done by another member of staff, a purchase by one of the employees appearing as a purchase by Miss Burchell, and an incident involving the purchase by another employee of a pair of expensive sunglasses which were charged by Miss Burchell at the cost of a less expensive type. During the company's investigations of these incidents Miss Burchell was implicated in statements made by a fellow employee. Management, in investigating these allegations, did not confront Miss Burchell with the employee who made such statements. It was put to the UK EAT, on behalf of Miss Burchell, that the employer should have confronted Miss Burchell with this employee and allowed her the opportunity of challenging the statements. Management had simply transmitted the statements to Miss Burchell without advising her who had made them or confronting her with the employee. The UK EAT held that it was not unreasonable on the part of the employer to resist such a confrontation. When the matter was put to Miss Burchell in general terms with an implication that she had acted dishonestly her reaction was to deny the allegation saying: 'You'll have to prove it.' She did not give any further explanation. It was put to the UK EAT, on behalf of Miss Burchell, that to effect a dismissal for a reason of this sort the employers were obliged to conclusively prove that Miss Burchell had been guilty of dishonesty.

The UK EAT held that the function of a tribunal faced with a problem of this sort is to decide every time whether the employer who discharged the employee on the ground of the misconduct in question (usually, though not necessarily, dishonest conduct) entertained a reasonable suspicion amounting to the belief in the guilt of the employee of that misconduct at that time. First there must be established by the employer the fact of that belief—that the employer did believe it. Secondly, the employer must show that in his mind reasonable grounds upon which to sustain that belief existed. Thirdly, the employer must prove that at the stage at which he formed his belief on those grounds he had carried out as much investigation into the matter as was reasonable in all the circumstances of the case. It is not relevant that the tribunal would itself have shared that view in those circumstances. It is not the function of the tribunal to examine the quality of the material which the employer had before him to see whether it was the sort of material, objectively considered, which would lead to a certain conclusion on the balance of probability or whether it was the sort of material which would lead to the same conclusions only upon the basis of being 'sure' in a criminal context or such as to put the matter 'beyond reasonable doubt'. The test all the way through is reasonableness. A conclusion on the balance of probabilities will in any surmisable circumstance be a reasonable conclusion.

8.25.3   IRISH CASE LAW

The leading Irish EAT case is *Hennessy v Read and Write Shop Ltd* UD 192/78.

The claimant, a shop assistant for the respondents, asked her manageress for a discount on a doll for her daughter who also worked in the shop. It was agreed that the discount would be from £8.49 to £7.50. The manageress heard the claimant asking her daughter if she had paid for the doll and the daughter replied that she had. The manageress somewhat concerned about the transaction went into the shop the following day (Sunday) and checked the till rolls but could not find an entry of £7.50 or an approximate figure. Enquiries were carried out by the manageress and manager as a result of which the claimant's daughter was dismissed the following Tuesday and the claimant was dismissed the following Wednesday. The EAT, in considering the evidence on foot of which the employer's decision was made, stated:

'. . . the Employment Appeals Tribunal is not a criminal court. It does not apply itself to establishing the guilt or innocence in the criminal sense of an employee dismissed fundamentally because of the employer's belief that at the time of dismissal a monetary transaction had been improperly handled by the employee resulting in a loss to the employer in financial terms and particularly in loss of confidence in the capacity of the employee to maintain a position of trust.'

In deciding whether or not the dismissal of the claimant was unfair a test of reasonableness is applied to:

(a) the nature and extent of the enquiry carried out by the respondent prior to the decision to dismiss the claimant; and

(b) the conclusion arrived at by the respondent that on the basis of the information resulting from such enquiry the claimant should be dismissed.

In the course of the investigation the claimant had first confirmed that she had handled the transaction and recalled her daughter paying for the doll. She examined the till roll and agreed that there was no entry for £7.50 on the roll. The employer stated to her that if she agreed that she handled the transaction and if she further agreed that there was no entry of £7.50 on the till roll he had no alternative but to draw the conclusion that there was collusion between the claimant and her daughter and that he would be forced to dismiss her. The EAT further stated:

'[I]n deciding whether or not the dismissal of the claimant was unfair we applied the test of reasonableness to the nature and extent of the inquiry made by the respondents prior to the decision to dismiss the claimant. We applied the same test to the conclusion arrived at by the respondent that on the basis of the information resulting from such inquiry the claimants should be dismissed.'

The EAT held:

'[W]e are satisfied that the claimant was an employee in a position of trust in the company . . . we are unanimous in our opinion that on the basis of the information resulting from the inquiry the conclusion arrived at by the respondents that the claimant should be dismissed was fair and reasonable in all the circumstances.'

For a further exposition of the standards required of an employer in effecting such a dismissal, see *Dunne v Harrington* M259 UD 166/77.

In *Looney & Co Ltd v Looney* UD 843/84 the EAT stated:

'It is not for the Tribunal to seek to establish the guilt or innocence of the claimant nor is it for the Tribunal to indicate or consider whether we in the employer's position would have acted as [he] did in his investigation or concluded as he did or decided as he did. To do so would be to substitute our own mind and decision for that of the employer. Our responsibility is to consider against the facts what a reasonable employer in [his] position and circumstances at that time would have done and decided and to set this up as a standard against which [his] actions and decision be judged.'

In *Georgopoulus v Beaumont Hospital Board* 4 June 1997 unreported the Supreme Court ruled on the standard of proof to applicable in a dismissal case. The Court held that as the case was a civil case not involving allegations of criminal offences and that as the standard of proving a case beyond reasonable doubt was confined to criminal trials and it had no application in procedures of a civil nature. The Supreme Court accepted that the charges against the plaintiff in that case were particularly serious and had serious implications for his reputation but held that this did not require that the facts upon which the allegations were based should be established 'beyond all reasonable doubt' and that they could be dealt with on the 'balance of probabilities'. The court held that the degree of probability required should always be proportionate to the nature and gravity of the issue being investigated.

See also *Pacelli v Irish Distillers* [2004] ELR 25.

8.26 Absence/Sickness Dismissals

8.26.1 GENERALLY

One of the commonest forms of dismissal is that relating to an employee's attendance record, usually involving a high level of absence due to illness.

Unlike most forms of dismissal, this area does not involve any fault on the part of the employee. In scrutinising such a dismissal a court or tribunal must balance the employee's welfare against the demands of the business, which is frequently a difficult task. The 1977 Act says very little other than the general statement in section 6(4)(a) that a dismissal shall not be unfair if it results wholly or mainly from the capability of the employee for performing work of the kind which he was employed by the employer to do.

Absence dismissal related to illness cannot be dealt with solely under unfair dismissal legislation and the case law under that legislation, but must now take account of the requirements of the Employment Equality Acts, 1998–2004. That legislation confers substantial protection on employees suffering from disability, a term which is very widely defined and is liable to cover most, if not all, forms of illness which might, or do, give rise to substantial absence from work, such as might trigger an investigation and a possible decision by the employer not to retain the employee in employment. That topic is dealt with in detail in Chapter 6: Equality and Discrimination in the Workplace and must be kept in mind when considering the following explanation of the law relating to absence dismissals under unfair dismissal legislation.

On the basic principles of such dismissals the jurisprudence is clear as in *Reardon v St Vincent's Hospital* UD 74/79 which is one of the earliest EAT cases to tackle the problem. In this case Mr Reardon was employed as a kitchen porter in St Vincent's Hospital. He had a serious problem with many prolonged absences, all due to illness and all covered by medical certificates. The employers wrote to Mr Reardon on several occasions informing him that his sick leave record was a source of concern and inconvenience and that if it did not improve the question of his continued employment would have to be reviewed. Mr Reardon's sick leave record did not improve and his employers decided to terminate his employment. It was argued on behalf of Mr Reardon that, as all absences were due to illness and covered by medical certificates, it was unfair of the employers to dismiss him. It was further stated on his behalf that his health had improved since his dismissal and as his doctor had, prior to the dismissal, suggested that a change of duties away from the kitchen might help, the employers should have transferred Mr Reardon away from the kitchen. The employers submitted that they did not have any suitable alternative vacancy for Mr Reardon. The EAT held that the dismissal was not unfair. The question was whether Mr Reardon was capable under section 6(4) of the 1977 Act of doing the work for which he was employed. In the view of the EAT Mr Reardon and the kitchen did not agree. The employers, following the doctor's recommendations, considered the possibility of moving him to another job but did not have a suitable alternative. The employers acted reasonably in dismissing Mr Reardon and the EAT emphasised that it was not Mr Reardon's fault that he was not capable of doing his job.

Before effecting such a dismissal, in common with all other forms of dismissal, an employer is obliged to afford fair procedures to an employee and warn the employee of the possibility that the employment may be terminated. The employer must afford to the employee all reasonable opportunities to improve on the attendance record but if it is clear that it is beyond the capacity of the employee to improve the attendance record the employer may dismiss if there is no other alternative, including contrived tolerance of the absence.

8.26.2 ILLNESS RECORDS GIVING RISE TO DISMISSAL

There are two main types of illness record which give rise to dismissal and each must be approached separately.

8.26.2.1 Frequent intermittent absences

The first type of such illness record is that of a large amount of absences covering a considerable number of short periods where the absence is medically certified to be for a number of different reasons.

The leading case on this type of dismissal is the English case *International Sports Co Ltd v Thomson* [1980] IRLR 340. Mrs Thomson was dismissed for persistent absenteeism. For the last 18 months of her employment she was absent on average for about 25 per cent of the time. Most of her absences were covered by medical certificates which referred to a large number of conditions such as dizzy spells, anxiety, nerves, bronchitis, virus infections, cystitis, dyspepsia and flatulence. The employers had an absence tolerance level of eight per cent. When Mrs Thomson exceeded this level she was warned. In all a total of four warnings were given to her, the last one stating that if there was no improvement in her attendance record dismissal would result. Before deciding to dismiss the company consulted a general practitioner employed by them. After looking at the employee's medical certificates the doctor advised no useful purpose would be served by examining the employee because she had not had an illness which could be subsequently verified. There did not appear to be any common link between the various illnesses and the doctor saw little point in examining the woman when the symptoms of the illnesses would undoubtedly have passed. At first instance an industrial tribunal held against the employers on the grounds that they had not acted reasonably in dismissing the employee for persistent sickness absence without carrying out a full and proper investigation including examination of the employee prior to making their decision. On appeal, the UK EAT overruled that decision and held:

> 'where an employee has an unacceptable level of intermittent absences due to minor illness what is required is firstly that there should be a fair review by the employer of the attendance record and the reasons for it and secondly appropriate warnings after the employee has been given an opportunity to make representations. If there is then no adequate improvement in the attendance record in most cases the employer will be justified in treating the persistent absences as a sufficient reason for dismissing the employee. It would be placing too heavy a burden on an employer to require him to carry out a formal medical investigation in such a case. Even if he did such an investigation would rarely be fruitful because of the transient nature of the employee's symptoms and complaints. There is no rule of law or practice to support the proposition that employers are bound to investigate the bona fides of medical certificates issued. It cannot realistically be said that any reasonable employer would investigate the position in order to query the authenticity or genuineness of medical certificates before reaching a decision. This is a case where the reasonable employer was entitled to say "enough is enough".'

The employers had investigated the employee's attendance record and issued warnings. The dismissal therefore was held to be fair.

8.26.2.2 Continuing problem or underlying condition

The second type of illness absence is either frequent short absences or lengthy absences related to one continuing problem or underlying condition. In this sort of case the employer in reviewing the position would normally be expected to obtain medical advice to find out:

(a) whether or not the problem will persist; and

(b) what is the likelihood of the employee being able to attend on a more regular basis in the future.

This sort of problem was addressed in the leading EAT case *Mooney v Rowntree Mackintosh Ltd* UD 473/474/475/478/90 which addressed both types of absence problem but in relation to the latter stated:

'. . . faced with the problem of prolonged absence due to illness an employer will seek to obtain a medical report on the employee's condition in order that he may evaluate the likelihood of his returning to work in the reasonable future or of his ability of ever being able to perform the work which he was employed to do and possibly consider alternative employment if he is not able to do such work. In any event having equated himself with the true medical position at the particular time he will be in a position to relate the needs of his business with the employee's need to recover from his illness and make an assessment of whether he can any longer keep the employee's position open for him.'

8.26.3 ONUS OF PROOF

The High Court in *Bolger v Showerings (Ireland) Ltd* [1990] ELR 184 upheld the dismissal of Mr Bolger by reason of absence from work and stated in allowing the appeal:

(a) for a dismissal on grounds of incapacity to be deemed fair the onus is on the employer to show that:

(i) it was the incapacity which was the reason for the dismissal;

(ii) the reason was substantial;

(iii) the employee received fair notice that the question of his dismissal for incapacity was being considered; and

(iv) the employee was afforded an opportunity of being heard;

(b) where there is no dispute between employer and employee as to the incapacity of the employee because of ill health it is not necessary for the employer to await the results of medical tests before deciding to dismiss the employee; and

(c) in this case the appellant had substantial grounds for the dismissal and the dismissal had been reasonable in all the circumstances.

8.26.4 MANAGEMENT DECISION

It should be noted that in seeking medical advice employers should always keep in mind that the decision to terminate is not a decision to be made by a doctor but is one to be made by management in light of medical advice.

In *Bergin v Easons Cash & Carry (Wholesale) Ltd* UD 669/81 the EAT addressed a case where the employee had in the last year of her employment a considerable record of sick leave, and from 3 July 1981 to the date of her dismissal on 25 September 1981, was on continuous sick leave. The employee's absence caused the employers concern because her medical certificates did not indicate the exact nature of her illness and when she would be likely to return to work. The employee was interviewed on 4 September 1981 and was asked to obtain more definite information on when she would be returning to work. It was pointed out to her that her job could not be kept open for her indefinitely and if she did not know when she would be returning her employment would have to be terminated. The employee promised to get a report from her doctor. A further meeting took place on 15 September 1981 when the employee was warned that her job would not be kept open indefinitely and was asked to contact the company doctor to arrange a medical examination. She was warned that if it was unfavourable she would be expected to return to work in a month. The employers refused to alter their decision to dismiss as they were relying on the report from their own doctor. At the hearing of the claim there was no dispute on the facts other than that the employee stated that her job did not involve any 'heavy cleaning work'. On the evidence the EAT held that the dismissal was unfair. The employers had given no reason for the dismissal other than the company doctor's report. The company doctor was not familiar with the work carried out by the employee and no effort was made by the employers to elaborate on what the employee meant by 'heavy cleaning work'. The employee had complied with the request of management and obtained a medical opinion from her own doctor which, when submitted, was totally ignored by management even though it stated that her condition was improving and it was anticipated that she would be returning to work in a month. The decision to dismiss had been abdicated by the employers to the company doctor who was not fully conversant with the facts. As the dismissal decision was one which should properly have been made by management in light of medical advice the dismissal was held to be unfair.

8.26.5 UP-TO-DATE MEDICAL OPINION

In *McLoughlin v Celmac (Ireland) Ltd* UD 799/84 the decision to dismiss was taken without getting an up-to-date medical opinion with regard to the employee's possible future availability for work. The EAT held that the employer should have had up-to-date medical evidence prior to making the decision to dismiss. The dismissal was held to be unfair.

In *Walsh v Arthur Guinness Son & Co (Dublin) Ltd* UD 871/85 the claimant had been warned about his unsatisfactory attendance and could not give an indication as to when he thought he would be fit for work. It was decided to dismiss him. He then made a submission through his trade union that he had been informed by his doctor that he would be fully fit to resume work in the very near future. The company went ahead with the dismissal. The EAT held it was unfair because the employers did not take steps to ascertain the fitness of the employee prior to making the decision to dismiss. This appears to be a clear case where, had the employee been examined by a doctor, it could have resolved the 'crystal ball gazing' that the company engaged in prior to making the decision to dismiss.

8.26.6 NEED TO DISMISS

One very important factor often overlooked by employers in making a decision to dismiss by reason of incapacity is the need to dismiss. Some employers take the view that because an employee has a poor attendance record, that justifies dismissal. That is not the case. The dismissal must be related to the requirements of the business. There will be many instances where employers are able to make alternative arrangements and can tolerate high levels of absence. They must therefore in all absence-related cases be able to show that dismissal was necessary for good commercial reasons.

In *McGrane v Mater Private Nursing Home* UD 369/85 the claimant was dismissed by reason of her high level of absence. The EAT noted that there was no pressure on the employer to replace the employee and there was effectively no reason to dismiss. The dismissal was held to be unfair.

In *McElhinney v Templemore Co-operative Society Ltd* UD 434/82 the EAT commented:

> 'In cases of ill health the basic question that has to be determined in every case is whether in all the circumstances the employer can be expected to wait any longer and, if so, how much longer. The nature of the illness, the likely length of the continuing absence, the need of the employers to have done the work which the employee was engaged to do—and these presumably will vary with the size of the employing organisation. In some cases four to six weeks may justify dismissal, in others six months may not. What is reasonable will depend on the circumstances.'

In *Cummins v Jurys Hotel Group plc* [1994] ELR 21 Ms Cummins was dismissed due to prolonged absence. There was medical opinion to the effect that her medical problems might be aggravated by the type of work she did for the company. The company did not have any suitable alternative work available for the claimant and dismissal was held to be fair.

In *Boyle v Marathon Petroleum (Ireland) Ltd* UD 787/93 the claimant had been out of work due to illness for over two years and the medical opinion was that he would not be fit to return to work. He was accepted under an income continuance plan. Under the terms of such plans beneficiaries usually have to remain legally employed by the employer, which occurred here. A replacement employee was recruited and the claimant's position was filled. Some two years later he sought to return to work on the basis that he was now fit. The company advised him that there was no position for him as his pre-accident position had been filled and there was no other work available. He claimed unfair dismissal. On the evidence the EAT came to the conclusion that the claimant's contract of employment was frustrated at a date earlier than when he informed the respondent he was fit to return to work and, as frustration automatically terminates a contract of employment, there was no dismissal.

It may happen that the employee is actually fit at the time the decision to dismiss is made in circumstances where the decision is made due to the history or pattern of absences (*Lynock v Cereal Packaging Ltd* [1988] IRLR 510).

8.26.7 EMPLOYEES INJURED OR ALLEGEDLY INJURED AT WORK

Absence from work may in some cases be caused by actual or alleged negligence of the employee causing injury or illness which in turn results in absence from work. In such circumstances an employer is entitled to dismiss given the incapacity of the employee. In *Caulfield v Waterford Foundry Ltd* [1991] ELR 137 the employee suffered a back injury at work and this made him unfit to do the heavy work required in the place of employment. His dismissal was held to be fair as he was not fit for any work in the respondent company.

8.26.8 INCOME CONTINUANCE/PERMANENT HEALTH INSURANCE

Many employers effect insurance policies to cover their employees during a period of prolonged absence due to illness. Normally these policies have a deferred period of six months or 12 months during which the employee will not receive benefit but on the completion of that period is entitled to apply to be covered. It is normally a condition of these policies that the employee remain an employee while in receipt of payments. If the employers therefore were to terminate the employment they would defeat the employee's rights under such a policy. That itself may give rise to a common law breach of contract action, probably based on an implied term that the existence of the policy gave the employee an implied right to remain in the employment, albeit ill, for the deferred period in order not to defeat his entitlement. Once accepted under the policy the money is paid by the insurer to the employer who processes it through the payroll in the normal way and passes the net amount to the employee. If the employee were to regain his health and seek to return to work after a prolonged absence while covered by such a policy the employer may have a problem, having effectively treated the employee for all practical purposes as having left employment, unless of course it was accepted that a *Boyle*-type frustration of the contract of employment applied.

The situation was considered in *McGrath v Euro Container Shipping plc* UD 819/92. In September 1990 the claimant became incapacitated and was accepted for permanent health insurance cover. He kept in sporadic contact with the company about his illness. The claimant was fit to return to work in April 1992 when his permanent health insurance payment ceased. The company had, while he was absent from work, 'no longer regarded him as an employee'. The EAT held that he was not dismissed and was at all material times an employee.

In *Adin v Sedco Forex International Resources Ltd* [1997] IRLR 280 the court of Session in Scotland held against an employer who sought to dismiss an employee who was entitled to claim under short-term and long-term disability plans but by reason of the dismissal was prevented from obtaining the benefit of the plans. The Court of Session accepted that where an employee is off work due to illness, and in receipt of sick pay, there was an implied term in the contract that the employee would not be dismissed on grounds of sickness or for an arbitrary reason since to do so would be to subvert the employee's entitlements to payments while sick.

In *Hill v General Accident Fire and Life Corporation* [1998] IRLR 64 the court did state, however, that the employer was not in breach of the employee's contract of employment in dismissing the employee on grounds of redundancy while he was off work ill and in receipt of sickness benefit with a prospective entitlement to long- term sickness benefit under an ill-health policy. The court held that there was no implied term that the employers would not use their contractual powers of dismissal where that would frustrate an accruing or accrued entitlement to sickness benefit or ill health and early retirement. The court refused to accept that there was an implied term that gross misconduct was the only cause that would warrant dismissal of an employee who was in receipt of sick pay. The court examined the implied term of mutual trust and confidence and held that an employer would be prohibited from terminating a sick employee's employment 'solely with a view to relieving themselves of the obligation to make such payment for a specious or arbitrary reason or for no cause at all. To do so would be to subvert the employee's entitlement to payment while sick'. This decision is arguably only of any use to an employee who can prove that the actual reason for dismissal was to deny him his entitlement to short-term or long-term sickness benefit and is unlikely to avail an employee where an employer dismisses for cause, e.g. misconduct or redundancy. It remains to be seen whether this decision or similar decisions could be extended to cover a situation where an employee is dismissed due to non-performance or inability to perform by reason of illness. Employers should ensure that their terms or conditions for sick pay or sick leave and the manner in which those conditions operate do not exclude pregnancy-or maternity-related illness, as to do so would be in breach of the Employment Equality Acts, 1998–2004 (*Mckenna v Northern Health Board* [2005] (C-191/03)).

8.26.9   LIGHT WORK

Where illness or incapacity is partial, rendering the employee unfit to do the work for which he was employed, but resulting in him still being in a position to do some work, an employer is under no obligation to provide alternative or light work unless there is a suitable alternative vacancy available. In *Gurr v Office of Public Works* UD 919/87 and *Corless v Steiner (Galway) Ltd* UD 535/82 the EAT stated:

'We are satisfied that the respondent was not unreasonable in deciding that there was no alternative employment available for the claimant. There is no legal obligation on an employer to provide light work for an employee.'

The EAT will, in any event, examine the facts of a dismissal to see if an employee could have been accommodated without undue difficulty.

In *Caulfield v Waterford Foundry Ltd* [1991] ELR 137 it was held that all employees of the foundry, being general operatives, could be called upon to do heavy work at any time. There were therefore no jobs in the foundry for which the claimant was fit on the basis of the medical report submitted. As the claimant was not fit for any work in the respondent company the dismissal was justified on grounds of incapacity.

8.26.10 DISCLOSURE OF OUTCOME OF MEDICAL EXAMINATION

In *Lawless v Dublin County Council* UD 335/89 the employer's medical officer examined the claimant and concluded that he was unfit for further work and should be retired on health grounds. The claimant was not advised by the doctor that he was intending to recommend his retirement and the claimant was not appraised of the outcome of the examination by the respondent's medical officer. The EAT held:

'Having heard the evidence presented the Tribunal is satisfied, while the respondent appears to have acted on a bona fide medical report, that because of the seriousness of the recommendation contained in that report a single medical report was not adequate. It is our view that a second report or indeed a specialist opinion should have been obtained before Mr Byrne contemplated his decision. It is our further view that there was an obligation on the respondent because of the medical report they had received to inform the claimant of the report and that his position was under review.'

The question of fitness for work was dealt with in some detail by the High Court in *Porter v Donegal County Council* [1993] ELR 101. The Department of the Environment introduced a requirement that all firemen should retire at the age of 55. The claimants at the time they were taken on had a normal retirement age of 60. The county council forcibly retired the employees who then claimed unfair dismissal. The justification for the forced retirement was the Department of Environment requirement and the practice that given the nature of the work, firemen should not be required to work after the age of 55. In holding that the dismissals were unfair because of the unilateral imposition of a new retirement age Flood J held that the employer could have resolved the problem of possible unfitness by requiring the employees to undergo regular medical examinations. He effectively held, albeit in an obiter dictum, that the employer had an implied right to require the employees to undergo a medical examination. An employer cannot normally oblige an employee to undergo a medical examination but in this case it was accepted that the employer might be in a position to suspend the employee from duty until such time as the employee had satisfied the employer as to his fitness.

8.26.11 ABUSE OF SICK LEAVE

Abuse of sick leave by working or otherwise acting inconsistently with being out sick and on sick leave may justify dismissal for misconduct or dishonesty. The general principles are well set out in *Lynch v P V Doyles Hotel Ltd* UD 89/89 and *Gildea v James Doherty (Production) Letterkenny Ltd* UD 680/84. The actual conduct of the employee will come under close scrutiny and the employer's grounds for believing that the employee had acted improperly will be examined carefully in situations such as this.

In *Malone v Burlington Industries (Ireland) Ltd* UD 947/82 the claimant was seen on his farm while medically certified ill. He was met near his hay shed. A tractor and trailer were loaded with bales of hay and the tractor's engine was still running nearby to him. When asked if he was working the claimant stated he was 'doing a bit'. At the EAT hearing the claimant denied he had been working and said that the tractor had not been running but was on loan from a neighbour and had broken down. The managers who met the claimant assumed from the scene that he had been doing heavy work. The EAT held, however, that it was not satisfied that the claimant's activities were in conflict with his declaration of inability to work for the company. It pointed out that there was a difference between being fit for industrial work for an eight-hour shift and 'doing a bit' around a farm or household. The dismissal was held to be unfair.

In *Hardy v Cadbury Ireland Ltd* UD 727/83 Hardy was dismissed because, while absent on sick leave, it was alleged that he was collecting clothes at a charge and bringing them to the dry-cleaners. His dismissal for breaching the sick pay scheme was upheld as being fair.

In absence cases procedures may be effectively redundant if the employee is accepted as actually being unfit. In *Fahy v Comhlucht Siuicre Éireann Teoranta* UD 607/82 it was held that fair procedures had not been following by the employer; however, the evidence was that the claimant was still unable to work at the time of the hearing and the decision would have been the same even if fair procedures had been followed and the dismissal was held to be fair. This contrasts with the dissenting opinion in *Caulfield v Verbatim* UD 938/93 referred to at **8.18.2.1** above.

8.27 Competition/Conflict of Interest

8.27.1 GENERALLY

An employer is entitled to dismiss where it is established that an employee is competing against him or acting against his interests and in breach of his duty of fidelity. An employer is entitled to defend himself against unfair competition from his employee and take whatever reasonable steps are necessary in order to achieve that end (*Davidson and Maillou v Comparisons* [1980] IRLR 360). In *Harris and Russell Ltd v Slingsby* [1973] IRLR 221 it was held that an employer cannot dismiss an employee who was seeking employment with a competitor unless the employer had grounds to show that the employee was doing so in order to abuse his confidential position. If an employee forms the intention of leaving to set up in competition that does not of itself justify termination (*Laughton and Hawley v Bapp Industrial Supplies Ltd* [1986] IRLR 245). That case should be contrasted with *Marshall v Industrial Systems and Controls Ltd* [1992] IRLR 294 where the managing director of the company was dismissed after it was discovered that he had planned with another manager to set up in competition and take away some of the company's best business. The managing director had also tried to induce another key employee to join in the new venture.

The Irish cases are interesting on this whole question. In *Preece v Irish Helicopters Ltd* UD 236/84 the employee had signed an acknowledgment in his terms and conditions of employment that he would not 'assist or support any activity by myself or with others which may be in conflict with or in competition with or contrary to the interests of Irish Helicopters Limited'. The company received information that the claimant was involved in setting up another company and seeking a licence. The claimant was interviewed. He was evasive and admitted nothing. He was asked to sign an undertaking that if he was in any way connected with the application for a licence he would withdraw from it. He refused to sign any such undertaking. The board of the company took the view that his failure to sign the undertaking had damaged the trust and confidence necessary between them. He was dismissed. The EAT held:

> 'An employer is entitled to insist that an employee does not interest himself in a company which will compete with the business of the employer. Failure of the claimant to

commit himself not to do anything while in the respondent's employment in pursuit of his own interest which might conflict with the interest of his employer was reasonably construed as a breach of duty or loyalty.'

The dismissal was held to be fair.

In *Mulchrone v Feeney* UD 1023/82 the employee worked for a confectioner in Westport. In her spare time she worked part-time for a direct competitor. She was dismissed because her employer believed that she 'was undermining his business and also that there was a danger she could be passing on trade secrets'. The EAT held, having regard to the size of the town of Westport, the direct competition in a limited market and the inadvertent possibility of the claimant passing on information, that the dismissal was justified.

8.27.2   FAMILY CONNECTIONS

In *Goggin Carroll & Co v Dineen* UD 106/85 the employers traded as insurance brokers in the town of Charleville, Co Cork. The employee was an office worker. The employers became aware that the employee's boyfriend was setting up a competing business in the town. While the employers had complete confidence that the employee would not knowingly breach confidentiality, they were concerned that information of a confidential nature could be inadvertently passed on. She was offered an alternative position in another branch some 30 miles away. She refused the offer and was dismissed. The EAT held that the dismissal was unfair as 'the fear of an inadvertent slip is not grounds for dismissal'.

The EAT took a different view in *Coffey v Alcan Metal Centres (Dublin) Ltd* UD 603/90. The respondent was a substantial company with two main competitors in Dublin. The pricing or rebating of products was highly sensitive and, if leaked to either competitor, could have caused considerable damage to the company. The appellant's brother and fiancé worked for the company. Both left within a short period of time to join one of the two competitors. The claimant subsequently married her fiancé. The company explained their concerns to the claimant about the possibility of breach of confidence while not aware of any actual breach of confidence. Discussions were had with the claimant about what could be done to avoid a dismissal. The company did not believe it had any other option. The claimant was unable to put forward any other option. The claimant was dismissed. The EAT held that where an employer had a real and significant concern held bona fide derived from circumstances which could reasonably justify it and that the employer's own circumstances did not reasonably permit the adoption of an alternative solution to that of dismissal, dismissal was justified.

A similar decision was reached in *Fitzgerald v Regsimm Ltd (t/a Doherty Print)* [1997] ELR 65 where the claimant, who was employed as a printer, became a director of a company owned by his brother who had himself left the employing company and set up a business in direct competition with the employer. The claimant denied his directorship, which the employer confirmed on foot of a Companies Office search. The claimant then claimed he had no involvement in the company but was a director only for legal reasons. The EAT held that the employer was justified in terminating the claimant's employment due to the breakdown of trust and confidence and the claimant's involvement in a competing company.

In *Fairbrother v Stiefel Laboratories (Ireland) Ltd* UD 665/85 the claimant was employed as director of research and development in a pharmaceutical company manufacturing dermatological products for skin disorders. The claimant's contract contained detailed confidentiality provisions. It came to the employer's attention that the claimant's wife, a trained pharmacist, had set up her own company and launched a new protective cream for sensitive skin. The company pointed out to the claimant the possibility of a conflict of interest. As the conflict could not be resolved the claimant was dismissed. The dismissal was held to be fair. The EAT stated:

'We accept that the claimant's wife cannot be restrained from using her own knowledge to set up a business but having regard to her husband's position of responsibility, authority and control in the respondent company we consider that the claimant had obligations to ensure the wellbeing of his own company and to act in its best interest by discouraging his wife from promoting a product which the respondents felt was competing with their own product. We accept that the respondents were mainly concerned with the protection of their legitimate interests and the extent of those interests depends on the nature of the business and the employee's position within it. In reaching our conclusions it is not necessary for us to determine whether or not there was a conflict of interest . . . the only point at issue is whether the respondents acted reasonably in treating the claimant's failure to have his wife's product withdrawn as a reason for his dismissal. The claimant was made aware of the likely consequences if the conflict of interests was not resolved and he was given every opportunity to resolve it.'

8.27.3 BEHAVIOUR INCONSISTENT WITH EMPLOYER'S BUSINESS

In *O'Donoghue v Carroll Group Distributors Ltd* UD 942/82 the claimant was dismissed for acting in a manner inconsistent with the employer's business. The claimant drove a van to work. The side of the van had two non-smoking stickers prominently displayed on it. The van was normally parked outside the employer's depot. It was in plain view of customers and fellow employees. Some of the claimant's fellow employees objected to the stickers. The claimant was asked to remove the stickers but refused. She was then asked to park her van on the public road or at the rear of the premises. She refused. She was then dismissed. The EAT held that the dismissal was fair, stating:

'We take the view that the stickers were a cause of serious embarrassment to the respondent and could have been detrimental to its business. We feel that the claimant refused a reasonable and important request and left the respondent with no option but to dismiss her.'

8.28 Criminal Convictions

Criminal convictions may justify dismissal if the offence is connected with the employment (*Singh v London County Bus Services* [1976] IRLR 176). The criminal act may affect the reputation of the business (*Robb v Mersey Insulation Co Ltd* [1972] IRLR 18).

In *O'Leary v Thomas Crosbie & Co Ltd* UD 1118/83 the claimant was convicted of indecent assault and subsequently dismissed from his employment. The EAT held:

'The critical factor in this case is whether or not the claimant's criminal conduct was such as to render him unsuitable for his employment with the respondent or unacceptable to other employees. The Tribunal is not satisfied that the latter onus was fully discharged by the respondent. Accordingly the respondent not having fully discharged the onus the Tribunal takes the view that the claimant must succeed on the primary issue namely that the dismissal was unfair.'

8.29 Lack of Competence and Poor Performance

8.29.1 TEST OF INCOMPETENCE

There are effectively two tests used in incompetence or poor performance dismissal cases, being:

(a) does the employer have an honest belief of the employee's incompetence?

(b) does the employer have reasonable grounds to sustain such a belief?

These tests were referred to in *McDonnell v Rooney (t/a Spar Supermarket)* [1992] ELR 214.

In *Cooke v Thomas Linnell & Sons Ltd* [1977] IRLR 132 it was held:

> 'When responsible employers have genuinely come to the conclusion over a reasonable period of time that the manager is incompetent we think that it is some evidence that he is incompetent. When one is dealing with routine operations which may be more precisely assessed there is no real problem. It is more difficult when one is dealing with such imponderables as the quality of management which as a last resort can only be judged by those competent in the field.'

In *Taylor v Alidair Ltd* [1978] IRLR 82 Denning LJ summarised the test of incompetence as being:

> 'Whenever a man is dismissed for incapacity or incompetence it is sufficient that the employer honestly believed on reasonable grounds that the man is incapable and incompetent. It is not necessary for the employer to prove that he is in fact incapable or incompetent.'

It is a matter for employers to set their own standards and they may therefore insist on levels of competence or higher standards than might pertain in comparable organisations.

8.29.2 MONITORING OF EMPLOYEE

The employer's actions will be examined carefully both in terms of procedure and the substantive action taken to remedy and monitor the poor performance.

It was held in *James v Waltham Holy Cross UDC* [1973] IRLR 202 that:

> '. . . the employer should be very slow to dismiss upon the grounds that the employee is incapable of performing the work which he is employed to do without first telling the employee of the respects in which he is failing to do his job adequately, warning him of the possibility or likelihood of dismissal on this ground and giving him an opportunity to improve his performance.'

In *Dowling v Niteout Ltd* UD 938/82, having examined the work done, the conclusion reached by the employer that the employee was incompetent was unfair given that the employer had not properly trained the employee for the job in respect of which he had been determined to be incompetent. Dismissal was held to be unfair.

Regular monitoring of an employee's performance is important (*O'Brien v Professional Contract Cleaners Ltd* [1991] ELR 143). The claimant had been warned, accepted the warnings and improved her performance. She was subsequently dismissed. The EAT held on the evidence that at the time of the dismissal she was adequately performing her duties and the employer had not kept himself fully appraised of her competence and the dismissal was held to be unfair.

It was held in *Sutton and Gates (Luton) Ltd v Boxall* [1978] IRLR 486:

> 'Where the poor performance is something over which the employee himself has control he should be warned probably several times and given plenty of opportunity to improve his performance. If it reaches the stage where it becomes obvious that he is incapable the employer, provided he handles the matter sensibly, is entitled to dismiss. But, in such circumstances, the employer should not dismiss without giving the employee a final opportunity to explain.'

8.29.3   INTRANSIGENT EMPLOYEES

In the case of intransigent employees who do not accept warnings, or do not accept that there is any justification for warnings, and who give no indication that they will heed the warning, dismissal may be justified at an earlier stage than otherwise. In *Retarded Children's Aid Society Ltd v Day* [1978] IRLR 128 Denning LJ stated:

'In some cases it may be proper and reasonable to dismiss at once, especially with a man who is determined to go his own way. It should be kept in mind of course that the employee must be advised that their conduct will lead to dismissal. If they then refuse to do anything about their conduct it appears that dismissal is justified at an early stage rather than at a later stage.'

8.29.4   TEMPORARY APPOINTMENT

In *Williams v Willis Oil Tool Ireland Ltd* UD 59/83 the employee was promoted to a senior position which he occupied together with another senior employee, both being under assessment to get the job in due course. The other employee was chosen and Mr Williams' employment was terminated. The dismissal was held to have been unfair. The EAT held that the appointment to the joint position was expressed to be temporary and the claimant therefore had a reasonable expectation that he could revert to his old position if he did not get the new job on a permanent basis. Failure to do so was a dismissal and an unfair dismissal.

8.30   Conduct

In *Parsons v Liffey Marine Ltd* [1992] ELR 136 the claimant had a medical certificate stating that he was unfit for work for a period of one week. He was offered a certificate by his doctor for a period of two weeks but stated that he wanted to go back to work and the certificate for one week would suffice. At the end of that one week, however, the claimant had a continuing problem and, rather than return to the hospital, he altered the date of the certificate. The employers claimed that this was a serious breach of trust. The EAT, however, ordered his re-engagement, the dismissal being held to be unfair on the grounds that 'while the Tribunal did not condone the claimant's actions in altering the certificate he had nonetheless ultimately admitted to this. The penalty of dismissal was disproportionate to the offence and was accordingly unfair'.

In *O'Mahony v Whelan (t/a Pallet Providers)* [1992] ELR 117 a scuffle took place close by a rotary saw which, while it had been switched off, was still moving. The employer, having investigated the matter, took the view that he could not take the risk that such an incident would not occur again and as there was a rule that fighting in the workplace would result in instant dismissal, he dismissed the claimant. The EAT held that the summary dismissal of the claimant was warranted as a recurrence of the incident could result in serious injury. The respondent was justified in making a rule which protected his workplace and a breach of this rule was a serious offence.

In *Costello v Gerard F May Roofing Ltd* [1994] ELR 19 the company issued a circular about the times at which holidays could be taken. The claimants ignored the circulars and booked holidays at a time when the employer had prohibited holidays. Their employment was terminated upon taking the holidays in contravention of their employer's instruction. The EAT held that the claimants were aware of the employer's position with regard to the taking of holidays and in disregarding the circulars were responsible for the resulting dismissals and their claims failed.

In contrast, in *Conroy v Iggy Madden Transport Ltd* [1991] ELR 29 the employer claimed that it had a standard holiday period and the claimant took her annual holidays against management wishes. The claimant, however, contradicted this and stated that she had been told, when she was originally offered the job, that she could take her annual leave at her own discretion. The EAT held that the dismissal was unfair as it was too severe a penalty for the claimant having taken holidays against the management's wishes.

The employer's terms and conditions were upheld in *McKenna v Farrell Brothers* [1991] ELR 77 where the claimant's contract had a requirement that he work overtime on request. He had done so for a period but subsequently refused to work overtime despite having been told that his refusal would cause problems in meeting orders. He persisted in his refusal and was dismissed. The dismissal was held to be a fair dismissal as the claimant was in breach of his contract by refusing to work overtime.

In *Creed v KMP Co-Op Society Ltd* [1991] ELR 140 the claimant worked in a meat factory. One of the terms of employment was that 'fighting, provoking or instigating a fight when on company premises' warranted immediate dismissal. Following an investigation of an incident where it was alleged that the claimant had thrown a piece of fat, which was dangerous behaviour and which the employer decided could lead to further horseplay and accidents, the claimant was dismissed. The EAT held that it was a fair dismissal, the employer having 'acted reasonably in all the circumstances. A thorough investigation was carried out by the respondent. The claimant did not act aggressively but his action caused risk of injury to others. Having regard to the dangerous environment the dismissal was not unfair'.

In *McArdle v Superquinn* [1991] ELR 171 the employer had in place strict requirements on checkout register procedures and impressed upon the staff the importance of the procedures and that breach of them was a dismissible offence. During a series of test purchases the claimant was observed to fail to register a number of items on different occasions and her explanations were deemed to be unacceptable. The EAT held the dismissal to be fair, the employer having acted reasonably in all the circumstances following a thorough investigation of the explanations given by the claimant and having afforded her sufficient time, information and opportunity to enable her to explain her actions.

In *O'Keefe Weber v Terence Casey & Co* [1997] ELR 71 the claimant was employed as a secretary and typing was her main function. The respondent became aware that she was doing typing unrelated to her work. The principal returned to the office unexpectedly and discovered the claimant occupied at the unofficial work whereupon she was dismissed summarily for breach of trust. The dismissal was held to be fair.

8.31   Penalty

Even where fair procedures are followed carefully and the employer has decided that the employee's behaviour was sufficiently serious to justify a severe penalty, the EAT will require the employer to assess a range of penalties and not just dismissal or retention in employment. Employers are frequently asked at hearings by EAT members, whether they considered any penalty other than dismissal. In *Bolger v Dublin Sport Hotel Ltd* UD 45/85 the claimant was dismissed for working for another employer on a day when he should have been at work for the respondent but had failed to attend. The EAT held that the dismissal was unfair because dismissal was not the appropriate penalty. It was held that the employer should have considered alternatives such as suspension without pay and/or a final written warning. While the claimant's conduct was clearly serious the EAT still determined that he should be re-engaged (*Fitzpatrick v Superquinn Ltd* UD 462/84).

It is a well-established principle that in determining whether a dismissal is unfair regard cannot be had to matters of which the employer was unaware at the time of dismissal. Any such facts, which later came to light, could not have formed part of the reason for dismissing the employee and therefore cannot be assessed in determining the basic fairness or otherwise of the decision (*Devis & Sons Ltd v Aitkins* [1977] IRLR 314). The effects of rigid adherence to that principle could possibly work an injustice where, immediately after the dismissal, information came to light that may have been relevant, such as absolute proof of the employee's guilt or the employee engaging in another form of misconduct possibly unknown to the employer at the time the decision was made. The EAT mitigates the effect of the rule by taking into account other facts not known at the time of dismissal in consideration, of the remedy, if any, which should be afforded to the employee. Section 7(1)(c) of the 1977 Act makes reference to awards of compensation and provides that compensation shall be in such amount '*in respect of any financial loss incurred ... as is just and equitable having regard to all the circumstances*'. In *Devis & Sons Ltd v Aitkins* the employee succeeded but received no compensation because he had contributed 100 per cent to his dismissal. The contribution was measured having regard to misconduct which came to light after the decision, which was held to be unfair, was made. In that case the House of Lords held:

(a) evidence of misconduct discovered since dismissal is irrelevant and inadmissible in deciding whether a dismissal is fair;

(b) in assessing compensation tribunals are entitled to take into account misconduct which came to light after the dismissal; and

(c) there is no inconsistency in coupling a finding of unfair dismissal with an award of no compensation.

See also *Fitzpatrick v Polygram Records Ltd* [1994] ELR 24.

8.32 Contracting Out and Settlement of Cases

8.32.1 CONTRACTING OUT

It is not possible for an employee to contract out of his rights under unfair dismissal legislation. Section 13 of the 1977 Act provides:

'*. . . a provision in an agreement (whether a contract of employment or not and whether made before or after the commencement of this Act) shall be void in so far as it purports to exclude or limit the application of or is inconsistent with any provisions of this Act.*'

If an employee were to reach an agreement with his employer at the time of a dismissal whereby the employer paid an amount of money to the employee which he stated to be in full and final discharge and settlement of all or any claim the employee may have the question must be asked as to whether or not such an agreement is defeated by section 13. It may well be. The circumstances in which the agreement was entered into will be examined.

In *Shortt v Data Packaging Ltd* [1996] ELR 7 the EAT heard evidence of the offer and payment of an ex gratia payment on condition that a letter of waiver was signed. The claimant was advised that he would not receive the money unless the waiver was signed. He stated he would sign the waiver on a without prejudice basis. The EAT held that on the evidence of the meetings leading up to the signing of the waiver and of the signing of the document it had jurisdiction to hear the claimant's claim.

Agreements entered into after the initiation of proceedings are rarely set aside under section 13 as to do so would be to defeat the settlement of cases and, where in practice, a very substantial amount of cases are actually settled. In *Fitzgerald v Pat the Baker* [1999] ELR 227 the claimant resigned from his employment because he was demoted and then signed a document accepting a payment which was stated to then preclude him from taking a claim against the employer. The claimant signed the document without professional advice. He then brought a claim for constructive dismissal. The employer sought to rely on the document, claiming that the claimant was precluded from bringing his claim as a result of what he had signed. The EAT drew a distinction between settlements of cases which followed negotiations, usually with professional advice, and settlements essentially imposed by one party on the other without negotiation or professional advice. The former are within the jurisdiction of the legislation and are valid whereas the latter are void under the legislation.

8.32.2 DUPLICATION OF CLAIMS

Section 15 of the 1977 Act provided that where an employee gave notice in writing to a rights commissioner or tribunal of intention to claim under the 1977 Act the employee could not then recover damages for wrongful dismissal at common law. Where proceedings for damages at common law for wrongful dismissal were initiated a claim could not then be brought under the 1977 Act. In both cases it was the initiation and notification of the claim that brought about the bar to the alternative remedy even where the claim initiated or notified was not proceeded with. That situation was changed in section 10 of the 1993 Act, which provides that the bar will only apply where a recommendation has actually been made by a rights commissioner, the hearing of a claim by the EAT has commenced or where the common law court proceedings have commenced. It is possible therefore for an employee to initiate claims for unfair dismissal and wrongful dismissal but be deemed to have abandoned one of the remedies under section 10 at the time specified. Section 15 of the 1977 Act was considered by the Supreme Court in *Parsons v Iarnród Éireann* [1997] ELR 203. The plaintiff had sought declaratory orders relating to the defendant's internal appeals and decision to dismiss and also claimed in those High Court proceedings 'damages for wrongful/unfair dismissal'. The Supreme Court held:

(a) the effect of section 15 was not to oust the jurisdiction of the High Court but to provide an employee with an additional statutory remedy. However, the Unfair Dismissals Act, 1977 provides that employees must choose between suing for damages at common law for wrongful dismissal and claiming relief under the Unfair Dismissals Act;

(b) the traditional relief at common law was a claim for damages and whereas the plaintiff may have had an entitlement to declarations, such declarations were in aid of his common law remedy and had no independent existence apart from it.

Section 15 of the 1977 Act also provided that a person who accepts redress under the Anti-Discrimination (Pay) Act, 1974, sections 9 or 10 cannot accept any redress under the Unfair Dismissals Act, 1977, section 7, as amended by the 1993 Act.

Apart from legal procedures there was the possible duplicity of proceedings where an employee brought an unfair dismissal claim and also referred the dispute regarding the dismissal to the Labour Court under the terms of the Industrial Relations Acts, 1946–2001. The EAT had, in a number of cases, indicated an unwillingness to rule on a dismissal where the Labour Court had dealt with the matter, and vice versa, but the problem of duplicity has now been resolved by virtue of the provisions of the 1993 Act, section 7, which amends the 1977 Act, section 8, and provides that a dispute in relation to a dismissal cannot be referred under the Industrial Relations Acts, where a recommendation has been made by a rights commissioner under unfair dismissal legislation or a hearing by the EAT has commenced. It also provides that if the matter has been referred under the Industrial Relations Acts and a recommendation has been made by a rights commissioner under that legislation or a hearing by the Labour Court has commenced then the employee cannot seek redress under unfair dismissal legislation.

8.32.3 DISCRIMINATORY DISMISSALS

Under the provisions of the Employment Equality Acts, 1998–2004, an employee may claim discriminatory dismissal for the reasons as set out in that legislation—Chapter 6: Equality and Discrimination in the Workplace. Where a claim has been made under that legislation and either a settlement has been reached or the Equality Tribunal has begun an investigation, the employee is not entitled to also seek redress under unfair dismissal legislation—unless the director having completed an investigation directs otherwise (section 101(2)(b) Employment Equality Act, 1998).

8.32.4 REMEDIES/REDRESS

8.32.4.1 Generally

Unfair dismissal legislation provides for three possible remedies as follows:

(a) reinstatement;

(b) re-engagement; or

(c) compensation.

8.32.4.2 Reinstatement

Reinstatement is to the position which the employee held immediately before the dismissal on the same terms and conditions as he enjoyed. The 1993 Act provides that if terms and conditions have been improved after the employee was dismissed and prior to the reinstatement order taking effect the employee must enjoy the improved or more beneficial terms and conditions. An employee who is reinstated will be entitled to back pay for the period he was out of work and all other benefits and perquisites to be brought up to date. The employee retains continuity of service if reinstated. For this reason tribunals have reinstated employees even where the employee may have been partly to blame for the original dismissal. In such cases the tribunal may vary the strict application or understanding of reinstatement by providing that part of the period the employee was out of work should be treated as a period of unpaid suspension.

8.32.4.3 Re-engagement

Re-engagement is where the tribunal orders that the employee resume work in the position he held immediately before his dismissal or in a different position which might be 'reasonably suitable . . . on such terms and conditions as are reasonable having regard to all the circumstances'. Re-engagement is very close to reinstatement but does not of itself guarantee continuity and payment of lost salary, perquisites and benefits. The tribunal may order re-engagement on the condition that continuity of service is not broken.

8.32.4.4 Compensation

Compensation is the most common form of remedy and frequently preferred by the parties. Remuneration is not simply basic salary but includes 'allowances in the nature of pay and benefits in lieu of or in addition to pay'. The term remuneration includes salary and all other cash payments such as commissions, bonuses and non-cash items such as company car, value of employer's contribution to pension scheme, share options, VHI and any other benefit provided to the employee at the employer's cost. Remuneration does not include expenses which are incurred in the carrying out of duties.

Remuneration may be awarded under the legislation up to a maximum of 104 weeks' gross entitlement.

Compensation itself may only be calculated on the basis of actual loss incurred by the employee as a result of the dismissal as opposed to damages. The Supreme Court considered the issue of contribution and the EAT's discretion in calculating loss in *Carney v Balkan Tours Ltd* [1997] ELR 102 and stated:

'1. The Employment Appeals Tribunal in determining the payment to be made by the respondent to the appellant of compensation by way of redress for unfair dismissal in respect of financial loss incurred by her and attributable to that dismissal were entitled to have regard to her contribution to the dismissal as one of the relevant circumstances in determining the amount to be so paid.

2. The discretion conferred on the Tribunal by section 7 is very wide. Section 7(2)(d) coupled with the discretion conferred upon the adjudicating tribunal in its widest terms would lead to the inference that the legislature intended that the body determining the nature or extent of the redress to which the employee was entitled should look at all the circumstances of the case including the conduct of the parties prior to the dismissal.'

8.32.4.5 Assessment of loss

Employees have an obligation to mitigate their loss once they are dismissed. Compensation may be reduced or may not be awarded at all if an employee has failed to mitigate his loss. Under the 1993 Act social welfare entitlement received following dismissal may not be taken into account in calculating actual loss. The actual loss of an employee will be examined carefully by a tribunal or court before making any compensatory award and a fairly strict line is taken in compensation being awarded only where there is real loss. An example of this is in *Coyle v Tipper House Trust Ltd* UD 904/93 where the employee won his unfair dismissal claim but was awarded no compensation under the legislation (it being prior to the 1993 Act), nor was he able to recover under the Minimum Notice and Terms of Employment Act, 1973, having suffered no loss. The employer's case was that the employee was redundant but this was rejected by the EAT. The EAT had heard evidence that, at the time of the dismissal and shortly thereafter, the claimant was unfit for work on medical grounds. His future prognosis was unclear. The EAT held, in the circumstances, of his unfitness and, in allowing his claim under the Unfair Dismissals Acts, made no award under that legislation 'as the Tribunal was told that the claimant has been unfit for work since his dismissal and it cannot be said when he will be fit for work, if ever, in the future. As the claimant was not available for work in the notice period due to illness his claim under the Minimum Notice and Terms of Employment Acts, 1973–1991 is dismissed'.

The 1993 Act also provides that if an employee has been held to have been unfairly dismissed and suffered no loss a basic award of up to four weeks' remuneration may be made.

8.32.4.6 Taxation of termination payments

All payments made to employees relating to the termination of employment, whether paid at the time of termination or thereafter, are subject to taxation of termination payments. Taxation applies whether the payments are agreed as part of a settlement or an ex gratia payment and also where awarded by a rights commissioner, EAT, Circuit Court, High Court, or Supreme Court. The taxation of such payments was originally provided for under the terms of the Income Tax Act, 1967, sections 114 and 115 as amended by subsequent Finance Acts. The applicable provisions are now contained in Chapter 5 of the Taxes Consolidation Act, 1997.

While the ceiling of 104 weeks' remuneration is based on the gross remuneration figure, compensation and actual loss are based on the net figure as the difference is not a loss to the employee. An example of the calculation of remuneration gross and net is as follows:

	€ *Gross*	€ *Net*
Salary	30,000	20,000
VHI	500	500
Car	3,000	2,000
Employer's pension contribution	5,000	5,000
Annual bonus	4,000	2,000
Telephone rental	500	400
Accommodation	4,000	2,500
Total remuneration	**47,000**	**32,400**

8.33   **Taxation**

The basic rules on taxation of termination payments are as follows:

(a)   basic exemption available to all employees on each and every occasion of termination of employment; and

(b)   rebate for each full year of service.

These deductions may be applied by the employer without Revenue consent.

The Finance Act also allows for an additional allowance which is available in whole or in part once every 10 years. Effectively therefore over a 10-year period an individual can use up this allowance to the maximum. This allowance, however, will not be available if the individual is a member of an occupational pension scheme with the right to receive a lump sum from such a scheme. The individual, however, can irrevocably give up the right to receive the lump sum from the pension scheme and therefore avail of this allowance. If the individual receives or is entitled to receive a pension lump sum then this additional allowance is reduced by the amount of the pension lump sum—most lump sums will be in excess of the additional allowance which makes the exercise academic but if it was less than the additional allowance then there would be a balancing allowance available to the individual.

To mitigate the effects of the above reliefs there is a further relief available to employees in respect of the taxation of termination payments. This is available as an alternative to the entitlements referred to above and it is as follows:

Standard capital superannuation benefit which is calculated as follows:

$$\frac{A \times B - C}{15}$$

where

A = average remuneration for the last 36 months of service.

B = number of complete years of service.

C = any tax-free lump sum received or receivable under an appropriate Revenue-approved pension scheme.

On the basis of the above the amount of relief is calculated. Tax is then applied to the taxable portion as if it was income in the year in which it was received. This will be at the standard rate or may, depending on the employee's income in that particular year, push the income into a higher tax bracket. To mitigate the effect of this the Revenue Commissioners allow the application of what is known as top-slicing relief which is computed as follows:

$$A - (P \times T)$$

where

A = the additional tax which would be payable if the taxable lump sum were treated as income earned in the year of assessment over and above the amount which would have been payable if the lump sum were not taxable.

P = the taxable lump sum.

T = the average rate of tax chargeable in respect of the income of the employee for the five preceding years.

8.34 Claims under Unfair Dismissal Legislation

8.34.1 TIME LIMITS

An employee must bring an unfair dismissal claim to a rights commissioner or the EAT within six months of the date of dismissal, extendable to 12 months under the 1993 Act where appropriate. In *Hogan v Quaid* [1996] ELR 210 the claimant's employment was terminated on 23 April 1994 and she lodged an unfair dismissal claim on 14 December 1994. She claimed that she thought there would be an offer of part-time employment so she had not lodged her claim. She was also unaware of the six-month time limit. On the evidence the EAT held that the circumstances did not prevent the claimant lodging her claim within six months of the date of her dismissal and declined jurisdiction under the provisions of section 8(2), as amended, of the Unfair Dismissals Acts, 1977–1993. The EAT also gave detailed consideration to what constitutes 'exceptional circumstances' in the decision of *McDonagh v Dell Computer Corporation* [2004] ELR 197 where the claimant had suffered a depressive illness caused by a work-related injury which, on the basis of medical evidence given to the tribunal, contributed to his inability to make his claim within the statutory time limit and held that this did constitute exceptional circumstances and allowed the claim to be made outside the six-month period but within the 12-month period provided for in the legislation.

If the employee chooses to lodge a claim with a rights commissioner the employer may object and require that the hearing be carried out by the EAT. The time limits remain the same.

8.34.2 DOCUMENTATION

There are pre-printed forms available for the making of claims to both the rights commissioner and the EAT. Once the claim form is served on the employer the employer must revert to the rights commissioner within 21 days advising of the objection or willingness to participate in the hearing. In the case of EAT hearings an appearance form will be forwarded by the tribunal to the employer and the employer must complete this and return it to the tribunal and file it on the employee or employee's representative within 14 days of receipt. Completion and service of all documentation is essential; otherwise the employer may not be entitled to participate in the hearing although the tribunal has a discretion to extend the time for the filing of an appearance form on application.

The EAT has issued guidelines on its procedures which are set out at **8.35.1** below.

8.35   Employment Appeals Tribunal

8.35.1   GUIDELINES FOR PERSONS REPRESENTING PARTIES BEFORE THE EAT

Guidelines have been prepared for the assistance of those who appear on behalf of clients before the EAT.

The EAT was established to provide a speedy, inexpensive and relatively informal means for resolution of disputes under the various legislation that comes within the tribunal's scope. All practitioners should bear this principle in mind when preparing and presenting cases and should avoid 'legalisms'.

- Practitioners trained in the adversarial method should remember that the EAT often uses the inquisitorial method and may raise matters that have not been raised by either of the parties.

- While the EAT is empowered to take evidence on oath, it is not essential to take sworn evidence, and evidence may be presented in a less formal manner. By and large, the EAT endeavours to limit the application of the oath to cases where it is necessary.

- Where cross-examination is considered necessary, practitioners are reminded that such cross-examination should be brief and to the point and they should also bear in mind that, at the end of the cross-examination, there may be further questions from EAT members. Re-examination, if required, may follow the members' questions.

- The EAT does not necessarily enforce the strict rules of evidence. The 'best evidence' rule does not always apply and hearsay evidence may be admitted by the EAT, subject to the rules of fair procedure.

- Parties should endeavour to reach agreement on uncontroversial issues of fact (wages, length of service etc). If possible, parties should try to reach a wider agreement so as to net down the issues to be decided by the EAT.

- There are no paper pleadings lodged in the EAT. However, the parties are expected to set out their respective cases in writing on the forms completed by the parties prior to hearing. A flexible approach, however, is taken to these papers and parties will not necessarily be confined to what is contained in them. This approach by the EAT is, however, governed by the rules of fair procedure.

- Documents to be used by the parties should be prepared in a booklet or booklets and sufficient copies should be made for the EAT and the other party.

- Both parties are entitled to make opening statements. Apart from outlining a party's case, these statements will help to eliminate areas of disagreement and bring the focus of the EAT onto the net issues involved.

- Witness summonses may be obtained on application to a sitting division of the EAT. Parties should bear in mind that it is the EAT which requires the attendance of a witness, and the issue of a summons is a matter within the EAT's discretion. Applications should be made in good time so as to allow the witness reasonable opportunity to make arrangements to attend. If the venue of the hearing requires a witness to travel some distance, this is a matter to which the EAT shall have regard in deciding whether to issue a summons. Professional witnesses and witnesses who are not closely involved with either party should not be unnecessarily detained.

- The EAT does not have power to order discovery of documents. It is, however, empowered to order a person to attend at a time and place and to bring such documents as are specified. An application for such a summons should state the nature of the documents involved with some particularity.

- By their very nature, adjournments cause delays to the EAT's schedule of hearings. While consideration will be given to all applications, the following conditions should at least be met when applying for an adjournment:
  — good cause should be shown as adjournments are only granted for very grave reasons;
  — the application should be at the earliest opportunity after receipt of the notice of hearing, save where the EAT for just cause dispenses with this requirement; and
  — the written consent of the other party must be obtained. Where same is not forthcoming or cannot be procured easily, the EAT nevertheless requires the application to be made at the earliest possible date.

- The EAT may not award costs against any party unless, in its opinion, a party has acted frivolously or vexatiously. Such costs are confined to a specified amount in respect of travelling expenses and any other costs or expenses reasonably incurred by that other party in connection with the hearing, but shall not include any amount for the attendance of counsel or solicitors, officials of a trade union, or of an employers' association.

8.35.2   STATUTORY FORMS TO BE USED IN APPLICATION TO EAT

T1-A: to be used for direct claims to the Tribunal under the following Acts:

- Redundancy Payments Acts, 1967–2003; and/or

- Minimum Notice and Terms of Employment Acts, 1973–2001; and/or

- Unfair Dismissals Acts, 1977–2001; and

- Organisation of Working Time Act, 1997.

T1-B: this form is to be used for appeals of a rights commissioner's recommendation to the Tribunal under the following legislation:

- Unfair Dismissals Acts, 1977–2003; and/or

- Payment of Wages Act, 1991;

- Terms of Employment (Information) Act, 1994;

- Maternity Protection Act, 1994;

- Adoptive Leave Act, 1995;

- Protection of Young Persons (Employment) Act, 1996;

- Parental Leave Act, 1998;

- European Communities (Safeguarding of Employees' Rights on Transfer of Undertakings) (Amendment) Regulations, 2000;

- European Communities (Safeguarding of Employment) Regulations, 2000;

- Carer's Leave Act, 2001.

T1-C: this form is to be used for appeals to the tribunal under the Protection of Employees (Employers' Insolvency) Acts, 1984–1991.

RP51B: this form is to be used for appeals against a decision of the Minister for Enterprise, Trade and Employment or a deciding officer in a matter of redundancy under the Redundancy Payments Acts, 1967–1991.

T2: this form is to be used by a respondent against whom a claim has been lodged to enter a notice of appearance before the tribunal.

These forms are available on the Department of Enterprise, Trade and Employment website in the downloadable forms page http://www.entemp.ie/forms/index.htm#eat.

All enquiries and forms must be addressed to

Employment Appeals Tribunal,
Davitt House,
65A Adelaide Road,
Dublin 2.

CHAPTER 9

REDUNDANCY

9.1 Introduction

The Redundancy Payments Act, 1967 came into operation on 1 January 1968. The Act was largely based on the UK Redundancy Payments Act 1965 and provides monetary compensation in the event that employees are made redundant. The Principal Act was amended by the Redundancy Payments Act, 1971 and Redundancy Payments Act, 2003. The collective citation is now known as the Redundancy Payments Acts, 1967–2003. The Redundancy Payments Acts apply to employees employed in employment which is insurable for all benefits under the Social Welfare Acts and to employees who are so employed in such employment in the period of four years ending on the date of termination of employment.

9.2 Definition of Redundancy

The statutory definition of redundancy is found in the Redundancy Payments Act, 1967, Section 7(2) as amended by section 4 of the Redundancy Payments Act, 1971 and section 5 of the Redundancy Payments Act, 2003, and provides that:

'. . . an employee who is dismissed shall be taken to be dismissed by reason of redundancy if for one or more reasons not related to the employee concerned the dismissal is attributable wholly or mainly to

(a) the fact that his employer has ceased, or intends to cease, to carry on the business for the purposes of which the employee was employed by him, or has ceased or intends to cease, to carry on that business in the place where the employee was so employed, or

(b) the fact that the requirements of that business for employees to carry out work of a particular kind in the place where he was so employed have ceased or diminished or are expected to cease or diminish, or

(c) the fact that his employer has decided to carry on the business with fewer or no employees, whether by requiring the work for which the employee had been employed (or had been doing before his dismissal) to be done by other employees or otherwise, or

(d) the fact that his employer has decided that the work for which the employee had been employed (or had been doing before his dismissal) should henceforward be done in a different manner for which the employee is not sufficiently qualified or trained, or

(e) the fact that his employer has decided that the work for which the employee had been employed (or had been doing before his dismissal) should henceforward be done by a person who is also capable of doing other work for which the employee is not sufficiently qualified or trained.'

This definition is quite broad, broader than the equivalent UK provision. Part of the reason for such a broad definition is that the 1967 and 1971 Acts sought to confer on a wide constituency of employees the right to a statutory redundancy payment.

In *Bates & Ors v Model Bakery Ltd & Ors* [1993] ILRM 22 the plaintiffs were employed by Model Bakery in the defendant's bakery in Letterkenny, County Donegal. As a result of the employer's failure to pay arrears in consequence of a Labour Court recommendation for a salary increase the plaintiff employees having issued strike notice duly commenced industrial action from 13 September 1987. On 18 January 1988 the defendant wrote to each of the plaintiffs alleging that they, by their unauthorised withdrawal of labour, had effectively frustrated their contracts of employment. On that basis the employees were not entitled to any payments pursuant to the Redundancy Payments Acts. The EAT held that the employees had not followed the grievance procedure and in those circumstances there had not been any dismissal which would entitle the plaintiffs to relief. The matter was appealed to the High Court on a point of law. Lardner J held that the plaintiffs' contracts of employment were terminated by the decision of the Bakery to close down which brought a redundancy situation into existence. On appeal to the Supreme Court, the Supreme Court upheld the High Court findings. O'Flaherty in considering the application of section 7(2) of the 1967 Act held that:

> '. . . the letter of 18 January to the plaintiffs constituted a dismissal of the employees: it was an unequivocal indication to them that their services were no longer needed. At that time the Bakery had ceased or intended to cease carrying on business.'

Accordingly, the statutory presumption, already quoted, section 7(2)(a), came into effect. O'Flaherty J went on to find that strike action did not satisfy any category of case within the doctrine of frustration of contract. Similarly, Egan J held:

> 'On 18 January 1988, the Bakery wrote to each of the plaintiffs alleging that they (the plaintiffs) by their unauthorised withdrawal of labour, had effectively frustrated their contract by not later than 31 December 1987. The Bakery, in fact, closed down about this time. For reasons already stated, the plaintiffs did not frustrate their contracts and I am satisfied that the letter of 18 January 1988 constituted a dismissal and that section 7(2) of the 1967 Act applies . . . there was an actual dismissal in this case and it was attributable to the statutory reason. A redundancy, therefore, arose.'

For further examples of actual dismissals which satisfy the definition of redundancy in the 1967 Act pursuant to section 7(2)(a) see *Hyde v Father Denis Kelleher as Nominee of the Sponsors of the Vermoy Schools' Project and Others* [2004] 15 ELR 145 which involved the complete cessation of a community scheme project run by virtue of a contract between FAS and the Community Scheme Project and *O'Briain v National Rehabilitation Board & Ors* [2002] 13 ELR 210 which concerned the dissolution of the National Rehabilitation Board.

An application of section 7(c) occurred in *Lillis v Kiernan* EAT 22 June 2004. The facts were that the respondent owned a pig farming business and that the claimant was the general manager. The general manager's wage was approximately 40 per cent more than each manager and a business decision was taken to make the claimant redundant and share his functions between himself and the other managers. It was also decided by the respondent to abandon some of the work done and to remove the respondent's time from certain tasks and put his time into other tasks, namely reorganisation. The claimant was not replaced and at the time of trial there was no general manager working for the respondent. The EAT held that the redundancy was in accordance with the requirements as set out in the Redundancy Payments Acts.

Section 7(d) was also found be satisfied in *Byrne v Trackline Crane Hire Ltd* EAT 2 May 2003. The facts were that the company was a crane hire business with cranes varying in size from 10 tonnes to 120 tonnes. It was the policy of the respondent that when a driver was employed he was assigned to a particular crane. The claimant was employed to drive an 18-tonne crane and the use of the crane became redundant because it was unprofitable. Evidence from the respondent was that an excessively long time would be required to train the claimant in the use of another more profitable crane.

The EAT in being satisfied from the evidence that a genuine redundancy existed at the company, said:

'Redundancy existed in a category of business which involved disposing of equipment and replacing it with more modern equipment. One particular machine was not making much money . . . Since the applicant had been for the greater part of his employment with the company driving this particular type of crane, which had to be sold, his position no longer existed.'

9.3 The Impersonality and Change Requirement

The EAT in *St Ledger v Frontline Distributors Ireland Ltd* [1995] ELR 160 said that the statutory definition of 'redundancy' has two important characteristics. Those being 'impersonality' and 'change'. The EAT held:

'. . . impersonality runs through the five definitions in the Acts. Redundancy impacts on the job and only as a consequence of the redundancy does the person involved lose his job.

    'Change also runs through all five definitions. This means change in the workplace. The most dramatic change of all is a complete closedown. Change may also mean a reduction in needs for employees, or a reduction in number. Definition (d) and (e) involve change in the way the work is done also another form of change in the nature of the job. Under these two definitions change in the job must mean qualitative change. Definition (e) must involve, partly, at least, work of a different kind, and that is the only meaning we can put on the words "other work". More work or less work of the same kind does not mean "other work" and is only quantitative change.'

The requirement for impersonality was reinforced by the EAT in *Moloney v Deacon and Sons Ltd* [1996] ELR 230. In that case the claimant had been dismissed for what was claimed to be a reason of redundancy. The company made a number of submissions to the EAT, including a written note of the reasons for discontinuation of employment. One of which was that the claimant did not satisfactorily complete a statutory probationary period, and made reference to a final warning letter. Reference was also made to a claim for back pay which Mr Moloney had withdrawn, having been found to have made a false statement. In the circumstances the EAT held:

'One of the essential features of redundancy is impersonality. One of the reasons given for dismissal refers to the claimant's personality.'

Accordingly, the EAT held that the dismissal was not to be one arising from a genuine redundancy situation.

9.4 Requisite Period of Employment

Section 7(1) provides the general right for an employee to receive a redundancy payment provided he has been employed for the 'requisite period'. The requisite period is defined by section 7(5) as being a period of 104 weeks' continuous employment within the meaning of Schedule 3 of the Act. Any period of employment with the employer before the employee had attained the age of 16 years is excluded.

In *Gormally v McCartin Brothers (Engineering) Ltd* [1982] IRLM 215 Mr Gormally commenced employment with McCartin Brothers on 26 February 1979. His employment was terminated by two weeks' notice expiring on the 20 February 1981. His period of employment was therefore short two days (Saturday and Sunday) of the requisite 104 weeks to qualify under the 1967 Act. Mr. Gormally contended that his working week was a five-day week from Monday to Friday and that he had exactly 104 working weeks' employment. The EAT in considering the definition of the word 'week' in the Interpretation Act, 1937 held that the Oireachtas intended the definition that was contained in the 1967 Act would apply. In so finding the EAT said:

> '[I]n our view the reference to weekly calculation of remuneration seems to contemplate a working week. It is commonplace for many five-day-week employees to have a day's wages deducted in respect of an absent day, and such deduction is, in our experience, one-fifth of the weekly rate. In respect of weekly paid employees, at least, the remuneration contemplated by both employer and employee, must be related to working days only.'

It did say, however in passing, that the position of a person whose remuneration is expressed in an annual salary might possibly be different. This passing comment is unhelpful as there is an increasing number of employees whose remuneration is expressed as an annual salary. The better view is that a working week is the correct definition in order to calculate the continuous employment of 104 weeks. On the issue of continuous employment see also the decision of Murphy J in *Irish Shipping Limited v Adams* High Court, 30 January 1987 unreported and *Carmel Raymond Hoey and ISPCA* EAT 24 September 2004 T Daly Chair for the impersonality requirement.

9.5   Dismissal by an Employer

It is perhaps obvious that for the purpose of attracting benefits under the Acts an employee must be dismissed by his or her employer. Section 9, as amended by section 6 of the 2003 Act provides that dismissal however will only arise where:

(a)   the employer terminates the employee's contract of employment; or

(b)   a fixed-term or specified-purpose contract either expires or the purpose ceases without the contract being renewed under the same or similar contract; or

(c)   the employee terminates the contract in circumstances such that the employee is entitled to terminate by reason of the employer's conduct.

A dismissal will not occur in circumstances where the employee's employment is either renewed or the employee is re-engaged by the same employer under a new contract and essentially the provisions of the contract do not differ from the previous contract. Similarly, an employee will not be dismissed for the purpose of the Acts if the employee is re-engaged by another employer immediately on the termination of his previous employment. Again, effectively on the same terms and conditions that the employee previously employed prior to the termination of his contract of employment. This includes continuity of service and can only occur in circumstances where there is agreement with the employee, the previous employer and the new employer.

In *Cahill v Knight's Cleaning Services Ltd* EAT 10 April 2003 the respondent was a cleaning company. The client company, where Ms Cahill worked, terminated their contract with Knight's Cleaning. Knight's Cleaning offered Ms Cahill alternative work at different locations. This was declined by her saying that it was unsuitable. Ms Cahill was offered work with the client company which had terminated the contract. The EAT held that:

> '. . . the contract with the respondent company and the shop owner had terminated and the claimant decided to accept an offer of direct employment with the shop owner rather than be located elsewhere with the respondent company.'

What is not apparent from the EAT decision is whether or not there was the requisite agreement between Ms Cahill, Knight's Cleaning Services and the client company. One can only assume that agreement was in existence and the other aspects of section 9(3) of the Act had been satisfied.

9.6 Resignation by Employee

Redundancy payments are not available where an employee resigns from their employment. In *Collins v Excel Property Services Ltd* EAT 31 December 1998, Ms Collins was employed by Excel as a cleaner to work at a school in Cobh under a cleaning contract between the Board of Management of the School and Excel. In June 1997 the school sought tenders for the cleaning contract for the school year beginning September 1997. In or about August 1997 the school advised Excel that its tender for the contract was unsuccessful and that the contract had been awarded to another cleaning contractor. By virtue of the Acquired Rights Directive 77/187/EEC, Ms Collins' employment transferred to the new cleaning contractor. Having commenced with the new cleaning contractor Ms Collins and her co-workers felt that the machines provided by the new contractor for cleaning the school were not of the same standard as those used by them in their previous employment with Excel and for this reason they resigned their employment. Ms Collins then claimed redundancy from Excel, her former employer. The EAT held that there was a transfer for the purposes of the Acquired Rights Directive and Ms Collins' contract of employment was transferred from Excel to the new cleaning contractor. Ms Collins resumed cleaning of the school at the commencement of the new school year but resigned after a few days. The EAT found that there was no case against Excel and further that there was not a redundancy situation with Ms Collins as the cleaning of the school still remained to be done.

9.7 Lay-off and Short-time

An employer is entitled to place their workforce on lay-off and short time in circumstances where the employer is unable to provide work. However, the employer is only entitled to do so where it is reasonable for the employer to believe that the lay-off or short time will not be permanent and that the employer gives notice to that effect to the employee prior to them being laid off or placed on short time. Short time occurs where an employee's pay is less than one half of his normal weekly pay or his hours of work are reduced to less than one half of his normal weekly hours (section 11).

An interesting issue which arises and on which the Act is silent is the right of an employer to deduct wages where employees are laid off or placed on short time. In Bowers, *Employment Law* (5th edition) at p 59 it says 'at common law, the employer is in breach of contract if he lays off an employee without pay unless there is an express or implied term permitting the lay-off'. The law is stated in similar terms in Rideout, *Principles of Labour Law* (4th edition) at p 267 and *Halsbury's Laws of England* (4th edition) Volume 16, para 581 n15.

In *Law v Irish Country Meats (Pig Meats) Ltd* [1998] ELR 266 White J, of the Circuit Court, held that an employer's fundamental obligation is to pay the agreed remuneration for the times of work during which the employee is prepared to work. There is no general right at common law to lay-off without pay. Such right may however, be established in very limited circumstances which may be established through custom or general usage. Such a custom must be reasonable, certain and notorious. Accordingly, an employer is not entitled to not pay wages during a lay-off or short time and prior agreement with the employees is required pursuant to the Payment of Wages Act 1991 to lawfully withhold wages during that time.

Where an employee has been laid off or kept on short time for four or more consecutive weeks, or within a period of 13 weeks for a series of six or more weeks of which not more than three weeks were consecutive and, after this period, he gives his employer notice in writing of his intention to claim redundancy payment, the employee will be entitled to redundancy (section 12). This enables an employee to claim redundancy pay where they have been laid off or kept on short time for a specified period of time. It prevents an employer keeping an employee on lay-off or short time for an indefinite period without having to make payments pursuant to the Act. An employer on receipt of notice from an employee pursuant to section 12 is entitled to give counter-notice pursuant to section 13 which must inform the employee that they will recommence employment not later than four weeks after the notification and for a period of not less than 13 weeks during which time he or she would not be laid off or kept on short time.

If an employee does not give his or her employer notice pursuant to section 12, their lay-off can arguably continue indefinitely. It is only the notice given by the employee which triggers the end of the lay-off on the employee's part. This can be met by counter-notice given by the employer pursuant to section 13.

In *An Post v Oliver McNeill* [1998] ELR 19 O'Sullivan J made some observations in respect of a lay-off period which exceeded 26 weeks. The facts in that case were that Mr McNeill argued that he was dismissed due to redundancy and that he had not received redundancy payment or the appropriate period of notice. An Post denied that the defendant had been dismissed or had been made redundant and argued that Mr McNeill's refusal to work had caused the termination of his employment. An Post further argued that there were breaks during his employment which would affect his continuity of employment. The EAT determined that Mr McNeill was continuously employed and that frequent breaks which had occurred during his period of employment were periods of lay-off. In relation to the period of lay-offs O'Sullivan J (on appeal to the High Court) made the following observation:

'. . . there is nothing in the statutory provisions to which I have referred which establishes that the period of lay-off may not exceed 26 weeks. In the context of the minimum notice legislation, a shorter period shall count as a period of service and in the context of the redundancy payments legislation; continuity of employment shall not be broken by a lay-off of a shorter period. There is nothing to say that a lay-off cannot exceed this period. Indeed, the specific provisions to which I have referred suggest that such can be the case.'

9.8   Disentitlement to Redundancy

An employee who has been dismissed is not be entitled to redundancy payment if his employer terminates the employee's employment because of misconduct. This does not apply if an employee has received their notice of proposed dismissal for redundancy and before the date of dismissal the employee takes part in a strike and the employer, by reason of the employee taking part in the strike, terminates the employee's contract of employment for misconduct (section 14).

When an employer is contemplating redundancy, it is often the case that alternative employment can be found for those employees who would otherwise be made redundant. The terms and conditions of employment on offer may or may not differ from the employment that the employee occupied and from which he was to be made redundant. An employee is not be entitled to redundancy payment if his employer has offered to renew his contract of employment or to re-engage him under a new contract of employment. That said, the provisions of the contract, as renewed, or of the new contract, insofar as the capacity and place in which he would be employed and as to other terms and conditions of his employment, cannot differ from the corresponding provisions of his previous contract. Also, the renewal or re-engagement must take effect on or before the date of the termination of his previous contract and the employee has unreasonably refused the offer. If all these conditions are met the employee is not entitled to a redundancy payment (section 15(11)).

Where the offer to the employee as to the capacity and place in which he would be employed and as to other terms and conditions of employment do differ wholly or in part from the corresponding provisions in his previous contract, different considerations apply. Importantly, in this regard the offer by the employer must constitute an offer of suitable employment in relation to the employee and if that is the case and the employee has unreasonably refused the offer, the employee is disentitled to redundancy payment (section 15(2)).

The area which has received much attention is the place of employment. Often, an employee will be made redundant but offered new employment with the employer at a different site. In *Broderick v Dorothea Fashions Ltd* EAT 1978 it was held that East Arran Street was not the same place as Churchtown and in *Early v Floorstyle Contracts Ltd* EAT 2003 that Skerries was not the same place as Swords.

9.9 Notice of Redundancy

The Redundancy Payments Acts require two weeks' notice of termination of employment for those persons who are entitled to redundancy payments, i.e. those employees who have not less than 104 weeks' service (section 17). The notice is given formally by the employer completing an RP50 form, a copy of which is given to the employee. The RP50 form combines the old forms RP1 (Notice of Redundancy), RP2 (Certificate of Redundancy), RP3 (Rebate Claim) and RP14 (Employee's Application for a Lump Sum from the Social Insurance Fund). Accordingly, in addition to notifying the employee of the redundancy, the form also records the receipt by the employee of the statutory redundancy amount from the employer and is used by the employee to claim a rebate from the Social Insurance Fund. The employer is then obliged to send to the Minister for Enterprise, Trade and Employment the original form. Failure to do so may result in the employer being fined and may affect the rebate to which an employer is entitled to having made the statutory redundancy payment.

Notwithstanding the provisions of section 17, long-serving employees will have longer notice entitlements under the Minimum Notice and Terms of Employment Act, 1973. In particular section 4(2) sets out the actual notice dependent upon length of service of an employee. Contractual notice entitlements should also be borne in mind, as they must be complied with in order to avoid claims of wrongful dismissal. It will suffice to give the longest period of notice which will itself subsume and cover the other periods of notice provided the RP50 form is issued by the employer at least two weeks before the redundancy takes effect.

9.10 Redundancy Payment

The amount of statutory redundancy pay is calculated by reference to Schedule 3 (as amended) of the Redundancy Payments Act, 1967. The payment is calculated by reference to weeks per year of service. The number of weeks to be applied to the years of the service was increased in 2003 following sustained pressure from the trade union movement.

The increased benefits were passed into law by virtue of the Redundancy Payments Act, 2003.

All earnings of an employee in excess of €600 are disregarded in making the statutory redundancy payments. This means that in calculating a week's pay, if an employee earns €600 or less gross per week then his actual weekly remuneration is used in formulating the amount due. If he earns in excess of €600 gross per week, the payment is capped at €600 gross per week. The formula for making the payment is as follows:

(a) two weeks' pay for each year of continuous employment over the age of 16 years; and

(b) an additional one week's normal earnings.

In order to determine the number of years of continuous employment, the number of weeks of continuous employment is divided by 52. For example, an employee with 208 weeks' service will have four continuous years. Where this calculation produces a remainder of 26 or more weeks the year will be rounded up. Where the calculation produces a reasonable service that is not an exact number of years, the 'excess' days will be credited as a proportion of a year.

The Department of Enterprise, Trade and Employment has a redundancy calculator on its website at http://www.entemp.ie/employment/redundancy/calculator.htm the purpose of which is to allow the user to calculate a statutory redundancy entitlement for a qualifying employee.

9.11 Continuous Employment

It is important to understand the concept of continuous employment having regard to the fact that it determines, to a significant extent, the amount of statutory lump sum an employee will be entitled to receive. In most cases continuous employment will be relatively easy to determine. Schedule 3 (as amended) to the Redundancy Payments Acts sets out what constitutes continuous employment. Put simply, employment shall be taken to be continuous unless terminated by dismissal or by the employee's voluntarily leaving the employment. The period of notice due to an employee under the Minimum Notice and Terms of Employment Act, 1973, if not given by the employer, is allowed as continuous service for the purpose of calculating redundancy payments.

When an employee's period of service has been interrupted by a period of sickness, lay-off, holidays, service in the reserve Defence Forces or any cause (other than the voluntary leaving of the employment concerned by the employee) authorised by the employer, continuity of employment is not broken. Also, a period during which an adopting parent was absent while on adoptive leave or additional adoptive leave or an employee was absent from work while on additional maternity leave, parental leave, force majeure leave or carer's leave will equally not amount to a break in an employee's continuity of employment. Any period during which an employee was absent from work because of a lockout by the employer or because the employee was participating in a strike will not affect an employee's continuity of time.

Similar to the provisions for continuous employment, the period during which an employee is absent on adoptive leave, additional maternity leave, parental leave, force majeure leave, carer's leave will be allowable as reckonable service. Reckonable service will not count where during, and only during this three-year period ending the date of termination of employment, an employee who is absent from work by reason of a strike on the business or industry.

9.12   Reckonable Service

Having established that an employee has the required continuous employment, within that period an employee must have reckonable service for the purpose of calculating the exact number of weeks of continuous employment. Schedule 3 (as amended) again provides the method by which reckonable service is calculated. None of the following absences from work during and only during, the three-year period ending with the date of termination of employment, is allowable as reckonable service:

(a)   absence in excess of 52 consecutive weeks by reason of an occupational accident or disease within the meaning of the Social Welfare (Consolidation) Act, 1993;

(b)   absence in excess of 26 consecutive weeks by reason of any illness not referred to in paragraph (a);

(c)   absence by reason of lay-off by the employer;

The difference between continuous employment and reckonable service can be illustrated as follows. In circumstances where an employee has four years' continuous employment by virtue of Schedule 3 and assuming that they were absent by reason of a strike for a period of 12 weeks, the calculation of statutory lump sum would be based on 246 weeks' reckonable service.

9.13   Normal Weekly Remuneration

Schedule 3 (as amended) also defines normal weekly remuneration for the purpose of calculating a lump sum. For employees who are paid wholly by an hourly time rate or by a fixed wage or salary the employee's normal weekly remuneration is taken to be his or her earnings (including any regular bonus or allowance which does not vary in relation to the amount of work done and any payment in kind) for his or her normal weekly working hours as at the date he or she was declared redundant together with the employee's average weekly overtime earnings to be calculated by ascertaining the total amount of overtime earnings of the employee concerned in the period of 26 weeks which ended 13 weeks before the date on which the employee was declared redundant and dividing that amount by 26.

There are also calculations required in respect of employees who are paid wholly or partly by piece rates, bonuses or commissions. If an employee has no normal working hours his or her normal weekly remuneration is taken to be the average weekly remuneration including any bonus, pay allowance or commission received over the period of 52 weeks prior to the date he or she was declared redundant.

9.14   Payments in Excess of Statutory Requirements

It is common practice in Ireland for employees and trade unions to negotiate extra statutory redundancy payments, usually calculated as a set number of weeks' pay—with no ceiling on the amount of a week's pay—for each year of service. In the case of long-service employees a cap is sometimes applied, e.g. no more than two years' remuneration payable. These payments in excess of the statutory redundancy payments will be subject to tax whereas statutory redundancy payments are tax-free. Where there are collective redundancies (**9.16** below) trade unions and/or staff on their own behalf negotiate redundancy agreements. Other employees may have a contractual right to enhanced redundancy benefits which had been agreed prior to the redundancy situation arising. In any event, there is no preclusion for an employer to agree to benefits in excess of the statutory redundancy benefits. In those circumstances, the enhanced redundancy benefits should be expressed to include the statutory redundancy benefits to avoid any argument that the redundancy benefits are cumulative.

9.15 Resolution of Disputes

Disputes on the application of the Redundancy Payments Acts, 1967–2003 are dealt with by the EAT.

9.16 Collective Redundancies

9.16.1 INTRODUCTION

Where an employer embarks on a programme of collective redundancies the Protection of Employment Act, 1977, the Protection of Employment Order, 1996, SI 370/1996, the Protection of Employment Act, 1977 (Notification of Proposed Collective Redundancies) Regulations, SI 140/1977 and the European Communities (Protection of Employment) Regulations, 2000, SI 488/2000 must be followed.

The Protection of Employment Act was Ireland's attempt to satisfy its obligations under Council Directive 75/129/EEC on the approximation of the law of the member States relating to collective redundancies. The Act only applies to establishments normally employing more than 20 persons. Those employing less than 20 persons cannot, by definition, effect collective redundancies.

9.16.2 DEFINITIONS

The term 'redundancy' in the Act is linked directly to the Redundancy Payments Acts, 1967–2003 and section 6(3) contains a comprehensive definition of the term 'establishment'. In the 1977 Act 'collective redundancies' are defined in section 6(1) as follows:

> '. . . where in any period of 30 consecutive days the number of such dismissal is—
> (a) at least 5 in an establishment normally employing more than 20 and less than 50 employees,
> (b) at least 10 in an establishment normally employing at least 50 but less than 100 employees,
> (c) at least 10% of the number of employees in an establishment normally employing at least 100 but less than 300 employees, and
> (d) at least 30 in an establishment normally employing 300 or more employees.'

Unlike the Redundancy Payments Acts, 1967–2003, the Protection of Employment Act, 1977 applied to all employees with a contract of service regardless of the length of time they are employed or the hours they work. If, therefore, employees under Irish legislation are not entitled to a statutory redundancy payment (or do not have the right to claim unfair dismissal, by virtue of not having the requisite continuous service required to make claims under that legislation) they must still be counted as employees for the purposes of the Act.

The number of employees normally employed in an establishment is taken to be the average of the number employed in each of the 12 months preceding the date on which the first dismissal takes effect.

9.16.3   CONSULTATION AND NOTIFICATION

In the event that the number of redundancies satisfy the definition of collective redundancies the employer must, with a view to reaching an agreement, initiate consultations with employees' representatives. The consultations must include the following matters:

(a) the possibility of avoiding the proposed redundancies, reducing the number of employees effected by them or mitigating their consequences by recourse to accompanying social measures aimed inter alia, an aid for redeploying or retraining employees made redundant;

(b) the basis on which it will be decided which particular employees will be made redundant.

These consultations must be initiated at the earliest opportunity and in any event at least 30 days before the first dismissal takes effect (section 9(2)).

'Employee representatives' are defined, by section 2 of the Act as inserted by the European Communities (Protection of Employment) Regulations, 2000, SI 488/2000 as:

'(a) trade union, staff association or accepted body with which it has been the practice of the employer to conduct collective bargaining negotiations, or

(b) in the absence of such a trade union, staff association or accepted body, a person or persons chosen (under an arrangement put in place by the employer) by such employees from amongst their number to represent them in negotiations with the employer.'

In circumstances where paragraph (a) above does not apply, it is a matter for the employer how they organise a person or persons to represent the employees as their representatives. Accordingly, it is a matter entirely for the employer but at the very least, some process should be undertaken where employees have a free say as to who will represent their interests. It is unlikely to be sufficient that persons are simply appointed by the employer. The persons at the very least must be chosen by the affected employees.

When an employer is consulting their employees as required by the Act, the employer must supply the employee's representatives with all relevant information relating to the proposed redundancy. This includes (but is not limited to):

(a) the reasons for the proposed redundancies;

(b) the number and descriptions or categories of employees whom it is proposed to make redundant;

(c) the number of employees and description of categories, normally employed;

(d) the period during which it is proposed to affect the proposed redundancies;

(e) the criteria proposed for the selection of the workers to be made redundant; and

(f) the method of calculating any redundancy payments other than those methods set out in the Redundancy Payments Acts, 1967–2003, section 10(2).

In addition, the employer must supply to the Minister for Enterprise Trade and Employment copies of all information supplied to the employees' representatives (section 10(3)).

Not only is the employer required to supply the Minister with information provided to the employees' representatives, an employer must notify the Minister, in writing, of his proposals to create collective redundancies at the earliest opportunity and in any event at least 30 days before the first dismissal takes effect. The employer must in turn copy the notification to the Minister to the employees' representatives (section 12). The Protection of Employment Act, 1977 (Notification of Proposed Collective Redundancies) Regulations, 1977, SI 140/1977 prescribed the particulars to be specified by an employer in a notification to the Minister. It would appear that the rationale behind the notification to the

Minister is to enable the Minister to intervene and discuss directly with the employer the potential redundancies and perhaps suggest solutions to avoid them.

The Act does not apply to redundancies resulting from the expired or fixed-term contract or specified-purpose contract on the cessor of the purpose. Employees employed by public administrative bodies or by establishments governed by public law in terms of civil service establishments are also excluded from the scope of the Act (*Griffin v South West Water Services Ltd* [1995] IRLR 15).

9.16.4 COMMENCEMENT OF COLLECTIVE REDUNDANCIES

The Act prohibits collective redundancies taking effect before the expiry of the period of 30 days beginning on the date of the relevant notification to the Minister (section 14). If an employer, notwithstanding the provisions of the Act, affects redundancies prior to the expiration of the 30-day period the employer is guilty of an offence and liable on conviction on indictment to a fine not exceeding €12,500. Indeed, section 15 of the Act contemplates further consultations with the Minister.

It may be possible to avoid the requirements under the Act in circumstances where an employer staggers the redundancies such that in any 30-day period there will not be the number of employees made redundant which would otherwise satisfy the definition of collective redundancy.

While section 9 requires the employer to consult employees' representatives, there is no prescription as to how long that consultation is required to take. The consultation may be conducted over a very short period of time (and certainly not over a period of 30 days). Even where consultation occurs over a short period of time, say within five days, while this may be not within the spirit of the Act, it is not unlawful.

9.16.5 RESOLUTION OF DISPUTES

The European Communities (Protection of Employment) Regulations, 2000, SI 488/2000 provides that where an employee, trade union, staff association or accepted body alleges that an employer has contravened sections 9 or 10 of the Act, they may present a complaint to a rights commissioner and the rights commissioner must give the parties an opportunity to be heard by him or her and to present to him or her any evidence relevant to the complaint. The rights commissioner must then make a decision to do one or more of the following:

(a) declare the complaint is, or as the case may be, is not well founded;

(b) require the employer to comply with the provisions of the Act; and/or

(c) require the employer to pay to the employee compensation of such amount (if any) as is just and equitable having regard to all the circumstances but not exceeding four weeks' pay (regulation 6(2)).

A rights commissioner cannot entertain a complaint if it is made outside a six-month period beginning on the date of the alleged contravention (regulation 6(3)).

The purpose of the 2000 Regulations was to more fully comply with the obligations of the Directive by providing for representation of and consultation with employees in the absence of a trade union or similar body and a right of complaint for an employer who is alleged to have contravened section 9 or 10 of the Act. The Regulations also increase the level of fines (regulation 5).

CHAPTER 10

TRADE UNIONS, TRADE DISPUTES AND INDUSTRIAL RELATIONS

10.1   Constitutional Position of Trade Union Membership

10.1.1   INTRODUCTION

Trade unions have been an integral part of the industrial relations scene in Ireland for a considerable period of time. They hold a privileged position in that they are bodies that are devoted in large part to fixing collective rates of pay for their members. On its face therefore, they are bodies that engage in restraint of trade and inhibit the free movement of supply and demand on fixing prices, in this case wage levels. That said, trade unions are protected from anti-competitive prosecutions and breaches of economic tort by virtue of statutory protection contained in the Trade Union Acts, 1871–1990. Indeed, section 2 of the Trade Union Act, 1871, 34 & 35 Vic c 31 provides:

> 'The purposes of any trade union shall not, by reason merely that they are in restraint of trade, be deemed to be unlawful so as to render any member of such trade union liable to criminal prosecution for conspiracy or otherwise . . .'

Given the protection provided by the Trade Union Acts, the legislation sets up an elaborate system of registration of trade unions. The property belonging to trade unions (which can be of substantial value) must be vested in trustees of the union for the use and benefit of the union and its members. The Acts regulate the rules of registered trade unions and require that those rules contain as a minimum, provisions in respect of several matters which are contained in the Act. The minimum requirements are contained in the first schedule to the Trade Union Act, 1871 and include:

- the name of the trade union and place of meeting for the business of the trade union;
- the whole of the objects for which the trade union is to be established;
- the manner of making, altering, amending and rescinding rules;
- a provision for the appointment and removal of a general committee of management, of a trustee or trustees, treasurer and other officers;
- a provision for the investment of the funds, and for an annual or periodical audit accounts;
- the inspection of the books and names of members of the trade union by every person having an interest in the funds of the trade union.

The Industrial Relations Act, 1990 extended the schedule to include the requirement that the rules of every trade union must contain certain provisions in respect of strikes and other industrial action (section 14(5)). In addition authorised trade unions are required to include in their rules 'provisions specifying the conditions of entry into and cesser of membership of such trade union' (Trade Union Act, 1941, section 12(1)(a)).

Trade unions by their very nature are political organisations. The Trade Union Act, 1913, 2 & 3 Geo 5 c 30 however restricts the application of trade union funds for certain political objects (section 3(3)). Those objects include expenditure of money:

- on the payment of any expense incurred by a candidate or prospective candidate for election;

- on the holding of any meeting or the distribution of any literature of documents in support of any candidate or prospective candidate;

- on the maintenance of any person who is a member of the Oireachtas or holds a public office;

- in connection with the registration of electors or the selection of a candidate for the Oireachtas or any public office;

- on the holding of political meetings of any kind, or on the distribution of political literature or political documents of any kind.

The Trade Union Act, 1941 requires any body of persons which wishes to carry on negotiations on the fixing of wages or other conditions of employment to hold a negotiation licence granted by the Minister for Enterprise, Trade and Employment. No body or persons shall be granted or hold a negotiation licence unless it is a trade union registered under the Trade Union Acts (or a trade union under the law of another country) and it has deposited with the High Court an 'appropriate sum'. The appropriate sum is a sliding scale depending on the size of the union and is no more than a nominal sum.

The Acts also provide for 'excepted bodies'. Excepted bodies are defined by the Trade Union Act, 1941 to in effect mean a body which carries on negotiations for the fixing of the wages or other conditions of employment of its own (but no other) employees. The Trade Union Act, 1942 extended the expression 'excepted body' to include a body of all the members of which are employed by the same employer and which carries on negotiations for the fixing of the wages or other conditions of employment. The most common example of an excepted body would be the staff association of a company. Excepted bodies are not required to hold a negotiating licence. The meaning of excepted body was extensively considered in *Iarnród Eireann v Holbrooke* [2000] ELR 109, [2001] ELR 65 (Supreme Court).

In that case the Irish Locomotive Drivers' Association, which was registered as a trade union, contended that it was also an 'excepted body' on the basis that all of its current members were employees of Irish Rail. The difficulty was that the constitution of the association permitted membership to locomotive drivers for the entire island of Ireland which in theory at least opened the membership to employees of Translink, the Northern Ireland railway company. In the High Court O'Neill J said it was essential that all the members of an 'excepted body' must at all times be employed by the same employer. He said that the appropriate test was potential membership and accordingly the association was not an 'excepted body'. In the Supreme Court however Fennelly J, speaking for the unanimous court disagreed with the conclusion of O'Neill J. He held that in respect of the association's Constitution:

'To read into the section words which would exclude bodies whose members could potentially include persons employed by another employer is not justified by any canon of construction of which I am aware.'

Notwithstanding the Supreme Court's disagreement with O'Neill J they did not hold the association to be an 'excepted body' because the legislation was couched in the present tense. Accordingly, an 'excepted body' was one which carries on negotiations for fixing wages and the Supreme Court was of the opinion that, since the association was not carrying on such negotiations at that time it could not be an 'excepted body'.

It is interesting to note O'Neill J's historical analysis of the necessity for excepted bodies. It was O'Neill J's view (one not challenged by the Supreme Court) that the reason for the intention of the legislature in creating the body designated as an 'excepted body':

> '. . . was to relieve an obvious hardship which might have arisen in the context of the enactment of section 6(1) of the Trade Union Act, 1941 in that many employees in small firms might have been deprived of the benefit of trade union representation in the carrying on of negotiations for the fixing of wages and other conditions of employment, where members of the staff of a particular employer did not wish to join a large outside union but whose members were too small to raise and maintain what in 1941 was a very substantial deposit of £1,000 which was required for the purpose of getting a negotiating licence.'

The Trade Union Act, 1975 attempts to facilitate the amalgamation of trade unions and in doing so reduce the number of unions in the State. Grants are paid under the Trade Union Act, 1975 to help unions defray certain additional costs (for example administrative expenses and specified salary and pension costs) they have incurred as a result of a merger. The grants are discretionary and applications made by unions are assessed on the basis of an administrative scheme of grants and are subject to the approval of the Minister for Finance.

10.1.2 UNION RECOGNITION

10.1.2.1 Unilateral right to join union

The employee who exercises a constitutional right to join a trade union cannot insist that they enjoy the full benefit of such membership, by in turn insisting that the employer recognise their union. The right conferred by the Constitution is an individual personal right and does not carry with it the concomitant obligation on an employer to recognise that trade union. In *Abbott and Whelan v ITGWU* [1982] 1 JISLL 56 the plaintiff's members of ITGWU joined the ATGWU. Their employer, the Southern Health Board, did not have a formal recognition agreement with the ATGWU. The plaintiffs sought to insist that their employer deal with the trade union of their choice. When the Board refused the plaintiffs brought the matter to the High Court. They claimed inter alia that the defendants were interfering with or obstructing them in the exercise of their constitutional right to join the trade union of their choice and, what they claimed, was the further right to be represented by such trade union in the conduct of negotiations with their employers, concerning wages and other conditions of employment. In his judgment McWilliam J referred to article 40.6.1(iii) and the rights conferred on the plaintiffs and other citizens by that provision and considered *Meskell v CIE* [1973] IR 121 and *Educational Company of Ireland v Fitzpatrick* [1961] IR 345, where active steps were taken to compel the citizens to forgo their constitutional rights. He held that there was no attempt to compel the plaintiffs to forgo their constitutional rights in this particular case:

> 'Insofar as the Board is concerned it appears to me to be clear that the plaintiffs have no constitutional right to compel the Board to engage in negotiations either with them or with their union . . .
> 'In the present case, the plaintiffs have joined ATGWU without first ascertaining whether that trade union would or would not be in a position to negotiate with the Board. Employers must frequently have refused to negotiate with employees or their unions and this may have led to industrial action but, outside the terms of the contract of employment, employers are not bound to take part in any, or any particular form of, negotiations.
> 'On the facts of this case I am of the opinion that the refusal of the Board to negotiate with ATGWU is not coercion to forgo a constitutional right within the principles which have been enunciated.'

In the earlier case of *EI Company Ltd v Kennedy* [1968] IR 69 Walsh J stated in an obiter dictum:

'In law an employer is not obliged to meet anybody as the representative of his worker, nor indeed is he obliged to meet the worker himself for the purpose of discussing any demand which the worker may make.'

10.1.3   IMPLIED RECOGNITION

In the absence of a specific contractual provision that the employee's trade union will be recognised it is arguable that, where an employee is a member of a trade union and the employer is dealing with or had dealt with that union, there is an implied term in the contract between the employer and the employee to the effect that the employee's union will be recognised. In the context of a transfer of an undertaking the employees may seek to rely on the provisions of Article 3 of the Directive by claiming that their right to have their union recognised is something that arises from the existence of an employment relationship at the date of transfer. In this regard, Article 3 refers to *'rights and obligations . . . arising from . . . an employment relationship'*.

However, regulation 4(i) of the European Communities (Protection of Employees on Transfer of Undertakings) Regulations, 2003 which transposes the Direction into Irish Law reads: *'The tranferor's rights and obligations arising from a contract of employment existing on the date of a transfer shall, by reason of such transfer, be transferred to the transferee.'* Accordingly, when transposed into national law, the rights and obligations *'arising from an employment relationship'* were excluded. On that basis, unless an employee has an implied or express right in their contract of employment relating to recognition of a trade union, it will not transfer as a consequence of a transfer of undertaking.

The absence of a system of formal recognition in Ireland allows that recognition may arise by express agreement but also by implied agreement. Recognition could be implied from a course of dealing between the parties and by the recognition, albeit in limited ways, of a trade union for certain purposes such as in disciplinary hearings.

As there is no system of formal recognition provided for in Irish law there is also no system of derecognition. An employer wishing to derecognise a trade union must have regard to the contractual position the employer has with the trade union and with its own employees as referred to above.

10.1.4   RELATIONSHIPS BETWEEN TRADE UNIONS

For trade unions who are affiliated to the Irish Congress of Trade Unions (ICTU) the constitution of the ICTU contains regulations for dealing with the maintenance of good relationships between its affiliated unions and has a disputes procedure which can be invoked to deal with disputes and rule on their resolution.

The provisions of this rule were considered against the backdrop of an individual's constitutional right to join or not to join a trade union by McWilliam J in *Abbott and Whelan v ITGWU* [1982] 1 JISLL 56 where he was invited to hold that the provisions of clause 47 were unconstitutional given the similarity between rule 47 and section 26 of the Trade Union Act, 1941 which had been held to be unconstitutional in *National Union of Railwaymen v Sullivan* [1947] IR 77. McWilliam J held that as clause 47(d) applied only between the trade unions concerned, the rule could not operate to deny the plaintiffs their constitutional rights which would remain enforceable 'despite any agreements to the contrary made between the two unions or anyone else'.

10.1.5   CLOSED SHOP PROVISIONS

Even where an employer does not recognise a union there is nothing to prevent the employees in their personal capacity being members of the trade union. While the judgment in *Abbott and Whelan v ITGWU* [1982] 1 JISLL 56 would indicate that in many situations the employees do not have the legal right to have their trade union recognised, they may still retain their membership, albeit in a situation where their trade union is very restricted as to what it can do for them. In European law an employee also has the right not to join a trade union and in the pre-entry closed shop case, *Sigurjonsson v Iceland* [1993] 16 EHRR 462, the European Court of Human Rights held that Article 11 of the European Convention on Human Rights encompassed 'a negative right of association'. In addition, any attempt to have transferred employees give up membership of their trade union of choice would be seen as an attempt to get them to surrender their constitutional right to join the trade union of their choice and is likely to be held as unconstitutional (*Meskell v CIE* [1979] IR 121). See also *Young, James and Webster v UK* [1983] IRLR 35 in relation to the post-entry closed shop.

The only course of action open to employees who have such a difficulty would be to seek to put pressure on either the employer or, indirectly, on their fellow employees by way of a trade dispute. A trade dispute engaged in by any party seeking to force membership of a particular trade union on any employee would itself be unconstitutional (*Murtagh Properties Ltd v Cleary* [1972] IR 330 and *National Union of Railwaymen v Sullivan* [1947] IR 77). Where an employee has a constitutional right to be, and remain, a member of a trade union any attempt to have that person surrender that right would fall foul of *Murtagh Properties* and the judgment of Budd J in *Educational Company of Ireland Ltd v Fitzpatrick (No 2)* [1961] IR 345 where he stated inter alia:

> 'The Court will therefore assist and uphold a citizen's constitutional rights . . . and it follows that if one citizen has a right under the Constitution there exists a correlative duty on the part of other citizens to respect that right and not to interfere with it.'

10.1.6   THE RIGHT TO STRIKE

The law of the European Union recognises the right to strike as enshrined in Article 13 of the European Community Social Charter, 1989. In Ireland there is no right to strike but rather there is a freedom in certain circumstances to strike, in that immunities from legal restrictions on strikes and industrial actions will be conferred, provided certain conditions are met. The legal system of the European Union goes a stage further and confers a right which implies an entitlement to infrastructural, legal and state support for the right to strike. It is suggested that the right to strike values the collective interest more than it values the individual interest which may be overridden by the collective (Barnard, *EC Employment Law*, pp 446–447).

10.2   Trade Disputes

10.2.1   INTRODUCTION

Irish law is still based on the individual contract and trade dispute law is no different. It recognises the position of trade unions, but more as supporters and advisers of the individual rather than the leaders of collective action. In many employments, particularly those with larger numbers of employees and which are unionised, employers deal with their employees on a collective basis and conclude agreements either with a group of employees or a trade union or staff association acting on their behalf. In this way terms and conditions of employment, pay rises etc are dealt with rather than meeting and dealing with each individual employee. There would still be individual contact, perhaps in relation to performance appraisal and performance issues, but in the main the employers deal with the employees on a collective basis.

Trade disputes are provided for in the Industrial Relations Acts, 1946–2004 and are defined in varying terms in the Acts depending on the relevant part of the legislation to which the definition will be applied. For example the definition of trade dispute in the Industrial Relations Act, 1946 is:

> *'Any dispute or difference between employers and workers or between workers and workers connected with the employment or non-employment, or the terms of the employment, or with the conditions of the employment of any person.'*

In *Ryanair V Irish Municipal Public and Civil Trade Union/Irish Airlines Pilots Association* DECP051 (25 January 2005), the Labour Court considered the differences between definitions of 'trade dispute'. They said in respect of the definition contained in the 1946 Act:

> 'This is a broader definition than that contained in the 1990 Act (or that previously contained in the now-repealed Trade Disputes Act, 1906) in that it includes a difference between employers and workers as well as a dispute. In the context in which it is used the term "difference" ' must mean something distinct from a "dispute". It would appear to have been included in the definition of the 1946 Act so as to allow the court to investigate a disagreement arising within an employment before positions became so entrenched as to constitute a dispute, in the sense that a strike or industrial action is in place or in contemplation.'

It is clear from the definition, and indeed decisions which have considered the definition, that the meaning of trade dispute is an extremely broad concept covering a multitude of issues that may arise in the workplace.

The Industrial Relations Act, 1969 permits the Labour Court to investigate trade disputes at the request of parties (section 20). During 2004, 142 cases were referred directly to the Labour Court under this section: a reduction of 21 from 2003. The end process of a referral under section 20 of the 1969 Act is a recommendation from the Labour Court. In circumstances where the worker concerned or their trade union request the Labour Court to investigate the dispute, they can undertake to accept the recommendation of the court and in those circumstances the court shall investigate the dispute. This can also apply where both parties undertake to accept a recommendation. If the employer does not undertake to accept the recommendation it is not binding on the employer.

The definitions of trade dispute are so broad that they can encompass circumstances which would otherwise amount to an unfair dismissal and be dealt with in accordance with the Unfair Dismissals Acts, 1977–2001. An employee who has the requisite service and satisfies the jurisdictional requirements of the Unfair Dismissal Acts, will tend to follow that course. The decision of the EAT is binding and the employee can be awarded up to two years' salary. It is only in circumstances where an employee does not meet the jurisdictional requirements of the Unfair Dismissal Acts, for example, they do not have the requisite 12-month continuous service, that they invoke a trade dispute. In effect, the application by that employee of the trade dispute is de facto an unfair dismissal claim.

The industrial relations system in Ireland operates primarily within the parameters of the Trade Union Acts and Industrial Relations Acts. This system is based on the premise that employers and employees are not compelled to use the vehicles of the State in order to resolve their (trade) disputes. Arguably, the Industrial Relations (Amendment) Act, 2001 and the Industrial Relations (Miscellaneous Provisions) Act, 2004 represent a departure from the voluntarist system. The Acts enable the Labour Court to make binding determinations on pay and conditions of employment regardless of the view of the parties to the hearing. The rational behind the legislation was to address union concerns in respect of union recognition where, after repeated attempts, employers refused to recognise the trade union and in particular, refused to negotiate with the trade unions on pay and condition affecting their employees and members respectively.

Disputes regarding trade union recognition are traditionally referred to the Labour Court via section 20 of the Industrial Relations Act, 1969. The employer has the option to either accept or reject any recommendation made by the Labour Court. A recommendation that an employer should recognise the trade union could simply be rejected and there was no right for the trade union to enforce the recommendation of the court.

Section 2 of the 2001 Act was substantially amended by the Industrial Relations (Miscellaneous Provisions) Act, 2004. It now provides strict guidelines to the Labour Court which must be met before the Labour Court may investigate a dispute.

Section 2 provides that at the request of a trade union or excepted body the court may investigate a trade dispute where the court is satisfied that:

- it is not the practice of the employer to engage in collective bargaining negotiations in respect of the grade, group or category of workers who are partied to the trade dispute, and internal dispute resolution procedures (if any) normally used by the parties concerned have failed to resolve the dispute (section 2(1)(a));

- the employer has failed to observe a provision of the code of practice on voluntary dispute resolution, or the dispute having been referred to the Labour Relations Commission for resolution in accordance with the provisions of the code have not produced a resolution to the dispute (section 2(1)(a));

- the trade union or the excepted body has not acted in a manner which has frustrated the employer in observing a provision of the code of practice (section 2(1)(c));

- the trade union or the excepted body have not had recourse to industrial action after the dispute was referred to the Labour Relations Commission in accordance for the provisions in the code of practice (section 2(1)(a)).

The court may hold a preliminary hearing to determine or not whether the requirements specified in section 2 have been met. In the case of *Ryanair v Irish Municipal, Public and Civil Trade Union/Irish Airline Pilots Association*, Ryanair requested the Labour Court to hold a preliminary hearing pursuant to section 3 of the 2001 Act to determine if the requirements of section 2 had been met. This followed an application by IMPACT requesting the court to investigate the trade dispute between it and Ryanair pursuant to the 2001 Act. Ryanair contended that the court lacked jurisdiction to investigate the dispute on three grounds, those being:

(1)   that there was no trade dispute within the meaning of section 2 of the Act;

(2)   that it was the practice of the employer to engage in collective bargaining negotiations in respect of the grade, group or category of workers who are parties to the trade dispute, if any;

(3)   that the internal dispute resolution procedures had not failed to resolve the dispute.

It was accepted that Ryanair had refused to negotiate with the trade union on the matters that had been referred to the Labour Court. It did submit that it did engage in extensive collective bargaining with its employees and employee representatives.

The Labour Court found that there was a valid trade dispute. In relation to whether or not Ryanair engaged in collective bargaining, Ryanair claimed to do so through its Employee Representative Committees (ERCs) and through what was described as townhall meetings. The court found that the townhall meetings constituted a form of consultation or information meetings and did not have the essential characteristics of collective bargaining. (See also *SIPTU* v *Ashford Castle* [2004] 15 ELR 214). Similarly the court was not satisfied that ERCs were engaged by Ryanair for the purposes of collective bargaining. The court said that it was satisfied:

'That whilst Ryanair communicates and consults with employees, including pilots in relation to their pay and condition of employment, it is not its practice to engage in collective bargaining negotiations as the court understands that expression. The Court has also found that there are no operative internal disputes resolution procedures.'

Accordingly, the Labour Court held that it did have jurisdiction to investigate the trade dispute referred to it by the pilots' trade union.

The Labour Court indeed went further in its decision having regard to the arguments before it. The Labour Court considered the provisions of section 2(1)(a) regarding collective bargaining negotiations and noted that collective bargaining negotiations must be in respect of 'the grade, group or category of employees who are parties to the trade dispute'. In considering this section the Labour Court held:

'The words grade, group and category must each mean something different otherwise the provision would be a tautology. In its submission IALPA told the court that the pilots whom it represents wish to negotiate with professional assistance of that Union and not otherwise (and there is nothing before the court which could indicate that IALPA is not faithfully representing the views of its members in that regard). Pilots as a body are clearly a category of employees. But those who wish to be represented by IALPA and are associated with the claims forming the subject matter of the dispute referred to the court are undoubtly a group within the category. The only body which this group has authorised to represent them in collective bargaining negotiations is IALPA.

'Ryanair, as is its right, will not negotiate with IALPA. It seems axiomatic that if Ryanair does not recognise the only body which the group of employees who are party to the trade dispute wish to represent them, it could not be its practice to engage in collective bargaining negotiations in respect of that group.'

In other words, the Labour Court held that pilots as a body were a category of employees. Within that category were a group of pilots who chose to be represented by the union and so long as Ryanair refused to negotiate with the union on behalf of those employees, Ryanair was not engaging in collective bargaining for the purposes of the 2001 Act. This would be the case even in circumstances where the Labour Court held that Ryanair had engaged in collective bargaining with its employees. In this regard the court went on to hold:

'Hence, even if the court is wrong in its main conclusion and it is the practice of Ryanair to engage in collective bargaining negotiations with an excepted body of pilots, it would hold that any such body could not lawfully do so in respect of the group of pilots who are party to the instant dispute.'

A similar decision was arrived at by the Labour Court in *M1 Northlink Limited v SIPTU*, Decision No 18307, 2 September 2005.

The decision of the Labour Court was the subject of a judicial review application to the High Court. The judicial review proceedings were not in a context of the substantive decision of the Labour Court but with the process in which the Labour Court engaged in coming to that decision. Hanna J unreported judgment—14 October 2005 did not find any deficiency in the process engaged by the Labour Court and accordingly the judicial review application was unsuccessful. Consequently the Labour Court decision stands. The High Court decision has been appealed to the Supreme Court.

In the event that the court does have jurisdiction to investigate the dispute, it is required by section 5 of the 2001 Act to investigate the dispute and may make a recommendation giving its opinion in the matter, and where appropriate, its view as to the actions that should be taken, having regard to the terms and conditions of employment and to dispute resolution and disciplinary procedures, in the employment concerned. Where, in the opinion of the court, a dispute that is the subject of a recommendation under section 5 has not been resolved, the court may at the request of a trade union or excepted body and following a review of all relevant matters, make a determination. The ability of the court to make a determination is by virtue of section 6 of the 2001 Act. Section 6(2) prohibits the Labour Court from making a determination in respect of arrangements for collective bargaining. The determination of the Labour Court can ultimately be enforced by the Circuit Court. In that regard, the trade union may apply to the Circuit Court for an order 'directing the employee to carry out the determination in accordance with its terms' (see Section 10).

10.2.2 TRADE UNION DISPUTES AND INDUSTRIAL ACTION

The law in relation to trade disputes in the the context of industrial action is contained principally in the Industrial Relations Act, 1990. Part II of the 1990 Act contains practical provisions relevant to trade disputes. Section 8 contains a number of definitions including:

> '"Trade dispute" means any dispute between employers and workers which is connected with the employment or non-employment or the terms or conditions of or affecting the employment of any person.
>
> '"Employer" means a person for whom one or more workers work or have worked or normally work or seek to work having previously worked for that person.
>
> '"Worker" means any person who is or was employed whether or not in the employment of the employer with whom a trade dispute arises but does not include a member of the Defence Forces or of the Garda Síochána.
>
> '"Industrial Action" means any action which affects, or is likely to affect, the terms or conditions, whether express or implied, of a contract and which is taken by any number or body of workers in combination or under a common understanding as a means of compelling their employer, to accept or not to accept terms or conditions of or affecting employment.'

10.2.3 PRECONDITIONS TO LAWFUL INDUSTRIAL ACTION

In order for workers and their trade unions to engage in an effective and lawful trade dispute within the terms of the 1990 Act the following conditions must be satisfied.

The immunities in the Act only apply to members and officials of authorised trade unions (section 9(1)). Given the constitutional right to join or not to join a trade union it appears that the exclusion of persons who are not members of an authorised trade union from significant immunities conferred by the 1990 Act is constitutionally suspect but to date has not been challenged.

If the dispute relates to an individual worker any agreed procedures in existence or normally availed of by custom or in practice, in the employment concerned, or provided for in a collective agreement, for the resolution of individual grievances, must be adhered to before the immunities may be relied on (section 9(2)–(4)).

If the strike or industrial action is to be supported, organised or participated in, by a trade union the union must hold a secret ballot as provided for in section 14 of the Act. This does not preclude workers from taking unofficial action without a secret ballot or without the support or involvement of their trade union. If they do so, however, the restrictions on an employer obtaining injunctive relief as provided for in section 19 of the Act will not apply (*Nolan Transport (Oaklands) Ltd v Halligan* [1998] ELR 177).

10.2.4 THE GOLDEN FORMULA

10.2.4.1 Introduction

The Industrial Relations Act, 1990 confers the immunities on workers and their representatives only if they are acting within what is known as the 'golden formula' (see Wedderburn, *The Worker and the Law*, p 222). This 'golden formula' is repeated in many sections of the 1990 Act and is the principal condition workers and their representatives must satisfy in order to benefit from the immunities, and be entitled to engage in industrial action, as provided in the 1990 Act and other industrial relations legislation. The formula provides that the actions of such persons must be 'done in contemplation or furtherance of a trade dispute'.

10.2.4.2 Statutory definitions

10.2.4.2.1 *Generally*

Part II of the 1990 Act commences with a definition section which provides as follows:

'In this Part, save where the context otherwise requires—

'"employer" means a person for whom one or more workers work or have worked or normally work or seek to work having previously worked for that person;

'"trade dispute" means any dispute between employers and workers which is connected with the employment or non-employment, or the terms or conditions of or affecting the employment, of any person;

'"trade union" means a trade union which is the holder of a negotiation licence under Part II of the Trade Union Act, 1941;

'"worker"' means any person who is or was employed whether or not in the employment of the employer with whom a trade dispute arises, but does not include a member of the Defence Forces or of the Garda Síochána;

'"industrial action" means any action which affects, or is likely to affect, the terms or conditions, whether express or implied, of a contract and which is taken by any number or body of workers acting in combination or under a common understanding as a means of compelling their employer, or to aid other workers in compelling their employer, to accept or not to accept terms or conditions of or affecting employment;

'"strike"' means a cessation of work by any number or body of workers acting in combination or a concerted refusal or a refusal under a common understanding of any number of workers to continue to work for their employer done as a means of compelling their employer, or to aid other workers in compelling their employer, to accept or not to accept terms or conditions of or affecting employment.'

10.2.4.2.2 *Employer*

The Trade Disputes Act, 1906 did not define the word 'employer'. The Act did use the word and it was considered in the notorious case of *Roundabout Ltd v Beirne* [1959] IR 423. A pub was purchased by Roundabout Ltd and all unionised staff were dismissed. When the pub opened under its new ownership it was run by officers of the company and not employees. An injunction was granted on the basis that as the company employed no employees it could not be an employer. It is likely nowadays that a court would take a more liberal view and if necessary lift the corporate veil (*Examite Ltd v Whitaker* [1977] IRLR 312).

In *McHenry Brothers Ltd v Carey* [1984] 3 JISLL 80 seasonal workers who worked for McHenry Brothers Coal Merchants were refused employment when the new season commenced and they then engaged in a picket. The company argued that as they were at that time unemployed they were not employees. The court did not accept that contention and held that as they were habitually engaged in employment and, in this particular case, with the company they were picketing then they were workers within the meaning of the 1906 Act and entitled to picket. The definition of worker in this section allows that a worker can be a person who is not in the employment of the employer with whom the trade dispute arises. The definition of 'employer' was enacted to give effect to the reasoning in the *McHenry Brothers* case. In *J Bradbury Ltd v Duffy* [1984] 3 JISLL 86 McWilliam J held that there had to be some restriction on who could picket an employer and he looked at the extreme case, which had very often been quoted by employers as being offensive to them, of a number of new job applications being received by an employer and the employer quite legitimately only having a set number of positions and rejecting some of the people concerned. If those people rejected were to picket there was no logic or fairness in treating that picket as being valid. It is suggested that the definition of 'employer', where it states that a person must be deemed in seeking work to have 'previously worked for that person', gives effect to the reasoning behind the *McHenry Brothers* decision but does not allow a person initially seeking employment, who fails, to engage in a valid trade dispute.

10.2.4.2.3   *Trade dispute*

The definition of 'trade dispute' is more restricted than that in the 1906 Act. The 1906 Act definition allowed disputes between worker and worker which were also most unpopular with employers. It is hard to argue with the logic of an employer's position where a dispute arises between two groups of workers and the employer's business can be validly and legally limited or totally restricted. At the same time, however, a trade dispute may now exist between an employer and persons who are not his employees as the definition states that the dispute may be with persons 'whether or not in the employment of the employer with whom a trade dispute arises'. Again it seems that this is more in the way of allowing secondary disputes than allowing that an employer's business be affected by total strangers with no nexus whatsoever. Considerable restrictions have been put on secondary picketing in section 11. See **10.2.4.5.6**.

The phrase 'connected with' in the definition of a trade dispute appears to allow for an indirect connection between the matters in dispute and the 'target' employer. The decision of Barron J in the High Court in *Nolan Transport (Oaklands) Ltd v Halligan* [1995] ELR 1 examined a number of aspects of the 1990 Act which are referred to throughout this chapter but, in relation to the definition of 'trade dispute', Barron J commented that the definition 'permits as a dispute anything affecting a worker in the course of his employment'.

10.2.4.2.4   *Observations on the definitions*

On the definitions generally Barron J made the interesting observation:

> '. . . it seems to me, that so far as the law is to be applied to industrial relations disputes, the right to take industrial action including the right to picket has been restricted essentially to a right to workers to take action against their own employer and no one else.'

He then allowed for the exception provided in section 11 which is dealt with at **10.2.4.5** below but commented on how restricted the right to secondary picketing is.

Barron J also held that 'it is now clear that as between employers and workmen everything which pertains to the terms and conditions of employment may be the subject of a trade dispute'. It is not a matter for a court to determine the reasonableness or otherwise of a dispute or a position either party might take in a dispute simply to determine whether there is a dispute and that it comes within the statutory definition. Section 5 of the Unfair Dismissals Act, 1977 (as amended) affords certain protections to employees dismissed for engaging in industrial action. In *Tuke v Coillte Teoranta* [1998] ELR 324 the claimants were held to have behaved unreasonably but it was determined that even though their actions were unreasonable, such actions did constitute industrial action within the meaning of the Unfair Dismissals Act, 1977 and they had available to them the protections afforded by the relevant sections. The EAT in that case, in examining the definition of industrial action in the Unfair Dismissals Acts, which is quite similar to the definition in the Industrial Relations Act, 1990, noted that the word 'lawful' was not used in the definition of 'strike' in the 1977 Act and went on to state 'a strike does involve a breach of contract (albeit a breach that is protected by law in certain circumstances)'.

It appears that a trade union cannot have a dispute with an employer within the meaning of the 1990 Act (*Ryan v Cooke and Quinn* [1938] IR 512, *Doran v Lennon* [1945] IR 315 and *Sheriff v McMullen* [1952] IR 236). The *Sheriff* case was referred to in the *Nolan* decision and Barron J held 'at the time when it is sought to rely upon the existence of a trade dispute there must be a member of the union employed by the employer 'on whose behalf the union is acting'.

10.2.4.3   Protection for trade unions

The definitions of 'industrial action' and 'strike' require 'a common understanding' and are framed in such a way as to exclude action by individual workers. This is mirrored in further provisions below. Picketing comes within the definition of industrial actions. Section 9 of the 1990 Act provides:

> '(1)   Sections 11, 12 and 13 shall apply only in relation to authorised trade unions which for the time being are holders of negotiation licences under the Trade Union Act, 1941, and the members and officials of such trade unions, and not otherwise.
>
> (2)   Where in relation to the employment or non-employment or the terms or conditions of or affecting the employment of one individual worker, there are agreed procedures availed of by custom or in practice in the employment concerned, or provided for in a collective agreement, for the resolution of individual grievances, including dismissals, sections 10, 11 and 12 shall apply only where those procedures have been resorted to and exhausted.
>
> (3)   Procedures shall be deemed to be exhausted if at any stage an employer fails or refuses to comply with them.
>
> (4)   The procedures referred to in subsection (2) may include resort to such persons or bodies as a Rights Commissioner, the Labour Relations Commission, the Labour Court, an Equality Officer and the Employment Appeals Tribunal but shall not include an appeal to a court.'

Subsection (1) mirrors the provisions of section 11 of the Trade Union Act, 1941 and as a result persons who are not union members cannot picket and do not have the protection of section 12 of the 1990 Act. They are, however, protected by section 10 which deals with conspiracy. It is only required that persons be members or officials of trade unions, not that they have specific trade union sanction, although sanction in essence is required by section 17 of the 1990 Act. The definition section does not define who is a trade union official but there is a definition given in section 11(5). That definition limits cover to paid officials as opposed to shop stewards.

Section 9(2) is the legislature's attempt to direct disputes through the voluntary problem-solving mechanism and provides that immunities will not be available unless agreed procedures, or those normally provided for 'by custom or in practice', for the resolution of individual grievances are resorted to and exhausted. An injunction was granted in 1991 in *Iarnród Éireann v Darby and O'Connor Irish Times*, 23 March 1991 which was a dispute relating to an individual worker who had not gone through agreed procedures and the picket was held not to enjoy any immunities under the 1990 Act. Subsection (4) allows for reference to a number of bodies but specifically excludes 'an appeal to a court'. It must be taken therefore that if the Labour Court were to be subject to a judicial review or an EAT subject to appeal to the Circuit Court an individual involved will not be deprived of the immunities by virtue of section 9(2).

10.2.4.4   The golden formula

10.2.4.4.1   *Statutory provision*

The golden formula appears for the first time in section 10 and from this section on the Act deals with the mechanics of actually taking industrial action. The golden formula has been considered in some detail by the courts here and in the UK. Section 10 provides:

> '(1) An agreement or combination by two or more persons to do or procure to be done any act in contemplation or furtherance of a trade dispute shall not be indictable as a conspiracy if such act committed by one person would not be punishable as a crime.
>
> (2) An act done in pursuance of an agreement or combination by two or more persons, if done in contemplation or furtherance of a trade dispute, shall not be actionable unless the act, if done without any such agreement or combination, would be actionable.
>
> (3) Section 3 of the Conspiracy, and Protection of Property Act, 1875, and subsections (1) and (2) of this section shall be construed together as one section.'

10.2.4.4.2 *Case law*

For a dispute to be in 'contemplation' the dispute must be either imminent or actual. Action may not be taken because of a possible dispute at some time in the future (*Esplanade Pharmacy Ltd v Larkin* [1957] IR 285 and *Crazy Prices (Northern Ireland) v Hewitt* [1980] NI 150). The use of the word 'furtherance' has given rise to consideration as to whether or not the actions of persons involved in the dispute are to be measured objectively or subjectively. The House of Lords held in *Express Newspapers Ltd v MacShane* [1980] AC 672 that immunity depends on the bona fides of a defendant and that what must be examined is the defendant's belief as to whether or not they were acting in furtherance of their dispute by engaging in the action complained of. The 1990 Act touches on the problem in section 13(2) dealing with immunity against action in tort where it provides that there is a defence available where a trade union can show that the act 'was done in the reasonable belief that it was done in contemplation or furtherance of a trade dispute'.

Although a trade dispute cannot be anticipated, it was held in *General Aviation Services (UK) Ltd v TGWU* [1985] ICR 615 that an action taken through fears for job security after an employer contracted services to an outside party was related to termination or suspension of employees and so it was taken in furtherance of a trade dispute with the employer even though redundancy notices had not been served at the time the dispute was engaged in.

The consequences of a conspiracy have been dealt with in Ireland and England in recent decisions. The UK Court of Appeal held in *Metall und Rohstoff AG v Donaldson Lufkin & Jenrette Inc* [1991] QB 391 that where two parties agreed to pressure a third party to cause that party economic loss, their actions do not give rise to liability unless their sole or predominant purpose is to injure the third party's interest. If their sole or predominant purpose is to advance their own commercial interests they are not liable. The Supreme Court took a different line in *Taylor v Smyth* 5 July 1990 unreported that liability for conspiracy would lie, if it was done by an individual, would be unlawful, regardless of the motive being solely of self interest.

In *Middlebrook Mushrooms Ltd v TGWU* [1993] IRLR 232 a trade union was in dispute with the plaintiffs who were mushroom producers. The union engaged in the distribution of leaflets urging supermarket customers to boycott the plaintiffs' produce. The plaintiffs sought an injunction against the union inducing breach of contract between it and its customers—the supermarkets—or from interfering with any such contract. The UK Court of Appeal held that in order for an action to amount to a direct inducement to break a contract it had to be aimed directly at one of the contracting parties. The action in this case had been aimed at shoppers and the effect such action had on the minds of the retailers was indirect and, there being no suggestion of any unlawful means, the union's actions were not therefore tortious. The court went on to hold that there was no evidence of any existing contracts between the supermarkets and the plaintiffs with which the union's actions could have interfered and this was not a situation in which the existence of contractual relations could or should be inferred from the surrounding facts.

10.2.4.5   Picketing

10.2.4.5.1   *Statutory provisions*

Section 11 provides a right to picket provided certain preconditions are met and certain conduct is observed while maintaining the picket.

No steps have been taken in section 11 to limit unofficial pickets. It may be seen that picketers must be acting 'in contemplation or furtherance of a trade dispute' and 'acting on their own behalf or on behalf of a trade union'.

10.2.4.5.2   *Number of pickets*

No attempt was made to limit the number of pickets but the courts have traditionally held that a dispute is not bona fide if excessive numbers of picketers 'go beyond what is reasonably permissible for the communication of information' or 'may amount to obstruction or nuisance or give rise to a reasonable apprehension of a breach of the peace' (*EI Company Ltd v Kennedy* [1968] IR 69 at p 91). The courts have granted a number of injunctions over the years where pickets were strategically located to cause maximum nuisance or where the numbers deployed in picketing were such as to interfere with day-to-day activity.

In *Tynan v Balmer* [1966] 2WLR 1181 it was held that where a group of pickets walking in a circle in the road outside a factory entrance blocked the highway and caused vehicles approaching to stop they were guilty of an unreasonable use of the highway and a nuisance at common law which overrode their possible immunities in respect of a trade dispute.

10.2.4.5.3   *Place*

The place at which picketing may be carried on has been limited in section 11(1). The 1906 Act allowed picketing 'at or near a house or place where a person resides or works or carries on business or happens to be'. It may be seen that picketing may now only be carried on 'at, or where that is not practicable, at the approaches to, a place where their employer works or carries on business'. Under the 1906 Act this right was limited despite the apparently explicit statutory provisions (*Irish Dunlop Ltd v Power* 10 and 23 September 1981, High Ct unreported). A problem can arise where the place sought to be lawfully picketed is located on private property to which access may be required but cannot be gained because the Act does not allow trespass. That situation has not changed in the 1990 Act.

Rathmines Town Hall Shopping Centre was picketed in 1982 as a result of a dispute between Power Supermarkets and some of its employees. The employees picketed, on public property, all entrances to the shopping centre. The owners and one of the tenants sought an injunction given the effect of the picket on other businesses in the shopping centre not involved in the dispute. An injunction was granted but on the basis of an undertaking by New Ireland to permit access to the complex for the purposes of picketing the supermarket. The 1990 Act does not resolve the conflict between the right of employees to picket their employers and the right of the employers and/or others to refuse to allow trespass. In *Rayware Ltd v Transport and General Workers Union* [1989] IRLR 134 it was held that the phrase 'at or near' a place of work had to be considered in the geographical sense having regard to the purpose of the legislation and the modern context in which the picketing arose. Picketing at the entrance to a trading estate almost a mile away from the employer's actual premises was conducted 'near' the place of work and was lawful within the statute, particularly given that the only means of access to the premises to be picketed were by way of a private road which could not be trespassed upon.

10.2.4.5.4   *Placards and documentation*

Placards or documentation handed out on the picket line must be true and accurate, otherwise the validity of the picket might be affected (*Brendan Dunne Ltd v Fitzpatrick*

[1958] IR 29). See also the observations of Barron J in *Nolan Transport* referred to at **10.2.5.4** below.

10.2.4.5.5   *Interpretation of 'employer'*

The High Court and Supreme Court took a surprisingly strict line on the use of the words 'their employer' in section 11(1) in *Westman Holdings Ltd v McCormack* [1992] 1 IR 151, [1991] ILRM 833 where the defendants had been employed as bar staff in a Dublin pub. The pub was sold to the plaintiff. Prior to the completion of the sale all the staff were dismissed by reason of redundancy. When the plaintiffs reopened the premises the staff sought employment and when this was refused they placed an official picket on the premises. It was argued that as the staff had never been employed by the plaintiff, the plaintiff was not 'their employer' within the meaning of section 11(1). An injunction was granted by the High Court and upheld by the Supreme Court on the basis that there was a fair question to be tried at the full hearing and because the balance of convenience favoured the plaintiff. While the decision is in itself restrictive, it appears to ignore the provisions of the Acquired Rights Regulations. See also *Daru Blocklaying V Building and Allied Trades Union* [2003] IRLM 227.

10.2.4.5.6   *Secondary picketing*

The 1906 Act did not specifically deal with secondary picketing. The right to engage in secondary picketing was distilled from the various definitions in the Act and the scheme of the Act itself. The 1990 Act addresses secondary picketing directly in section 11(2). It can be seen that the secondary dispute has been greatly circumscribed.

The subsection may be paraphrased as follows:

> Action can be taken against an employer who is not a party to the trade dispute if but only if it is reasonable to believe at the commencement of attendance and throughout the continuance of attendance that that employer has directly assisted their employer who is a party to the trade dispute for the purpose of frustrating the strike or other industrial action.

It will undoubtedly prove difficult for secondary picketers to show that the employer they are picketing has directly assisted the employer with whom there is a dispute for the purpose of frustrating their action. Employers support for each other tends to be commercial and not out of any sense of idealism or brotherhood. A third-party employer may, however, by its actions constitute a considerable barrier to the resolution of a dispute in favour of the workers.

In *Nolan Transport (Oaklands) Ltd v Halligan* [1995] ELR 1 Barron J stated:

> '[I]t seems to be that so far as the law is to be applied to industrial relations disputes the right to take industrial action including the right to picket has been restricted essentially to a right to workers to take action against their own employer and no one else. An exception to that does exist in section 11 but it is only intended to permit secondary picketing when the person being picketed has acted out of its ordinary course of business and solely for the purpose of making the primary picketing ineffective. It is not applicable in the present case nor is it submitted that it is. The right which emerges is that workmen may take action against their employer in relation to a dispute between others. In other words workmen may picket their own employer in order to urge that employer to bring pressure on the employer involved in the primary dispute.'

10.2.4.5.7   *Inducing or threatening breach of contract*

Section 12 is effectively a re-enactment of section 3 of the 1906 Act but, in addition, deals with the previously grey area of those who threaten to induce breach of contract of employment or threaten to breach their own contracts of employment. Section 12 provides:

338

'An act done by a person in contemplation or furtherance of a trade dispute shall not be actionable on the ground only that—

(a)   it induces some other person to break a contract of employment, or

(b)   it consists of a threat by a person to induce some other person to break a contract of employment or a threat by a person to break his own contract of employment, or

(c)   it is an interference with the trade, business, or employment of some other person, or with the right of some other person to dispose of his capital or his labour as he wills.'

It should be noted from this section that protection is only afforded where there is a threat to break one's own contract of employment and inducing breach of or threatening to induce breach of a commercial contract is not protected.

The section does not specifically address itself to indirect inducement of the breach of a commercial contract. It remains the case that lawful industrial action may, and often does, result in the breach of a commercial contract. The question must still be addressed as to whether or not that is actionable.

British decisions indicate a division of opinion (*J T Stratford & Son Ltd v Lindley* [1965] AC 269 and *Hadmor Productions Ltd v Hamilton* [1983] 1 AC 191).

In *The Trade Union and Industrial Relations Acts of Ireland* by Tony Kerr, he gives an example as follows:

'B Limited is in dispute over terms and conditions of employment with its employees.

'B Limited is party to a commercial contract with A Limited whereby A Limited has agreed to deliver goods to B Limited.

'A trade union official representing employees of B Limited induces A Limited's employees to break their contracts of employment by persuading them to refuse to deliver the goods to B Limited. Consequently there is breach of the commercial contract.

'Can either party sue the trade union official? If there has been inducement it is indirect and it relates to the context of employment of A Limited's employees.

'Section 12 renders the inducement of breach of the contracts of employment "not actionable".

'The trade union official appears immune in respect of an action by A Limited.

'Is the trade union official immune in respect of an action brought in respect of the indirect inducement of the breach of the commercial contract?'

The Supreme Court ruling at injunction stage in *Talbot (Ireland) Ltd v Merrigan* 1 May 1981, unreported appears to have taken the view that the trade union official would possess no immunity as against either A Limited or B Limited. As Tony Kerr states at p 194, in the Dáil Debate on this Bill the phrase 'shall not be actionable' was stated to mean that it shall not be actionable 'by any person'.

10.2.4.5.8   *Immunity in tort*

Section 13 is substantially a re-enactment of section 4 of the 1906 Act but this time the immunity in tort is limited to torts committed in contemplation or furtherance of a trade dispute. The immunity in section 4 of the 1906 Act was against all actions in tort regardless of how they occurred. The immunity is strictly limited to actions in tort and not any of the other areas of law. Section 13 provides:

'(1)   An action against a trade union, whether of workers or employers, or its trustees or against any members or officials thereof on behalf of themselves and all other members of the trade union in respect of any tortious act committed by or on behalf of the trade union in contemplation or furtherance of a trade dispute, shall not be entertained by any court.

(2)   In an action against any trade union or person referred to in subsection (1) in respect of any tortious act alleged or found to have been committed by or on behalf of a trade union it shall be a defence that the act was done in the reasonable belief that it was done in contemplation or furtherance of a trade dispute.'

It may be seen that section 13(2) uses the subjective approach favoured in *Express Newspapers Ltd v McShane* [1980] AC 672 that the immunity will lie where the act was done 'in the reasonable belief' that it was in contemplation or furtherance of a trade dispute.

In *Nolan Transport (Oaklands) Ltd v Halligan* [1995] ELR 1 the union sought to avoid liability by relying on section 13. Barron J dealt with it by reference to both subsections as follows:

(a) in relation to section 13(1) it did not avail the union because he held that there was no bona fide trade dispute in existence and the protection of this subsection was therefore lost; and

(b) under section 13(2) he held that the defence lay under two different circumstances. He said on the facts there may have been a doubt about reasonable belief but, he emphasised, where there was no trade dispute how could there be a reasonable belief that a dispute existed? He commented that the fact that the creation of the dispute and the commencement of the industrial action in this particular case was not bona fide did not of itself mean that subsequent action by the union or branches of the union were necessarily mala fide. He held that the onus of proof lay on the union to establish such a reasonable belief and that there was no evidence available to him on this point and held that as a result the union was liable for the tortious activity established.

In considering the whole question of reasonableness regard must be had to the position, which has always been the case with the courts, that it is not a matter for the courts to examine whether or not a trade dispute has any merit. It is simply the function of the courts to establish the fact of a dispute no matter how outrageous the position of either party might be. Barron J in *Nolan* stated:

'[I]t is no function of this court to determine whether or not the conditions under which the drivers of the plaintiff company worked were fair or unfair, were favourable or unfavourable, having regard to other employments of a similar nature.'

Presumably, however, in now having to assess the reasonable belief of the existence of a trade dispute regard might well be had to the nature of the dispute and its bona fides. It will be very difficult for judges to avoid the temptation of taking that route towards a decision.

It was also held in *NWL Ltd v Woods and Nelson* [1979] 3 All ER 614 that a demand is not prevented from being a dispute or being the basis for a dispute connected with terms and conditions of employment by reason of the fact that it is unreasonable and commercially impracticable.

10.2.4.6   Secret ballots

10.2.4.6.1   *Statutory provisions*

Section 14 of the Act came into effect on 18 July 1992 as provided for in section 14(1). Section 14 provides that the rules of every trade union shall contain a provision for the holding of secret ballots and that the union shall not organise, participate in, sanction or support a strike or other industrial action without a secret ballot.

Section 14 is one of the more novel provisions of the 1990 Act. Although similar in intent to UK balloting provisions it is not similar in terms of the draftsmanship.

10.2.4.6.2   *Deficiencies in statutory provisions*

While a secret ballot is now required to sanction industrial action the blessing of the union is still not required, so unofficial action is still valid industrial action in Irish law. The whole process of balloting was examined closely in the *Nolan* decision and some of the evidence given in relation to the ballot and, in particular, its outcome in that case attracted very considerable attention. It is a constant source of frustration with Irish legislation that provisions are enacted setting out legal theory without proper regard being had to the practical consequences of the legislative provisions. It is difficult to understand why the legislature in this case did not seek to deal with the mechanics of balloting. Simply to provide that a ballot should take place and not deal with how it should take place, or the consequences of it not taking place in accordance with the statutory requirements, is most unsatisfactory and has already given, and will continue in the future to give, rise to problems.

10.2.4.6.3   *Irregularities in balloting procedures*

Section 14(3) provides that the rights conferred by the previous subsection dealing with the mechanics of a secret ballot are conferred only on members of the trade union concerned and on no other person. What is to happen therefore if a trade union ignores some or all of the provisions of a secret ballot and an employer is on the receiving end of what is effectively unlawful action by virtue of the breach of section 14?

Barron J went some way towards addressing this difficult issue. He stated that the protections of sections 10, 11 and 12 are lost when the action is in disregard of the outcome of a secret ballot. He then said: 'These latter words are significant and suggest that the validity of the secret ballot is dependent upon proof that those voting were aware of the issue or issues involved.' Who is to provide this proof and who may call for such proof?

Barron J went on to state that the defendants made the case that the declared result of a secret ballot cannot be questioned by the plaintiff (section 14(3)). Barron J admitted evidence as to how the secret ballot was carried out in the *Nolan* case and as to how individuals voted. He stated:

> 'There are both rights conferred and obligations imposed on the union for the benefit of its members. Although no one else can claim such benefits the subsection does not mean that a secret ballot could only be investigated at the instance of the members. In so far as there are rights conferred upon the members voting "and no other person" the members by giving sworn evidence are availing of such rights there is no proviso on the subsection that such rights can only be availed of in proceedings to which they are parties. Nor can the union avoid the obligation imposed upon it as to how the ballot should be conducted. Finally the allegation that the result was not properly declared is an allegation of fraud. In my view a section in an enactment cannot be used as an instrument of fraud so that the defendants will not be entitled in refuting the allegation of fraud to rely solely upon subsection (3).'

Barron J was reversed by the Supreme Court in its decision in *Nolan Transport (Oaklands) Ltd v Halligan* [1998] ELR 177 where the court accepted Barron J's findings as to the facts that the declared result of the ballot did not properly reflect the votes cast and that there was an irregularity in the ballot but held, despite the provisions of section 17 which provide that individuals lose immunities when they act in disregard of, or contrary to the outcome of secret ballot, the defendants in this case individually did not lose the benefits of the immunities. While the irregularities may have been a matter for the union it was held by the Supreme Court that the union did not lose immunity from actions in tort conferred by section 13 since that immunity is not made conditional upon a secret ballot, and the individual defendants, who were engaged in the picketing, could not be held liable for irregularities in the ballot carried out by the trade union.

In *RJB Mining (UK) Ltd v National Union of Mineworkers* [1997] IRLR 621 the RJB Group operated a number of coal mines. RJB did not formally recognise the NUM which had a substantial membership amongst RJB employees. The union proposed a series of one-day strikes by all of their members working at RJB collieries in support of its claim for recognition and conducted a secret ballot on the question of industrial action. Section 227(1) of the UK Trade Union and Labour Relations (Consolidation) Act 1992 provides:

'Entitlement to vote in the ballot must be accorded equally to all members of the trade union who it is reasonable at the time of the ballot for the union to believe will be induced to take part or, as the case may be, to continue to take part in the industrial action in question, and to no others.'

The Act also provides that where there are employees at different work locations, separate ballots should be held for each location. The results of the ballot may, however, be aggregated in a single ballot which was done by the NUM. The ballot took place and resulted in a decision in favour of strike action and strike notice was served. The employers sought an injunction on the basis of irregularities in the ballot arguing that the statutory balloting requirements had been contravened. One section of the workforce, members of the Colliery Officials and Staff Association (COSA), a part of the NUM, were not balloted. The employers argued that they should have been balloted. The union argued they did not have to be balloted but the employers countered that if that was the case then why were some 200 members of COSA balloted? The UK High Court granted an interlocutory injunction on the following basis.

'1. [I]t was at least highly arguable that the union was in breach of the requirements of [the 1992 Act] in omitting from the ballot on the proposed industrial action a significant number of its members who would be called on to take part in the action and including in the ballot a number of others who would not.

2. It is the duty of the union to ensure that all those and only those entitled to vote in a ballot on industrial action are given the opportunity of doing so. A union is not expected to achieve 100 per cent perfection in conducting such ballots and has the protection of the de minimis rule and the test of reasonable practicability since there will always have been some changes with which the best of paperwork or computer systems will not have kept pace. However the fact that the structure of a particular union is likely to be more productive of error than a different structure of another union is not an acceptable excuse for non-compliance with the statutory requirements. If the structure of an organisation makes it impossible or difficult to comply with new legislation the organisation must give consideration to how compliance can be better achieved.'

In *West Midlands Travel Ltd v Transport and General Workers Union* [1994] IRLR 578 a ballot paper asked two questions, as follow.

'(1) Are you prepared to take part in strike action?
(2) Are you prepared to take part in industrial action short of a strike?'

In relation to question (1) 1,265 answered yes, 1,225 answered no with 147 blanks. On the second question 1,059 voted yes and 1,156 voted no and there were 427 blanks. The total members who took part was 2,642.

The employers claimed that 1,265 was not a majority in favour of strike action and claimed that the action was not valid. The UK Court of Appeal held that the action was valid where there was a majority who answered question (1) in favour of strike action.

10.2.4.6.4   *Who may be balloted*

Section 14(2)(a) seems to allow a fairly wide electorate for a strike ballot and does not appear to limit the right to ballot to those employed by the employer or in the place where the dispute is proposed to take place. In *University of Central England v National and Local Government Officers Association* [1993] IRLR 81 the plaintiffs were former polytechnics. They negotiated with NALGO on terms and conditions of employment of their employees. A dispute arose and the union balloted all of its members affected by the negotiations who were employed in all the former polytechnics and colleges covered by the plaintiffs' organisation. The ballot allowed industrial action and allowed it against any of the individual employers. The plaintiffs sought an injunction against the union on the grounds that the ballot did not comply with the statutory requirements and that in order to do so, the ballot had to be a ballot of each individual employer's employees. The UK High Court rejected the plaintiffs' contention and held that the union was entitled to ballot the wider electorate provided that in the terms of the statute:

'... the union could show that it was reasonable for it to believe and it did believe that there was some common factor relating to the terms and conditions of employment in respect of which the industrial action was called, it was entitled to hold a ballot of all its members affected by that factor, whether or not they were employed by the same employer.'

Section 14(2)(a) also provides that a union 'shall not organise, participate in, sanction or support a strike or other industrial action without a secret ballot'. It would appear that this does not place the union in a neutral position and that the union is entitled to actively involve itself in preparation for such action prior to the taking of a ballot. See *London Borough of Newham v National and Local Government Officers Association* [1993] IRLR 83 where NALGO was involved in a wide-ranging dispute with the borough and held various ballots of various branches. Some ballots took place at a time when other branches were already in dispute and NALGO had involved itself in direct support of the other employees in dispute and was not obliged to call off all existing industrial action until the final of the ballots was completed. The court stated that where there was a series of disputes 'the fact that the earlier action would be subsumed in a broader industrial action did not mean that the later ballot was in any way concerned with the earlier action'.

In *London Underground Ltd v NUR* [1989] IRLR 341 a ballot paper referred to four areas of dispute, only one of which constituted a current dispute with the employers. The court held that the wording of a ballot of whether or not to take industrial action must not refer to matters which do not constitute a current trade dispute with an employer. Although it is permissible to gather into one general question separate issues which form separate trade disputes it is not permissible to refer to extraneous issues even if the ballot paper does also refer to a genuine and existing trade dispute.

In *Post Office v Union of Communication Workers* [1990] IRLR 143 the question was asked on a ballot as to whether or not members were willing to take industrial action up to and including strike action. There is a statutory provision in the UK to the effect that unions must ask separate questions in this regard. The court held that separate questions must be set down on the ballot form and, following the ballot, the union could then legally endorse only the type of action for which they secured a yes vote from the majority of members.

In *British Railways Board v NUR* [1989] IRLR 349 200 members of the NUR were accidentally not given the opportunity to vote. The court held that this did not render the ballot invalid.

In *Daru Blocklaying Ltd v Building and Allied Trades Union* [2003] ILRM 227, the plaintiff building company sought an injunction against BATU and named individuals in respect of pickets placed on a construction site. An argument contended by the company was that the union had failed to ballot the appropriate persons. Kelly J in granting the injunction held:

'The ballot ought to have been conducted in circumstances where the entitlement to vote would be accorded equally to all members whom it was reasonable at the time of the ballot for the union concerned to believe would be called on to engage in the strike or other industrial action. Only three persons were balloted. On the day the picketing commenced it is accepted by the defendants that there may have been as many as nine persons attending on the picket ... The union is obliged to ensure that all members whom it is reasonable at the time of the ballot for the union concerned to believe will be called upon to engage in the strike or other industrial action be balloted ... In my opinion the onus is upon the defendants to satisfy the court as to compliance with the provisions of the Section 14.'

10.2.4.6.5 *Miscellaneous*

Section 14(2)(c) allows that the officers of a trade union are not obliged to take industrial action simply because a secret ballot sanctions it.

Subsection (2)(d) allows a second trade union to support another trade union's dispute where that other trade union has had a valid secret ballot in favour of such dispute but where the first union does not.

Subsection (2)(e) requires the Irish Congress of Trade Unions to sanction its 'All Out Picket' before another trade union actively supports a dispute. The ICTU policy is that if a trade union wants to call on members of another union or unions to support strike action it must make its request through ICTU. Congress circulates this request to all affiliated unions and those directly concerned and the matter is given consideration by the Industrial Relations Committee of Congress. The provision provides therefore in multi-union disputes or wide-ranging disputes that not only must a secret ballot take place but ICTU authorisation must be given, which is again an indication of the support the 1990 Act gives to existing structures and practices which have proven useful in trade disputes.

10.2.4.6.6   *Employers' rights to injunctions*

Section 19 provides:

'(1)   *Where a secret ballot has been held in accordance with the rules of a trade union as provided for in section 14, the outcome of which or, in the case of an aggregation of ballots, the outcome of the aggregated ballots, favours a strike or other industrial action and the trade union before engaging in the strike or other industrial action gives notice of not less than one week to the employer concerned of its intention to do so, that employer shall not be entitled to apply to any court for an injunction restraining the strike or other industrial action unless notice of the application has been given to the trade union and its members who are party to the trade dispute.*

(2)   *Where a secret ballot has been held in accordance with the rules of a trade union as provided for in section 14, the outcome of which or, in the case of an aggregation of ballots, the outcome of the aggregated ballots, favours a strike or other industrial action and the trade union before engaging in the strike or other industrial action gives notice of not less than one week to the employer concerned of its intention to do so, a court shall not grant an injunction restraining the strike or other industrial action where the respondent establishes a fair case that he was acting in contemplation or furtherance of a trade dispute.*

(3)   *Notice as provided for in subsection (1) may be given to the members of a trade union by referring such members to a document containing the notice which the members have reasonable opportunity of reading during the course of their employment or which is reasonably accessible to them in some other way.*

(4)   *Subsections (1) and (2) do not apply—*

(a)   *in respect of proceedings arising out of or relating to unlawfully entering into or remaining upon any property belonging to another, or unlawfully causing damage or causing or permitting damage to be caused to the property of another, or*

(b)   *in respect of proceedings arising out of or relating to any action resulting or likely to result in death or personal injury.*

(5)   *Where two or more secret ballots have been held in relation to a dispute, the ballot referred to in subsections (1) and (2) shall be the last such ballot.'*

Under the 1906 Act a large number of injunctions were granted to employers, due consideration having been given to the two determining factors governing the grant of all injunctions be they in trade dispute situations or otherwise:

(a)   had the applicant established that there was a fair issue to be tried?

(b)   whom did the balance of convenience favour?

It is difficult to conceive in any trade dispute situation where the balance of convenience would not favour the employer. Employees choose to take action and give up their rights to remuneration and therefore bring about their own loss, whereas the employer may be seen as the victim whose business could be irreparably damaged if a trade dispute was to be effective. The workers' position was more difficult where employers made applications for ex parte injunctions. McCarthy J was particularly critical of the situation in *Bayzana Ltd v Galligan* [1987] IR 241 where he made the point that the granting of an ex parte injunction and the consequent removal of a picket at its early stages could prove fatal to the entire industrial action sought to be engaged in and that the injunction was therefore resolving the dispute which was not the intention of the court or the purpose of the injunction. This was a view shared by Lardner J in *Draycar v Whelan* [1993] ELR 119.

Section 19 has sought to limit an employer's right to apply for an injunction to a situation where the employer has given notice of application to the trade union and the members and where there has been a secret ballot. Then the court cannot grant an injunction as long as the trade union can establish 'a fair case' that it was 'acting in contemplation or furtherance of a trade dispute'. Subsection (2) alters the normal legal rules relating to interlocutory injunctions in so far as they apply to trade dispute situations. Once the applicant establishes there is a fair question to be decided the court must then establish whether the defendants can establish a fair case that they were acting in contemplation or furtherance of a trade dispute, in which event the injunction will not be granted. If the defendants cannot establish that they were acting in contemplation or furtherance of a trade dispute, then and only then will the court consider the balance of convenience. See also *Daru Blocklaying Ltd v Building and Allied Trades Union* [2003] ILRM 227.

10.2.5 TWO CASE STUDIES

10.2.5.1 *G & T Crampton Ltd v Building and Allied Trades Union*

10.2.5.1.1 *The facts*

The plaintiff, Crampton, was building a science block at Dublin City University. Crampton had contracted for a specific completion date and was subject to penalty clauses providing for payment of £30,000 per week in the event of default on its part in completing the building on time. Certain of the defendants were employed as bricklayers on the site by a sub-contractor M J Lambe & Sons Ltd. Lambe had a specific sub-contract which it completed, and then terminated the employment of all of its bricklayers on the site. A second sub-contractor, Colm Murphy, was then engaged on a further sub-contract for other works but did not re-employ the bricklayers who had previously worked for Lambe on the site. The defendant trade union, BATU, contended that the bricklayers were actually employees of Crampton at all material times. Laffoy J in the High Court stated that the core issue between Crampton and BATU was BATU's objection to Crampton's practice of sub-contracting blocklaying and bricklaying work on its construction sites and of not employing blocklayers and bricklayers, members of BATU, directly. The union placed a picket at the entrance to the DCU site which effectively brought a stop to all work on the site. Crampton sought an injunction against the industrial action engaged in by BATU and some of its members who, in turn, relied on section 11 of the 1990 Act and contended that the court was precluded from granting the relief sought by virtue of section 19 of the Act. Laffoy J quoted section 19(2) in relation to secret ballots and stated that in applying that provision:

> 'I must determine whether three pre-conditions—that a secret ballot was held, that its outcome favoured industrial action and that the requisite notice was given—stipulated in the provision have been fulfilled and, if they have, I must then decide whether the defendants have established a fair case that they were acting in contemplation or furtherance of a trade dispute and if they have I must refuse the plaintiff's application.'

10.2.5.2 High Court decision

In giving her decision Laffoy J referred to a decision of Keane J in an early interlocutory application in the *Nolan Transport* case (22 March 1994) where Keane J commented that there appeared to be no authority on section 19 but that as a matter of first impression the onus must be on the person resisting an injunction application to establish that the provisions of section 14 have been complied with and that the court must be satisfied on the evidence before it that section 14 has been complied with. Laffoy J agreed with Keane J.

In a grounding affidavit on behalf of Crampton it was stated that not all of the members likely to be affected by the strike had been balloted, that union members employed by Murphy on the site had not been balloted, and if they had the result may well have been different. It was also claimed that although notification of the intention of the union to ballot its members was issued in advance of a Labour Court recommendation, one of the grounds claimed to justify the picket was the rejection by the union of the said Labour Court recommendation. In a replying affidavit on behalf of the defendants there was what Laffoy J called 'a bald statement' simply to the effect that the ballot had been carried out in accordance with the rules of the union as required by the 1990 Act. Given the conflicting statements in various affidavits Laffoy J concluded:

> '[T]here is no evidence whatsoever before the court as to the outcome of the secret ballot conducted by the union and, in particular, there is no evidence that the outcome favoured picketing the site. On this ground alone I am satisfied that there is no evidence before the court, that one of the pre-conditions stipulated in section 19(2) has been complied with. . . . Accordingly the defendants have not established that they are entitled to rely on section 19(2) and the plaintiff's application falls to be decided on the basis of the ordinary principles applicable to applications for interlocutory injunctions.'

Laffoy J went on to hold that there was a fair issue to be tried, the picketers were not entitled to the protection of section 11 and, on the balance of convenience, held that damages would not adequately compensate Crampton for loss suffered between the time of the application and the trial of the action. Conversely, if an injunction was granted, damages would adequately compensate the defendants should they be successful at the trial in respect of any loss suffered due to the injunction being in force pending the trial.

10.2.5.3   On appeal to the Supreme Court

The matter then went to the Supreme Court on appeal ([1998] ELR 4). Hamilton CJ delivered a judgment with which Flaherty J and Barrington J concurred. Reference was made by the Supreme Court to the letter giving strike notice to Crampton which was notice of 'strike or other industrial action' and did not purport to particularise the nature of the industrial action sought to be taken. A question arose therefore on the interpretation of sections 14 and 19 as to whether it is sufficient merely to have a proposal before members on the question of strike or other industrial action without specifying the nature of the action for which the members' approval is sought and necessary by virtue of the terms of sections 14 and 19.

The court held 'on this issue alone there is a fair question to be tried'. The court also held there is a fair question to be tried as to the need for the entire circumstances of the ballot to be investigated for the purpose of ascertaining whether or not the members whom it was reasonable to expect at the time would be called upon to engage in the strike or other industrial action were given a fair opportunity of voting. While it was alleged on behalf of the defendants that all members who were likely to be affected were notified, it was contended on behalf of Crampton that they were not all given an opportunity of voting and that there was an issue to be tried therefore as to the adequacy of the ballot. The adequacy of the ballot paper was also questioned by the court because the ballot paper did not contain the details of any proposal upon which the members were being called to ballot. It was merely described as an official ballot on a proposal to engage in strike or other industrial action but there was no detail of the actual 'proposal' with members simply being asked to vote either 'in favour' or 'against'.

The court held there was also a fair issue to be tried as to whether Crampton was or had been the employer of some of the defendants as provided for in the definition of employer in the 1990 Act, section 8. Citing the judgment of Finlay CJ in *Westman Holdings Ltd v McCormack* [1992] 1 IR 151, the court held that there was a fair question to be tried and 'the learned trial judge was entitled to come to the conclusion that the condition precedent to the implementation of section 19 was not established'.

The Supreme Court therefore held:

(a) the learned trial judge was entitled to conclude that the conditions precedent to the implementation of the 1990 Act, section 19 were not established;

(b) there was a fair issue to be tried as to whether the ballot satisfied the terms of sections 14 and 19 of the 1990 Act since the proposal before the members failed to particularise the kind of industrial action contemplated;

(c) there was a fair issue to be tried as to whether or not all members whom it was reasonable to expect at the time would be called upon to engage in the strike or other industrial action were given a fair opportunity of voting;

(d) there was a fair issue to be tried whether the provisions of section 11(1) applied to the defendants.

The learned trial judge was entitled to conclude that damages would be an inadequate remedy if an injunction were refused and that the balance of convenience was in favour of granting an injunction.

10.2.5.4   *Nolan Transport (Oaklands) Ltd v Halligan*

10.2.5.4.1   *Background*

The first- and second-named defendants were employed as drivers by the plaintiffs with a family-run haulage company. They were both members of SIPTU. A dispute arose over pay and conditions. Some of the drivers in the employ of the company joined SIPTU. SIPTU wrote to the company seeking a meeting 'to set in train the necessary steps to establish what we hope will be a good working relationship'. The day after the letter was sent three of the drivers met the father of the Nolan family and on the following day met other members of the family involved in running the company. As a result of the discussions with the father and the conduct of the father and other members of the family on those days the drivers contended that they had been dismissed from employment with the company. This contention, however, was rejected in the High Court by Barron J who held also that the father did not have authority to dismiss and the defendants 'recognised that this was so'.

Subsequently meetings of the membership of the trade union were held, attended by only a small number of persons, and a decision was made to hold a ballot for industrial action. The ballot was held over a number of days at locations where the company traded or where their drivers were located. Twenty-three members of the union voted in the ballot. The union initiated a trenchant campaign in support of the planned industrial action but the overwhelming majority of the drivers (48) expressed dissatisfaction with it. Eleven of the drivers subsequently claimed that they had voted against industrial action and evidence was adduced to the High Court that a 12th driver had also voted against industrial action which would have given a majority against such industrial action. The Supreme Court stated 'as the evidence of the drivers was accepted by the learned trial judge it necessarily followed that the result of the ballot ... was dishonest and the inescapable conclusion reached that the ballot had been "rigged" '. A bitter dispute followed, some drivers working, others striking and bitter claims, counterclaims and allegations passing between those involved.

Following a 28-day hearing of nearly a hundred witnesses Barron J held in the High Court [1995] ELR 1 that there was no bona fide trade dispute and that the union was not entitled to authorise strike action on the basis of what he found as a fact to be a false ballot result. Substantial damages were awarded to the company attributed to defamation and malicious falsehood, loss of profits and additional costs. The Supreme Court per Murphy J (Denham Barrington and Lynch JJ concurring) and per O'Flaherty J considered the following issues.

10.2.5.4.2 *Was there a trade dispute?*

The court held that the issue of whether there was a trade dispute depended on the question as to whether Halligan, Nolan or their union believed that the three employees, or some of them, had been dismissed as claimed. The court accepted that Barron J had effectively held that Mr Halligan had an honest belief that he had been dismissed but went on to state that the existence of a trade dispute based on that belief did not in the circumstances confer immunities under the 1990 Act on the employees and trade unions because he was of the view that the dispute was not:

> '. . . in truth or in substance the injustice which the union sought to remedy by the industrial action and secondly that the true purpose of that industrial action was to coerce all of the employees of the plaintiff into membership of the union.'

The Supreme Court disagreed with that conclusion stating:

> 'Part of the difficulty arises from the fact that lawyers and judges have used the words "bona fide trade dispute" with different meanings and in different contexts. If employers and workers both acknowledge themselves to be engaged in a trade dispute there is no difficulty in describing it as a bona fide trade dispute. A bona fide trade dispute may also exist where one party denies that there is any dispute and the other believes that he has been wronged and is in dispute as a result. On the other hand an outside party or "meddler" who had no legitimate interest of his own to protect but who stirred up trouble in a business for reasons of malice or spite could not claim to be engaged in a bona fide trade dispute.'

The court went on to state:

> 'If however a bona fide trade dispute does exist between an employer and workers, some of whom happen to be members of a trade union the trade union is entitled within the Constitution and the law to support its members who are in dispute. That, in doing this, it may be partly motivated by the aim of impressing its members and other workers and enhancing its own reputation and membership appears to me to be quite irrelevant as long as it acts within the law and does not attempt to infringe the constitutional right of each worker to join or not to join a trade union as he himself thinks best.'

On this reasoning the court held that the appellants were entitled to the statutory immunities conferred by the 1990 Act.

10.2.5.4.3 *Was the union entitled to authorise strike action?*

In considering this question the court examined the provisions of the 1990 Act in relation to the carrying out of secret ballots, the effect of a secret ballot and how the immunities provided for in the 1990 Act would be affected or not as a result of an impugned secret ballot. Reference was made to the decision reached at the interlocutory stage in the *Nolan* case by Keane J on 22 March 1994 where he held that there was not evidence before him of sufficient weight to indicate that section 14 had been complied with and therefore the benefit of section 19(2) was unavailable to the trade union. It was emphasised by Murphy J, however, that he made that determination on the balance of probabilities and in relation to the substantive issue between the parties and that he was merely concerned to determine whether there was a serious issue to be tried. Reference was also made to *Crampton*, the judgment of Laffoy J and the fact that it was upheld by the Supreme Court but this was qualified by stating that those judgments related to particular and limited circumstances. Murphy J went on to state:

'In the circumstances it may be said that there has not been a definitive interpretation of section 19(2) of the 1990 Act but I would find it difficult to escape the conclusion reached by Keane J and accepted by Laffoy J that the onus lies upon the party resisting an application for an interlocutory injunction to show that a secret ballot as envisaged by section 14 has been held.'

10.2.5.4.4 *Supreme Court decision*

Murphy J went on to state that compliance with section 14 on the part of the trade union movement would obviate any problems in relation to the interpretation of section 19 but he reserved his position as to the interpretation of section 19 'until a case directly involving it comes before the Court'.

Murphy J concluded that a trade dispute existed in the *Nolan* case and that the statutory immunities were available to the appellants and overturned the decision of the High Court.

O'Flaherty J in his judgment made a number of interesting comments. On the two questions he held:

(a)   whether or not a trade dispute existed: 'The evidence is clear that there was a trade dispute. The men, at the very least, had good grounds for thinking themselves dismissed.'

(b)   on whether or not the union was entitled to authorise strike action, having regard to the manner in which the 'secret ballot' was conducted and the manner in which those voting actually voted, he stated in the course of his judgment that section 14 was designed primarily to strengthen the role of union management against the actions of maverick members. He said this was borne out by the wording of subsection (3) which refers to the rights being conferred by subsection (2) on the members of the trade union *'and on no other person'*.

He went on to state that section 13 is unaffected by whether there has or has not been a ballot as the trade union immunity in tort is conferred regardless of whether there has been a ballot. On the status of secret ballots and in particular faulty or improper secret ballots he stated:

'[W]hile I agree that the legislation touching the holding of secret ballots is there primarily as a matter of internal trade union management, I reject the submission that once such a shambles, as is disclosed as regards the ballot that was held here occurs, that we should simply turn a blind eye to it. The duty to observe the law devolves on everyone—I have already said that simply because the obligation comes through the rules rather than directly from the legislation is of no great importance—so there is a serious obligation on union management to give proper example to the rest of the people by ensuring that the requirements concerning the holding of a proper secret ballot are always observed. . . . the legislation solidifies and, indeed, expands the privileged position afforded by the law to trade unions. Privilege carries duties as well as rights. That said however the essential position is that there was here a trade dispute and those engaged in it are protected and the union has its statutory immunity from suit.'

The Supreme Court ([1998] ELR 177) held the following.

(1)   The court would not set aside any of the findings of primary fact made by the trial judge. The judge had ample evidence on which to base his conclusions and enjoyed the benefit of judging the credibility of witnesses.

(2)   The contention made by the plaintiff that the dismissals were contrived by the employees was not supported by any version of the facts.

(3)   The finding that the union was conducting affairs with the sole purpose of getting a foothold in the company to unionise the whole workforce could not stand. Such

an inference was unjustified. The expressed aims of the industrial action and the mandate expressly sought by the union related to the reinstatement of employees who the union claimed were dismissed.

(4) If a bona fide trade dispute exists between an employer and employees, some of whom happen to be members of a trade union, the trade union is entitled, within the Constitution and the law, to support its members who are in dispute. That in doing this it may be partly motivated, in engaging in successful industrial action, by the aim of impressing its members and other workers and enhancing its own reputation and membership, is irrelevant as long as the union acts within the law and does not attempt to infringe the constitutional right of each worker to join or not to join a trade union as he himself thinks best.

(5) In determining whether a bona fide trade dispute exists the court is not entitled to review the conduct of those engaged in industrial action to determine their motivation or ultimate ambitions. The court's function is to decide whether there is a reasonable basis for an honest belief in the existence of a trade dispute.

(6) The trade dispute in the instant case was bona fide. There was evidence which justified the employees' and the union's belief that they had been wrongfully dismissed and it was genuine in that it represented the immediate quarrel between the parties.

(7) The employees did not lose the benefits of the statutory immunities of the 1990 Act pursuant to section 17 of the Act. Either no secret ballot was held or else the secret ballot in its outcome authorised the industrial action. Obiter: even if the evidence justified the conclusion that the majority of the employees who were members of the union voted against industrial action the reconstruction of the resolution in pursuance of the decision of the court would not be 'the outcome' of the ballot and it could not be suggested that striking union members acted in disregard of it.

(8) Neither did the union lose the benefit of the statutory immunity given by section 13 of the 1990 Act. Under section 17 of the Act the union's immunity under section 13 would remain unaffected whether or not a secret ballot were held and regardless of the manner in which the ballot was held. It might, however, risk the loss of its negotiating licence in accordance with section 16 of the Act.

10.3 Industrial Relations

10.3.1 INSTITUTIONS

Ireland has a well-established and effective tradition of dispute resolution based largely on the voluntary structure created and governed, by the Industrial Relations Acts, 1946–1990.

The legislation established the existing structures of Irish industrial relations—initially the Labour Court, Joint Labour Committees and Joint Industrial Councils, the establishment of the function of rights commissioner in 1969 and later the Labour Relations Commission under the 1990 Act. Trade disputes, low pay and the necessity for flexible forms of conciliation and arbitration, are all dealt with within the framework established by this legislation.

The 1946 Act established the Labour Court and defines its functions and those of its various officers, set up Joint Labour Committees and Joint Industrial Councils and provides for the registration of certain employment agreements. The 1969 Act extended the functions of the Labour Court and created the office of rights commissioner. The 1976 Act brought agricultural workers within the scope of the two earlier Acts.

10.3.2   SCOPE

The Acts apply to any person aged 15 years or more who has 'entered into or works under a contract with an employer' to do any form of work—clerical, manual or otherwise. Excluded are various public service employees, civil servants, members of the Defence Forces and the Garda Síochána, officers of vocational education committees, teachers, etc who have their own conciliation and arbitration schemes on agreements. See section 23 Industrial Relations Act, 1990.

10.4   The Labour Court

10.4.1   GENERALLY

Established by the 1946 Act and extended in both size and functions by the 1969 and 1976 Acts, the Labour Court sits in divisions of three, consisting of an independent chairman and one employer and one trade union representative. The members of the court are full-time. The court has extensive powers to summon witnesses, to require evidence on oath if it wishes and to determine its own working procedures. It is obliged to submit a general report to the government each year.

Labour Court hearings are relatively informal and normally consist of the parties making a written submission in advance of the hearing which is exchanged at, or immediately prior to, the hearing and then at the hearing itself one representative for each side acts as spokesperson taking the court through their submission and responding to the other side's submission and dealing with any questions or points of information raised by the members of the court. The court does not apply rules of evidence such as would be applied in a court of law or at EAT hearings but will have regard to fair procedures and the rules of natural and constitutional justice and is very protective of the interests of all parties appearing before it. Recommendations of the court are not legally binding (*State (St Stephen's Green Club) v Labour Court* [1961] IR 85).

Under the normal law of contract there is nothing to prevent the parties to a Labour Court reference agreeing in advance of the hearing to be bound as between themselves by the recommendation of the court. While the recommendation would not of itself thereby become legally binding it could be open to one or other of the parties to seek to enforce its terms by bringing a breach of contract action against the other party. Some confusion over the legal status of Labour Court recommendations has arisen in light of the provisions of section 13(9)(a) of the Industrial Relations Act, 1969. Section 13 creates the office of rights commissioner and sets out the functions of, and procedures to be adopted by, rights commissioners including the right to appeal a rights commissioner's recommendation to the Labour Court. Section 13(9)(a) provides:

> 'A party to a dispute in relation to which a Rights Commissioner has made a recommendation may appeal to the court against the recommendation and the parties to the dispute shall be bound by the decision of the court on the appeal.'

There is no legal mechanism to enforce the decision of the Labour Court on appeal from a rights commissioner and, as the court has no jurisdiction to make legally binding recommendations, the parties are not bound in law by the decision of the court. It appears that this section was intended to indicate a finality to the court's recommendation rather than to confer on it a legal status it does not have.

The Labour Court is empowered to make legally binding decisions when ruling on appeals from equality officers under the terms of the Anti-Discrimination (Pay) Act, 1974 and the Employment Equality Act, 1977. Despite the fact that Labour Court recommendations are not legally binding in industrial relations matters it is usual for the parties to accept such recommendations as failure to do so tends to contribute to ongoing industrial relations difficulties and may be to the discredit of the party rejecting the recommendation. See Kerr, *The Trade Union and Industrial Relations Acts of Ireland Commentary*, pp 207–208.

The Industrial Relations (Amendment) Act, 2001 and the Industrial Relations (Miscellaneous Provisions) Act, 2004 enable the court having investigated the dispute to make a recommendation. In the event that the recommendation does not resolve the dispute, the court is entitled to make a determination, which in turn is enforceable in the Circuit Court.

10.4.2   SPECIAL INVESTIGATION PROCEDURES

The court must consider any matter referred to it by the Minister for Enterprise, Trade and Employment concerning 'the employment conditions prevailing as regards the workers of any class and their employers' and must furnish a report on the results of its investigation to the Minister (1946 Act, section 24).

If the workers or their union, as party to a dispute, ask the court to investigate and undertake to accept the court's recommendation, the court must investigate and the union is bound to accept its conclusions. If all parties to a dispute ask the court to investigate, and if they all agree to be bound by the recommendation, the court must investigate and the parties are bound to accept its conclusions. These investigations are to be given priority over the other business of the court (1969 Act, section 20).

The court may, unasked, investigate a dispute in which no trade union is involved if a stoppage of work has already occurred. In such cases, the court must publish its intentions and take evidence from all persons wishing to testify. The court may then decide to issue a recommendation, or take no action, or make an award having force for three months and whose terms (as regards conditions of employment, including pay) are legally enforceable (1946 Act, section 71).

In exceptional circumstances, which the court feels warrant its direct intervention in a dispute without being asked to do so by a party, it may conduct an investigation and issue a recommendation (1946 Act, section 67; 1969 Act, section 18).

10.4.3   CONCILIATION

The court appoints industrial relations officers (known as 'conciliation officers' under the 1946 Act, but renamed in the 1969 Act) who, as independent mediators between the parties to trade disputes, are responsible for seeking to reconcile them. Such conciliation is a necessary preliminary to most investigations by the court except in circumstances which the court considers require its direct intervention (1969 Act, section 18).

10.4.4   ARBITRATION

Where a trade dispute has occurred or is feared, the court may, with the consent of the parties refer the dispute to an arbitrator, or may itself arbitrate (1946 Act, section 70). This power has not yet been used by the court. Arbitration of employment disputes in Ireland is virtually unknown. Section 5 of the Arbitration Act, 1954 provides that the Act shall not apply to 'arbitration of any question relating to the terms or conditions of employment or the remuneration of any employees'. This appears to exclude all employment disputes from the scope of arbitration. Section 5 provides that the restrictions contained in that section do not apply to the 1946 Act, section 70.

10.4.5   FAIR EMPLOYMENT RULES

The court has power, after consulting the organisations representing the employers and workers in question, to make rules providing for 'fair employment conditions'.

10.4.6   STANDARD WAGES FOR AREAS

Having given due notice of its intention, the court may (on its own initiative or at the request of any interested party) fix a weekly wage which, in its opinion, should be paid to adult, unskilled workers in any given area.

10.4.7   APPEAL

If a party is in disagreement with a Labour Court recommendation, they may refer the matter to the High Court on a point of law only. Such reference is normally made by way of judicial review. This is a quick and relatively inexpensive procedure whereby administrative bodies such as the Labour Court are subject to having their decisions scrutinised (mainly for procedural fairness) by the High Court to ensure that they are legally correct. Questions of fact are determined by the Labour Court and cannot be reviewed by the High Court. If the Labour Court has determined the facts of a case the findings of fact are not subject to review (*North Western Health Board v Martyn* [1987] IR 565, [1988] ILRM 519 and *State (St Stephen's Green Club) v The Labour Court* [1961] IR 85 and *Ryanair v IMPACT/IALPA* unreported 25 January 2005).

10.5   Rights Commissioners

The 1969 Act created the office of rights commissioner and empowers the Minister for Labour to appoint rights commissioners.

Where a trade dispute, other than a dispute connected with the rates of pay, hours or times of work, or annual holidays of a body of workers exists or is apprehended, a party to the dispute may refer it to a rights commissioner. A rights commissioner cannot investigate a trade dispute if:

(a)   the Labour Court has already made a recommendation on it; or

(b)   a party to the dispute notifies the commissioner in writing that he objects to the dispute being investigated by a rights commissioner (in which event either party is free to bring the dispute before the Labour Court).

In addition, rights commissioners have been conferred with functions and powers by other legislation in respect of which their decisions are legally binding, such as unfair dismissal legislation and the Payment of Wages Act, 1991, Protection of Employees (Part-Time Work) Act, 2001 and Protection of Employees (Fixed-Term Work) Act, 2003. Rights commissioners have power to provide for the conduct of proceedings before them; in general, such proceedings tend to be less formal than proceedings in the Labour Court. Investigations are held in private.

Although the recommendations of a rights commissioner are not legally binding on the parties to a dispute, they are frequently sufficient to resolve it. If either party is dissatisfied, however, they may appeal to the Labour Court. The decision of the Labour Court is then final, although no penalties exist for refusing to comply (section 13(9) Industrial Relations Act, 1969). Except by way of such appeal, the court cannot investigate a dispute on which a rights commissioner has already issued a recommendation. Rights commissioners have had their functions greatly expanded to cover the resolution of disputes under a much wider body of legislation (eg unfair dismissal claims).

10.6 Joint Labour Committees

The 1946 Act empowers the Labour Court to set up Joint Labour Committees ('JLCs'), whose purpose is to regulate conditions of employment and minimum rates of pay for all workers engaged in the type of activity of which the members of the committee are representative. Joint Labour Committees tend to exist in sectors where wages and conditions have traditionally been below the general norm. Some 26 JLCs now exist. Once the Labour Court approves the creation of a JLC whose members (employers and workers) the court believes to be representative of employers and workers in that trade or industry, the JLC is free to submit proposals to the court for an employment regulation order setting down proposals for minimum rates of pay and for other minimum conditions of employment. These proposals are then published by the Labour Court which may then, at its discretion, make an employment regulation order. The wages or conditions specified in the order thereupon become the legal minimum for all employees in that trade or industry whether or not they took part in the process or are even aware of the making of the order. The observance by employers of relevant employment regulation orders is enforced by inspectors appointed by the Minister for Labour. The inspectors have power to examine any data on wages, conditions of work, etc relevant to such order (eg wage books or employee registers).

10.7 Joint Industrial Councils

A Joint Industrial Council (JIC) is an association of persons which:

(a) is substantially representative of workers of a particular class, type or group and their employers;

(b) has the object of promoting harmonious relations between such employers and workers;

(c) provides by its rules that if a trade dispute arises, no strike or lockout will take place until the dispute has been considered by the association.

The Labour Court, when satisfied these conditions are fulfilled, registers the association as a 'Registered Joint Industrial Council' (1946 Act, Part V). Registration of a JIC facilitates the subsequent registration of employment agreements (**10.8** below) and also authorises the JIC to engage in negotiations to fix wages and/or conditions of employment even though it has no negotiation licence.

10.8 Registered Employment Agreements

10.8.1 GENERALLY

The parties to any agreement on pay and/or conditions of employment of any class or group of workers may apply to the Labour Court to 'register' the agreement.

Once registered, the agreement becomes a legally enforceable statement of minimum pay rates and/or conditions of employment and is directly applicable to every worker (and his employer) of the type, class or group to which it is expressed to apply including workers and employers within the type, class or group who are not parties to the agreement. (*National Union of Security Employers v Labour Court Ireland and Attorney General* 10 JISLL 97). The terms, conditions and provisions of a registered employment agreement would automatically transfer to a transferee under the provisions of Article 3(1) and (2) of the Transfer of Undertakings Directive and regulations 3 and 4(1) of SI 306/1980.

10.8.2 CONDITIONS OF REGISTRATION

The Labour Court will register an agreement if satisfied that the employers and workers' representative of the class of employment concerned are in agreement as to registration. The agreement must provide that no strike or lockout will occur until the appropriate negotiating procedures have been utilised. Before registering an agreement, the court must first publish notice of it and hear any objections made by any person affected. Employment agreements and their registration are dealt with in Part III of the 1946 Act.

10.9 Industrial Relations Act, 1990

Part I of the 1990 Act consists of seven sections dealing with preliminary issues and interpretation and repeals. Part II as has been seen, contains the law relating to trade disputes. Part III of the Act is headed 'Industrial Relations Generally'. It contains a definition of 'worker' in section 23 which is somewhat different from the definition adopted for the purposes of trade union and trade dispute laws contained in Part II of the same Act. It is not as wide a definition as the one contained in section 8 and defines the term 'worker' only for the purposes of the Industrial Relations Acts, 1946–1976 and Part III of the 1990 Act and contains the requirement that the contract is one whereby the worker contracts 'personally to execute any work or labour'. As personal service is an essential feature of a contract of service independent contractors are thereby by their nature excluded from the legislation relating to industrial relations.

The definition of a worker was expanded in July 1998 to include officers of local authorities and health boards by the deletion of the exclusion of such persons in the 1990 Act, section 23(1)(d). This brought officers of local authorities and health boards within the remit of the 1990 Act and gave them access to the Labour Relations Commission, Labour Court and Rights Commissioners in respect of industrial relations matters. Industrial Relations Act, 1990 (Definition of Worker) Order, 1998, SI 264/1998.

Section 24 established the Labour Relations Commission (LRC). The constitution of and ground rules for the LRC are contained in the 1990 Act, Schedule 4.

Section 25 sets out the functions of the Commission which are to:

(a) provide a conciliation service;

(b) provide an industrial relations advisory service;

(c) prepare codes of practice relevant to industrial relations in consultation with the unions and employer organisations;

(d) offer guidance on codes of practice and help to resolve disputes concerning the implementation of such codes;

(e) appoint equality officers and rights commissioners and provide staff and facilities for those services;

(f) conduct or commission research into industrial relations matters and review and monitor developments in that area; and

355

(g)   assist JLCs and JICs in the exercise of their function.

The section provides that except where there is specific provision for the direct reference of trade disputes to the Labour Court trade disputes must first be referred to the Commission or its appropriate services.

Section 26 helps to demarcate the functions of the Labour Court and the LRC. The Labour Court cannot investigate a trade dispute unless it receives a report from the Commission that it cannot do anything further to advance the resolution of the dispute and the parties request the court to investigate. The chairman of the Commission may, however, refer a matter to the court for investigation.

10.10   Codes of Practice

Section 42 of the 1990 Act obliges the LRC to prepare draft codes of practice concerning industrial relations for submission to the Minister and to seek the views of interested parties on behalf of workers and employers. The draft code of practice is submitted to the Minister who then, by order, declares the code a statutory code under this Act. After that, in any proceedings before a court, the Labour Court, the Commission, the EAT, a rights commissioner or the Equality Officer the code of practice is admissible in evidence and any of its provisions of relevance may be taken into account in determining the question at issue. Failure by a person to observe any provision of the code of practice is not of itself an offence and does not render a person liable to any civil or criminal proceedings but obviously a breach of the code will have considerable bearing on the outcome of the determination.

The Labour Court has a function under section 43 to give an opinion as to the interpretation of a code of practice on application by any party on notice to any other party. Like its normal functions the Labour Court only makes a recommendation in relation to breach of codes of practice and there is nowhere stated to be a legally binding function for the court in this regard.

CHAPTER 11

TRANSFER OF UNDERTAKINGS

11.1 The Transfer of Undertakings Directives

11.1.1 TRANSFER OF UNDERTAKINGS DIRECTIVE 77/187/EEC

On 14 February 1977 pursuant to Article 100 of the EC Treaty the Council of the European Community enacted the Transfer of Undertakings Directive 77/187/EEC for the purpose of protecting certain rights of employees in the event that the business in which they were employed was transferred to a new employer.

The Directive became part of Irish domestic legislation by virtue of the European Communities (Safeguarding of Employees' Rights on Transfer of Undertakings) Regulations, 1980, SI 306/1980.

11.1.2 DIRECTIVE 2001/23/EC OF 12 MARCH 2001

Council Directive 2001/23/EC of 12 March 2001 deals with the approximation of the laws of the Member States relating to the safeguarding of employees' rights in the event of transfers of undertakings, businesses or parts of undertakings or businesses.

11.1.3 THE EUROPEAN COMMUNITIES (PROTECTION OF EMPLOYEES ON TRANSFER OF UNDERTAKINGS) REGULATIONS, 2003, SI 131/2003

The Regulations revoke and repeal the previous legislation on the transfers of undertakings, SI 306/1980 and SI 487/2000. The Regulations also effect compliance with EC Council Directive 2001/23/EC of 12 March 2001 (which itself consolidates Acquired Rights Directives 77/187 and 98/50). All law relating to the transfer of undertakings is now contained within a single statutory instrument.

11.1.4 SCOPE OF DIRECTIVE AND REGULATIONS

11.1.4.1 Application

11.1.4.1.1 *Directive*

The Directive applies to *'undertakings, businesses or parts of undertakings or businesses'*. This raises the question as to what is meant by an undertaking and what constitutes the transfer of part of an undertaking. The term 'undertaking' is not defined in the Directive or the Regulations.

11.1.4.1.2 *Regulations*

The Regulations apply to:

(i) any transfer of an undertaking, business, or part of an undertaking or business from one employer to another employer as a result of a legal transfer (including the assignment or forfeiture of a lease) or merger (reg 3(1)). The Regulations still require a change of employer and therefore share sale takeovers are still not covered by the new Regulations;

(ii) the Regulations include a transfer by way of assignment or forfeiture of a lease. This gives effect to the case of *Foreningen Af Arbejdsledere I Danmark v Daddy's Dance Hall A/S* [1988] IRLR 315 in which the European Court of Justice decided these transactions were covered by the Directive. The definition of 'legal transfer' also has the benefit of the broad definition given in the broad definition set out in the case of *Dr Sophie Redmond Stichting v Bartol* [1992] IRLR 366;

(iii) 'transfer' also means 'the transfer of an economic entity which retains its identity' (reg 3(2)). This gives effect to the European Court case of *Spijkers v Gebroeders Benedik Abbatoir CV* [1986] 2 CMLR 296 which set out certain factors to be considered in considering if a transfer was being effected, including: the type of undertaking or business concerned; whether assets, tangible or intangible are transferred; whether employees are taken over; whether customers are transferred; and the degree of similarity between activities carried on before and after the transfer and the period if any for which those activities are suspended.

The transfer must involve a change of employer. In most cases it is easy to identify that there has been a change of employer; however, in some cases it may be difficult to ascertain. It is essential to establish if there has been a change of employer; if not the Directive and Regulations will not apply as a change of employer is a fundamental prerequisite.

The change of employer may come about by the takeover by a new owner but may also apply where full ownership does not change but management responsibility transfers including management of subsidiary activities. This is of particular importance in the contracting out of certain services which form part of a business where the main business itself remains in place with the same ownership and therefore, of itself, not subject to the provisions of the Directive and the Regulations. A transfer of employees within the context of an intra-group transfer may therefore constitute a transfer within the meaning of the Regulations, as was held in European Court of Justice decision, *Allen v Amalgamated Construction Co Ltd* [2000] IRLR 119.

Employee and trade union contractual entitlements survive post-transfer by virtue of the Directive and Regulations regardless of whether the purchaser is aware of the existence of such obligations or commitments. All rights and entitlements of employees who transfer must be honoured by the purchaser or transferee both individually and collectively.

There must be continued recognition of employee representatives. In much the same way that employment relationships are entered into by agreement of the parties an employer in Ireland is only obliged to recognise a trade union where the employer confers specific recognition rights on that trade union. The Directive and Regulations provide for automatic continuance of trade union representation.

The parties to a transfer have obligations to notify, inform and possibly to consult with employees and their representatives before the transfer takes effect. Given the importance to employees of a change in their employer it is essential in order for employees to protect their own interests that they get advance notice of any proposed change and the Directive and Regulations make specific and wide-ranging provisions in this regard. These provisions are particularly important to anyone entering into negotiations for the purchase or transfer of a business.

Pension entitlements do not have to be continued by a transferee. Regulation 4(1) and (2) provide that all rights and obligations arising from a contract of employment transfer from transferor to transferee and require a transferee to continue to observe the terms and conditions agreed in any collective agreement on the same terms applicable to the transferor until the date of termination or expiry of the collective agreement or the entry into force or application of another collective agreement. In this regard, the new regulations do not alter the existing situation.

Regulation 4(3) deals with rights under or in connection with occupational pension schemes. Again, this is not substantially different from the position applicable under the 1980 Regulations. The exclusions from the Regulations are therefore employees' rights conferring on them immediate or prospective entitlement to old age or survivors' benefits under supplementary or inter-company pension schemes falling outside the Social Welfare Acts. However, regulation 4(4)(b) provides for an obligation on the part of a transferee to ensure that the interests of employees and of persons no longer employed in the transferor's business are protected in respect of rights conferring on them immediate or prospective entitlement to old-age benefits including survivors' benefits. It should be noted that the Regulations renew the obligation on the transferee contained in the 1980 Regulations to make good any deficit in respect of a pension scheme.

Where the Directive and/or Regulations are breached, liability falls on the transferee or purchaser. It is not possible for the parties to a commercial agreement to anticipate all liabilities that may arise in the future. It is therefore usual for commercial agreements for the sale or transfer of a business to provide that the purchaser will be indemnified in respect of certain liabilities whether specifically anticipated or not. Failure to make proper provision for future liabilities could mean a significant negative impact on the transferee or purchaser of a business. Proper advance planning and due diligence enquiries are particularly important.

It does not apply to transfers in the context of an insolvent transferor. If an employer ceases to trade by reason of insolvency and the business is subsequently transferred the provisions of the Directive and Regulations will not apply. Regulation 6 excludes the transfer of an undertaking, business or part of an undertaking or business where the transferor is the subject of bankruptcy or insolvency proceedings. However, if the sole or main reason for the institution of bankruptcy or insolvency proceedings in respect of a transfer is the evasion of an employer's legal obligation under the Regulations, the Regulations apply to a transfer effected by that transferor.

They apply to all undertakings. The Regulations apply to public and private undertakings engaged in economic activities whether or not they are operating for gain (reg 3(3)). But the administrative reorganisation of public administrative authorities or the transfer of administrative functions between public administrative authorities is not a transfer for the purposes of the Regulations, as provided for by the European Court in *Henke v Gemeinde Schierke and Verwaltungsgemeinschaft 'Brocken'* [1996] IRLR 701.

11.1.4.2 How businesses change hands

Businesses usually change hands in one of three ways.

1. *Sale of shares*

   The Regulations do not apply to a share-sale takeover.

2. *Sale of the assets and goodwill of business to a new operator*

   A business may be sold wholly or partly to a new owner, be it a person or a company, who continues to operate it even with certain changes. The employees of the business are consequently employed by a new person or legal entity, the Regulations come into effect and govern the rights and obligations of the parties to the transaction, the seller, the buyer, the employees and their representatives. There is a change of employer and the Regulations apply.

3. ***Transfer of ownership by operation of law or indirect means***

    The legal ownership of a business may change on the occurrence of something that does not require the specific agreement of the contracting parties such as the surrender of a lease or franchise. In these circumstances case law on the Directive has shown that if the business is continued by the person or body to whom it is surrendered or transferred there is a transfer of an undertaking and the transferee becomes liable not only to the employees, but for the employees, and may have a duty to continue them in employment depending on how the transferee plans to run the business.

11.1.5   WHO IS COVERED BY THE DIRECTIVE AND REGULATIONS?

11.1.5.1   Directive

The Directive uses the term 'employee' throughout but also refers to persons having an 'employment relationship', which must be taken to be intended to cover most categories of persons carrying out work for another.

11.1.5.2   Regulations

'Employee' is defined under the Regulations as a person of any age, who has entered into or works under (or, where the employment has ceased, entered into or worked under) a contract of employment. Other persons deemed to be employees for the purpose of the Regulations are:

(i)   a person holding office under, or in the service of, the State;

(ii)   a civil servant within the meaning of the Civil Service Regulation Act, 1956 (No 46 of 1956) shall be deemed to be an employee employed by the State or government;

(iii) an officer or servant of a harbour authority, health board or vocational education committee shall be deemed to be an employee employed by the authority, board or committee.

11.1.5.3   Agency workers

Agency workers being used by a transferor do not automatically transfer from a transferor to a transferee. The definition of 'employer' means, a person with whom the employee has entered into or for whom the employee works under a contract of employment. The employer under the contract of employment in the case of an agency worker is the person paying the wages of the individual concerned. So only if the agency worker is paid by the transferor is he deemed to be part of the transferor's undertaking. An employment contract means a contract of service or apprenticeship or contract with an agency worker (within the meaning of the Employment Agency Act, 1971) whereby he or she performs personally any work or service for a third person whether or not the third person is a party to the contract.

11.1.5.4   Public bodies

In *Henke v Gemeinde Schierke & Verwaltungsgemeinschaft 'Brocken'* [1996] IRLR 701 the ECJ examined a situation where a public administrative entity, the Municipality of Schierke, was transferred to a new local government body and the municipal administration of

Schierke was dissolved. Ms Henke was secretary to the mayor of Schierke. One of the matters that arose for consideration in the case was whether or not Ms Henke and people like her, who were employees of a public body, came within the scope of the term 'employee' as used in the Directive. In the course of his opinion Advocate-General Lenz considered submissions made by the German government that a local authority was not an undertaking within the meaning of the Directive. The Advocate-General stated (at paragraph 22): 'It is not contested . . . that a municipality can generally carry out economic activities.' He went on to refer to a number of areas of normal economic activity engaged in by local authorities and said that:

'. . . even if exercise of an economic activity were to be regarded as a precondition for the application of the Directive a municipality could definitely be treated as being an undertaking within the meaning of the Directive. It is therefore questionable whether the municipality and its employees should be excluded from the scope of application of the Directive simply because the municipality also acts in the exercise of powers of a public authority.'

The Advocate-General in his reasoning allowed that in its purest form a State agency or an emanation of the State could be excluded from the scope of the Directive when carrying out governmental or quasi-governmental or local authority functions which are not among the activities of the European Community governed by the EC Treaty. He did, however, point out the type of economic activities that may be engaged in by such bodies in respect of which they can or may employ 'employees' who would be covered by the Directive. He also pointed out the difficulty in ascertaining the type of bodies that may be excluded from the definition of undertaking and commented:

'[T]he criterion of activity in the exercise of public powers is very difficult to pin down since it is subject to cost and change. What is today regarded as purely public may in even only a few years be carried out by a private undertaking with a view to profit. It also cannot be ruled out that functions carried out by a private undertaking will not be regarded after a time as being again functions of the public authorities. It is therefore possible to justify the employees carrying out these activities being covered at one time by the protection of the Directive and then following a change of view as to the public character of their activities, no longer enjoying that protection. In addition it is questionable how an employee carrying out both activities in the exercise of public powers and economic activities would have to be classified.'

He went on to say that while an 'undertaking' must be defined having regard to whether or not it employs employees the definition of 'employee' cannot have regard to whether or not the persons are employed in an 'undertaking'. He referred to *Redmond Stichting v Bartol* [1992] IRLR 366 and *Mikkelsen v Danmols Inventar A/S* [1986] 1 CMLR 316 and stated that the applicability of the Directive must be decided 'based solely on the concept of an employee'. He concluded by stating:

'Accordingly, the Directive is applicable whenever employees within the meaning of the national protective provisions are employed in an undertaking or an organisational entity. It is irrelevant whether the undertaking is engaged in the sphere of public administration or in the private sector. This means that the Directive may also be applied to a municipality where workers are employed within the meaning of the national protective provisions.'

In its subsequent judgment in *Henke v Gemeinde Schierke* the ECJ appeared to be in little doubt that governmental or public functions did not of themselves come within the terms of the Directive. The court made reference to the Preamble to the Directive where the protection of the Directive is stated to relate to 'changes in the structure of undertakings resulting from economic trends' and without any further analysis concluded: 'The reorganisation of structures of the public administration or the transfer of administrative functions between public administrative authorities does not constitute a "transfer of an undertaking" within the meaning of the Directive.'

The ECJ disagreed with the Advocate-General as to whether the local authority concerned was an undertaking within the meaning of the Directive. The court held that it was not an undertaking. The court did not make any observation on whether or not the status of the persons employed therein, as determined under national law, would disqualify them from the coverage of the Directive if they did not have a 'contract of service'. Regard must be had to Article 3 of the Directive when it refers to 'employment relationships' and given that, while civil servants do not have coverage of all employment legislation in Ireland and indeed are excluded from much of it, they do have legal protections and it appears therefore that while they are not 'protected as an employee under the national legislation' as referred to by Advocate-General Van Gerven in *Redmond Stichting v Bartol* their employment relationship must transfer. It appears from the decision of the court in *Henke v Gemeinde Schierke* that if there is determined to be in existence an 'undertaking' within the meaning of the Directive and there is a 'transfer' within the meaning of the Directive then the persons employed in the undertaking to be transferred have the protection of the Directive.

11.2 Interpreting the Directive and Regulations

The long title of the Directive is:

> *'On the approximation of the laws of the Member States relating to the safeguarding of employees' rights in the event of transfers of undertakings, businesses or parts of undertakings or businesses.'*

11.2.1 THE PREAMBLE

11.2.1.1 Directive

The Preamble makes reference to the manner in which the Directive became law and refers to Article 100 of the EC Treaty.

The Preamble has been quoted in cases to assist in interpreting the scope of the Directive as in *Henke v Gemeinde Schierke* [1996] IRLR 701 where the ECJ referred to the use of the words 'economic trends' to support the view that the Directive does not apply to governmental or civil service activities.

11.2.1.2 Regulations

Regulation 1 gives the title of the Regulations. The introduction to the Regulations refers to Directive 2001/23/EC of 12 March 2001 and defines the Minister for the purposes of the Regulations as being the Minister for Trade, Enterprise and Employment.

Regulation 2(2) provides:

> *'A word or expression that is used in these Regulations and which is also used in the Council Directive has, unless the context otherwise requires, the same meaning in these Regulations that it has in the Directive.'*

11.2.2 TERRITORIAL SCOPE

11.2.2.1 Directive

The territorial scope of the EC Treaty is as set out generally in the European Communities Act, 1972 and covers Ireland and its territorial waters. Article 1(2) provides that the undertaking must be within the territorial scope of the EC Treaty.

The question of residence in Ireland was considered in *Roche v Sealink Stena Line Ltd* [1993] ELR 89. See also *Davis v Sealink Stena Line Ltd* UD 874/93.

11.2.2.2   Regulations

It is by no means certain what happens in this jurisdiction in the event of an international transaction involving the transfer of employees. If the transfer is into another country in the EEA where the equivalent of the Regulations apply, that law must be applied. If the transfer is outside the EEA then it is arguable that employees have no rights to transfer to the new employer, if foreign-based.

11.2.3   THE PURPOSIVE APPROACH

The Directive and Regulations are broadly drafted and, in the absence of clear definitions, interpretation has been difficult. The approach adopted by courts and tribunals has been to ensure the social purpose of the Directive is met, albeit thereby causing difficulty for employers, employees and their advisers in trying to interpret the precise scope and application of the Directive's provisions and ordering their affairs accordingly. Rather than limiting themselves to the interpretation of the precise words and phrases used in the Directive the courts have adopted what is called the 'purposive approach'. In his opinion in *JMA Spijkers v Gebroeders Benedik Abattoir CV* [1986] 2 CMLR 296 Advocate-General, Sir Gordon Slynn stated (at p 489):

'It is clear that the overriding objective of the Directive is to protect workers in a business which is transferred. . . . In deciding whether there has been a transfer . . . all the circumstances have to be looked at. Technical rules are to be avoided and the substance matters more than the form.'

In *Spijkers* the full court (at p 492) also made reference to the aim and context of the Directive which is referred to in the Preamble to the Directive as being:

'To provide for the protection of employees in the event of a change of employer, in particular, to ensure that their rights are safeguarded.'

In *Landsorganisationen i Danmark v Ny Molle Kro* [1989] IRLR 37 the court stated again in quoting the Preamble and referring to Articles 1(1), 3(1), (2) and 4(1) of the Directive (p 39):

'[T]he purpose of the Directive is to safeguard, as far as possible, the rights of workers in the event of a change of employer by enabling them to remain in employment with the new employer on the same conditions agreed with the transferor.'

Also in *Ny Molle Kro* the court, referring to its decision in *Mikkelsen v Danmols Inventar A/S* [1986] 1 CMLR 316, stated (at p 40):

'The objective of the Directive is to ensure as far as possible the continuation without change of the contract of employment or the employment relationship with the transferee in order to avoid the worker concerned being placed in a less favourable position by reason of the transfer alone.'

The courts in Ireland have, in common with courts in the UK, adopted this purposive approach which is not their traditional approach to the interpretation of legislation. Blaney J in *Bannon v Employment Appeals Tribunal and Drogheda Town Centre Ltd* [1992] ELR 203 quoted the ECJ in its reference to the aim and context of the Directive as being to protect employees, and went on to find that there was a transfer in that particular case and the employee concerned was protected by the provisions of the Directive and Regulations.

Irish law must have regard to the ECJ interpretation of Directives to ensure that the implementation of the domestic equivalent of the relevant European law meets the requirements of the European Union.

11.2.4   IRISH POSITION

Blayney J commented in B*annon v Employment Appeals Tribunal and Drogheda Town Centre Ltd* [1992] ELR 203 at p 207, referring to both *Spijkers v Gebroeders Benedik Abattoir CV* [1986] 2 CMLR 296 and *Landsorganisationen i Danmark v Ny Molle Kro* [1989] IRLR 37:

'[T]he Court has indicated very clearly what the objective of the Directive is and it has also set out the criteria in the light of which the National Courts should determine if the Directive is applicable.'

He also quoted with favour (at p 209) the ECJ's judgment in *Ny Molle Kro* on the purposive approach to be adopted in Irish law.

The EAT took a wide and purposive approach in its determination in *Morris v Smart Brothers Ltd* UD 688/93. In that case the EAT was faced with a factual situation where on the transfer of a business certain employees had their employment terminated by the transferor by reason of redundancy and claimed unfair dismissal against the transferor and the transferee. In the absence of proper Irish regulations implementing the Directive and interlinking it with existing Irish employment law, the EAT was left to wrestle with the difficulties posed in giving effect to the Directive. The EAT quoted Barrington J in *Mythen v Employment Appeals Tribunal* [1990] ELR 1 when he commented that the provisions of the Directive and Regulations 'have revolutionary implications for the relationship between employers and employees' and went on to state in relation to the effect of the Directive on Irish employment law:

'In using the word "revolutionary" Barrington J did not understate the significance of the changes to the law involved in the Directive. [It] did indeed revolutionise the law in relation to contracts of employment. In effect it obliges the new owner of a business to enter a contract of employment with any employee who was working in the business at the date of transfer. This obligation flies in the face of the Common Law principles governing the creation of contracts of any kind. Given the primacy of EC law the Common Law must, of course, give way.

'Moreover, if the new owner of a business does not engage such an employee his failure to do so may be regarded as dismissal. This leads to the major conceptual problem that one is deemed to have dismissed someone whom one never employed. In Common Law terms one is deemed to have terminated a contract that never existed.

'There are other conceptual problems involved in the Directive's use of the word "dismissal". Apart from the liability placed on the new owner of a business who never engaged the employee concerned there is another difficult legal question. If the transferee declines to engage the employee what is the position of the transferor? Closely related to this is another question as to the separate liabilities of the old employer and the new employer.'

11.3   Undertakings

The Directive and Regulations apply only to the transfer of an 'undertaking'. There is no definition given of the term 'undertaking' in the Directive or the Regulations, nor is there any definition given in any of the EU Treaties. The term is, however, used in Article 85 of the EC Treaty which deals with competition law and provides:

'The following shall be prohibited as incompatible with the common market: all agreements between undertakings, decisions by associations of undertakings and concerted practices which may affect trade between Member States and which have as their object or effect the prevention, restriction or distortion of competition within the common market.'

The Regulations apply to public and private undertakings engaged in economic activities whether or not they are operating for gain. Economic activity is not to be equated with profitable, or profit-making, activity. In order for an economic entity to be regarded as an undertaking it does not have to be engaged in activity which is carried on with a view to making a profit. This definition has the effect of allowing within the ambit of the Directive/ Regulations:

(a)   charities;

(b)   local authorities;

(c)   health boards;

(d)   State and semi-State bodies;

(e)   schools, colleges, educational and medical establishments and foundations;

(f)   trade associations; and

(g)   trade unions.

But the administrative reorganisation of public administrative authorities or the transfer of administrative functions between public administrative authorities is not a transfer for the purposes of the Regulations.

11.4   Economic Entity/Undertaking

11.4.1   INTRODUCTION

The way in which the ECJ has approached the concept of an economic entity indicates that the term 'economic entity' is interchangeable with the term 'undertaking'. Undertakings are economic entities and vice versa. In *Suzen v Zehnacker Gebaudereinigung GmbH Krankenhausservice* [1997] IRLR 255 the ECJ observed:

'The aim of the Directive is to ensure continuity of employment relationships within an economic entity. . . . The decisive criterion for establishing the existence of a transfer within the meaning of the Directive is whether the entity in question retains its identity as indicated inter alia by the fact that its operation is actually continued or resumed. For the Directive to be applicable the transfer must relate to a stable economic entity whose activity is not limited to performing one specific works contract. The term entity thus refers to an organised grouping of persons and assets facilitating the exercise of an economic activity which pursues a specific objective.'

In the UK case of *Isles of Scilly Council v Brintel Helicopters Ltd and Ellis* [1995] IRLR 6 the EAT observed:

'An economic entity may well just comprise activities and employees. In the service industry tangible assets may be unimportant or possibly non-existent. Thus for example the economic entity may consist of the provision of services where the real asset may be goodwill or possibly just the right to provide the service in question.'

'Economic entity' is described in the Regulations (reg 3(2)) as meaning 'an organised grouping of resources which has the objective of pursuing an economic activity whether or not that activity is for profit or whether it is central or ancillary to another economic or administrative entity'.

It was held prior to the enactment of the Regulations that the fact that the activity is not for profit does not mean that the Directive does not apply (see *Dr Sophie Redmond Stichting v Bartol* [1992] IRLR 366).

11.4.2 STABLE ECONOMIC ENTITY

In *Ledernes Hovedorganisation (Rygaard) v Dansk Arbejdsgiverforening (Stro Mølle Akustik) A/S* [1996] IRLR 51 the ECJ created the concept of the transfer of an undertaking of part of a business needing to be a transfer of 'a stable economic entity'—see the decision in *Suzen*, referred to at **11.4.1** above, also dealt with in more detail at **11.8.6.1.1**.

An undertaking or economic entity the subject matter of a transfer comes within the scope of the Directive and Regulations. Where a transaction involves the transfer of the whole or a substantial part of a business or economic entity it may be easily observed that there is a transfer of an undertaking involved. Where part of the economic entity or undertaking transfers the question arises as to whether that part of itself forms an economic entity and is a severable part of the undertaking. This topic is dealt with in more detail at **11.8** below, which deals with service providers and highlights the difficulties associated with carving out part of an economic entity or undertaking, transferring it, and then seeking to determine whether or not the Directive and Regulations apply in establishing whether or not there is an economic entity which is capable of being the subject of a transfer.

In *Botzen v Rotterdamasche Droogdok Maatschappij BV* [1986] ECR 519 certain departments of the main undertaking transferred and those departments were held to be in themselves an economic entity forming part of an undertaking capable of being the subject matter of a transfer for the purposes of the Directive and Regulations. That was a straightforward and predictable decision.

The position was far less straightforward and less predictable in *Schmidt v Spar und Leihkasse der Fruheren Amter Bordesholm* [1994] IRLR 302, which is also examined at **11.8.1.2**. In that case Ms Schmidt was employed by the bank concerned as a full-time employee to carry out cleaning of the branch that employed her. She was the only cleaner. The bank subsequently contracted out its cleaning work to an independent contract cleaning company. In the *Schmidt* case the question arose as to whether the cleaning activity of a branch of a bank constituted an economic entity or part of a business. Quite clearly the bank was itself an economic entity.

The question arose as to whether part of that economic entity transferred. Basic logic suggests that there is a transfer of part of the economic entity in such circumstances. The *Schmidt* case was therefore determined more on the question of part of the banking economic entity rather than by classifying the cleaning operations as an economic entity in themselves capable of being the subject matter of a transfer. The ECJ held (at p 303):

> 'The decisive criterion for establishing whether there is a transfer for the purposes of the Directive is whether the business in question retains its identity. This is indicated, inter alia, by the actual continuation or resumption by the new employer of the same or similar activities. In the present case the similarity in the cleaning work performed before and after the transfer, which was reflected in the offer to re-engage the employee in question, was typical of an operation which comes within the scope of the Directive.'

11.5 Transfer

11.5.1 INTRODUCTION

11.5.1.1 Directive

The Directive requires that there be a transfer of some nature, of the whole or part of an undertaking. The rights, duties and obligations governed by the Directive crystallise, or are triggered, by the occurrence of a transfer.

One of the earliest decisions of the ECJ interpreting the terms of the Directive, and one which continues to maintain seminal importance in the law relating to the transfer of undertakings, is the decision given by the court on 18 March 1986 in *JMA Spijkers v Gebroeders Benedik Abbatoir CV* [1986] 2 CMLR 296. Mr Spijkers worked for a company known as Colaris at their slaughterhouse located in the inappropriately named Ubach über Worms. Colaris agreed to sell the slaughterhouse together with offices, land and specified equipment to Benedik CV on 27 December 1982. From that date Colaris ceased trading. No trading was carried out until Benedik commenced trading on 7 February 1983. There was, therefore, at the time Benedik commenced business, no goodwill in the business. Benedik did not commence the identical trade as Colaris but carried on a similar type of trade using all of the Colaris employees, whom it re-employed under contracts agreed with those employees, with the exception of Mr Spijkers and one other employee who was too ill to work. Spijkers claimed that there had been a transfer of an undertaking and that Benedik should pay him from 27 December 1982 and provide him with work. Advocate-General Slynn made the following observations in his opinion (at pp 120–121):

'It is clear that the overriding objective of the Directive is to protect workers in a business which is transferred. In deciding whether there has been a transfer . . . all the circumstances have to be looked at. Technical rules are to be avoided . . . the substance matters more than the form. The essential question is whether the transferee has obtained a business or an undertaking (or a part thereof) which he can continue to operate. That at the time of transfer the business is still active, that machinery is being used, customers supplied, workers employed and that all the physical assets and goodwill are sold are strong indications that a transfer . . . has taken place. But these are not all necessary prerequisites of a transfer in every case . . . the fact that at the date of transfer trading has ceased or has been substantially reduced does not prevent there being a transfer of a business if the wherewithal to carry on the business such as plant, building and employees are available and are transferred. Nor is the fact that goodwill or existing contracts are not transferred conclusive against there being a transfer.'

The court followed that line of reasoning and held that in order for a business activity to come within the definition of the transfer of an undertaking 'the business in question . . . [must] . . . retain its identity'. The court held that there did not need to be a transfer of goodwill and that there could be cessation and resumption of the same or similar economic activities and stated (at p 493):

'Consequently it cannot be said that there is a transfer of an enterprise, business or part of a business on the sole ground that its assets have been sold. On the contrary, in a case like the present, it is necessary to determine whether what has been sold is an economic entity which is still in existence and this will be apparent from the fact that its operation is actually being continued or has been taken over by the new employer, with the same economic or similar activities.

'To decide whether these conditions are fulfilled it is necessary to take account of all the factual circumstances of the transaction in question including the type of undertaking or business in question, the transfer or otherwise of tangible assets such as buildings and stocks, the value of intangible assets at the date of transfer, whether the majority of the staff are taken over by the new employer, the transfer or otherwise of the circle of customers and the degree of similarity between activities before and after the transfer, and the duration of any interruption in those activities. It should remain clear however that each of these factors is only a part of the overall assessment which is required and therefore they cannot be examined independently of each other.'

While reference is made to the transfer of assets, as is seen at **11.8.5** below, asset transfer is not essential in order for there to be a transfer of an undertaking or part of an undertaking. In *Schmidt v Spar und Leihkasse* [1994] IRLR 302 no assets transferred and in *Merckx and Neuhuys v Ford Motor Co Belgium SA* [1996] IRLR 467 the ECJ said (at p 467):

'That there had been no transfer of tangible assets did not prevent the application of the Directive.'

The *Spijkers* tests for identifying the existence of a transfer have survived the passage of time and are still relevant but it must be kept in mind that each of the tests is in itself merely for guidance and when each test has been answered the totality has to be assessed to see whether or not it adds up to there being a transfer.

11.5.1.2 Regulations

The Regulations provide at regulation 4(1):

> 'The transferor's rights and obligations of the transferor arising from a contract of employment existing on the date of a transfer shall, by reason of such transfer, be transferred to the transferee.'

'Transfer' also means 'the transfer of an economic entity which retains its identity' (reg 3(2)). This refers back to the European Court case of *Spijkers v Gebroeders Benedik Abbatoir CV* [1986] 2 CMLR 296. In this case, it was stated that it is important to consider in each case whether some or all of the following factors are involved namely:

(i) consideration of the type of undertaking or business concerned;

(ii) whether assets, tangible or intangible are transferred;

(iii) whether employees are taken over;

(iv) whether customers are transferred;

(v) the degree of similarity between activities carried on before and after the transfer;

(vi) the period if any for which those activities are suspended.

These are all single factors in the overall assessment which must be made and therefore cannot be considered in isolation.

11.5.2 CESSATION AND LATER RESUMPTION

The fact that a transferor ceases the business entirely and there is then a lapse of time before the transferee resumes the business does not prevent there being a transfer of the undertaking or business concerned. Advocate-General Slynn went on to observe in *Spijkers* (at p 489):

> 'That after the sale there is a gap before trading is resumed is a relevant fact but it is not conclusive against there being a transfer within the meaning of the Directive. The transferee may well want to spend time reorganising or renovating the premises or equipment . . . the fact that the business is carried on in a different way is not conclusive against there being a transfer—new methods, new machinery, new types of customer are relevant factors but they do not of themselves prevent there being in reality a transfer of a business or undertaking. Though it is plain that a sale may take place simply of the physical assets or part of them with no intention in any real sense that the business should thereafter be carried on care must be taken to ensure that such a sale is not a disguise to avoid obligations to the workers.'

11.5.3 CHANGE OF OWNERSHIP

11.5.3.1 *Daddy's Dance Hall*

Spijkers is a straightforward case of a business changing hands and it was understood initially that it was only on a change of ownership that the Directive applied. The decision in *Foreningen af Arbejdsledere i Danmark v Daddy's Dance Hall A/S* [1988] IRLR 315 delivered by the ECJ on 10 February 1988 showed that the Directive could apply where there was no change in the legal owner of a business but rather a change in the person or body responsible for the management or day-to-day operation of the business which the court held constituted a transfer for the purposes of the Directive.

Irma Catering, a company, leased restaurants and bars from another company, Palads Teatret. The lease was determined on 28 January 1983 with effect from 25 February 1983. Mr Tellerup was an employee of the business operated by Irma Catering and was dismissed on notice to expire on 30 April 1983. On 25 February 1983, a new lease was granted by Palads Teatret to a different company, Daddy's Dance Hall. Mr Tellerup was re-engaged by Daddy's Dance Hall. He was later dismissed by Daddy's Dance Hall on 26 April 1983. A dispute arose about the terms of Mr Tellerup's employment at the date of termination and the length of notice to which he was entitled from Daddy's Dance Hall. It was held that Daddy's Dance Hall must carry the liabilities of Irma Catering to Mr Tellerup. The ECJ held that the Directive applies to a situation where, after the termin-ation of a lease, the owner of the undertaking leases it to a new lessee who continues to run the business and held: 'It is of no importance to know whether the ownership of the undertaking has been transferred.' It should be noted that there was no contractual nexus between Irma Catering and Daddy's Dance Hall. The court held (at paras 9 and 10, p 317):

> 'The Directive therefore applies as soon as there is a change, resulting from a con-ventional sale or from a merger, of the natural or legal person responsible for operating the undertaking who consequently enters into obligations as an employer towards the employees working in the undertaking and it is of no importance to know whether the ownership of the undertaking has been transferred.
>
> 'It follows that when the lessee who has the capacity of proprietor of the undertaking at the termination of the lease loses this capacity and a third person acquires it under a new lease concluded with the owner the resulting operation is capable of falling within the scope of application of the Directive as defined in Article 1(1). The fact that in such case the transfer takes place in two phases in the sense that as a first step the undertak-ing is transferred back from the original lessee to the owner who then transfers it to the new lessee, does not exclude the applicability of the Directive as long as the economic unit retains its identity. This is the case in particular when as in the instant case the business continues to be run without interruption from the new lessee with the same staff that was employed in the undertaking before the transfer.'

11.5.3.2   *Ny Molle Kro*

A similar line of reasoning to the *Daddy's Dance Hall* decision was followed in two further cases. In *Landsorganisationen i Danmark v Ny Molle Kro* [1989] IRLR 37 the owner of a tavern business, Mrs Hannibalsen, leased the tavern to Mrs Larsen. Mrs Larsen ran the tavern until such time as she was in breach of the lease whereupon the business reverted to the owner. The owner continued to manage the business without interruption to the employees. The reversion to the owner took place in January 1981. In May 1983 an employee was taken on and later that year when she left employment she claimed that she was entitled to a higher rate of wages than were actually paid to her by virtue of a collect-ive agreement to which the lessee had been party. The question arose as to whether or not the lessee's obligations under the collective agreement transferred to the owner on her taking back the operation of the tavern business from Mrs Larsen. The court held that the resumption of the business by the owner constituted a transfer in so far as the lessee lost the capacity of employer and that capacity was reacquired by the lessor. The court held that there was a transfer within the meaning of the Directive 'whenever as a result of a legal transfer or merger there was a change in the natural or legal person responsible for the running of the undertaking'.

This applies regardless of whether ownership of the undertaking has been transferred. The employees of an undertaking in which the employers change, without a transfer of owner-ship, are in need of the same protection afforded to employees of an undertaking which has been sold. Following that line of reasoning the court held that the takeover by Mrs Larsen as managing lessee meant that under the terms of the lease she acquired the capacity of employer and that in turn constituted a transfer of an undertaking and, further, that where the owner of the lease took back the running of the undertaking that resumption also constituted a transfer in so far as the lessee lost the capacity of employer and that capacity was reacquired by the lessor.

11.5.3.3   *Berg and Busschers v Besselsen*

In *Berg and Busschers v Besselsen* [1989] IRLR 447 Berg was employed as the manager of a bar/disco owned by Besselsen. In 1983 Besselsen transferred the operation of the establishment to a commercial partnership by means of a lease purchase agreement. Under Dutch law this type of transaction is defined as a 'sale of deferred payments by which the parties agree that objects sold shall not become the property of the purchaser by mere transfer'. This involves a change of management but no change of ownership until the deferred payments have been made, not dissimilar to a retention of title clause in the sale of goods. The commercial partnership in this case failed to perform its obligations under the lease purchase agreement, which was consequently terminated on foot of a court ruling obtained by Besselsen. The court ordered the restoration of the bar/disco to Besselsen. Following the logic of *Ny Molle Kro* referred to at **11.5.3.2** above the court held that the transfer of an undertaking pursuant to a lease purchase agreement such as that recognised under Netherlands law and to the retransfer of that undertaking on the termination of the agreement by a judicial decision came within the scope of the Directive.

11.5.3.4   *Guidon v Hugh Farrington*

In *Guidon v Hugh Farrington and Ushers Island Petrol Station* [1993] ELR 98 the claimant worked with Local Stores (Trading) Ltd trading as Seven-Eleven. Seven-Eleven had a branch in the Ushers Island Petrol Station which was owned by Mr Farrington. Seven-Eleven went into receivership and its lease at Ushers Island was surrendered on 14 June 1991, which was a Friday and a normal day of work for the claimant. The claimant returned to work at Ushers Island on 17 June 1991 and was advised that her employment had terminated. She claimed unfair dismissal against the respondent and claimed he was a transferee within the meaning of the Directive and Regulations, the lease having been surrendered and the business reverting to him. The EAT had regard to the decisions of the ECJ in *Ny Molle Kro* and *Berg v Besselsen* and held that there had been a transfer of the undertaking of the Seven-Eleven shop to the respondent Mr Farrington and that the dismissal of the claimant on the grounds of transfer was prohibited by the Directive and Regulations and in the circumstances was deemed to be unfair.

11.5.4   CONTRACTUAL NEXUS BETWEEN TRANSFEROR AND TRANSFEREE

The *Daddy's Dance Hall, Ny Molle Kro* and *Berg* cases illustrate how a transfer may result from actions of or affecting the parties without there being a contractual nexus between them. This lack of a contractual nexus came into even sharper focus in *Redmond Stichting v Bartol* [1992] IRLR 366. The Dr Sophie Redmond Foundation provided assistance to drug addicts, including those of a particular ethnic origin, in the Netherlands. The foundation was funded by grants from the Groningen local authority. The local authority terminated the grants to the Redmond Foundation and instead funded another foundation, the Sigma Foundation, which provided general assistance to those who had problems with drug dependency on condition that that foundation would be accessible to drug addicts. The clients/patients of the Redmond Foundation were transferred to the Sigma Foundation. The local authority had been leasing a building to the Redmond Foundation which they transferred to Sigma. Some of the Redmond employees transferred to the Sigma Foundation on foot of offers of new contracts of employment from Sigma.

Some of those employees not transferred to the Sigma Foundation who had been employed by the Redmond Foundation claimed that there had been a transfer of an undertaking within the meaning of the Directive and that their employment should transfer also. The ECJ held that the Directive did apply. The main points to note from the judgment are as follow.

(1) There is a transfer where a public body terminates a subsidy paid to one legal entity as a result of which the activities of that entity are terminated and transferred to another legal entity with similar aims.

(2) The Directive does not exclude non-profit-making bodies such as charities or foundations. The Directive applies to all employees who are covered by protection against dismissal under national law even if it be limited.

(3) The fact that the termination of the subsidy to the Redmond Foundation was a unilateral act of the local authority does not affect the determination as to whether or not there has been a transfer. This finding is of particular relevance to transfers of parts of undertakings such as canteen and cleaning services as was highlighted in more detail in the *Christonsen and Schmidt* cases dealt with at **11.8.1.2**.

(4) The decisive criterion for establishing whether there is a transfer of an undertaking is whether the unit in question retains its identity after the transfer. In order to ascertain whether or not there is a transfer it is necessary to determine whether the functions performed are in fact carried out or resumed by the new legal entity with the same or similar activities. This provision has had the effect of bringing the whole area of privatisation of hitherto publicly provided services within the scope of the Directive and Regulations.

The *Redmond* case focused attention on the fact that employees may follow the activity upon which they were working if that activity transfers from one employer to another. This could be the case even where their employer did not sell the business as a going concern and indeed may have played no active part in the transfer. The transfer of its activities was not effected by the foundation itself but by the funding authority. The activity then followed the funding and the employees followed the activity.

These concepts did not fit easily into Irish law. In Irish law, prior to the Directive taking effect, ownership and the status of employer and employee only changed or varied by or as a result of the conclusion of a specific agreement between the parties or implied in a situation or transaction where the parties were active. The *Redmond* case showed how the obligations of an employer towards an employee could transfer from one employer to another as a result of actions taken, not by those parties or in circumstances in which they had an input, but by others over whom they may have had no influence, or as result of a decision into which they had no input, and possibly against their wishes. However, in order to give full effect to the purpose of the Directive, the transfer must be looked at from the level of the employee and the effect on the employee rather than at the level of the employer and what the employer might seek or wish to do.

As was seen the Directive requires that there be the transfer of an undertaking or part of an undertaking 'as a result of a legal transfer or merger'. This would seem to imply that there must be a contractual nexus between the parties to a transfer. No guidance is given in the Directive as to what is meant by 'a legal transfer or merger', nor is there any reference to the term in the explanatory memorandum. Case law has shown that a very loose definition will be applied requiring, not that there be any legal formality to the transfer, but rather that the transfer take place within the context of an arrangement which has aspects of legality and enforceability to it. Advocate-General Van Gerven in *Redmond* stated (at p 373, paragraph 18):

'I would like to stress that, in assessing the question whether, in a given situation, there has been a transfer resulting from a "legal transfer or merger" within the meaning of the Directive, the court has generally taken as its starting point the principle that the question must be examined in the light of the final result of the operation in question.'

11.5.5 TRANSFER OF ACTIVITY

Advocate-General Van Gerven has indicated in *Redmond* the thinking that will apply, which is to ascertain what is the activity for which the employees were employed in the first place, and examine it then in light of what has occurred. If the activity is seen to be continuing, even with some differences, there is likely to be deemed to be, or have been, a transfer of an undertaking within the meaning of the Directive. Not all of the activity has to transfer. It was argued in *Redmond* that Sigma did not do everything the Redmond Foundation had done, nor did all of the Redmond employees transfer, and that there were differences in the way in which certain other services would or would not be provided. In light of this it was argued that as the activity that transferred was not identical to that carried out by Redmond the Directive then did not apply. The court rejected that argument and indicated that what did and did not transfer must be examined and weighed within the overall context of what occurred to determine on balance whether or not the business retained its identity and was transferred. The court set out a list of criteria to be examined but stressed that each criterion is merely a single factor in the overall assessment and none of them are determining factors. When the factors are weighed it is for the national court to decide in light of that exercise whether or not the business in question retained its identity. In quoting its own judgment in *Spijkers v Gebroeders Benedik Abbatoir CV* [1986] CMLR 296 the court held in *Redmond* (at p 369, paragraphs 23 and 24):

'[T]he decisive criterion for establishing whether there is a transfer within the meaning of the Directive is whether the business in question retains its identity as would be indicated, in particular, by the fact that its operation was actually continued or resumed.

'. . . in order to determine whether those conditions are fulfilled, it is necessary to consider all the factual circumstances characterising the transaction in question, including the type of undertaking or business concerned, whether the business's tangible assets such as buildings or moveable property are transferred, the value of its intangible assets at the time of the transfer, whether or not the majority of its employees are taken over by the new employer, whether or not its customers are transferred and the degree of similarity between the activities carried on before and after the transfer and the period, if any, for which those activities are suspended. It should be noted, however, that all those circumstances are merely single factors in the overall assessment which must be made and cannot therefore be considered in isolation.'

11.6 Franchises or Dealerships

When a franchise or dealership changes hands is this transfer of an undertaking? In *Merckx and Neuhuys v Ford Motor Co Belgium SA* [1996] IRLR 467 Mr Merckx and Mr Neuhuys were employed as salesmen with Anfo Motors which sold motor vehicles as a Ford dealer in and around Brussels. Ford was the main shareholder in Anfo Motors. On 8 October 1987 Anfo Motors informed Mr Merckx and Mr Neuhuys that it would discontinue all its activities on 31 December 1987 and that with effect from 1 November 1987 Ford would have its interests looked after by an independent dealership, Novarobel, which was then in existence and trading. Novarobel took on 14 of the 64 employees of Anfo. Anfo wrote to all of its customers informing them of the discontinuance of its activities and recommending the services of Novarobel. Mr Merckx and Mr Neuhuys were proposed to move to the employment of Novarobel but for various reasons they objected and sought compensation for breach of contract, unlawful dismissal and redundancy together with outstanding bonus payments. Anfo counterclaimed. The court stated that there were two questions to be dealt with. The first question was whether Article 1(1) of the Directive must be interpreted as applying where an undertaking holding a motor vehicle dealership for a particular territory discontinues its business and the dealership is then transferred to another undertaking which takes on part of its staff and is recommended to customers, without any transfer of assets.

Reaching its decision the court had regard to a number of decisions including *Redmond Stichting v Bartol* [1992] IRLR 366, and *Foreningen af Arbejdsledere i Danmark v Daddy's Dance Hall A/S* [1988] IRLR 315. In answer to the first question the court stated inter alia (at p 474):

> 'It is clear from the case law that for the Directive to apply it is not necessary for there to be a direct contractual relationship between the transferor and the transferee. Consequently, where a motor vehicle dealership concluded with one undertaking is terminated and a new dealership is awarded to another undertaking pursuing the same activities the transfer of undertaking is the result of a legal transfer for the purposes of the Directive as interpreted by the court.'

On the facts of this particular case it was found that Ford had concluded an agreement and guarantee with Novarobel under which Ford undertook 'to bear the expenses relating to certain payments for breach of contract, unlawful dismissal or redundancy which might be payable by Novarobel to members of the staff previously employed by Anfo Motors'. The court held that fact confirmed there was a legal transfer within the meaning of the Directive. The court answered the first question by determining that the Directive did apply. See also *Clark and Tokeley Ltd* (*t/a Spellbrook*) *v Oakes* [1997] IRLR 564.

11.7 Transfer of Employees

11.7.1 UNDERLYING PHILOSOPHY

The underlying philosophy of the Directive was well explained by the UK EAT in *Birch v Nuneaton and Bedworth Borough Council* [1995] IRLR 518 when it stated:

> 'If similar activities are continued in different hands the identity of the undertaking is retained, a transfer occurs, the employees follow the work and protection is enjoyed by the employees.'

11.7.2 TRANSFER OF PART OF AN UNDERTAKING

The Directive provides that it shall apply not just to the transfer of an undertaking or business but also to the transfer of part of an undertaking or business. It has been seen that where part of a business is an economic entity in itself that part may be easily identifiable as the subject matter of a transfer of part of a business. Difficulties may arise where the part sold off or transferred was not a readily identifiable economic entity prior to the transfer as it depended for its existence on being part of a larger economic entity. Difficulty may arise in identifying the transferor and whether particular employees are employed in the part of the business transferred.

In *Michael Peters Ltd v Farnfield and Michael Peters Group plc* [1995] IRLR 190 Mr Farnfield was chief executive of the Michael Peters Group plc, a holding company for some 25 subsidiaries. When the parent company and its subsidiaries went into receivership and four subsidiaries were sold off, the parent company was not a party to the sale agreement. It was held, however, by an industrial tribunal that Mr Farnfield's employment transfer was on the basis that in reality the four subsidiary companies, together with that part of the parent company's assets belonging to those companies, formed part of a 'single economic unit'. Part of the parent company was transferred and Mr Farnfield was protected because he was employed by the transferor of the business. The UK EAT, however, overruled the industrial tribunal, holding that it was inappropriate to apply a concept of a 'single economic unit' that the transferors were not the parent company and Mr Farnfield was not therefore an employee of the transferor.

In *Sunley Turriff Holdings Ltd v Thomson* [1995] IRLR 184 there was a detailed analysis of the particular transfer concerned and it was decided that the part of the business in relation to which Thomson was employed by the transferor was actually transferred, and therefore the Directive/Regulations applied. The twist in this case was that Thomson continued to work for the transferor after the transfer. He was not designated as one of the employees transferred and continued to work for a receiver for some two months after the transfer until he was dismissed. The tribunal held that a mistaken belief of the employee cannot defeat the principle of automatic transfer under the Directive/Regulations. The contract transferred as a matter of law and there was no actual dismissal by the transferees or resignation from their employment.

In *Botzen v Rotterdamsche Droogdok Maatschappij* [1986] ECR 519 the ECJ considered a situation where Mr Botzen and his seven co-plaintiffs were assigned to parts of a business which were not the subject matter of transfer. One of the questions addressed to the court was:

'Does the scope of the Directive also extend to the rights conferred upon and the obligations imposed upon the transferor by contracts of employment which exist at the date of transfer and which are made with employees whose duties are not performed exclusively with the aid of assets which belong to the transferred part of the undertaking?'

Advocate-General Slynn dealt with the transfer of a part of an undertaking in *Botzen* at p 521 as follows:

'I do not consider that it is necessary or desirable in this case to seek to define comprehensively what is "part of" a business. That is largely a question of fact though it will usually involve the transfer of a department or factory or facet of the business. It may perhaps also involve the sale of a fraction of a single unit of business. Once it is decided as a fact that part of the business is transferred then those workers who during their working hours are wholly engaged in that part are entitled to rely on the terms of the Directive. It will of course cover the full-time and part-time workers. A basic working test, it seems to me, is to ask whether, if that part of the business had been separately owned before the transfer the worker would have been employed by the owners of that part over the owners of the remaining part. The only exception I would admit to the requirement that an employee must be "wholly" engaged in that part of the business would be where an employee was required to perform other duties to an extent which could fairly be described as de minimis. On the other hand if a worker in fact is engaged in the activities of the whole business or in several parts then he cannot be regarded for the purpose of the Directive as an employee "of" the part of the business transferred.'

The decision of the full court in *Botzen* is not particularly helpful in that the court held that the test to be applied was whether or not there had been a transfer of the part of the business for which the employee was 'assigned and which formed the organisational framework within which their employment relationship took effect'.

11.7.3   PART OF AN UNDERTAKING OR A MERE ACTIVITY?

The subject matter of a transfer is not always easily distinguishable as being part of the undertaking from which it is transferred. The question may arise as to whether or not it is an integral part of the economic entity constituting the undertaking or, alternatively, whether it is merely an activity of the undertaking which activity in itself is not an economic activity capable of being the subject matter of a transfer within the meaning of the Directive.

In *Schmidt v Spar und Leihkasse der Fruheren Amter Bordesholm* [1994] IRLR 302, the bank which employed Ms Schmidt, which of itself was clearly an 'undertaking', decided that it no longer wished to employ Ms Schmidt as an employee to carry out the daily cleaning work of the bank and decided to contract out the work to a contract cleaning company. This case is dealt with in more detail at **11.8.1.2** below. The question arose, however, as to whether or not the cleaning work constituted part of the undertaking of the bank so transferred. The bank contended that the performance of the cleaning operations was neither the main function nor an ancillary function of the undertaking and therefore did not involve the transfer of an economic unit and did not come within the definition of transfer of an undertaking within the terms of the Directive. In its submissions to the court the Commission took the view that if the cleaning was carried out by staff of the undertaking it was a service which the undertaking itself performed and the fact that such work was merely an ancillary activity not necessarily connected with the main objects of the undertaking could not have the effect of excluding the transfer from the scope of the Directive. The court held in this regard (p 636):

> 'The decisive criterion for establishing whether there is a transfer . . . is whether the business in question retains its identity. This is indicated inter alia by the actual continuation or resumption by the new employer of the same or similar activities.
>
> 'The fact that the activity in question was performed by a single employee prior to the transfer is not sufficient to preclude application of the Directive.'

11.7.4   STABLE ECONOMIC ENTITY

What might in day-to-day terminology be termed as an ancillary activity of an undertaking may be deemed to be part of the undertaking and therefore be classified as a transfer within the terms of the Directive. The activity must, however, be classifiable as a stable economic entity as per *Ledernes Hovedorganisation (Rygaard) v Dansk Arbejdsgiverforening (Stro Mølle Akustik) A/S* [1996] IRLR 51 ('*Rygaard*') which is dealt with in detail at **11.8.4**. See also *Wynnwith Engineering Co Ltd v Bennett* [2002] IRLR 170 and *Temco Service Industries SA v Imzilyen* [2002] IRLR 214.

11.7.5   *SPIJKERS* CRITERIA

In ascertaining whether or not there has been a transfer of an undertaking, and keeping in mind that it must be a stable undertaking with an ongoing life rather than a short-term contractual enterprise as per *Rygaard*, the following are the *Spijkers* criteria to be judged in an overall context in ascertaining has there been a transfer:

— has the entity retained its identity?

— have assets transferred (although it is not essential that they do so)?

— what has happened to the intangible assets, such as goodwill, and have they transferred?

— have some or all of the staff been taken over by the new employer?

— has the customer base transferred?

— are the activities carried on post-transfer similar to those carried on pre-transfer?

— an interruption in the operation of the undertaking or economic entity is not fatal to the fact of transfer, but a consideration, and dependent on the duration and effect of such interruption;

— if there is no transfer of assets and the transferee does not take over a major part of the workforce and the combined entity of the group of employees and assets they used to carry on the economic activity is not transferred, in circumstances where the economic entity needs assets to continue in existence there may not be a transfer as per the qualifications laid down by the ECJ in *Suzen v Zehnacker Gebaudereinigung GmbH Krankenhausservice* [1997] IRLR 255.

11.8   Service Providers

11.8.1   GENERALLY

The approach adopted by the EAT in Ireland adopts a strict test in this area, in contrast with the UK Court of Appeal which adopts a more flexible, employee-oriented approach.

Many businesses have services provided for them by outside agencies, companies or individuals none of whom are, or can be, classified as employees but which themselves have employees who may be committed wholly or in substantial part to the provision of the services. These services also can be in respect of core activities or ancillary activities. They could be core activities in the sense of having sub-contract manufacturing done, or ancillary activities, such as the provision of canteen services to employees of the business, the cleaning of the premises or the provision of security services.

Whether subsidiary or ancillary activities which are transferred are covered by the Directive/Regulations will depend on whether or not they are classified as an economic entity or a mere activity. What constitutes an economic entity has proven to be particularly difficult to distinguish from a mere activity in the area of service providers and subsidiary or ancillary services.

The starting point in determining the tests to be applied has to be *JMA Spijkers v Gebroeders Benedik Abbatoir CV* [1986] 2 CMLR 296. The *Spijkers* criteria are merely indiciae of what might be an economic entity or an economic unit within or attached to an undertaking. While *Spijkers* is the starting point subsequent case law has both fine-tuned the definition of the economic entity or activity that may be the subject of a transfer of an undertaking or part of an undertaking and has added new tests, most notably in *Ledernes Hovedorganisation (Rygaard) v Dansk Arbejdsgiverfovenig Stro Mølle Akinskik A/S* [1996] IRLR 51.

The position of service providers and the transfer or movement of services and service contracts and whether they are covered by the Directive and Regulations will depend on the facts of the situation and how employees are affected.

The position of employees affected by the contracting out of services is governed in the main by two fact situations that may arise:

(a)   where the principal is providing the service itself and determines to transfer the service to an outside agency, which henceforward will provide the service, as an independent contractor, usually a company that is in the particular line of business providing a service to a number of principals; or

(b)   where a company is already contracting out services, which it may or may not have itself provided in the past, to an independent contractor and changes independent contractors. The question arises as to what happens to staff providing the service where their employer loses the contract to provide the service and the contract is awarded to another independent contractor employer, who is not the principal.

11.8.1.1 *Rask and Christensen v Iss Kantineservice A/S*

The first situation arose and was considered by the ECJ in *Rask and Christensen v ISS Kantineservice A/S* [1993] IRLR 133.

The principal, Philips A/S, a Danish company which had provided a canteen service for its staff and employed a number of people to provide that canteen service, decided to contract out the running of its staff canteen to ISS, which was an independent catering company providing canteen services to various companies. Philips agreed to pay ISS a fixed monthly fee to cover costs relating to management, wages, insurance and the provision of work clothing. Philips also agreed to provide, free of charge, premises, equipment, electricity and certain other services. Some basic assets such as tableware were sold at cost price to ISS. ISS undertook to offer employment on the same rates of pay to the Philips' staff who were engaged in the provision of the service and would transfer into the employment of ISS consequent on the awarding of the contract. Rask and Christensen transferred to ISS but complained about certain changes in their working conditions made by ISS. Following on from that dispute Rask refused to work under the new conditions and as a consequence was dismissed. Rask and Christensen claimed compensation for the changes in their terms and conditions and Rask also claimed compensation in respect of her dismissal. They claimed against ISS and the question as to whether or not the transfer between Philips and ISS came within the meaning of Directive 77/187 (and the domestic Danish law implementing that Directive) was referred to the ECJ for consideration. ISS put forward two main arguments to the court.

(a) An agreement of the type concluded with Philips A/S does not effect any transfer within the meaning intended by the Directive since it does not confer either full and entire responsibility for the provision of the services, particularly in so far as the customers and the fixing of prices is concerned, nor does it confer legal ownership of assets necessary for the provision of the services.

(b) An agreement such as concluded between ISS and Philips A/S relates to services which themselves could not be described as an 'undertaking' within the meaning of the Directive by reason of the fact that they are ancillary activities and not part of the main core activity of the transferor.

In addressing the two points the ECJ referred to its decision in *Berg and Busschers v Besselsen* [1989] IRLR 447 where it held that the Directive was applicable in any case where, following a legal transfer or merger, there is a change in the legal or natural person responsible for carrying on the business and who, by virtue of that fact, incurs the obligation of an employer vis-à-vis the employees of the undertaking, regardless of whether or not ownership of the undertaking is transferred. The ECJ also referred to *Botzen v Rotterdamsche Droogdok Maatschappij* [1986] ECR 519 and its finding that the employment relationship 'is essentially characterised by the link existing between the employee and the part of the undertaking to which he is assigned to carry out his duties'. The ECJ went on to state that the fact that the activity transferred 'is only an ancillary activity of the transferor undertaking not necessarily related to its objects cannot have the effect of excluding that transaction from the scope of the Directive'. The court also held that the restricted form of agreement between the transferor and the transferee was not such as could operate to exclude the provisions of the Directive either.

On the principal question referred to it the ECJ held inter alia:

'Where the responsibility for providing a service is, by agreement, entrusted by the owner of an undertaking to the owner of another undertaking who assumes the obligations of an employer in respect of the employees who are engaged in the provision of that service, that transaction is capable of falling within the scope of Article 1(1). Neither the fact that the activity transferred is only an ancillary activity of the transferor nor the fact that the agreement relates to the provision of services provided exclusively for the benefit of the transferor in return for a fee the form of which is fixed by the agreement, prevents the Directive from applying.'

11.8.1.2   *Schmidt v Spar*

The issue of the contracting out of services came into sharper focus in another decision of the ECJ in *Schmidt v Spar und Leihkasse der Fruheren Amter Bordesholm*, [1994] IRLR 302. In this case a branch of a bank employed Schmidt to do the cleaning work required by that branch. Following refurbishment and extension the bank decided to terminate the employment of Schmidt and contract out the cleaning work to a contract cleaning company which was already responsible for cleaning most of the other branches of the bank. Schmidt was offered employment by the contract cleaning company at a higher monthly wage but she turned down the offer on the grounds that she would be receiving in essence a lower hourly wage, since there was a larger area to clean as a result of the extension of the premises.

Schmidt claimed under the terms of the Directive. It was argued by the German government and the bank that cleaning was not a business carried on by the bank and that there was not therefore a transfer of an undertaking or part of an undertaking. The bank contended that the cleaning operations were neither the main function nor an ancillary function of the undertaking. What occurred in *Schmidt* was similar in principle to what happened in *Rask and Christensen v ISS Kantineservice A/S* [1993] IRLR 133 and, not surprisingly therefore, the court held that there had been a transfer. What caused the surprise expressed at the time the *Schmidt* decision issued was the fact that the actual work done by Schmidt was not as substantial as that done by the employees in *Rask and Christensen* and there was no transfer of assets or infrastructure surrounding *Schmidt*, but rather a transfer of the actual service itself which was provided by one individual employee. Many commentators construed the work done by Schmidt as merely an activity carried on in or by the bank. Many could not understand how such an activity could be in itself deemed an economic entity or part of a larger economic entity being the bank itself. The ECJ held in *Schmidt*:

(a)   the cleaning operations of a branch of an undertaking may be treated as part of the business of that undertaking within the meaning of the Directive;

(b)   where a transfer relates only to part of a business, the protection provided by the Directive applies to employees assigned to that part of the undertaking;

(c)   when an undertaking contracts out the responsibility for operating one of its services, such as cleaning, to another undertaking which thereby assumes the obligations of an employer towards employees assigned to those duties, that operation may come within the scope of the Directive;

(d)   the decisive criterion for establishing whether there is a transfer for the purposes of the Directive is whether the business in question retains its identity. This is indicated, inter alia, by the actual continuation or resumption by the new employer of the same or similar activities, as the ECJ had held in both *Spijkers v Gebroeders Benedik Abbatoir CV* [1986] 2 CMLR 296 and *Redmond Stichting v Bartol* [1992] IRLR 366; and

(e)   the fact that only one employee was assigned to the part of the undertaking transferred does not preclude the application of the Directive, nor does the absence of any transfer of tangible assets even though this is normally a factor taken into account by national courts in assessing when there has in fact been a transfer of an undertaking.

In its decision the ECJ refers to the cleaning work of the bank being part of the undertaking of the bank. It based its decision on the applicability of the Directive to the transfer of part of an undertaking. Previous case law, however, had distinguished parts of an undertaking so covered by the Directive by reference to there being an economic entity in itself capable of being transferred. In *Schmidt* the ECJ made reference to its decision in *Botzen*. Most of the confusion in the minds of commentators on *Schmidt*, and the difficulties caused by the subsequent application of the *Schmidt* criteria, have been caused by the failure to accept or understand that the cleaning work carried out in *Schmidt* was in itself an economic entity which became the subject of a transfer.

11.8.2   ECONOMIC UNIT

Using a term such as 'economic entity' to describe the cleaning services provided by Schmidt has caused confusion. It is difficult for many people to understand how the activity of cleaning one branch of a bank by one person could constitute an economic entity within the scope of the Directive. A somewhat more understandable and acceptable term 'economic unit' was adverted to by Advocate-General Van Gerven in his opinion in *Schmidt* when he stated:

> 'the court recognises a common denominator underlying three concepts of "undertaking", "business" and "part of a business", namely that of an "economic unit" or a "business", terms which, in my opinion, refer to a unit with a minimum level of organisational independence which can exist by itself or constitute part of a larger undertaking.'

He also stated:

> 'From all this I infer that the phrase "undertaking, business or part of a business" within the meaning of the Directive is underpinned by the concept of an economic unit which refers to an organised whole consisting of persons and (tangible and/or intangible) assets by means of which an economic activity is carried on having an objective of its own, albeit one that is ancillary to the objects of the undertaking; a whole which, moreover, can be part of an even larger corporate whole.'

Advocate-General Van Gerven was of the view that cleaning operations constituted an economic activity within the meaning of the Directive. He also emphasised in reaching his decision that the fact situation in *Schmidt* involved an undertaking ceasing cleaning operations previously performed by its staff in order to contract them out to a separate undertaking. It must be kept in mind in any analysis of the *Schmidt* decision that that is the particular fact situation giving rise to the decision. In *Schmidt* it was also argued to the ECJ that entrusting cleaning operations to an outside firm did not involve the transfer of an economic unit. In arriving at its decision the ECJ quoted with favour the argument put forward on behalf of the Commission which was:

> '[I]f the cleaning is carried out by the staff of the undertaking, it is a service which the [undertaking] performs itself and the fact that such work is merely an ancillary activity not necessarily connected with the objects of the undertaking cannot have the effect of excluding the transfer from the scope of the Directive.
>
>   'According to the case law of the court . . . the Directive is applicable where, following a legal transfer or merger, there is a change in the legal or natural person who is responsible for carrying on the business and who by virtue of that fact incurs the obligations of an employer vis-à-vis the employees of the undertaking, regardless of whether or not ownership of the undertaking is transferred.'

The protection provided by the Directive applies in particular by virtue of Article 1(1) where the transfer relates only to a business or part of a business; that is to say, a part of an undertaking. In those circumstances the transfer relates to employees assigned to that part of the undertaking since, as the ECJ held in its judgment in *Botzen v Rotterdamsche Droogdok Maatschappij* [1986] 2 CMLR 50, an employment relationship is essentially characterised by the link between the employee and the part of the undertaking or business to which he is assigned to carry out his duties.

Thus, when an undertaking entrusts by contract the responsibility for operating one of its services, such as cleaning, to another undertaking which thereby assumes the obligations of an employer towards employees assigned to those employees, that operation may come within the scope of the Directive. As the ECJ held at paragraph 17 of its judgment in *Rask and Christensen v ISS Kantineservice* [1993] IRLR 133 the fact that in such a case the activity transferred is for the transferor merely an ancillary activity not necessarily connected with its objects cannot have the effect of excluding that operation from the scope of the Directive.

In retrospect, and in particular in light of its subsequent decision in *Suzen v Zehnacker Gebaudereinigung GmbH Krankenhausservice* [1997] IRLR 255, it would have been more helpful had the ECJ specifically referred to the cleaning activity as being an economic entity in itself and how it was held to be so.

11.8.3 RESTRICTING TRANSFERS

In view of the wide and purposive approach taken by the courts to the application of the Directive employers and their advisers were finding that it was becoming increasingly difficult to ascertain exactly where the Directive did or did not apply. Apart from the very many obvious cases when it would apply it was being found that its provisions were arising in situations that no one had anticipated as being relevant to them. The application to service contracts and service providers caused enormous practical difficulties and business people were becoming more and more vocal in their criticism of the Directive and the domestic regulations in the Member States. It appears that the members of the ECJ became aware of the practical difficulties their decisions were causing. Their response was to issue two judgments which introduced fine, and indeed not so fine, points of distinction as to what would or would not constitute a transfer of an undertaking, thereby restricting the application of the Directive and domestic regulations and leading in *Betts v Brintel Helicopters Ltd* [1997] IRLR 361 to a reversal of the UK High Court decision.

11.8.4 STABLE ECONOMIC ENTITY—*RYGAARD*

In *Ledernes Hovedorganisation (Rygaard) v Dansk Arbejdsgiverforening (Stro Mølle Akustik) A/S* [1996] IRLR 51 Rygaard was employed by Svend Pedersen A/S, a firm of carpenters. Pedersen had a contract with SAS Service Partner to build a canteen. Pedersen informed SAS that it wanted part of the work it was contracted to do to be completed by Stro Mølle Akustik. Stro Mølle submitted a tender to SAS and it was accepted. Pedersen and Stro Mølle then entered into an agreement to effect a takeover of the works transferred. The agreement provided that Stro Mølle was liable to reimburse Pedersen the expenditure, including wages, which Pedersen had already incurred with regard to the works transferred. It also provided that two of Pedersen's apprentices would be transferred to Stro Mølle. On the day after the agreement Pedersen terminated Rygaard's contract of employment. Rygaard continued to work for Stro Mølle until he was given notice of dismissal by them. Meanwhile Pedersen was declared bankrupt. Rygaard brought wrongful dismissal proceedings against Stro Mølle and the question arose as to whether or not the Directive applied to the transfer of Rygaard's employment from Pedersen to Stro Mølle. The ECJ held that:

(a) the taking over with the view to completing, with the consent of the awarder of the main building contract, works started by another undertaking, consisting of two apprentices and an employee together with the materials assigned to those works, does not constitute a transfer of an undertaking within the meaning of the Directive;

(b) in order to be a transfer of an undertaking the transfer must relate to a stable economic entity whose activity is not limited to performing one specific works contract. That is not the case where there is a transfer from one undertaking to another of building works with a view to their completion and the transferor undertaking merely makes available to the new contractor certain workers and material for carrying out the works in question. Such a transfer could come within the terms of the Directive only if it included the transfer of a body of assets enabling activities of the transferor undertaking to be carried on in a stable way.

11.8.5 ASSET TRANSFER

In *Spijkers v Gebroeders Benedik Abattoir CV* [1986] 2 CMLR 296 the ECJ had held that the fact that physical assets were sold was a strong indication that a transfer within the meaning of the Directive had taken place. In *Rask and Christensen v ISS Kantineservice* [1993] IRLR 133 the ECJ held that consideration of whether a business's tangible assets were transferred is one of the circumstances to be considered in determining whether or not there was a transfer of undertaking but was merely a single factor in the overall assessment which must be made and could not be considered in isolation. In *Schmidt v Spar und Leihkasse der Fruheren Amter Bordesholm* [1994] IRLR 302 the ECJ also confirmed that the transfer of assets was one of the factors to be considered in the overall judgment as to whether or not an undertaking has in fact been transferred but stated that the absence of a transfer of assets does not preclude the existence of part of the undertaking. In *Ledernes Hovedorganisation (Rygaard) v Dansk Arbejdsgiverforening (Stro Mølle Akustik) A/S* [1996] IRLR 51 ('*Rygaard*') the ECJ, reaffirming its view on the transfer of assets as being one of the factors to be considered, then gave the 'asset test' a particular importance in the circumstances of this by holding that the cases of *Spijkers* and *Schmidt* presupposed that the transfer related to a stable economic entity whose activity was not limited to performing one specific works contract. In *Schmidt* the cleaning work needed to be done for as long as the bank was in use. In *Rygaard*, however, once the carpentry sub-contract had come to an end the economic entity effectively ceased to be. In determining whether or not an economic entity was stable and long-term the ECJ held that the transfer of a specific works contract 'would only come within the terms of the Directive if there was a transfer of a body of assets' but further qualified that requirement by stating 'the assets must enable the activities of the transferor undertaking, or the part transferred, to be carried on in a stable way'. It must be taken that what is meant by 'stable' in this context is the same as 'long-term' or 'ongoing'.

11.8.6 LEGAL TRANSFER OR MERGER AND SERVICE PROVIDER

11.8.6.1 What is legal transfer?

Article 1(1) of the Directive states that it shall apply to the transfer of an undertaking, business or part of an undertaking or business to another employer 'as a result of a legal transfer or merger'.

In *Rygaard* Advocate-General Cosmas examined the facts in the case in detail in light of the case law and his views may be summarised as follows.

(a) The case law of the ECJ has established that there must be a change in the person responsible for the operation of the undertaking in order for there to be a transfer.

(b) The economic entity transferred must continue to exist and retain its identity. The ECJ has accepted that an undertaking retains its identity where its operation is in fact continued or taken over by the new employer with the same economic activities or analogous activities.

(c) The Directive is applicable only when the change in the person responsible for the operation of the undertaking is based on a contract, that is to say, stems from a contractual transfer or from a merger and transfers by operation of the law or resulting from a unilateral act of dispositions are thus excluded. This is a questionable finding given the approach taken by the ECJ in *Redmond Stichting v Bartol* [1992] IRLR 366 where it could be said that the Redmond Stichting played no part in the transfer and from where they stood the transfer was a unilateral act. In *Redmond* the ECJ held that the term 'legal transfer' covers the situation in which a public body decides to terminate a subsidy paid to one legal person as a result of which the activities of that legal person are fully and definitively terminated and to transfer to another legal person with similar aims.

11.8.6.1.1 *The* Suzen *case*

On 11 March 1997 the ECJ issued a decision directly relating to change of service providers which greatly qualified the general understanding of previous decisions of the court. The case was *Suzen v Zehnacker Gebaudereinigung GmbH Krankenhausservice* [1997] IRLR 255. Two questions were referred to the court and were considered together. They asked whether the Directive applies to a situation in which a person, who had entrusted the cleaning of his premises to a first undertaking, terminates that contract and for the performance of similar work enters into a new contract with a second undertaking without any concomitant transfer of tangible or intangible business assets from one undertaking to the other. The following points were made by the court.

(a) The aim of the Directive is to ensure continuity of employment relationships within an economic entity irrespective of any change of ownership.

(b) For the Directive to be applicable the transfer must relate to a stable economic entity whose activity is not limited to performing one specific works contract (see *Rygaard*).

(c) The mere fact that the service provided by the old and the new awardees of a contract is similar does not support the conclusion that an economic entity has been transferred. An entity cannot be reduced to the activity entrusted to it. Its identity also emerges from other factors, such as its workforce, its management staff, the way in which its work is organised, its operating methods or, indeed, where appropriate, the operational resources available to it.

(d) The mere loss of a service contract to a competitor cannot therefore by itself indicate the existence of a transfer within the meaning of the Directive. In those circumstances the service undertaking previously entrusted does not, on losing a customer, cease fully to exist, and a business or part of a business belonging to it cannot be considered to have been transferred to the new awardee of the contract.

(e) Since, in certain labour-intensive sectors, a group of workers engaged in a joint activity on a permanent basis may constitute an economic entity it must be recognised that such an entity is capable of maintaining its identity after it has been transferred where the new employer does not merely pursue the activity in question but also takes over a major part in terms of the numbers and skills of the employees specially assigned by his predecessor to that task. In those circumstances the new employer takes over a body of assets enabling him to carry on the activities or certain activities of the transferor undertaking on a regular basis.

The ECJ held:

'The Directive . . . is to be interpreted as meaning that the Directive does not apply to a situation in which a person who had entrusted the cleaning of his premises to a first undertaking terminates his contract with the latter and for the performance of similar work enters into a new contract with a second undertaking, if there is no concomitant transfer from one undertaking to the other of significant tangible or intangible assets or taking over by the new employer of a major part of the workforce in terms of their numbers and skills assigned by his predecessor to the performance of the contract.'

The application of the principles and the finding in *Schmidt v Spar und Leihkasse der Fruheren Amter Bordesholm* [1994] IRLR 302, together with the guidance given in other cases, had led to the conclusion that, in both example situations as set out above where service providers were retained or changed, the Directive would apply. That was greatly qualified by the decision in *Suzen*. The *Schmidt* case had set out general principles of interpretation but its finding was based on the particular facts.

The *Suzen* decision caused considerable confusion when it first issued. Many commentators thought that the ECJ had overruled itself. Advocate-General La Pergola in *Suzen* certainly invited the court to contradict previous findings, but the court took a more subtle approach and found on the particular facts of the case leaving *Schmidt* intact.

In *Schmidt* the bank was clearly an economic entity. The cleaning of the bank was held to be part of that economic entity. That part of the undertaking transferred to the outside cleaning company retained to do the cleaning work. That outside cleaning company took over part of the economic entity and it did not take a great jump of logic to conclude that the employee assigned to the part transferred came within the Directive and was herself transferred.

In *Suzen* the cleaning work did not form part of the economic entity that was the school. The school had separated it and given it to an outside company. When the contract between them came to an end, a new contract was granted to a new service provider. The new service provider was in the cleaning business and simply got the commercial benefit of being able to use its existing assets and workforce to do the cleaning. The first cleaning company who had lost the contract remained in existence and continued working. Its contract with the school could not be deemed to be part of its undertaking, merely one of its assets. When the contract transferred it was therefore not a transfer of part of the undertaking of that first contract cleaning company but a transfer of one of its assets and, as Advocate-General Cosmas stated in *Rygaard*, 'the mere disposal of assets of an undertaking does not constitute a transfer of that undertaking within the meaning of the Directive'.

11.8.6.1.2 Suzen *applied in Ireland*

The EAT has generally applied *Suzen* in Ireland, as the following cases illustrate.

- *Cannon v (1) Noonan Cleaning Ltd (2) CPS Cleaning Services Ltd* RP 324/97, UD 200/97 and MN 591/97: here, a contract for the cleaning of the Balbriggan Garda station was lost to CPS Cleaning. No tangible assets transferred between the two contractors. The claimant turned up for work with the contractor after the ending of the first contractor's contract and she was sent away by the second contractor who thereafter declined to employ her. By an application of the *Suzen* case it was found there was no transfer of an undertaking.

- *Mary Shiels, Dawn Flanigan, Hannah McMahon and Julie Dunne v Noonan Cleaning and ISS Contract Cleaners Ltd* UD 461/97, RP 180/97, MN 754/97: the claimants were employed by ISS Contract Cleaners Ltd on a cleaning contract on a site in Shannon. On re-tendering, ISS lost the contract and was succeeded by Noonan Cleaning Ltd with effect from 19 May 1997. The employees were told that the contract had been lost to Noonan Cleaning and were told to report to work with Noonan. The employees did so but were told by Noonan that they would not be employed by them. ISS's original view was that all employees would automatically transfer to the new company under SI 306/1980. However, it was acknowledged that the legal position had changed following the ECJ's ruling in *Suzen* and this was subsequently applied in Ireland by the Employment Appeals Tribunal in *Cannon v Noonan Cleaning Ltd*. Accordingly, as a result, ISS accepted that the employees had redundancy claims against ISS and had no right to transfer because no assets transferred between the two cleaning companies and Noonan declined to employ the employees. Noonan also relied upon *Suzen* to resist any liability to the employees. The EAT unequivocally applied *Suzen* and held in the circumstances that no claim lay against Noonan Cleaning and that all the employees were dismissed by reason of redundancy and were entitled to notice monies and redundancy payments under respectively the Minimum Notice in Terms of Employment Acts, 1973–1991 and the Redundancy Payments Acts, 1967–1991.

- *Maria Bruton v Knights Cleaning Services Ltd* B25/97, UD 803/97, MN 2001/97: in this case, a supermarket changed cleaning contractors providing cleaning services to a supermarket. The outgoing cleaning contractor forwarded details of employees to the new cleaning contractor and expected the employees to be employed by the new contractor. The claimant was on holiday at the time of the transfer and due to commence maternity leave. She was not employed by the new contractor. None of the other employees employed by the old contractor were taken on by the new contractor and therefore the Employment Appeals Tribunal, applying the *Suzen* case, decided that there was no transfer of an undertaking from transferor to transferee. See also *Cullen v United Cargo Services Ltd* RP 517/2003.

- *Collins v Excel Property Services Ltd RP 27/98:* Collins was employed by Excel as a cleaner to work at the Colaiste Mhuire in Cobh under a cleaning contract between the board of management of the school and Excel. The school sought tenders for a contract to clean the school. Excel lost the opportunity to perform that contract in that tendering exercise and the contract was given to a new contractor. Four employees employed on the contract, including the applicant, transferred to the new contractor. However, Mrs Collins and her colleagues felt that the machines provided by Mr Carter for cleaning the school were not of the same standard used by them in their previous employment and for that reason, they terminated their employment. Mrs Collins then claimed a redundancy payment from Excel, her former employer. Excel contended that there was no liability therefore and that the obligations of Excel were transferred to Mr Carter under the provisions of SI 306/1980. The question was whether the changeover of contractors providing cleaning services to the school amounted to a transfer of an undertaking. The EAT considered *Suzen* and concluded that the transfer of cleaning contracts did not preclude the application of the Acquired Rights Directive. Nor did it matter, following the ECJ decision in *Merckx* [1996] IRLR 467, that there was no contractual relationship between transferor and transferee. The court recognised that there would not be a transfer of an undertaking if there was no transfer of significant tangible or intangible assets of a taking over by the new employer of a major part of the workforce in terms of numbers and skills.

- In *Digan v Sheehan Security Corporation Ltd* UD235/ 2003 the EAT was asked to look at the question of a transfer of an undertaking on the changeover of security contractors providing security services at the Athlone Accommodation Centre, securing a building with some four hundred or so residents. The facts were that Sheehan took over a contract from a previous contractor. No assets transferred from outgoing contractor to incoming contractor but Sheehan took over 13 of the 14 security staff. Only the former site supervisor was the one out of the 14 who did not transfer to Sheehan. The claimant was offered a job on the transfer but worked for only four weeks before being dismissed, raising the issue of his continuity of service.

- One of the respondent's main arguments was that it conducted the security service in a manner different from the way it had been conducted by its predecessor. The EAT accepted that whilst the activities were not identical, especially in the way those activities were managed or supervised, they were conducted in a broadly similar way and would properly be described as 'similar activities'. The EAT therefore ruled against Sheehan on this point. However, the Employment Appeals Tribunal felt bound by the case of *Ayse Suzen v Zehnacker Gebaudereinigung GmbH Krankenhausservice* [1997] ECR I-1259 which stipulated that a changeover of contractors per se does not amount to a transfer of an undertaking unless there is a concomitant transfer from one undertaking to the other of significant tangible or intangible assets or the taking over by the new employer of a major part of the workforce. The EAT conceded that most of the existing workforce was taken on but there was no transfer of assets. The majority of the tribunal therefore concluded that as the previous contractor had transferred no assets, plant, book debts, buildings or trade in goodwill, this meant that there was no transfer of an undertaking and the case was more akin to the mere loss of a service contract and continuation of activity than the transfer of an economic entity.

11.8.6.1.3   Schmidt *and* Suzen *distinguished*

Subsequent decisions in Ireland and the UK have helped to clarify the distinction between *Schmidt* and *Suzen*, most notably by the Irish EAT in *Power v St Paul's Nursing Home and T & M Cleaning Ltd* [1998] ELR 212 and the UK EAT in *ECM (Vehicle Delivery Service Ltd) v Cox* [1998] IRLR 416.

In *Power* the claimants were employed as cleaners at St Paul's Nursing Home. The nursing home decided to contract out the cleaning duties in respect of which the claimants were employed. The claimants were made redundant. St Paul's then entered into a contract with T & M Cleaning Ltd to carry out the cleaning duties. Cleaning equipment and other ancillary minor assets which St Paul's utilised in the cleaning operations were transferred to T & M Cleaning Ltd. The respondents submitted the basis of case law, including the *Suzen* decision, that they had no liability for the claimants whom, they maintained, had no rights under the Directive and Regulations as a result of the transfer of the cleaning activities. In referring to the *Suzen* decision the EAT held:

> 'For the Directive to be applicable the court held that the transfer must relate to a stable economic entity whose activity is not limited to performing one specific works contract and the term entity referring to an organised grouping of persons and assets . . . there were tangible assets such as any could be identified in cleaning services. Employees would have been taken over by the new employer, the activities were exactly the same before and after the transfer. . . . It is the opinion of this Tribunal that the Directive applies to these particular sets of circumstances and in fact it would be most artificial if it was held that the case was otherwise.'

The most succinct explanation of the distinction between the ECJ decisions in *Schmidt* and *Suzen* was given by the UK EAT in *ECM (Vehicle Delivery Service Ltd) v Cox*. Axial Ltd employed the applicants as drivers and yardmen. Axial had a contract with VAG Ltd to deliver cars imported into the UK. VAG changed service provider and Axial lost the contract which was given by VAG to ECM. ECM carried out the contract from a different site and used a different delivery system with different administrative arrangements. ECM did not employ any of the applicants who had worked on the contract prior to the change of the contractor. The applicants claimed that the transfer was covered by the Directive and Regulations and that they had been unfairly dismissed as a consequence. The industrial tribunal held in their favour. The tribunal found that there was a relevant transfer within the meaning of the appropriate UK Regulations and stated that the 'undertaking which was transferred amounted to the VAG contract itself and the activities that surrounded that contract'. Subsequent to the industrial tribunal decision the ECJ issued its decision in *Suzen*. On appeal to the EAT it was argued, on behalf of the employers, that in light of the *Suzen* decision the industrial tribunal had erred in equating the transfer of a service contract with the transfer of an undertaking and that all that had been transferred in this particular case was a particular activity. The UK EAT under the chairmanship of Morison J dismissed the appeal and held inter alia the industrial tribunal did not err in finding that there was a transfer of an undertaking when the applicants' employers lost a car delivery contract on which they were employed to ECM and the applicants were not employed by ECM.

11.8.6.2   Factors to be considered

The following factors should be considered in measuring a given fact situation as being a transfer or not as the case may be.

11.8.6.2.1 *Assets or resources*

It is relevant to consider whether or not assets or resources are taken over (see the judgment of the court of Appeal in *Betts v Brintel Helicopters* [1997] IRLR 361). The ECJ, however, in *Merckx and Neuhuys v Ford Motor Co* [1996] IRLR 467 held that there could still be a transfer even though the premises at which the motor dealership was carried on did not change hands, and stated that it was 'irrelevant that the principal place of business is situated in a different area of the same conurbation provided that the contract territory remains the same'. It should also be noted that there were no assets involved in *Schmidt*.

11.8.6.2.2 *Transfer of goodwill*

Goodwill is such an intangible thing, and so limited in many modern situations where the goodwill may be invested in customers who could disappear on a transfer of a business, that while consideration must be given to the transfer of goodwill and/or customers not a lot of weight will be given to this particular test. The UK Court of Appeal did, however, suggest, in *Betts* that the right to provide a service which is an intangible asset comparable to goodwill, is a 'significant asset', and is probably at the very least a 'reserve'.

11.8.6.2.3 *Employees*

Following *Suzen* consideration will now have to be given to whether or not a major part of the workforce has been taken over by the new employer. The ECJ, in referring to what is or is not a major part of the workforce, stated in its judgment:

> 'In labour-intensive sectors a group of workers engaged in the joint activity on a permanent basis may constitute an economic entity and such an entity is capable of maintaining its identity after it has been transferred where the new employer does not merely pursue the activity in question but also takes over a major part in terms of the numbers and skills of the employees specially assigned by his predecessor to that task. In those circumstances the new employer takes over a body of assets enabling him to carry on activities of the transferor undertaking on a regular basis.'

It would appear, therefore, that a major part of the workforce may be defined as being a numerical minority of the workforce where the skills of that minority are the determining factor in their retention. Failure or refusal to take on part of the workforce in an attempt to circumvent the Directive and Regulations will not avail a transferee as held in *Power v St Paul's Nursing Home and T & M Cleaning Ltd* [1988] ELR 212 and *ECM (Vehicle Delivery Service Ltd) v Cox* [1998] IRLR 416.

11.8.6.2.4 *Existence of organisational structure or organised grouping of resources*

The assets, goodwill, resources and employees must be underpinned or marked out by an organisational structure giving them a unity or making them capable of being construed as an economic entity or unit in themselves. The infrastructure of management operating methods and operational resources will act as the glue to bind assets, goodwill and employees together as an identifiable entity capable of being the subject matter of a transfer, as highlighted in the *Suzen* decision. The infrastructure and method of operation may change, provided there remains an organisational structure marking out the business or part of the business transferred as an economic entity in itself.

The interesting concept of a 'grouping of resources' was introduced, for the first time, in Article 1(1)(b) of the amending Directive.

11.8.6.3   Further case law

The ECJ issued decisions in five service provider cases consolidated into two separate decisions.

11.8.6.3.1   Hernandez v Gomez Perez

Hernandez v Gomez Perez [1999] IRLR 132 involved bringing back in-house cleaning work which had previously been contracted out. The question arose as to whether the employees of the service provider were entitled to transfer into the employment of the principal when the principal terminated the service contract and took upon itself the carrying out of the work previously contracted out. The ECJ held:

'Directive 77/187 applies to a situation in which an undertaking which contracted out the cleaning of its premises to another undertaking decides to terminate the contract which it had with that other undertaking and to carry out that cleaning work itself provided that the operation is accompanied by the transfer of an economic entity between the two undertakings.

'The aim of Directive 77/187 is to ensure continuity of employment relationships within an economic entity irrespective of any change of ownership. The term "economic entity" refers to an organised grouping of persons and assets enabling an economic activity which pursues a specific objective to be exercised. While such an entity must be sufficiently structured and autonomous it will not necessarily have significant tangible or intangible assets. In certain sectors such as cleaning the activity is essentially based on manpower. Thus an organised grouping of wage earners who are specifically and permanently assigned to a common task may, in the absence of other factors of production, amount to an economic entity.

'It is for the national court to determine whether the maintenance of the premises of the undertaking which awarded the contract was organised in the form of an economic entity within the outside cleaning firm before the firm awarding the contract decided to carry out the work itself.'

11.8.6.3.2   Sanchez Hidalgo v Associacion de Servicios Aser *and* Ziemann v Ziemann Sicherheit GmbH

The second decision was in *Sanchez Hidalgo v Associacion de Servicios Aser* and *Ziemann v Ziemann Sicherheit GmbH* [1999] IRLR 136, the first of which involved two cases on the change of one service provider for another on the ending of a contract. Mrs Sanchez Hidalgo was one of five employees employed by a contracting firm which provided home-help services to persons in need on foot of a contract it held with the municipality of Guadalajara. When the contract expired the municipality awarded a new contract to Aser. The ECJ was posed the question as to whether there was a transfer of undertaking as between the first company, Minerva, and the second company, Aser. The second case involved the transfer of security or surveillance services between service providers. The ECJ held:

'Directive 77/187 applies to a situation in which a public body which contracted out its home-help service for people in need or awarded a contract for the surveillance of some of its premises, decides on expiry of the contract or its termination to contract out the service to a different undertaking provided that the operation is accompanied by the transfer of an economic entity between the two undertakings.

'The aim of Directive 77/187 is to ensure continuity of employment relationships within an economic entity irrespective of any change of ownership. The term "economic entity" refers to an organised grouping of persons and assets enabling an economic activity which pursues a specific objective to be exercised. Whilst such an entity must be sufficiently structured and autonomous it will not necessarily have significant tangible or intangible assets. In certain sectors such as cleaning and surveillance the activity is essentially based on manpower. Thus an organised grouping of wage-earners who are specifically and permanently assigned to a common task may, in the absence of other factors of production, amount to an economic entity.

'It is for the national court to determine whether the home-help service and the surveillance of the medical supplies depot were organised in the form of an economic entity within the first undertaking, to which provision of the service in question was contracted out.'

11.8.6.3.4   Keenan v Professional Contract Services Ltd

The EAT appears to have changed the position it took in *Cannon v Noonan Cleaning Ltd* in *Keenan v Professional Contract Services Ltd* UD 454/455/456/98. The facts of the case were that Professional Contract Services Ltd took over a cleaning contract from Grosvenor Cleaning at Dublin City University. Meetings were held prior to the takeover which the claimants attended. The facts are not set out in any particular detail in the EAT determination but it appears that the employees of Grosvenor were asked to fill out forms to confirm their interest in transferring but it is not stated in the determination why it was that the three claimants did not transfer. The respondents submitted to the EAT that they required forms to be filled out because of certain restrictions being placed on them by the university and the need to change the work rota from a two-shift to a one-shift operation. It appears that the claimants' failure to submit the forms referred to 'left the respondents with the impression that for some reason . . . the claimants no longer wished to work for them'. Following the late submission of the forms the respondents offered alternative employment to the claimants but this was rejected. The EAT held:

> 'The Tribunal determines that there was a transfer of undertaking in this case which was accepted by the respondents. The recommendation of the Rights Commissioner is therefore overturned. The Tribunal is not satisfied that the claimants were made sufficiently aware of their entitlements under the transfer of undertaking to the extent that the respondents did not fulfil their obligation to their employees. Consequently the Tribunal finds that the claimants were unfairly dismissed. The Tribunal is however unanimous in finding that the claimants contributed substantially by not making their position sufficiently clear to the employer.'

The employees' contribution was taken into account in calculating the modest amounts of compensation awarded by the EAT.

11.8.6.4   What is transferred?

Regulation 4 provides:

> 'The transferor's rights and obligations of the transferor arising from a contract of employment existing on the date of a transfer shall, by reason of such transfer, be transferred to the transferee.'

These provisions give rise to the question as to what precisely is transferred when the transfer of an undertaking occurs. Contracts of employment and the terms and conditions that apply between an employer and an employee or worker are not easily ascertainable. The nature of employment relationships is such that the terms, conditions, rights and obligations of the parties are rarely clearly laid out and arise from a number of sources, some giving rise to legal rights and obligations which may only be altered at the instance of, and with the consent of, both parties, and others which are merely prescriptive or arise for administrative convenience which may be altered, varied or removed at the instance of one of the parties, often the employer.

In order to appreciate the full scope of the Directive and Regulations regard must be had to existing Irish law and practice on terms and conditions of employment and how they can be changed or varied.

In *Rask and Christensen v ISS Kantineservice A/S* [1993] IRLR 133 ISS had made some relatively minor changes to the terms and conditions of employment of the plaintiffs when they transferred. Instead of paying salaries on the last Thursday of the month they paid them on the last working day of a month and employees no longer received allowances for laundry or for shoes, which they claimed were part of their pay prior to the transfer. In *Rask* the ECJ held (at p 134):

388

'Article 3 of the Directive must be interpreted as meaning that on the transfer the terms of the contract of employment or of the employment relationship relating to salary, and in particular to its date of payment and composition, may not be varied, notwithstanding that the total amount remains unchanged.

'The Directive does not however preclude a variation of the employment relationship with the new employer insofar as national law allows the employment relationship to be altered in a manner unfavourable to employees in situations other than the transfer of an undertaking provided that the transfer of the undertaking itself is not the reason for the alteration. The Directive is intended to extend the protection guaranteed to workers independently by the laws of Member States to cover the case where an undertaking is transferred. It is not intended to establish a uniform level of protection throughout the Community. Thus the Directive can be relied on only to ensure that the employee concerned is protected in his relations with the transferee to the same extent as he was in his relations with the transferor under national law.'

It may be seen therefore that where the laws of Member States within the European Union allow for contracts, terms or conditions of employment to be changed or alterations made in employment relationships, then, provided that the transferor could do so, there is nothing to prevent the transferee doing so. Regard must be had, however, to regulation 5 as dealt with at **11.9.1** below which precludes changes arising directly as a result of the fact of the transfer. These situations will, however, be rare.

11.8.7 DATE OF TRANSFER AND EXISTENCE OF RIGHTS AND OBLIGATIONS

The rights of employees which become subject to transfer and the obligations of the transferee consequent on the transfer depend on what rights and obligations were in existence as of the date of transfer as per regulation 4(1). In order to ascertain the full extent of such rights and obligations the existence of a contract of employment or employment relationship as of the date of transfer must be established and there must then be an analysis of the terms and conditions applying as between the parties to ascertain what exactly transfers.

In *Secretary of State for Employment v Spence* [1986] IRLR 248 the UK Court of Appeal held that where a company was in receivership and employees were dismissed at 11.00 a.m. on 28 November 1983 and an agreement for the sale of the business was concluded at 2.00 p.m. on 29 November 1983, the contracts of employment of the employees did not subsist at the moment of transfer and their contracts of employment did not therefore transfer on the sale of the business. This decision was greatly qualified in *Litster v Forth Dry Dock and Engineering Co Ltd* [1989] IRLR 161 referred to at **11.8.8.1** below, albeit directly related to the interpretation of UK regulation 5. The ECJ has effectively confirmed Litster and the potential liability of a transferee for dismissals effected immediately before transfer by a transferor in *Dethier v Dassy and Sovam SPRL (in liquidation)* 12 March 1998 (unreported).

Where an employment relationship does not exist at the date of transfer the transferee has no liability for the former employee of the transferor. In *Wendelboe v LJ Music ApS (in liquidation)* [1985] ECR 457 Mr Wendelboe and two colleagues were employed by LJ Music, a company which made cassette recordings, until 28 February 1980 on which date they were made redundant with immediate effect as the company was in financial difficulty. On 4 March 1980 the company was declared insolvent. At the bankruptcy hearing on 4 March a director of the company, who had been one of its employees, proposed that the business including premises, stock and machines be purchased by another company, SPKR. The final agreement on the transfer was concluded on 27 March 1980. The Bankruptcy Court did, however, authorise SPKR to use the insolvent business's premises and equipment as and from 5 March 1980. The final agreement of 27 March specified that the company's business was deemed to have been carried out on behalf of and at the risk of SPKR from 4 March 1980. On 6 March 1980, six days after their dismissal, Mr Wendelboe and his two colleagues were engaged by SPKR. Wendelboe and his colleagues brought an action against the insolvent company which argued inter alia that as there was a continuing employment relationship the transferee company, SPKR, was liable in respect of any damages for unfair dismissal. In considering the issues put to it the ECJ in the course of its judgment held that the Directive does not apply to rights and obligations of workers whose contract of employment or employment relationship had terminated or ceased at the time of transfer. The court in *Wendelboe* did not analyse the actual date of transfer in any particular detail but it is implicit from the judgment that the date of transfer must have been held to be 27 March. The judgment is a general one and does not specifically deal with Mr Wendelboe but does make it clear that if an employee is not employed in an undertaking on the date of transfer—and date of transfer is a matter of fact to be decided by national courts—there is then no obligation on the transferee in respect of rights or obligations arising from the contract of employment or employment relationship with the transferor.

11.8.8 TIME OF TRANSFER OR DATE OF TRANSFER?

11.8.8.1 Time of transfer and date of transfer distinguished

In *Wendelboe* the ECJ used the expressions 'date of transfer' and 'time of transfer' as if they were identical terms. They are clearly not. Commercial arrangements and transfers may take place in phases or in stages rather than at a precise moment. In order to ensure that the purpose of the Directive is achieved it would appear that 'time of transfer' would allow more scope than the more precise term 'date of transfer'. Article 3(1) is, however, quite clear in its use of the term 'date of transfer'. The Irish Regulations also use the term date of transfer. A more purposive approach than that taken in *Secretary of State for Employment v Spence* [1986] IRLR 248 was taken by the House of Lords in *Litster v Forth Dry Dock and Engineering Co Ltd* [1989] IRLR 161. In *Litster* the transferor and transferee arrived at an agreement prior to the transfer that the transferor would dismiss employees in order that the transferee would benefit from the hiring of other and cheaper labour after the transfer. In order to continue the business employees were needed and therefore, under regulation 5, the employees were held to be entitled to transfer and liability under the Directive and UK Regulations was held to be that of the transferee. As of the actual date of transfer there were no contracts of employment or employment relationships in existence. Adopting the 'date of transfer' terminology in the Directive would have allowed the aim of the Directive to be defeated in situations such as arose in *Litster*. To ensure that the purpose of the Directive was met the House of Lords was prepared to imply into the terminology of the UK Regulations a term that the rights conferred by those regulations on persons 'employed immediately before the transfer' also cover persons who 'would have been so employed if they had not been unfairly dismissed in the circumstances'.

11.8.8.2 Transfer over period of time

Case law indicates that courts and tribunals are prepared to allow that a transfer may take place over a period of time, thereby giving the coverage of the Directive and Regulations to employees who were employed in the undertaking at any time over that period (*A & G Tuck Ltd v Bartlett* [1994] IRLR 162 and *Dabell v Vale Industrial Services (Nottingham) Ltd* [1988] IRLR 439).

In *Dabell* there had been dealings between the proposed transferor and transferee over a period of time but the proposed transfer was subsequently abandoned. Dabell was employed by Vale Industrial Services which became technically insolvent. Nofotech made an offer for the purchase of Vale's business. An agreement was reached in principle and various assets, machines, materials, orders and debtors transferred. Three employees of Vale, including Mr Dabell, worked for Nofotech for a short period during which time they were paid by Nofotech. A short time later Dabell tendered his resignation to Nofotech claiming constructive dismissal. The negotiations between Nofotech and Vale subsequently ran into difficulty and the proposed merger was abandoned. Dabell maintained his claim against Nofotech. In the circumstances of that case the UK Court of Appeal held:

> '[T]here had been a transfer of the business of Vale Industrial Services to Nofotech prior to the appellant's resignation from Nofotech notwithstanding that the merger was subsequently called off.
>
> 'Whether or not there has been a transfer of a business must be decided as at the date when the act of which the employee complains occurred. In the present case at the date of the appellant's resignation Vale had closed its premises and everything had been handed over to Nofotech—machines, customer connection, goodwill, existing contracts and employees. There was clearly a transfer of the undertaking on the ordinary meaning of the words.'

In *Dabell* Balcombe LJ in an obiter dictum stated (at p 443):

> 'The argument on behalf of the respondents that there had not been a final and conclusive transfer of ownership at the date of the appellant's resignation would mean that, even if the deal had come to full fruition as in most cases it probably would have, the appellant would not have been entitled to claim unfair dismissal by Nofotech. That would make no kind of sense on the facts of the present case.'

In *Longden and Paisley v Ferrari Ltd* [1994] IRLR 157 the second-named respondent purchased the business of Ferrari Ltd from receivers by way of a single sale of assets agreement which had been concluded on foot of a course of dealing over a period of weeks. At the time of the conclusion of the sale of assets agreement the appellants were not employed in the business. Their claims under the Transfer of Undertaking Regulations failed because they were not employed in the transfer of business 'immediately before' the transfer of the undertaking. In this case the UK EAT looked at the transactions engaged in between the transferee and the receivers and held that, while there existed a series of linked transactions, the transfer of the undertaking was not 'effected' by the series of transactions but was effected by the conclusion of the final agreement and at the time it was effected the appellants were not in employment and therefore not subject to transfer. The UK EAT held inter alia:

> 'In the present case although there was a succession of events which could be described as causally linked to one another and to the ultimate conclusion of the sale agreement the transfer was not effected by those earlier transactions. The transfer took place on completion of the agreement.'

11.8.8.3   Purposive approach by courts

Courts and tribunals have tended to take a more purposive approach to the construction of the date of transfer then was taken in the *Longden and Paisley* case following the lead given by the House of Lords in *Litster*. In *Macer v Abafast Ltd* [1990] IRLR 137 a transfer took place through a series of transactions which involved a 12-day gap in employment for Mr Macer. The UK EAT closed that gap by following *Litster* and as it had been admitted by Abafast Ltd that it had engineered the 12-day gap in employment to break Mr Macer's statutory continuity of service which was not allowed by the UK EAT. What the employee actually does during the gap in service may be relevant to the determination as to whether or not he was employed at the date or time of transfer.

In *Justfern Ltd v Skaife D'Ingerthorpe* [1994] IRLR 164 the UK EAT held that where an employee was in receipt of unemployment benefit for a period of one week between the closing of a business and its subsequent purchase he was on a liberal construction of the words 'at the time of the transfer' available for work and therefore effectively still in employment and stated:

'The receipt of unemployment benefit is not inconsistent with availability for employment in the business in which an employee had been lately employed. A liberal construction of the words "at the time of the transfer" accords with the evident policy of the legislature to preserve continuity of employment . . . regulation 17(2) is capable of operating a cross and interval greater than a week. It followed that it is capable of bridging a similar period of uncertainty as to whether or not an employee will be re-employed by the purchaser of the business. The receipt of unemployment benefit does no more than create such uncertainty. It does not eliminate the possibility even on a short-term basis of such employment. There is a major distinction between applying for and receiving unemployment benefit because wages have ceased and taking on another job. Accordingly, the employee's application for and receipt of unemployment benefit did not result in an interruption in his employment such as to make it impossible to treat his employment with the [transferee] . . . as continuous with his employment with the [transferor].'

Article 3(4), in referring to pension rights and the necessity to protect the interest of employees and of persons no longer employed, refers to 'at the time of the transfer'. The wording of the Directive does not therefore draw a distinction between the terms 'date of transfer' and 'time of transfer' and it appears to be left to the ECJ to give some further interpretation as to how strictly the term 'date of transfer' will be applied and whether or not the expression 'time of transfer' allows for a widening of the timing of the occurrence of the transfer from the 24-hour period clearly provided within the expression 'date of transfer'.

11.8.9 CAN EMPLOYEES AGREE CHANGES PRIOR TO OR AT TIME OF TRANSFER?

11.8.9.1 Introduction

While it may appear commercially desirable, and indeed desirable in the context of ongoing industrial relations, that the parties to an employment relationship should remain free to agree changes in terms and conditions of employment regardless of whether or not a transfer is or has taken place within the meaning of the Directive, the legality of agreed changes in the event that there is a transfer within the meaning of the Directive is unclear. While there are no contracting-out provisions in the Directive or Regulations the application of the Directive is mandatory and therefore it is not open to the parties to a transfer to avoid its provisions. If the parties reach agreement that something should occur, such as a variation in terms and conditions, which the transferor and transferee are prohibited by the Directive from doing themselves, is such variation valid?

In *Foreningen af Arbejdsledere i Danmark v Daddy's Dance Hall A/S* [1988] IRLR 315 the ECJ set out the general principle which suggests that an employee cannot agree a change even where it may be advantageous holding as referred to above and qualified in *Rask and Christensen v ISS Kantineservice A/S* [1993] IRLR 133, also referred to at **11.8.1.1** above.

In two joined appeals the UK Court of Appeal considered whether or not the Directive prohibited agreed changes in terms and conditions between the transferee and the employees whose employment had been or was about to be transferred. The court considered the question in the cases of *Wilson v St Helens Borough Council and Meade and Baxendale v British Fuels Ltd* [1977] IRLR 505.

The facts of the two cases were different and, while the appeals were joined as one, different conclusions were reached in each case.

11.8.9.2 *Wilson v St Helens Borough Council*

In *Wilson v St Helens Borough Council* the employees were employed in a home for boys with behavioural problems. They were employed by Lancashire County Council which gave notice, to the trustees of the home, that they would cease to manage the home due to funding problems. St Helens Council agreed to take over responsibility on certain terms. Lancashire County Council entered into negotiations with the trade union which was representative of the staff and it was agreed that staff numbers would be reduced from 162 to 72 and that those transferring to St Helens would be appointed to new posts with different job descriptions. Those not transferring were redeployed by Lancashire. The staff to be transferred were dismissed by Lancashire by reason of redundancy and were re-employed with immediate effect by St Helens Council but on different terms and conditions from they had enjoyed with Lancashire. Some of the employees brought claims that the changed terms and conditions worked a detriment on them as compared to the terms and conditions they had enjoyed.

The UK EAT held that if the operative reason for an agreed variation in terms and conditions is the transfer of an undertaking the variation is ineffective and the terms of the original contract of employment remain in force. The UK EAT held that the principle of automatic transfer contained in the Directive is mandatory and precludes even a consensual variation.

The UK Court of Appeal, however, did not address that very important issue and took a different approach to the facts of the situation. The court focused on the reason for the change and sought to categorise it within the category of 'economic, technical or organisational reasons entailing changes in the workforce' which allows, in certain circumstances, for termination of employment in the context of a transfer within the meaning of the Directive. In doing so the UK Court of Appeal avoided answering the question as to whether terms and conditions may be consensually varied at the time of or immediately after a transfer. The court held that the termination by Lancashire County Council of the employment of Wilson and the other applicants was a permissible termination and therefore St Helens Council was starting from a position of having no obligations transferred to it. There was therefore not a variation but rather a termination by Lancashire, which was permitted within the terms of the Directive, and the creation of new contracts on new terms and conditions between St Helens and the employees concerned. St Helens therefore did not have liability to the employees for detriment suffered arising from or in comparison with the terms and conditions they enjoyed with Lancashire.

11.8.9.3   *Meade and Baxendale v British Fuels Ltd*

Meade and Baxendale had similar facts but arrived at a different conclusion. The two men worked for National Fuel Distributors (NFD) which merged with the British Fuels Group to form British Fuels Ltd (BFL). NFD gave notice of dismissal on grounds of redundancy to both men. On the same day they received notice they were offered employment with BFL on less favourable terms and conditions including a lower rate of pay. The letter of offer noted that their previous service had been 'bought out' by the redundancy and severance payments made by NFD. BFL were unaware that the Directive applied. Meade and Baxendale took up employment with BFL and some months later signed statements of terms and conditions reflecting their new terms. A year later they sought declarations that they were still employed on the terms and conditions they had enjoyed with NFD.

The UK Court of Appeal held that, on the evidence, the transfer of the undertaking itself was the reason for the dismissal of both Meade and Baxendale. The purported dismissal was ineffective within the terms of the Directive and the original contracts of employment continued as if made with the transferee BFL. Subsequent agreement with BFL on different terms and conditions could not limit the operation of the terms of the Directive since the transfer or a reason connected with it remained the principal reason for the alteration.

While the ECJ appears to have left some discretion to courts in Member States to determine whether or not changes to a contract are allowable within the law of that Member

State, *Meade and Baxendale* was not determined on whether or not the employees had validly agreed changes to their contract within the contract law of the UK but rather allowed the two employees to argue either that there was no real intention to change their contracts, or they did so under a mistaken belief that they may have had no option or, indeed, even been obliged to do so and the Directive applied to set aside their apparent consensual variation in their contracts of employment. The UK Court of Appeal reasoned that there was a direct causal link between the transfer and the dismissal of Meade and Baxendale; therefore the dismissal was a nullity as also effectively was the variation of terms and conditions, which was, on the face of it, valid at common law, because it too had a causal link to the transfer.

11.8.9.4   Conclusion

It appears therefore that changes may only be agreed or imposed where the first pre-transfer contract has come to an end for economic, technical or organisational reasons. Following this line of reasoning employers will encounter considerable practical difficulties where the terms and conditions of a workforce which is merged with or added to an existing workforce are considerably different from the existing workforce and it will take considerable time and effort to reach a position of harmonisation of both. It would appear, however, following *Wilson* and *Meade and Baxendale* that the employer is not in a position to negotiate or agree changes with employees unless their contracts are validly terminated within the terms of the Directive and domestic regulations prior to the transfer in which event the transferee is starting with a clean slate. See the House of Lords decision in these joined cases: *Wilson v St Helens Borough Council* and *British Fuels Ltd v Baxendale and Meade* [1998] IRLR 706.

11.8.10   NO OBLIGATION ON EMPLOYEES TO TRANSFER

It should be kept in mind at all times in contemplating a purchase of a business or effecting a transfer that employees are not obliged to transfer. In *Katsikas v Konstantinidis and Skreb* [1993] IRLR 179 the ECJ held that, in the event of a transfer, employees were entitled to object to the transfer. What then happens to the contract of employment is a matter for each Member State to determine. The ECJ has made its view as to what happens very clear in a number of cases, notably *Mikkelsen v Danmols Inventar A/S* [1986] 1 CMLR 316 where the court stated (para 16):

> 'The protection which the Directive is intended to guarantee is however redundant where the person concerned decides of his own accord not to continue the employment relationship with the new employer after the transfer. That is the case where the employee in question terminates the employment contract or employment relationship of his own free will with effect from the date of the transfer or where that contract or relationship is terminated with effect from the date of the transfer by virtue of an agreement voluntarily concluded between the worker and the transferor or the transferee of the undertaking. In that situation Article 3(1) of the Directive does not apply.'

The ECJ further stated in *Merckx and Neuhuys v Ford Motor Company Belgium SA* [1996] IRLR 467:

> 'Article 3(1) of Directive 77/187 does not preclude an employee employed by the transferor at the date of the transfer of an undertaking from objecting to the transfer to the transferee of the contract of employment or the employment relationship. In such a case it is for the Member States to determine what the fate of the contract or employment relationship with the transferor should be.'

11.9 Trade Unions

11.9.1 LEGISLATIVE PROVISIONS

The status and rights of trade unions and employee representatives are sought to be protected in the transfer of undertakings by virtue of the provisions of Article 5 of the Directive, which the explanatory note states was intended not to interfere 'with existing national arrangements and structures of workers' representative bodies'.

Regulation 7 provides as follows:

'Where an undertaking or business or part of a undertaking or business the subject of a transfer, preserves its autonomy after the transfer, the status and function of the representatives or of the representation of the employees affected by the transfer shall be preserved by the transferee concerned On the same terms and subject to the same conditions as existed before the date of the transfer as specified in any enactment, or in any agreement between the employer and the employee's representatives.'

11.9.2 UNION RECOGNITION

Employees who exercise a constitutional right to join a trade union cannot insist that they enjoy the full benefit of such membership by in turn insisting that the employer recognise their union. The right conferred by the Constitution is an individual personal right and does not carry with it the concomitant obligation on an employer to recognise that trade union, according to the judgment of McWilliam J in *Abbott and Whelan v ITGWU* [1982] 1 JISLL 56. The plaintiffs were members of a trade union, the ATGWU. Their employer, the Southern Health Board, had a formal recognition agreement with the ITGWU. The plaintiffs sought to insist that their employer deal with the trade union of their choice and, when the board refused, the plaintiffs brought the matter to the High Court claiming inter alia that the defendants were interfering with or obstructing them in the exercise of their constitutional right to join the trade union of their choice and what they claimed was the further right to be represented by such trade union in the conduct of negotiations with their employers concerning wages and other conditions of employment. In his judgment McWilliam J referred to article 40.6.1(iii) of the Constitution and the rights conferred on the plaintiffs and other citizens by that provision, considered in *Meskell v CIE* [1973] IR 121 and *Educational Company of Ireland v Fitzpatrick* [1961] IR 345 where active steps were taken to compel the citizens to forgo their constitutional rights, and held that there was no attempt to compel the plaintiffs to forgo their constitutional rights in this particular case stating (at p 60):

'Insofar as the Board is concerned it appears to me to be clear that the plaintiffs have no constitutional right to compel the Board to engage in negotiations either with them or with their union . . .

'In the present case, the plaintiffs have joined ATGWU without first ascertaining whether that union would or would not be in a position to negotiate with the Board. Employers must frequently have refused to negotiate with employees or their unions and this may have led to industrial action but, outside the terms of the contract of employment, employers are not bound to take part in any, or any particular form of, negotiations.

'On the facts of this case I am of the opinion that the refusal of the Board to negotiate with ATGWU is not coercion to forgo a constitutional right within the principles which have been enunciated.'

11.9.3   IMPLIED RECOGNITION

In the absence of a specific contractual provision that the employee's trade union will be recognised it is arguable that, where an employee is a member of a union and the employer is dealing with or had dealt with that union, there is an implied term in the contract between the employer and the employee to the effect that the employee's union will be recognised. In the context of a transfer of an undertaking the employee could then seek to rely on the provisions of the Directive by claiming that his right to have his union recognised is something that arises from the existence of an employment relationship at the date of transfer. In this regard the Directive refers to 'rights and obligations . . . arising from . . . an employment relationship'. The employment relationship could be deemed to involve a trade union where a person is a member and is actively represented by such union.

The absence of a system of formal recognition in Ireland allows that recognition may arise by express agreement but also by implied agreement. Recognition could be implied from a course of dealing between the parties and by the recognition, albeit in limited ways, of a trade union for certain purposes such as in disciplinary hearings. In *National Union of Tailors and Garment Workers v Charles Ingram & Co Ltd* [1977] IRLR 147, the UK EAT, in a case relating to recognition of a trade union for the purpose of redundancy consultations, held in relation to recognition:

> 'Recognition implies agreement which involves consent. Where, as in the present case, there is neither a written agreement that the union should be recognised nor an express agreement which is not in writing it is sufficient if the established facts are clear and unequivocal and give rise to the clear inference that the employers have recognised the union. This will normally involve conduct over a period of time and the longer that state of facts has existed the easier it is to reach a conclusion that the employers have recognised the union.'

11.9.4   PICKETING BY EMPLOYEES OF A TRANSFEROR

The High Court, and on appeal the Supreme Court, granted an interlocutory injunction to the purchaser of a pub to restrain a picket placed by employees of the former owners in *Westman Holdings Ltd v McCormack* [1992] 1 IR 151. The defendants in the case had been employed in a pub which was sold to the plaintiff. Before the completion of the sale the defendants and all other members of staff were dismissed. The defendants sought employment with the new owner, the plaintiff, but were refused. When the new owners re-opened the premises an official picket was placed on the pub. As none of the defendants had ever been employed by the new owner, the plaintiff, it was argued that the plaintiff could not constitute their 'employer' within the meaning of section 11(1) of the 1990 Act.

The High Court granted an interlocutory injunction restraining the picketing on the basis that the plaintiff had raised a fair question and because the balance of convenience was in its favour. That decision was upheld by the Supreme Court. The case did not appear again before either the High Court or the Supreme Court and therefore the benefit of their observations on the effect of the Directive and Regulations on the transfer of a trade dispute is not available. From the available information it is not clear if the Directive and Regulations were referred to at all in either hearing and it appears that the case was dealt with purely as a trade dispute under the 1990 Act.

It appears that following the ECJ decisions *d'Urso v Ercole Marelli Elettromeccanica Generale SpA* [1992] IRLR 136 and *Rotsart de Hertaing v J Benoidt SA (in liquidation)* [1997] IRLR 127 picketing by employees of a transferor directed against a transferee must be held to be valid and protected, provided all of the other requirements of the 1990 Act are complied with. Injunctive relief may still be available to a transferee under the 1990 Act provided the applicant for injunctive relief can establish that there is a fair question to be tried at the hearing of the action and that the balance of convenience is in favour of granting such relief (*Bayzana Ltd v Galligan* [1987] IR 241).

11.9.5 TRANSFER-RELATED DISMISSALS AND ORGANISATIONAL CHANGES ARISING FROM TRANSFER

In the Directive Article 4 allows for dismissals to take place for ecomonic, technical or organisational reasons entailing changes in the workforce. No guidance is given as to what is meant by any of the terms 'economic', 'technical' or 'organisational', nor is there any guidance given as to the extent of 'changes in the workforce' which may or must result following on such dismissals. It is left to the individual Member States and their courts and tribunals to determine what is or is not allowable.

Article 4 does not provide for sanctions against an employer who breaches its terms. That is again left to the Member States and courts and tribunals within those Member States.

Regulation 5 of the Irish Regulations provides similar protection but with some important difference in wording and emphasis as follows:

> '(1) *The transfer of an undertaking, business or part of an undertaking or business shall not in itself constitute grounds for dismissal by the transferor or the transferee and such a dismissal, the grounds for which are such a transfer, by a transferor or a transferee is prohibited.*
>
> (2) *Nothing in this Regulation shall be construed as prohibiting dismissals for economic, technical or organisational reasons entailing changes in the work force.*
>
> (3) *If a contract of employment is terminated because the transfer involves a substantial change in working conditions to the detriment of the employee concerned, the employer concerned shall be regarded as having been responsible for termination of the contract of employment.'*

11.9.6 TRANSFER-RELATED DISMISSALS

It is not uncommon in trying to circumvent the Directive and Regulations that the transferee of a business will require that the transferor terminate the employment of some or all of the employees prior to the transfer. The ECJ held in *P Bork International A/S (in liquidation) v Foreningen af Arbejdsledere i Danmark* [1989] IRLR 41 that where employees were dismissed on 22 December 1981, when a company ceased operation, and were re-employed on 30 December 1981 by the purchaser of the business the reason for the termination was the transfer itself. The court found this as a fact in light of the evidence to the effect that the dismissals took place at a time close to the date of transfer and the workers concerned were subsequently re-engaged. The court held that in order to give effect to the Regulations the workers must be considered as still employed in the undertaking on the date of the transfer with the consequent effect that the Regulations/Directive apply to them. The ECJ stated in its judgment:

> '[I]t is appropriate to take account of all the factual circumstances surrounding the transaction which may include in particular whether the tangible and intangible assets have been transferred as well as a major part of the staff of the undertaking, the degree of similarity between its activities before and after the transfer and the duration of any period of stoppage connected with the transfer. The fact that the undertaking was temporarily closed and did not have any employees at the time of the transfer was a factor to be taken into consideration for the purpose of determining whether an economic entity which was still in existence had been transferred. However it was not in itself sufficient to preclude the existence of a transfer within the meaning of Article 1(1) particularly in a situation such as the present case in which the undertaking ceased its

operations for only a short period which also coincided with the end-of-the-year holidays.'

'Hiving down' or requiring pre-transfer dismissals is prohibited.

11.9.7 SLIMMING DOWN AND LIABILITY FOR SEVERANCE COSTS

Any attempt by a purchaser or transferee to negotiate or deal with a transferor and procure that the transferor bring about structural or organisational changes in order that the transferee can take over a slimmed-down or reduced workforce will clearly impact on the transferee and, having regard to the automatic transfer of liabilities as referred to in *Rotsart de Hertaing v J Benoidt SA* [1997] IRLR 127, the only possibility the transferee has of mitigating the effect of these provisions is to secure sufficient effective indemnities. Such indemnities will only apply as between the transferor and the transferee. As far as the employees are concerned the transferee is the one who will carry liability to them. It is therefore advisable that reorganisation, restructuring or reduction of a workforce should be carried out by the transferee, leaving the transferee in the best position to justify its own actions in terminating the employment of certain of the workforce. That will not help the transferee, however, in costing the takeover of the business from the transferor. The transferee will not want to carry potentially substantial severance payments immediately after purchasing a business but again this is a matter it will have to plan for in its negotiations with the transferor.

A transferee should not seek to have liability for such payments imposed on the transferor by having the transferor reduce or reorganise the workforce on the basis of someone else's (the transferee's) reasons or plans for doing so. The transferee is better placed to deal with all issues arising consequent on termination of employment of any of the workforce as a result of the transfer. If the transferee does not want to be exposed to the cost of having to do so, provision may be made to recover the cost from the transferor or make some provision for the reservation of sufficient funds for this purpose; however, the level of severance payments the workforce might seek may not be easily predictable. If the workforce were to hold out for substantially higher payments than may have been paid in the past, and the parties have done their calculations based on such historical payments, difficulties may arise and great care must be taken by both parties in planning for the costs of rationalisation or reduction in the workforce consequent on a transfer.

11.10 The ETO Defence

11.10.1 GENERALLY

The Directive and Regulations provide that nothing shall prohibit dismissal for economic, technical or organisational ('ETO') reasons entailing changes in the workforce. In the main this may be construed as coming within the statutory definition of redundancy. It does, however, appear to go a stage further. In *Anderson v Dalkeith Engineering Ltd* [1984] IRLR 429, on similar facts to *Litster v Forth Dry Dock and Engineering Co Ltd* [1989] IRLR 161, new owners employed many of the workforce dismissed by a receiver prior to a transfer. Those not re-employed complained of unfair dismissal. It was held that the dismissals were not unfair. It was held that the motives of the purchaser in seeking the dismissals were irrelevant to the consideration of whether the vendor had acted fairly. The UK EAT held that what was relevant was the reasons of the receiver, not the acquiring company. The reasons of the receiver were economic. In order to get the best price for the business the receiver was obliged to dismiss the workforce.

It appears the effect of this decision is that if the transferor can satisfactorily show that in order to sell the business he had no option but to dismiss some or all of the workforce those dismissals will not be unfair. It may well be that the transferor/vendor of the business can anticipate generally what an as-yet-unknown transferor or purchaser would look for in such a business and, indeed, if the business is in poor commercial health it may be prudent to make such changes regardless of whether the business is ever sold or transferred, but in many cases the vendor or transferor will know who the likely purchaser/transferee is. They will very often have discussions and negotiations with that party and the prospective purchaser/transferee is very likely to give an indication as to the type of business structure or numbers employed that they would consider to be ideal. In that instance it would be very difficult for a vendor/transferor to claim, as their own, the reasons for restructuring and effecting dismissals albeit within domestic redundancy laws. The best practice would seem to be for the transferee to effect the necessary changes and accommodate the cost of doing so in their contract with the vendor/transferor.

Where a transferee requires the imposition of pre-transfer manpower structures or requirements it is prudent that a transferor enquire into the reasons of the transferee for doing so; otherwise it may well be held that the transferor did not have a reason of substance by virtue of his unquestioning acceptance of the requirements of the transferee. The change in judicial approach to, and interpretation of, the Directive and Regulations in recent years is such that liability will almost always be deemed to be that of the transferee. The reasoning should therefore be that of the transferee. Employers have found it difficult to justify making changes prior to a transfer in order to make their business more saleable or more attractive (*Wheeler v Patel* [1987] IRLR 211, *Gateway Hotels Ltd v Stewart* [1988] IRLR 287 and *Ibex Trading Co Ltd v Walton* [1994] IRLR 564).

11.10.2 CHANGES IN THE WORKFORCE

11.10.2.1 Harmonisation of terms and conditions

It is essential that the ETO reasons must entail 'changes in the workforce'. This normally requires a change in the numbers of people employed to perform particular functions, not merely a change in their terms and conditions (*Berriman v Delabole Slate Ltd* [1985] IRLR 305). Where a transferee purchases a business or part of a business to add to a pre-existing business, difficulties may arise where attempts are made to harmonise terms and conditions as between the two groups of employees.

11.10.2.2 Employees surplus to requirements

If, after a transfer, employees are surplus to the transferee's requirements and could in a non-transfer situation be properly regarded as redundant, then the ETO defence will apply (see *Gorictree Ltd v Jenkinson* [1984] IRLR 391 and *Trafford v Sharpe & Fisher (Building Supplies) Ltd* [1994] IRLR 325).

11.10.2.3 Economic reasons

Where an employer seeks to justify changes on economic grounds this does not entitle the employer to reduce the employee's remuneration. In *Meikle v McPhail* [1983] IRLR 351 the new owner of a pub, who had accepted liability for existing employees when he took over the premises, realised after he took control of the business that substantial economies would have to be made and, as a result, made all of the staff, with one exception, redundant. Mrs Meikle challenged the decision to make her redundant and, in the absence of being able to show that she should have had preference over an employee who was retained, she failed in her claim as the employer relied on the economic defence available in the Directive and Regulations.

The UK EAT has held that the economic reason for the dismissal must relate to the conduct of the business, and therefore a desire to obtain an enhanced price for the business or to achieve a sale is not a reason which relates to the conduct of the business, and is therefore not an economic reason. In that particular case the reason for the dismissal was the vendor's wish to comply with the requirements of the intending purchaser who wanted the workforce reduced and this was held not to be capable of coming within the term 'economic'. The UK EAT also stated in that case that the word 'economic' cannot be read on its own as to do so would be to give the term very wide meaning and would allow for dismissals in far more situations than had been envisaged by the Directive and Regulations. The UK EAT suggested that the approach that might be taken would be to limit the meaning of the word and stated 'the adjective economic' must be construed ejusdem generis with the adjectives 'technical' and 'organisational'. The approach to the construction of the word 'economic' adopted in *Wheeler v Patel* [1987] IRLR 211 was followed by the UK EAT in *Gateway Hotels Ltd v Stewart* [1988] IRLR 287.

Gateway operated a hotel which was making a loss and they agreed the sale of the hotel as a going concern to another company which made it a condition of the sale that Gateway would terminate the employment of all of the employees in the business prior to takeover. Gateway were very unhappy with this and tried to persuade the purchaser to remove the condition, but as they were anxious not to lose the sale, they ultimately had to agree to the term and dismissed all of the staff. The staff claimed against Gateway on the basis of their belief that there should have been an automatic transfer of their employment to the purchaser. Gateway pleaded that there was an 'economic' reason for the terminations. The UK EAT upheld the decision of the industrial tribunal that the reason for the dismissals was the transfer of the undertaking and not on 'economic' grounds.

Attempts by transferors to facilitate transferees by dismissing staff before the transfer are unlikely to survive the tests laid down by the ECJ, particularly in *Rotsart de Hertaing v J Benoidt SA* [1997] IRLR 127 coupled with *Litster v Forth Dry Dock and Engineering Co Ltd* [1989] IRLR 161, and even if the employees were to be re-engaged it could still be held to be a breach of the Directive as commented on by Advocate-General Slynn in *Wendelboe v LJ Music ApS* [1985] ECR 457 when he stated:

> 'When employees are dismissed, with a view to, and before, a transfer falling within the Directive and are re-engaged immediately by the transferee thereafter, their dismissal must be regarded as contrary to Article 4(1) subject to the exceptions specified in that paragraph.'

11.10.3   REASON FOR DISMISSAL—TRANSFER OR ETO?

It is a feature of many of the cases where the ETO defence is pleaded that employees claim the reason for their dismissal was the transfer per se and therefore their dismissal was prohibited, whereas the transferor or transferee claims that the reasons were economic, technical or organisational.

In *Porter and Nanayakkara v Queens Medical Centre* [1993] IRLR 486 the plaintiffs were employed by a health authority as consultant paediatricians. The authority had contracts with two hospitals for the provision of paediatric services. The authority decided to reorganise the service and terminated the arrangement with the two hospitals, entering into a new contract with the defendants. The defendants looked at alternative ways of providing the paediatric service and decided to restructure by creating four new consultant paediatrician posts. These posts carried different responsibilities and obligations from the consultant posts previously held by the plaintiffs with the health authority. The plaintiffs applied for two of the 'new' posts but were unsuccessful. As a result of the restructuring of the transferee the plaintiffs were made redundant. The plaintiffs claimed that they were dismissed by reason of the transfer of the undertaking. The UK High Court held that the transfer of the service to the defendants was a transfer of an undertaking stating:

'Although the dismissal of the plaintiffs on the grounds of redundancy was a consequence of the transfer of the undertaking the termination was not invalidated by Article 4(1) of the Directive which provides that the transfer of an undertaking "shall not in itself constitute grounds for dismissal by the transferor or the transferee".

'The changed methods which the defendants intended to introduce to provide the services required amounted to a reorganisation entailing changes in the workforce. Since the defendants were introducing a new organisation which required that they should be free to make an uninhibited choice in filling the posts concerned the change in the workforce which was entailed by organisational reasons was the termination of the existing contracts.'

See also *Ibex Trading Co Ltd v Walton* [1994] IRLR 564.

11.10.4 MOTIVATION FOR CHANGE

In order for employers to rely on the ETO defence they must be able to show that their decision was a bona fide decision to make changes and that those changes entailed changes in the workforce. The motivation factor mirrors the requirement in redundancy law that the dismissal must be 'wholly or mainly' by reason of redundancy (Redundancy Payments Act, 1967, section 7(2)).

11.10.5 ETO AND REDUNDANCY

11.10.5.1 *Morris v Smart Brothers Ltd*

The Irish cases have tended to equate the ETO defence with the concept of redundancy, particularly decisions of the EAT. In *Morris v Smart Brothers Ltd* UD 688/93 the EAT examined a situation where Smart Brothers had operated eight retail clothing outlets in Dublin together with a head office, warehouse and wholesale business. When the company ran into trading difficulties it was broken up and various of the shops were sold off, some to co-respondents of Smart Brothers in this particular case. The EAT had to consider the position of employees in some of the stores which had changed hands and continued to operate and where the employees had claimed they were entitled to remain in employment in the stores by reason of the protections afforded by the Directive and Regulations. The EAT held that there had been transfer of an undertaking in the sale of shops to some of the co-respondent companies by Smart Brothers, which itself ceased to trade, and the EAT held inter alia:

(a) the employment of all of the staff ended by reason of redundancy when Smart Brothers ceased to carry on business. There was therefore no claim of unfair dismissal against Smart Brothers as redundancy is a substantial ground justifying dismissal under unfair dismissal legislation;

(b) individual shops which had been subsidiaries of Smart Brothers continued operating as clothing shops under various new owners. The EAT held that, notwithstanding the application of the Directive and Regulations, in those circumstances no liability for staff remained with Smart Brothers in respect of the failure of transferees to engage staff who previously had worked at those locations. The dismissal of the employees by Smart Brothers was not grounded in the transfer 'in itself' but arose because that company ceased trading, leading to the redundancy of its employees. That is an economic reason as permitted by the Directive;

(c) while one of the shops retained its identity it retained a greatly reduced workforce and moved from being 100 per cent retail to 50 per cent retail, 50 per cent wholesale. Two people remained employed in the business: one was the owner and the other was an individual moved from another branch because of his experience of the wholesale trade. The EAT held that the reduction in staff numbers on the retail side and the introduction of wholesale business amounted to 'economic, technical or organisational reasons entailing changes in the workforce';

(d) in respect of one of the shops that retained its identity with the same trade as had been carried on by Smart Brothers, an employee succeeded in his claim of unfair dismissal when he was not engaged by the transferee whom the EAT held had failed to show an economic, technical or organisational reason to justify the non-employment of the individual concerned.

11.10.5.2 *Cunningham v Oasis Stores Ltd*

In another EAT case, *Cunningham v Oasis Stores Ltd* [1995] ELR 183, the EAT examined a complicated factual situation where a retail clothing business had been run by a succession of companies operating retail shops. The last transfer involved the purchase of four of the shops by Oasis Stores Ltd, a British company, which operated its own retail clothing business. Oasis planned to add the four shops to its chain of stores. Mrs Cunningham and Mrs O'Connor, the claimants in the case, were senior executives involved in managing the business and operating the four shops. The legal owners of the shops licensed them to the operators who employed Mrs Cunningham and Mrs O'Connor. Oasis purchased the legal interest in the shops and the licences were in due course surrendered to Oasis. On assuming ownership and responsibility for the shops Oasis managed them from an area office in the north of England. Senior management functions were based at the Oasis head office in London. The claimants argued that there was a transfer of an undertaking and that the failure to retain them in employment was a prohibited dismissal. The respondents argued that there was no transfer because Oasis had most of its clothing stock specially manufactured to its own specification, but that if there was a transfer the claimants' work was not referable solely to the part of the business transferred, and, further that the manner in which Oasis structured the management of the business and carried it on from a different location by persons who were already working for them was an economic, technical or organisational justification for the termination of the claimants' employment.

11.10.6 SCOPE OF THE ETO DEFENCE

- The reasons must be those of the transferee.

  — Dismissal by a transferor at the request or behest of a transferee immediately prior to the transfer in circumstances where it is abundantly clear that there is an obvious ETO reason why the employee should not physically transfer on the basis that his employment would inevitably be terminated by the transferee may constitute a valid defence.

- There must be a change or changes in the workforce.

  — Normally numbers will reduce but not necessarily. If a function is done away with this could be a change in the workforce but if a new function is created the numbers may not drop and yet the ETO defence could justify the termination of the employment of the employee carrying out the function which has been done away with.
  — A transferee cannot use the ETO defence to simply change terms and conditions of employment. If an employee's function is no longer required the employment of that employee may come to an end. In the employer's restructuring a new post could be created with different terms and conditions.

- Economic grounds must relate to the conduct of the business post-transfer and will relate to the cost of running the business.

- Technical grounds must also relate to the conduct of the business after transfer and will relate to skills and manner of operation of the business and the use of technical skills, whether abilities and qualifications, mental or physical.

- Organisational grounds again must relate to the business post-transfer and must be linked to the manner in which the business is run in terms of structural, departmental, administrative or managerial functions.

- Redundancy as recognised by Irish law will meet the requirements of the ETO defence.

11.11   Information and Consultation

11.11.1   LEGISLATIVE REQUIREMENTS

Regulation 8 of the Irish Regulations may be summarised as providing the following.

(1)   An obligation to inform.

   (a)   The obligation lies on both the transferor and transferee.

   (b)   Both transferor and transferee must inform the employee representatives of the employees who are affected by the transfer not just the employees themselves, of the matters set out at regulation 8(1)(a)–(c), not later than 30 days before the transfer is carried out or in any event in good time before the transfer is carried out.

   (c)   Where there are no employee representatives in either or both workforces the employer concerned must facilitate the election of employee representatives.

   (d)   The information must cover the following:
   (i)   the date or proposed date of the transfer. This is a new provision;
   (ii)   the reasons for the transfer;
   (iii)   the legal, economic and social implications of the transfer for the employees; and
   (iv)   the measures envisaged in relation to the employees.

   (e)   The information must be given not later than 30 days before the transfer is carried out or in any event in good time before the transfer is carried out.

(2)   An obligation to consult.

   (a)   Applies only where there are measures envisaged by either the transferor or the transferee in relation to his employees.

   (b)   Consultation must take place not later than 30 days before the transfer is carried out or in any event in good time before the transfer is carried out.

   (c)   Consultation must be carried out 'with a view to seeking agreement'.

11.11.2   TIMING

Regulation 8(1) provides a joint liability on both the transferor and the transferee to 'inform' all employees of the matters referred to therein 'where reasonably practicable' not later than 30 days before the transfer is carried out and in any event 'in good time' before the transfer. Regulation 8(2) provides that if measures are envisaged in relation to the employees then the transferor or the transferee, whichever is appropriate, shall consult with the employee representatives, within the same timeframe but, very importantly, must do so 'with a view to seeking agreement.'

Do these obligations crystallise when the transfer is a possibility or a probability? Does there have to be a legally binding agreement in place in order for the obligations to crystallise? If heads of agreement are signed, does the obligation crystallise, even though the heads of agreement are not legally binding and the transfer may never take place, as happened in *Dabell v Vale Industrial Services Ltd* [1988] IRLR 439? Some assistance can be derived from the decision of the UK High Court, in *Griffin v South West Water Services Ltd* [1995] IRLR 15. In that case, the court considered the EC Collective Redundancies Directive 75/129/EEC (as amended). Article 2 of that Directive provides:

> *'Where an employer is contemplating collective redundancies, he shall begin consultations with the workers' representatives in good time with a view to reaching an agreement.'*

The court, when considering the obligation to consult with workers' representatives, in that context, stated that:

> 'The obligation to consult only arises when the employer's contemplation of redundancies has reached the point where he is able to identify the workers likely to be affected and can supply the information which the Article requires him to supply. Provided he does this in sufficient time to enable consultation to take place with the workers' representatives "with a view to reaching an agreement" (or, as it is put in the amended Article, "in good time with a view to reaching an agreement") I cannot see that the Article requires the employer to embark upon the process of consultation at any particular moment, much less as soon as he can be said to have in mind that collective redundancies may occur. The essential point, to my mind, is that the consultation must be one where, if they wish to do so, the workers' representatives can make constructive proposals and have time in which to do so before the relevant dismissal notices are sent out.'

It may be open to employers who have compelling reasons not to comply with regulation 8, and where those compelling reasons constitute emergency or force majeure, to seek a type of exemption afforded by the ECJ in the collective redundancies case of *Dansk Metalarbejderforbund v Nielsen* [1985] ECR 553.

The Scottish EAT in *Association of Patternmakers and Allied Craftsmen v Kirvin Ltd* [1978] IRLR 318 considered a situation where the employer in the face of financial difficulties continued to trade in what was held to be 'the genuine and reasonable expectation that redundancies will be avoided' and in that case that was held to be a 'special circumstance' which absolved the employer from the obligation to inform and consult under the UK Employment Protection Act 1975.

These cases, however, were cases where redundancies were forced on the employers by circumstances outside their control. It is hard to envisage a situation where a transfer could affect an employer so quickly and with a suddenness that would justify failure to inform and consult employees to be affected by the transfer. Employers may well have a dilemma where commercial confidentiality is essential; they inform and consult their employees at the first available opportunity but the transfer takes effect immediately or very soon thereafter.

11.11.3   NOTICES

The Irish Regulations provide a method of notifying employees directly where they do not have representatives. Regulation 8(6) requires the transferor and/or the transferee, as appropriate, to furnish each employee with written notices containing particulars, in terms of subparagraphs (a), (b) and (c) of regulation 8(1).

11.11.4   INJUNCTIVE RELIEF

One of the most effective remedies for an employee is to obtain injunctive relief preventing any steps being taken in the transfer by either or both of the transferor and transferee until the employee's rights under regulation 8 are honoured. The question of injunctive relief as an effective remedy under the Collective Redundancies Directive was sought to be referred to the ECJ in *Griffin v South West Water Services Ltd* [1995] IRLR 15 but the court of Appeal refused to refer questions to the ECJ when requested to do so by the union in that case.

Where an employer fails to comply with the requirements of regulation 8, it may be open to an employee or a representative union to obtain injunctive relief, preventing the implementation of the transfer, pending compliance with regulation 8. In the decision of Blayney J in *Maybury v Pump Services Ltd and Eldea Ltd* 2 May 1990, High Ct unreported the first-named defendant had encountered financial difficulties. The second-named defendant was a company specifically formed with the intention of purchasing the assets, business and goodwill of the first defendant. The plaintiff was advised by his employer, Pump Services Ltd, that his employment would not continue after the transfer, unless he was offered employment by the second-named defendant, the purchaser of the business. The second-named defendant was unable to give the plaintiff any assurances regarding the terms of continued employment or any indication of the implications of the transfer of the business for him personally. The plaintiff made an ex parte application to the High Court, seeking injunctive relief on the grounds that both defendants had failed to comply with regulation 8. The High Court made an interim order, restraining the first-named defendant from selling or completing the sale of the assets and goodwill of the business to the second-named defendant until further order. The case settled at the interlocutory stage without any further order.

Since then the UK High Court has refused to grant injunctive relief in *Betts v Brintel Helicopters Ltd; Betts v KLM ERA Helicopters (UK) Ltd* [1997] IRLR 361, which was based on an interpretation of the relevant UK regulations which specifically provide that the remedy for a breach of the relevant section referring to transfer of undertakings be by way of complaint to an industrial tribunal. The court refused the injunction in *Betts* on the basis that the remedy available to the employee was by way of complaint to an industrial tribunal.

There are no remedies for employees provided for in the Irish Regulations. It is a matter for the State to impose the penalties provided for in the Regulations. Employees may plead the Regulations in seeking to enforce the rights created thereunder but there is no right to any remedy. Whatever about employees covered by unfair dismissal legislation, employees who are refused information or consultation and whose employer simply ignores regulation 8 cannot be left without any remedy, which would be the case were injunctive relief to be refused in all cases.

The High Court in Ireland refused injunctive relief in *Hyland Shipping Agencies* 2 February 1996, High Ct unreported but not in a situation involving Article 6 or regulation 8. Various reliefs were sought in *Hyland*, one of which was a mandatory injunction directing the defendants to comply with their obligations to inform and consult; however, at the time of the hearing the transfer had taken place and the judgment was therefore taken up with consideration of the failure to employ, or dismiss the plaintiffs consequent on the transfer. Seeking to injunct a dismissal is a considerably more complicated matter than seeking to injunct a transfer, at least until such time as information is furnished and/or consultation takes place. The courts might in time prove to be more amenable to regulation 8 injunctions given that employers are well placed to have the injunction removed by the relatively simple act of complying with the regulation and, in many cases, would be in a position to furnish an undertaking to this effect on the making of an injunction application.

It should also be remembered that no consultation, or inadequate consultation, in breach of regulation 8, may give rise to valid industrial action protected by the provision of the Industrial Relations Acts.

In *Moran v Bloxhams Stockbrokers UD 377/2002* Bloxhams took over the private client department of a stockbroking company and acquired a team of brokers and its client base. This proposed transfer was to take place the applicant was about to go on maternity leave.

She became aware that her employing division might be closed down and there was talk of merging with a private bank. However, a number of issues had to be clarified before the employee would move. No details of the job were given to her in writing and her maternity leave and severance pay were not agreed. There were no details of holidays, car allowance or pension.

The applicant was put under pressure to make up her mind but it was clear to her that in terms of overall remuneration she would be earning considerably less. In May 2001 she commenced her maternity leave, knowing that her division was closing down and severance packages were issued. In view of the uncertainty she informed Bloxhams she was not joining as part of the transfer. She sought employment with another brokerage firm.

The applicant claimed constructive dismissal/unfair dismissal arising out of failure of the potential employer adequately to inform her of her employment terms in a situation where her employment was being taken over by Bloxhams in a transfer of an undertaking. It was held that the employer was at fault in failing to outline the terms of her transfer to her and in guaranteeing that those terms were commensurate to those to which she enjoyed with the transferor. No consideration was given to her personal circumstances and it was held that the applicant was entitled to resign and claim constructive dismissal and was awarded €12,000 under the Unfair Dismissals Acts, 1977–2001.

11.11.5   TRANSFER OF RESTRICTIVE COVENANTS

Given that regulation 4(1) provides that the rights of a transferor arising from a contract of employment or from an employment relationship transfer to the transferee then it is to be expected that if restrictive covenants are otherwise effective in law the benefit of those restrictive covenants and contractual obligations must pass to the transferee. This is a comparatively rare situation in which an employer may seek to invoke the terms of the Regulations in its favour.

In the UK case *Morris Angel & Son Ltd v Hollande* [1993] IRLR 169, the UK Court of Appeal considered what happens to a clause prohibiting employees from soliciting the employer's customers, on the transfer of a business. In such circumstances, the transferor and the transferee inevitably will have different customer lists. There are two issues to be considered:

(1)   does the restriction transfer automatically?

(2)   if it transfers what does it restrict? If, for example, a restriction applied to customers of the transferor it would appear that after the transfer, and provided the transferee has acquired the part of the business which still deals with those customers, the restriction will apply in respect of those customers. If, however, the employee has started to deal with customers of the transferee in his new employment can the restriction he had with the transferor be read as including the transferee's customers? It would seem logical and practical that it must do so but given the strict interpretation applied to restrictive covenants this is unlikely to be the case. The covenant is likely to be interpreted exactly as it was drafted with the transferor and only be effective in the context in which it was actually put in place.

In *Morris Angel & Son Ltd v Hollande* the UK Court of Appeal considered regulation 5(1) of the UK Regulations which provides:

'A relevant transfer shall not operate so as to terminate the contract of employment of any person employed by the transferor in the undertaking or part transferred but any such contract which would otherwise have been terminated by the transfer shall have effect after the transfer as if originally made between the person so employed and the transferee.'

The equivalent Irish regulation 4, as has been seen at **11.8.6.4** above provides:

'The transferor's rights and obligations arising from a contract of employment existing on the date of a transfer shall, by reason of such transfer, be transferred to the transferee.'

The UK Court of Appeal, in overturning the earlier UK High Court decision, interpreted this regulation as having a retrospective effect, in the sense that it should be 'read as referring to the transferee as the owner of the undertaking transferred or in respect of the undertaking transferred'. The practical result, where the employee continues in the transferee's employment, is that, in most cases, the new owners will have to renegotiate restrictive covenants with the employees concerned. Otherwise, it appears that the scope of the prohibition could remain frozen as at the date of transfer, despite the employee's ongoing dealings with customers of the transferee. The alternative interpretation would give rise to a situation whereby an employee who, having joined a small company and having undertaken not to solicit that company's customers, could find himself in a position where a much larger entity takes over his company and, consequently, the prohibition on soliciting customers covers a much larger number of such customers. The court pointed out that such interpretation would:

'... turn the obligation on the employee ... into a quite different and possibly much wider obligation than the obligation which bound him before the transfer. ... Such an obligation was not remotely in contemplation when the service agreement was entered into.'

The UK Court of Appeal would not allow the covenant to operate to cover the business of the transferee which had not been in contemplation or existence at the time the restriction was concluded with the transferor but did allow that the restriction would continue to apply post-transfer in relation to the clients of the transferor stating:

'The better construction is that the covenant can be enforced in respect of clients of the undertaking transferred of which Morris Angel Ltd are deemed as a result of the transfer retrospectively to have been the owner.'

The UK Court of Appeal held that restrictive covenants do transfer but only in certain circumstances and subject to certain qualifications.

11.11.6   EXTENT OF RESTRICTION

In *Morris Angel & Son Ltd v Hollande* [1993] IRLR 169 the restriction took effect after employment ended and restricted the employee for a period of one year after ceasing to be employed from directly or indirectly seeking to procure orders from or do business with 'any person, firm or company who has at any time during the one year immediately preceding such cesser done business with the group'. When the business transferred Mr Hollande was dismissed. The transferee then sought to enforce the restrictive covenant in respect, not only of persons, firms or companies Mr Hollande had done business with while employed by the transferors, but also sought to restrain him from doing or seeking to do business with anyone who had done business with the plaintiffs during the relevant period. That clearly was an extension of the obligation Hollande had entered into.

But could an employee who remains in employment with the transferee seek to avoid the restriction continuing into his future employment with the transferee? It appears that this will largely depend on the wording of the restriction transferred. If somebody in Hollande's position, for example, worked for a period of six months with the transferee and then left employment could the transferee restrict him from doing business with everyone with whom he had dealt in the 12 months prior to the termination? This would include, in the example given, six months of the transferor's customers and six months of the customer base of the merged business of the transferor and the transferee. It is unlikely that a difficulty will arise if the post-transfer customer base is largely the same or similar to the pre-transfer base but if the transferee is a larger company and mixes the transferor's business with its own thereby giving the restriction much wider scope will it still be upheld?

It is to be expected that the temporal, product and geographical restrictions on restrictive covenants will continue to apply but could the employee argue that at the time he agreed the original restriction he did not contemplate there being a transfer, and the consequent widening of its scope, thereby escaping its effects? That question remains to be answered. One answer would be to follow the line of the UK Court of Appeal in *Morris Angel v Hollande* and strike down the restriction as applying to the wider business on the grounds that it constituted 'an obligation ... not remotely in contemplation when the service agreement was entered into' but upholding the general concept that such a covenant, indeed all contractual covenants, prima facie do transfer.

11.12 Automatic Transfer of Liabilities, Rights and Obligations

11.12.1 GENERALLY

The ECJ held in *Berg and Busschers v Besselsen* [1989] IRLR 447 that, in circumstances where Member States have not determined that the transferor and the transferee shall be severally liable after the transfer, Article 3(1) must be interpreted as meaning that, after the date of a transfer, the transferor is, by virtue of the transfer alone, discharged from liability.

11.12.2 BENEFITS TRANSFERRED

The extent of potential liabilities that may be the subject of a transfer is considerable and includes all contractual liabilities such as remuneration, holidays and other benefits including benefits in kind. In *O'Donovan v Ryanair Ltd and Servisair (Ireland) Ltd* [1997] ELR 63 the claimant claimed in respect of the loss of travel concessions when moving from the employment of Ryanair to Servisair. The EAT did not give any definitive views on whether or not travel concessions were transferred by the Directive/Regulations but did accept that the claimant had a grievance regarding the withdrawal of travel concessions. His claim failed on other grounds.

Neither the Directive nor the Regulations nor any of the existing case law deal with the problem posed to a transferee where the transferee is incapable of meeting all of the contractual terms and conditions existing on the date of transfer. If an airline carried out its own baggage handling and employed baggage handlers to do that work and those baggage handlers enjoyed travel concessions what would be the position if the baggage handling transferred to another independent company which was not an airline and could not provide, and did not have access to, travel concessions which it could confer on its employees? None of the existing case law answers such a troublesome question. If the line were to be taken that the liability to provide all benefits and benefits in kind transfer and the obligation to provide travel concessions transfers to the transferee is the transferee obliged to subsidise travel engaged in by its new employees?

In *Donnelly v Value Homes* RP 448/2002 an employee who began working for Newcomen Builders Ltd and transferred following its closure to Value Homes Ltd and who was promised that his redundancy rights were protected and carried over to Value Homes, successfully sued for a redundancy payment when ultimately made redundant by Value Homes, based on length of service with Newcomen and Value Homes combined.

One of the most difficult areas for practitioners in the area of the Regulations is the rule that an employee may not waive rights under the Directive and therefore may not even agree to a change in terms and conditions of employment to his or her detriment if the reason for the change is the transfer itself (see *Wilson v St Helens Borough Council* [1981 IRLR 706). In order to change terms and conditions of employment by consent it must therefore be demonstrated that the reason for the change is not the transfer itself.

The ECJ issued an important ruling in November 2004 in the case of *Boor v Ministre de la Fonction publique et de la Reforme administrative Case C–425/02* in relation to the employer's ability to harmonise terms and conditions. In this case Johanna Boor was employed by a private sector not for profit organisation concerned with training activities for the unemployed. The organisation's function was transferred to the State of Luxembourg. There was thus a transfer of the function in which she worked from the private sector to the public sector. However, public sector pay rates are set by legislation. This meant that under the statutory pay scales she was allocated a lower remuneration than she had received with her previous, private sector employer.

The ECJ indicated that if the change amounted to a substantial reduction in her remuneration she would be able to resign and claim constructive dismissal. However, the interesting part of the case is that the ECJ said that there is nothing in principle in the event of the transfer of an undertaking from the private sector to the public sector to prevent the new employer from reducing the amount of remuneration of the employee concerned in order to comply with national rules in force for public employees. The public sector employer responsible must take into account as far as possible the employee's length of service in allocating the correct pay scale for the employee but in principle, the change could be made.

This is a very significant development and is a departure from the rule of the ECJ in *Daddy's Dance Hall* [1988] IRLR 315 that an employee may not agree to a change in his or her terms and conditions if the change is by reason of the transfer.

11.13   Pensions

11.13.1   GENERAL EXCLUSION FOR PENSIONS

Article 4(4) of the Directive qualifies the general principle set out in Article 3(1) and (2) that all rights and obligations arising from the contract of employment or the employment relationship shall transfer by providing that *'employees' rights to old-age, invalidity or survivors' benefits under supplementary company or inter-company pension schemes outside the statutory social security schemes in Member States are not included'*.

Regulation 4(3) is not materially different from the position applicable under the 1980 Regulations. The Regulations do not apply to employees' rights to old age, invalidity or survivors' benefits under supplementary or inter-company pension schemes falling outside Social Welfare Acts. Regulation 4(4)(b) continues, however, the obligation of a transferee to ensure that the interests of employees and of persons no longer employed in the transferor's business are protected in respect of rights conferring on them immediate or prospective entitlement to old-age benefits including survivors' benefits.

11.14   Insolvency

Regulation 6 excludes the transfer of an undertaking business or part of an undertaking where the transferor is the subject of bankruptcy proceedings or insolvency proceedings. The Regulations however include the proviso in Directive 98/50 which seeks to control employers' avoidance schemes. Thus if the sole or main reason for the institution of bankruptcy or insolvency proceedings in respect of a transfer is the evasion of an employer's legal obligation under the Regulations, the Regulations apply to a transfer effected by that transferor (see *HBM Abels v Administrative Board of Bedrijfsvereniging Voor de Metaal-Industrie en de Electrotechnische Industrie* [1987] 2 CMLR 406). The Irish High Court has confirmed this view in *Re Castle Brand Ltd (in liquidation)* and *Re the Companies Acts, 1963–1983* 25 March 1995, Hamilton J unreported.

The EAT in Ireland has taken the view that a voluntary liquidation does not come within the exclusion of insolvent undertakings from the terms of the Directive and Regulations. In *Kelly v Cavanagh Hiester Ltd (in liquidation) and Dubshad Ltd* UD 222–224/96 the EAT held inter alia:

> 'As the liquidation of Hiester Ltd was a voluntary liquidation the Tribunal holds that the . . . Regulations, SI 306/1980 apply and in this instance there was a transfer of the business to Mr Brian Cavanagh when Hiester Ltd went into liquidation. Accordingly there was no break in the claimant's service.'

The High Court in *Mythen v Employment Appeals Tribunal* considered the scope of the *Abels* decision and, while not making a definitive statement, did indicate that Abels would be restricted to a sale by a liquidator when holding (at p 2):

> 'It could not be assumed that because the court of Justice of the European Communities had held that the Directive does not apply to a sale by a liquidator, it would also hold that the Directive would not apply to a sale by a receiver appointed by a debenture holder—*Abels* considered.'

In *Mythen* Barrington J analysed the views of Advocate-General Sir Gordon Slynn and the reasoning of the ECJ in *Abels* and appeared to take the view that the *Abels* principle could only apply in an enforced liquidation of a bankrupt company and stated (at p 10):

> 'It follows that the reasons for not applying the directive to transfers of undertakings taking place in liquidation proceedings are not applicable to proceedings of this kind taking place at an earlier stage.'

See also the ECJ decision in *Dethier v Dassy and Sovam SPRL (in liquidation)* 12 March 1998 (unreported).

11.15 Due Diligence

11.15.1 INTRODUCTION

Having formed the preliminary intention to transfer the undertaking the transferor and transferee must at an early stage have regard to their obligations under regulation 4 and carry out detailed preparatory work to ascertain the full nature and extent of the obligations arising under the Directive and Regulations consequent on the proposed transfer.

The sort of practical difficulties that may arise in the sale of a business and transfer of employees are indicated by the case of *Walsh and Cotter v Demford Taverns Ltd and Bowler* UD 436/437/97. Demford Taverns ran a pub which they agreed to sell to John Bowler. The claimants were barmen employed by Demford. After the sale the claimants reported for work with Mr Bowler who told them that they would have to apply for any jobs that might be available. Mr Bowler believed that the employees were the responsibility of Demford as they were their employees and believed that Demford had 'taken care' of them. The claimants sued both the transferor, Demford, and the transferee, Bowler, for unfair dismissal. Mr Bowler argued that the business he had purchased and was operating was very different from the business that had been carried out by Demford prior to the sale because he had modernised it, refurbished the building and was carrying it out in a very different fashion. The EAT, however, held that the identity of the business was still the same and had not changed as a result of the transfer. It was still a pub serving both food and drink and running a late-night bar in a similar fashion to its operation by Demford Taverns. The EAT accordingly held that there had been a transfer of undertaking within the meaning of the Directive and Regulations and that the claimants should succeed in their claim.

Some suggested steps to be followed in order to assist with complying with the obligations under the Directive and Regulations and to ensure that the transferee is fully informed and in a position to deal with all eventualities that may arise are set out below.

11.15.2   PRELIMINARY PERSONNEL AUDIT

A comprehensive audit of the target business should be carried out at an early stage, prior to the due diligence process, and a listing of the transferring employees should be made, with as much consideration as possible given individually to each of the employees concerned, as regards his/her future in the new entity. Where it is not possible to plan for individual employees or specific numbers a general assessment of manpower requirements must be carried out.

A similar audit of the transferee's business should be carried out in order to see whether there will be duplication of function, as the addition of the 'new' employees may impact on the purchaser's own staff.

11.15.3   THE DUE DILIGENCE PROCESS

Legal and financial advisers will play a significant role with their clients in the due diligence process itself, and it is incumbent on them to obtain from their opposite number, or the transferor directly, as much necessary information as possible. Where queries are raised and answered, the transferee will have secured representations from the transferor, which may be relied on in the future, in the event of difficulties arising. Failure to raise the queries may fix the transferee with additional liability or cause confusion, where liability cannot be established, at a later stage. The nature of the business will dictate the type of employee requisitions raised. The general structure will be the same in most cases, but the specific level of detail will vary, depending on the nature of the business. Businesses with highly skilled employees of a technical or professional nature, will require more in-depth enquiry than might otherwise be the case.

The transferee should seek confirmation that the transferor has complied with his obligations under regulation 8.

11.15.4   TRADE UNIONS

While trade union involvement in the undertaking may be dealt with in the queries raised regarding each individual employee, it is better to categorise union affairs on a separate basis. Most unionised companies have various agreements with trade unions and tend to keep this sort of information on separate files, which must be opened to the purchasers. Queries should be raised as to meetings held with the trade unions in the months, and indeed years, prior to the transfer, in order to establish the type of issues that tend to be raised by the unions. It might be the case that individual employees have contractual obligations, and answers given to queries in that context might indicate that the employees perform those obligations without difficulty. However, if it transpired that the unions had been making various claims, prior to the transfer, to have the situation changed, it is most important that a transferee be on notice of that fact. It could have a significant effect on the manner in which the work is done and the cost of having it done. In particular, where a target undertaking is in some difficulty, trade unions may have gone quiet, immediately prior to the transfer, not wishing to rock the boat. The arrival of a potential transferee who is bigger and wealthier, may lead to the resurrection of claims which had been thought to have disappeared. There are loose traditions in certain industries and services that an employer who sells out gives the employees who remain some form of 'bonus'. That has to be anticipated, where at all possible, and steps taken to ensure that the purchaser does not, unknowingly, become liable for such payments or unwittingly purchase the business, without an indemnity against any such claim being made.

11.15.5   INDEMNITIES AND WARRANTIES

The actual nature of indemnities and warranties sought and obtained will vary from case to case. While it is easy to advise that indemnities and warranties be obtained, in practice, they can be very difficult to secure. Where they are secured, it is vitally important to ensure that the wording is correct. A transferee might be indemnified against any award that might be made to an employee, but may not be indemnified against the legal costs of having to defend themselves. Where, for example, there are redundancies to be effected as a result of the transfer and given that the ETO defence is likely to be more available to the transferee than the transferor it being the reasons of the transferee that have given rise to termination, the question of meeting the cost of redundancy payments, both statutory and ex gratia, will have to be considered. In practice it is more likely that the transferee will have to carry such cost and it may require to provide for the cost in consideration paid to the transferor, if any. It may not be possible to measure the full extent of such costs at the time of transfer and therefore some form of indemnity will usually be sought from the transferor. The transferor, on the other hand, will not wish to furnish an open-ended indemnity and allow the transferee to spend his money at will so the nature, extent and effectiveness of these indemnities and warranties will usually fall to negotiations between the parties. Having followed the above steps the parties and, in particular, the transferee will be better able to assess what is required by way of indemnity and warranty.

11.15.6   SOCIAL PLAN

Having followed the above steps the transferee may need to prepare a social plan, particularly where there are measures envisaged that may impact negatively on employees, either those transferred or those not being transferred or, in certain circumstances, the existing workforce of the transferee.

11.15.7   INSURANCE

It is essential that a transferee carry out a comprehensive review of its existing insurance arrangements and what insurance may be required in the future consequent on the transfer of the responsibilities and liabilities created by the Directive and Regulations.

11.15.8   ENFORCEMENT OF AND REMEDIES UNDER THE REGULATIONS

Regulation 10 of the Regulations provides for a complaints procedure as set out below.

> '10. (1) A complaint that an employer has contravened any of these Regulations (other than Regulations 4(4)(a) and 13 in relation to an employee may be presented to a rights commissioner by:

    (a)   *the employee, or*

    (b)   *a trade union, staff association or excepted body on behalf and with the consent of the employee.*

(2)   *A complaint under paragraph (1) shall be presented by giving notice of it in writing to a rights commissioner and the notice shall contain such particulars and be in such form as may be specified from time to time by the Minister.*

(3)   *A copy of a notice under paragraph (2) shall be given to the other party or parties concerned, by the rights commissioner concerned.*

(4)   *Where a complaint is presented to a rights commissioner under paragraph (1), the rights commissioner shall—*

    (a)   *give the parties an opportunity to be heard and to present any evidence relevant to the complaint;*

    (b)   *give a decision in writing in relation to the complaint; and*

    (c)   *communicate the decision to the parties.*

(5)   *A decision of a rights commissioner under paragraph (4) shall do one or more of the following:*

    (a)   *declare that the complaint is or, as the case may be, is not well founded;*

    (b)   *require the employer to comply with these Regulations and, for that purpose, to take a specified course of action; or*

    (c)   *require the employer to pay to the employee compensation of such amount (if any) as in the opinion of the rights commissioner, is just and equitable in the circumstances, but—*

        (i)   *in the case of a contravention of Regulation 8, not exceeding 4 weeks remuneration and,*

        (ii)   *in the case of a contravention of any other Regulation, not exceeding 2 years remuneration,*

    in respect of the employee's employment calculated in accordance with Regulations made under section 17 of the Unfair Dismissals Act 1977,

and a reference in this paragraph to an employer shall be construed, in a case where ownership of the relevant undertaking or business, or the part concerned of that undertaking or business, of the employer changes after the contravention to which the complaint relates occurred, as a reference to the person who, by virtue of the change, becomes entitled to such ownership.

(6)   *A rights commissioner shall not entertain a complaint under this Regulation unless it is presented to the commissioner within the period of 6 months beginning on the date of the alleged contravention to which the complaint relates, or where the rights commissioner is satisfied that exceptional circumstances prevented the presentation of the complaint within that period, such further period, not exceeding 6 months from the expiration of the first-mentioned period, as the rights commissioner considers reasonable.*

(7)   *Proceedings under this Regulation before a rights commissioner shall be conducted otherwise than in public.*

(8)   *A rights commissioner shall furnish the Tribunal with a copy of each decision given by the commissioner under paragraph (4).*

(9)   *A rights commissioner shall maintain a register of all decisions made by him or her under this Regulation and shall make the register available for inspection by members of the public during normal office hours.'*

CHAPTER 12

REDRESS, REMEDIES AND FORUMS

12.1 Introduction

An important aspect in advising clients is to advise them on what redress and remedies they have available to them. In the context of employment law the issue of redress is a vexed and complex question. There are a number of forums to which an employee and employer can turn in order to enforce their rights under common law and relevant legislation. This chapter concludes with a table that identifies which forum is available in relation to each piece of legislation dealt with in this book. The table also deals with time limits, the remedies available to the person making the claim, and the forum which will entertain a right of appeal.

In respect of the table, the following institutions are relevant.

12.2 Rights Commissioner

The Industrial Relations Act 1969 established the office of the 'rights commissioner'. Rights commissioners are appointed by the Minister for Enterprise, Trade and Employment. They are required to deal with trade disputes under the Industrial Relations Acts, 1969–1990 and also have functions under the Adoptive Leave Acts, 1995–2005, the Carer's Leave Act, 2001, Competition Act, 2002, the Industrial Relations (Miscellaneous Provisions) Act, 2004, the Maternity Protection Acts, 1994–2004, the National Minimum Wage Act, 2000, the Organisation of Working Time Act, 1997, the Parental Leave Act, 1998, the Payment of Wages Act, 1991, the Protection of Employees (Fixed-term Work) Act, 2003, the Protection of Employees (Part-time Work) Act, 2001, the Protection of Young Persons (Employment) Act, 1996, the Protections for Persons Reporting Child Abuse Act, 1998, the Safety, Health and Welfare at Work Act, 2005, the Terms of Employment (Information) Acts, 1994 and 2001, the Unfair Dismissals Acts, 1977–2001 and the European Communities (Protection of Employment) Regulations, 2000, SI 488/2000 and the European Communities (Protection of Employees on Transfer of Undertakings) Regulations, 2003, SI 131/2003.

More information on the functions and procedure of the Rights Commissioners Service can be found on the Labour Relations Commission website www.lrc.ie. Complaint forms are also available for downloading.

12.3   Employment Appeals Tribunal

The EAT was established by section 39 of the Redundancy Payments Act, 1967 and is the traditional forum for unfair dismissal claims. However, the EAT is also the forum for determining complaints both at first instance and on appeal in a number of employment law areas. In particular the EAT has functions under the Minimum Notice and Terms of Employment Acts, 1973–2001, Payment of Wages Act, 1991, Terms of Employment (Information) Act, 1994 and 2001, Organisation of Working Time Act, 1997, Adoptive Leave Act, 1995, Maternity Protection Acts, 1994–2004, Protection of Young Persons (Employment) Act, 1996, Unfair Dismissal Acts, 1977–2001, Carer's Leave Act, 2001, Redundancy Payments Act, 1967–2001, Parental Leave Act, 1998, European Communities (Protection of Employees on Transfer of Undertakings) Regulations, 2003, and the Protection of Employees (Employees Insolvency) Acts, 1984–2001.

More information on the functions and procedure of Employment Appeals Tribunal is available on the Tribunal website www.eatribunal.ie. Again complaint forms are available for downloading.

12.4   The Labour Court

The Labour Court was established by the Industrial Relations Act, 1946 and is involved traditionally with industrial relations' matters. However, the Labour Court is the forum for redress at first instance or on appeal in a number of areas. The Labour Court has functions in the Organisation of Working Time Act, 1997, Industrial Relations Acts, 1946–2001, Protection of Employees (Part-time Work) Act, 2001, Protection of Employees (Fixed-term Work) Act, 2003, Employment Equality Act, 1998–2004, and the National Minimum Wage Act, 2000.

More information on the functions and procedure of the Labour Court is available on the Labour Court website www.labourcourt.ie. Labour Court recommendations are readily available on this site.

12.5   The Labour Relations Commission

The Labour Relations Commission was established under the Industrial Relations Act 1990, section 24. It was essentially established to promote the improvement of industrial relations and to provide the Rights Commissioner Service. The LRC insofar as it is required to provide good industrial relations has its functions and powers contained in the Industrial Relations Acts, 1946–2001.

More information on the functions of the Labour Relations Commission may be found on its website www.lrc.ie.

12.6   Office of Director of Equality Investigation (Equality Tribunal)

The Equality Tribunal (Office of the Director of Equality Investigations) was established under the Employment Equality Act, 1998. The tribunal oversees the Employment Equality Acts, 1998–2004 which make discrimination in the workplace unlawful on the grounds of gender, marital status, family status, sexual orientation, religion, age, disability, race or membership of the traveller community. Claims taken pursuant to this Act may be the subject of mediation through equality mediation officers. Failing mediation, the matter will be determined by equality officers whose decisions may be appealed to the Labour Court.

More information on the functions and procedures of the Equality Tribunal are available on their website www.equalitytribunal.ie. A number of forms and a database of decisions are also easily accessible.

12.7 The Civil Courts

The Civil Courts remain available to employees for the determination of common law actions such as wrongful dismissal, breach of contract and injunctive relief. They also are available in certain circumstances as an appellate body from decisions made by various tribunals and courts under statute.

12.8 The Health & Safety Authority

The Health & Safety Authority was established under the Safety Health and Welfare at Work Act, 1989. Its responsibility is for the promotion and enforcement of workplace health and safety in Ireland. The Authority monitors compliance with occupational health and safety legislation and in that regard, in the event of breaches, conducts prosecutions. The Authority has also taken responsibility for bullying and harassment intervention and has issued a code of practice on the prevention of workplace bullying.

The code of practice and more information is available on the Authority's website www.hsa.ie.

REDRESS EMPLOYMENT LAW

Legislation	Forum/ statutory authority	Time limit	Remedy	Appeal	Enforcement (where no appeal is made and the decision/ determination is not carried out)
Adoptive Leave Acts, 1995–2005	Rights commissioner section 32	Six months (12 in exceptional circumstances section 34(1)	• Decision in relation to the dispute • Directions for resolution of dispute • Compensation up to 20 weeks remuneration section 33(3)	• EAT within four weeks • High Court on a point of law only section 36(2)	Circuit Court section 39
Carer's Leave Act, 2001	Rights commissioner section 19	Six months (12 in exceptional circumstances) section 19(3) & (8)	• Decision section 19 • Grant of leave section 21(1) • Compensation up to 26 weeks remuneration section 21(2)	• EAT within four weeks section 20(1) & (2) • High Court on a point of law only section 23(2)	Circuit Court section 39
Common law civil proceedings	The courts	Six years	• Damages resulting from breach of contract (usually notice the employee ought to have received) • Injunction restraining termination of employment		
Data Protection Act, 1988 & 2003	Data Protection Commissioner section 9	Investigate whether a complaint is made or not section 10	Serve: • enforcement/information or notice requiring compliance with the Act • prohibition notice on transfer of personal data section 10 • note section 31 penalties	• Circuit Court within 21 days • High Court on a point of law section 26	Prosecution/penalties in District/Circuit Court

Legislation	Forum/ statutory authority	Time limit	Remedy	Appeal	Enforcement (where no appeal is made and the decision/ determination is not carried out)
Employment Equality Acts, 1998–2004	Director of Equality Tribunal (where individual is in employment)	Six months (12 in exceptional circumstances)	• Director issues a decision • Equal pay • Arrears of remuneration for up to three years before the date of referral • Compensation in respect of discrimination or victimisation occurring during six years prior to referral, up to two years' remuneration if employed otherwise up to €12,697 • Equal pay • Order for equal treatment • Order to take specified action section 82	Labour Court within 42 days	Circuit Court
Equal Status Act, 2000–2004	Director of Equality Tribunal section 21(1)	Six months (12 in exceptional circumstances) section 21(6) Must notify service provider of intention to make complaint within two months of incident section 21(2)	• Decision • Compensation up to €6,349 • An order to take a specified course of action section 27	• Circuit Court within 42 days section 28 • No further appeal lies other than to the HC on a point of law section 28(3)	Circuit Court section 31
European Communities (Protection of Employment) Regulations, 2000 (Protection of Employment Act, 1977), SI 488/2000	Rights commissioner section 6(1)	Six months (12 in exceptional circumstances) section 6(3)	• Decision requiring compliance with Protection of Employment Act, 1977 Act and to take a specified course of action section 6(2) • Compensation up to four weeks' remuneration section 6(2)(c)	• Appeal to EAT within six weeks • Appeal to High Court on point of law sections 7, 8, 10 Terms of Employment Information Act	

Legislation	Forum/statutory authority	Time limit	Remedy	Appeal	Enforcement (where no appeal is made and the decision/determination is not carried out)
European Communities (Protection of Employees of Transfer of Undertakings) Regulation, 2003 SI 131/2003	Rights commissioner reg 10(1)	Six months (12 in exceptional circumstances) reg 10(6)	• Decision requiring the employer to comply with the regulations and to take a specified course of action • Compensation up to four weeks' remuneration (if contravene reg 8)	• EAT within six weeks reg 11(1) & (2) • High Court on a point of law reg 12 within 10 days • Compensation up to two years' remuneration (if contravene any other reg)	Circuit Court reg 14
Industrial Relations Acts, 1946–2004	• Rights commissioner • Labour Court		• Recommendation on the merits of dispute • Recommendation • Determination	• Labour Court within six weeks • HC on a point of law	Circuit Court (section 10, 2001 Act)
Maternity Protection Acts, 1994–2004	Rights commissioner section 31	Six months (12 in exceptional circumstances) section 31	• Decision in relation to the dispute • Directions for resolution of dispute • Grant leave • Compensation up to 20 weeks' remuneration section 32	• EAT (four weeks) section 33 • High Court on a point of law only section 34	Circuit Court section 37
Minimum Notice and Terms of Employment Acts, 1973–2001	Employment Appeals Tribunal section 11(1)	Six years	Compensation up to eight weeks' pay	High Court within 10 days on a question of law only section 11(2)	Contract debt in appropriate court section 12(2)
National Minimum Wage Act, 2000	Rights commissioner section 24(1)	Six months (12 in exceptional circumstances) section 24(2)	• Decision • Arrears • Reasonable expenses • Require an employer to remedy any breach of the Act section 26	• Labour Court within six weeks section 27 • High Court on a point of law section 30(2)	• Labour Court section 31 • Circuit Court section 32

Legislation	Forum/statutory authority	Time limit	Remedy	Appeal	Enforcement (where no appeal is made and the decision/determination is not carried out)
Organisation of Working Time Act, 1997	Rights commissioner section 27(2)	Six months (12 in exceptional circumstances) section 27(4) & (5)	• Decision requiring compliance with the Act • Compensation up to two years' remuneration section 27(3)	• Labour Court within six weeks section 28(1) & (2) • High Court on a point of law only section 28(6) within 10 days	• Labour Court section 29 • Circuit Court
Parental Leave Act, 1998	Rights commissioner section 18	Six months section 18(5)	• Rights decision section 21(1) • Grant of parental leave section 21(2)(a) • Compensation up to 20 weeks' remuneration section 21(2)(b) & (3)	• EAT within four weeks section 19(1) & (2) • High Court on point of law section 20	Circuit Court may direct the party to comply with decision or determination section 22
Payment of Wages Act, 1991	Rights commissioner section 6(1)	Six months (12 in exceptional circumstances) section 6(4)	• Decision section 6(1) • Reasonable compensation up to the net amount of wages in respect of deduction or payment section 6(2)	• EAT within six weeks section 7(2) • High Court on a point of law only section 7(4)	Circuit Court section 8(1)
Protection of Employees (Part-Time Work) Act, 2001	Rights commissioner section 16(1)	Six months (12 in exceptional circumstances) section 16(5) & (4)	• Decision requiring compliance with Act • Compensation up to two years' remuneration section 16(2)	• Labour Court within six weeks section 17(1) & (2) • High Court on a point of law only section 17(6) within 10 days	Circuit Court section 18

Legislation	Forum/ statutory authority	Time limit	Remedy	Appeal	Enforcement (where no appeal is made and the decision/ determination is not carried out)
Protection of Employees (Fixed-Term Work) Act, 2003	Rights commissioner section 14(1)	Six months (12 in exceptional circumstances) section 14(3) & (4)	• Decision requiring compliance with Act • Require the employer to re-instate or re-engage the employee (including on a contract of indefinite duration) • Compensation up to two years' remuneration section 14(2)	• Labour Court within six weeks section 15(1) & (2) • High Court on a point of law only section 15(6) within 10 days	Circuit Court section 16
Protection of Employees (Employer's insolvency) Act, 1984–2001	Employment Appeals Tribunal section 9	Six weeks section 9	Declaration that Minister is liable to make payment (out of social insurance fund) and specify amount	High Court within 10 days on point of law only	
Protection of Young Persons (Employment) Act, 1996	Rights commissioner section 18(1)	Six months (12 in exceptional circumstances) section 18(4)	• Recommendation ordering a specific course of action • Compensation as is just and equitable section 18(3)	• EAT within six weeks section 19(1)&(2) • High Court on a point of law section 19(4)	• EAT • District Court section 20
Redundancy Payments Acts, 1967–2003	Employment Appeals Tribunal	Six months (12 in exceptional circumstances)	Determination as to: • entitlement to lump sum payment • entitlement to rebates • what is 'continuous employment' • whether offer of alternative employment was reasonable section 36	High Court within 10 days on a point of law only section 40 as amended by section 9 of 1971 Act	

Legislation	Forum/ statutory authority	Time limit	Remedy	Appeal	Enforcement (where no appeal is made and the decision/ determination is not carried out)
Safety, Health & Welfare At Work Act, 2005	Health & Safety Authority		Serve: • direction requiring improvement plan to be submitted • improvement notice • prohibition	District Court	Prosecution/penalties in District/Circuit/High Court may restrict or prohibit use of place of work where there is a risk to health and safety
Terms of Employment (Information) Act, 1994 and 2001	Rights commissioner section 7(1)	Six months section 7(3)	• Recommendation to correct statement section 7(2) • Compensation up to four weeks' remuneration section 7(2)(d)	• EAT within six weeks section 8(1) • High Court on a point of law only section 8(4)	District Court section 9
Unfair Dismissals Acts, 1977–2001	• Rights commissioner (only where no objection is lodged by either party) • Employment Appeal Tribunal • Circuit Court • High Court section 7	Six months (12 in exceptional circumstances) section 8 and section 8(1A)	• Rights commissioner may issue a recommendation/EAT makes a determination section 8(11A)(a)&(b) • EAT may award re-instatement, re-engagement or compensation up to two years' remuneration section 7 • Circuit Court may award damages for wrongful dismissal	• EAT within six weeks section 9(1) & (2) • Circuit Court within six weeks section 11 UD (Amend) Act, 1993 • High Court on a point of law	Circuit Court section 10

INDEX

INDEX

INDEX

INDEX

Job functions
changes in
constructive dismissal, 8.6.6.5
contract of employment, 1.5.3
Job location
change of
constructive dismissal, 8.6.6.5
Job sharing
employment equality
indirect discrimination, 6.5.4
Job title, 1.1.2
Joint Industrial Councils
role of, 10.7
Joint Labour Committees
background to, 10.6
Joint Safety and Health Agreements, 5.8.2

Knowledge acquired in course of employment
types of, 1.5.17.4

Labour Court
appeals from, 10.4.7
arbitration, 10.4.4
conciliation, 10.4.3
fair employment rules, 10.4.5
historical background, 10.4.1
powers of, 10.3.2
special investigation procedures, 10.4.2
standard wages for areas, 10.4.6
statutory provisions, 12.4
Labour Relations Commission
statutory provisions, 12.5
Lack of personal control over work
identified as causing stress, 5.10.2.4
Law Reform Commission
proposals on corporate killing, 5.21.4
Layoffs, 9.7
Leave, 1.1.2
Legal representation
disciplinary hearings, 8.24
Legal transfer
transfer of undertakings, 11.8.6.1
Legitimate interests
employers, 1.5.17.10
Length of service qualification
fixed-term employees, 4.3.4.5
Letter of appointment, 1.1
Liabilities
transfer of undertakings
automatic transfer, 11.12.1
Light work
provision in relation to illness and incapacity, 8.26.9
Like work
definition of, 6.6.4.1
equal pay
case law, 6.6.4.2
statutory provisions, 6.6.4.1
Liquidation
contract of employment, 1.5.26
Local authorities
defined as undertakings, 11.3

Lock-outs
unfair dismissal, 8.17
Loyalty
duty of, 1.5.17.2

Machine-paced work
identified as causing stress, 5.10.2.4
Machinery, responsibility for
contract of employment, 1.5.26
Manual handling of loads
definition of, 5.10.6.1
health and safety at work
statutory provisions, 5.10.6.1
training, 5.10.6.2
Manufacturers
health and safety at work, 5.5.4
Marital status
discriminatory interview questions regarding, 1.3.2
employment equality
case law, 6.2.4
statutory provisions, 6.2.2
Maternity leave
allocation of minimum period of leave, 3.4.2.2
additional leave, 3.4.2.5
extension, 3.4.2.4
unexpected early confinement, 3.4.2.6
variation, 3.4.2.3
death of mother, 3.4.8
entitlement, 3.4.2.1
contract of employment, 1.5.26
hospitalisation of child, 3.4.4
notification of intention to return to work, 3.4.11
payment during, 3.4.5
postponement of, 3.4.4
resolution of disputes relating to, 3.4.14
right to return to work, 3.4.10.2
suitable alternative work, 3.4.10.3
sickness of employee, 3.4.3
statutory provisions, 3.4.1, 3.4.15
Maternity protection
health and safety at work, 5.11
Medical establishments
defined as undertakings, 11.3
Medical examinations, 1.3.3.4
disclosure of results, 8.26.10
refusal to undergo, 5.5.1.2
Medical fitness to work, 5.8.1
Medical foundations
defined as undertakings, 11.3
Medical practitioner
duty of care to prospective employee, 1.3.3.4
Mental strain, 3.2.3.6.4
Migrant workers
definition of, 4.5
employment protection, 4.5
Minister for Enterprise, Trade and Employment
health and safety at work
powers of, 5.20.1.1
Mutual trust and confidence
employment injunctions, 7.6

434

INDEX

INDEX